Some Genealogy Keys
to Some
Georgia Family Trees

Histories and Genealogies of Assorted Jackson,
Fricks, Neel, Anderson, Jordan, Gravatt, Hudgins,
Tanner, Pettyjohn and Rogers Family Lines

By R. Olin Jackson III
B.A., M.Ed.

Published by Whippoorwill Publications, LLC
Roswell, GA 30075

ISBN (hardback): hardback 979-8-9872286-0-9
ISBN (softcover): 979-8-9872286-1-6

Library of Congress Cataloguing-in-Publication Data: 2022922387

Also by R. Olin Jackson:
Mystery & History in Georgia, Volume I (2021)
Mystery & History in Georgia, Volume II (2023)

Some Genealogy Keys To Some Georgia Family Trees is available online from Amazon.com, Barnes and Noble.com and other fine booksellers

Foreword

Detailed here for the first time is an in-depth analysis of the genealogy of ten associated family lines in Georgia. These include the **Jackson**, **Fricks**, **Neel**, **Anderson**, **Jordan**, **Gravatt**, **Hudgins**, **Tanner**, **Pettyjohn**, and **Rogers** families, whose ancestors, all originating from Western Europe, immigrated to the "New World" in the 17th, 18th, and 19th Centuries seeking personal, religious and political freedom from oppressions existent in their home countries. The ports of immigration of these families into America ranged from Delaware, New Jersey and New York, to Pennsylvania, Virginia and Rhode Island, from whence they migrated westward through the Carolinas, Tennessee, Kentucky, Alabama, Georgia, and ultimately throughout the nation all the way to California.

Award-winning author and editor R. Olin Jackson has gathered together an array of census records, family trees, marriage records, death records, wills, private papers, family photographs, military records, photos of various family members and historic family homes, and much more, creating a potpourri of historic information on the above families for interested relatives. This material paints a vivid picture of the origin of these families, their lives, legacies, and remaining landmarks in the United States.

In addition to these materials, the author has also researched, compiled, and written extensive histories of each of these family lines, providing a startling amount of information in the captivating back-stories provided herein. Along with these family histories, detail-specific genealogies are outlined for each of these families.

Although this book was compiled to serve as a genealogical source for relatives and researchers of the families contained herein, the author acknowledges in advance the inevitability of errors and omissions which are inherent in a work of this nature. Accordingly, this book should not be considered to be a comprehensive genealogical reference guide. Whether done by accident, or intentionally due to space constraints, errors and omissions are unavoidable in any genealogical work. As a famed singer/songwriter once penned, *"Please don't remind me of my failures. . . . I'm aware of them."* Nevertheless, all the information on the pages which follow – gathered over the span of many years – has been heavily researched, compiled and presented here to the best of the author's ability.

Table of Contents

Neel Family History in Georgia

The Neel family was among the first settlers in Bartow County, Georgia, and instrumental in the re-establishment of order and civility in that area following the devastation wrought by the U.S. Civil War. At various times, family members were elected to public office, serving in posts such as representatives to the Georgia State Legislature and U.S. Presidentially-appointed positions; and received Georgia state gubernatorial appointment to judgeship.

The 1850 Federal Census of District 40, St. Clair, Alabama, lists Joseph H. "Neal," age 57, as head of his household and a native of Georgia, farming real estate valued at $750.00. His household members include his wife, Nancy, age 52, and children Elizabeth E. ("Emerline"), age 21, and James M. *(not to be confused with the later James Monroe Neel, son of Joseph Lockhart Neel)*, age 17. The other family members, David Washington, born 1817; Florah Hawthorn, born 1821; William M., born 1823; and Joseph Lockhart, born 1826; are not mentioned, but they all obviously were young adults well into their 20s and 30s and already departed from the home nest by 1850.

Joseph Lockhart Neel (09/22/1826 – 03/09/1909) came first to Adairsville (ne Gordon County) in the early 1840s and was prominent in the foundation of that community. He appears in the *1850 Federal Census of Gordon County*. There, on November 2, 1848, he married Mary Ann Swain and began business as a merchant. This early involvement in northwest Georgia occurred barely ten years after the Cherokee Indians had been removed from this and other regions of Georgia on the infamous *"Trail of Tears."*

According to the *History of Bartow County* (1933) by Lucy Josephine Cunyus Mulcahy, *"Adairsville was incorporated in February, 1854, with D.A. Crawford, Joseph Lockhart Neel, H.G. Lawrence, A.C. Trimble, and John W. Parrot appointed as town commissioners."* On page 85 it also states that in 1857-1858, Joseph Lockhart Neel was elected to and served in the Georgia State Legislature, and also as a member of the Masonic Lodge in both Adairsville and Cartersville.

In 1862, shortly after the onset of the war, "Captain" Neel organized, at Adairsville, a company of volunteers for service in the Confederate Army as a part of Company H ("Veach Guards," Bartow County, GA), 40th Regiment, Georgia Volunteer Infantry, Army of Tennessee, C.S.A., commanded by Col. Abda Johnson.

According to historic records at the Georgia Department of Archives & History in Atlanta, Captain Neel's unit was assembled with other northwest Georgia contingents at Camp McDonald near Big Shanty (present-day Kennesaw), Georgia, and initially brigaded with the 41st, 42nd, 43rd, and 52nd Georgia Infantry Regiments.

Engagements

The 40th was first sent to Tennessee, then Mississippi, where it was placed in Barton's Brigade, Department of Mississippi and East Louisiana. The 40th participated in the conflicts at Chickasaw Bayou and Champion's Hill, and were part of the garrison which was forced to surrender during the siege of Vicksburg on July 4, 1863. Captain Neel, as were many others, was wounded in this conflict. It is worth noting, that while the Union forces were able to surround and starve the Confederates into surrender, they were less able to actually defeat them in battle during the early years of the war. However, as disease, malnutrition, starvation and other deprivations began taking a toll upon the Confederates during the later years of the war, their losses began to accumulate progressively.

After undergoing a prisoner exchange, the 40th Georgia was reorganized and attached to General Stovall's Brigade, which again included the 41st, 42nd, 43rd, and 52nd Georgia Infantry Regiments and, the 1st Georgia State Line Troops.

The 40th (including Capt. Neel) ultimately served on numerous battlefields from Chattanooga to Nashville and in many of the major engagements in the Georgia Campaign, including the brutal clashes at Shiloh, Chattanooga, Resaca, Chickamauga, Missionary Ridge, the Hundred Days Battles, New Hope Church, Kennesaw Mountain, Peachtree Creek, and the Battle of Atlanta.

According to Sam Watkins, author of the now well-known book, *Company Aytch*, and a line soldier of Company H of the First Tennessee Infantry Regiment, Army of Tennessee from the opening of the war until its close, some 5,100 troops who originally composed the First Tennessee had been reduced to roughly 125 officers and men at the conclusion of the conflict in 1865, such was the bloody and destructive nature of the engagements in which this army served.

The other infantry units of the Army of Tennessee fared little better. During this time, Captain Neel was one of many individuals in this group who found themselves fighting through their own towns and communities and, indeed, their own shattered homes and former properties, as they sought – though severely outnumbered – to turn back the tide of invasion by Union General William T. Sherman whose army was relentlessly ransacking, thieving, pillaging and burning its way down through Georgia in the spring and summer of 1864. It is still a point of pride among many Southerners, that

despite the fact that Sherman's troops – according to the general's own figures – numbered approximately 100,000 or more troops during his march through Georgia, and the Confederate forces confronting him numbered less than 60,000 troops at best, the Federal forces still were unable to consistently defeat the men in gray in head to head combat, and were forced to perform incessant flanking movements in order to reach and ultimately surround Atlanta to lay siege to the city.

After his withdrawal from Atlanta with the 40th, Captain Neel later also saw action in the horrendous desperate engagements at Franklin and Nashville, Tennessee, and finally, at Bentonville, North Carolina, where he witnessed the conclusion of the war, surrendering on April 26, 1865. By this point, only a handful of the original enlistees in the 40th Georgia remained to return to northwest Georgia where they found their families scattered, their homes and farms totally destroyed, and their way of life erased from the landscape forever. Many once-prosperous towns and communities of northwest Georgia, including Van Wert in Polk, Cassville in old Cass County, Etowah, Stilesboro, and Allatoona in Bartow – among numerous others – never recovered from the devastation, some of them disappearing completely from the landscape.

Watkins described the terrible Battle of Franklin (in which Captain Neel participated) near the end of the war as *"the blackest page in the history of the war of the Lost Cause. It was the bloodiest battle of modern times in any war. It was the finishing stroke upon the independence of the Confederacy. I was there. I saw it. My flesh trembles and creeps and crawls when I think of it today. . . It beggars description. It was four o'clock on that dark and dismal December day when the line of battle was formed. . . As we marched on down through an open field toward the rampart of blood and death, the Federal batteries began to open and mow down our men. . . a scene so sickening and horrible*

In 1857-'58, Joseph Lockhart Neel was elected to the Georgia State Legislature.

that it is impossible for me to describe it. . . A sheet of fire was poured into our very faces, and for a moment, we halted as if in despair as the terrible avalanche of shot and shell laid low those brave and gallant heroes. . . Never on this earth did men fight against such terrible odds. . . The earth was red with blood. It ran in streams, making rivulets as it flowed. . . Dead soldiers filled the entrenchments. The firing was kept up until midnight when it gradually died away."

Wounded In Action

Such was the dramatic and terrible specificity of Watkins' recollections and observations, that they have been quoted numerous times, not only in every segment of **The Civil War**, the acclaimed 1990 television series by noted Civil War authority Ken Burns, but also frequently in the multi-volume **Time-Life** series **The Civil War**. Captain Neel fought in all of these engagements.

Where many of the Southern troops joined for only a one or two-year enlistment and then returned home, Neel and others like Watkins endured what undeniably were unbelievable hardships in their day-to-day quest for survival for the entire duration of the war. From the day he volunteered his services, Captain Neel never hesitated nor wavered in his military commitment, serving long after many others had quit.

It would, in fact, have been quite easy for Captain Neel to simply retire from the field and return home as did many of his compatriots. He suffered from a number of wounds and literally passed right by what was left of his home in Adairsville during the Army of Tennessee's retreat in the face of the overwhelming numeric superiority of Sherman's Army in July of 1864. Neel, however, remained resolutely devoted to his unit. Quitting was not an option.

According to the official Muster Roll of Company H, 40th Regiment, Georgia Volunteer Infantry, Army of Tennessee, CSA, Captain Joseph Lockhart Neel – as was also the case with countless of these noble souls – was wounded at Vicksburg, Mississippi, on July 4, 1863; in Atlanta, Georgia (during the Battle of Atlanta) on July 22, 1864; and in Bentonville,

North Carolina on March 19, 1865. He was listed in the Greensboro, North Carolina hospital on April 26, 1865, and paroled at Charlotte, North Carolina, on May 6, 1865.

According to reminiscences of his experiences which were written down prior to his death by his daughter, Leonora Neel, Captain Neel was directed by Col. Abda Johnson of the 40th Regiment to *"take charge"* one day. *"After several color bearers had been shot down before another could be appointed, Capt. Neel could not bear to see the (Confederate) flag trail in the dust any longer,"* Ms. Neel recorded. *"Of course the enemy frequently aimed at the color-bearer* (since he served as the rallying point for the troops and attracted significant attention) *and he* (Capt. Neel) *was therefore wounded in the hand on this occasion. Many times he was in hard-fought battles, and was wounded no less than three times."* On one occasion (date unknown) Captain Neel was photographed in uniform with his arm held aloft, showing the missing portion of his hand which had been shot away.

One incident – somewhat humorous today if such is possible of so terrible an event – recorded by Ms. Neel of Captain Neel's reminiscences involved a fellow soldier. *"When falling back during Sherman's campaign through Georgia, one of Capt. Neel's soldiers became so exhausted – or stubborn about giving up his homeland – that he stopped and stated that he would not go another step further, and subsequently dropped down into a fence corner. It was at about that time, as fate would have it, that a shell struck the fence (near) where this soldier was resting, causing him to immediately resume the march – double-quick – running ahead of Capt. Neel who asked him in passing why he was running so fast. The startled soldier reportedly paused only briefly to reply, 'Because I can not fly!'"*

After the war, according to records, since Adairsville had not been completely destroyed, Captain Neel rejoined his wife, Mary, in that community to engage in farming and the mercantile business once again with his brother-in-law, W. Jesse Swain, helping to rebuild that shattered community. He was active in educational, civic, and political affairs locally, and was elected once again to represent his region in the Georgia General Assembly for the 1876-1877 term.

In 1882, Mr. Neel removed to live in Cartersville, near his son who had become prominent in the development of that community. Though he had remained active in his community endeavors even after returning from the terrible experiences of the war, Captain Neel, reportedly, was never the same man, his spirit reportedly broken. He died 27 years later in 1909 at the age of 83, in his home on "Neel Street" in Cartersville.

It quite possibly was Captain Neel, as a farmer upon the Neel lands in Cartersville – or possibly even one of the field-hands tilling his land – who discovered a large Native American hand-axe/tomahawk today in the possession of one of Mr. Neel's descendants. This hand-axe was kept in the Neel family at their home – coincidentally not far from present-day Etowah Indian Mounds in Cartersville – for many years. Mr. Neel's granddaughter, Isabelle Neel Jackson, often told family members prior to her death that her mother and father, interestingly (and ironically), had used the stone "to tenderize steaks."

James Monroe Neel

Captain Neel's eldest surviving son, James Monroe Neel (01/22/1850 – 11/30/1930) was a young boy during the days of the Civil War in Georgia. He attended the common schools of Bartow and then the University of Kentucky. He taught school for two years while studying law with his great-uncle, David W. Neel of Gordon County, and was admitted to the Georgia Bar on February 1, 1874.

Records indicate that in 1875, James had opened a law office in Adairsville, but soon relocated to Cartersville where he became associated with the firm of Gen. W.T. Wofford. Approximately two years later, he became a partner with Judge Robert B. Trippe.

In 1881, James became principal owner of the law firm of Neel, Conner and Neel (W.J.) of Cartersville, but this partnership was dissolved when his brother, W.J., received a government appointment from President Grover Cleveland. During a later period,

James was the principal of Neel & Peeples (O.T.) of Cartersville.

Also in 1875, James married Anna Anderson of Adairsville. Their children were Ella, born in 1876, Joseph Francis, born in 1878, and Oliver Anderson, born in 1881. To James' utter despair, Anna died from what was described as "child-bed fever" 26 days after Oliver's birth. From that point forward, Oliver was devotedly raised by James' spinster sister, "Aunt Nora" (Leonora).

On January 4, 1883, James married once again, this time to Julia Margaret Anderson, the sister of his beloved late wife, Anna. According to

Neel, James Monroe – Photographed circa 1880-1885.

1902 NEEL FAMILY PHOTOGRAPH
The extended Neel family was photographed at 119 South Avenue in Cartersville, Georgia, in 1902 during a family reunion. (REAR, STANDING) (L-R): Blanch Hall Neel (Joe Neel's wife); Juliet Anderson "Dootz" Neel-McClatchey; Oliver Anderson "Uncle Poly" Neel; Mary Ella Neel; James Monroe "Syl" Neel, Jr.; Robert William "Bob" Neel; Julia Anderson Neel (James Monroe Neel's wife); and Joseph Francis Neel. (SEATED IN CHAIRS, L-R): Joseph Norris Neel (eldest son of James Monroe holding baby Gladys); Gladys Neel; Roland Hall Neel; Susan Gaines Anderson (O.D. Anderson's wife); Oliver Davis (O.D.) Anderson; James Monroe Neel; and Joseph Lockhart Neel (far right). (SEATED ON THE GROUND): Frederick Donald Neel; Blanche Neel; and Isabelle Neel (Jackson) (beside pillow). Some quarters maintain the gentleman seated in the center [identified as Oliver Davis (O.D.) Anderson] and the female seated on his right are in fact Joseph Lockhart Neel and Leonora "Aunt Nora" Neel, with O.D. Anderson seated instead on James Monroe Neel's left.

genealogical notes by Jule Brooke which she transcribed from conversations sometime in the mid-1900s with James' three daughters – Ella ("Aunt Neely"), Juliet ("Aunt Dootz"), and Isabelle ("Izzie") – James and Julia Margaret were married *"in the Hedden's home on Bartow Street"* in Cartersville. More children were born into the family from Julia Margaret. Bob was born in 1890, Isabelle in 1894, and Fred in 1898.

Life on South Avenue

As his law practice prospered and family grew, James knew that a larger home would be necessary, so he contracted with a builder for the construction of a substantial residence on South Avenue (present-day 119 South Avenue) in Cartersville. This fine structure was within easy walking distance of James' law offices downtown, and still stands today. It has been said that James' wife, Julia Margaret, could always tell in later years when James was homeward bound as she could hear his walking cane tapping on the sidewalk as he walked up South Avenue.

On one side of the large Neel home stood another home where the Foute family lived. Julia Margaret's other sister, Laura Anderson, had married Augustus Marcellus Foute who was a cousin. Augustus had lost an arm in the war, but he never allowed this handicap to slow him in the least. He and Laura produced four children: Augustus, Jr.; Anna; Julia; and Mary.

On the other side of the Neel home (toward rear?) stood the final abode of Captain Neel where he, his wife, Mary; his daughter, Leonora ("Aunt Nora"); and Oliver Neel lived. As indicated earlier, Oliver was the third child of James Monroe and his first wife, Anna, and was raised by Aunt Nora.

Two magnolia trees which ultimately grew to a substantial height were planted in the front yard of the 119 South Avenue home. This yard also contained pink oleander, parina, double violets, tulips, white ferns or asparagus, and a 3 to 4-foot lemon tree that reportedly produced delicious fruit "as large as oranges."

To the rear of the home was a large field for the family cow. The Neel sisters vividly remembered one occasion when they were sent hunting for the cow – which had "escaped" on a rainy day – and their irritation with Grandpa Neel at sending them off to fetch the wayward beast.

The smokehouse where corn shucks were burned to smoke sides of bacon, hams, and sausage, was located to the rear of the home. The hogs were kept in a pen nearby. The barn to the rear of the home was the domain of "Plugola," an aged, dark-coated horse once used to pull the wagon which provided transportation in earlier days.

In the 1920s, mischievous grandchildren – who were constantly exploring the grounds – chanced upon a keg of whiskey which had been secreted away in the barn. It was a discovery which became a part of the family lore in those days of "abstinence," particularly in a community which sported the likes of nationally-famous and fiery evangelist Sam Jones who lived just a few blocks away in his elegant mansion.

The big Neel home was the center of much activity over the years with the advent of all the children and grandchildren and cousins. The home had shutters on the windows, but no screens except in the dining room. A large sofa in the living room was remembered as being "hard," and due to its lack of use, the hounds were allowed to sleep on it. Upstairs there were double-beds in every room for the many children who lived, laughed, loved, and played throughout this happy domain until they reached the age to go out into the world on their own.

The children were all devout Baptists, just as were their parents, and were regulars in the nearby Baptist Church. Judge Neel was a member and a deacon there for many years, but the elder Captain Neel strangely did not attend church. He often explained that he had decided to abstain from church services ever since the day he had fallen into a deep ditch alongside one of the dark streets while walking home after attending a prayer meeting one night. He always claimed he was shocked to still be alive, and insisted it was a "sign" that he should avoid church from that point forward.

Community Service

In 1892, James, just like his father before him, ran for and was elected to the Georgia State Legislature. During the 1893 session, he wrote and introduced the *Neel Pleading Act* which was passed into law (Acts of 1893, page 56) in Georgia. It regulated the pleading procedure in civil actions in Georgia courts, and is still in use in the courts today (as of this writing, 2023).

By 1907, James Monroe Neel was recognized as one of the foremost legal minds in the state. He was appointed by Governor McDaniel in 1885 as the first judge of the City Court of Cartersville. A retiring and modest man in public, James, according to records, was masterful in the courtroom and highly respected as a legal force who was always supremely-prepared when trying a case.

James' counsel eventually was widely sought throughout the state, and indeed, in some corners nationally. His clients were many and varied, and included the Seaboard Airline Railway, the North

Neel, Joseph Lockhart – Photographed circa 1865-1870. The awkward appearance of Joseph in this print is due to the fact that he is displaying his hand to show where several of his fingers were severed in wounds suffered in battle. The dark appearance (instead of the traditional butternut or Confederate gray) of his heavy uniform coat may be due simply to the inaccurate color tone of the photo. *(See the Neel Family History for a more detailed description of Joseph's Civil War record and experiences.)*

Carolina and St. Louis Railway ("N.C. & St. L."), the Louisville and Nashville Railroad ("L. & N."), the First National Bank of Cartersville, the American Textile Company, and many others.

The year 1909 must have been a difficult one for James. Oliver Davis ("O. D.") Anderson (Julia Margaret's and Anna's father who was 85 years of age) fell off the porch of the Neel home on January 25th, and died three days later. Captain Neel – who had weathered many a storm, not the least of which was his service through almost four years of deadly combat in the Civil War – died in March of that year at the age of 83, in his home next to James' home.

As is the case ultimately with all men, James Monroe Neel eventually reached the age at which he was forced to retire, and his tapping cane was no longer heard on South Avenue. His legal practice was carried on by two of his sons – James Monroe Neel Jr. ("Syl") and Fred – and by a grandson, James Monroe Neel III. Descendants of the family still practice law under the Neel banner in Cartersville even today.

The 1883-1884 Cartersville City Directory states as follows: *"J.M. Neel – attorney at law. Judge Neel is one of the most talented lawyers of north Georgia. He is a native of Bartow, was raised in Adairsville, and studied Blackstone in Calhoun, being admitted to practice in 1874. He has since built up a large clientage among the leading people of this and adjoining counties. He has a neat and comfortable office to the north of the hotel on the public square. In his two years' service as City Judge he has shown fine judgement and profound knowledge of law. He is a member of the State Bar Association and is one of the energetic citizens of Cartersville."*

(Joseph Lockhart Neel is the great-great-grandfather of the children of the late Ralph Olin Jackson, Jr. and the late Marilyn Jordan Jackson formerly of Rockmart, Georgia, as well as many other branches of the family, including the McClatchey, Brooke, and Aldred families to name just a few.)

Neel Genealogical Line
(Ancestry of One Neel Family Line in Georgia)
(Country of Origin of Neel Family Line: Ireland)

The name "Neel" an identity of long-standing in Ireland, reportedly was brought to England in the great wave of migration following the Norman Conquest of 1066. The Neel family domiciled, among other spots, in Berkshire where Willelmus *filius* Nigelli was listed in the Domesday Book of 1086. The name was carried to Iceland by Scandinavians as Njáll, taken to Norway, then back to France before being brought to England by the Normans. It was also introduced into northwestern England and Yorkshire, interestingly, by Norwegians – from *Ireland*

Great-great-great-great-great-grandfather: Samuel Neel

b.   ?
m.   ? Issue: David
d.   ?

Great-great-great-great-grandfather: David Neel

b.   circa 1774, Colleton, SC
m.   Florilla Hawthorn (b. 1781, South Carolina). Issue: **James Hawthorn**, Finis E., Sally and Laura
d.   Alabama

> **Note #1:**   In 1798, David Neel was issued a land grant in Elbert County, Georgia. David's father-in-law, James Hawthorn, was from Monaghan Co., Ireland. James purchased land in Elbert County in 1792. He was married to Florilla "Flora" Cameron, and died circa 1826.

Great-great-great-grandfather: James Hawthorn Neel

b.   03/25/1797 in Elbert County, GA
m.   1817 in Morgan County, GA to Nancy Morrow (b. 07/19/1797, Mecklenberg, N.C., d. 02/04/1877, Gordon Co., GA). Issue: [David Washington (b. 10/12/1817); Florah Hawthorn (b. 10/23/1821); William M. (b. 06/22/1823); **Joseph Lockhart**; Elizabeth Emerline (b. 12/28/1828, Alabama); James Monroe (b. 10/01/1831, Alabama); and Mary (b. 10/12/1834)
d.   08/16/1872, Gordon Co., GA

Great-great-Grandfather: Joseph Lockhart Neel

b.   9/22/1826, Jefferson Co., Alabama
m.   11/02/1848, Bartow Co., GA to Mary Ann Swain (b. 03/07/1824, Anderson, SC, d. 09/27/1901, Cartersville, Bartow Co., GA). Issue: **James Monroe**, Sarah Elizabeth (b. 3 June 1851, Cassville, GA, d. 21 December 1855); Leonora (b. 16 Sept 1853, Cassville, GA, d. 19 June 1935, GA), Joseph Norris (b. 14 Nov 1857, GA, d. 11 Nov 1950, GA); and William Jesse (b. 15 Feb 1860, GA, d. 24 March 1908, GA)d.03/09/1909, Cartersville, Bartow Co., GA.

> **Note#2:**   In1862, "Capt." Neel organized at Adairsville a company of volunteers for service in the Confederate Army as part of Company H, 40th Georgia Infantry Regiment commanded by Col. Abda Johnson. Capt. Neel first saw service in the Kentucky Campaign under General Braxton Bragg, and later was in the siege of Vicksburg. He also was with the Army of Tennessee in all the battles of the Georgia Campaign, including hard fighting at Resaca, New Hope, Kennesaw Mountain, and in the Battle of Atlanta. He saw later action at Franklin and Nashville, and finally at Bentonville, North Carolina where he witnessed the conclusion of the war. According to the official Muster Roll of Company H, 40th Regiment, GA Volunteer Infantry, Army of Tennessee, Capt. Joseph Lockhart Neel was wounded at Vicksburg, Mississippi on July 4, 1863, in Atlanta, GA (during the Battle of Atlanta) on July 22, 1864, and at Bentonville, NC, on March 19, 1865. He was listed in the Greensboro, NC hospital on April 26, 1865, and paroled at Charlotte, NC, May 6, 1865.

d.   03/1909, Cartersville, Bartow Co., GA. Buried: Cartersville

Great-Grandfather: James Monroe Neel

b.   01/22/1850, Adairsville, Bartow Co., GA
m.   1st   1875 in Bartow Co., GA, to Anna Anderson (b. 1850, d. 1881). Issue: Ella Mary (b. 08/28/1877, Adairsville, Bartow Co., GA, d. 26 June 1962, Adairsville, Bartow Co.); Joseph Francis (b. 11/25/1878, Cartersville, Bartow Co., d. 17 February, 1934); and Oliver Anderson (b. 09/1881, Cartersville, Bartow Co., d. 23 Jan 1972).
     2nd   1883 (Jan. 4) in Bartow Co., GA, to Julia Margaret Anderson (Anna Anderson's sister) (b. 01/25/1856, Adairsville, Bartow, GA. d. 05/12/1909, Cartersville, Bartow Co., GA). Issue: Laurie A. (b. 22 Nov 1883, Cassville, GA, d. 28 Nov 1970); Juliet (b. 03 June 1885, Cassville, d. 06/25/1960); James Monroe, Jr. (b. 22 Feb 1887, Cassville, d. 28 Dec 1958); Robert William (b. 12 Aug 1890, Cassville, d. 31 Oct 1975); **Isabelle**; and Frederick Donald (b. 15 May 1898, Cassville, d.17 September 1959).
d.   11/30/1930, Cartersville, Bartow Co., GA. Buried Cartersville, Bartow Co., GA

Grandmother: Isabelle Neel Jackson

b.   02/25/1894, Cartersville, Bartow Co., GA
m.   02/23/1921 in Cartersville, Bartow Co., GA to Ralph Olin Jackson, (b. 10/15/1893, Cartersville, Bartow Co., GA, d. 01/01/1986, Rockmart, Polk Co., GA). Issue: Mary Ann (b. 04/20/1922, Rockmart, GA); **Ralph Olin, Jr.**; and Julia (b. 1925, Rockmart).
d.   12/04/1981, Rockmart, Polk Co., GA. Burial: cremated; ashes buried Rose Hill Cemetery, Rockmart, GA.

STATE of GEORGIA.

469

By His Excellency *James Jackson* Captain-General, Governor, and Commander in Chief in and over the said State, and of the Militia thereof.

To all to whom these Presents shall come, GREETING:

KNOW YE, That, in pursuance of the Act for opening the Land-Office, and by virtue of the powers in me vested, I HAVE given and granted, and, by these presents, in the name and behalf of the said state, DO give and grant unto *David Neel his* heirs and assigns forever, ALL that tract or parcel of land, containing *two hundred and fifty* acres, situate, lying, and being in the county of *Elbert* in the said state, and butting and bounding *South West by unknown land North East by Vacant land South East by Borders land and North West by unknown land*

having such shape, form, and marks, as appear by a plat of the same hereunto annexed; together with all and singular the rights, members, and appurtenances thereof, whatsoever, to the said tract or parcel of land belonging, or in any wise appertaining; and also all the estate, right, title, interest, claim, and demand of the state aforesaid, of, in, to, or out of, the same: TO HAVE AND TO HOLD the said tract or parcel of land, and all and singular the premises aforesaid, with their and every of their rights, members, and appurtenances, unto the said *David Neel his* heirs and assigns, to *his* and their own proper use and behoof forever, in Fee simple.

GIVEN under my hand, and the great seal of the said state, this *Sixteenth* day of *May* in the year of our Lord one thousand seven hundred and ninety *eight*; and in the *Twenty Second* year of American Independence.

Signed by his Excellency the Governor, the } *16th* day of *May* 1798 } *Jas. Jackson*

49₇   Registered, the *17th* day of *May* 1798.

1798 LAND GRANT, ELBERT COUNTY, GEORGIA

<u>Neel, David</u> – David Neel was granted this parcel of land in Elbert County by the governor of the state of Georgia. The reason for the grant is unknown, but quite likely involved military service of some special capacity.

[handwritten marriage record]

State of Georgia / Cass County — To any minister of the Gospel, Judge of the Superior Court, Justice of the Inferior court or Justice of the Peace, you are hereby authorised to Join Joseph L Neal and Mary Ann Swain in lawful bonds of Matrimony agreeable to the Constitution and Laws of this State. Given under my hand and Seal this 23rd day of October 1848

Georgia / Cass County — J S Phillips C C O — I certify the foregoing was duly Solemnized before me this 2nd day of November eighteen hundred and forty eight — David Morrow J.P.

Recorded 18th June 1849
Jonathan S Phillips C C O

[handwritten marriage record]

State of Georgia / Cass County — To any minister of the Gospel, Judge of the Superior Court, Justice of the Inferior Court or Justice of the Peace, You are hereby authorised to Join Ezekiel J. Phillips and Mary Hilton in lawful bonds of Matrimony agreeable to the Constitution and Laws of this State. Given under my hands and Seal This 26th day of December 1848

J S Phillips C C O

Georgia / Cass County — I certify the foregoing was duly Solemnized before me this Second day of January eighteen hundred and forty nine — Nathan Howard J.P.

Recorded 26th June 1849
Jonathan S Phillips C C O

1849 MARRIAGE ROLLS, CASS COUNTY, GEORGIA

Neel, Joseph Lockhart and Swain, Mary Ann – The happy couple were joined in marriage in old Cass County – quite possibly in Cassville – in one of the churches which still stand in that now forgotten community virtually erased forever during the U.S. Civil War. Joseph Lockhart possibly had a moment to remember that blissful day as he marched back through Cassville some fifteen years later while defending the state against the advance forces of Union Gen. William Sherman.

SCHEDULE I.—Free Inhabitants in *District* 40 in the County of *St Clair* State of *Alabama* enumerated by me, on the *14th* day of *November* 1850. *Aby Wolley* Ass't Marshal.

		The Name of every Person whose usual place of abode on the first day of June, 1850, was in this family.	Age	Sex	Color	Profession, Occupation, or Trade of each Male Person over 15 years of age.	Value of Real Estate owned.	Place of Birth, Naming the State, Territory, or Country.				Whether deaf and dumb, blind, insane, idiotic, pauper, or convict.	
1	2	3	4	5	6	7	8	9	10	11	12	13	
		Rimer Williams	44	F				S. Carolina	1		1		1
		Emeline P "	10	F				Ala					2
97	97	*Spencer Hurd*	40	M		Farmer	210	N Carolina	1				3
		Catharine "	36	F				"					4
		Sarah "	17	F				"					5
		Nancy "	15	F				"					6
		Thomas "	6	M				"					7
		Sidney "	4	M				Ala					8
		James "	3	M				"					9
		John "	2/12	M									10
98	98	*John P Herring*	39	M		Farmer	1600	S Carolina	1				11
		Hester "	40	F				Tennessee	1		1		12
		Johnathan Williams	20	M		"		N Carolina	1				13
		James F McLaughlin	20	M		"		Ala					14
		Catharine Strange	19	F				"					15
99	99	*James H Neal*	53	M		Farmer	750	Georgia	1				16
		Nancy "	52	F				"					17
		Elizabeth E "	21	F				Ala					18
		James M "	17	M		"		"					19
100	100	*Mitchell Mize*	37	M		Farmer		S Carolina	1				20
		Rebecca "	29	F				"					21
		Nancy "	7	F				Ala					22
		Thomas M "	6	M				"					23
		James "	3	M				"					24
		Rebecca Simpson	65	F				N Carolina	1		1		25
101	101	*Henry H Courson*	25	M		Farmer	700	Georgia	1				26
		Elizabeth J "	23	F				Ala					27
		Elizabeth "	2	F				"					28
		Sarah Ann "	1	F				"					29
102	102	*Charles P Courson*	26	M		Farmer	500	Georgia	1	1			30
		Julia "	20	F				Ala		1			31
103	103	*Hubbard H Strange*	36	M		Blacksmith		S Carolina	1				32
		Margaret "	29	F				Ala					33
		Benjamin F "	10	M				"		1	1		34
		Sarah E "	8	F				"			1		35
		Mary C "	6	F				"					36
		Joseph E "	4	M				"					37
		John Q "	2	M				"					38
		Alamath B "	2/12	M				"					39
104	104	*Amos S Posey*	27	M		Farmer	250						40
		Frances A "	27	F									41
		William A "	3	M									42

1850 FEDERAL CENSUS, DISTRICT 40, ST. CLAIR, ALABAMA

"Neal," James Hawthorn – This Census lists James H. "Neal," age 53, as head of his household farming real estate in Alabama valued at $750.00. It notes he is a native of Georgia. His household members include his wife, Nancy, age 52, and children Elizabeth E. (Emerline), age 21, and James M. (not to be confused with the James Monroe Neel of 1850-1930, son of Joseph Lockhart Neel), age 17. The other older children: David Washington, (1817); Florah Hawthorn, (1821); William M., (1823); and Joseph Lockhart (1826-1909) are not mentioned, since they were all obviously young adults well into their 20s and 30s by 1850, and already departed from the home nest. Joseph Lockhart has moved to Georgia where he lives in Gordon County.

SCHEDULE I.—Free Inhabitants in The 12th Division in the County of Gordon State of Georgia enumerated by me, on the 25th day of Nov 1850. Alex Stamp Ass't Marshal.

Dwelling-houses numbered in order of visitation	Families numbered in the order of visitation	The Name of every Person whose usual place of abode on the first day of June, 1850, was in this family.	Age	Sex	Color	Profession, Occupation, or Trade of each Male Person over 15 years of age.	Value of Real Estate owned	Place of Birth, Naming the State, Territory, or Country.	Married within the year	Attended School within the year	Persons over 20 who cannot read & write	Whether deaf and dumb, blind, insane, idiotic, pauper, or convict.	
201	202	Joseph L. Neel	24	M		Farmer	300	Ala					1
		Mary A.	25	F				S.C.					2
		James M.	½	M				Geo					3
202	203	Andrew J. Kinman	26	M				Tenn					4
		Harriet	18	F				Ala					5
		Frances	8	F				Geo					6
		James H.	4	M							1		7
203	204	Ingram Score	33	M									8
		Susan	25	F									9
		Georgia A.	6	F									10
		John W.	4	M									11
		Martha C.	3	F									12
		Robert Carter	2	M									13
204	205	Andrew J. Cooper	34	M				Geo					14
		Pamela	36	F				Ala					15
		William C.	12	M				Geo					16
		Josiah R.	10	M				Geo					17
		Elizabeth I.	3	F				Geo					18
205	206	Jesse Campbell	30	M				Ala			1		19
		Rebecca	25	F				Geo					20
		Julius	4	F				Geo					21
206	207	John S. Kennedy	21	M		Laborer		Geo					22
		Eliza	25	F				Geo					23
		Infant	5m	M				Geo					24
207	208	Alex Strickland	21	M				Geo					25
		Mary J.	20	F				Tenn					26
		Infant	½	F				Geo					27
208	209	Joseph J. Neel	30	M		Farmer	300	Ala					28
		Susanna	22	F				Ala					29
		Frances E.	4	F				Geo					30
		Obadiah	1	M				Geo					31
209	210	Jesse P. Stalling	24	M				Geo					32
		Martha	22	F				Geo					33
		George W.	2	M				Geo					34
		Joseph A.	1	M				Geo					35
		Nancy Bailey	24	F				Geo					36
210	211	James J. Mason	36	M				Ala					37
		Elizabeth	30	F									38
		Harris J.	16	M									39
		Amanda	13	F							1		40
		Jonas	8	M									41
		Sarah	6	F									42

1850 FEDERAL CENSUS, DIVISION 12, GORDON COUNTY, GEORGIA

Neel, Joseph Lockhart - Joseph Lockhart Neel, head of his household, is 24 years of age, and is now living in Georgia. He is listed as a farmer with real estate valued at $300.00. His listed place of birth is "Alabama." His household includes: his wife, Mary A., age 25 and a native of South Carolina; and his son, James M. (Monroe), not yet a year old. Joseph came first to Adairsville (ne Gordon County) in the early 1840s and was prominent in the foundation of that community. He married his wife – Mary Ann Swain – there on November 2, 1848, and, in addition to his farming endeavors, began business as a merchant. The financial outlook in the agrarian South is still very promising with the U.S. Civil War not yet on the horizon.

Page No. 17   179

SCHEDULE 1.—Free Inhabitants in _Township 16~17 & 18_ in the County of _St Clair_ State of _Alabama_ enumerated by me, on the _29th_ day of _June_ 1860. _Hubbard H. Strange_ Ass't Marshal

Post Office _Round Pond_

Dwelling-houses numbered	Families numbered	The name of every person whose usual place of abode on the first day of June, 1860, was in this family.	Age	Sex	Color	Profession, Occupation, or Trade	Value of Real Estate	Value of Personal Estate	Place of Birth	Married	School	Read/write	Whether deaf and dumb, blind, etc.	
		Margaritt Godwin	63	f		House wife			Geo					1
		Mary "	29	f		Domestic			Ala			1		2
		Margarito "	23	f		do			do					3
		Marilla "	21	f		do			do			1	1	4
		William "	19	m		Farmer			do			1		5
		Palmelia "	17	f		Domestic			do			1		6
		James Godwin	15	m		Farm labor			do			1		7
110	110	James McLaughlin	62	m		Farmer	800	600	Geo					8
		Kijiah "	60	f		House wife			do			1		9
		Louiza "	38	f		Domestic			Ala			1		10
		Marion "	24	m		Farmer			do			1		11
		John "	17	m		do			do			1		12
		Mary "	17	f		Domestic			do			1		13
111	111	James H. Neel	63	m		Farmer	800	2000	G.A.					14
		Nancy "	63	f		House wife			do					15
		Elizabeth "	31	f		Domestic			Ala					16
112	112	Thomas J. Stubbs	29	m		Farmer	2000	1093	S.C.					17
		Permelia "	28	f		House wife			do			1		18
		William "	16	m		Farmer			Ala			1		19
		Malissa "	14	f					do			1		20
		Louiza "	12	f					do			1		21
		James "	10	m					do			1		22
		Lewis "	8	m					do			1		23
		Mary "	4	f					do					24
		Joseph "	3	m					do					25
113	113	Morgan McLaughlin	28	m		Farmer		292	do					26
		Mary "	23	f		House wife			do					27
		George "	7/12	m					do					28
114	114	Robert McSwayer	26	m		Farmer		375	do					29
		Jane "	23	f		House wife			do				1	30
		Luvena "	7/12	f					do					31
115	115	Charles Maguire	32	m		Farmer		400	Ala					32
		Sarah "	26	f		House wife			N.C.					33
		Isaac "	4	m					Ala					34
		Robert "	1	m					do					35
		William "	7/12	m					do					36
116	116	Ann Phelps	49	f		Farmer	500	278	S.C.				1	37
		Jane "	32	f		Domestic			do			1	1	38
		William "	19	m		Farmer			do			1		39
		Abija "	8	m					Ala					40

No. white males, 20   No. colored males, ___   No. foreign born, ___   No. blind, ___   4100   5238   No. idiotic, ___   No. convicts, ___

No. white females, 20   No. colored females, ___   No. deaf and dumb, ___   No. insane, ___   No. paupers, ___

1860 FEDERAL CENSUS, ROUND POND, ST. CLAIR COUNTY, ALABAMA

Neel, James Hawthorn – James, now age 63, continues to reside in Alabama where he is still the head of his household. He is listed as a "Farmer," with real estate valued at $800.00 and personal property valued at $2,000.00. He again lists his place of birth as "Georgia" (Elbert County). Also listed in his household are his wife, Nancy, age 63; and daughter, Elizabeth, age 31, identified as a "domestic."

Page No. 78

SCHEDULE 1.—Inhabitants in *Subdivision No 144* , in the County of *Bartow* , State of *Georgia* , enumerated by me on the *17* day of *August* 1870.

Post Office: *Adairsville*

Francis M. Walker, Ass't Marshal.

1	2	3 The name of every person whose place of abode on the first day of June, 1870, was in this family.	4	5	6	7 Profession, Occupation, or Trade of each person, male or female.	8	9	10 Place of Birth	11	12	13	14	15	16	17	18	19	20
1		Rudd Sefronia	9	F	W				Ga										
2		Mary	2	F	W				Ga										
3	604 604	Bruce James	24	M	W	Farm Labor			Ga					1					
4		Missnar	23	F	W	Keeping house			Ga										
5		James A	2	M	W				Ga										
6	605 605	Compton Wilson	20	M	W	Farm Laborer		100	Ga					1					
7		Rebecca	54	F	W	Keeping house			N.C.										
8		Reed Elizabeth	29	F	W	Keeping house			Ga										
9		Sarah	10	F	W	at home			Ga										
10		Susan	9	F	W				Ga										
11	606 606	Willie Francis	25	M	W	R.R. Sec hand			Ga									1	
12		Louisa C	21	F	W	Keeping house			Ga										
13	607 607	Neel James He	74	M	W	Retired Farmer		300	Ga									1	
14		Nancy	72	F	W	Keeping house			Ga										
15		Emiline	39	F	W	Asst Keeping house			Ala										
16		Fannie	65	F	B	house servant			Va					1	1	b			
17	608 607	Bradford David H	45	M	W	Farmer	1200	700	S.C.									1	
18		Sarah E	37	F	W	Keeping house			Ga										
19		Mary M	17	F	W	at home			Ga										
20		Martha A	15	F	W				Ga						1				
21		Samuel	13	M	W				Ga						1				
22		Sarah E	11	F	W	at home			Ga						1				
23		Lola C	9	F	W				Ga						1				
24		Charles M	6	M	W				Ga										
25		George D	3	M	W				Ga										
26	609 609	Johnson Thomas	39	M	W	Ret Grocer	1000	800	N.C.									1	
27		Eliza J	31	F	W	Keeping house			Ga										
28		Eugenia b	18	F	W	at home			Ga										
29		Edma b	11	F	W	"			Ga										
30		Eulalie	4	F	W				Ga										
31	610 610	Strawn William J	30	M	W	R.R. Sec Boss	300	300	Ga									1	
32		Elizabeth	38	F	W	Keeping house			Ga										
33		Isabella	15	F	W	at home			Ga										
34		Luella	13	F	W	"			Ga										
35	611 611	Mansing George	33	M	W	Boot & Shoe Maker	175	700	Ga									1	
36		Francis A	30	F	W	Keeping house			Ga										
37		Robert	11	M	W				Ga						1				
38		Laura	10	F	W				Ga						1				
39		Charlie	8	M	W				Ga										
40		Lela	6	F	W				Ga										

1870 FEDERAL CENSUS, ADAIRSVILLE, BARTOW COUNTY, GEORGIA

Neel, James Hawthorn – Now listed as 74 years of age and with the economy of the South devastated by the U.S. Civil War, James has moved from Alabama to Georgia near to his son, Joseph Lockhart – quite likely for survival purposes – and lists his profession as "retired farmer." Despite the dire circumstances of 1870, James, nevertheless lists the value of his personal assets at $300.00, which would be equivalent to the purchasing power of approximately $6,784.00 in 2023 dollars. This represented a substantial nest-egg, so though he was elderly and without visible means of support, he was not destitute. Also listed here in James's household are his wife, Nancy, 72; Emerline, age 38, *"keeping house"*; and Fannie, age 65, a blind servant.

Page No. 71

Inquiries numbered 3, 16, and 17 are not to be asked in respect to infants. Inquiries numbered 11, 12, 15, 16, 17, 19, and 20 are to be answered merely by an affirmative mark, as /.

SCHEDULE 1.—Inhabitants in *Subdivision No 144*, in the County of *Bartow* , State of *Georgia*, enumerated by me on the *16* day of *August*, 1870.

535

Post Office: *Adairsville*

Francis M Walker, Ass't Marshal.

		The name of every person whose place of abode on the first day of June, 1870, was in this family.	Age	Sex	Color	Profession, Occupation, or Trade of each person, male or female.	Value of Real Estate	Value of Personal Estate	Place of Birth	Father of foreign birth	Mother of foreign birth	If born within the year	If married within the year	Attended school within the year	Cannot read	Cannot write	Whether deaf and dumb, blind, insane, or idiotic	19	20	
1		Hibberts Ellen	17	F	W	at home			Ga											1
2		— Thomas	10	M	W	at home			Ga											2
3	538 538	Ayar Joel W	34	M	W	Dry goods & grocs merchant ret	4000	830	Ga									1		3
4	539 539	Neel Joseph L	43	M	W	Farmer	1500	1500	Ala									1		4
5		— Mary A	45	F	W	keeping house			S.C											5
6		— James	20	M	W	at School			Ga					1						6
7		— Lenora	17	F	W	at home			Ga											7
8		— Joseph N	13	M	W	clerk in Ret dy			Ga											8
9		— William J	10	M	W	at home			Ga											9
10	540 540	Rush Lane	29	M	M	Shoe Maker	150	100	Ga						1	b		1		10
11		— Louvena	20	F	M	keeping house			Ga							b				11
12		Runnels Jack	25	M	B	farm laborer			S.C						1	1	B	1		12
13	541 541	Borden Joseph P	41	M	W	Clerk in Ret dry	1500	500	Ga									1		13
14		— Elizabeth L	39	F	W	keeping house			Ga											14
15		— Leyhedia L	18	F	W	at home			Ga											15
16		— Joseph P	4	M	W				Ga											16
17	542 542	Biddy John	60	M	W	Farmer	1500	2000	S.C						1	b		1		17
18		— Elijah	20	M	W	farm laborer			Ga						1	b				18
19		McCane John	9	M	W				Ga											19
20	543 543	Mann John L	68	M	W	Farmer	1000	500	Ga									1		20
21		— Catherine	66	F	W	keeping house			N.C											21
22		— Sallie A	38	F	W	at home			Ga											22
23		— Calvin	20	M	W	farm laborer			Ga											23
24	544 544	Johnson John J	47	M	W	Farmer	1200	400	S.C									1		24
25		— Mary	29	F	W	keeping house			Ga											25
26		— Martha J	13	F	W	at home			Ga											26
27		— Henry W	9	M	W				Ga			c								27
28		— Lula	5	F	W				Ga											28
29		— Robert Lee	4	M	W				Ga											29
30	545 545	Anderson Oliver P	45	M	W	Mcht Ret dy goods	4000	2725	Tenn									1		30
31		— Amelia	44	F	W	keeping house			S.C											31
32		— Leaura J	22	F	W	at home			Ga											32
33		— James	21	M	W	asst clerk Ret dy g			Ga									1		33
34		— Annah M	18	F	W	at home			Ga											34
35		— Julia	13	F	W	at home			Ga											35
36		— Frank	4	M	W				Ga											36
37		Hodges Francis M	29	M	W				Ga								Blind	1		37
38	546 546	Gray John W	41	M	W	Mcht Ret dy good	4000	5000	Ga											38
39		— Sarah A	37	F	W	keeping house			Ga											39
40		— Frank P	16	M	W	at School			Ga											40

No. of dwellings, ____ No. of white females, ____ No. of males, foreign born, ____ 18,850 13,075 No. of insane, ____
" " families, ____ " " colored males, ____ " " females, " ____ ____
" " white males, ____ " " females, ____ " " blind, ____

1870 FEDERAL CENSUS, ADAIRSVILLE, BARTOW COUNTY, GEORGIA

Neel, Joseph Lockhart – At age 43, Joseph, still the head of his household, lists his profession as *"farmer,"* and the value of his real estate as *$1,500.00* and his personal property as $1,500.00. Despite the desperate lawless times – which were severe in the Deep South from 1865-1880 – Joseph Neel appears to have prospered. In 1870, $3,000.00 was equivalent to the purchasing power of approximately $67,830.00 in 2023 dollars. Also listed in Joseph's household are: his wife, Mary, age 45, *"keeping house"*; James, age 20, *"away at school"* (at the University of Kentucky); Lenora, age 17; Joseph N. (Norris), 13, employed as a *"clerk in ret. dry gds"* (clerk in retail dry goods); and William J. (Jesse), 10, *"at home."*

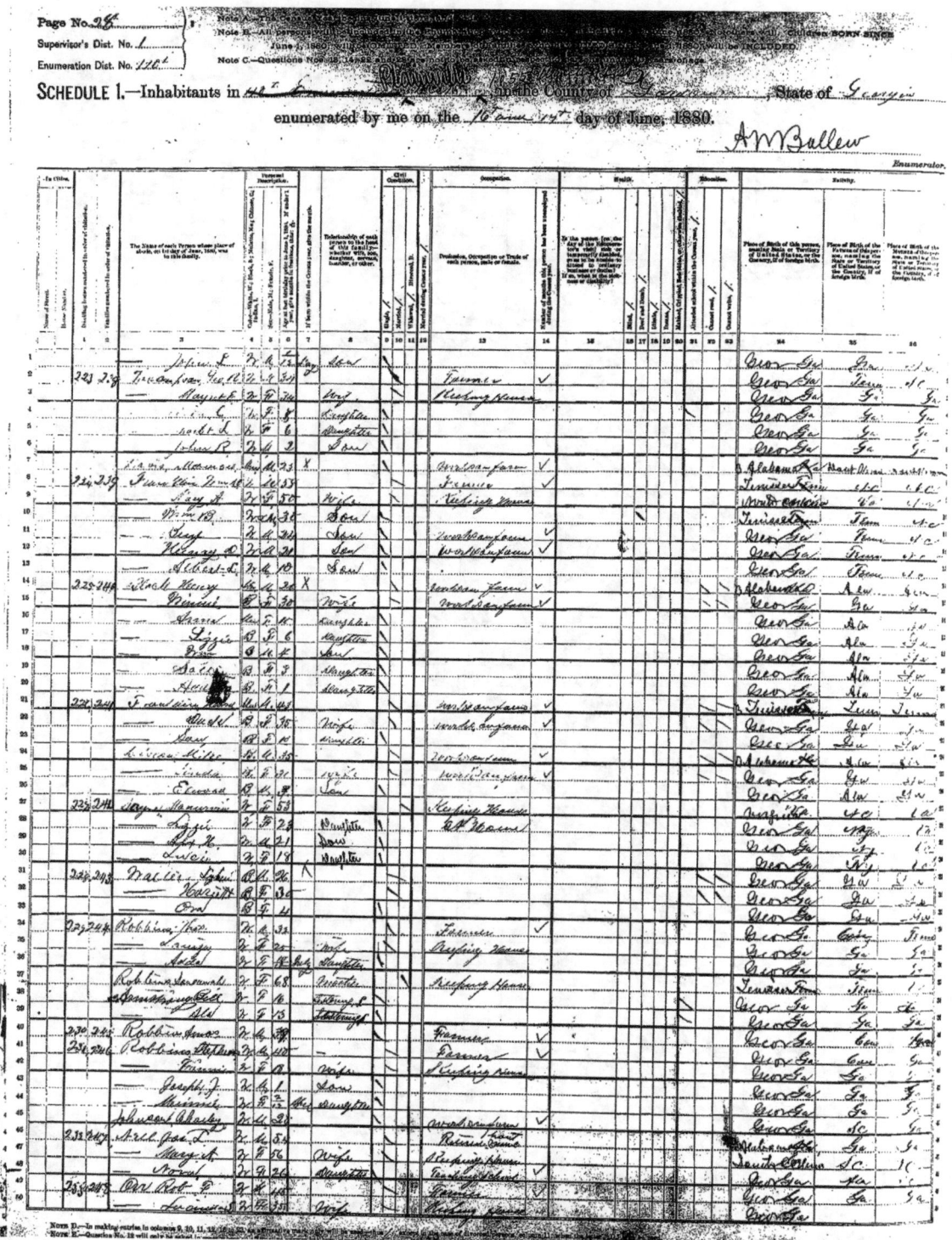

1880 FEDERAL CENSUS, PLAINVILLE, GORDON COUNTY, GEORGIA

Neel, Joseph Lockhart – Joseph is now 54 years of age and listed as "retired." His spinster daughter, Nora, age 26, yet lives with him, as does his wife, Mary Ann (Swain), age 56. Nora is listed as "teaching school." Mary Ann is listed as "keeping house." Joseph's address here in Gordon County obviously preceded his eventual move to "Neel Street" in Cartersville behind his son, James Monroe's home on South Avenue.

7—224.

TWELFTH CENSUS OF THE UNITED STATES.　　　B

SCHEDULE No. 1.—POPULATION.

| Supervisor's District No. | 7 | Sheet No. |
| Enumeration District No. | 5 | 2 |

State _Georgia_
County _Bartow_

Township or other division of county _822d District Coosalitie_　Name of Institution, _____

Name of incorporated city, town, or village, within the above-named division, _Cartersville_　Ward of city, _3d_

Enumerated by me on the _4th_ day of June, 1900. _William R. Mountcastle_, Enumerator.

1900 FEDERAL CENSUS, DISTRICT 822, CARTERSVILLE, BARTOW COUNTY, GEORGIA

Neel, James Monroe – Now age 50, James is listed as the head of his household at the large home which he had contracted for construction on South Avenue in Cartersville (which still stands as of this writing in 2023). Also listed in his household are: his wife, Julia Margaret, age 43 [whom James had married in 1883 following the heart-breaking death of his first wife, Anna (Julia's sister) in 1881]; Ella M., 23; Joseph F., 21; Laurie A., 16; Juliette, 14; James M., 13; Robert W., 9; and Isa, 6; and Frederick, 2.

Neel, Joseph Lockhart – Also listed separately in this same 1900 Federal Census for District 822, Cartersville, Joseph is now 73 years of age, but is still listed as the head of his household. He now lives on Neel Street, in a small home to the rear of James's larger Neel home on South Avenue. Listed with him in this Neel Street home are: his wife, Mary, 76; his unmarried daughter, Leonora, age 46 (known in the family as "Aunt Nora"); and Oliver A., the third and invalid child of James Monroe and wife Anna who was lovingly raised by Aunt Nora. Nine years from this date, Joseph Lockhart will be gone.

17

STATE Georgia
COUNTY Bartow
TOWNSHIP OR OTHER DIVISION OF COUNTY Cartersville No. 822 Militia District

DEPARTMENT OF COMMERCE AND ...
THIRTEENTH CENSUS OF THE UNI...
NAME OF INCORPORATED ...

NAME OF INSTITUTION _____

	LOCATION			NAME	RELATION	PERSONAL DESCRIPTION								NATIVITY	
						Sex	Color	Age	Marital					Place of birth of this Person	Place of Birth of Father
1	2	190	147	Attaway Lutie	Head	F	W	49	M1			1	1	Georgia	Georgia
2				Augustine W.	Son	M	W	15	S					Georgia	Arkansas
3				Ashland Eula	Sister	F	W	42	S					Georgia	Georgia
4	6	142	198	Neese Wiley	Head	M	B	58	M2 23					South Carolina	South Carolina
5				Hattie	Wife	F	B	38	M2 23			2	2	Georgia	United States
6	10	193	199	Shepherd Robert	Head	M	B	23	M1 4					Georgia	Georgia
7				Curtis	Wife	F	Mu	22	M1 4			4	0	Alabama	Alabama
8				Harris Hubbard	Brother in law	M	B	20	M1 0					Alabama	Alabama
9				Annie M.	Sister in law	F	B	20	M1 0			0	0	Tennessee	Tennessee
10	100	194	200	Guyton David J.	Head	M	W	69	M1 47					Georgia	South Carolina
11				Rebecca J.	Wife	F	W	67	M1 41			1	1	South Carolina	South Carolina
12	104	195	201	Bartlett Ernest C.	Head	M	W	31	M1 4					Tennessee	Tennessee
13				Ida M.	Wife	F	W	30	M1 4			0	0	Tennessee	Tennessee
14	111	196	202	Griffin Clark H.	Head	M	W	30	M1 6					Georgia	Georgia
15				Ora B.	Wife	F	W	32	M1 6			2	2	Georgia	Virginia
16				James H.	Son	M	W	4	S					Georgia	Georgia
17				Margear E.	Daughter	F	W	2	S					Georgia	Georgia
18	307	197	203	Neel James M.	Head	M	W	60	Wd					Georgia	United States
19				Ella	Daughter	F	W	30	S					Georgia	Georgia
20				Juliet	Daughter	F	W	24	S					Georgia	Georgia
21				James M.	Son	M	W	22	S					Georgia	Georgia
22				Robert N.	Son	M	W	19	S					Georgia	Georgia
23				Ira	Daughter	F	W	16	S					Georgia	Georgia
24				Frederick	Son	M	W	11	S					Georgia	Georgia
25	9	198	204	Smith Norilla	Head	F	Mu	28	S			2	1	Georgia	Alabama
26				Albert	Son	M	Mu	14	S					Georgia	Georgia
27				Gottheigh Jean	Boarder	M	B	13						Georgia	Georgia
28			205	White Hattie	Head	F	B	48	Wd			4	1	North Carolina	United States
29	10	199	206	Washington Hettie	Head	F	B	26	M1 2			1	1	Georgia	Georgia
30				Clifford	Son	M	B	7	S					Georgia	Georgia
31	414	240	247	Allison Jacob S.	Head	M	W	39	M2 7					Georgia	North Carolina
32				Minnie	Wife	F	W	57	M2 7			1	1	Georgia	Georgia
33				Mashell S.	Son	M	W	2	S					Georgia	Georgia
34				Sarah	Mother	F	W	82	Wd			7	6	North Carolina	North Carolina
35				Paralee	Sister	F	W	43	S					Georgia	North Carolina
36	420	201	248	Tikkle John E.	Head	M	W	42	S					Georgia	United States
37	379	242	249	Moore Charlie	Head	M	B	37	M1 15					Georgia	United States
38				Loretta	Wife	F	Mu	30	M1 15			3	3	Georgia	South Carolina
39				Frank	Son	M	B	13	S					Georgia	Georgia
40				Percy	Son	M	B	9	S					Georgia	Georgia
41				Laura	Daughter	F	Mu	6	S					Georgia	Georgia
42				Franklin Allen	Brother in law	M	Mu	25	S					Georgia	South Carolina
43				Jim	Brother in law	M	Mu	19	S					Georgia	South Carolina
44	327	203	250	Hilburn John C.	Head	M	W	61	M1 43					Georgia	South Carolina
45				Mercy C.	Wife	F	W	54	M1 43			12	8	Alabama	Alabama
46				Paul	Son	M	W	18	S					Georgia	Georgia
47				Lela	Daughter	F	W	14	S					Georgia	Georgia
48	321	204	251	Prince James K.	Head	M	W	43	M1 21					Georgia	Georgia
49				Mary E.	Wife	F	W	40	M1 21			6	2	Georgia	United States
50				Fred P.	Son	M	W	18	S					Georgia	Georgia

1910 FEDERAL CENSUS, CARTERSVILLE, BARTOW COUNTY, GEORGIA

Neel, James Monroe – In a testament to the hard times being experienced – with harder times yet to come – six of the Neel children are still living at the big Neel home on South Avenue in Cartersville. James, now 60 years of age, has out-lived both his wives, his second – Julia Margaret Anderson – passing away in 1909, barely two months after the death of James's father – Joseph Lockhart Neel.

LABOR—BUREAU OF THE CENSUS   95   SUPERVISOR'S DISTRICT NO. _1_   SHEET NO. _10_ A

TED STATES: 1910—POPULATION   ENUMERATION DISTRICT NO. _5_

PLACE _Cartersville City (part of)_   WARD OF CITY _3_

ENUMERATED BY ME ON THE _22_ DAY OF _April_ 1910.   _Emory H Gilreath_ ENUMERATOR.

Place of Birth of Mother of this person.	True or naturalized	Whether able to speak English; or, if not, give language spoken.	Trade or profession of, or particular kind of work done by this person	General nature of industry, business, or establishment in which this person works	Whether employer, or working on own account	If an employer	Number of weeks out of work during 1910	Attend school	Able to read	Able to write	Owned or rented	Free or mortgaged	Farm or house	Number of farm schedule		
Georgia		English	Librarian	Public Library	W	no	0	Yes	Yes		O	F	H			1
Georgia		English	None					Yes	Yes	Yes						2
Georgia		English	None					Yes	Yes							3
South Carolina		English	Laborer	General Farm	W	no	O	No	No		R		H			4
United States		English	Washerwoman	At Home	O A			Yes	Yes							5
Georgia		English	Laborer	Ware House	W	no	O	Yes	Yes		R	4 15 5	2 X			6
Alabama		English	Washerwoman	At Home	O			Yes	Yes							7
Alabama		English	Miner	Ochre Mine	W	no	O	Yes	Yes			7 8 0 6				8
Tennessee		English	Dressmaker	At Home	O A			Yes	Yes							9
South Carolina		English	Own Income					Yes	Yes		O	F	H			10
South Carolina		English	None					Yes	Yes							11
Tennessee		English	Cd Cashier	Iron Railroad Office	W	no	O	Yes	Yes		R	H 10 6 X 5				12
Tennessee		English	None					Yes	Yes							13
Georgia		English	Dentist	General Practice	O A			Yes	Yes		O	F	H			14
South Carolina		English	None					Yes	Yes							15
Georgia			None													16
Georgia			None								O	F	H			17
United States		English	Lawyer	Gen. Practice	O A			Yes	Yes							18
Georgia		English	Music Teacher	At Home	O A			Yes	Yes			7 0 6 X				19
Georgia		English	None					Yes	Yes							20
Georgia		English	Lawyer	General Practice	O A			Yes	Yes							21
Georgia		English	None					Yes	Yes	Yes						22
Georgia		English	None					Yes	Yes	Yes						23
Georgia		English	None					Yes	Yes	Yes						24
Alabama		English	None					No	No		R		H			25
Georgia		English	Laborer	Odd Jobs	W	no	O	No	No	No		15 5 9 8				26
United States		English	Delivery Boy	Grocery Store	W	no	O	No	No	No		14 3 3 X				27
United States		English	Washerwoman	At Home	O A			No	No		R		H			28
Georgia		English	Cook	Private Family	W	no	O	Yes	Yes				H			29
Georgia			None							Yes						30
North Carolina		English	Farmer	Gen. Farm	O A			No	No		R	F 5				31
Georgia		English	None					Yes	Yes							32
Georgia			None													33
North Carolina		English	None					Yes	Yes							34
North Carolina		English	None					Yes	Yes							35
South Carolina		English	Superintendent	Electric Light Plant	W	no	O	Yes	Yes		R	4 10 2 0 4				36
United States		English	None					No	No		R		H			37
Georgia		English	Washerwoman	At Home	O A			No	No							38
Georgia		English	Laborer	Gen. Farm	W	no	O									39
Georgia			None							No						40
Georgia			None							No						41
Georgia		English	Laborer	Ore Mine	W	no	O	Yes	Yes			15 5 0 4				42
Georgia		English	Laborer	Odd Jobs	W	no	O	No	No	No		15 5 9 8				43
Georgia		English	Contractor	Houses	Emp			Yes	Yes		R	H 4 0 9 8				44
Alabama		English	None					Yes	Yes							45
Alabama		English	Carpenter	House	W	no	5	Yes	Yes	No						46
Alabama		English	None					Yes	Yes	No						47
Georgia		English	None					No	No		R		H			48
United States		English	None					No	No							49
Georgia		English	Laborer	Planing Mill	W	no	O	No	No	No						50

Right portion of document on facing page

STATE *Georgia*

COUNTY *Bartow*

9—137

DEPARTMENT OF COMMERCE—

FOURTEENTH CENSUS OF THE UNIT

TOWNSHIP OR OTHER DIVISION OF COUNTY: *Cartersville*

NAME OF INCORPORA

NAME OF INSTITUTION

ENUM

	PLACE OF ABODE.			NAME	RELATION.	TENURE		PERSONAL DESCRIPTION				CITIZENSHIP.			EDUCATION.			Place of birth of each person
1	301	25	27	Story, Ann Mrs	Head	R		F	W	64	Wd				yes	yes	Tennessee
2	307	24	28	Neel, James M.	Head	O	F	M	W	69	Wd				yes	yes	Georgia
3				— Nora	Sister			F	W	53	S				yes	yes	Georgia
4				— Ella	Daughter			F	W	38	S				yes	yes	Georgia
5				— Isabel	Daughter			F	W	24	S				yes	yes	Georgia
6	321	27	29	Chitwood, Daniel B.	Head	R		M	W	67	M				yes	yes	Georgia
7				— Melissa	Wife			F	W	65	M				yes	yes	Georgia
8				— Carl	Son			M	W	80	S				yes	yes	Georgia
9	419	28	30	Rogers, William C.	Head	R		M	W	41	M				yes	yes	Georgia
10				— Susan	Wife			F	W	37	M				yes	yes	Georgia
11				— Pearl	Daughter			F	W	22	S				yes	yes	Georgia
12				— Sam	Son			M	W	16	S			no	yes	yes	Georgia
13				— Gudson	Daughter			F	W	11	S				yes	yes	Georgia
14				— Griffin	Son			M	W	9	S				yes	yes	Georgia
15				— Lula Bell	Daughter			F	W	6	S			yes	yes		Georgia
16				— J Cy	Son			M	W	4½	S				no	no	Georgia
17				— Wilson	Son			M	W	1½	S				no	no	Georgia
18				— L. A.	Father			M	W	70	Wd				yes	yes	Georgia
19				Pruitt, Paul	Brother-in-law			M	W	25	S				yes	yes	Georgia
20	428	29	31	Chambers, Fulton	Head	R		M	B	30	M				yes	yes	Georgia
21				— Eva	Wife			F	B	24	M				no	no	Georgia
22				— Australia	Daughter			F	B	10	S			yes	yes	yes	Georgia
23				— Jessie	Daughter			F	B	8	S			yes	yes	yes	Georgia
24				— Lottie	Daughter			F	B	7	S			yes	yes	yes	Georgia
25				— Pauline	Daughter			F	B	5	S			no	no	no	Georgia
26				— Mattie	Daughter			F	B	4½	S				no	no	Georgia
27				— John Willie	Son			M	B	1½	S				no	no	Georgia
28	216	30	32	Rogan, John R.	Head	O	F	M	W	50	M				yes	yes	Tennessee
29				— Fannie	Wife			F	W	50	M				yes	yes	Georgia
30				— Sarah	Daughter			F	W	25	S				yes	yes	Tennessee
31	207	31	33	Hull, Harvard S	Head	O	F	M	W	66	M				yes	yes	Georgia
32				— Allora	Wife			F	W	64	M				yes	yes	Illinois
33	302	32	34	McPeever, Davis J.	Head	R		M	W	58	M				yes	yes	Georgia
34				— Alice	Wife			F	W	57	M				yes	yes	Georgia
35				— John	Son			M	W	22	S				yes	yes	Georgia
36	329	33	35	Summers, Sam	Head	R		F	Mu	45	M				no	no	Georgia
37				— Tualva	Daughter			F	Mu	20	S			no	yes	yes	Georgia
38				— Robert	Son			M	Mu	17	S			no	yes	yes	Georgia
39				— Carrie	Daughter			F	Mu	7	S			yes	yes	yes	Georgia
40				Balinger, Jim	Badger			M	B	45	S				yes	yes	Georgia
41	323	34	36	Crow, Ira A.	Head	R		M	W	30	M				yes	yes	Georgia
42				— Pollie	Wife			F	W	39	M				no	no	Georgia
43				— Jason	Son			M	W	21	S			no	no	no	Georgia
44				— Bufford	Son			M	W	7	S			no	no	no	Georgia
45	321	35	37	Hass, Olef	Head	R		M	W	27	M				no	no	Georgia
46				— Edna	Wife			F	W	24	M				yes	no	Georgia
47				— Claire	Daughter			F	W	11	S			yes	yes	yes	Georgia
48				— Willie	Son			M	W	9	S			no	no	no	Georgia
49				— Mac	Son			M	W	5	S			no	no	no	Georgia
50				— Edna Sue	Daughter			F	W	2½	S				no	no	Georgia

1920 FEDERAL CENSUS, CARTERSVILLE, BARTOW COUNTY, GEORGIA

Neel, James Monroe – By 1920, most all of the members of this once exceedingly-large family had departed the nest to seek their fortunes on their own. James is getting up in years now himself, being 70 years of age. His father, Joseph Lockhart, passed away in 1909. Still left at home with James are Aunt Nora, and James's children Ella and Isabelle. In a brief ten years, James himself will be gone.

20

BUREAU OF THE CENSUS   207   [D1—578]

~ED STATES: 1920—POPULATION

SUPERVISOR'S DISTRICT No. 7   SHEET No. 2

ENUMERATION DISTRICT No. 6

~TED PLACE _Cartersville_   (Insert proper name and, also, name of class, as city, village, town, or borough. See instructions.)   WARD OF CITY _3_

~MERATED BY ME ON THE _2d_ DAY OF _January_ 1920.   _Wm H Felton_   ENUMERATOR.

	NATIVITY AND MOTHER TONGUE.				Whether able to speak English.	OCCUPATION.			
	FATHER.		MOTHER.						
Mother tongue.	Place of birth.	Mother tongue.	Place of birth.	Mother tongue.		Trade, profession, or particular kind of work done, as spinner, salesman, laborer, etc.	Industry, business, or establishment in which at work, as cotton mill, dry goods store, farm, etc.	Employer, salary or wage worker, or working on own account.	Number of farm schedule.
20	21	22	23	24	25	26	27	28	29
English	Tennessee	English	Tennessee	English	yes	None			
English	Alabama	English	South Carolina	English	yes	Attorney	At Law	OA	
English	Alabama	English	South Carolina	English	yes	None			
English	Georgia	English	Georgia	English	yes	None			
English	Georgia	English	Georgia	English	yes	None			5
English	Georgia	English	Virginia	English	yes	Laborer	Farm	W	6 80½
English	South Carolina	English	Georgia	English	yes	None			7
English	Georgia	English	Georgia	English	yes	Laborer	Farm	W	8 80½
English	Georgia	English	Georgia	English	yes	Farmer	General	OA 2	9 00
English	Georgia	English	Georgia	English	yes	None			10
English	Georgia	English	Georgia	English	yes	None			11
English	Georgia	English	Georgia	English	yes	None			12
English	Georgia	English	Georgia	English	yes	None			13
English	Georgia	English	Georgia	English	yes	None			14
English	Georgia	English	Georgia	English	yes	None			15
English	Georgia	English	Georgia	English	yes	None			16
English	Georgia	English	Georgia	English	no	None			17
English	Tennessee	English	South Carolina	English	yes	None			18
English	Georgia	English	Georgia	English	yes	Farmer	General	OA 9	19
English	Georgia	English	Georgia	English	yes	Laborer	Ore Mine		20
English	Georgia	English	Georgia	English	yes	None			21
English	Georgia	English	Georgia	English	yes	None			22
English	Georgia	English	Georgia	English	yes	None			23
English	Georgia	English	Georgia	English	yes	None			24
English	Georgia	English	Georgia	English	yes	None			25
English	Georgia	English	Georgia	English	yes	None			26
English	Georgia	English	Georgia	English	w	None			
English	Tennessee	English	Tennessee	English	yes	Postman	RFD Mail	S	
English	South Carolina	English	South Carolina	English	yes	None			30
English	Tennessee	English	Georgia	English	yes	Teacher	Public School	S	
English	Georgia	English	Georgia	English	yes	Bookkeeper	Grocery Store	W	31 988
English	Germany	English	Germany	English	yes	Merchant	Grocery	OA	32
English	Georgia	English	Georgia	English	yes	None			33 767
English	Georgia	English	North Carolina	English	yes	None			34
English	Georgia	English	Georgia	English	yes	None			35
English	Georgia	English	Georgia	English	yes	Servant	General	W	36 960
English	Georgia	English	Georgia	English	yes	None			37
English	Georgia	English	Georgia	English	yes	None			38
English	Georgia	English	Georgia	English	yes	None			39
English	Georgia	English	Georgia	English	yes	Fireman	Gas Plant	W	40 176
English	Georgia	English	Georgia	English	yes	Oiler	Oil Mill	W 390	41 390
English	Georgia	English	Georgia	English	yes	None			42
English	Georgia	English	Georgia	English	no	None			43
English	Georgia	English	Georgia	English	yes	None			44
English	Georgia	English	Georgia	English	yes	Fireman	Oil Mill	W	45 176
English	Georgia	English	Georgia	English	yes	None			46
English	Georgia	English	Georgia	English	yes	None			47
English	Georgia	English	Georgia	English	yes	None			48
English	Georgia	English	Georgia	English	yes	None			49
English	Georgia	English	Georgia	English	no	None			50

Right portion of document on facing page

State **Georgia**

County **Bartow**

Township or other division of county **X**

Incorporated place **Cartersville** city town

Ward of city **4**   Block No.

Unincorporated place

Institution

DEPART
FIFTEENTE

	House number	Num-ber of dwell-ing house	Num-ber of family	NAME of each person whose place of abode on April 1, 1930, was in this family	RELATION Relationship of this person to the head of the family	Home owned or rented	Value of home, if owned, or monthly rental if rented	Radio set	Does this family live on a farm	Sex	Color or race	Age at last birthday	Marital con-dition	Age at first marriage	Attended school since Sept. 1, 1929	Whether able to read and write	PLACE OF BIRTH PERSON	PLACE OF BIRTH FATHER
1	208	155	182	Broughton, Ulysses	Son				no	M	Neg	10	S		yes	yes	Georgia	Georgia
2				" Myrtiel S	Daughter				V	F	Neg	7	S		yes		Georgia	Georgia
3				" Clara	Daughter				V	F	Neg	6	S		yes		Georgia	Georgia
4				" Kathleen	Daughter				V	F	Neg	4	S		no		Georgia	Georgia
5				" Alma	Daughter				V	F	Neg	2	S		no		Georgia	Georgia
6			183	Chisholm, Georgia	Head	R	8		no	F	Neg	40	Wd		no	yes	Georgia	Georgia
7				" Annie M.	Daughter				V	F	Neg	13	S		yes	yes	Georgia	Georgia
8				" Mamie	Daughter				V	F	Neg	16	S		no	yes	Georgia	Georgia
9				" William	Son				V	M	Neg	20	S		no	no	Georgia	Georgia
10	204	156	184	Pruitt, Lucy M	Head	R	6		no	F	Neg	42	Wd		no	yes	Georgia	South Carolina
11				" Lillian	Daughter				V	F	Neg	14	S		yes	yes	Georgia	Georgia
12				" Wynene	Daughter				V	F	Neg	12	S		no	yes	Georgia	Georgia
13				" Lucilen	Daughter				V	F	Neg	8	S		yes		Georgia	Georgia
14		157	185	Rucker, Vashti	Head	R	6		no	F	Neg	43	Wd		no	yes	Georgia	Georgia
15				" Tilla Me	Daughter				V	F	Neg	16	S		no	yes	Georgia	Georgia
16				" Willie R	Daughter				V	F	Neg	13	S		yes	yes	Georgia	Georgia
17				" Beautiful C.	Daughter				V	F	Neg	9	S		yes		Georgia	Georgia
18				" Reba	Daughter				V	F	Neg	8	S		yes		Georgia	Georgia
19	112	158	186	Erwin, Ella M	Head-H	O	1000		no	F	Neg	30	Wd		no	yes	Georgia	Georgia
20				Congus, Georgia	Aunt				V	F	Neg	50	Wd		no	yes	Georgia	Georgia
21				Smith, Nancy	Lodger				V	F	Neg	28	S		no	yes	Georgia	Georgia
22	104	159	187	Sproull, Ella	Head	O	150		no	F	Neg	49	Wd		no	yes	Georgia	South Carolina
23				" Capitola	Daughter				V	F	Neg	21	S		no	yes	Georgia	Georgia
24				" Willie	Daughter				V	F	Neg	19	S		no	yes	Georgia	Georgia
25		208	333	Towns, Mary	Head-H	O	1000		no	F	Neg	60	Wd		no	no	Georgia	Alabama
26	7	160	188	Neel, J. Monroe Jr	Head	O	6000	R	no	M	W	43	M	29	no	yes	Georgia	Georgia
27				" Sarah H.	Wife-H				V	F	W	36	M	22	no	yes	Georgia	Georgia
28				" Holmes	Son				V	M	W	12	S		yes	yes	Georgia	Georgia
29				" James M Jr	Son				V	M	W	5	S		yes		Georgia	Georgia
30				" William	Son				V	M	W	1 4/12	S		no		Georgia	Georgia
31	9	161	189	Vaughan, Francis J	Head	O	6000		no	M	W	30	M	23	no	yes	Georgia	Georgia
32				" Marie	Wife-H				V	F	W	29	M	22	no	yes	Sweden	Sweden
33				" Alfred	Son				V	M	W	4 1/2	S		no		Georgia	Georgia
34	11	162	190	Shaw, Robert A.	Head	O	7500		no	M	W	31	M	23	no	yes	Georgia	Georgia
35				" Martha C.	Wife-H				V	F	W	25	M	17	no	yes	Georgia	Georgia
36				" Robert W	Son				V	M	W	7	S		yes		Georgia	Georgia
37				" Thurman	Son				V	M	W	5	S		no		Georgia	Georgia
38	101	163	191	Demry, Will	Head	O	1300		no	M	Neg	53	M	23	no	yes	Georgia	Georgia
39				" Mary J	Wife-H				V	F	Neg	55	M	25	no	yes	Georgia	Georgia
40	105	164	192	Kemp, Asbury	Head	R	12		no	M	Neg	70	M	20	no	no	Georgia	Georgia
41				" Lou	Wife-H				V	F	Neg	64	M	14	no	yes	Georgia	South Carolina
42	115	165	193	Carnes, Mattie	Head-H	O	1325		no	F	Neg	49	Wd		no	yes	Georgia	Georgia
43	201	166	194	Harris, Lucy	Wife-H	R	6		no	F	Neg	40	M	32	no	yes	Georgia	Georgia
44				" George	Head				V	M	Neg	41	M	33	no	yes	Alabama	Georgia
45				" Mollie	Daughter	R			V	F	Neg	14	S		no	yes	Georgia	Georgia
46	200	167	195	Moon, Sylvia	Head-H	R	7.50		no	F	Neg	36	Wd		no	yes	Georgia	Georgia
47				Sayon, Perry	Father				V	M	Neg	69	Wd		no	yes	Georgia	United States
48				Moon, Albert	Daughter				V	F	Neg	17	S		no	yes	Georgia	Georgia
49	205	168	196	Brawner, Lloyd	Head	R	6		no	M	W	21	M	20	no	yes	Georgia	Georgia
50				" Ola	Wife-H				V	F	W	21	M	20	no	no	Georgia	Georgia

ABBREVIATIONS TO BE USED IN COLUMNS INDICATED:

1930 FEDERAL CENSUS, CARTERSVILLE, BARTOW COUNTY, GEORGIA

Neel, James Monroe, Jr. – The Neel family patriarch – James Monroe, Sr. – had passed away earlier in the year, and James Monroe, Jr. is now listed as "Head" of the household on South Avenue. Listed with him are his wife, Sarah, and sons Holmes, James III (?), and William A.

Form 15-6
MENT OF COMMERCE—BUREAU OF THE CENSUS
CENSUS OF THE UNITED STATES: 1930
POPULATION SCHEDULE

Enumeration District No. 8-23 Supervisor's District No. 21

Sheet No. 8 A

Enumerated by me on April 7, 1930, Mrs. Paul C. Franklin, Enumerator.

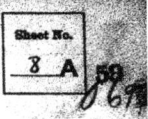

MOTHER	Language spoken in home (21)	A	B	C	22	23	24	OCCUPATION (25)	INDUSTRY (26)	CODE (D)	Class of worker (27)	28	29	30	31	32	#
Georgia		78					yes	none									1
Georgia		78						none									2
Georgia		78						none									3
Georgia		78						none									4
Georgia		78						none									5
Georgia		78					yes	Laundress	At home	8596	W	yes					6
Georgia		78					yes	none									7
Georgia		78					yes	Cook	Private family	6096	W	yes					8
Georgia		78					yes	Service boy	Garage	7673	W	no	34				9
South Carolina		78					yes	Cook	Private home	6096	W	yes					10
Georgia		78					yes	Child's nurse	Private Home	9596	W	yes					11
Georgia		78					yes	Delivery boy	Grocery Store	8690	W	yes					12
Georgia		78						none									13
Georgia		78					yes	Cook	Boarding House	609V	W	yes					14
Georgia		78					yes	None									15
Georgia		78					yes	none									16
Georgia		78						none									17
Georgia		78						none									18
Georgia		78					yes	Cook	Private home	6096	W	no	35				19
Georgia		78					yes	Cook	Private home	6096	W	yes					20
Georgia		78					yes	Nurse practical	Independent	8796	6	yes					21
South Carolina		78					yes	Laundress	At home	8596	W	yes					22
Georgia		78					yes	Cook	Private home	6096	W	yes					23
Georgia		78					yes	Nurse-Child's	Private family	9596	W	yes					24
Alabama		78					yes	Cook	Private Family	6096	W	yes					25
Georgia		78					yes	Lawyer	Independent	5X94	O	yes		no			26
Georgia		78					yes	None									27
Georgia		78					yes	none									28
Georgia		78						none									29
Georgia		78						none									30
Georgia		78					yes	Manager	Dry Goods Store	8491	W	yes		yes	WW		31
Georgia		78					yes	none									32
Georgia		78						none									33
Georgia		78					yes	Cashier	Bank	8583	W	yes		no			34
Georgia		78					yes	none									35
Georgia		78						none									36
Georgia		78						none									37
Georgia		78					yes	Cook	Hotel	609V	W	yes		no			38
Georgia		78					yes	none									39
Georgia		78					yes	none						no			40
South Carolina		78					yes	laundress	At home	8596	W	yes					41
Georgia		78					yes	Merchant	Grocery Store	9X91	O	yes					42
Georgia		78					yes	laundress	At Home	8596	W						43
Georgia		82					yes	Laborer	Odd Jobs	7899	W	yes		no			44
Georgia		78					yes	none									45
Alabama		78					yes	Cook	Private family	6096	W						46
South Carolina		78					yes	Carpenter	Odd jobs	O6X	W	no	36	no			47
Georgia		78					yes	Child's nurse	Private family	9596	W	yes					48
Georgia		78					yes	Laborer	Golf links	787V	W	yes		no			49
Georgia		78					yes	none									50

ENTRIES ARE REQUIRED IN THE SEVERAL COLUMNS AS FOLLOWS:

Mrs. Paul C. Franklin

Right portion of document on facing page

State _Georgia_ Incorporated place _____ 1041 Ward of city _____ Unincorporated place _____

County _Bartow_ Township or other _Wolf Pen_ Block Nos. _____ Institution _____
division of county

Line No.	LOCATION	HOUSEHOLD DATA	NAME	RELATION	PERSONAL DESCRIPTION	EDUCATION	PLACE OF BIRTH		RESIDENCE	
1	23 R 4 no	Benham, Arthur F	head	O m neg 23 m no 2		Georgia		R	Bartow
2		Nellie	wife	1 F neg 20 m no 5		Georgia		R	Bartow
3		Katie B.	daughter	F neg 3 5 no 0		Georgia			
4		Odell	son	m neg 1 5 no 0		Georgia			
5	24 O 5000 no	Neel, J. Monroe	head	O m w 94 m no	90	Georgia		Cartersville Bartow
6		Sarah H	wife	1 F w 46 m no 2 2		Georgia		Cartersville Bartow
7		Holmes	son	m w 22 5 no C1 4		Georgia		Cartersville Bartow
8		J. Monroe Jr.	son	m w 15 5 no H2 1		Georgia		Cartersville Bartow
9		William A	son	m w 11 5 no 5		Georgia		Cartersville Bartow
10	25 R 4 no	Warde, Fred	head	O m w 36 m no 4 4		Georgia		R Bartow
11		Noreen	wife	1 F w 26 m no 5 5		Georgia		R Bartow
12		Lankford	son	m w 8 5 no 0		Georgia		R Bartow
13		Noreen	daughter	F w 2 5 no		Georgia			
14	26 R 8 no	Yancey, Lawrence	head	O m w 49 m no 6 6		Georgia		same place
15		Emmie	wife	1 F w 40 m no 9 9		Georgia		same place
16		Cleese	daughter	F w 17 5 no 9 9		Georgia		same place
17	27 R 4 no	Evans, George	head	O m w 28 m no 7 7		Georgia		same place
18		Maxie	wife	1 F w 23 m no 9 9		Georgia		same place
19		Willie Sue	daughter	F w 4 5 no 0		Georgia		same place
20		Jack	son	m w 2 5 no		Georgia		
21	28 R 10 yes	McEver, Homer	head	O m w 32 5 no 6		Georgia		same place
22		John	father	m w 63 wd no		Georgia		same place
23	31 R 8 no	Heath, George	head	O m w 56 m no 7		Georgia		son in laws
24		Cora	wife	1 F w 48 m no 2		Georgia		same house
25		Joe	son	m w 22 5 no 8		Georgia		same house
26		Francis	daughter	F w 16 5 no 9 9		Georgia		same house
27	32 R 8 no	Clark, Mervin A	head	O m w 34 m no 9 9		Georgia		same place
28		Mary Kate	wife	1 F w 26 m no 8		Georgia		same place
29		Mary E	daughter	F w 2 5 no 0		Georgia		
30	33 R 4 no	Teague, John L Jr	head	O m w 54 m no 7 7		Georgia		same house
31		Ida Mae	wife	1 F w 50 m no 7 7		Georgia		same house
32	34 R 4 no	Warde, Merida	head	O m w 34 m no 4 4		Georgia		same place
33		Pauline	wife	1 F w 30 m no 5 5		Georgia		same place
34		LaNell	daughter	F w 13 5 no 6 6		Georgia		same place
35		Lud	son	m w 12 5 no 3		Georgia		same place
36		Jr. C	son	m w 7 5 no 1		Georgia		same place
37	35 R 8 no	Hawkins, Mark	head	O m w 45 m no 8		Georgia		same place
38		Bessie	wife	1 F w 42 m no 2		Georgia		same place
39		Herbert	son	m w 18 5 no 6 6		Georgia		same place
40		Clyde	son	m w 16 5 no 5 5		Georgia		same place

SUPPLEMENTARY QUESTIONS
For Persons Enumerated on Lines 14 and 29

Line No.	NAME	PLACE OF BIRTH OF FATHER AND MOTHER		MOTHER TONGUE (OR NATIVE LANGUAGE)	VETERANS	SOCIAL SECURITY	USUAL OCCUP
		FATHER	MOTHER				
14	Yancey, Lawrence	Georgia	Georgia	English		yes	Truck d
29	Clark, Mary E	Georgia	Georgia	English		no	O

SYMBOLS AND EXPLANATORY NOTES

Col. 5. VALUE OF HOME, IF OWNED: Col. 10. COLOR OR RACE: Col. 12. AGE AT LAST BIRTHDAY: Col. 14. HIGHEST GRADE OF SCHOOL COMPLETED:

1940 FEDERAL CENSUS, CARTERSVILLE, BARTOW COUNTY, GEORGIA

Neel, James Monroe, Jr. – James, Jr. continues to preside over the family with wife Sarah and children Holmes, James Monroe, and William A.

DEPARTMENT OF COMMERCE—BUREAU OF THE CENSUS
SIXTEENTH CENSUS OF THE UNITED STATES: 1940

POPULATION SCHEDULE

S.D. No. 7   E.D. No. 8-22   Sheet No. 1 A

Enumerated by me on April 11, 1940.

214   Mrs Nida C. Liscomb, Enumerator.

19	20	D	21	22	23	24	25	E	26	27	28 (Occupation)	(Industry)	30	F	31	32	33	34	Line No.
Georgia	yes		yes						1	50	Farmer	Farming	Ow			52	365	Yes		1
Georgia	yes		no	no	no	no	H													2
																				3
																				4
Georgia	no		yes		—	—	—		60		Lawer	law	Oa			0		Yes		5
Georgia	no		no		—			H									0		Yes		6
Georgia	no		yes		—			H	1					Su					Yes		7
Georgia	no		no	no	no	no	S							2			0	0	Yes		8
Georgia	no		no	no	no	no	S	6											Yes		9
Georgia	yes		yes		—	—	—		24		Laborer	manganese mine	Ow			57	0	No		10
Georgia	yes		no	no	no	no	H														11
Georgia			yes																		12
																					13
			yes		—	—	—		40		Truck driver	mining	Ow			26	312	No		14
			no	no	no	no	H											No		15
			yes		—				32		Operator	mine	Oa			0		No		16
			no	no	yes		—		0	40	miner	mine	Oa			24		No		17
			yes								machine operator	mine	Oa			0		No		18
																				19
																				20
			yes		—				40		Farming	Farming	Oa			51	0	No		21
			yes						40		Farmer	Farming	Oa			52		No		22
			yes		—				30		Slag operator	manganese mine	Ow			48	540	No		23
			no	no	no	no	H										0	0	No		24
			yes		—			H	40		Odd jobs	manganese mine	Ow			48	540	No		25
			no	no	no	no	S										0		No		26
			yes		—				40		miner	manganese	Oa			52	0	No		27
			no	no	no	no	H										0	0	No		28
																				29
			no	no	7	no	U		6		mining	manganese	Ow			48	500	No		30
			no	no	no	no	H												No		31
			no	no	no	no	U				miner		73			52	0	No		32
			no	no	no	no	H										0	0	No		33
																				34
																				35
																				36
			no	no	no	no	U			35	miner	manganese	Oa							37
			no	no	no	no	H											No		38
			yes		—	—	—		40		Truck driver	manganese mine	Ow			0	0	No		39
			yes						40		Laborer	mine	Ow					No		40

PERSONS 14 YEARS OLD AND OVER

FOR ALL WOMEN WHO ARE OR HAVE BEEN MARRIED

FOR OFFICE USE ONLY—DO NOT WRITE IN THESE COLUMNS

USUAL INDUSTRY	47	J	48	49	50	K	L	M	N	O	P	Q	R	S	T	U	V	W	X	Y	Z	Line No.
46																						
driver mining	Ow				1																	14
																						29

Right portion of document on facing page

25

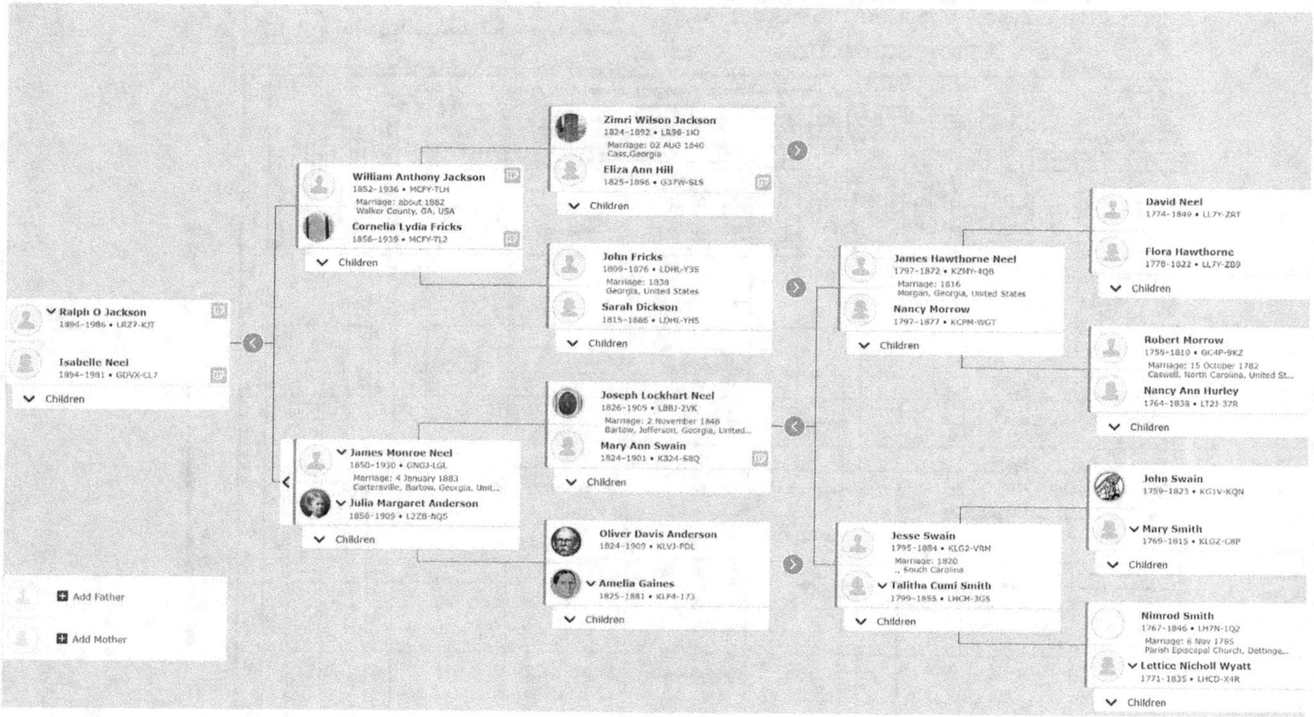

Chart 1

Ralph O Jackson
1894–1986 • LRZ7-KJT

Isabelle Neel
1894–1981 • GDVX-CL7

∨ Children

➕ Add Father

➕ Add Mother

William Anthony Jackson
1852–1936 • MCFY-TLH
Marriage: about 1882
Walker County, GA, USA

Cornelia Lydia Fricks
1856–1959 • MCFY-TL2

∨ Children

James Monroe Neel
1850–1930 • GNGJ-LGL
Marriage: 4 January 1883
Cartersville, Bartow, Georgia, Unit...

∨ **Julia Margaret Anderson**
1856–1909 • L2ZB-NQ5

∨ Children

Zimri Wilson Jackson
1824–1892 • LR98-1KO
Marriage: 02 AUG 1840
Cass,Georgia

Eliza Ann Hill
1825–1896 • G37W-SLS

∨ Children

John Fricks
1809–1876 • LDHL-Y3S
Marriage: 1838
Georgia, United States

Sarah Dickson
1815–1886 • LDHL-YH5

∨ Children

Joseph Lockhart Neel
1826–1909 • L8BJ-2VK
Marriage: 2 November 1848
Bartow, Jefferson, Georgia, United...

Mary Ann Swain
1824–1901 • K324-S8Q

∨ Children

Oliver Davis Anderson
1824–1909 • KLVJ-FDL

∨ **Amelia Gaines**
1825–1881 • KLF4-173

∨ Children

James Hawthorne Neel
1797–1872 • KZMY-4QB
Marriage: 1816
Morgan, Georgia, United States

Nancy Morrow
1797–1877 • KCPM-WGT

∨ Children

Jesse Swain
1795–1884 • KLG2-VBM
Marriage: 1820
., South Carolina

∨ **Talitha Cumi Smith**
1799–1855 • LHCH-3GS

∨ Children

David Neel
1774–1849 • LL7Y-ZRT

Flora Hawthorne
1778–1822 • LL7Y-ZB9

∨ Children

Robert Morrow
1755–1810 • GC4P-9KZ
Marriage: 15 October 1782
Caswell, North Carolina, United St...

Nancy Ann Hurley
1764–1838 • LT2J-37R

∨ Children

John Swain
1759–1823 • KG1V-KQN

Mary Smith
1769–1815 • KLGZ-C8P

∨ Children

Nimrod Smith
1767–1846 • LH7N-1Q2
Marriage: 6 Nov 1795
Parish Episcopal Church, Dettinge...

∨ **Lettice Nicholl Wyatt**
1771–1835 • LHCD-X4R

∨ Children

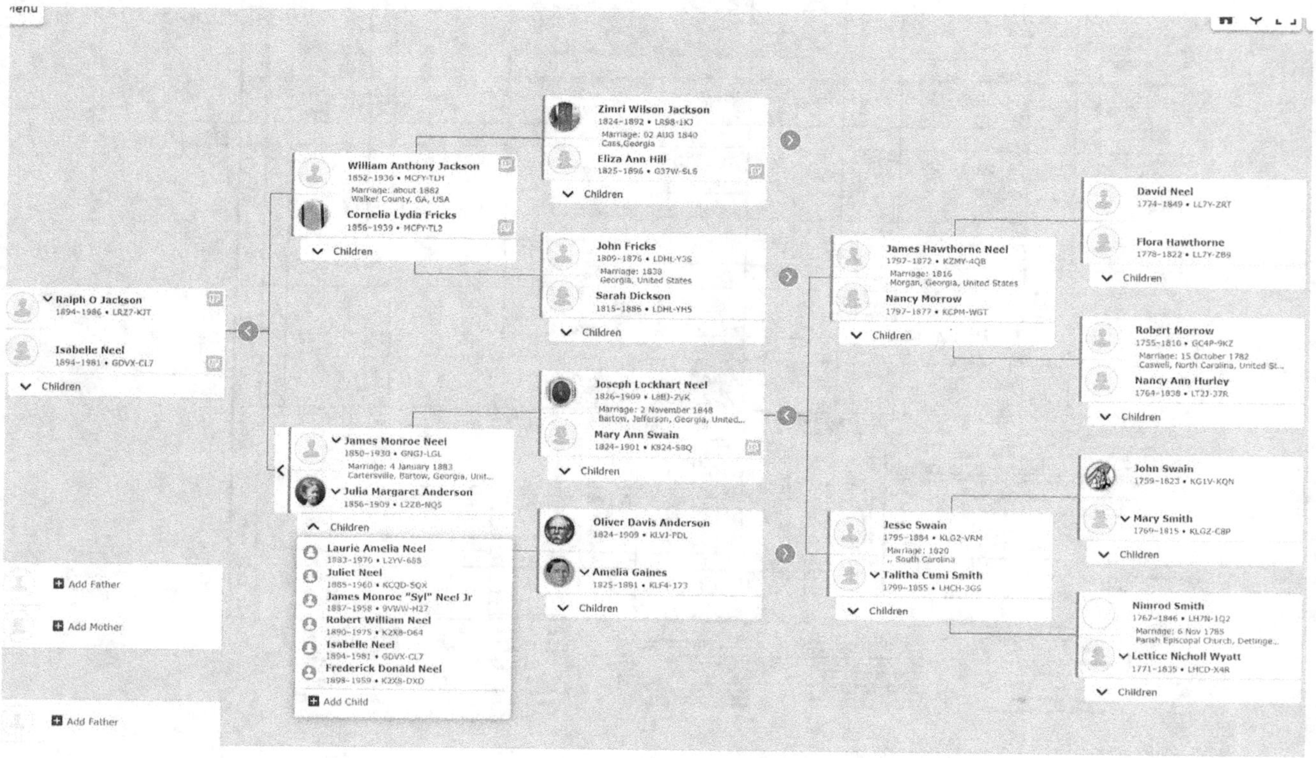

Chart 2

enu

Ralph O Jackson
1894–1986 • LRZ7-KJT

Isabelle Neel
1894–1981 • GDVX-CL7

∨ Children

➕ Add Father

➕ Add Father

William Anthony Jackson
1852–1936 • MCFY-TLH
Marriage: about 1882
Walker County, GA, USA

Cornelia Lydia Fricks
1856–1959 • MCFY-TL2

∨ Children

James Monroe Neel
1850–1930 • GNGJ-LGL
Marriage: 4 January 1883
Cartersville, Bartow, Georgia, Unit...

∨ **Julia Margaret Anderson**
1856–1909 • L2ZB-NQ5

∧ Children

Laurie Amelia Neel
1883–1976 • L2YV-688

Juliet Neel
1885–1960 • KCQD-SQX

James Monroe "Syl" Neel Jr
1897–1958 • 9VWW-H27

Robert William Neel
1890–1975 • K2K8-D64

Isabelle Neel
1894–1981 • GDVX-CL7

Frederick Donald Neel
1899–1959 • KXX9-DXD

➕ Add Child

Zimri Wilson Jackson
1824–1892 • LR98-1KO
Marriage: 02 AUG 1840
Cass,Georgia

Eliza Ann Hill
1825–1896 • G37W-SL6

∨ Children

John Fricks
1809–1876 • LDHL-Y3S
Marriage: 1838
Georgia, United States

Sarah Dickson
1815–1886 • LDHL-YH5

∨ Children

Joseph Lockhart Neel
1826–1909 • L8BJ-2VK
Marriage: 2 November 1848
Bartow, Jefferson, Georgia, United...

Mary Ann Swain
1824–1901 • K324-S8Q

∨ Children

Oliver Davis Anderson
1824–1909 • KLVJ-FDL

∨ **Amelia Gaines**
1825–1881 • KLF4-173

∨ Children

James Hawthorne Neel
1797–1872 • KZMY-4QB
Marriage: 1816
Morgan, Georgia, United States

Nancy Morrow
1797–1877 • KCPM-WGT

∨ Children

Jesse Swain
1795–1884 • KLG2-VRM
Marriage: 1820
., South Carolina

∨ **Talitha Cumi Smith**
1799–1855 • LHCH-3GS

∨ Children

David Neel
1724–1849 • LL7Y-ZRT

Flora Hawthorne
1778–1822 • LL7Y-ZB9

∨ Children

Robert Morrow
1755–1810 • GC4P-9KZ
Marriage: 15 October 1782
Caswell, North Carolina, United St...

Nancy Ann Hurley
1764–1838 • LT2J-37R

∨ Children

John Swain
1759–1823 • KG1V-KQN

∨ **Mary Smith**
1769–1815 • KLGZ-C8P

∨ Children

Nimrod Smith
1767–1846 • LH7N-1Q2
Marriage: 6 Nov 1795
Parish Episcopal Church, Dettinge...

∨ **Lettice Nicholl Wyatt**
1771–1835 • LHCD-X4R

∨ Children

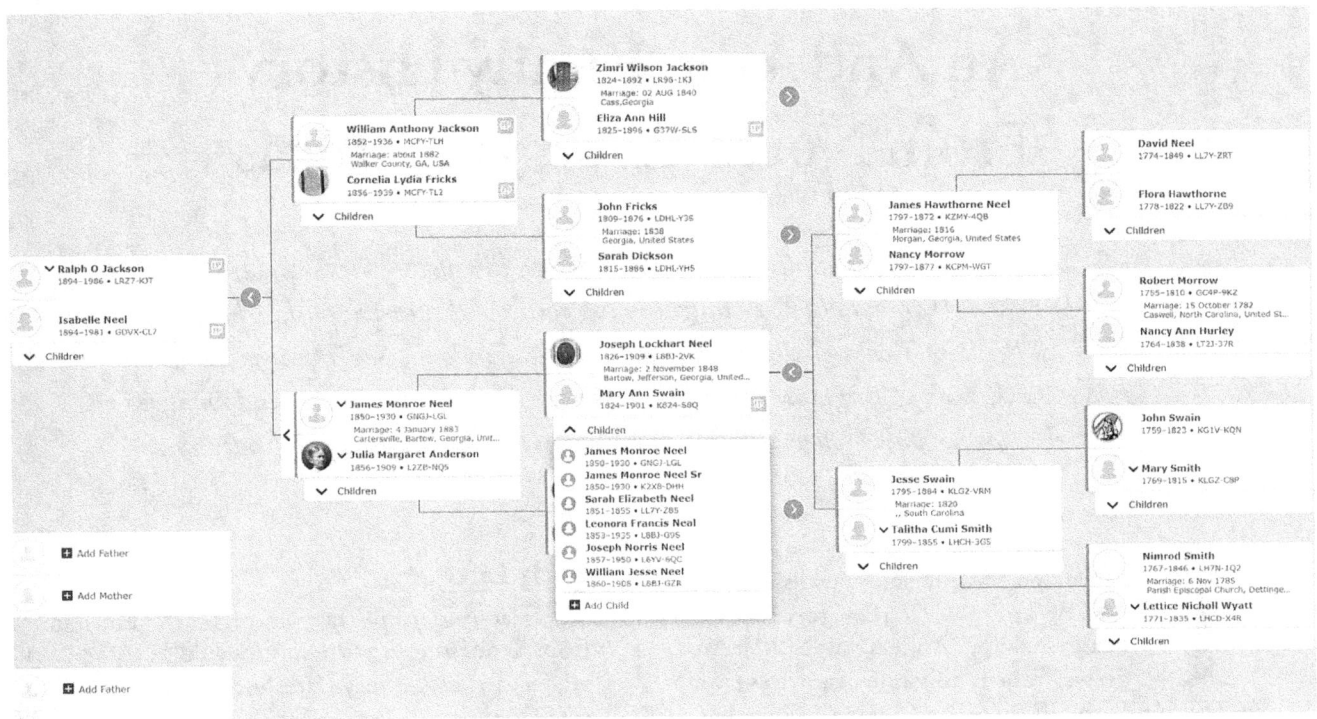

Ralph O Jackson
1894-1986 • LRZ7-K3T

Isabelle Neel
1894-1981 • GDVX-CL7

∨ Children

William Anthony Jackson
1852-1936 • MCFY-TLH
Marriage: about 1882
Walker County, GA, USA

Cornelia Lydia Fricks
1856-1939 • MCFY-TL2

∨ Children

James Monroe Neel
1850-1930 • GNGJ-LGL
Marriage: 4 January 1883
Cartersville, Bartow, Georgia, Unit...

Julia Margaret Anderson
1856-1909 • L2ZB-NQ5

∨ Children

Zimri Wilson Jackson
1824-1892 • LR98-1KJ
Marriage: 02 AUG 1840
Cass,Georgia

Eliza Ann Hill
1825-1896 • G37W-SLS

∨ Children

John Fricks
1809-1876 • LDHL-Y3S
Marriage: 1838
Georgia, United States

Sarah Dickson
1815-1886 • LDHL-YH5

∨ Children

Joseph Lockhart Neel
1826-1909 • LBBJ-2VK
Marriage: 2 November 1848
Bartow, Jefferson, Georgia, United...

Mary Ann Swain
1824-1901 • K824-S8Q

∧ Children

- **James Monroe Neel** 1850-1930 • GNGJ-LGL
- **James Monroe Neel Sr** 1850-1930 • K2XB-DHH
- **Sarah Elizabeth Neel** 1851-1855 • LL7Y-ZB5
- **Leonora Francis Neal** 1853-1925 • LBBJ-Q9S
- **Joseph Norris Neel** 1857-1950 • L6YV-6QC
- **William Jesse Neel** 1860-1908 • L883-GZR

➕ Add Child

James Hawthorne Neel
1797-1872 • KZMY-4QB
Marriage: 1816
Morgan, Georgia, United States

Nancy Morrow
1797-1877 • KCPM-WGT

∨ Children

Jesse Swain
1795-1864 • KLG2-VRM
Marriage: 1820
,, South Carolina

Talitha Cumi Smith
1799-1855 • LHCH-3GS

∨ Children

David Neel
1774-1849 • LL7Y-ZRT

Flora Hawthorne
1778-1822 • LL7Y-ZB9

∨ Children

Robert Morrow
1755-1810 • GC4P-9KZ
Marriage: 15 October 1782
Caswell, North Carolina, United St...

Nancy Ann Hurley
1764-1838 • LT23-37R

∨ Children

John Swain
1759-1823 • KG1V-KQN

Mary Smith
1769-1915 • KLGZ-C8P

∨ Children

Nimrod Smith
1767-1846 • LH7N-1Q2
Marriage: 6 Nov 1785
Parish Episcopal Church, Dettinge...

Lettice Nicholl Wyatt
1771-1935 • LHCD-X4R

∨ Children

➕ Add Father

➕ Add Mother

➕ Add Father

Ralph O Jackson
1894-1986 • LRZ7-K3T

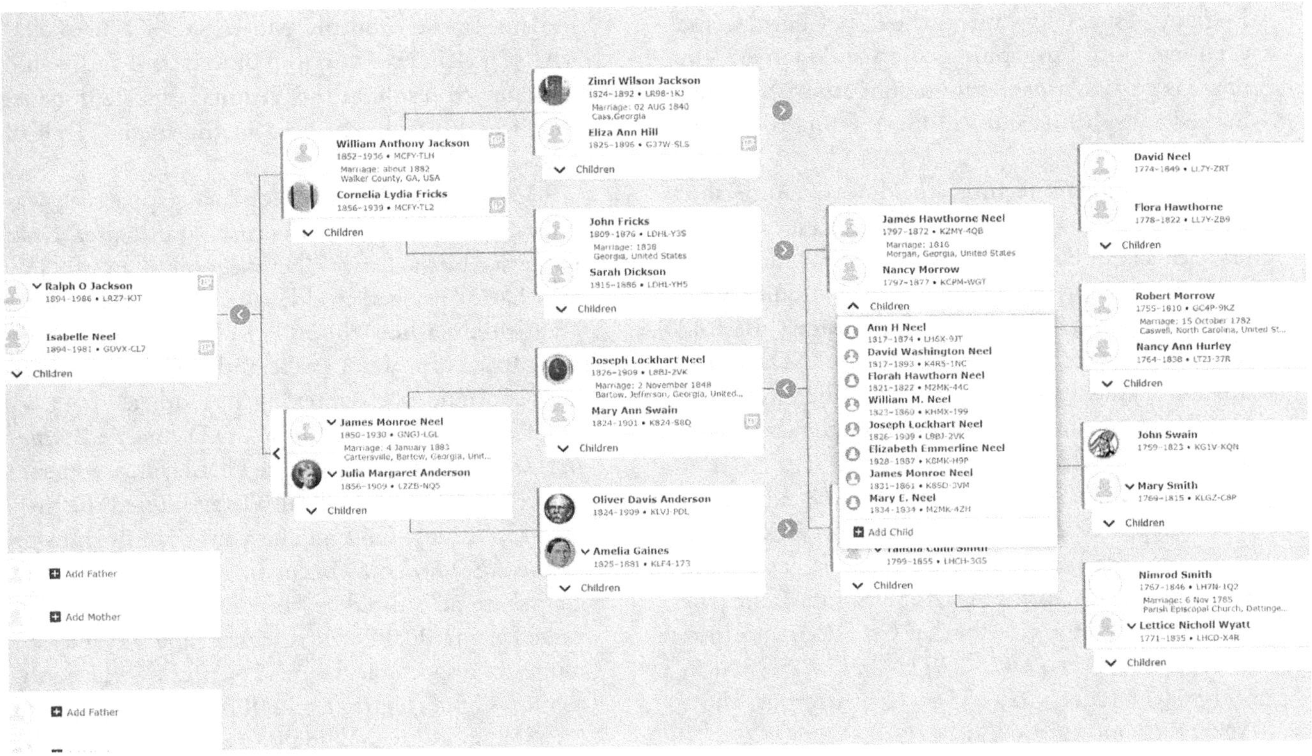

Isabelle Neel
1894-1981 • GDVX-CL7

∨ Children

William Anthony Jackson
1852-1936 • MCFY-TLH
Marriage: about 1892
Walker County, GA, USA

Cornelia Lydia Fricks
1856-1939 • MCFY-TL2

∨ Children

James Monroe Neel
1850-1930 • GNGJ-LGL
Marriage: 4 January 1883
Cartersville, Bartow, Georgia, Unit...

Julia Margaret Anderson
1856-1909 • L2ZB-NQ5

∨ Children

Zimri Wilson Jackson
1824-1892 • LR98-1KJ
Marriage: 02 AUG 1840
Cass,Georgia

Eliza Ann Hill
1825-1896 • G37W-SLS

∨ Children

John Fricks
1809-1976 • LDHL-Y3S
Marriage: 1838
Georgia, United States

Sarah Dickson
1815-1886 • LDHL-YH5

∨ Children

Joseph Lockhart Neel
1826-1909 • LBBJ-2VK
Marriage: 2 November 1848
Bartow, Jefferson, Georgia, United...

Mary Ann Swain
1824-1901 • K824-S8Q

∨ Children

Oliver Davis Anderson
1824-1909 • KLVJ-PDL

Amelia Gaines
1825-1681 • KLF4-173

∨ Children

James Hawthorne Neel
1797-1872 • KZMY-4QB
Marriage: 1816
Morgan, Georgia, United States

Nancy Morrow
1797-1877 • KCPM-WGT

∧ Children

- **Ann H Neel** 1817-1874 • LH6X-9JT
- **David Washington Neel** 1817-1893 • K4R5-1NC
- **Florah Hawthorn Neel** 1821-1822 • M2MK-44C
- **William M. Neel** 1823-1860 • KH4X-199
- **Joseph Lockhart Neel** 1826-1939 • LBBJ-2VK
- **Elizabeth Emmerline Neel** 1928-1987 • KDMK-H9P
- **James Monroe Neel** 1831-1861 • K8SD-3VM
- **Mary E. Neel** 1834-1934 • M2MK-4ZH

➕ Add Child

Talitha Cumi Smith
1799-1855 • LHCH-3GS

∨ Children

David Neel
1774-1849 • LL7Y-ZRT

Flora Hawthorne
1778-1822 • LL7Y-ZB9

∨ Children

Robert Morrow
1755-1610 • GC4P-9KZ
Marriage: 15 October 1782
Caswell, North Carolina, United St...

Nancy Ann Hurley
1764-1838 • LT23-37R

∨ Children

John Swain
1759-1823 • KG1V-KQN

Mary Smith
1769-1815 • KLGZ-C8P

∨ Children

Nimrod Smith
1767-1846 • LH7N-1Q2
Marriage: 6 Nov 1785
Parish Episcopal Church, Dettinge...

Lettice Nicholl Wyatt
1771-1935 • LHCD-X4R

∨ Children

➕ Add Father

➕ Add Mother

➕ Add Father

An Anderson Family History From North Georgia to Texas

O.D. Anderson and his family were fated to not only live during the dark days of the U.S. Civil War, but also to be caught in the vortex of the terrible onslaught of General William Tecumseh Sherman's infamous "March to the Sea" through Georgia in 1864. Like many Georgians of that day, they were made of strong stock, and managed to find a way not only to survive, but to persevere in those unbelievably difficult times.

The name "Anderson" translates to "son of Andrew." Variant forms of the name include "Anders" and "MacAndrews." The family line originates from Ireland, and usually is of immigrant origin, having been introduced into Ulster Province by settlers and traders who arrived from Scotland and England, especially during the 17th Century, and then later into burgeoning colonial America. The name is particularly common of Scots-Irish settlers in the Pennsylvania and Virginia sections of the 18th Century.

According to records, the line of Andersons from which Oliver Davis Anderson descends – as far back as can be traced by this writer – did in fact originate in Scotland, and prior to that quite likely from an ancient Celtic tribe in pre-history. Beyond the above-quoted possible sources, the O.D. Anderson family ancestors undoubtedly – as did multitudes of early American settlers – simply sought a better life in the New World.

Isaac Anderson was born in 1668, and married *Martha Bell*, born in Ireland in 1703. From them descended *James* (b. 1720, Ireland); James' son, *Robert* (b. 1763, York, PA); Robert's son, *Isaac (the younger)* (b. 1795, Rockbridge Co., VA); and then Isaac's son, *Oliver Davis "O.D."* (b. 04/05/1824 in Maryville, Blount Co., TN). As is obvious, these Andersons "moved around."

Early Life

Isaac Anderson (the younger) moved his family from Tennessee to what soon would become Cassville and Cass County (later incorporated into Bartow County), Georgia, in 1834, when O.D. was still a small boy. Growing up in what then was the American frontier, the Andersons lived among the native Indians (most probably Muscogee or Cherokees) who still claimed ownership of that land and would continue to reside in this vicinity until 1838 when they were forcibly removed in the tragic "Trail of Tears."

O.D., possessing very blond hair, apparently was one of the first – if not the first – fair-haired child witnessed by the native Cherokees there. In later life, after having reached an elder age, O.D. would tell his grandchildren how the Indians had picked him up and carried him about exuberantly upon their shoulders, continuously frightening his mother.

Upon reaching maturity, O.D. married *Amelia Gaines* in 1845, moving to Adairsville to operate a hotel there (1847). He also later entered the mercantile business. O.D. and his young family show up in the *1850 Federal Census* in Cass County, Georgia, where he is listed as *"merchant,"* with real estate valued at $1,000.00, which at that time was at least a modestly-respectable financial portfolio – the equivalent of slightly less than $34,000.00 in 2023 dollars.

Sometime around 1858, O.D. decided to move

Anderson, O.D. – In addition to serving as the Postmaster of Adairsville, O.D. Anderson also became a vital cog in the management of the Western & Atlantic Railroad (W&A RR) in Georgia during the U.S. Civil War. Pictured is the locomotive "General" and train from that era on the W&A RR. In 1962, one hundred years after the war's famed "Great Locomotive Chase," the General went on tour, retracing the route of the incident from Marietta to Ringgold, Georgia. (Photo courtesy of Adairsville History Museum).

his family to Arkansas to follow his parents who were migrating westward. Life in the harsh realities of the west, however, apparently did not agree with O.D., though he spent nearly a year there with his family before returning to Georgia.

O.D. next appears in the *1860 Federal Census* of Adairsville, Cass County, Georgia, where he is listed as *"Postmaster."* At the time of the U.S. Civil War, O.D. – in addition to serving as postmaster – was depot agent of the newly-completed Western & Atlantic (W&A) Railroad at Adairsville.

As one might imagine, the W&A was vitally important to the war effort, and O.D.'s job shortly became a very busy post. He was refused service by the regular Confederate Army because he had a defective eye, but he did serve as a member of what was called "the Georgia State Troops," possibly a home-guard unit. It, however, was his talent in the manipulation and management of railroad rolling stock which shortly was recognized by Confederate authorities and put to use.

As the war progressed, O.D. – in addition to his other responsibilities with the W&A – was kept busy as a purchasing agent, acquiring and shipping supplies for the Confederacy via the railroad. As the battle front moved inexorably southward toward Adairsville in the war's later years, in part naturally following the route of the vital supply line of the W&A, it soon became apparent to O.D. that his home was about to be caught within the teeth of the conflict, and he and his family would have no choice but to refugee southward down into Georgia.

Fleeing In A Boxcar

While the *Battle of Resaca* was taking place – where, incidentally, the father (***Capt. Joseph Lockhart Neel***, C.S.A.) of O.D.'s future son-in-law (***James Monroe Neel***) was involved in desperate fighting – O.D. was preparing his family to flee southward. Due no doubt to his employment with the W&A, and the vital necessity of his professional manipulation of the rail line's Georgia rolling stock in the war effort, O.D. and his family, interestingly, were permitted to have a W&A railroad boxcar for their personal use. They loaded this unique conveyance with household goods and were soon being transported by rail southward toward Atlanta and into the lower reaches of Georgia.

Due no doubt to the severe limitations of space within the confines of the boxcar, O.D.'s young son, James, who is believed to have been approximately 13 years of age at the time, amazingly traveled **on foot** with the family's slaves through what then was the very densely-forested north Georgia countryside. Making this feat even more unbelievable for a youngster of James' age is the fact that north Georgia in the 1860s was a trackless wilderness with virtually no roads whatsoever other than occasional game trails and a few very crude wagon roads, and, of course, travel aids such as road signage – or any directional guidance of any type for a youngster or adult – were nonexistent in those dark days. It is unknown today just how James was able to navigate his way southward and ultimately reach the vicinity of Atlanta, let alone locate his family whose boxcar had been taken eastward from Atlanta to Stone Mountain, Georgia, but locate them he did.

When the Anderson family had reached Atlanta

and their boxcar sent eastward on the Georgia Railroad – no doubt at the direction of O.D. – the railroad management responsibilities of the family patriarch had required him to chart a course separate from that of his family. While they went east, he went south.

According to family records, after reaching Stone Mountain, the Andersons spent approximately two months on a railroad siding in that small town living within the strict confines of the boxcar. It is unknown by this writer if these circumstances involved freezing winter weather within the boxcar, or the unbearable heat generated by a harsh Georgia summer. Either way, their stark existence under these circumstances is almost unthinkable – but those were anything but "normal" times, and thousands of war-weary refugees had no roof over their heads whatsoever.

Nevertheless, the Andersons reportedly eventually tired of the harsh environment of their boxcar home, and set out northeastward on foot to Monroe, Georgia, where they somehow obtained a home in that locality – either by renting or squatting. They remained at this location until the raids by Federal troops became so frequent and deadly that they decided to move on once again – no doubt fleeing with retreating Confederate troops – into South Carolina, still amazingly traveling on foot.

After reaching South Carolina and finding the accommodations and options for survival even worse in that realm, Amelia and her children decided to return to Monroe where they remained until the end of the war. The children reportedly even went to a rustic school in Monroe and made many friends there.

Meanwhile, O.D., according to family records and lore, was in South Georgia (quite likely Barnesville), where he continued to manage what remained of the Georgia state railroad rolling stock for the Confederacy – a task at which he apparently had become quite adept, moving it continuously around the state on the rails which remained in existence, keeping as much of it as possible out of the hands of Federal troops. His work in this capacity did not cease – nor did his separation from his family – until the end of the war.

After The War

With the war concluded, both Amelia and her family in Monroe, and O.D. in south Georgia, traveled back across the war-torn, lawless, and devastated Georgia countryside to return to their home in Adairsville to see what – if anything – remained to salvage. It is unknown today how the family members communicated with each other while separated (almost certainly not at all), or what they discovered when they arrived back at their home in Adairsville. No family lore or ancient letter has been discovered which recorded those circumstances for posterity. Suffice it to say that historic records of the war which do exist describe a totally devastated north Georgia, particularly along the route of the Western & Atlantic Railroad which would include their home in Adairsville and present-day Bartow County.

Just as did many others, the Anderson family found shelter of one sort or another, and somehow struggled along, scratching out a meager existence in what was left of a culture literally *"gone with the wind."* O.D. initially attempted to survive by farming, but when that failed, he turned back to something about which he knew a bit more – the mercantile business. Interestingly, it was the same pursuit in the same town as the father (Joseph Lockhart Neel) of his future son-in-law (James Monroe Neel).

O.D. was able to survive within that profession, no doubt due to his many and close relationships with the people of his community. At that point after the war, hard currency was nonexistent in Georgia – or anywhere in the South for that matter – so a system of "barter" took over. Those in need of items of necessity took other items of value to barter for the materials they needed. O.D. and his family survived in this same manner.

Bessie Bevins, one of O.D.'s grandchildren, described him during those days as follows: *"He had many noble characteristics. He was much more intelligent than the average man of his time, and his tiny frame bore a heart of gold. Kind and considerate of everyone, he was a very polite man and a devout Christian."*

Raised as a Presbyterian, O.D. joined the Baptist Church with his wife and was staunch in his belief.

He was clerk of Oothcaloga Baptist Church outside Adairsville for many years. A friend once told him he made himself poor feeding preachers. He was a great believer in Sunday school and a faithful attendant for many years.

A description of the life these Georgians were forced to lead in these dark days during and following the war would not do justice to the struggles and horrors they faced. The marauding Union Armies had pillaged and stolen everything in sight during the months and years of the war. Anything of value was taken – particularly foodstuffs, tools, draft animals, and any valuables which had not been hidden.

After the Union army departed, lawlessness – which had already existed in abundance during the war years – descended upon the region with a vengeance. Law enforcement was nonexistent, and the defense of the family and its remaining pitiful possessions fell to the few male heads of household who had survived the war. This task usually fell to the younger males in the family, since most of the older men were either dead or disabled.

As such, life in north Georgia – and most of the rest of the old South – was an extremely dangerous undertaking at best. There also were very few items with which to barter for food and other necessities until gardens and livestock could be rebuilt, so hunger and lack of shelter constantly plagued the general population. For this reason, many families simply picked up what little they owned and departed for the West – usually to Texas – to begin life anew. O.D. and his family chose to remain in Georgia and struggle on.

Family Marriages

Anna Anderson, the future wife of James Monroe Neel later of Cartersville, was the third of O.D.'s six children. James Monroe Neel also grew up in Adairsville, probably in the same church as the Andersons. A daguerreotype described by the Neel sisters once showed a very pretty Anna with brown hair and eyes. She talked of wrapping bandages around the poor and desperate Confederate soldiers during the war.

Ella, O.D.'s eldest child, married *Zachariah McReynolds* in 1869, and began the flight of some of

the family to Texas with her husband – such was the desperate nature of circumstances in Georgia. Some of their descendants can still be found in that state today.

Julia Margaret Anderson who was six years younger than sister Anna, was a pretty 19-year-old at the time of Anna's marriage to James Monroe Neel. She would later marry James herself following the untimely death of her sister.

In February of 1875, sister *Laura Anderson* married a Confederate veteran and cousin, *Augustus Marcellus Foute*. They eventually moved to Cartersville, an "up and coming" town on the W&A, ultimately building a fine home there next to the home

Anderson, O.D. – Oliver Davis Anderson was photographed here in 1902 at the Neel residence on South Avenue in Cartersville, GA.

of sister Anna and her husband, James Monroe Neel, at 119 South Avenue.

Old Cass County in which Adairsville had existed prior to the war had been totally devastated, with its county seat of government – Cassville – reduced to a charred ruin, never to be rebuilt. Cartersville, also on the newly-rebuilt Western & Atlantic Railroad, was the progressive community selected as the new county seat of government, offering hope to the remaining populace of the area, including both the Anderson and Neel families.

Brother *Jimmy Anderson* who had married the previous year carried a reputation as the family mischief-maker, and was continuously keeping things lively. He lived in Kingston with his wife *Hepatia Bowden Anderson*.

O.D. Anderson shows up in the *1880 Federal Census* of Cartersville, Bartow County, Georgia, with Julia Margaret and Frank still living at home with him and wife Amelia. O.D. is listed in this headcount as *"furniture merchant."*

Several years after the death of his wife Amelia in 1881, O.D. married her sister, *Susan Gaines*. With the struggles he had endured in Georgia since the war's end, O.D. apparently decided that he was ready to move on to a new horizon. No one had ever accused O.D. of being a "risk-taker," but he apparently saw in Susan the same lust for life which he had enjoyed in Amelia, and it wasn't long before he had made the decision to uproot his family and leave Georgia himself.

One Final Adventure

No one can ever claim O.D. was not adventurous. With all of his experiences behind him to date, he chose – at almost 60 years of age – to strike out yet again in one last professional adventure. He and Susan apparently sold their Adairsville property and purchased, of all things, an orange grove in Apopka, Florida, and moved there to raise and market oranges. Both O.D. and Susan show up in the *1885 Federal Census of Orange County, Florida* where he is identified as *"orange grower."*

No one ever accused O.D. of being lazy either, and following what must have been great labors, his orange groves flourished initially, but "Lady Luck" just did not favor the hard-working transplanted Georgian. Nothing could save him from the "great freeze of 1892." O.D. lost his entire livelihood for the second time in a little over 25 years, a situation which would have crushed and devastated a lesser man.

O.D. and Susan, however, picked up the remaining pieces of their life together and struggled onward once again. They ultimately were forced to move back to Cartersville to live with his daughter and her husband – the Foutes – next door to his daughter and son-in-law James Monroe Neel.

Those were family-centered times, when family stood strongly beside those who were struggling, and "took in" those who were homeless. Such was the case with O.D. and what remained of his family when the Foutes rescued them with domicile following their Florida losses.

After that, the seasons came and went more quickly for O.D. The year 1909 undoubtedly was yet another difficult one for the Anderson family. O.D., who had by then reached the ripe old age of 85, tragically tumbled off the high front porch of James Monroe Neel's home (which still stands on South Avenue in Cartersville as of this writing), possibly as the result of a stroke. He lingered for three days before passing.

Though the method of his death was tragic, O.D. nevertheless had enjoyed a full and rich – if oftentimes difficult – life with a large and extended family. He lived out his final years next door to the substantial Neel homestead and many nieces, nephews, and grandchildren in Bartow County.

O.D.'s lust for life had caused it to be filled with adventure – some of it good and some of it not so good – and he was remembered fondly by all who knew him. His name has been passed down more than favorably from generation to generation of family descendants. In a turn-of-the-century photograph of the extended family taken in front of the old Neel home circa 1902, O.D. Anderson is the one with the broadest smile.

(Grateful appreciation is extended to the late Marvin R. and Sally Bruce McClatchey for information contained in this article.)

Anderson Genealogical Line
(Ancestry of One Anderson Family Line in Georgia)
(Country of Origin of Anderson Family Line: Scotland & Ireland)

On the Scottish west coast, the Anderson family was born among the ancient Dalriadan clans. The surname derives from a patronymic meaning "son of Ander/Andrew" (itself derived from the Greek name "Andreas," meaning "man" or "manly"). Anderson is the eighth-most frequent surname in Scotland and 52nd-most common in England. *The surname Anderson was first found in the Great Glen and Strathspey regions, where the Anderson family is descended from Mac Ghille Andreis, servant of St. Andrew, Scotland's Patron Saint.*

Great-great-great-great-great-great-grandfather: Isaac Anderson

- **b.** 1668, Scotland
- **m.** Martha Bell (b. 1703, Ireland; d. 1749, probably Augusta, VA, USA). Issue: **James**
- **d.** 1747, Augusta, VA

Great-great-great-great-great-grandfather: James Anderson

- **b.** 1720, Ireland
- **m.** 1749 in Augusta, VA, Jane Jennett Ellison (b. 1730, Augusta, VA, d. 1779). Issue: Capt. John (b. 1740, d. 1817); James (b. 1742, d. 1813); Jacob (b. 1744, d. 1834); Martha (b. 1745 or 1750, York, PA, d. 1834); Jean (b. 1735 or 1747, Augusta, VA); Margaret (b. 1750, d. 1817); John (1752 or 1753, York, d. 1817); Isaac (1754, York); James (1756, York, d. 1832); Jacob (b. 1760); Jane (b. 1760); John Henderson (b. 1765); **Robert Baxter**; Margaret (b. 1769, d. 1800); Martha (b. 1770); James (b. 1777, d. 1850); and James (d. 1797).
- **d.** 1798

Great-great-great-great-grandfather: Robert Baxter Anderson

- **b.** 1766, Augusta, Virginia, British colonial America
- **m.** 10/13/1791, Margaret Walker (b. 1770, Rockbridge Co., VA, d. 20 Sept 1806, Cedar Grove, Rockbridge Co., VA). Issue: William (b. circa 1792, Rock Bridge, VA, d. circa 1793, Rock Bridge, VA); Mary (b. ca. 1792, Rockbridge Co., VA, d. 1793, Rockbridge Co., VA); William (b. ca. 1794, Rockbridge, VA); **Isaac** (b. 29 Nov 1795, Rockbridge, VA, d. 10 Dec 1881, Cherry Grove, Saline Co., Ark); Jane (b. 24 March 1797, Rockbridge, VA, d. 4 April 1848, Rockbridge, VA); Martha (b. 1798, Rockbridge, VA, d. 1803, Rockbridge, VA); George M. (b. 1798, Rockbridge Co., VA); William Silas (b. 1800, Rockbridge, VA, d. 15 July 1857, Webster, West VA); Elizabeth W. (b. 1801, Rockbridge, VA, d. 1875, Camden, Missouri); John M. (b. 1804 Rockbridge, d. 17 Sept 1823); Col. William Walker (b. 10 June 1804, d. 29 Oct 1886, Chattanooga, Hamilton Co., TN); and Margaret (b. 20 Sept 1806, Cedar Grove, Rockbridge Co., TN, d. 30 Sept 1806, Cedar Grove, Rockbridge Co., TN).
- **d.** 08/07/1823, Rock Bridge Baths, Rockbridge Co., VA.

Great-great-great-grandfather: Isaac Anderson

- **b.** 11/29/1795, Rockbridge Co., VA
- **m.** 10/13/1821 in Kingston, Roane Co., TN to Julianne Foute (b. 09/10/1802, Dandridge, Jefferson Co., TN, d. after 1882, Sheridan, Grant, Arkansas, USA). Issue: Adolphus A. (b. circa 1822, Blount, TN); **Oliver Davis**; Margaret Elizabeth (b. 01/20/1831, Kingston, Roane, TN, d. 08/19/1913, Terrell, TX); Thomas Jefferson (b. 7 May 1829, White, TN, d. 27 Sept 1897, Choctaw, Van Buren, Arkansas); Major Aloysius Adolphus (circa 1834, Floyd Co., GA, d. 1895 Texarkana, Miller, Ark); Robert Newton (b. 1835, Floyd Co., GA, d. 1905 Arkansas); Jacob F. (b. 1842, Floyd Co., GA, d. 1905 Arkansas); Cornelia Jane (b. 11 January 1843, d. 15 Dec 1910, Clark, Arkansas); Hannah Amlice "Ann" (b. 1847, Floyd Co., GA, d. 1922, Arkansas); and Ann Lee.
- **d.** 10 December 1881, Cherry Grove, Saline Co., Arkansas, USA

Great-great-grandfather: Oliver Davis Anderson

- **b.** 04/05/1824, Maryville, Blount Co., TN
- **m.** 09/09/1845 in Cassville, Bartow Co., GA to Amelia Gaines (b. 1826, Laurens Co., SC, d. 12/15/1881, Cartersville, Bartow Co., GA). Issue: Ella Sue (b. 1846, Virginia, d. 25 July 1925, Palestine, Anderson, TX); Laura Jane (b. 27 June 1846, Adairsville, Bartow Co., GA, d. 28 January 1917, Cartersville, Bartow); Frank (b. 1847, Virginia); James Marcellus (b. 9 March 1850, Cass Co., GA, d. 12 April, 1922, Adairsville, Bartow); Anna Mary (b. 16 May 1850, GA, d. 29 Sept 1881, Cartersville, Bartow Co.); **Julia Margaret**; and Francis Robert (b. 24 Jan 1865, Bartow Co., GA, d. 27 Nov 1944).
- **d.** 01/28/1909, Cartersville, Bartow Co. Buried 01/29/1909, Cartersville.

> **Note #1:** Oliver Davis Anderson was raised in Cassville, his family having moved there from Tennessee when Oliver, or "O.D." was a small boy. Born in 1824, he was very blond, and apparently the first fair-haired child the native Indians of the Cassville region had ever seen. Cherokees still resided there at that time, since they were not removed to reservations in the West until 1838.

> **Note #2:** During the U.S. Civil War, O.D. was depot agent and postmaster at Adairsville on the Western & Atlantic Railroad (W&A). He was considered vital to the war effort with his service on the W&A. Due to this employment, he and his family were permitted a railroad boxcar for their personal use. As the war reached Resaca, O.D. had the boxcar loaded with household goods and his family was taken southward by rail to Atlanta, then to Stone Mountain, GA, where the boxcar was parked on a side-track. The family spent approximately two months living in this boxcar. Tiring eventually of this life, they traveled northeastward to Monroe, Georgia, where they rented a house and remained until Federal raids – and the criminals which followed them – became so dangerous, that they moved on to South Carolina. At war's end, they traveled back to their devastated home in Adairsville.

Note #3: In 1862, Capt. Joseph Lockhart Neel organized at Adairsville, a company of volunteers for service in the Confederate Army as part of Company H, 40th Georgia Infantry Regiment, commanded by Col. Abda Johnson (CSA). Capt. Neel first saw service in the Kentucky Campaign under General Braxton Bragg (CSA), and later in the siege of Vicksburg. He also was with the Army of Tennessee in all of the Georgia Campaign, including hard fighting at Resaca, New Hope, Kennesaw Mountain, and the Battles of Peachtree Creek and Atlanta. He saw later action at Franklin and Nashville, TN, and finally at Bentonville, NC, where he witnessed the conclusion of the war. According to the official *Muster Roll* of Company H, 40th Volunteer Infantry, Army of Tennessee, CSA, Capt. Joseph Lockhart Neel was wounded at Vicksburg, Mississippi July 4, 1863, in Atlanta, GA (during the Battle of Atlanta) July 22, 1864, and in Bentonville, NC, on March 19, 1865. He was listed in the Greensboro, NC hospital on April 26, 1865, and paroled in Charlotte, NC on May 6, 1865.

Note #4 Several years after the death of his first wife Amelia Gaines in 1881, O.D. married her sister, *Susan Gaines*.

Great-grandmother: Julia Margaret Anderson Neel

b. 01/25/1856, Adairsville, Bartow Co., GA
m. 01/04/1883 in Bartow Co., GA, to James Monroe Neel (b. 1/22/1850, Adairsville, Bartow Co., GA, d. 11/30/1930, Cartersville, Bartow Co., buried Cartersville, Bartow). Issue: Laurie A. (b. 11/1883, Cassville, GA, d. 1970); Juliet (b. 07/1885, Cassville, d. 1965); James Monroe, Jr. (b. 02/1887, Cassville, d. 1958); Robert William (b. 08/1890, Cassville, d. 1976); **Isabelle**; and Frederick Donald (b. 05/1898, Cassville, d. 1959).
d. 05/12/1909, Cartersville, Bartow Co. Buried Cartersville, Bartow.

Grandmother: Isabelle Neel Jackson

b. 02/25/1894, Cartersville, Bartow Co., GA
m. 02/23/1921 in Cartersville, Bartow Co., GA to Ralph Olin Jackson, (b. 10/15/1893, Cartersville, Bartow Co., GA, d. 01/01/1986, Rockmart, Polk Co., GA). Issue: Mary Ann (b. 04/20/1922, Rockmart, GA); **Ralph Olin, Jr.**; and Julia (b. 1925, Rockmart).
d. 12/04/1981, Rockmart, Polk Co., GA. Buried: Rose Hill Cemetery, Rockmart, Polk Co., GA.

Notes:

1850 FEDERAL CENSUS, SUBDIVISION 30, FLOYD COUNTY, GEORGIA

<u>Anderson, Isaac</u> - Isaac is listed as the head of his family, being 54 years of age and a merchant, with real estate valued at $2,500.00. He lists the location of his birth as "Virginia." His family members are listed as: Julia Ann, age 46; Robert, age 15; Elizabeth, age 10; Jacob, age 8; Jane, age 6; and Amlice, age 4. Isaac was somewhat of a nomad, moving from Virginia to Tennessee to Georgia to Arkansas (and possibly other states) during his lifetime. He married Julia Ann Foute in Tennessee in 1821 where Oliver Davis was born in 1824. Oliver Davis married Amelia Gaines in 1845, in Cassville, Cass County, Georgia, to live.

SCHEDULE I.—Free Inhabitants in _____ in the County of _____ State of Georgia enumerated by me, on the 31 day of Oct 1850. _____ Ass't Marshal.

		The Name of every Person, whose usual place of abode on the first day of June, 1850, was in this family.	Age	Sex	Color	Profession, Occupation, or Trade of each Male Person over 15 years of age.	Value of Real Estate owned.	Place of Birth, Naming the State, Territory, or Country.				Whether deaf and dumb, blind, insane, idiotic, pauper, or convict.	
1	2	3	4	5	6	7	8	9	10	11	12	13	
		Thomas Mullenax	8	M				Ga					1
		Oliver "	6	M				"					2
		James "	4	M				"					3
		Andrew "	1	M				"					4
		Andrew Mullenax	22	M		Labr		Ga					5
		Leah "	½	F				"					6
1652	1653	B. H. L. Bomer	26	M		Physician	6000	S C					7
		Martha "	19	F				Ga					8
		James L "	2	M				"					9
		William "	1	M				"					10
1653	1654	John L. McAlister	52	M		Depo Agent	2000	S C					11
		Mary "	50	F				Ga					12
		Jacob Dyer	45	M		Merchant		Tenn					13
		Montreville King	20	M		Clerk		N C					14
		John Boren	21	M		H Carpenter		Tenn					15
		Elizabeth Whitcomb	28	F				S C					16
		George Shaw	60	M		Merchant		Ga					17
		George W Walker	40	M		"		N Y					18
1654	1655	O. D. Anderson	26	M		Merchant	1000	Ga					19
		Amelia "	21	F				S C					20
		Laura J "	5	F				Ga					21
		James "	3	M				"					22
		Mary A "	8/12	F				"					23
		Thomas I Anderson	21	M		Clerk		Ga					24
1655	1656	John R. Hale	34	M		Grocery Keeper		Tenn					25
		Mary "	31	F				Ga					26
		Thomas H. "	12	M				"					27
		Eliza J "	10	F				"		1		Blind	28
		L. H. "	8	M				"					29
		John R. "	6	M				"					30
		Sarah E "	4	F				"					31
1656	1657	Elias Black	28	M		Labr		Ga					32
		Malinda "	21	F				"					33
		Sarah J "	5	F				"					34
		George W "	1	M				"					35
1657	1658	S. M. Nored	34	M		Labr		S C					36
		Mary "	26	F				"					37
1658	1659	Robert Craighead	35	M		Teacher		Tenn					38
		Louisa I "	36	F				Ga					39
		Thomas "	10	M				"		1			40
		William "	6	M				"		1			41
		Sarah "	6	F				"					42

27 m

1850 FEDERAL CENSUS, DIVISION 17, CASS COUNTY, GEORGIA

Anderson, O.D. – Oliver Davis is listed as the head of his household, being 26 years of age and a merchant, with real estate valued at $1,000.00. He lists the location of his birth as "Georgia." His household members are listed as: Amelia, age 25, born in South Carolina; Laura J., age 5; James, age 3; Mary A., age eight months; and Thomas I., age 21, listed as a "clerk." (The identity of this Thomas I. is a mystery.)

Page No. 21

SCHEDULE 1.—Free Inhabitants in *Calvert Township* in the County of *Saline* State of *Arkansas* enumerated by me, on the *11th* day of *June* 1860. *Henry A. Bean* Ass't Marshal.

Post Office *Town*

1	2	3	Description			Profession, Occupation, or Trade of each person, male and female, over 15 years of age.	Value of Estate Owned.		Place of Birth, Naming the State, Territory, or Country.	11	12	13	14	
Dwelling-houses numbered in the order of visitation.	Families numbered in the order of visitation.	The name of every person whose usual place of abode on the first day of June, 1860, was in this family.	Age	Sex	White, black, or mulatto.		Value of Real Estate.	Value of Personal Estate.		Married within the year.	Attended School within the year.	Persons over 20 y'rs of age who cannot read & write.	Whether deaf and dumb, blind, insane, idiotic, pauper, or convict.	
125	125	John W. Smith	23	M		farm labor	200	175	Tennessee					1
		Mary J.	20	F					Ark's					2
		William D.	2	M					Ark's					3
		James R.	4/12	M										4
126	126	Thomas M. Crutchfield	25	M		farmer	200	250	Alabama					5
		Olivia A.	23	F		"			Mississippi					6
		Sarah J.	1	F					Mississippi					7
127	127	John M. Dumont	33	M		Blacksmith	960	500	Alabama					8
		Ann E.	30	F		House wife			Tennessee					9
		William H.	3	M					Ark's					10
		Henry H.	2	M					"					11
		Susy A.	1/2	F					"					12
		Trinity	34	F		Laborer			Alabama					13
		Lewis O. Wright	23	M		Mechanic		100	"					14
128	128	James Will B. Parker	38	M		Farmer	800	500	"					15
		Mary	33	F		"			Tennessee					16
		Sarah J.	3	F					Ark's					17
		John M.	1	M					"					18
		Eliza J.	1/2	F					"					19
		Mary White	15	F		Laborer			Tennessee					20
129	129	John Medcalf	41	M		Farmer		150	North Carolina					21
		Frances	54	F					North Carolina					22
130	130	Joseph Hodge	50	M		Laborer			Tennessee					23
131	131	Archer Murdick	33	M		farmer		500	New York					24
		Nancy	33	F					Tennessee					25
132	132	Joseph A. Ford	28	M		farmer	200	200	Virginia					26
		Martha E.	23	F		"			"					27
		Cornelia D.	5	F					"					28
		Joseph H.	3	M					Ark's					29
		Oliver S.	2	M					"					30
133	133	Isaac Anderson	64	M		farmer	1000	5000	Virginia					31
		Julia A.	56	F		"			Tennessee					32
		Jacob	20	M		"			Georgia					33
		Cornelia J.	17	F					Georgia					34
		Hannah	14	F					Georgia					35
134	134	Lewis J. Mauney	35	M		Merchant	200	500	North Carolina					36
		Nancy	25	F					Georgia					37
		Anna	6	F					"					38
		George	3	M					"					39
		Robert Guimarin	49	M		Gardner			France					40
40		No. white males 21 No. colored males ___ No. foreign born 1 No. blind ___ No. white females 19 No. colored females ___ No. deaf and dumb ___ No. insane ___					7,840	16,175	No. idiotic ___ No. pauper ___				No. convict ___	

1860 FEDERAL CENSUS, CALVERT TOWNSHIP, SALINE COUNTY, ARKANSAS

Anderson, Isaac – Isaac is listed as the head of his household, being 64 years of age and a farmer, with real estate valued at $1,000.00 and personal property valued at $5,000.00. He lists the location of his birth as "Virginia." His household members are listed as: Julia A., 56, born in Tennessee; Jacob, age 20, born in Georgia; Cornelia J., age 17, born in Georgia; and Hannah, age 14, born in Georgia.

Page No. 88

SCHEDULE 1.—Free Inhabitants in *The Town of Adairsville* in the County of *Cass* State of *Georgia* enumerated by me, on the *15th* day of *Aug* 1860. *Wm. H. Rod.* Ass't Marshal.

Post Office *Cassville Ga*

899

		The name of every person whose usual place of abode on the first day of June, 1860, was in this family.	Age	Sex	Color	Profession, Occupation, or Trade of each person, male and female, over 15 years of age.	Value of Real Estate	Value of Personal Estate	Place of Birth, Naming the State, Territory, or Country.	Married within the year	Attended School within the year	Persons over 20 y'rs who cannot read & write	Whether deaf and dumb, blind, insane, idiotic, pauper, or convict.	
1	2	3	4	5	6	7	8	9	10	11	12	13	14	
1	602 602	John P. Ayers	39	m		Farmer	5000	2.000	Georgia					1
2		Martha	33	f					"					2
3	603 603	O. D. Anderson	35	m		Post Master		400	Tennessee					3
4		Amelia "	33	f					S. C.					4
5		Laura J. "	13						Georgia		1			5
6		James "	11	m					"		1			6
7		Anna M. "	9	f					"		1			7
8		Ella S. "	7	"					"					8
9		Julia M. "	5	"					"					9
10		Joseph L. Gash	23	m		Gentleman		3.500	N. C.					10
11	604 604	John O. Middlebrooks				Farmer		8.300	Ga.					11
12		Delitha "	32	f					"					12
13		Adolphus "	11	m					"					13
14		Emma "	4	f					Ga.					14
15	605 605	John O. H. McLin	45	m		Carpenter		500	S. C.					15
16		Julia A. "	32	f					Tennessee					16
17		Berner "	6	m					Ga.					17
18	606 606	William H. Eames	76	"		No Occupation		250	S. C.					18
19		Susan "	41	f					Tennessee					19
20		Luther "	5	m					Ga.					20
21		Sina "	3	f					"					21
22		William "	2	m					"					22
23	607 607	James G. Grace	27	"		Farmer		350	"					23
24		Isabella "	26	f					N. C.					24
25		Lucinda "	7	f					Ga.					25
26		William "	5	m					"					26
27		Newton "	2	"					"					27
28		Thomas J. Grace	33	"		Day Labor			"					28
29	608 608	William M. Osburn	27	"		Farmer		1500	S. C.					29
30		Martha "	23	f					Ga.					30
31		Milton T. "	4	m					"					31
32	609 609	Benjamin F. Smith	22	"		Day Labor		100	S. C.					32
33		Elizabeth "	23	f					"					33
34	610 610	Joseph Reed	57	m		No Occupation		20	N. C.					Blind	34
35		Sarah "	25	f					Ga.					35
36		George O. "	22	m		Banker Sin't		400	"					36
37	611 611	Thomas Reed	39	"					"					Blind	37
38		Nancy "	19	f					"					38
39		California "	4	f					"					39
40	612 612	Jackson Reed	36	m		Day Labor			"					40

No. white males, 24. No. colored males, ____. No. foreign born, ____. No. blind, 2. 5000 9.420 No. idiotic, ____.
No. white females, 16. No. colored females, ____. No. deaf and dumb, ____. No. insane, ____. No. pauper, ____.

1860 FEDERAL CENSUS, ADAIRSVILLE, CASS COUNTY, GEORGIA

Anderson, O.D. – Oliver Davis is listed as the head of his household, being 35 years of age and occupation listed as "Postmaster," with personal property valued at $400.00. He lists the location of his birth as "Tennessee." His household members are listed as: Amelia, age 33, born in South Carolina; Laura, age 13; James, age 11; Anna M., age 9; Ella S., age 7; Julia Margaret, age 5; and Joseph L. Gash, age 23, listed as a "gentleman" born in North Carolina, with personal property valued at $3,500.00.

38

Page No. 71

☞ Inquiries numbered 3, 16, and 17 are not to be asked in respect to infants. Inquiries numbered 11, 12, 15, 16, 17, 19, and 20 are to be answered merely by an affirmative mark, as /.

SCHEDULE 1.—Inhabitants in *Subdivision No 144* , in the County of *Bartow* , State *

of *Georgia* , enumerated by me on the *16* day of *August*, 1870.   535

Post Office: *Adairsville*   *Francis M Walker*, Ass't Marshal.

1	2	3	4	5	6	7	8	9	10	11	12	13	14	15	16	17	18	19	20	
		Hibberts Ellen	17	F	W	at home			Ga											1
		— Thomas	10	M	W	at home			Ga											2
3	538	538	Dyar Joel H	34	M	W	Dry Goods + groc Merchant Ret	4000	850	Ga								1		3
4	539	539	Neel Joseph L	43	M	W	Farmer	1500	1500	Ala									1	4
		— Mary A	45	F	W	Keeping house			S.C											5
		— James	20	M	W	at School			Ga				1							6
		— Lenora	17	F	W	at home			Ga											7
		— Joseph N	13	M	W	clerk in Ret dry g			Ga											8
		— William T	10	M	W	at home			Ga											9
0	540	540	Rush Lane	29	M	W	Shoe Maker	150	100	Ga						1	k		1	10
		— Louvena	20	F	W	Keeping house			Ga								k			11
		Runnels Jack	25	M	B	Farm laborer			S.C						1	1	B		1	12
3	541	541	Bowden Joseph A	41	M	W	clerk in Ret dry g	1500	500	Ga									1	13
4			— Elizabeth C	39	F	W	Keeping house			Ga										14
5			— Hephedia C	18	F	W	at home			Ga										15
6			— Joseph P	4	M	W				Ga										16
7	542	542	Biddy John	60	M	W	Farmer	1500	2000	S.C							k	1		17
8			— Elijah	20	M	W	Farm laborer			Ga							k			18
9			McCane John	9	M	W				Ga										19
0	542	543	Mora John L J	68	M	W	Farmer	1000	500	Ga								1		20
		— Catherine	66	F	W	Keeping house			N.C											21
		— Sallie A	38	F	W	at home			Ga											22
		— Calvin	20	M	W	Farm laborer			Ga											23
	544	544	Johnson John J	47	M	W	Farmer	1200	400	S.C								1		24
		— Mary	29	F	W	Keeping house			Ga											25
		— Martha J	13	F	W	at home			Ga											26
		— Henry W	9	M	W				Ga		c									27
		— Lula	5	F	W				Ga											28
		— Robert Lee	4	M	W				Ga											29
	545	545	Anderson Oliver D	45	M	W	Mcht Ret dry goods	4000	2725	Tenn								1		30
		— Amelia	44	F	W	Keeping house			S.C											31
		— Laura I	22	F	W	at home			Ga											32
		— James	21	M	W	Asst clerk Ret dry g			Ga									1		33
		— Anna M	18	F	W	at home			Ga											34
		— Julia	13	F	W	at home			Ga											35
		— Frank	4	M	W				Ga											36
		Hodges Francis M	29	M	W				Ga									Blind	1	37
	546	546	Gray John W	41	M	W	Mcht Ret dry goods	4000	5000	Ga										38
		— Sarah A	37	F	W	Keeping house			Ga											39
		— Frank P	16	M	W	at School			Ga											40

No. of dwellings, ____   No. of white females, ____   No. of males, foreign born ____   18857 13,075   No. of insane, ____

" families, ____   " colored males, ____   " females, ____

" white males, ____   " females, ____   " blind, ____

1870 FEDERAL CENSUS, SUBDIVISION 144, ADAIRSVILLE, BARTOW COUNTY, GEORGIA

Anderson, O.D. – Oliver Davis is listed as the head of his household, being 45 years of age and occupation listed as "Mcht. (Merchant) Ret. Dry goods" with real estate valued at $4,000.00 and personal property valued at $2,725.00. He lists the location of his birth as "Tennessee." His household members are listed as: wife, Amelia, age 44, born in South Carolina; and children Laura I, age 22; James, age 21, with occupation listed as "Assist. Clerk, Ret. Drg" (Assistant Clerk of Retail Dry Goods); Anna M., age 18; Julia Margaret, age 13; Frank, age 4; and Francis M. Hodges, age 29, listed as "blind."

39

.15.

Page No. __22__

Supervisor's Dist. No. _1_

Enumeration Dist. No. _1_

Note A.—The Census Year begins June 1, 1879, and ends May 31, 1880.
Note B.—All persons will be included in the Enumeration who were living on the 1st day of June, 1880. No others will. Children BORN SINCE June 1, 1880, will be OMITTED. Members of Families who have DIED SINCE June 1, 1880, will be INCLUDED.
Note C.—Questions Nos. 13, 14, 22 and 23 are not to be asked in respect to persons under 10 years of age.

SCHEDULE 1.—Inhabitants in _Cartersville_ in the County of _Bartow_, State of _Georgia_, enumerated by me on the _8th_ day of June, 1880.

Robert M. Pattillo, Enumerator.

			Name	Color	Sex	Age	Relationship				Occupation			Health							Education		Nativity		
1	✓	212 223	Montgomery William	W	M	11	Son	✓			At School										✓		Ga	N.Y.	N.Y.
2			William E	W	M	95	Father	✓			At Home		Broken Leg					✓				N.Y.	N.Y.	N.Y.
3			Sarah	W	F	73	Mother	✓			At Home											N.Y.	Eng	N.Y.
4	✓	213 224	Anderson Oliver	W	M	56					Furniture Merchant											Tenn	Va	Tenn
5			Amelia	W	F	54	wife				Keeping House		Rheumatism									S.C.	Va	S.C.
6			Julia M	W	F	22	daughter	✓			Keeping House											Ga	Tenn	S.C.
7			Frank A	W	M	15	son				Printer	✓										Ga	Tenn	S.C.
8	✓	214 225	Hix Deaborn	W	M	30					Furniture Maker	✓										Ga	Ga	Tenn
9			Malinda	W	F	59	Mother				Keeping House								✓			Tenn	Va	Tenn
10			Robert L	W	M	2	Son															Ga	Ga	Ga
11			Mary	W	F	30	wife				Keeping House											Ga	Eng	Tenn
12	✓	215 226	Head Lucy E	W	F	41					Keeping House											S.C.	N.C.	S.C.
13	✓		John D	W	M	17	son				Clerk in Store											Ala	Ky	S.C.
14	✓		Gertrude	W	F	10	daughter				At School								✓			Ga	Ky	S.C.
15	✓		Lena	W	F	6	daughter															Ga	Ky	S.C.
16	✓	216 227	Gilbert William	W	M	58					Grocer	✓										Ga	Ga	Ga
17			Mary J	W	F	50	wife				Keeping House											Ga	Ga	Ga
18			Alfred	W	M	15	son				Grocer	✓										Ga	Ga	Ga
19			Lizzie	W	F	23	daughter				At Home											Ga	Ga	Ga
20			Maline	W	F	20	daughter				At Home											Ga	Ga	Ga
21			Katy	W	F	15	daughter				At School								✓			Ga	Ga	Ga
22			Lea	W	F	8	daughter															Ga	Ga	Ga
23			William J	W	M	7	son															Ga	Ga	Ga
24			Eliza H	W	F	78	Mother				Keeping House											Ga	Ga	Ga
25	✓	217 228	White Warren	W	M	57					Carpenter	✓										S.C.	S.C.	S.C.
26			Sarah	W	F	61	wife				Keeping House											S.C.	S.C.	S.C.
27	✓	218 229	Cooper Ralph	W	M	61					Carpenter	✓										S.C.	S.C.	S.C.
28			Cornelia	W	F	60	wife				Keeping House											Ga	Ga	S.C.
29			Morris Ralph	W	M	2	grandson															Ga	Ga	Ga
30	✓	219 230	Jackson Albert	W	M	30					Grocer											Ga	Ga	Ga
31			Katy E	W	F	19	wife				Keeping House											Ark	Tenn	Tenn
32	✓	220 231	Murray Peter	B	M	55	X				Blacksmith								✓			Ga	Va	Va
33			Cathrine	B	F	50	wife				Keeping House								✓			Ga	S.C.	S.C.
34	✓	221 232	Lynn William	B	M	19	boarder				Laborer	✓										Ga	Ga	Ga
35	✓	222 233	Trammell Conrad	W	M	57					Farmer											Ga	N.C.	N.C.
36			Nancy	W	F	52	wife				Keeping House											Ga	Ga	Va
37			Mary	W	F	23	daughter				Keeping House											Ga	Ga	Ga
38			Thomas	W	M	15	son				Farmer	✓										Ga	Ga	Ga
39			Lee	W	M	16	son				At School											Tenn	Ga	Ga
40			James	W	M	12	son				At School											Ga	Ga	Ga
41	✓		Bell Minnie	B	F	12	servant				Servant											Ga	Ga	Ga
42	✓		Trammell Cherry	W	F	21	daughter				School Teacher		Asthma									Ga	Ga	Ga
43	✓	223 234	Flemming Francis	W	M	55					Farmer											S.C.	S.C.	S.C.
44			Mary	W	F	52	wife				Keeping House		Pregnant mind									S.C.	S.C.	S.C.
45			Maretta	W	F	20	daughter				At Home											Ga	S.C.	S.C.
46			Julia	W	F	23	niece				At Home											Ga	S.C.	S.C.
47	✓	224 235	Giner Augustus	W	M	50					Baker											Ohio	Ohio	Ohio
48			Sarah	W	F	23	wife				Keeping House								✓			Ga	Ga	Ga
49			Saml	W	M	3	son															Ga	Ohio	Ga
50	✓		Fausett Adaline	W	F	29	boarder				Keeping House											Ga	Va	S.C.

1880 FEDERAL CENSUS, CARTERSVILLE, BARTOW COUNTY, GEORGIA

Anderson, O.D. – Oliver Davis is listed as the head of his household, being 56 years of age and occupation listed as *"furniture merchant."* He lists the location of his birth as Tennessee, with his father born in Virginia and mother born in Tennessee. His household members are listed as: Amelia, age 54; Julia M. (Margaret), age 22; and Frank A., age 15, is listed as a *"printer."*

1885 FLORIDA STATE CENSUS, DISTRICT 11, ORANGE COUNTY, FLORIDA

Anderson, O.D. – Several years after the death of his first wife Amelia Gaines in 1881, O.D. married her sister, *Susan Gaines.* O.D., 60 years of age by the time of this 1885 Florida State Census, is listed as the head of his household, with an occupation listed as *"orange grower."* He lists the location of his birth as Tennessee, but this time he lists his father and mother as both born in Virginia. His household members are listed as: Susan Anderson, age 60.

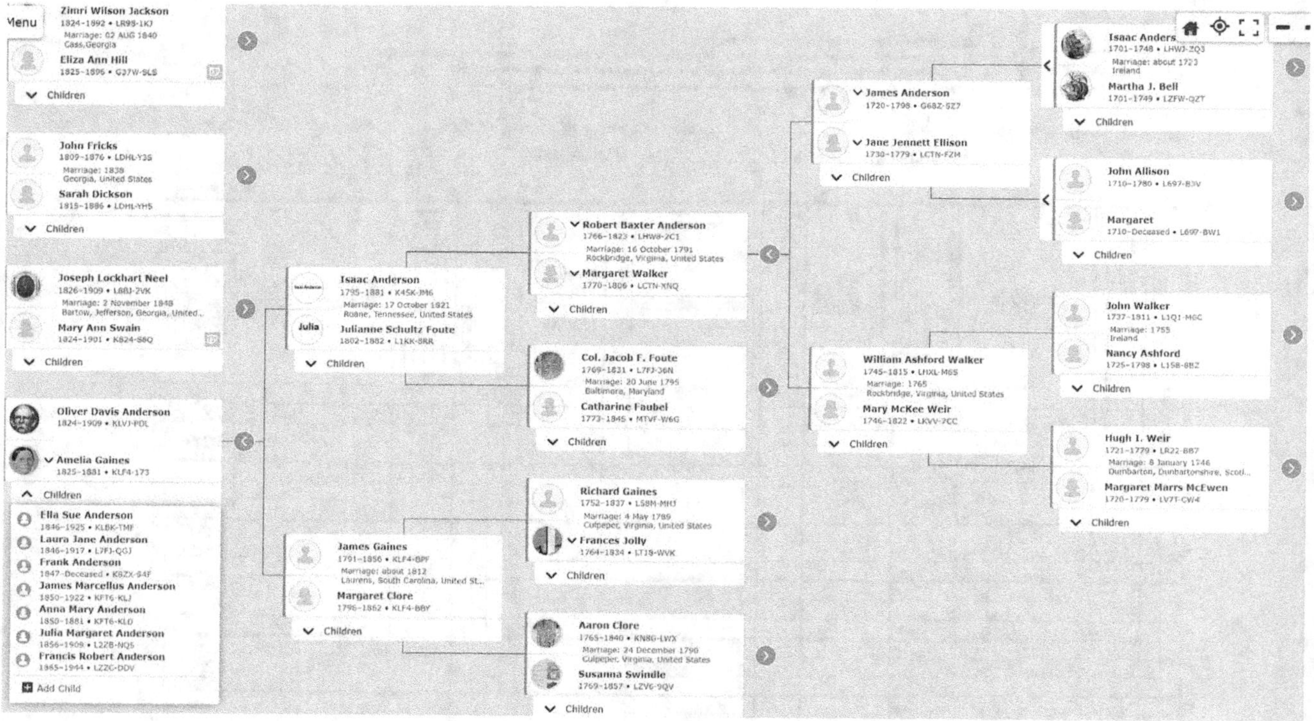

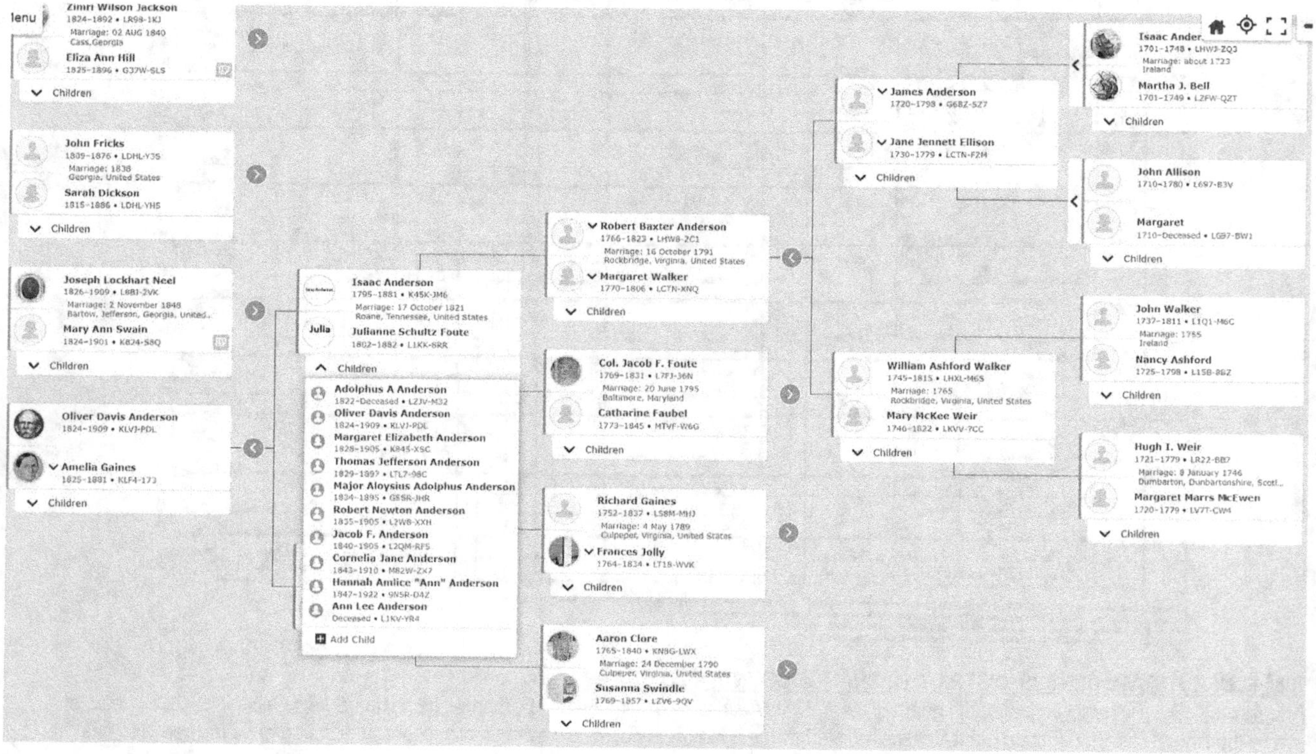

Menu

Zimri Wilson Jackson
1824–1992 • LR99-1KJ
Marriage: 02 AUG 1840
Cass,Georgia
Eliza Ann Hill
1825–1896 • G37W-SLS
∨ Children

John Fricks
1809–1876 • LDHL-Y3S
Marriage: 1838
Georgia, United States
Sarah Dickson
1815–1896 • LDHL-YHS
∨ Children

Joseph Lockhart Neel
1826–1909 • L68J-2VK
Marriage: 2 November 1848
Bartow, Jefferson, Georgia, United...
Mary Ann Swain
1824–1901 • K824-S8Q
∨ Children

Oliver Davis Anderson
1824–1909 • KLVJ-PDL
∨ **Amelia Gaines**
1825–1881 • KLF4-173
∧ Children
○ **Ella Sue Anderson** 1846–1925 • KL8K-TMF
○ **Laura Jane Anderson** 1846–1917 • L7FJ-QGJ
○ **Frank Anderson** 1847–Deceased • K8ZX-94F
○ **James Marcellus Anderson** 1850–1922 • KFT6-KLJ
○ **Anna Mary Anderson** 1850–1881 • KFT6-KLO
○ **Julia Margaret Anderson** 1856–1909 • L2ZB-NQS
○ **Francis Robert Anderson** 1865–1944 • LZZG-DDV
⊕ Add Child

Isaac Anderson
1795–1881 • X45K-JM6
Marriage: 17 October 1821
Roane, Tennessee, United States
Julia
Julianne Schultz Foute
1802–1882 • L1KK-BRR
∨ Children

James Gaines
1791–1856 • KLF4-BPY
Marriage: about 1812
Laurens, South Carolina, United St...
Margaret Clore
1796–1882 • KLF4-BBY
∨ Children

∨ **Robert Baxter Anderson**
1766–1823 • LHW9-2C1
Marriage: 16 October 1791
Rockbridge, Virginia, United States
∨ **Margaret Walker**
1770–1806 • LCTN-XNQ
∨ Children

Col. Jacob F. Foute
1769–1821 • L7FJ-36N
Marriage: 20 June 1795
Baltimore, Maryland
Catharine Faubel
1773–1845 • MTVF-W6G
∨ Children

Richard Gaines
1752–1837 • LS8H-MHJ
Marriage: 4 May 1789
Culpepec, Virginia, United States
∨ **Frances Jolly**
1764–1934 • LTJ9-WVK
∨ Children

Aaron Clore
1765–1840 • KN8G-LWX
Marriage: 24 December 1790
Culpepec, Virginia, United States
Susanna Swindle
1769–1857 • LZV6-9QV
∨ Children

∨ **James Anderson**
1720–1798 • G6BZ-5Z7
∨ **Jane Jennett Ellison**
1730–1779 • LCTN-FZH
∨ Children

William Ashford Walker
1745–1815 • LHXL-M6S
Marriage: 1765
Rockbridge, Virginia, United States
Mary McKee Weir
1746–1822 • LKVV-7CC
∨ Children

Isaac Anders
1701–1748 • LHW3-ZQ3
Marriage: about 1723
Ireland
Martha J. Bell
1701–1749 • L2FW-QZT
∨ Children

John Allison
1710–1780 • L697-B3V
Margaret
1710–Deceased • L697-BW1
∨ Children

John Walker
1737–1811 • L1Q1-M6C
Marriage: 1755
Ireland
Nancy Ashford
1725–1798 • L158-8BZ
∨ Children

Hugh I. Weir
1721–1779 • LR22-BB7
Marriage: 8 January 1746
Dumbarton, Dunbartonshire, Scoti...
Margaret Marrs McEwen
1720–1779 • LV7T-CW4
∨ Children

---

lenu

Zimri Wilson Jackson
1824–1892 • LR99-1KJ
Marriage: 02 AUG 1840
Cass,Georgia
Eliza Ann Hill
1825–1896 • G37W-SLS
∨ Children

John Fricks
1809–1876 • LDHL-Y3S
Marriage: 1838
Georgia, United States
Sarah Dickson
1815–1896 • LDHL-YHS
∨ Children

Joseph Lockhart Neel
1826–1909 • L68J-2VK
Marriage: 2 November 1848
Bartow, Jefferson, Georgia, United...
Mary Ann Swain
1824–1901 • K824-S8Q
∨ Children

Oliver Davis Anderson
1824–1909 • KLVJ-PDL
∨ **Amelia Gaines**
1825–1881 • KLF4-173
∨ Children

Isaac Anderson
1795–1881 • K45K-JM6
Marriage: 17 October 1821
Roane, Tennessee, United States
Julia
Julianne Schultz Foute
1802–1882 • L1KK-BRR
∧ Children
○ **Adolphus A Anderson** 1822–Deceased • LZJV-MJ2
○ **Oliver Davis Anderson** 1824–1909 • KLVJ-PDL
○ **Margaret Elizabeth Anderson** 1828–1905 • K845-XSC
○ **Thomas Jefferson Anderson** 1829–1897 • L7L7-98C
○ **Major Aloysius Adolphus Anderson** 1834–1895 • G89R-JHR
○ **Robert Newton Anderson** 1835–1905 • L2W8-XXH
○ **Jacob F. Anderson** 1840–1905 • L2QM-RFS
○ **Cornelia Jane Anderson** 1843–1910 • M82W-ZX7
○ **Hannah Amilce "Ann" Anderson** 1947–1922 • 9N5R-D4Z
○ **Ann Lee Anderson** Deceased • L1KV-YR4
⊕ Add Child

∨ **Robert Baxter Anderson**
1766–1823 • LHW8-2C1
Marriage: 16 October 1791
Rockbridge, Virginia, United States
∨ **Margaret Walker**
1770–1806 • LCTN-XNQ
∨ Children

Col. Jacob F. Foute
1769–1831 • L7FJ-36N
Marriage: 20 June 1795
Baltimore, Maryland
Catharine Faubel
1773–1845 • MTVF-W6G
∨ Children

Richard Gaines
1752–1837 • LS8H-MHJ
Marriage: 4 May 1789
Culpeper, Virginia, United States
∨ **Frances Jolly**
1764–1834 • LT18-WVK
∨ Children

Aaron Clore
1765–1840 • KN9G-LWX
Marriage: 24 December 1790
Culpeper, Virginia, United States
Susanna Swindle
1769–1857 • LZV6-9QV
∨ Children

∨ **James Anderson**
1720–1798 • G6BZ-5Z7
∨ **Jane Jennett Ellison**
1730–1779 • LCTN-FZH
∨ Children

William Ashford Walker
1745–1815 • LHXL-M6S
Marriage: 1765
Rockbridge, Virginia, United States
Mary McKee Weir
1746–1822 • LKVV-7CC
∨ Children

Isaac Ander
1701–1748 • LHW3-ZQ3
Marriage: about 1723
Ireland
Martha J. Bell
1701–1749 • L2FW-QZT
∨ Children

John Allison
1710–1780 • L697-B3V
Margaret
1710–Deceased • LG97-BW1
∨ Children

John Walker
1737–1811 • L1Q1-M6C
Marriage: 1755
Ireland
Nancy Ashford
1725–1798 • L158-8GZ
∨ Children

Hugh I. Weir
1721–1779 • LR22-BB7
Marriage: 8 January 1746
Dumbarton, Dunbartonshire, Scoti...
Margaret Marrs McEwen
1720–1779 • LV7T-CW4
∨ Children

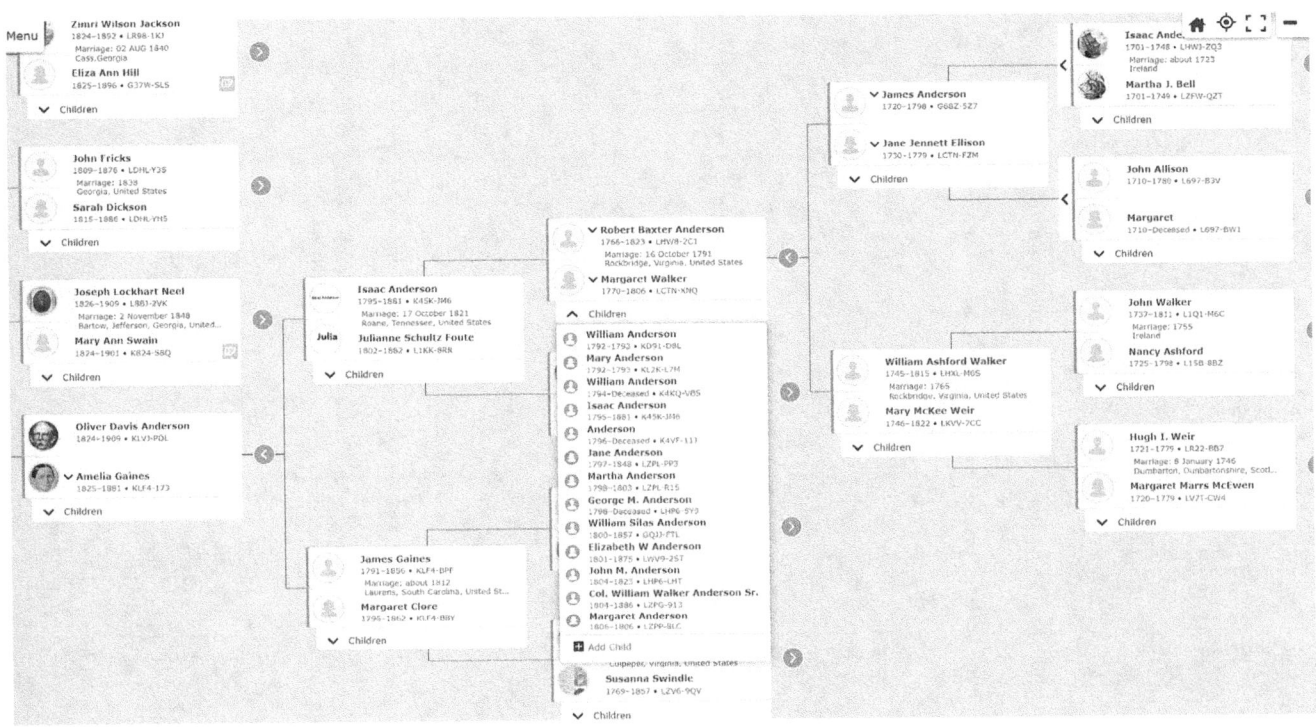

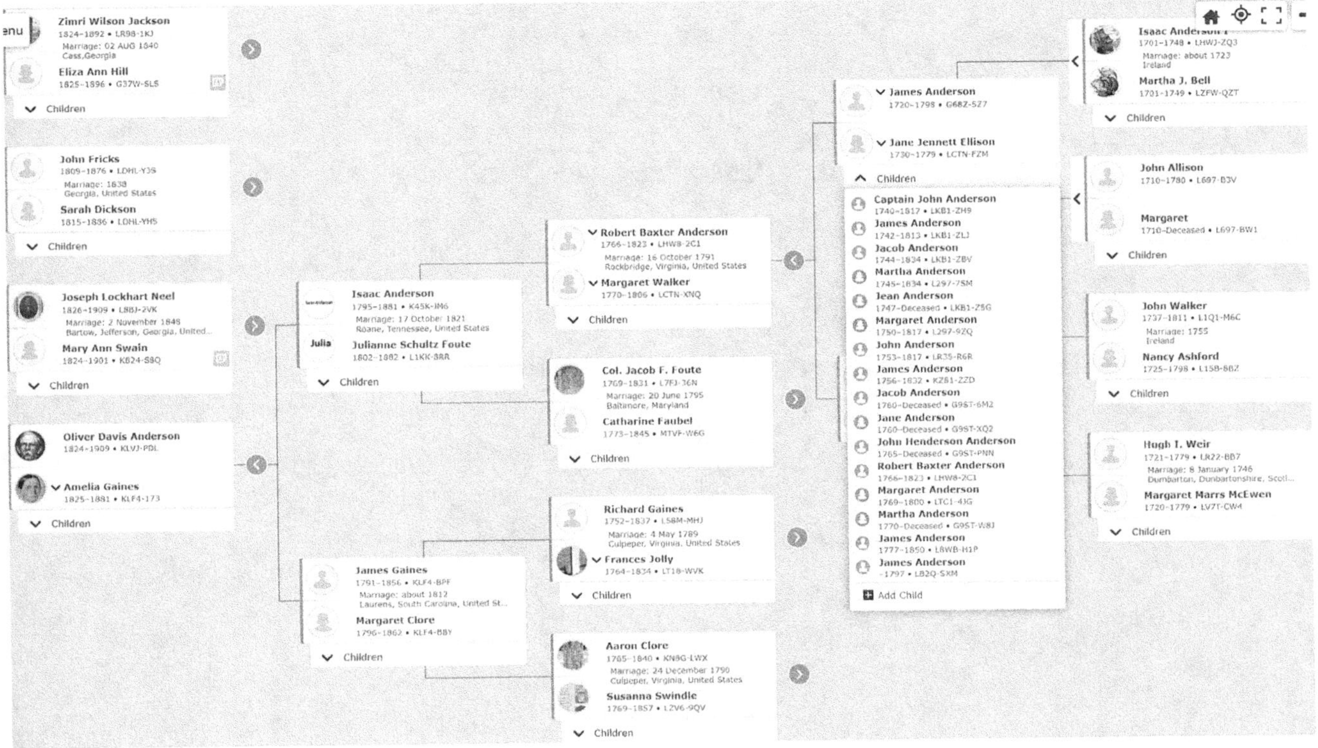

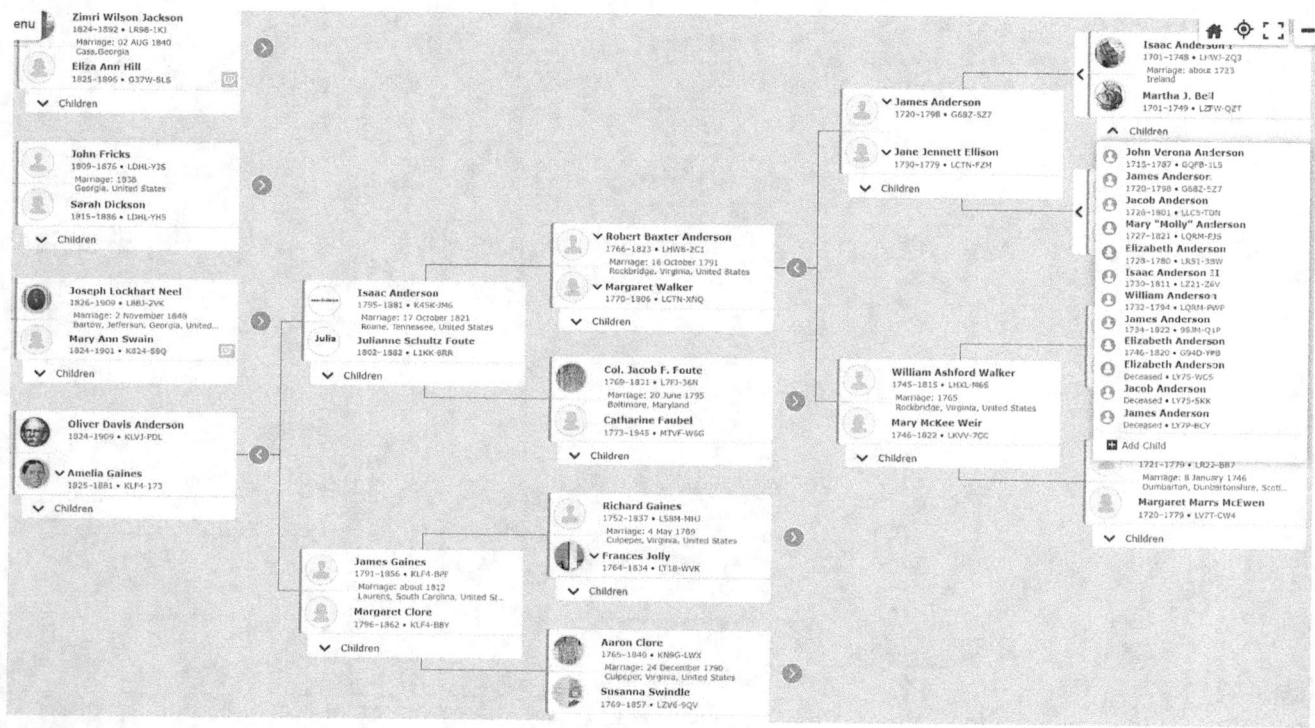

Family Tree of Anderson Family, pages 42-44 – progressing from most recent to most historic.

Jackson Family History
In Bartow Co., Georgia

They were prominent in the construction industry in Bartow County as early as the 1850s – almost 175 years ago as of 2023. The Jackson brothers left a standing legacy which is visible in many of the wonderful antebellum and post-bellum homes which still grace the landscape of the county even today.

A solitary entry on a page from an ancient receipts book (which, as of this writing in 2023, still hangs on the wall of the **Bartow History Center** in downtown Cartersville, Georgia) lists the donors to the construction of the first county courthouse in the city. *"Milton C. Jackson"* is listed among those donors, and, as is explained below, undoubtedly was at least one of the original builders of that historic structure. In fact, he and his brother, Zimri, were instrumental in the construction of a number of the early commercial and residential structures of Bartow.

According to records, Milton was a skilled designer, and the "architect" side of a contracting partnership with his equally-skilled builder-brother, Zimri. Their trademark was large two-story homes with soaring gables and fancy trim-work ("gingerbread") on the porches and around the eaves of the homes. These homes were also often built with distinctive pointed Gothic Revival windows.

Zimri W. Jackson (1824 -1894), was born in North Carolina, and migrated southward circa 1835-1840 with his father, Thomas Frederick Jackson (1782-1850) and the rest of Thomas Frederick's family to the tiny north Georgia mountain community of Hinton. At that time, Hinton was located in what then was Gilmer County, but what later (1853) was incorporated into Pickens County, Georgia.

By the time of the **1850 Federal Census of Cass County**, Zimri had married and moved his family to Division 12 in that domicile (present-day Bartow County), where, at age 26, he is listed as a *"carpenter,"*

with real estate valued at $300. His household in this census includes: his wife, Elizabeth, 25; his son, James W., age 5; and an individual named Newton McLure, age 19, also listed as a *"carpenter"* from South Carolina, who perhaps was an apprentice.

Just prior to his death in 1850, Thomas Frederick was enumerated in the September, **1850 Federal Census of Gilmer County** in Subdivision 33. He is listed there – at age 67 – as a *"farmer,"* with real estate valued at $400. His wife, Elizabeth, age 63, is listed with him, as are his daughters Nancy, age 22, and

TRAMMEL HOUSE, CARTERSVILLE, GEORGIA
Located at 124 Enota Drive, the structure known today as the Trammel House was built by the Jackson brothers, and carries the distinctive triple-gabled Gothic Revival lines which was a hallmark of their style. (Photo by Olin Jackson)

GEORGE JACKSON HOME, CARTERSVILLE, GEORGIA
At 2 Cedar Lane, the impressive and immense home of George Jackson - one of builder Zimri Jackson's sons - still stands as of this writing (2023). It is not known positively that this home was built by the Jackson brothers, but it carries all the same distinctive Jackson architectural features such as soaring gables and pointed cathedral Gothic Revival windows which were difficult to install and even more difficult to build. These unusual windows were extremely durable when properly installed, a quality to which the age of these homes attest. (Photo by Olin Jackson)

Margaret, age 19. Two others listed in this Gilmer County household are Jacob Collins Jackson, age 5, and Samuel Eaton, age 17, listed as a *"farmer."*

Since daughter Margaret is but 19 years of age at this juncture, this means that she was born when Elizabeth was 44 years old. Young Jacob's mother is unknown today. She might possibly have been Margaret, though age 14 is a bit young for bearing children.

Both Thomas Frederick and his wife, Elizabeth Ann Patterson, lived out their lives in Hinton, and are buried in old Hinton Cemetery in Pickens. As recently as the late 1980s, Thomas Frederick's sizeable historic family home – complete with the classic "soaring 'Jackson' gables" – still stood in Hinton before later being tragically consumed by a fire reportedly set by vandals.

By 1849, Cassville, the seat of government of old Cass (present-day Bartow) County, had grown into the largest town in northwest Georgia, with four hotels, two colleges, four churches, a two-story brick courthouse, and many commercial and private business endeavors. Business was booming there and it was a powerful magnet for young men searching for their destinies. It was a place in particular which offered many new construction opportunities for builders such as the Jacksons.

Cassville therefore would have held untold attraction for young men such as Zimri and his brothers. His entrepreneurial carpentry skills no doubt had been learned at his father's knee, judging from the impressive Hinton home which still survives today in photographs. In all early censuses in which Zimri appears, his profession is listed as either *"master carpenter,"* or *"builder,"* or *"master builder."*

ATTAWAY HOME, CARTERSVILLE, GEORGIA
At 23 Attaway Drive, the Jackson partners built the Attaway family
- Jeffie Gilreath home which is situated impressively upon a soft
knoll in town. (Photo by Olin Jackson)

On page 21 of the ***Bartow County Heritage Book***, ***Volume I***, Zimri W. Jackson is listed as *"among the important persons entering the Civil War from Bartow County."* He had enlisted circa 1862 in Company I, 40th Regiment, Georgia Volunteer Infantry, but when his prowess as a builder was discovered, he, according to tradition, was sent instead to Savannah, Georgia, where he reportedly built ships for the Confederate Navy.

Meanwhile, as the war raged in the Southeast, total destruction prevailed in its aftermath. Back in Cassville, between May 19 and November 5 of 1864, the entire town – including most of the residential homes – was all but erased forever, after being torched by federal troops. Only the churches and a smattering of homes used for hospitals and the quartering of troops survived. Following this utter devastation, the town was never re-built, the charred remnants standing in mute testimony to the unconscionable destruction wreaked in Sherman's infamous *"March to the Sea."*

For many years – even well into the 20th Century – the innumerable scorched chimneys in the former downtown area of Cassville were a stark reminder of the dead town. Though Cass County had been absorbed into and renamed Bartow County in 1861, and though the town of Cassville had been relieved of its designation as the county seat of government,

it nevertheless had continued to persevere until being burned to the ground by Sherman. Nearby Cartersville on the commerce-producing *Western & Atlantic Railroad* was named the new county seat.

Zimri's home, built in 1861 on the Cassville Road, was one of the few in the Cassville area which miraculously survived the war and the heavy fighting which had occurred in and around old Cass County. The talented builder returned to this home – which still stands today – and resided there for the remainder of his life after the war.

Several federal censuses of the late 1860s list the births of several of Zimri's children in "Cassville." The ***1870 Federal Census***, however, actually identifies his residence as "Cartersville." Since Zimri had built his Cassville Road home (513 Cassville Road) approximately mid-way between Cassville and Cartersville, his "new" address listed in the *1870 Census* undoubtedly resulted simply from the fact that Cassville proper had essentially disappeared, and the nearby growing Bartow township of "Cartersville" had become the new county seat of government, as well as Zimri's new census address of record.

Among the earliest of the exceptional homes built by Zimri and Milton was this Cassville Road home. It has been owned for many years by the Joe L. Myers family. The late Mrs. Joe Myers is the granddaughter of Thomas Patterson Jackson, a younger brother of Zimri and Milton. This impressive home – as of this writing in 2022 – is yet owned and occupied by Joel Myers and his wife Camille.

The huge 10 by 8-inch hand-hewn sills of this home are constructed with mortised and tenon joints, and pegged with wooden pegs. The corner posts are all heart pine and all the doors were hand-planed and constructed with pegs. All the floors – even the front porch floor – are basically still composed of the original wide boards laid down over 150 years ago.

To the rear of the aged Jackson-Myers home, evidence existed for many years of a ditch which was hastily dug by the Jacksons to hide their valuables from the advancing Union troops. Mrs. Jackson reportedly also hid her nearly-grown son, along with the family livestock, in the woods to the rear of the home.

Another historic structure credited to the Jacksons is the original Bartow County Courthouse on the old Cartersville town square. In their youth in the 1950s, a number of the Jackson descendants of the area were told by grandparents and other long-time residents of Bartow on numerous occasions that their ancestors had been the builders of that structure (which today houses the **Bartow History Center**). There is substantive evidence to support this claim.

An article on Zimri and Milton entitled *"Builders of Cartersville – the Jackson Brothers"* was published on November 11, 1975, in the **Cartersville Daily Tribune News**. This article documents their construction legacy in the county. The writer, Mr. Clyde Jolley, was well-known with that publication for many years, and a very active member of the **Etowah Valley Historical Society** (EVHS). Mr. Jolley describes in great detail the numerous homes in Cartersville – many of which are still standing – which were built by the Jacksons, and in his article he credits them with construction of the courthouse as well.

"By 1869, they (the Jackson brothers) *had completed Bartow County's new courthouse which was to remain the county seat of government until 1902,"* Jolley wrote. His reference for this statement is unknown today, but his historical society credentials and his detailed article imply he researched the topic in depth.

Jolley also knew where the Jackson brothers' shop once had stood (corner of Carter and Railroad Streets) in Cartersville, a detail which had been thought by most to have been lost through time. A follow-up article in the May, 1994 issue of the EVHS's periodical again identifies the Jackson brothers as

WILLIAM ANTHONY JACKSON PLANTATION HOME, CARTERSVILLE, GEORGIA
On Mission Road in Bartow, the brothers built Zimri's son, William Anthony, this classic plantation-style dwelling with its distinctive "planters porch" from which instructions were often given in the mornings to field hands. This home, as of this writing (2023) is still owned by the Jackson family today. (Photo by Olin Jackson)

JACKSON-MYERS HOME, CARTERSVILLE, GEORGIA
Located at 513 Cassville Road, Zimri built this home for himself in 1861, living here until he died suddenly one morning at the breakfast table. It is one of the few homes in the Cassville, Georgia, vicinity which were not destroyed by contingents of Gen. William Sherman's troops as they wantonly devastated Georgia in 1864. This structure was also still in the Jackson family as of this writing (2023), owned by Joel and Camille Myers. (Photo by Olin Jackson)

builders of the Bartow County Courthouse *"which remained the county seat of government until 1902."*

Even more compelling is an article published in **The Courant American** of Cartersville on May 26, 1892, page 4, which announced Zimri's death to the county. Among the many laudable accomplishments reviewed in this article, it states very clearly, *"Mr. Jackson was a successful farmer during his latter days, but earlier a prominent contractor, and was connected with the construction of Bartow's courthouse besides a number of Cartersville's business structures."*

As noted by the ancient receipts book page hanging today on the Bartow History Center wall in downtown Cartersville, Milton Jackson's name on this document clearly indicates he was a major donor to the courthouse construction at the height of his

contracting partnership with his brother. Since he and Zimri literally "made their living" by building such structures in Bartow, it is highly unlikely they would have been contributing to the coffers of a competitor in the building trade in their own community.

To the contrary, Milton and Zimri almost certainly were in fact making a contribution toward a construction project with which they undoubtedly expected to be involved. In the **Bartow County Heritage, Volume I**, printed in 1995 and compiled by the **Bartow County Genealogical Society**, page 25 states as follows: *"The construction of the two-story brick courthouse began in 1867. There were contract disagreements between Wallis-McElreath (the presumed initial builders) and the county's building committee which caused a legal battle that stalled work that was* *stretched into 1869. Work started up again in 1870. The work was probably completed in 1873."*

At that point, since construction is listed as beginning in 1867, and ceased in 1868 – with the courthouse uncompleted – and since solid evidence on the History Center wall today lists Milton C. Jackson as a major donor to the construction, logic would dictate that the Jackson brothers almost certainly took over the project sometime in late 1869 or early 1870, following the legal settlement, and completed construction of the courthouse. After a substantial legal battle such as this which occasionally occurs in small town politics, it is highly unlikely the town fathers would have retained the Wallis-McElreath builders to continue work on the project, particularly if they had a "master builder" such as Zimri and his talented architect brother waiting in the wings who were even willing to donate to the construction cost.

Regarding the home-building talents of the Jackson brothers, evidenced today by the numerous historic structures still extant, one needs only to drive around the city and the outlying county to begin recognizing the signature marks of the Jacksons with the soaring gables, Gothic Revival windows, and unique "ginger bread" trimmings upon these homes.

In *Historic Bartow County*, *Circa 1828 – 1866*, published in 1981 by the *Etowah Valley Historical Society*, it states, *"One style of architecture popular in the county just before and immediately after the Civil War was the gabled, early Victorian or Gothic Revival house, two stories high and embellished with fancy scrollwork on the balustrades and around the eaves; usually the gables of these houses were topped with carved finials. Pre-Civil War homes in the area (thought to be the products of contractors Zimri and Milton Jackson) that are in the Gothic Revival mode include the Jackson-Myers house, the Billy Jackson house, the Munford house and the Dr. Wilson Hardy house."*

According to records, the unique construction skills of the Jackson brothers were employed in a variety of ways in the county, but were most instrumental in the construction of very eye-pleasing residences. Among the many homes they built, those still standing as of this writing (2023) include:

On Mission Road, they built the former residence of William A. "Billy" Jackson, Zimri's son, which still remains in the Jackson family today. This fine plantation-style structure has the classic "Planter's Porch" from which instructions were given each morning to the field hands. Though this home is slightly in disrepair as of this writing, it once was a show-piece of the county.

At 124 Etowah Drive, the Jackson brothers built a signature home for the Trammel family.

At 118 North Erwin Street, they built Milton's spacious home which was owned in later years by the Rowland family and is occupied as of this writing by Strands Salon.

At 23 Attaway Drive, the partners built yet another eye-pleasing creation for the Attaway family which was later owned by the Jeffie Gilreath family and, as of this writing, by Mr. Jim Hunter.

On West Avenue, they built a fine home for the Lumpkin family. When a fire partially destroyed the upper level of this residence, the Jacksons' trademark soaring gables were replaced by a conventional roofline. This home, having lost its architectural beauty lines, was later torn down to make room for new construction.

At 2 Cedar Lane and West Avenue, George Jackson, another of Zimri's sons, lived in an impressive domicile which still stands. It is not known positively

MILTON JACKSON HOME, CARTERSVILLE, GEORGIA
On North Erwin Street in what today is downtown Cartersville, the Jackson brothers built partner Milton's spacious home which was owned in later years by the Rowland family and is occupied as of this writing (2023) by Strand's Salon. (Photo by Olin Jackson)

today whether or not this home was built by the Jackson brothers, but it has all the ear-marks of their work, right down to the soaring gables and pointed cathedral Gothic windows, both of which were clearly their trademarks appearing on their other homes.

On Cherokee Avenue, they built a home for the Gaz White family which was later owned by City Manager Walter Mahone. This home later incurred a major fire in 1987, and was relocated to an unknown location.

Out in Peeples Valley, the Jackson brothers built, in 1859, a home for Lewis Martin Munford later owned by Oscar Peeples. It was subsequently sold and moved to a site in Cobb County, Georgia, circa 1983.

An imposing nine-room home located east of Cassville on White Road was built in the 1850s for Dr. Weston C. Hardy. It was one of only three Cassville homes spared by federal troops during the war, and a compelling case can be made for its construction by Zimri and Milton. This home, which was used as a hospital by both the Confederacy and federal troops during engagements, was built only a very short distance from Zimri's Cassville Road home. It also has unusual front porch pillars which are identical to the ones which appear in the photograph of the Hinton, Georgia, home of Frederick Jackson, father to Zimri and Milton. The Hardy home also has the identical single soaring front gable so often incorporated into the Jackson creations.

Milton was the younger of the two brothers in the Jackson partnership, but he passed away relatively early in life at the age of 45 on February 14, 1872. Knowing that death was eminent, Milton designed an elaborate tomb which was constructed according

OLD BARTOW COUNTY COURTHOUSE, CARTERSVILLE, GEORGIA
According to the best indications and records, the building firm of Wallis-McElreath began construction of the original Bartow County Courthouse (pictured) in 1867. Following contractual disagreements between them and the county's building committee, a legal battle ensued and construction ceased in 1868. In 1870, the Jackson brothers assumed the mantle of builders of the courthouse and construction was renewed, being completed circa 1873. It was photographed here in 2020. (Photo by Olin Jackson)

FREDERICK JACKSON HOMESTEAD, HINTON, PICKENS COUNTY, GEORGIA

The dilapidated home of Frederick and Elizabeth Jackson in Hinton, Georgia, was built circa 1840s, and was the home in which Zimri and Milton were raised. It is not difficult to discern the Jackson trademark soaring gables in this structure. This photograph was taken in the 1980s, just prior to the tragic destruction of this historic home by a fire set reportedly by vandals. (Photo by Joe Myers. Reprinted with permission.)

to his specifications to house his last remains on the summit of historic Oak Hill Cemetery in Cartersville.

Zimri lived considerably longer, dying of what appears to have been a heart attack or stroke on May 20, 1892, at the age of 70, while seated at the breakfast table of his Cassville Road home. He reportedly reached the table on the morning of his death, sat down and stated that he felt ill, and then simply collapsed into his morning meal. Interestingly, he is buried in Cassville Cemetery, not Oak Hill in Cartersville.

There no doubt were other homes built by the Jacksons in the vicinity of Bartow which were either destroyed during the Civil War or later by fire, neglect and other causes. Nevertheless, travelers and residents alike often still encounter impressive two-story historic homes in the Bartow County vicinity with either one, two or three "soaring gables," fancy trimwork, and oftentimes "pointed" Gothic windows. These homes invariably may be credited to the long-ago efforts of the Jackson brothers who were instrumental in the development of the county in the last half of the 19th Century.

(Zimri W. Jackson is the great-great-grandfather of the children of the late Ralph Olin Jackson, Jr. and the late Marilyn Jordan Jackson of Rockmart, Georgia, as well as of many other Jackson descendants in the Polk, Bartow and Hall County, Georgia areas.)

[Subtext Note: The surname "Jackson" is a baptismal name meaning "son of Jack," and a name of great antiquity. It is a pet form of the popular name in antiquity of "John," meaning "God has favored." Its European heritage is of Anglo-Saxon descent spreading to the Celtic countries of Ireland, Scotland and Wales in early times and is found in many mediaeval manuscripts throughout these countries. Interestingly, in its greatest antiquity, the name derives from the Ancient Greek Iōánnēs (Ἰωάννης), which in turn is a form of the Hebrew name Yôchânân / Yehochanan which means "graced by Yahweh," ("God is gracious"). It was the given name of Yochanan ben Zechariah, an ancient Jewish prophet known in English as "John the Baptist."]

ZIMRI JACKSON PHOTO, CARTERSVILLE, GEORGIA

Jackson Family History In Polk County, Georgia

*Ralph Olin Jackson, Sr., never advanced beyond the 4ᵗʰ grade in school,
but when it came to finances, he simply had an uncanny knack for making money.*

Ralph Olin Jackson, Sr., born on October 23, 1893, moved from Bartow County to Polk County in 1920, approximately 33 years after the town of Rockmart was founded. He was the son of William Anthony Jackson and Cornelia Fricks Jackson, and had already been a successful farmer even before moving to Polk County where he sought new opportunity.

Just prior to his move to Rockmart, Mr. Jackson had married Isabelle Neel, and he and his new bride traveled with the couple's possessions via six or seven mule-drawn wagons to a 300-acre farm Mr. Jackson had purchased on the dusty dirt trail between Rockmart and Aragon, Georgia, near the present-day entrance to a quarry.

Mr. Jackson initially raised cotton – with which he had been very successful Bartow – in the rolling pastureland opposite his large home. However, following the onslaught of the boll weevil plague of the late 1920s and early 1930s, he converted his business into a dairy farm.

When Goodyear Mills opened a large facility in Rockmart in the 1930s, Mr. Jackson was able to obtain a contract to sell milk to the residents in the mill's associated mill village. He also sold his products to the residents of Rockmart and nearby Aragon.

The farm Mr. Jackson had purchased was not only a productive farm, but a historic tract of property as well. During the U.S. Civil War, a contingent

His laborious, but perceptive farming practices proved successful in Bartow.

of the troops of General William T. Sherman camped for a period of time on the property. In the years the property was owned by Mr. Jackson, a Union Army bayonet, as well as a bullet mold (both in the possession today of Mr. Jackson's grandson, Olin), were unearthed on a gentle prominence on the property. These relics had obviously been lost or forgotten by the troops who camped there in the 1860s.

Mr. Jackson had what was known as a "three-team farm" in its early days, keeping up to three teams of mules busy plowing, sowing, and harvesting the crops he grew. His laborious, but perceptive farming practices proved successful once again.

By 1943, assisted by a number of successful real estate investments and a limited but shrewd acumen for stock investments (He purchased shares of a product called "Coca Cola" a few years before it found markets worldwide), Ralph was able to retire at the age of 50 and live on the income from his investments. He sold the Aragon Highway farm property to Southern States Portland Cement Company, then purchased a residence on Elm Street adjacent to the First Baptist Church in Rockmart.

At about this same time, Ralph also purchased - for taxes - a 700-acre farm south of Rockmart known as "the old Simpson place" at the foot of Vinson Mountain. This property - used by Mr. Jackson to raise beef cattle - also included a substantial residence, a large barn, historic Simpson waterfalls and

R.O. Jackson Farm, Polk County, GA – Photographed circa 1930s is the "three-mule-team" farm of Ralph O. Jackson, Sr., on the road (foreground) between Rockmart and Aragon, Georgia. The fine paved road today was but a very dusty narrow byway in the 1930s.

the remains of Simpson Falls Gristmill, a pioneer-era water mill used to grind corn and other grains into flour. It is believed that a pre-Civil War government-licensed distillery as well as a tannery and a cobbler's shop, also once existed in the vicinity of the gristmill.

In 1947, Mr. Jackson built a substantial lake and lakeside cabin on this property. He and Isabelle used this residence during the summer months. As of this writing, this 700-acre tract of property is owned by Mr. Jackson's grandchildren, as well as several other private owners.

Ironically, though he never advanced any further than the 10th grade (in an 11-grade school system), Mr. Jackson was destined to become an active participant in the development of Rockmart's education system. He was a member of the Polk County Board of Education for twenty years, serving as chairman for more than a decade. He served on the board which initiated the first county-wide, nine-month school system, and was chairman when the board consolidated the school system, eliminating the tiny sub-standard classrooms which had been used for decades.

Mr. Jackson was also a charter member of both the Cedar Valley Farmers' Club and the Rockmart Rotary Club, serving as a director of the charter Rotary. He was a deacon of the First Baptist Church in Rockmart and instrumental in its development from the 1940s thru the 1960s.

Mr. and Mrs. Jackson became the parents of two girls, Mary Ann (1922) and Julia (1925), and a boy, Ralph, Jr. (1923). All three children ultimately were graduated from high school and college. Isabelle passed away in 1982. Mr. Jackson passed away in 1986, and their children have long since passed away as well. At this writing in 2023, many of the grandchildren had passed as well.

Jackson Genealogical Line
(Ancestry of One Jackson Family Line in Georgia)
(Country of Origin of Jackson Family Line: ancient Israel and later Western Europe)

Jackson, a name of great antiquity, is a baptismal name meaning 'son of Jack.' It is a pet-name derivative of the name "John" in antiquity, meaning "God has favored." Its European heritage is of Anglo-Saxon descent spreading to the Celtic countries of Ireland, Scotland and Wales in antiquity and is found in many mediaeval manuscripts throughout these countries. Interestingly, the name derives from the Ancient Greek Iōánnēs (Ἰωάννης), which in turn is a form of the Hebrew name Yôchânân / Yehochanan which means "graced by Yahweh" or "God is gracious." It was the given name of Yochanan ben Zechariah, an ancient Jewish prophet known in English as <u>John the Baptist</u>. . .

Great-great-great-great-grandfather: Frederick Jackson

b. 1750 in North Carolina, possibly in Edgecombe County. Census records show Edgecombe residence 1790-1820.

m. ? Issue: **Thomas Frederick**

d. ca. 1830, probably Edgecombe County, NC

> **Note #1:** According to a roster of soldiers from North Carolina who served in the American Revolution (compiled by the Daughters of the American Revolution in 1932), Frederick Jackson was enumerated among this select cadre.

Great-great-great-grandfather: Thomas Frederick Jackson

b. 1782 in North Carolina, probably in Edgecombe County, NC, since his father, Frederick, was enumerated there in the 1790 Census. Thomas Frederick later lived in Lincoln County (latter-day Cleveland County), NC.

m. Elizabeth Ann Patterson (b. 01/1788, d. 12/1860, Pickens County, GA) Issue: Nathaniel Abernathy (b. 1815, NC); Thomas Frederick (b. 1817, NC); James W. (b. 1819, NC); Mary E. (b. 1821, NC); Sarah (b. 1824, NC); **Zimri Wilson** (b. 01/26/1824, NC); Milton C. (b. 1827, NC, d. 02/14/1872 in Bartow); Nancy (b. 1828, NC); Margaret (b. 1831, NC); Mathias and Jencie.

d. 1850 in Pickens County, GA

> **Note #2:** It is unknown today exactly when and why Thomas Frederick left North Carolina to settle in north Georgia. The fine home he built there in Gilmer (later becoming Pickens) County, unfortunately was destroyed by vandals circa late 1980s. It survives today in a photograph, and its quality indicates Thomas Frederick undoubtedly was in good health when it was built. Since his last child was born sometime in the 1830s in North Carolina, and since he (Thomas Frederick) died in 1850 in Pickens County, Georgia, he likely moved to Pickens circa 1840s to build the home. The quality and size of this home also indicates Thomas Frederick either was reasonably successful in North Carolina with ample funds to build the substantial Georgia home, or else he was an exceptionally talented builder himself, with the ability to construct fine homes – with the assistance of his sons.

> **Note #3:** At least two of Thomas Frederick's sons – Zimri Wilson and Milton C. – ultimately became renowned builders in nearby Bartow County, Georgia, constructing numerous beautiful antebellum and post-bellum homes and commercial buildings in the area, many of which still stand today. All of the homes are characterized by soaring gables and fancy trim-work, very similar to the family home in Pickens County. It is therefore believed that their father – Thomas Frederick – due to the quality of the Pickens home, taught his sons architecture and the art of building fine homes. During the U.S. Civil War, Zimri served in Company I, 40th Regiment, Georgia Volunteer Infantry, CSA. When his prowess as a builder was learned by Confederate officials, he reportedly was sent to Savannah, Georgia, to construct ships for the Confederacy.

Great-great-grandfather: Zimri Wilson Jackson

b. 01/26/1824 in North Carolina, possibly in Lincoln County

m. Eliza Ann Hill (b. 02/10/1825 in South Carolina, d. 05/1896 in Georgia). Issue: James Walter (b. 1850, Cassville, Bartow County, GA, d. Oklahoma); **William Anthony** (b. 05/25/1852, Cassville, Bartow Co., d. 04/14/1936, Cartersville, Bartow Co.); George Milton (b. 11/08/1854, Cassville, Bartow Co., d. 09/24/1940); Fannie (b. 1860, Cassville, Bartow Co.); Robert Zimri (b. 06/1864); Eddie L. (b. 1867, Cassville, Bartow Co.); and Thomas Arthur (b. Cassville, Bartow).

d. 05/20/1894 at his home on the old Cassville Road in Bartow County, GA.

> **Note #4:** According to records, of the many homes and buildings constructed by Zimri Wilson and Milton C. Jackson in Bartow, one was the original county courthouse which still stands (as of this writing in 2022) in downtown Cartersville. Zimri was also associated with industrialist Mark David Cooper of the Cooper Iron Works which once existed near Cartersville prior to the U.S. Civil War. The homes of both Zimri and Milton also still stand (as of this writing) in Bartow County, Zimri's on the old Cassville Road and Milton's somehow surviving in downtown Cartersville.

Great-Grandfather: William Anthony Jackson

b. 05/25/1852, Cassville, Bartow County, GA

m. 12/20/1881 in Bartow Co., GA, Cornelia Lydia Fricks (b. 1856, Pond Spring Dist, Walker Co, GA d. 03/06/1939, Bartow Co., GA) Issue: Asa D. (b. 02/04/1884, d. 07/11/1885, Cass Station, Bartow); Robert Wilson (b. 09/27/1885); Arthur Flavius (b. 09/07/1886, Cass Station, Bartow, d. 10/03/1966, Taylorsville, GA); Sally Maud (b. 04/10/1890, Cass Station, Bartow, d. 02/21/1950, Cartersville, Bartow Co.); **Ralph Olin** (b. 10/15/1893, Cartersville, Bartow Co.); and Annie Lee (b. 06/25/1896, Cartersville, Bartow Co., d. 09/21/1944).

d. 04/14/1936, Cartersville, Bartow Co., GA

> **Note #5:** Despite his limited education, Ralph Sr. possessed an uncanny knack for financial investments. In the late 1930s he began buying up quantities of scrap metal which he later sold to the U.S. government for a substantial profit during WW II. He purchased considerable stock in a little-known company called "Coca Cola" during its formative years, and it soon found markets worldwide. As a result of his financial acumen, he was able to retire at the age of 50. He was a founding member of the Rockmart Rotary Club and a deacon in the First Baptist Church of Rockmart for over 20 years, serving as Sunday School Superintendent from 1939 to 1951. Also in the 1950s, Ralph purchased some 700+ acres of prime mountain property by shrewdly paying only a tax lien owed by the previous owner. During the period of the 1950s thru the 1970s, Ralph was considered one of the wealthiest men in Polk County.

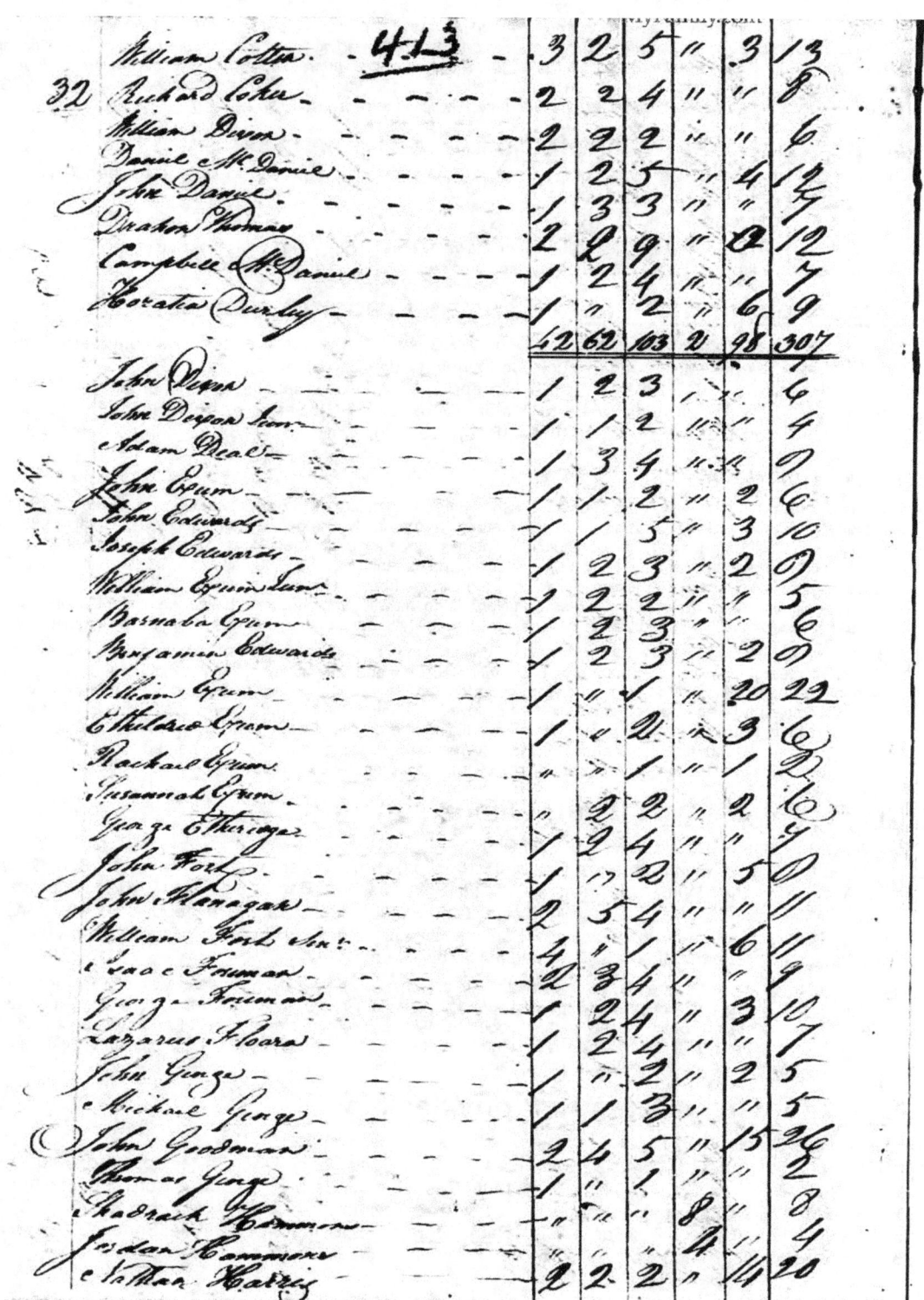

1790 FEDERAL CENSUS, EDGECOMBE COUNTY, NORTH CAROLINA

<u>Jackson, Frederick</u> – This is possibly the earliest census record on which Frederick appears. Details about the children are undiscernible from this record.

Name						
William Hare	3	5	8	"	4	11
Nicholas Hare	1	1	8	"	"	5
Randolph Hancock	2	"	8	"	4	14
John Howard	1	2	2	"	"	7
John Hail	1	3	3	"	"	1
	38	50	83	12	86	26a
Matthew Kinchin	2	4	2	"	23	31
Nathaniel Howell	2	1	2	"	"	5
Andrew Hamilton	1	2	3	"	3	9
Joseph Ing	1	1	4	"	2	11
Frederick Jackson	1	"	"	"	"	1
Shier Knight	1	4	2	"	"	7
Thomas Landingham	1	6	4	"	"	11
Isaac Morgan	1	2	2	"	"	5
John Mills	3	3	2	"	"	8
Hadly Morris	1	3	2	"	3	9
William Manning, senr	2	3	4	"	"	12
James Nelson	2	1	3	"	"	6
Elizabeth Williams	2	1	3	"	12	10
Malakiah Nicholson	2	3	4	"	4	13
John Nicholson	4	3	10	"	25	42
Elizabeth Pittman	3	3	4	"	12	22
William Powell	1	3	4	"	10	10
Francis Parker	2	5	5	"	4	16
John Ryland	1	3	2	"	2	8
Malakiah Penny	1	"	2	"	"	3
William Pittman	2	2	3	"	"	7
John Pace	1	2	4	"	"	7
Arthur Philips	"	2	3	"	15	21
Samuel Price	1	2	4	"	"	7
Stephen Pace	1	2	4	"	"	7
John Penny	1	"	"	"	"	1
Moses Powell	1	2	3	"	"	6
Reddick Smith	1	5	3	"	"	9
Philip Spier	2	2	2	"	5	16
Christian Spier	4	1	6	"	"	5
Wright Lynch	1	2	2	"	"	3
	18	73	03	"	108	331

Right portion of document on facing page

Amt. brought forward	558	247	333	300	170
Jordan Joshua	"	"	2	1	"
Jordan Henry		"		1	"
Jordan Cornelious		"	1	"	"
Jordan Eolie	"	2	"	"	"
Johnson Nathan	1	1	"	"	1
Jordan Gray	2	"	"	1	"
Jackson Charlotte	"	"	"	1	"
Jones Reuben	"	1	1	1	"
Jones James	1	"	1	"	"
Johnson Willis	2	"	"	1	"
Jones David	1	1	"	1	"
Johnson Jacob	"	"	1	"	"
Joshua Johnson	"	1	1	"	"
Josey William	1	1	"	"	1
Johnson James	"	1	1	"	1
Jackson Mary	"	"	"	"	"
Jones James	"	1	1	1	"
Jackson William	1	"	"	"	1
Jackson Frederick	"	"	"	"	"
Jones William	"	1	1	1	"
Johnson William	"	1	"	1	"
Jones Abram	1	"	2	1	"
Jones Jesse	"	"	"	1	"

1800 FEDERAL CENSUS, EDGECOMBE COUNTY, NORTH CAROLINA

Jackson, Frederick – Frederick also appears on this 1800 Census, but once again, it lists only the number of children, and no other information.

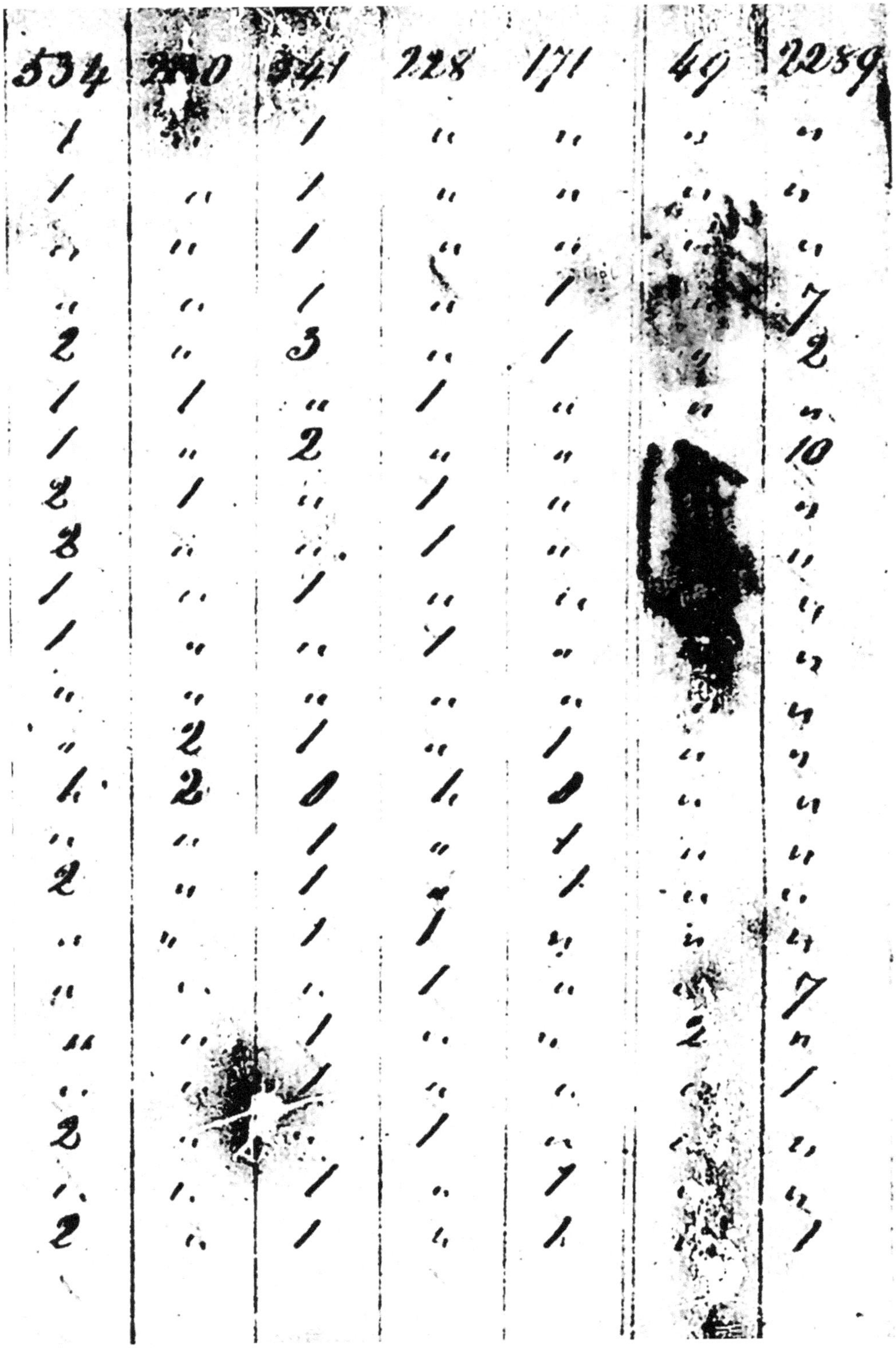

534	[illegible]	341	228	171	49	2289
1	[illegible]	1	"	"	"	"
1	"	1	"	"	"	"
"	"	1	"	"	[illegible]	"
"	"	1	"	1	[illegible]	7
2	"	3	"	1	[illegible]	2
1	1	"	1	"	"	"
1	"	2	"	"	[illegible]	10
2	1	"	1	"	[illegible]	"
3	"	"	1	"	[illegible]	"
1	"	1	"	"	[illegible]	"
1	"	"	1	"	[illegible]	"
"	"	"	"	"	[illegible]	"
"	2	1	"	1	"	"
4	2	0	4	1	"	"
"	"	1	"	1	"	"
2	"	1	"	1	"	"
"	"	1	1	"	"	"
"	"	"	1	"	"	7
"	"	1	"	"	2	"
"	[illegible]	1	"	"	[illegible]	1
2	"	"	1	"	[illegible]	"
"	"	1	"	1	[illegible]	"
2	"	1	"	1	[illegible]	1

Right portion of document on facing page

Frederick Jackson	2	"	"	
James Cross Sin	"	"	1	"
James Savage	"	"	"	1
Thomas Drummon	"	"	"	"
Penelope Nicholson	"	"	"	"
Henry Wall	"	"	1	"
John Banks	"	"	1	"
Elizabeth Dixon	"	"	"	"
William Anderson	1	2	3	"
James Anderson	"	"	"	"
Bartholomew Brown	"	"	"	1
Ann Yana	"	"	1	"
William Jones	"	"	1	1
Thomas Price	"	"	"	1
Priscilla Exum	"	1	1	1
John Boon	1	1	"	1
Smiths District Lazarus Oneil	"	"	"	1
Britton Jones	"	"	1	1
William Foxhall	"	"	1	1
Carried forward	712	327	419	408

1810 FEDERAL CENSUS, PINCHES DISTRICT, EDGECOMBE COUNTY, NORTH CAROLINA

<u>Jackson, Frederick</u> – In this census, it appears that within Frederick's household, there are two children (probably males) under the age of five, two individuals between the ages of 20 and 30, and one individual between 60 and 70 years of age. No other information is provided.

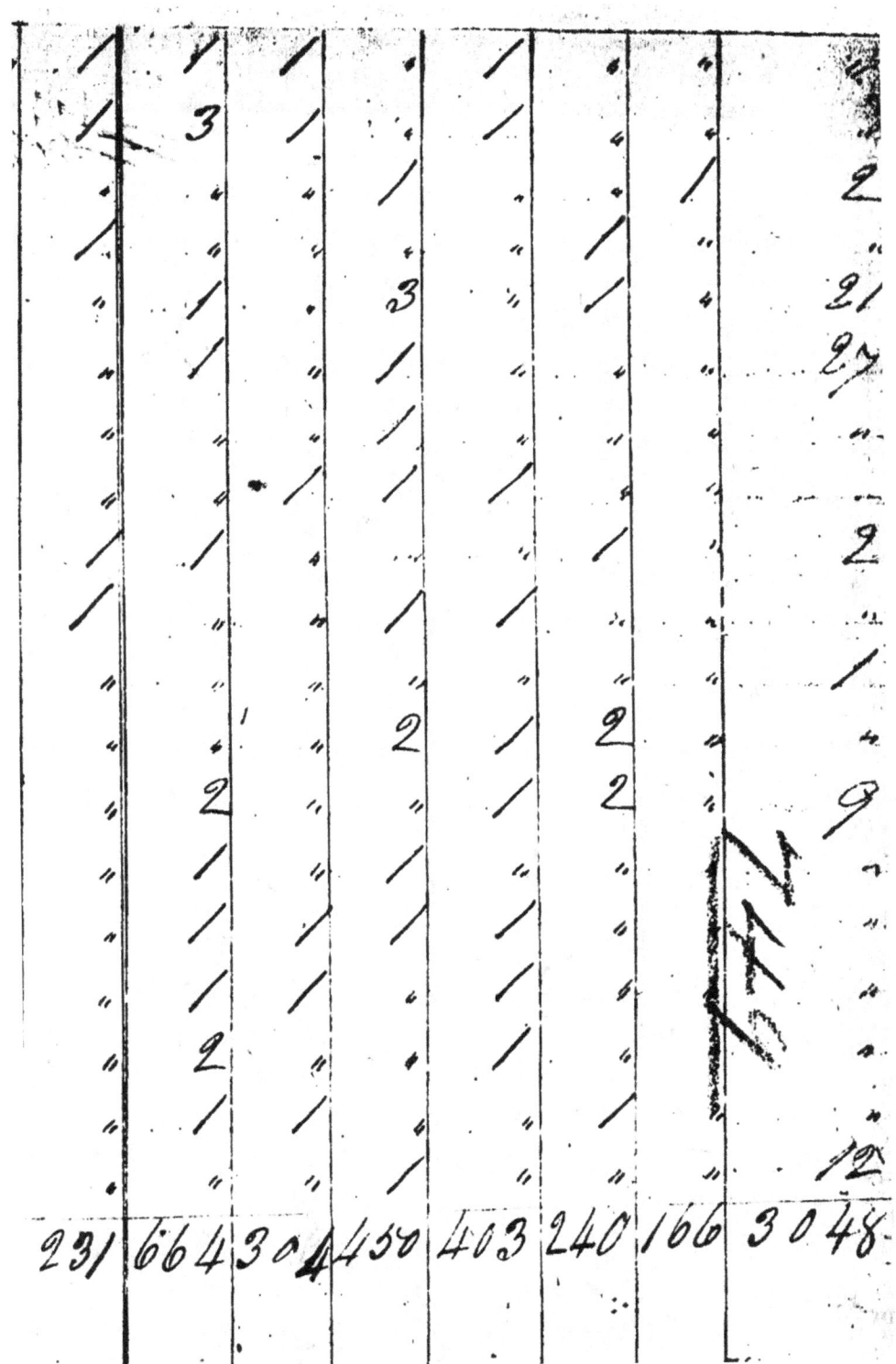

Right portion of document on facing page

Name													Total
Richard Paiter	1			1		1			1				2
Grisham C. Pitman	1		1	1	1				1	1			8
William Pitman				1		2			1				1
John Banks	3			1		1				1			
Elizabeth Cofield				1					1	1			26
Caleb Etheridge			1	3		1			1		1		6
Thomas Etheridge				1		2			1				2
James Etheridge				1									2
John Exum				1									2
Hardy King	1					3			1				2
Exum Lewis	3	2	1	2	1	1	2	2					13
Stephen Bradley					1				1	1	1		1
Susanna Boney						1				1			4
Samuel Dew	1	2			1	3							1
Joseph Pitman	2			1		2	1		1				1
Martin Wilkins													
Edmond Oneal	2	1			1	2	1		1				4
Joseph Abraham					1			2					1
Penelope Dixon	1					2			1				
Eli B. Whitaker, ngrs													9
Elizabeth Nicholson, ngrs													7
Richard Bradley				1	1	4			3	1			3
Susanna Danfs			1			1	2	1					
Thomas King			1						1				2
Frederick Jackson													2
Thomas Lyon	1	2		1	1	1			1				8
Alexander Cotten			1	1		2				1			8
Eaton Finch	3				1								2
Thomas Banks	5			1	1				1	1			5

1820 FEDERAL CENSUS, EDGECOMBE COUNTY, NORTH CAROLINA

<u>Jackson, Frederick</u> – Again only the Census Taker knew the interpretation of his numbers in this Census, since no specificity is provided across the top margin of the page.

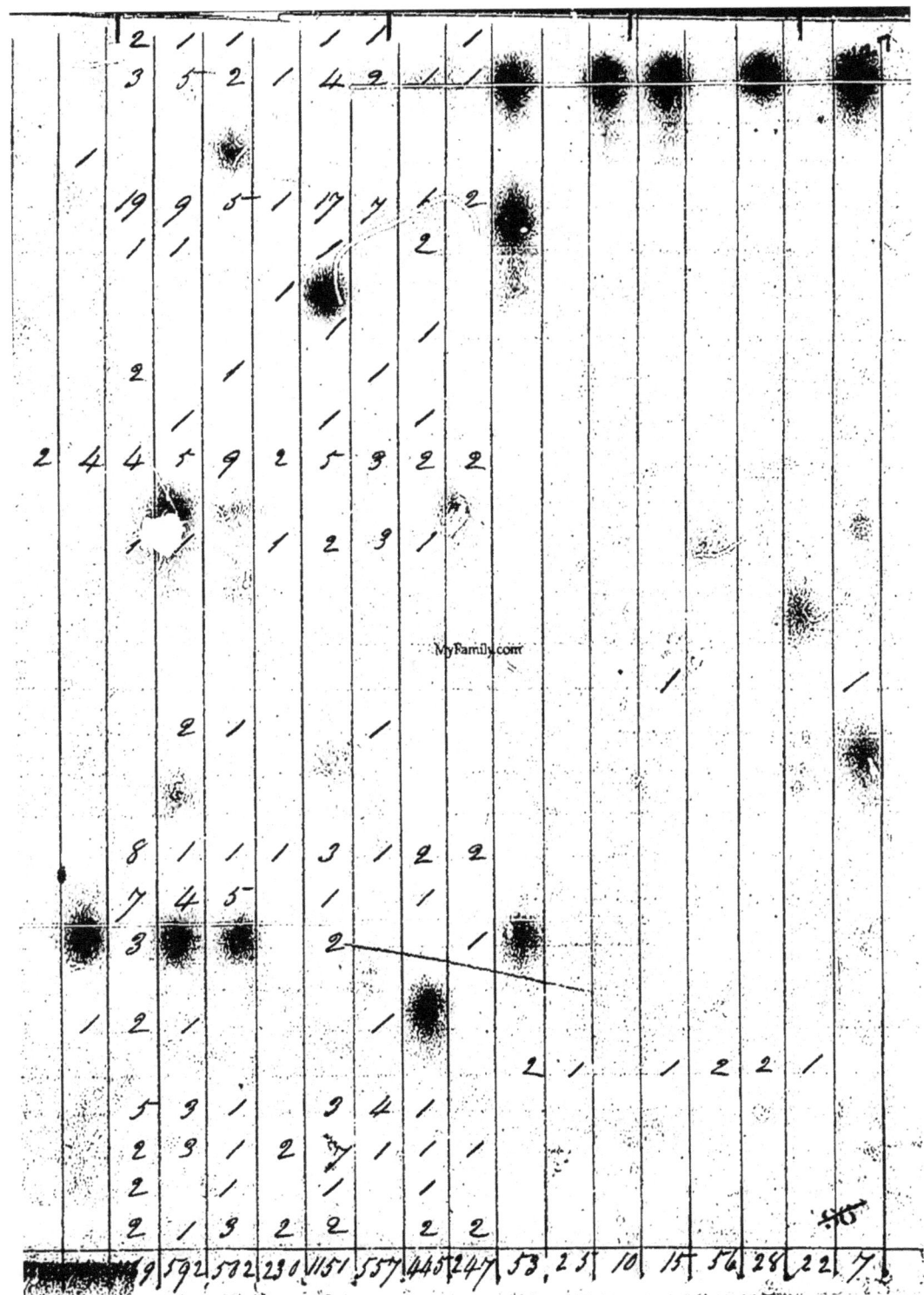

Right portion of document on facing page

(N° 4.) 160

SCHEDULE of the whole number

Name of County, City, Ward, Town, Township, Parish, Precinct, Hundred, or District	NAMES of HEADS OF FAMILIES.	MALES								
		Under five years of age	Of five and under ten	Of ten and under fifteen	Of fifteen and under twenty	Of twenty and under thirty	Of thirty and under forty	Of forty and under fifty	Of fifty and under sixty	Of sixty and under seventy
9	Wm Logan			1	2	2			1	
	John Rippy		1						1	
	James Ivings	1	2	1	1			1		
	John Adams	1				1				
	Francis Adams	1	1			1				
	Abednego Adams			1						1
	Zechariah Carly			2			1			
	Martin Rippy	1		1		1				
	Alfred Moore	1	1	1			1			
	William Martin Esq		1	2	2				1	
	William Powell	2	1	3	2			1		
	Richard Eskridge	2			1	1				
	William Williams	1	1			1				
	Betsy Y. Glenn									
	Hampton Collier					1				
	Benj Wilson					1				
	Fielding Bell	1				1				
	Benjamin Hardin			2						
	Thomas Hardin	1				1				
	Thomas Lowrie	1	1				1			
	Frederick Jackson	1	2	2	1			1		
	Alfred Carroll	1				1				
	William Ivings	2						1		
	Isaac Milenose	1	1	2			1			
	Isaac Wells		1		1					
	William Burke	1	1			1				
	Thomas Patterson					1				
	Peter Harmon	1	3	1		1				
		19	17	19	9	13	8	4	5	1

1830 FEDERAL CENSUS, LINCOLN COUNTY, NORTH CAROLINA

Jackson, Frederick – This 1830 Census for Frederick's family may be interpreted as follows: One at least can make some speculative assumptions about this Census. The *"one male under age five"* means a birth between 1825 and 1830, which possibly means Milton (1827). The *"two males between five and ten years of age"* means a birth between 1820 and 1825, which probably means Zimri (1824) and another unknown individual. The *"two males between ten and fifteen years of age"* means a birth between 1815 and 1820, and only Thomas Frederick, Jr. (1817) and James W. (1819) fall into that category. And the *"one male between fifteen and twenty years of age"* means a birth between 1810 and 1815, which could only be Nathaniel Abernathy (1815). The *"one female under five years of age"* again means a birth between 1825 and 1830 which would be Nancy (1828). The *"one female between five and ten years of age"* means a birth between 1820 and 1825, which would be either Mary (1821) or Sarah (1824). The *"one female between 15 and 20 years of age"* is unknown. Therefore, the individuals listed on this Census possibly included: Nathaniel Abernathy (1815); Thomas Frederick (1817); James W. (1819); Mary E. (1821); Sarah (1824); Zimri (1824); Milton (1827); and Nancy (1828). The fact that both Sarah and Zimri are listed as having been born in 1824 obviously is conflicting information.

of Persons within the Division allotted to

	FREE WHITE PERSONS, (INCLUDING HEADS OF FAMILIES.)								FEMALES.						
Of seventy and under eighty.	Of eighty and under ninety.	Of ninety and under one hundred.	Of one hundred and upwards.	Under five years of age.	Of five and under ten.	Of ten and under fifteen.	Of fifteen and under twenty.	Of twenty and under thirty.	Of thirty and under forty.	Of forty and under fifty.	Of fifty and under sixty.	Of sixty and under seventy.	Of seventy and under eighty.	Of eighty and under ninety.	Of ninety and under one hundred.
70 to 80	80 to 90	90 to 100	100, &c.	under 5	5 to 10	10 to 15	15 to 20	20 to 30	30 to 40	40 to 50	50 to 60	60 to 70	70 to 80	80 to 90	90 to 100
	1					1		1			1				1
					1				1						
				1		1	1		1						
				2	1			1							
				1			1								
							1				1				
					2	1	1	2	1						
				1	2			1							
				2	1	1		1							
						1	1		1	1					
				2	2		1								
					1			1							
				1				2	1		1				
				2											
				2				1							
				1				1							
				1				1	1	1					
				2	1			1							
				1	1	1		1							
				1	1		1		1						
								1							
					2	1		1							
				1	1	1		1							
				2	2				1					♠	
							1								
							1								
				1	1										
1	1			21	19	11	6	13	10	3	4	1		1	

Right portion of document on facing page

SCHEDULE I.—Free Inhabitants in _Subdivision No 33_ in the County of _Gilmer_ State of _Georgia_ enumerated by me, on the _23_ day of _September_ 1850. _Cole A. Ellington_ Ass't Marshal

		The Name of every Person whose usual place of abode on the first day of June, 1850, was in this family.	Age	Sex	White, black, or mulatto	Profession, Occupation, or Trade of each Male Person over 15 years of age.	Value of Real Estate owned	Place of Birth, Naming the State, Territory, or Country.				Whether deaf and dumb, blind, insane, idiotic, pauper, or convict.
1	2	3	4	5	6	7	8	9	10	11	12	13
		Jane Dillinger	30	F				N.C	1		1	
		Marcus "	13	M				"	1		1	
		John "	10	M				"	1			
		Sarah "	3	F				"				
		Mary M. "	2	F				"				
422	422	Washington Jackson	35	M		Farmer		S.C	1		1	
		Lucinda Jackson	22	F				"			1	
		William A. "	3	M				Ten				
		Thomas I. "	2	M				Ga				
423	423	Sanford Owens	26	M		Farmer		S.C	1			
		Martha Owens	34	F				"			1	
		Caroline "	17	F				Ga				
		James Clark	14	M				"			1	
		Anal "	9	M				"				
424	424	William H. Collins	38	M		Farmer	1500	N.C	1		1	
		Nancy Collins	36	F				S.C				
		Martin "	14	M				"			1	
		Elvy "	13	F				Nc	1		1	
		Emaline "	11	F				"	1		1	
		Enoy I "	7	F				"	1		1	
		Mary E "	5	F				Ga				
		Martha "	3	F				"				
		Roxanna "	2/12	F				"				
425	425	Daniel Hood	38	M		Farmer		S.C	1			
		Mary A. Hood	38	F				"			1	
		Julia A	18	F				"			1	
		Elizabeth I "	17	F				"			1	
		Nancy D "	14	F				"			1	
		Mary A "	13	F				N.C			1	
		Martha C "	11	F				"			1	
		Lydia A "	9	F				Ga			1	
		Richard M "	4	M				"				
		Silas B "	2	M				"				
426	426	Frederick Jackson	67	M		Farmer	400	N.C	1			
		Elizabeth Jackson	63	F				"	1			
		Nancy "	22	F				"				
		Margaret "	19	F				"				
		Jacob Collins "	5	M				"				
		Samuel Eaton	17	M		Farmer		Ga				
427	427	Amos Moss	58	M		Farmer	2500	S.C	1		1	
		Elizabeth Moss	58	F				"			1	
		Nancy "	20	F				"			1	

17m
25f

44.00

13.8

1850 FEDERAL CENSUS, GILMER COUNTY, GEORGIA

Jackson, Frederick – At some point in the 1840s, Frederick moved from North Carolina (where he reports he was born) to Georgia with his family. Listed as his household in this September, 1850 Census for Gilmer are: Frederick at 67 years of age; his wife, Elizabeth, 63; his daughter Nancy, 22; daughter Margaret, 19; another child, Jacob, age 5; and an individual named Samuel Eaton, age 17, with a profession listed as *"farmer."* Frederick's sons – Nathaniel, Zimri, Milton, Thomas, James and possibly Mathias – also departed North Carolina for Georgia in the 1840s, possibly living with Frederick until they could obtain their own property and livelihoods.

Jackson, Washington – Listed in a separate entry on this *1850 Federal Census for Gilmer* are Washington, age 35, with a profession as a *"farmer"*; Lucinda, age 22; William A., age 3; and Thomas I., age 2. The relationship, if any, of this family to the Frederick Jackson line is unknown.

158
51

SCHEDULE I.—Free Inhabitants in *The 12 Division* in the County of *Cass* State of *Georgia* enumerated by me, on the *2* day of *Oct* 1850. *Aly. Stroup* Ass't Mars

		The Name of every Person whose usual place of abode on the first day of June, 1850, was in this family.	Age	Sex	White, black, or mulatto	Profession, Occupation, or Trade of each Male Person over 15 years of age.	Value of Real Estate owned.	Place of Birth. Naming the State, Territory, or Country.	Married within the year	Attended School within the year	Persons over 20 who cannot read & write	Whether deaf and dumb, blind, insane, idiotic, pauper, or convict.
1	2	3	4	5	6	7	8	9	10	11	12	13
1		Columbus A Jones	17	M				Tenn				
2		Martha A "	14	F				Ga				
3		Mary E "	12	F				"				
4	988 1000	Eliza Hawks	33	F			1000	SC				
5		Kinion "	12	M				Ga		1		
6		Mary "	10	F				"		1		
7		Chester "	9	M				"		1		
8		Julius "	5	M				"				
9	989 1001	H A Wilson	45	M		Carriagemaker	500	Tenn				
10		Jane "	44	F				"				
11		Elizabeth "	19	F				"		1		
12		Josephine "	16	F				"		1		
13		Robert J T "	14	M				"		1		
14		Jane M B "	12	F				Ga		1		
15		Dorcas C "	10	F				"				
16		Augustus "	6	M				"				
17		Hiram W "	1	M				"				
18	990 1002	Robert McLure	45	M		Wheelwright	300	SC				
19		Elizabeth "	47	F				Va				
20	991 1003	D L Millholen	24	M		Bl. Smith		No. Carolina				
21		Nancy "	17	F				Ga				
22	992 1004	Leroy S Count	25	M		Wheelwright		NC				✓
23		Mary A "	23	F				"				
24		M S Matthews	22	M		"		NC				
25	993 1005	Zimri Jackson	26	M		H Carpenter	300	NC				
26		Eliza "	25	F				"				
27		James W "	5	M				Ga				
28		Newton McClure	19	M		Carpenter		SC				
29	994 1006	William T Hassel	35	M		Carpenter	700	SC				
30		Katharine "	34	F				Ga				
31		James "	16	M				"				
32		Malissa "	13	F				"				
33		Caroline Baker	18	F				"				
34	995 1007	Jonathan P Phillips	26	M		Lawyer	200	Ga				
35		Martha "	30	F				"				
36		Charles A "	6	M				"				
37		James "	4	M				"				
38		John "	2	M				"				
39	996 1008	Polly Phillips	64	F			2000	Ga				
40		Jas S S "	21	M				"			1	
41		Mary "	23	F				"				
42		Sarah "	13	F				"				

42no.   Amt of B..b

1850 FEDERAL CENSUS, CASS COUNTY, GEORGIA

<u>Jackson, Zimri</u> – By the time this October, 1850 Census was taken, Zimri had moved his family to Division 12 in Cass County (present-day Bartow). Zimri, age 26, is listed as a *"carpenter,"* with real estate valued at $300. His household includes: his wife, Elizabeth, 25, his son, James W., age 5, and an individual named Newton McLure, age 19, listed as a *"carpenter"* from South Carolina.

Page No. 39

SCHEDULE 1.—Free Inhabitants in 838 Dist. G.M. in the County of Cass State of Georgia enumerated by me, on the 14 day of June 1860. Wm. H. Rich Ass't Marshal.

Post Office Cassville Georgia.

849

Dwelling-houses numbered in the order of visitation	Families numbered in the order of visitation	The name of every person whose usual place of abode on the first day of June, 1860, was in this family.	Age	Sex	Color	Profession, Occupation, or Trade of each person, male and female, over 15 years of age.	Value of Real Estate	Value of Personal Estate	Place of Birth, Naming the State, Territory, or Country.	Married within the year	Attended School within the year	Persons over 20 years of age who cannot read and write	Whether deaf and dumb, blind, insane, idiotic, pauper, or convict.	
267	267	Mary Watson	42	F		Cook Lady		10	Georgia					1
		Nancy Watson	22	"					"				Blind Pauper	2
		Lucky "	18	"					"					3
		Mary "	14	"					"					4
		Isabella "	8	"					"					5
		John "	3	M					"					6
		Elliot "	3	M	+				"					7
		Nancy Carroll	64	"					Kentucky		1			8
268	268	Alfred Cross	21	M		Farmer		30	Tennessee		1			9
		Sarah "	18	F					"					10
		James M. "	1	M					Georgia					11
269	269	John Smith	53	"		"	1	4000	700	S.C.				12
		Nancy "	30	F					" "					13
		Robert "	17	M		"	1			" "					14
		Samuel "	17	"		"	1			" "		1			15
		John "	14	F					Georgia					16
		William "	14	"					"		1			17
		Milly "	13	F					"					18
		Nancy "	7	"					"		1			19
		Jane "	5	"					"					20
		Thomas "	3	M					"					21
		James M. "	1	M					"					22
		Levi Lawless	17	M					"					23
270	270	Hosey Byers	31	M		Farmer		40	S.C.					24
		Sarah "	17	F					Tennessee					25
		James M. "	12	M					Geo.					26
271	271	George F. Mines	38	"		"	1	4000		S.C.					27
		Francis J. "	29	F					" "					28
		Eliza A. "	7	"					" "					29
		Henry "	5	M					"					30
		Belle Y. "	3	F					"					31
272	272	Zemariah Jackson	36	M		Master Carpenter	1	4000	6405	R.C.					32
		Eliza A. "	35	F					S.C.					33
		James "	10	M					Geo.		1			34
		William A. "	8	"					"		1			35
		George M. "	5	"					"		1			36
		Thomas A. "	3	"					"					37
		Francis F. "	1/2	F					"					38
		William Harrison	23	M		Carpenter			Tennessee					39
		Green Suitty	19	"		Farmer	1			Georgia					40

No. white males, 19 No. colored males,   No. foreign born,   No. blind, 1   8660   8985   No. idiotic, 1
No. white females 21 No. colored females,   No. deaf and dumb,   No. insane,

1860 FEDERAL CENSUS, CASS COUNTY, CASSVILLE, GEORGIA

Jackson, "Zemariah" – With a listed age of 36, Zimri is apparently becoming somewhat prosperous. He is identified on this census as a *"master carpenter."* The Census Taker notes that Zimri has real estate valued at $4,000.00 and personal property valued at $6,405.00. Zimri therefore was approaching the point of considerable wealth for his day and time, but the U.S. Civil War with all its lawlessness and trauma will soon eliminate that financial comfort. Also listed in his household at this time are: his wife, Eliza, age 35; his sons James W. (Walter), 10; William A. (Anthony), 8; George M. (Milton), 5; Thomas A. (Arthur), 3; and infant daughter Frances, one month old.

1870 FEDERAL CENSUS, BARTOW COUNTY, 4TH DISTRICT, CARTERSVILLE, GEORGIA

Jackson, "Zimariah" – The 1870 Census finds Zimri, age 46, with a profession listed as "*builder.*" To be listed as a "*builder*" rather than "*carpenter*" implies a step up professionally in livelihood. Zimri lists real estate valued at $12,000.00, but personal property valued at only $500. The severely diminished value of Zimri's personal property is an indication that virtually everything of value had been stolen by Union Army contingents five years earlier during the U.S. Civil War. Anything of value which remained in the family's possession was used as "barter" since the general economy in the South – based upon Confederate dollars – had completely collapsed in 1864. Also listed in Zimri's household in this 1870 Census are: his wife, Ann, age 44; sons James W. (Walter), age 20; Anthony W. (William Anthony), age 18; George M. (Milton), age 16; Thomas A. (Arthur), 14, listed as "*in hi school*"; a daughter, Frances J., 11, "*hi school*"; and an infant son "*Little E*" (Eddie L.), age 2. Non-family members listed in this household include William Warriant (?), age 23, with profession listed as "*Carpenter,*" and Green Beatty, 17, listed as a "*farmer.*"

1880 FEDERAL CENSUS, BARTOW COUNTY, CARTERSVILLE, GEORGIA

Jackson, Z. W. – Zimri Wilson Jackson, age 56, interestingly, is identified on this census not as a *"builder,"* but as a *"farmer."* His death was still a good 14 years in the future at this point, but brother Milton – the "architect" side of the *Jackson Brothers Builders* partnership – had passed away somewhat prematurely on February 14, 1872. Zimri, therefore, had semi-retired from the builder profession, choosing to focus instead upon farming. Others listed in this household are: Zimri's wife, Eliza A., age 55, stating that her mother was born in South Carolina, and her father in Ireland; Zimri's son, Thomas A. (Arthur), age 23, listed as a *"laborer"*; daughter Fanni (Frances), age 20; and son, *"Little E.,"* age 12, listed as *at school.* Non-family members listed in this household include Cila Craig, age 35, a Black *"Cook"*; and Ida Craig, age 10, a Black *"Laborer."* Zimri's son <u>William Anthony</u>, now 28 years of age, had left the fold to seek his own profession. In a little over a year, he will marry Cornelia Fricks of Walker County, Georgia. The method in which they met is unknown today, since Bartow and Walker are several days apart distance-wise by horseback.

D.

Page No. 8

Note A.—The Census Year begins June 1, 1879, and ends May 31, 1880.
Note B.—All persons will be included in the Enumeration who were living on the 1st day of June, 1880. No others will. Children BORN SINCE June 1, 1880, will be OMITTED. Members of Families who have DIED SINCE June 1, 1880, will be INCLUDED.
Note C.—Questions Nos. 13, 14, 22 and 23 are not to be asked in respect to persons under 10 years of age.

Supervisor's Dist. No. 1

Enumeration Dist. No. 8

SCHEDULE 1.—Inhabitants in Cassville D No 828, in the County of Bartow, State of Georgia enumerated by me on the Third day of June, 1880.

J H Walker Jr. Enumerator

		Name of each Person	Personal Description			Civil Condition		Occupation	Health	Education		Nativity		
1	59 60	Smith Robert	B m 21	Mess-mate		1		Laborer on RR					NC	NC	NC
2		Clarke Steve	B m 34	" "		1		Laborer "					Ga	Ga	Ga
3		Cannon Sam	B m 24			1		Laborer "	✓						
4		Cannon Nathan	M m 44	" "		1		Laborer "	✓				SC	SC	SC
5		Johnson Brooks	B m 21	" "		1		Laborer "	✓		1 1	Ga	Ga	Ga
6		Lindsey George	B m 21	" "		1		Laborer "	✓			Virginia	Va	Va
7		Black Reese	B m 24	" "		1		Laborer "	✓			Ga	Ga	Ga
8		Roberson Emanuel	B m 27	" "		1		Laborer "	✓			NC	NC	NC
9		Fry John	B m 22	" "		1		Laborer "	✓					
10		Oaks Anderson	B m 21	" "		1		Laborer "	✓		1 1	NC	NC	NC
11	60 61	Clayton Kennedy	W m 38			1		Farmer				Ga	Virginia	Ga
12		— Constance	W f 28	Wife		1		Keeping house				Ga	Ga	Ga
13		— William	W m 6	Son		1						Ga	Ga	Ga
14		— George	W m 3	Son		1						Ga	Ga	Ga
15		— Lois	W f 1	Daughter		1						Ga	Ga	Ga
16		— Esther	W f 4/12 Feb	Daughter								Ga	Ga	Ga
17		Lee Margaret	W f 33	Servant		1		Servant			1 1	Ga	Ga	Ga
18		Ogle Jackson	W m 40	Boarder		1						Ga	Ga	Ga
19		Miller Andy	B m 20					Laborer		✓		Ga	Ga	Ga
20	61 62	Erwin Milton	B m 29				1	Blacksmith	✓		1 1	Ga	Ga	Ga
21		— Frank	B m 6	Son								Ga	Ga	Ga
22	62 63	Wheeler Marcus	W m 36			1		Farmer	✓			New York	NY	NY
23		— Mary	W f 35	Wife		1		Keeping house				NY	NY	NY
24		— Junilian	W m 13	Son		1		At School				NY	NY	NY
25		— Charles	W m 11	Son		1		At School				NY	NY	NY
26		— Lewis	W m 7	Son		1						Ga	NY	NY
27		— George	W m 5	Son		1						Ga	NY	NY
28		— Leroy	W m 2	Son		1						Ga	NY	NY
29	63 64	Morris Samuel	B m 34			1		Laborer	✓		1 1	Ga	Ga	Ga
30		— Polly	B f 29	Wife		1		Keeping house			1 1	Ga	Ga	Ga
31		— John	B m 13	Son		1		Laborer			1 1	Ga	Ga	Ga
32		John Wofford	B m 12	Stepson		1		Laborer			1 1	Ga	Ga	Ga
33		Wofford Ed	B m 8	Son		1						Ga	Ga	Ga
34		Morris Sam	B m 4	Son								Ga	Ga	Ga
35	64 65	Morris Benjamin	B m 36			1		Laborer	✓		1 1	Ga	Ga	Ga
36		— Virginia	B f 38	Wife		1		Keeping house			1 1	Ga	Ga	Ga
37		McDow Robert	B m 18	Step Son		1		Laborer				Ga	Ga	Ga
38	65 66	Price Robert	B m 33			1		Laborer				Ga	Ga	Ga
39		— Sophia	B f 24	Wife		1		Keeping house			1	SC	SC	SC
40		— Bessie	B f 7	Daughter								Ga	Ga	SC
41		— Beatrice	B f 5	Daughter								Ga	Ga	SC
42		— Mary	B f 3	Daughter								Ga	Ga	SC
43		— Anna	B f 1	Daughter								Ga	Ga	SC
44	66 67	Jackson William	W m 28			1		Farmer	✓			NC	NC	SC
45	67 68	Brown Peter	B m 25			1		Laborer			1 1	Miss	Miss	Miss
46		— Emma	B f 20	Wife		1		Keeping house			1 1	Ga	Ga	Ga
47		— Willie	B m 4	Son								Ga	Miss	Ga
48	68 69	Mitchell James	B m 24			1		Laborer	✓		1 1	Tenn	Ga	Ga
49		— Mary	B f 24	Wife		1		Keeping house			1 1	Ga	Ga	Ga
50		— George	B m 4	Son								Ga	Tenn	Ga

1. 6
3. 4

1880 FEDERAL CENSUS, BARTOW COUNTY, CASSVILLE, GEORGIA

<u>William A. Jackson</u> – In this separate 1880 Census, William is living alone and listed simply as being 28 years of age and working as a "farmer." He has listed the location of birth of his father as in North Carolina and mother in South Carolina.

1-226.

TWELFTH CENSUS OF THE UNITED STATES.

SCHEDULE No. 1.—POPULATION.

222 A

State Georgia
County Bartow

Supervisor's District No. 7
Enumeration District No. 7

Sheet No. 11

Township or other division of county Cassville

Name of Institution, X

Name of incorporated city, town, or village, within the above-named division,

Ward of city, X

Enumerated by me on the 12 day of June, 1900, James D Pittard, Enumerator.

1900 FEDERAL CENSUS, BARTOW COUNTY, CARTERSVILLE, GEORGIA

Jackson, William Anthony – By 1900, William Anthony was 48 years of age and had been living for quite some time in the large plantation-style home constructed for him years earlier on the outskirts of Cartersville by his father's Jackson Brothers Builders firm. Also listed in this household are: William's wife, Cornelia Fricks, age 44, born in Georgia (Walker County). This listing also indicates her father was born in Tennessee, and her mother in South Carolina. William's sons, Robert W., age 17, and Arthur, age 13; daughter, Sally M. (Maud), age 10; son, Ralph O. (Olin), age 6; and daughter, Annie L. (Lee), age 4, are also listed.

1910 FEDERAL CENSUS, DISTRICT 822, BARTOW COUNTY, CARTERSVILLE, GEORGIA

Jackson, William Anthony – Listed as 57 years of age, William Anthony – or "Willie" as many knew him – is yet the head of his household. Others listed here are: his wife, Cornelia F., age 54; his daughter, Sally M., age 20; his son, Ralph O., age 16; his daughter, Annie L., age 13; an individual named "Arthur," age 23, who is described interestingly NOT as William Anthony's son (as was actually the case), but rather as a "border" (boarder). William Anthony was remembered by his son, Ralph, as a stern taskmaster. At the relatively youthful age of 16, Ralph is listed on this census not as "son," but as "farm labor."

STATE _Georgia_

COUNTY _Bartow_

9–137

DEPARTMENT OF COMMERCE—BUREAU OF

FOURTEENTH CENSUS OF THE UNITED STATES

TOWNSHIP OR OTHER DIVISION OF COUNTY _822 Militia District_   NAME OF INCORPORATED PLACE ____

NAME OF INSTITUTION ____   ENUMERATED BY ME

			NAME	RELATION													Place of birth	
51			Hardin Iris	Daughter		F	W	17	S						Yes	Yes	Alabama	
52			— Printis	Son		M	W	14	S					Yes	Yes	Yes	Alabama	
53			— Hazel	Daughter		F	W	1½	S								Georgia	
54	For 170 177	Wade William	Head		K	M	W	42	Wd				No	No		Georgia	
55		— Jessie	Daughter			F	W	16	S				No	Yes	Yes	Georgia	
56		— Ronnie	Daughter			F	W	13	S				Yes	Yes	Yes	Georgia	
57	X 171 175	Palmer John	Head		R	M	W	26	M				Yes	Yes	Yes	Alabama	
58		— Maude	Wife			F	W	19	M				No	Yes	Yes	Alabama	
59	Fra 172 179	Cane Joseph P	Head		R	M	W	22	M				Yes	Yes	Yes	Georgia	
60		— Birtie	Wife			F	W	20	M				No	Yes	Yes	Georgia	
61	Fm 173 180	Cane Joseph F	Head		R	M	W	42	M				Yes	Yes	Yes	Georgia	
62		— Ida	Wife			F	W	58	M				Yes	Yes	Yes	Georgia	
63		— Elizabeth	Daughter			F	W	18	S				No	Yes	Yes	Georgia	
64	Fm 174 181	Padgett Paul	Head		R	M	W	23	M				Yes	Yes	Yes	Georgia	
65		— Nellie	Wife			F	W	20	M				No	Yes	Yes	Georgia	
66		— James H	Son			M	W	2¾	S							Georgia	
67		— Thelma E	Daughter			F	W	1¾	S							Georgia	
68		— Sarah D	Daughter			F	W	4/12	S							Georgia	
69	Fm 175 182	Harvell Duffie	Head		R	M	W	32	M				Yes	Yes		Georgia	
70		— Oraline	Wife			F	W	26	M				Yes	Yes		Georgia	
71		— Henry R	Son			M	W	7	S				Yes			Georgia	
72		— Willie	Son			M	W	5	S				No			Georgia	
73		— Odis	Son			M	W	3 9/12								Georgia	
74		— Metalene	Daughter			F	W	1½	S							Georgia	
75	Fm 176 183	Head Nathan	Head		R	M	W	39	M				Yes	Yes		Georgia	
76		— Nancy	Wife			F	W	26	M				Yes	Yes		Georgia	
77		— W Hixil M	Daughter			F	W	10	S				Yes	Yes	Yes	Georgia	
78		— James M	Son			M	W	7	S				Yes			Georgia	
79		— Floyd	Son			M	W	6	S				No			Georgia	
80		— Jack	Son			M	W	13/12	S							Georgia	
81		— William E	Son			M	W	2½	S							Georgia	
82		— Lois V	Daughter			F	W	14/12	S							Georgia	
83	Fm 177 156	Jackson William A	Head	1	O	M	W	67	M				Yes	Yes		Georgia	
84		— Cornelia L	Wife			F	W	63	M				Yes	Yes		Georgia	
85		— Annie L	Daughter			F	W	23	S				Yes	Yes		Georgia	
86	Fm 178 185	Jackson Robert W	Head	1	O	M	W	36	M				Yes	Yes		Georgia	
87		— Willie	Wife			F	W	33	M				Yes	Yes		Georgia	
88		— Louis W	Son			M	W	9	S				Yes			Georgia	
89		— Robert M	Son			M	W	5	S				No			Georgia	
90		— Milton	Son			M	W	2½	S							Georgia	
91	Fm 179 156	Bailey Presley	Head	1	R	M	Mu	47	M				Yes	Yes		Georgia	
92		— Della	Wife			F	Mu	23	M				No	No		Georgia	
93		— Benham Elizabeth	Mother in Law			F	B	50	Wd				No	No		Georgia	
94	Fm 180 187	Clark Ed L	Head	1	R	M	W	24	M				Yes	Yes		Georgia	
95		— Lizzie	Wife			F	W	22	M				Yes	Yes		Georgia	
96		— Buster	Son			M	W	4½	S							Georgia	
97		— Robert	Son			M	W	1½	S							Georgia	
98		— Holland Mattie	Mother in Law			F	W	54	Wd				No	No		Georgia	
99		— Bennett Jane	Grand Mother			F	W	72	Wd				No	No		Georgia	
100	Fm 181 188	Phillips Manuel	Head	1	R	M	W	30	M				Yes	Yes		Georgia	

1920 FEDERAL CENSUS, DISTRICT 822, BARTOW COUNTY, CARTERSVILLE, GEORGIA

Jackson, William Anthony – Willie is 67 years of age now, and slowing down, but is still the head of his household. Listed with Willie are wife, Cornelia F., age 64, and his daughter, Annie Lee, age 23. Entered below Willie's listing is that of his eldest living son, Robert Wilson, age 36; his wife, Willie, age 33; his sons Louis W., (9); Robert M., (5); and Milton, (2).

F THE CENSUS   [D1—878]

TES: 1920—POPULATION

SUPERVISOR'S DISTRICT No. 7   SHEET No.

ENUMERATION DISTRICT No. 3   9   B

WARD OF CITY   X   39 of

ON THE 13 DAY OF January, 1920.   George H Unu   ENUMERATOR 5970

					OCCUPATION.				
FATHER		**MOTHER**							
Place of birth.	Mother tongue.	Place of birth.	Mother tongue.		Trade, profession, or particular kind of work done, as spinner, salesman, laborer, etc.	Industry, business, or establishment in which at work, as cotton mill, dry goods store, farm, etc.			
21	22	23	24	25	26	27	28	29	
Alabama		Alabama		Yes	None				51
Alabama		Alabama		Yes	None				52
Alabama		Alabama			None				53
Georgia		Georgia		Yes	Farmer	General Farm		127	54
Georgia		Georgia		Yes	None				55
Georgia		Georgia		Yes	None				56
Alabama		Alabama		Yes	Labor	Stave Cunshu	co	21	57
Alabama		Georgia		Yes	None				58
Georgia		Georgia		Yes	Farmer	General Farm	oa	128	59
Georgia		Georgia		Yes	None				60
Georgia		Georgia		Yes	Farmer	General Farm		139	61
Georgia		Georgia		Yes	None				62
Georgia		Georgia		Yes	None				63
Georgia		Georgia		Yes	Farmer	General Farm	oa	130	64
Georgia		Georgia		Yes	None				65
Georgia		Georgia			None				66
Georgia		Georgia			None				67
Georgia		Georgia			None				68
Georgia		Georgia		Yes	Farmer	General Farm	oa	131	69
Georgia		Georgia		Yes	None				70
Georgia		Georgia			None				71
Georgia		Georgia			None				72
Georgia		Georgia			None				73
Georgia		Georgia			None				74
Georgia		Georgia		Yes	Farmer	General Farm	Em	132	75
Georgia		Georgia		Yes	None				76
Georgia		Georgia		Yes	None				77
Georgia		Georgia			None				78
Georgia		Georgia			None				79
Georgia		Georgia			None				80
Georgia		Georgia			None				81
Georgia		Georgia			None				82
North Carolina		South Carolina		Yes	None				83
North Carolina		South Carolina		Yes	None				84
Georgia		Georgia		Yes	None				85
Bahama		Georgia		Yes	Farmer	General Farm	Em	133	86
Georgia		Georgia		Yes	None	Do			87
Georgia		Georgia			None				88
Georgia		Georgia			None				89
Georgia		Georgia			None				90
Georgia		Georgia		Yes	Farmer	General Farm	oa	134	91
Georgia		Georgia		Yes	None				92
Georgia		Georgia		Yes	None				93
Georgia		Georgia		Yes	Farmer	General Farm	oa	135	94
Georgia		Georgia		Yes	None				95
Georgia		Georgia			None				96
Georgia		Georgia			None				97
Georgia		Georgia		Yes	None				98
Georgia		Alabama		Yes	None				99
Georgia		Georgia		Yes	Farmer	General Farm	oa	136	100

Right portion of document on facing page

75

1930 FEDERAL CENSUS, DISTRICT 822, BARTOW COUNTY, CARTERSVILLE, GEORGIA

Jackson, William Anthony – Now 77 years of age, only Willie and wife "Lydia C." (73) remain at home. All the others have departed. His son, Ralph Olin, will later often relate to his grandsons that though his father was considered a wealthy man, he provided little if anything in the way of financial assistance in life for Ralph.

Form 15-4

MENT OF COMMERCE—BUREAU OF THE CENSUS

I CENSUS OF THE UNITED STATES: 1930

POPULATION SCHEDULE

Enumeration District No. 8-4

Supervisor's District No. 2

Sheet No. 19 B

Enumerated by me on *April 4*, 1930, *John W Johnston*, Enumerator. 1754

MOTHER TONGUE (OR NATIVE LANGUAGE) OF FOREIGN BORN				CITIZENSHIP, ETC.			OCCUPATION AND INDUSTRY				EMPLOYMENT		VETERANS			
MOTHER	Language spoken in home before coming to the United States	CODE				Whether able to speak English	OCCUPATION	INDUSTRY	CODE	Class of worker	Whether actually at work	If not, line number on Unemployment Schedule	Yes No	What war or exped.		
20	21	A	B	C	22	23	24	25	26	D	27	28	29	30	31	32	23
Georgia		78				yes	none							no			51
Georgia		78				yes	Farmer	General Farm	VVVV	O	yes		yes	2x8	5	52
Georgia		78				yes	none										53
Georgia		78					none										54
Georgia		78					none										55
Georgia		78					none										56
Georgia		78					none										57
Georgia		78				yes	Farmer	General Farm	VVVV	O	yes		no		6	58
Georgia		78				yes	none										59
Georgia		78				yes	Teacher	Public School	9494	W	yes					60
Georgia		78				yes	none										61
Georgia		78				yes	Cashier	Bank	8583	W	yes		no		7	62
Tennessee		78				yes	none										63
Georgia		78				yes	none										64
Georgia		78				yes	none										65
Georgia		78					none										66
Georgia		78				yes	Farmer	General Farm	VVVV	O	yes		no		8	67
Georgia		78				yes	none										68
Georgia		78				yes	none										69
Georgia		78				yes	none										70
Georgia		78					none										71
Georgia		78					none										72
Georgia		78					none										73
Georgia		78				yes	none										74
Georgia		78				yes	none										75
South Carolina		78				yes	Farmer	General Farm	VVVV	O	yes		no		9	76
So. Carolina		78				yes	none										77
Georgia		78				yes	Farmer	General Farm	VVVV	O	yes		no		10	78
Georgia		87				yes	none										79
Texas		78				yes	Farm Laborer	General Farm	VIVV	W						80
Texas		78				yes	none										81
Texas		78				yes	none										82
Georgia		78				yes	none							no			83
Georgia		78				yes	none										84
Georgia		78				yes	none										85
Georgia		78				yes	Farmer	General Farm	VVVV	O	yes		no		11	86
Georgia		78				yes	none										87
Georgia		78					none										88
Georgia		78					none										89
Georgia		78					none										90
Georgia		78				yes	none										91
Georgia		78				yes	Farmer	General Farm	VVVV	O	yes		no		12	92
Georgia		78				yes	none										93
Georgia		78					none										94
Georgia		78					none										95
Georgia		78					none										96
Georgia		78					none										97
Georgia		78				yes	Farm Laborer	General Farm	VIVV	W	yes		no			98
Georgia		78				yes	Farmer	General Farm	VVVV	O	yes		no		13	99
Georgia		78				yes	none										100

Col. 25—World War _____ WW
Civil War _____ Civ
Spanish-American War _____ Sp
Philippine Insurrection _____ Phil
Boxer Rebellion _____ Box
Mexican Expedition _____ Mex

ENTRIES ARE REQUIRED IN THE SEVERAL COLUMNS AS FOLLOWS:

Cols. 6, 11, 12, 13, 14, 16, 18, 22, and 25—For all persons.
Cols. 7, 8, & 9, and 15—For heads of families only. (Col. 8 requires no entry for a farm family.)
Col. 10—For persons 10 years of age and over.
Col. 23—For all persons 10 years of age and over.

Cols. 21, 22, and 23—For all foreign-born persons.
Col. 14—For all persons 10 years of age and over.
Cols. 28, 27, and 29—For all persons for whom an occupation is reported in Col. 25.
Col. 30—For all males 21 years of age and over.

Right portion of document on facing page

1930 FEDERAL CENSUS, POLK COUNTY, ROCKMART, GEORGIA

Jackson, Sr., Ralph Olin – Willie's youngest son, Ralph Olin, has married. Around 1923, he purchased property where he intends to grow cotton. When the boll weevil makes cotton production untenable, Ralph will turn to dairy farming. He is listed here at age 36, with his family: wife, Isabelle, age 34; daughter, Mary Ann, age 7; son Ralph Jr., age 6; and daughter, Julia, age 4. Ralph becomes a very successful farmer and businessman, rising to status as one of the wealthiest individuals in Polk County.

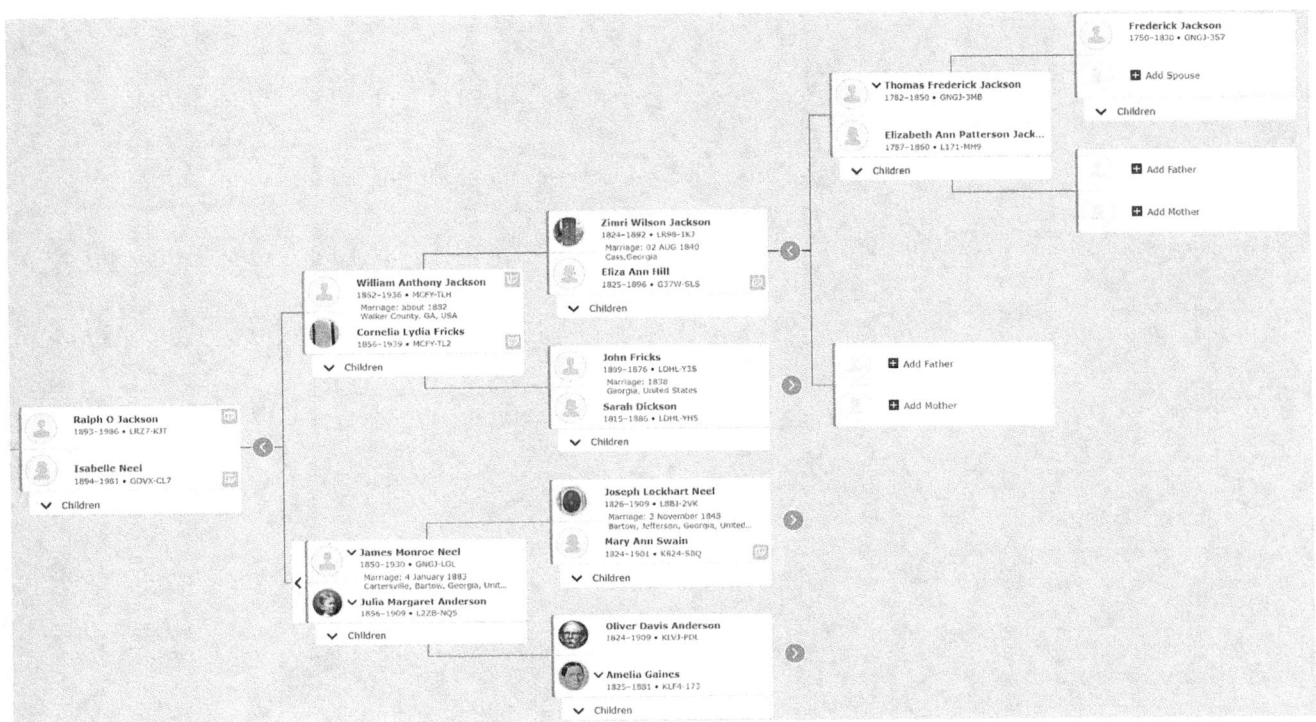

Frederick Jackson
1750–1830 • GNGJ-3S7

Add Spouse

Children

Thomas Frederick Jackson
1782–1850 • GNGJ-3MB

Elizabeth Ann Patterson Jack...
1787–1860 • L171-MH9

Children

Add Father

Add Mother

Zimri Wilson Jackson
1824–1892 • LR9B-1KJ
Marriage: 02 AUG 1840
Cass,Georgia

Eliza Ann Hill
1825–1896 • G37W-SLS

Children

William Anthony Jackson
1852–1936 • MCFY-TLH
Marriage: about 1892
Walker County, GA, USA

Cornelia Lydia Fricks
1856–1939 • MCFY-TL2

Children

John Fricks
1809–1876 • LDHL-Y3S
Marriage: 1838
Georgia, United States

Sarah Dickson
1815–1886 • LDHL-YH5

Children

Add Father

Add Mother

Ralph O Jackson
1893–1986 • LRZ7-KJT

Isabelle Neel
1894–1961 • GDVX-CL7

Children

Joseph Lockhart Neel
1826–1909 • L8BJ-2VK
Marriage: 2 November 1848
Bartow, Jefferson, Georgia, United...

Mary Ann Swain
1824–1901 • K824-SBQ

Children

James Monroe Neel
1850–1930 • GNGJ-LGL
Marriage: 4 January 1883
Cartersville, Bartow, Georgia, Unit...

Julia Margaret Anderson
1856–1909 • L2ZB-NQ5

Children

Oliver Davis Anderson
1824–1909 • KLVJ-PDL

Amelia Gaines
1825–1881 • KLF4-173

Children

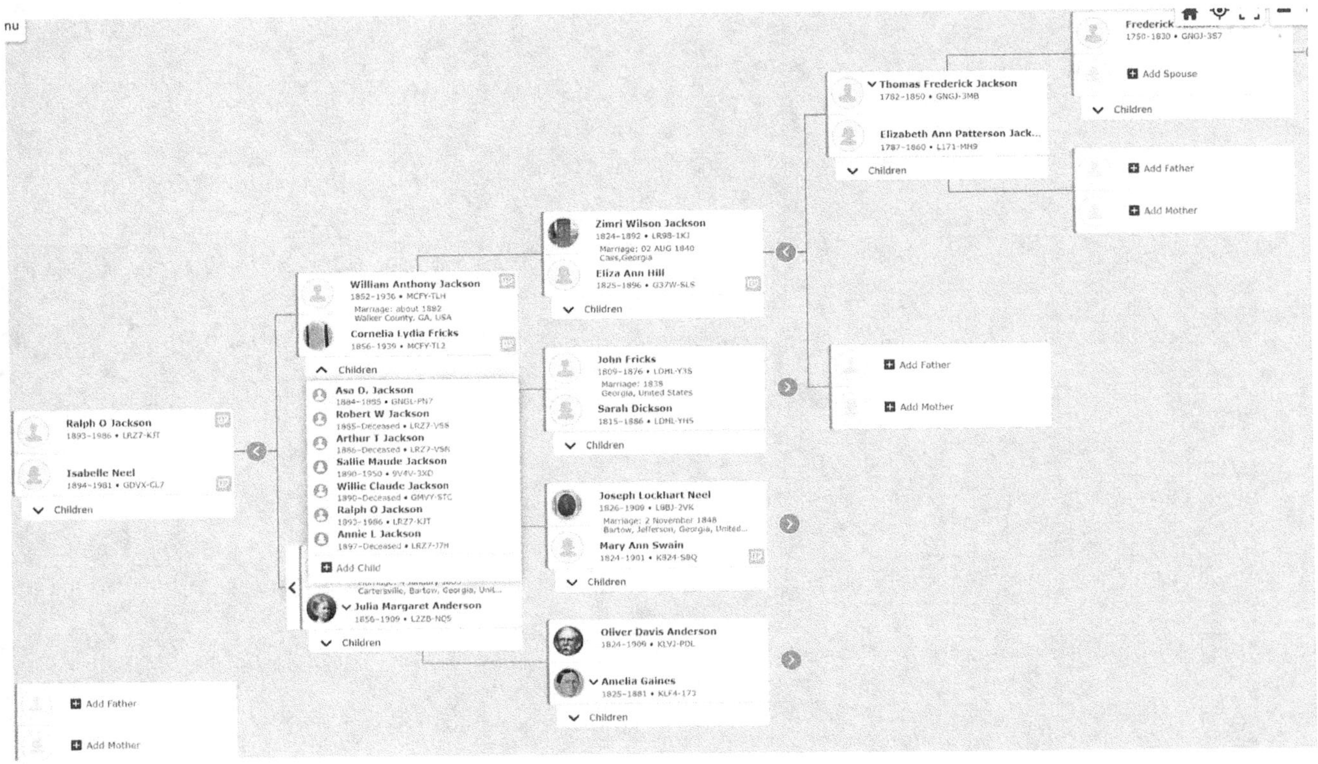

---

nu

Frederick Jackson
1750–1830 • GNGJ-3S7

Add Spouse

Children

Thomas Frederick Jackson
1782–1850 • GNGJ-3MB

Elizabeth Ann Patterson Jack...
1787–1860 • L171-MH9

Children

Add Father

Add Mother

Zimri Wilson Jackson
1824–1892 • LR9B-1KJ
Marriage: 02 AUG 1840
Cass,Georgia

Eliza Ann Hill
1825–1896 • G37W-SLS

Children

William Anthony Jackson
1852–1936 • MCFY-TLH
Marriage: about 1892
Walker County, GA, USA

Cornelia Lydia Fricks
1856–1939 • MCFY-TL2

Children
- Asa D. Jackson
  1884–1895 • GNGL-PN7
- Robert W Jackson
  1885–Deceased • LRZ7-VS8
- Arthur J Jackson
  1886–Deceased • LRZ7-VSN
- Sallie Maude Jackson
  1890–1950 • 9V4V-3XD
- Willie Claude Jackson
  1890–Deceased • GMVY-STC
- Ralph O Jackson
  1893–1986 • LRZ7-KJT
- Annie L Jackson
  1897–Deceased • LRZ7-7ZH

Add Child

Marriage: 4 January 1883
Cartersville, Bartow, Georgia, Unit...

Julia Margaret Anderson
1856–1909 • L2ZB-NQ5

Children

John Fricks
1809–1876 • LDHL-Y3S
Marriage: 1838
Georgia, United States

Sarah Dickson
1815–1886 • LDHL-YH5

Children

Add Father

Add Mother

Ralph O Jackson
1893–1986 • LRZ7-KJT

Isabelle Neel
1894–1961 • GDVX-CL7

Children

Joseph Lockhart Neel
1826–1909 • L8BJ-2VK
Marriage: 2 November 1848
Bartow, Jefferson, Georgia, United...

Mary Ann Swain
1824–1901 • K824-SBQ

Children

Oliver Davis Anderson
1824–1909 • KLVJ-PDL

Amelia Gaines
1825–1881 • KLF4-173

Children

Add Father

Add Mother

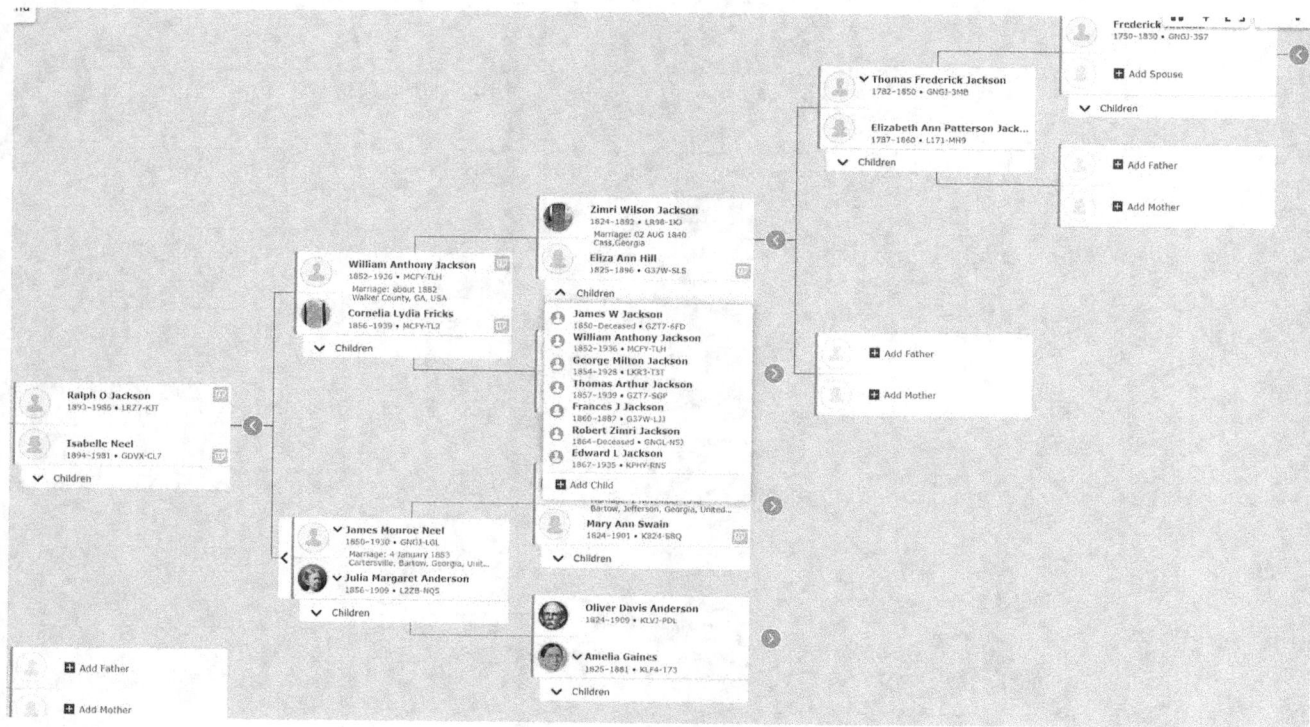

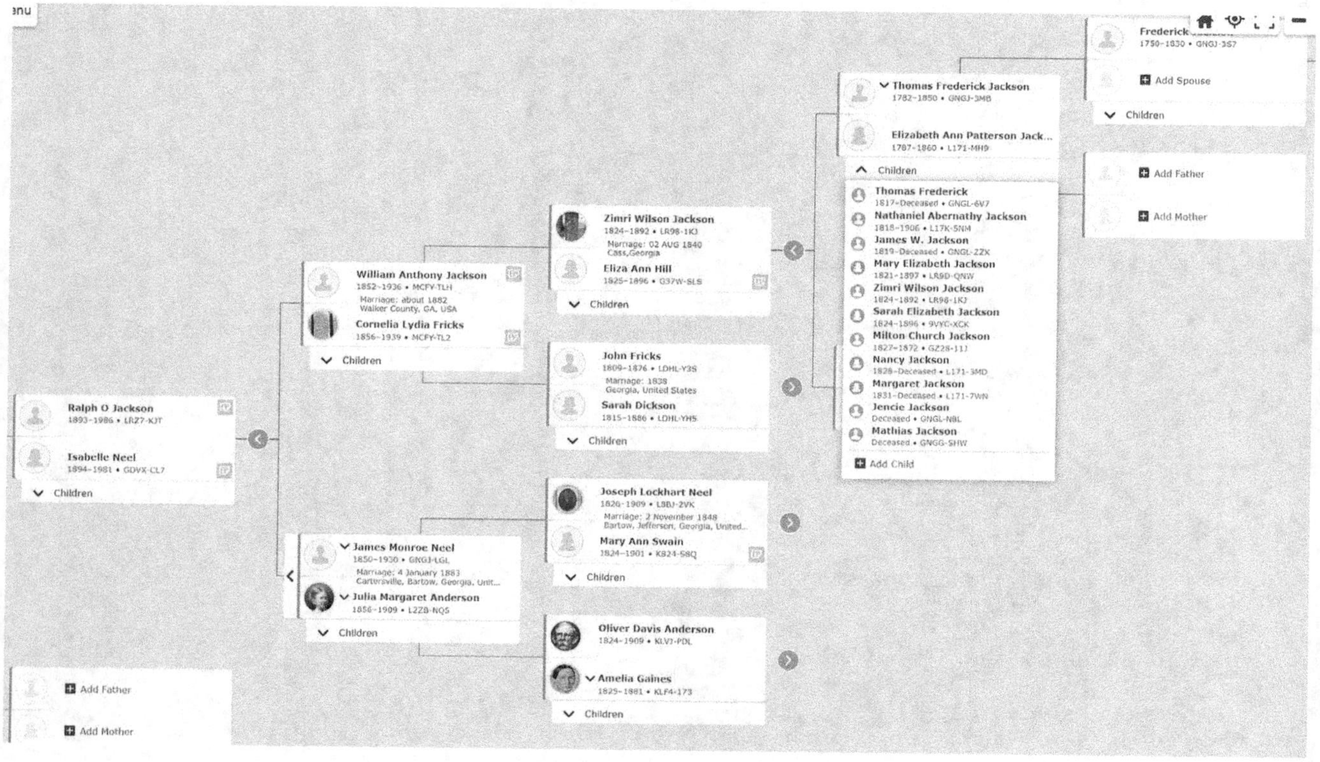

The Fricks Family History
From The Alps of Switzerland
To Pigeon Mountain in Georgia

The Fricks genealogical line originates in Germany and Switzerland. The family, many of whose male members specialized in carpentry and wood-working, emigrated to America in the early 1700s, no doubt seeking the same things as that of most early European settlers – religious, political, and general freedom from want and oppression. Today, their descendants can be found throughout the eastern United States.

The surname "Frick" or "Fricks" and sometimes "Fritz" first appeared among the Germanic peoples of Europe in the earliest days of their civilization. It is a shortened version of the name "Frederick," which is composed of the Germanic elements "fred," meaning "peace," and "ric," meaning "power."

The Frederick or "Frick" surname later became more prominent as numerous branches of this genealogical line acquired distant estates, some of which were located in other countries such as Switzerland. Through these acquisitions, as well as their important contributions to society in general, the family unerringly elevated its social status over the centuries.

The name is mentioned in a document in the year 1113 which states that the district of *"Frickthal,"* in northern Switzerland was administered – by appointment of the German emperor – by two brothers, Rudolph and Werner, counts von Frick. The records of both Zurich and Basel maintain that the descendants of these brothers were also men of distinction until the dissolution of the bonds between the German Empire and the Swiss Confederation when, owing to religious persecution and financial ruin, they (Counts Rudolph and Werner von Frick) were reduced to small land owners and farmers in the vicinity of Zurich.

In the Art Gallery in Zurich, Switzerland, there is still today a stained glass window to Gregor and Jacob Frick dated 1595, as they had regained a notable reputation for the family's contributions to the emerging European mediaeval society. Like many early names, the Fricks surname owed a portion of its popularity to a special early identity – that being the fact that there was a saint ("St. Frederick") who, as the Bishop of Utrecht (in modern-day Holland), labored continuously to end paganism and idolatry among the early Germanic peoples.

The "Fricks" genealogical line associated with the Jackson family in Georgia (USA) undoubtedly originates with the Swiss Fricks. One very early reference in this line flows from **"Oswald" Frick** who, according to records, was born in 1585 in Knonau, Uttenberg, Switzerland. He died in 1624 in Knonau.

The *Peace of Westphalia* signed in 1648 which ended the *Thirty Years War* in Europe established the right of individual princes to regulate the legality of churches in each German state. However, the increase in French (Catholic) power during the 17th Century diminished once again the Protestant authority in the Rhineland. Many of the Reformed Christian Churches (Lutheran, Moravian, Mennonites, the Amish, etc.) therefore began to migrate to Holland, and, from there, to the safer religious climes of the American colonies during the early portion of the 18th Century.

At least one branch of the descendants of Oswald Frick immigrated to the British colony of Pennsylvania, then down the eastern seaboard of the United States into North Carolina, South Carolina, Tennessee and Georgia. According to the Fricks family report of Ardath Katsenis, the Pennsylvania line of Fricks lived in Bucks and Lancaster counties in that colony until the latter portion of the 18ᵗʰ Century (1770s-1780s). Jacob Frick(s) was recorded as obtaining passage to Philadelphia on the *"Pennsylvania Merchant"* on September 18, 1733.

Land records indicate that a Henry and **Jacob Fricks** – who are believed to have been brothers with family ties in Pennsylvania – migrated from Bucks County, PA to Rowan County, NC where they purchased property prior to the American Revolution. Surry County, North Carolina, was formed from Rowan County in 1770, and thus is the reason for early Fricks records in both these counties. Many of these Fricks were descendants of carpenters and known for their woodworking prowess.

Born in Bucks County, Pennsylvania about 1751/52, Jacob Fricks was in Rowan County, North Carolina by 1776 where he volunteered for service in the Revolution. He married Elizabeth Earnhard (Ehrenhardt) in September of 1788. The couple moved to Union County, Illinois around Christmas of 1823.

Henry D. Fricks was the first of approximately eleven children born to Jacob and Elizabeth. He is believed to have been the first Fricks to have settled (just prior to 1840) in old Cass County (present-day Bartow), Georgia. Henry was somewhat of a vagabond – a very difficult lifestyle in those days of travel by foot or horseback – and had previously lived in North Carolina (Rowan County), South Carolina, north Georgia (Rabun County), and south Tennessee (Marion County) prior to moving to Cass County, Georgia.

The *1830 Federal Census* of Marion County, Tennessee, lists a Henry Fricks and his family. Subsequently, the *1840 Federal Census* of Cass (present-day Bartow) County, Georgia, lists Henry D. Fricks as a manufacturer (probably furniture or homebuilding) with a family of the size and age equal to that of the Henry Fricks listed in the 1830 Marion, Tennessee census.

This Henry D. Fricks purchased 40 acres of land in District 17 of Cass County, Georgia, in 1837. This property was later sold in a *Sheriff's Sale* to Henry's son, Joel G. Fricks, on February 8, 1850.

John Fricks was the fourth child of Henry D. Fricks and Mary Treece. He was born December 9, 1809, and married Sarah Dickson, daughter of Col. John Dickson in 1838. Sarah had been born in September of 1815.

John and Sarah eventually "pulled up stakes" and, in the Fricks vagabond tradition, moved to another locale northwestward in Walker County, Georgia. The reason for this relocation quite possibly lies in John's former acquaintance with a Scotsman by the name of McLemore, who had moved from the Battle Creek area of Marion County, Tennessee (where incidentally, John Fricks had also previously resided) sometime after 1819 to Walker County, Georgia.

The exact date of John Fricks's move to Walker is unknown today, but he and Sarah were there at least by 1840 since they were recorded in the *1840 Federal Census*. John is one of the original settlers of what once was known as the *"Lisbon District."* The later tiny community of Cooper Heights in Walker was originally known as *"Fricks Gap."*

The *1850 Federal Census* shows John and Sarah living with the Richard Partain family. John quite possibly was in the process of construction the home mentioned in August 17, 1899 issue of the *Walker County Messenger*, which reported as follows: *"G.R. Smith house painted. It is the house that John Fricks, Sr. built and lived in 50 years ago."*

John eventually owned at least 270 acres in the militia district once known as *"Pond Springs."* He was a justice of the peace there, and records indicate that in this capacity in 1866, he married his nephew, N.B. Fricks to Elizabeth Connally.

The early settlers of Walker County considered all the area in and around Pond Springs (Cassandra, Kensington, Shaw/Estelle, and Cedar Grove) as "McLemore Cove," and most often referred to it simply as "the cove." Nestled between Lookout Mountain and its spur, Pigeon Mountain, it was named for the Scotsman McLemore who had married a young Cherokee of that vicinity.

It is unknown by this writer if John Fricks enlisted in the Confederate or Union cause during the U.S. Civil War. What is known, however, is that in the very near vicinity of John's property, one of the Confederacy's greatest opportunities was lost. On September 17, 1863, a large number of Union troops passed the night near Cedar Grove Methodist Church, having entered the area via Dougherty's Gap. The following day, according to reports, they advanced a few miles north to Bailey's Cross Roads at Cassandra, joining even more troops who had come through Stephens Gap. In this confined capacity, had the Confederates acted, they might have decisively defeated this very large Federal force, but the opportunity slipped away. Whether John Fricks was involved in any capacity in any of this intrigue is unknown today, but it bordered his property.

Due to John's semi-successful business and social successes in this area, he no doubt was viewed as a semi-prominent citizen. This causes his ultimate demise to be all that more mysterious.

Though the exact details are unknown today, it appears that some severe misfortune must have befallen John not long after 1866, since, in his listing in the **1870 Federal Census** the census taker has described John's occupation as *"attends to no business,"* and in the space for *"Remarks,"* he sadly describes John as *"insane."* Perhaps the elder Fricks had been swiftly overtaken by some illness such as Alzheimer's Disease or suffered some tragic injury or setback during the war and/or its accompanying lawless years. This mystery undoubtedly will remain unsolved.

Whatever might have occurred, John Fricks, Sr. did not last many years beyond this point. He passed away six or seven years after whatever tragedy had befallen him on June 16, 1876. Sarah (Sallie) Fricks, his beloved wife, died almost exactly ten years after that on July 13, 1886, while visiting her daughter, Cornelia, in Bartow County, where reports indicate she had fallen ill.

During this illness in Cartersville, Sarah, apparently aware of her eminent demise, executed her *Last Will & Testament*. It was probated in Dade County. John and Sarah were both buried in the LaFayette Cemetery in Walker County.

John and Sarah Fricks had six children:

Mary Elizabeth, born October 29, 1837. She married Philemon McGuffey in October of 1861. She died in Walker County prior to July in 1886.

Flavius Josephus was born in 1839 and died in 1923 in Walker.

John Dickson was born in 1844 and died sometime between 1880 and 1886 in Walker. He married Sarah C. Lee.

Asa Tortoulette was born April of 1847 and suffered the misfortune of being murdered on Aug. 10, 1901 in Dade County. He married Virginia Park circa 1870.

Alexander Shaw was born May of 1849 and married Dora B. Connally.

Cornelia Lydia was born in 1856, and married William Anthony Jackson of Bartow County.

The Fricks of Walker County, Georgia, have now long departed, but their mark on that vicinity remains in *"Fricks Gap,"* as well as a deep cavern into one of the mountains of that locale still known even today as *"Fricks Cave."*

Fricks, Cornelia Lydia – Born in 1856, Cornelia was the daughter of John Fricks and Sarah Dickson. She married William Anthony Jackson on December 20, 1881 in Bartow County, Georgia. Prior to moving to Walker County, her family had lived in the Cassville area, at which the Jackson family also resided. This water-color is one of the few known representations of her image. She is buried with her husband in Cartersville, GA.

Fricks Genealogical Line
(Ancestry of One Fricks Family Line in Georgia)
(Country of Origin of Fricks Family Line: Germany and Switzerland)

The surname "Fricks" is a shortened version of the name "Frederick," which is composed of the Germanic elements "fred," meaning "peace," and "ric," meaning "power." The name seems to have begun very humbly, but gradually gained a notable reputation for its contribution to the emerging European mediaeval society. Like much early nomenclature, the Fricks surname owed its popularity to the fact that there was a saint ("St. Frederick") who, as the Bishop of Utrecht (in modern-day Holland), labored to end paganism and idolatry among the early Germanic peoples. The Fricks later acquired distant estates, some located in neighboring localities such as Switzerland.

Great-great-great-great-great-great-grandfather: Felix Frick
b. 06/06/1669, Knonau, Switzerland

m. 12/27/1695, Knonau, Uttenberg, Switzerland, to Barbara Grob (b. 11/09/1673, Knonau, Canton Zurich, Switzerland, d. 04/22/1744, Knonau, Uttenberg, Switzerland.) Issue: Elizabeth (b. 02/13/1698, Knonau, Switzerland); Heinrich (b. 01/01/1703, Knonau, Switzerland); Verena (b. 02/01/1705, Knonau, Switzerland); and Rudolf.

d. 02/11/1738, Knonau, Canton Zurich, Switzerland

Great-great-great-great-great-grandfather: Rudolf Frick
b. 09/15/1709, Knonau, Canton, Switzerland

m. 1749, Bucks Co., PA, Veronica Frick (b. 1728, PA, d. 1750, Rowan, NC). Issue: William Heinrich (b. 1750, Bucks Co., PA, d. 1801, Rowan, NC); **Jacob**; Henry (b. 1750, Bucks, PA, d. 02/1801, Rowan, NC; Elizabeth Ann (b. 1751, d. 1810); Mathias (b. 1760, Bucks, PA, d. 1833, Rowan, NC); Anna (b. 1762, Bucks, PA, d. 1861) and Sarah (b. 1762, d. 1803).

d. 1769, Pennsylvania, North Carolina

Great-great-great-great-grandfather: Jacob Frick
b. 1751, Bucks, PA

m. 09/1788, Rowan, NC, Eve Elizabeth Earnhard (Ehrenhardt) (b. 05/12/1771, Lowhill Township, Southampton, PA, d. 09/09/1852, Jonesboro, Union Co., IL). Issue: **Henry D.** ; George (b. 1790, Rowan, NC, d. 05/25/1841, Rowan); Elizabeth (b. 08/24/1795, Rowan, NC, d. 11/03/1858, Carroll Co, TN); Susanna (b. 1797, Rowan, d. 03/08/1869, Jonesboro, Union Co., IL); Jacob (b. 02/04/1801, Rowan, d. 03/03/1883, Jonesboro, Union, IL); Isaac (b. 1804, Rowan, d. 01/29/1840, Union, IL); Catharine (b. 02/03/1804, Rowan, d. 03/26/1864, Wetaug, IL); Caleb (b. 05/23/1809, Rowan, d. 05/17/1869, Union, IL); Nancy (b. 09/05/1811, NC, d. 09/10/1879, Dongola, Union, IL); Alexander (b. 05/03/1812, Rowan, d. 02/12/1852, Union, IL); and Paul (b. 07/09/1816, Rowan, d. 09/1897, Union, IL).

d. 01/27/1839, Union, IL

Great-great-great-grandfather: Henry D. Fricks
b. 1784, Rowan Co., NC

m. 1804, Rowan Co., NC, Mary Treece (b. 1785 in PA, d. 1865, Cass Co., GA) Issue: Michael Treece (b. 12/31/1804, Grassy Creek, Ashe, NC, d. 04/19/1872, Gordon Co., GA); Sarah (b. 1806, d. 1873); Pleasant (b. 05/1807 or 1808, Surry, NC, d. 1885 or 1895, Gordon GA); **John** (b. 09/09/1809, Surry, NC, m. 1838, Sarah Dickson, Walker Co, GA, d. 06/16/1876, Walker Co, GA); Martin Armstrong (b. 12/24/1811, Surry, NC, d. 07/11/1887, Hempstead, ARK); S. Davis (b. 02/16/1813, Warren, TN, d. 02/05/1898, McGregor, McLellan Co, TX); Joel G. (b. 02/02/1816, Pendleton, SC, d. 10/04/1898, Gordon, GA); Mary A. (b. 1817, Warren, TN, d. 1842 or 1859, TN); Permelia S. (b. 07/24/1818, Pendleton, SC, d. 05/29/1898, Bartow Co., GA); Elizabeth J. (b. 1818, Pendleton, SC, d. 1900); Napoleon B. (b. 1819 or 1821, Pendleton, SC, d. 09/11/1861, Centerville, VA); Lucelleus W. (b. 1821, Warren, TN, d. 1863, Ouachita, ARK); Isaac C. (b. 1822 or '23, Pendleton, SC, d. 02/1850, Cass Co., GA); Henry Reuben (b. 1823, Pendleton, SC, d. 05/08/1876 or 1879, Pickens Co., GA); Marcus Lafayette (b. 12/19/1825, Marion TN, d. 09/02/1904, Walker Co., GA).

d. 06/1849, Cass County, GA

Great-great-grandfather: John Fricks
b. 12/09/1809 (also found as 09/09), Surry Co., NC

m. 1838, Sarah Dickson (b. 09/1815, SC) Issue: Mary Elizabeth (b. 10/29/1837 or 1838); Flavius Josephus (b. 10/1839 d. 1923); John Dickson (b. 1844, Walker Co., GA); Asa Tortoulette (b. 1847, GA, d. 08/1901, Dade Co., GA); Alexander Shaw (b. 05/1849); and **Cornelia Lydia**.

d. 06/16/1876, Walker Co., GA

> **Note:** The John Fricks family lived in Cassville, Georgia, prior to moving to Walker County. They may have returned on occasion to revisit friends or family who remained in Cassville. This endeavor was a two to three-day trip by horseback or horse & buggy, but the trip time might have been reduced to one day via the Western & Atlantic Railroad which passed through both localities. It quite likely was on one of these return trips to Cassville (where, incidentally, lived also the Jackson family) that daughter Cornelia met her future husband, William Anthony Jackson.

Great-grandmother: Cornelia Lydia Fricks Jackson
b. 1856, Cassville, Bartow, GA

m. 12/20/1881, Cassville, Bartow Co., GA, William Anthony Jackson. Issue: Asa D. (b. 02/04/1884, d. 07/11/1885, Cass Station, Bartow); Robert Wilson (b. 09/27/1885); Arthur Flavius (b. 09/07/1886, Cass Station, Bartow, d. 10/03/1966, Taylorsville, GA); Sally Maud (b. 04/10/1890, Cass Station, Bartow, d. 02/21/1950, Cartersville, Bartow Co.); **Ralph Olin, Sr.** (b. 10/15/1893, Cartersville, Bartow Co.); and Annie Lee (b. 06/25/1896, Cartersville, Bartow Co., d. 09/21/1944).

d. 03/06/1939, Cartersville, Bartow, GA.

No. 4.)   SCHEDULE of the whole number of persons within the division allotted to *William Thedford*

NAMES OF HEADS OF FAMILIES.	FREE WHITE PERSONS, INCLUDING HEADS OF FAMILIES.																								FREE COLORED PERSONS.												
	MALES.												FEMALES.												MALES.						FEMALES.						
	Under 5	5 under 10	10 under 15	15 under 20	20 under 30	30 under 40	40 under 50	50 under 60	60 under 70	70 under 80	80 under 90	90 under 100	100 and up.	Under 5	5 under 10	10 under 15	15 under 20	20 under 30	30 under 40	40 under 50	50 under 60	60 under 70	70 under 80	80 under 90	90 under 100	100 and up.	Under 10	10 under 24	24 under 36	36 under 55	55 under 100	100 and up.	Under 10	10 under 24	24 under 36	36 under 55	55 under 100	100 and up.
Rebecca Smith				1												1	3			1																	
William Tidmore	2				1									2	2			1																			
John Burnett		2				1									1	1		1																			
A. McSloan				1	1									1				1																			
M. E. Rhodes				1	1									1				1																			
Floyd Rutherford	2				1													1	1																		
Flat Eaton		1			1									1	2																						
A. McCready		2			1									2		1				1																	
John Fricks	1				1									1				1																			
William Quillian					1									1				1																			
William Harris				1										1	2			1																			
A. Alexander	2				1										2			1																			
John Caldwell	2	1			1	1	1		1									1																			
John Hinton					1													1																			
C. B. Smith			2		1													1																			
L. W. Earnett	2	1			1													1																			
Mary Speir		2			1													1																			
Richard King				1	1		1											1		1																	
Mile Davis	1	1	2											1				1		1																	
Jonathan Davis							1																														
Andrew E. Bonds	1			1										2				1																			
James Quillian	1	2			1									2				1																			
Noah Meritt				1										2				1																			
Archibald Kease	1	2	1		1									2				1																			
C. W. Siebt					1												1	1																			
James Soumes	1				1									2				1																			
John King	2	2			1									2	1			1																			
William F. Keating	2	1	1			1									1	1		1																			
John McWhirter	1				1									1	1	2		1																			
Ezekiel McWhirter		3			1									3				1																			
Thomas Baily			1		1									2																							
	21	19	10	3	12	13	6		2	1				24	17	11	6	11	12	3	1	2															

1840 FEDERAL CENSUS, WALKER COUNTY, GEORGIA

Fricks, John – The household of John is listed as follows: one male under 5 years of age (Flavius, age 3 months); one male between ages 30 and 40 (John); one female under 5 years of age (Elizabeth, age 2); and one female between ages 20 and 30 (Sarah, age 25).

SCHEDULE I.—Free Inhabitants in _Main Dow_ in the County of _Walker_ State of _Georgia_ enumerated by me, on the _26th_ day of _October_ 1850. _A. B. Mi..._ Ass't Marshal.

Dwelling-houses numbered in the order of visitation	Families numbered in the order of visitation	The Name of every Person whose usual place of abode on the first day of June, 1850, was in this family.	Age	Sex	Color (White, black, or mulatto)	Profession, Occupation, or Trade of each Male Person over 15 years of age.	Value of Real Estate owned	Place of Birth. Naming the State, Territory, or Country.	Married within the year	Attended School within the year	Persons over 20 y'rs of age who cannot read & write	Whether deaf and dumb, blind, insane, idiotic, pauper, or convict.	
1		Asias F Grubbs	12	m				Geo.		/			1
		Mary A "	11	f				"		/			2
		John R "	8	m				"		/			3
		Hannah M "	6	f				"		/			4
1711	1711	James Ryan	27	m		farmer	800	Ten					5
		Denesia "	27	f				"					6
		William M "	6	m				Geo					7
		Martha I "	4	f				"					8
		Mary A "	1	f				"					9
12	12	Jesey Stephens	48	m		"		S C					10
		Ara "	46	f				Geo			/		11
		Elijas "	22	f				"		/			12
		Marinda "	16	f				"		/			13
		Ara I "	13	f				"					14
		Louis C "	8	m				"					15
		Jesey D "	6	m				"					16
		Leander "	3	m				"					17
		Nancy Haynes	70	f				"					18
13	13	Willis P Luker	35	m		"		Ten					19
		Elizabeth "	25	f				Geo					20
		Joseph A "	4	m				"					21
		Robert H "	3	m				"					22
		Nancy A "	1	f				"					23
14	14	Edward Cox	46	m		"		S C					24
		Polly "	44	f				"					25
		William "	22	m		"		"					26
		Freem "	17	m		"		"		/			27
		Joshua "	14	m				"					28
		Caroline "	11	f				"					29
		Adaline "	8	f				"			/		30
		Lowe "	3	m				Geo					31
15	15	Richmond Partin	58	m		"		"					32
		Jane "	33	f				S C					33
		James H "	4	m				Ten					34
		John Fricks	40	m			3800	N C		/			35
		Sarah "	35	f				S C					36
		Elizabeth "	12	f				Geo		/			37
		Flavius "	10	m				"		/			38
		John D "	6	m				"		/			39
		Asa T "	3	m				"					40
		Alexander S "	1	m				"					41
16	16	Jesey H Mankll	28	m		"	400	N C					42

1850 FEDERAL CENSUS, WALKER COUNTY, GEORGIA

Fricks, John – John Fricks is listed as the head of his household, being 40 years of age, with real estate valued at $3,500.00, which is the rough equivalent of $132,895.00 in 2022 dollars. He lists his place of birth as North Carolina. His household members are listed as: Sarah, age 35, born in South Carolina; Elizabeth, age 12, born in Georgia; Flavius, age 10, born in Georgia; John D., age 6, born in Georgia; Asa T., age 3; and Alexander S., age 1. Elizabeth, Flavius and John D. all attended school in 1850.

SCHEDULE 1.—Free Inhabitants in _Pond Spring District_ in the County of _Walker_ State of _Georgia_ enumerated by me, on the _10th_ day of _Aug_ 1860 _Wilson Lumpkin_ Ass't Marshal

Post Office _Pond Spring_

1	2	3	4	5	6	7	8	9	10	11	12	13	14
Dwelling-houses numbered in the order of visitation.	Families numbered in the order of visitation.	The name of every person whose usual place of abode on the first day of June, 1860, was in this family.	Age.	Sex.	White, black, or mulatto.	Profession, Occupation, or Trade of each person, male and female, over 15 years of age.	Value of Real Estate.	Value of Personal Estate.	Place of Birth, Naming the State, Territory, or Country.	Married within the year.	Attended School within the year.	Persons over 20 y'rs of age who cannot read & write.	Whether deaf and dumb, blind, insane, idiotic, pauper, or convict.
		Francis M	3	m					Ga				
		Elizabeth Lumpkin	50	F					N.C.				
983	956	William Shaw	39	m		Farmer	5600	864	Ga				
		Harriette	35	F					"				
		Kirjath A H	15	m					"			1	
		James B	12	m					"				
		S. Aman L	11	m					"				
		Cytha H	9	m					"				
		Hatriah L	7	m					"			1	
		George W	6	m					"				
		Annis C	3	F					"				
		Asa C	2	m					"				
984	957	James McNealy	36	m		Farmer		150	Tenn				
		Caroline	36	F					"				
		Sarah	14	F					"		1		
		Bethia	9	F					"		1		
		Mary H	7	F					Ga		1		
		John	4	m					"				
		Elizabeth	1	F					"				
985	958	Jesse Smith	36	m		Farmer		750	S.C.			1	
		Hannah	27	F					Ga				
		Francis J	12	m					"				
		Cornelius	6	m					"				
		Marian	3	m					"				
		Paville	2	F					"				
986	959	Alex McHenry	37	m		Farmer		75	Tenn			1	
		Polly	37	F					"				
		McFamily con.	7	F					"				
		George	6	m					"				
		Barnibus	12	m					Ga				
987	960	John Fricks	50	m		Farmer Preacher Methodist	5600	9600	N.C.				
		Sarah	44	F					S.C.				
	-	Mary E	22	F					Ga				
		John D	16	m					"		1		
		Asa T	13	m					"		1		
		Alexander S	11	m					"		1		
		Cassandra L	3	m					"				
		Martha Quillen	21	F			Instone Sarja			"				
988	961	Sack A Force	38	m		Farmer	3000	1000	Tenn				
		Sarah M	32	F					Ga				

No. white males, _21_ No. colored males, ____ No. foreign born, ____ No. blind, ____ No. idiotic, ____ No. convicts, ____

No. white females, _18_ No. colored females, ____ No. deaf and dumb, ____ No. insane, ____ No. paupers, ____

Value of Real Estate: _11,900_ Value of Personal Estate: _11,839_

1860 FEDERAL CENSUS, POND SPRING DISTRICT, WALKER COUNTY, GEORGIA

Fricks, John – John is listed as the head of his household and 50 years of age, with real estate valued at $5,600.00 and personal property valued at $9,600.00, which is quite an accumulation of assets for an individual listed as "Preacher Farmer." His household members are listed as: Sarah, age 44; Mary E., age 22; John D., age 16; Asa T., age 13; Alexander S., age 11; Cassandra L., 3; and Martha Quillen, age 21.

Page No. 2

Inquiries numbered 7, 16, and 17 are not to be asked in respect to infants. Inquiries numbered 11, 12, 15, 16, 17, 18, and 20 are to be answered (if at all) merely by an affirmative mark, as /.

SCHEDULE 1.—Inhabitants in *Subdivision No 128*, in the County of *Walker*, State of *Georgia*, enumerated by me on the *2nd* day of *June*, 1870.

Post Office: *Fricks Gap*.   *Leander K. Dickey*, Ass't Marshal.

1	2	3 The name of every person whose place of abode on the first day of June, 1870, was in this family.	4 Age	5 Sex	6 Color	7 Profession, Occupation, or Trade of each person, male or female.	8 Value of Real Estate	9 Value of Personal Estate	10 Place of Birth, naming State or Territory of U.S.; or the Country, if of foreign birth.	11	12	13	14	15	16	17	18 Whether deaf and dumb, blind, insane, or idiotic.	19	20	
1		— Parker J	3	M	W				Georgia											1
2		— Susan	2	F	W				Georgia											2
3		— Minnie	7/12	F	W				Georgia			Aug								3
4		Wiley Sandy	18	M	W	Farm laborer			South Carolina					/	/					4
5	9 8	Moreland John H	36	M	W	Farm laborer	350	150	Tennessee							/				5
6		— Mary M C	33	F	W	Keeping house			Tennessee					/	/					6
7		— William C	10	M	W	Farm laborer			Georgia					/	/	/				7
8		— James M	8	M	W	Farm laborer			Georgia						/	/				8
9		J William R	8	M	W	Farm laborer			Georgia						/	/				9
10		— Sarah C	6	F	W				Georgia											10
11		— Julia	2	F	W				Georgia											11
12		— Lula	4/12	F	W				Georgia			June								12
13	10 9	Fowler Joel A	46	M	W	Farmer	3600	1200	South Carolina							/				13
14		— Mary A	12	F	W	Attending School			Georgia					/						14
15		— Martha P	10	F	W				Georgia					/	/					15
16		— Ada	8	F	W				Georgia											16
17		— Edward	6	M	W				Georgia											17
18		— Adolphus	4	M	W				Georgia											18
19		— William	4	M	W				Georgia											19
20		— Joel	1	M	W				Georgia											20
21		Jones Whitfield S	20	M	W	Farm laborer			Georgia											21
22		Fowler Sarah	42	F	W	Keeping house			Georgia											22
23	11 10	Broom John L	31	M	W	Farm laborer		250	Georgia					/		/				23
24		— Mary A	28	F	W	Keeping house			Georgia											24
25		— William	5	M	W				Tennessee											25
26		— David	3	M	W				Georgia											26
27		— Nancy	7/12	F	W				Georgia			Aug								27
28	12 11	Fricks John	61	M	W	Retired Carpenter Attends to no business	2800	820	North Carolina								Insane	/	/	28
29		— Sarah	54	F	W	Keeping house			South Carolina											29
30		— John D	25	M	W	Farmer	1000	300	Georgia							/				30
31		— Alexander S	21	M	W	Farm laborer	500	100	Georgia					/		/				31
32		— Cornelia	13	F	W	Attending school			Georgia					/						32
33	13 12	Fricks Lela	40	F	B	Keeping house			Georgia						/	/				33
34		— George	17	M	B	Farm laborer			Georgia						/	/				34
35		— Rose	17	F	B	Keeping house			Georgia						/	/				35
36		— Benjamin	5	M	B				Georgia					/						36
37	14 13	Shaw William	48	M	W	Farmer	3520	1578	Georgia							/				37
38		— Harriet	46	F	W	Keeping house			Georgia											38
39		— James	22	M	W	Farm laborer			Georgia	May			/			/				39
40		— Jane	26	F	W				South Carolina	May										40

No. of dwellings, _____. No. of white females, _____. No. of males, foreign born, _____. No. of insane, _____.
6 " families, _____. " colored males, _____. " females, _____.
" white males, _____. " " " females, _____. " blind, _____.

1870 FEDERAL CENSUS, FRICKS GAP, WALKER COUNTY, GEORGIA

Fricks, John – John is 61 on this census. As with other families suffering from the devastation of the U.S. Civil War, both his estate and personal circumstances have taken a severe turn for the worse. The Census taker values John's real estate at $2,800.00, but his personal property at a mere $820.00. His former sizeable financial fortune has disappeared. Worse, his occupation at this stage is listed as "*Retired carpenter. Attends to no business,*" and he is described as "*insane.*" Curiously, this census also states that John is a "*Male Citizen of the U.S. of 21 years of age and upwards whose right to vote is denied or abridged on other grounds than rebellion or other crime.*" Perhaps this was a result of his perceived insanity, although in those days, there were no physicians or specialists qualified to accurately adjudge one as insane. Also listed in this household are: Sarah, 54; John D., 25, "*farmer,*" and real estate valued at $1,000.00 and personal property at $300.00; Alexander S., 21, "*farm laborer*" with real estate valued at $500.00 and personal property at $100.00; and Cornelia, age 13, listed as "*attending school.*"

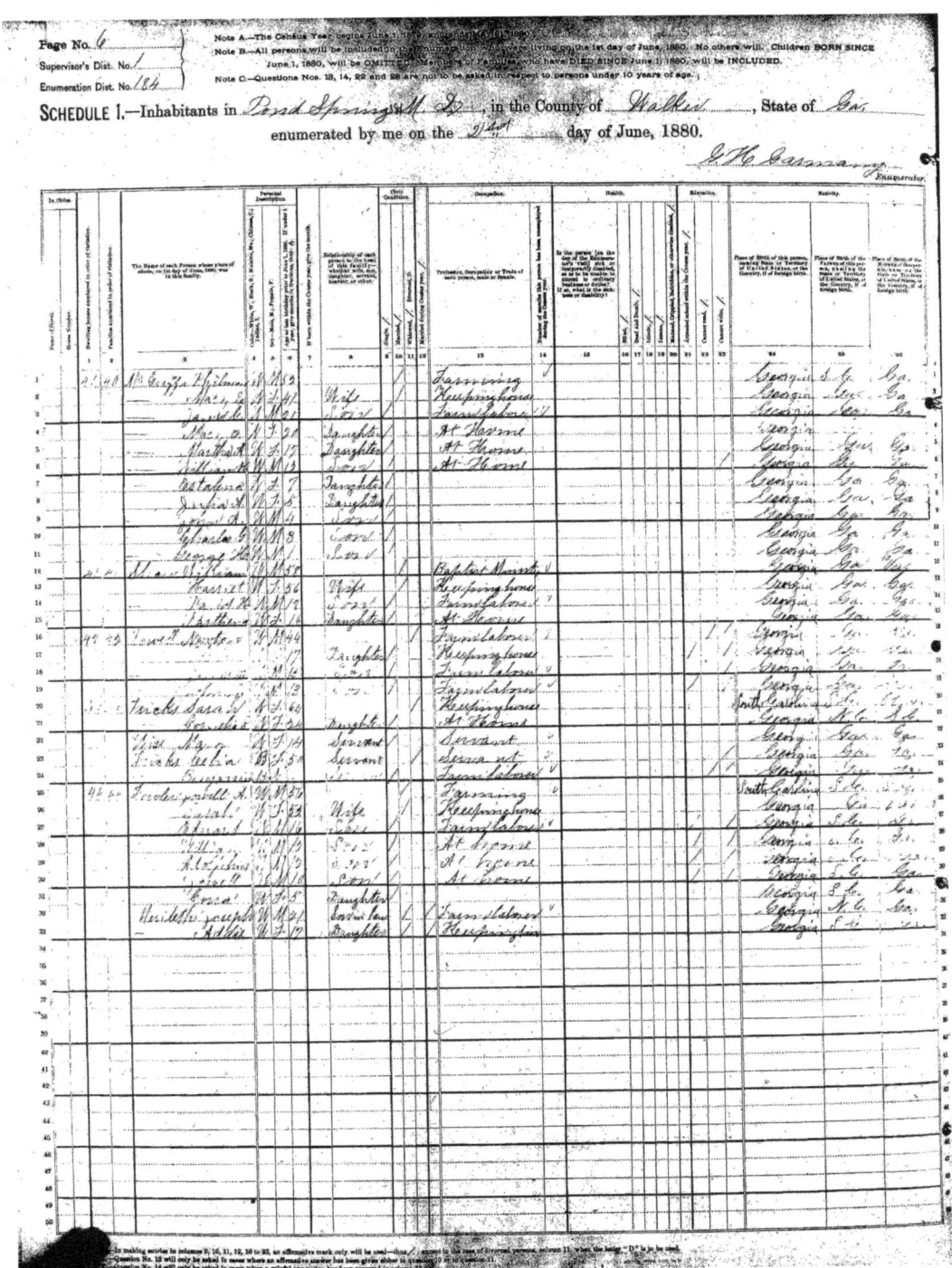

1880 FEDERAL CENSUS, POND SPRINGS, WALKER COUNTY, GEORGIA

Fricks, Sarah – At 64 and with her husband, John, now gone, Sarah is the effective head of the household although she is not granted identity of that distinction in the census. Cornelia, at 24, is listed simply as *"At home."* In just over a year, Cornelia will marry William Anthony Jackson of Cartersville (Bartow Co.) and move away from Fricks Gap forever. Interestingly, despite the U.S. Civil War having ended some 15 years earlier, three other members of this household are listed yet as *"servant"*: Margie Wise, a White female, age 14; Celia Fricks, a Black female, age 50; and Benjamin Fricks, a Black male, age indecipherable, listed as *"farm labor."*

STATE _Georgia_
COUNTY _Bartow_

DEPARTMENT OF COMMERCE AND [...]

THIRTEENTH CENSUS OF THE UNI[...]

TOWNSHIP OR OTHER DIVISION OF COUNTY _Cartersville militia district No 822_

NAME OF INCORPORATED [...]

NAME OF INSTITUTION

Location	Name	Relation	Personal Description						Nativity	
51 238 260	Griffin John R	Head	M W 37 M 15				Georgia	Alabama
52	Sula	Wife	F W 34 M 16 2 2				Georgia	Georgia
53	Flora	Daughter	F W 14 S				Georgia	Georgia
54	Robert	Son	M W 8 S				Georgia	Georgia
55 239 261	Garda Edd M	Head	M W 34 M 8	South Carolina	Spain
56	Florence	Wife	F W 26 M 8 2 2	South Carolina	South Carolina
57	Carl	Son	M W 6 S	South Carolina	South Carolina
58	Essie L	Daughter	F W 4 S	South Carolina	South Carolina
59 240 262	Hawkins James T	Head	M W 34 M 12	Alabama	Alabama
60	Nora	Wife	F W 33 M 12 1 1	Georgia	Georgia
61	Ralph	Son	M W 9 S	Georgia	Alabama
62 241 263	Padget Newman	Head	M W 24 M 5	Georgia	Georgia
63	Cora	Wife	F W 22 M 5 1 0	Georgia	Georgia
64	Wallace Alice	Boarder	F W 18 S	Utah	Louisiana
65 242 264	Bennett John	Head	M W 38 M 23	Georgia	Georgia
66	Martha	Wife	F W 47 M 23 8 4	Georgia	Georgia
67	Page	Son	M W 18 S	Georgia	Georgia
68	Julia	Daughter	F W 16 S	Georgia	Georgia
69	Burniss	Son	M W 12 S	Georgia	Georgia
70 243 265	Crow Bernard M	Head	M W 40 M 22	Georgia	Georgia
71	Martha J	Wife	F W 43 M 22 8 5	Georgia	Georgia
72	William A	Son	M W 15 S	Georgia	Georgia
73	John P	Son	M W 11 S	Georgia	Georgia
74	Jennie Lee	Daughter	F W 7 S	Georgia	Georgia
75 244 266	Street Anse	Head	M W 42 M 2	South Carolina	South Carolina
76	Louise	Wife	F W 33 M 2 10 1 1	Georgia	Georgia
77	Mack	Daughter	F W 12 S 10	Georgia	Georgia
78 245 266	Philip John	Head	M W 37 M 4	Georgia	Georgia
79	Amanda L	Wife	F W 33 M 4 3 1	Georgia	Georgia
80	Edna	Daughter	F W 13 S	Georgia	Georgia
81	Lucia	Daughter	F W 10 S	Georgia	Georgia
82	Ethel	Daughter	F W 7 S	Georgia	Georgia
83	John	Son	M W 4 S	Georgia	Georgia
84	Orpha	Mother	F W 61 M 17 5	Georgia	Georgia
85	Craton	Father	M W 68 M 41	Georgia	Georgia
86 X 246 267	Philips Vernon	Head	M W 21 M 1	Georgia	Georgia
87	Minnie	Wife	F W 17 M 1 1 0	Georgia	Georgia
88 247 268	Long Jasper N	Head	M W 38 M 6	Alabama	Georgia
89	Mae	Wife	F W 25 M 6 3 1	Georgia	Georgia
90	Ethel	Daughter	F W 2 S	Georgia	Alabama
91	Laurie J	Aunt	F W 70 S	Georgia	North Carolina
92 248 269	Jackson William A	Head	M W 57 M 28	Georgia	North Carolina
93	Cornelia L	Wife	F W 54 M 28 6 5	Georgia	North Carolina
94	Sallie M	Daughter	F W 20 S	Georgia	Georgia
95	Ralph O	Son	M W 16 S	Georgia	Georgia
96	Annie L	Daughter	F W 13 S	Georgia	Georgia
97	Arthur	Son	M W 23 S	Georgia	Georgia
98 249 270	Jackson Robert W	Head	M W 27 M 0	Alabama	Georgia
99	Willie	Wife	F W 33 M 0 0 0	Alabama	Georgia
100 250 271	Berry Floyd	Head	M B 33 M 1	Georgia	Georgia

1910 FEDERAL CENSUS, DISTRICT 822, CARTERSVILLE, BARTOW COUNTY, GEORGIA

Fricks, Cornelia – Cornelia Fricks (54) by this point has been married to William Anthony Jackson (57) and living in Cartersville (Bartow) for just under 30 years. This census also states that Cornelia's father was born in North Carolina and her mother in South Carolina. Other Jackson household members listed on this census are: Sallie M. (Maud), age 20; Ralph O. (Olin), age 16; Annie L. (Lee), age 13; and Arthur, 23, who was farming the land with brother Ralph.

LABOR—BUREAU OF THE CENSUS
TED STATES: 1910—POPULATION

SUPERVISOR'S DISTRICT NO. 7
ENUMERATION DISTRICT NO. 3
SHEET NO. 14 B

4501

) PLACE   X

WARD OF CITY   X

UMERATED BY ME ON THE 27th + 28th DAY OF April 1910.   George H. Uren   ENUMERATOR.

Place of birth of Mother of this person	Citizenship		Whether able to speak English; or, if not, give language spoken	Trade or profession of, or particular kind of work	General nature of industry, business, or establishment	Occupation		Education		Ownership of home			
Georgia			English	Laborer	Cotton mill	W	No	O	Yes Yes		O F H		
Georgia			English	None					Yes Yes				
Georgia			English	None					Yes Yes Yes				
Georgia				None					Yes				
South Carolina			English	Foreman	Cotton mill	W	No	O	Yes Yes		O F H		
South Carolina			English	None					Yes Yes				
South Carolina				None					Yes				
South Carolina				None									
Alabama			English	Foreman	Cotton mill	W	No	O	Yes Yes		O M H		
Georgia			English	None					Yes Yes				
Georgia				None					Yes				
Georgia			English	Laborer	Cotton mill	W	No	O	Yes Yes		O M H		
Georgia			English	None					Yes Yes				
Utah			English	Spooler	Cotton mill	W	No	O	Yes Yes No				
Georgia			English	Weaver	Cotton mill	W	No	O	Yes Yes		O M H		
Georgia			English	None					Yes Yes				
Georgia			English	Laborer	Cotton mill	W	No	O	Yes Yes No				
Georgia			English	Spinner	Cotton mill	W	No	O	Yes Yes No				
Georgia			English	Laborer	Cotton mill	W	No	O	Yes Yes Yes				
Alabama			English	Retail Merchant	Groceries	R			Yes Yes		H		
Georgia			English	None					No No				
Georgia			English	Farm labor	Working out	W	No	O	Yes Yes No				
Georgia			English	None					Yes Yes No				
Georgia				None					Yes				
South Carolina			English	Weaver	Cotton mill	W			Yes Yes		H	H	
Georgia			English	Weaver	Cotton mill	W			Yes Yes				
Georgia			English	None					Yes Yes Yes				
Georgia			English	Farmer	General farm				Yes Yes		F F 111		
Georgia			English	None					No No				
Georgia			English	Home labor	Home farm	W	No	O	Yes Yes Yes				
Georgia			English	Farm labor	Home farm	W	No	O	Yes Yes Yes		Yes		
Georgia				None									
Georgia				None									
Georgia			English	None					No No				
Georgia			English	None									
Georgia			English	Farmer	General farm	O			Yes Yes		F F 112		
Georgia			English	None					Yes Yes				
Alabama			English	Farm labor	Working out	W			Yes Yes		F F		
Georgia			English	None					Yes Yes				
Georgia				None									
North Carolina			English	None					Yes Yes				
North Carolina			English	Farmer	General farm	O mp			Yes Yes		O F F 113		
South Carolina			English	None					Yes Yes				
Georgia			English	None					Yes Yes No				
Georgia			English	Farm labor	Home farm	W	No	O	Yes Yes Yes				
Georgia			English	None					Yes Yes				
Georgia			English	Farmer	General farm	O mp			Yes Yes		F		
Georgia			English	Farmer	General farm	O mp			Yes Yes		F F 115		
Georgia			English	None					Yes Yes				
Georgia			English	Farm labor	Working out	W	No	O	Yes Yes		M H		

Right portion of document on facing page

91

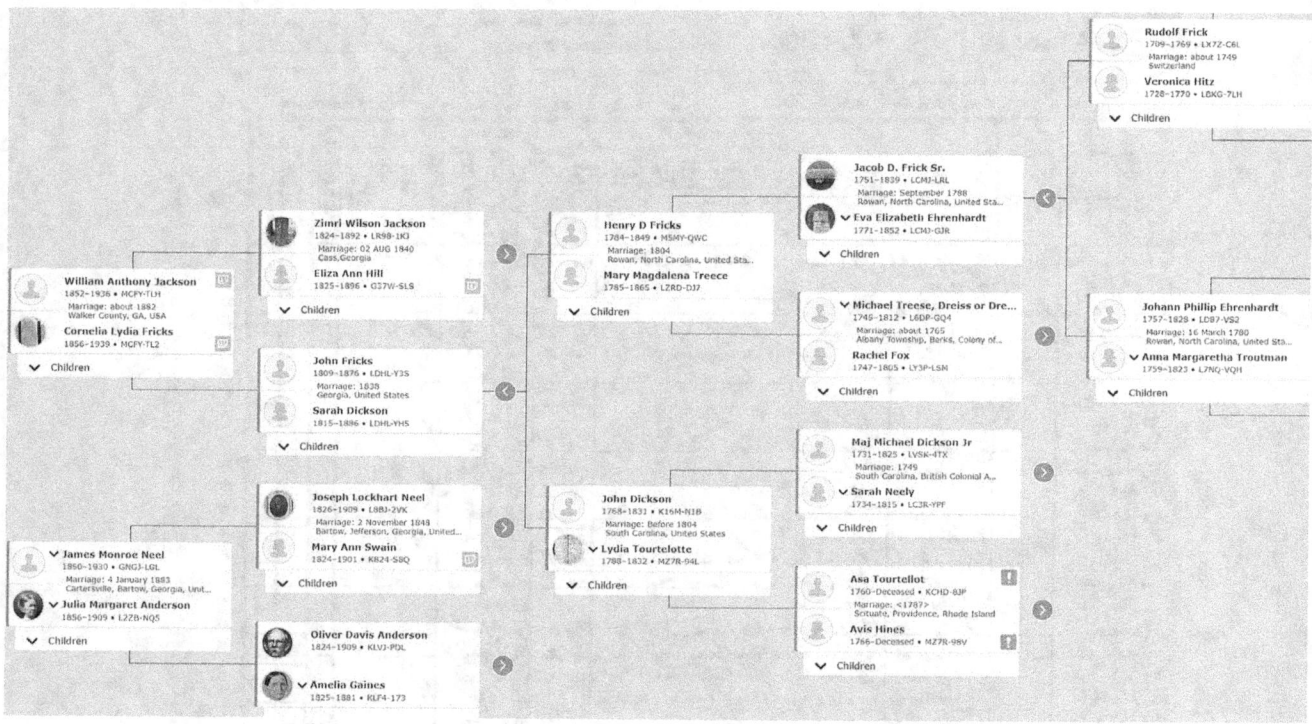

William Anthony Jackson
1852–1936 • MCFY-TLH
Marriage: about 1882
Walker County, GA, USA

Cornelia Lydia Fricks
1856–1939 • MCFY-TL2

∨ Children

Zimri Wilson Jackson
1824–1892 • LR98-1KJ
Marriage: 02 AUG 1840
Cass, Georgia

Eliza Ann Hill
1825–1896 • G37W-SLS

∨ Children

John Fricks
1809–1876 • LDHL-Y3S
Marriage: 1838
Georgia, United States

Sarah Dickson
1815–1896 • LDHL-YHS

∨ Children

Henry D Fricks
1784–1849 • MSHY-QWC
Marriage: 1804
Rowan, North Carolina, United Sta...

Mary Magdalena Treece
1785–1865 • LZRD-DJ7

∨ Children

John Dickson
1768–1831 • K16M-N1B
Marriage: Before 1804
South Carolina, United States

∨ **Lydia Tourtelotte**
1788–1832 • MZ7R-94L

∨ Children

Jacob D. Frick Sr.
1751–1839 • LCMJ-LRL
Marriage: September 1788
Rowan, North Carolina, United Sta...

∨ **Eva Elizabeth Ehrenhardt**
1771–1852 • LCMJ-GJR

∨ Children

∨ **Michael Treese, Dreiss or Dre...**
1749–1812 • L6DP-GQ4
Marriage: about 1765
Albany Township, Berks, Colony of...

Rachel Fox
1747–1805 • LY3P-LSM

∨ Children

Maj Michael Dickson Jr
1731–1825 • LVSK-4TX
Marriage: 1749
South Carolina, British Colonial A...

∨ **Sarah Neely**
1734–1815 • LC3R-YPF

∨ Children

Asa Tourtellot
1760–Deceased • KCHD-8JP
Marriage: <1787>
Scituate, Providence, Rhode Island

Avis Hines
1766–Deceased • MZ7R-98V

∨ Children

Rudolf Frick
1709–1769 • LX7Z-C6L
Marriage: about 1749
Switzerland

Veronica Hitz
1728–1770 • L8KG-7LH

∨ Children

Johann Phillip Ehrenhardt
1757–1829 • LD87-VS2
Marriage: 16 March 1780
Rowan, North Carolina, United Sta...

∨ **Anna Margaretha Troutman**
1759–1823 • L7NQ-VQH

∨ Children

James Monroe Neel
1850–1930 • GNG3-LGL
Marriage: 4 January 1883
Cartersville, Bartow, Georgia, Unit...

Julia Margaret Anderson
1856–1909 • L2ZB-NQ5

∨ Children

Joseph Lockhart Neel
1826–1909 • L9BJ-2VK
Marriage: 2 November 1848
Bartow, Jefferson, Georgia, United...

Mary Ann Swain
1824–1901 • KB24-5BQ

∨ Children

Oliver Davis Anderson
1824–1909 • KLVJ-PDL

∨ **Amelia Gaines**
1825–1881 • RLF4-173

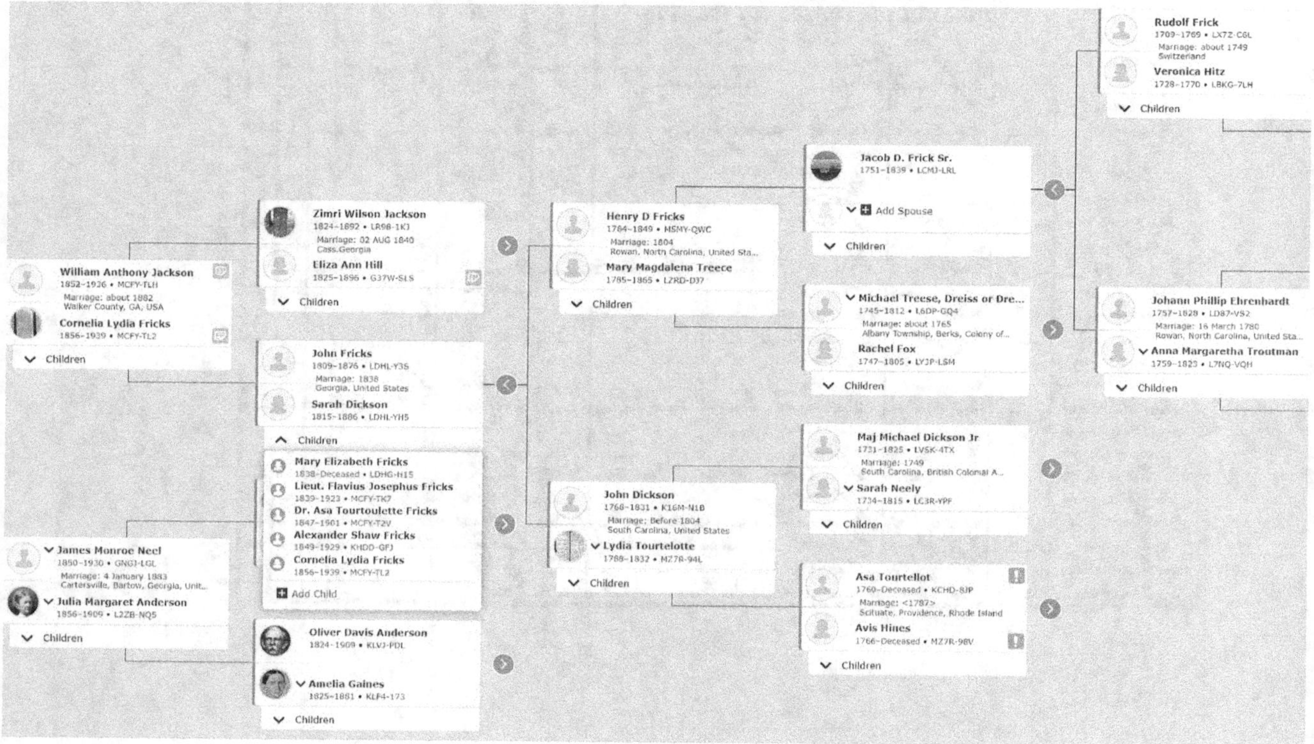

William Anthony Jackson
1852–1926 • MCFY-TLH
Marriage: about 1882
Walker County, GA, USA

Cornelia Lydia Fricks
1856–1939 • MCFY-TL2

∨ Children

Zimri Wilson Jackson
1824–1892 • LR98-1KJ
Marriage: 02 AUG 1840
Cass, Georgia

Eliza Ann Hill
1825–1896 • G37W-SLS

∨ Children

John Fricks
1809–1876 • LDHL-Y3S
Marriage: 1838
Georgia, United States

Sarah Dickson
1815–1886 • LDHL-YHS

∧ Children

○ **Mary Elizabeth Fricks**
1838–Deceased • LDHG-H15
○ **Lieut. Flavius Josephus Fricks**
1829–1923 • MCFY-TK7
○ **Dr. Asa Tourtoulette Fricks**
1847–1901 • MCFY-T2V
○ **Alexander Shaw Fricks**
1849–1929 • KHDD-GFJ
○ **Cornelia Lydia Fricks**
1856–1939 • MCFY-TL2
⊕ Add Child

Henry D Fricks
1764–1849 • MSHY-QWC
Marriage: 1804
Rowan, North Carolina, United Sta...

Mary Magdalena Treece
1785–1865 • LZRD-DJ7

∨ Children

John Dickson
1768–1831 • K16M-N1B
Marriage: Before 1804
South Carolina, United States

∨ **Lydia Tourtelotte**
1788–1832 • MZ7R-94L

∨ Children

Jacob D. Frick Sr.
1751–1839 • LCMJ-LRL

∨ ⊕ Add Spouse

∨ Children

∨ **Michael Treese, Dreiss or Dre...**
1745–1812 • L6DP-GQ4
Marriage: 1765
Albany Township, Berks, Colony of...

Rachel Fox
1747–1805 • LYJP-LSM

∨ Children

Maj Michael Dickson Jr
1731–1825 • LVSK-4TX
Marriage: 1749
South Carolina, British Colonial A...

∨ **Sarah Neely**
1734–1815 • LC3R-YPF

∨ Children

Asa Tourtellot
1760–Deceased • KCHD-8JP
Marriage: <1787>
Scituate, Providence, Rhode Island

Avis Hines
1766–Deceased • MZ7R-98V

∨ Children

Rudolf Frick
1709–1769 • LX7Z-C6L
Marriage: about 1749
Switzerland

Veronica Hitz
1728–1770 • L8KG-7LH

∨ Children

Johann Phillip Ehrenhardt
1757–1829 • LD87-VS2
Marriage: 16 March 1780
Rowan, North Carolina, United Sta...

∨ **Anna Margaretha Troutman**
1759–1823 • L7NQ-VQH

∨ Children

∨ **James Monroe Neel**
1850–1930 • GNG3-LGL
Marriage: 4 January 1883
Cartersville, Bartow, Georgia, Unit...

Julia Margaret Anderson
1856–1909 • L2ZB-NQ5

∨ Children

Oliver Davis Anderson
1824–1909 • KLVJ-PDL

∨ **Amelia Gaines**
1825–1861 • KLF4-173

∨ Children

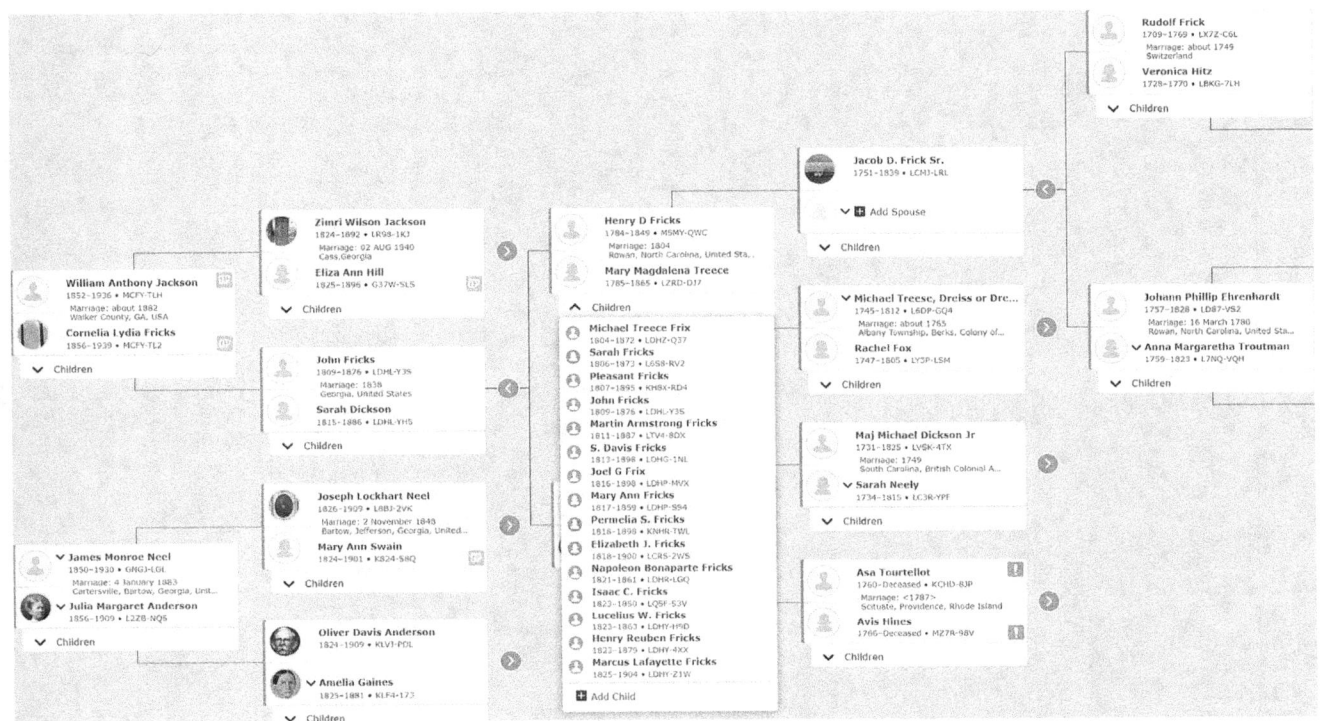

William Anthony Jackson
1852-1936 • MCFY-TLH
Marriage: about 1882
Walker County, GA, USA
Cornelia Lydia Fricks
1856-1939 • MCFY-TL2
⌄ Children

Zimri Wilson Jackson
1824-1892 • LR98-1KJ
Marriage: 02 AUG 1940
Cass,Georgia
Eliza Ann Hill
1825-1896 • G37W-SLS
⌄ Children

John Fricks
1809-1876 • LDHL-Y3S
Marriage: 1838
Georgia, United States
Sarah Dickson
1815-1886 • LDHL-YH5
⌄ Children

Henry D Fricks
1784-1849 • MSMY-QWC
Marriage: 1804
Rowan, North Carolina, United Sta...
Mary Magdalena Treece
1785-1865 • LZRD-DJ7
⌃ Children

Michael Treece Frix
1804-1972 • LDHZ-Q37
Sarah Fricks
1806-1872 • L6S8-RV2
Pleasant Fricks
1807-1895 • KHBX-RD4
John Fricks
1809-1876 • LDHL-Y3S
Martin Armstrong Fricks
1811-1887 • LTV4-BDX
S. Davis Fricks
1813-1898 • LDHG-1NL
Joel G Frix
1816-1898 • LDHP-MVX
Mary Ann Fricks
1817-1859 • LDHP-SS4
Permelia S. Fricks
1818-1896 • KNH6-TWL
Elizabeth J. Fricks
1818-1900 • LCRS-2WS
Napoleon Bonaparte Fricks
1821-1861 • LDHR-LGQ
Isaac C. Fricks
1821-1857 • LQSF-S3V
Lucelius W. Fricks
1823-1863 • LDHY-FMD
Henry Reuben Fricks
1823-1879 • LDHY-4XX
Marcus Lafayette Fricks
1825-1904 • LDHY-Z1W
➕ Add Child

Jacob D. Frick Sr.
1751-1839 • LCMJ-LRL
⌄ ➕ Add Spouse
⌄ Children

Michael Treese, Dreiss or Dre...
1745-1812 • L6DP-GQ4
Marriage: about 1765
Albany Township, Berks, Colony of...
Rachel Fox
1747-1805 • LY5P-LSM
⌄ Children

Maj Michael Dickson Jr
1731-1825 • LVSK-4TX
Marriage: 1749
South Carolina, British Colonial A...
⌄ **Sarah Neely**
1734-1815 • LC3R-YPF
⌄ Children

Asa Tourtellot
1760-Deceased • KCHD-8JP
Marriage: <1787>
Scituate, Providence, Rhode Island
Avis Hines
1766-Deceased • MZ7R-98V
⌄ Children

Rudolf Frick
1709-1769 • LX7Z-C6L
Marriage: about 1749
Switzerland
Veronica Hitz
1728-1770 • LBKG-7LH
⌄ Children

Johann Phillip Ehrenhardt
1757-1828 • LD87-VS2
Marriage: 16 March 1780
Rowan, North Carolina, United Sta...
⌄ **Anna Margaretha Troutman**
1759-1823 • L7NQ-VQH
⌄ Children

James Monroe Neel
1850-1930 • GNGJ-LGL
Marriage: 4 January 1883
Cartersville, Bartow, Georgia, Unit...
⌄ **Julia Margaret Anderson**
1856-1909 • L22B-NQS
⌄ Children

Joseph Lockhart Neel
1826-1909 • L8BJ-2VK
Marriage: 2 November 1848
Bartow, Jefferson, Georgia, United...
Mary Ann Swain
1824-1901 • KB24-S8Q
⌄ Children

Oliver Davis Anderson
1824-1909 • KLVJ-PDL
⌄ **Amelia Gaines**
1825-1881 • KLF4-173
⌄ Children

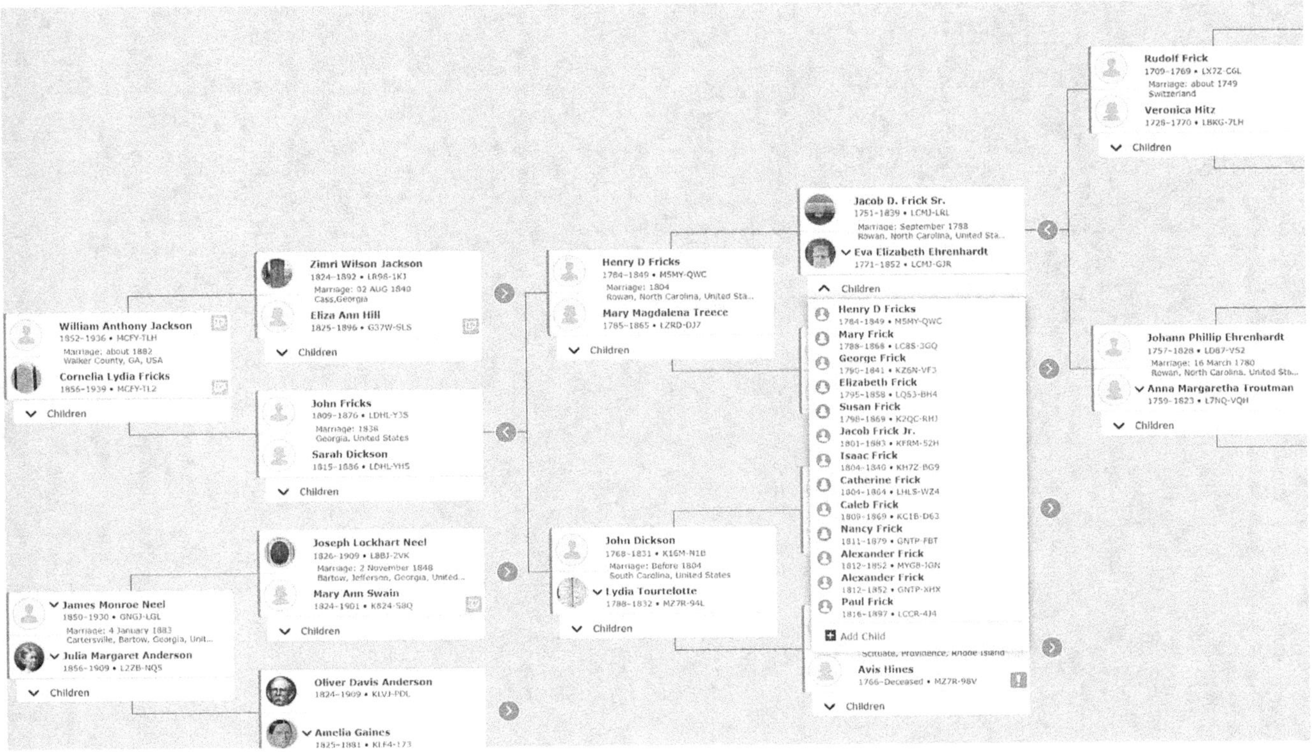

William Anthony Jackson
1852-1936 • MCFY-TLH
Marriage: about 1882
Walker County, GA, USA
Cornelia Lydia Fricks
1856-1939 • MCFY-TL2
⌄ Children

Zimri Wilson Jackson
1824-1892 • LR98-1KJ
Marriage: 02 AUG 1840
Cass,Georgia
Eliza Ann Hill
1825-1896 • G37W-SLS
⌄ Children

John Fricks
1809-1876 • LDHL-Y3S
Marriage: 1838
Georgia, United States
Sarah Dickson
1815-1886 • LDHL-YH5
⌄ Children

Henry D Fricks
1784-1849 • MSMY-QWC
Marriage: 1804
Rowan, North Carolina, United Sta...
Mary Magdalena Treece
1785-1865 • LZRD-DJ7
⌄ Children

John Dickson
1768-1831 • K16M-N1B
Marriage: Before 1804
South Carolina, United States
⌄ **Lydia Tourtelotte**
1788-1832 • MZ7R-94L
⌄ Children

Jacob D. Frick Sr.
1751-1839 • LCMJ-LRL
Marriage: September 1788
Rowan, North Carolina, United Sta...
⌄ **Eva Elizabeth Ehrenhardt**
1771-1852 • LCMJ-GJR
⌃ Children

Henry D Fricks
1784-1849 • MSMY-QWC
Mary Frick
1789-1868 • LC8S-3GQ
George Frick
1790-1841 • KZ6N-VF3
Elizabeth Frick
1795-1858 • LQS3-BH4
Susan Frick
1798-1869 • K2QC-RHJ
Jacob Frick Jr.
1801-1883 • KFRM-52H
Isaac Frick
1804-1846 • KH7Z-BG9
Catherine Frick
1804-1864 • LHLS-WZ4
Caleb Frick
1809-1869 • KC18-D63
Nancy Frick
1811-1879 • GNTP-FBT
Alexander Frick
1812-1852 • MYG8-1GN
Alexander Frick
1812-1852 • GNTP-XHX
Paul Frick
1816-1897 • LCCR-4J4
➕ Add Child

Rudolf Frick
1709-1769 • LX7Z-C6L
Marriage: about 1749
Switzerland
Veronica Hitz
1728-1770 • LBKG-7LH
⌄ Children

Johann Phillip Ehrenhardt
1757-1828 • LD87-VS2
Marriage: 16 March 1780
Rowan, North Carolina, United Sta...
⌄ **Anna Margaretha Troutman**
1759-1823 • L7NQ-VQH
⌄ Children

Scituate, Providence, Rhode Island
Avis Hines
1766-Deceased • MZ7R-98V
⌄ Children

James Monroe Neel
1850-1930 • GNGJ-LGL
Marriage: 4 January 1883
Cartersville, Bartow, Georgia, Unit...
⌄ **Julia Margaret Anderson**
1856-1909 • L22B-NQS
⌄ Children

Joseph Lockhart Neel
1826-1909 • L8BJ-2VK
Marriage: 2 November 1848
Bartow, Jefferson, Georgia, United...
Mary Ann Swain
1824-1901 • KB24-S8Q
⌄ Children

Oliver Davis Anderson
1824-1909 • KLVJ-PDL
⌄ **Amelia Gaines**
1825-1881 • KLF4-173

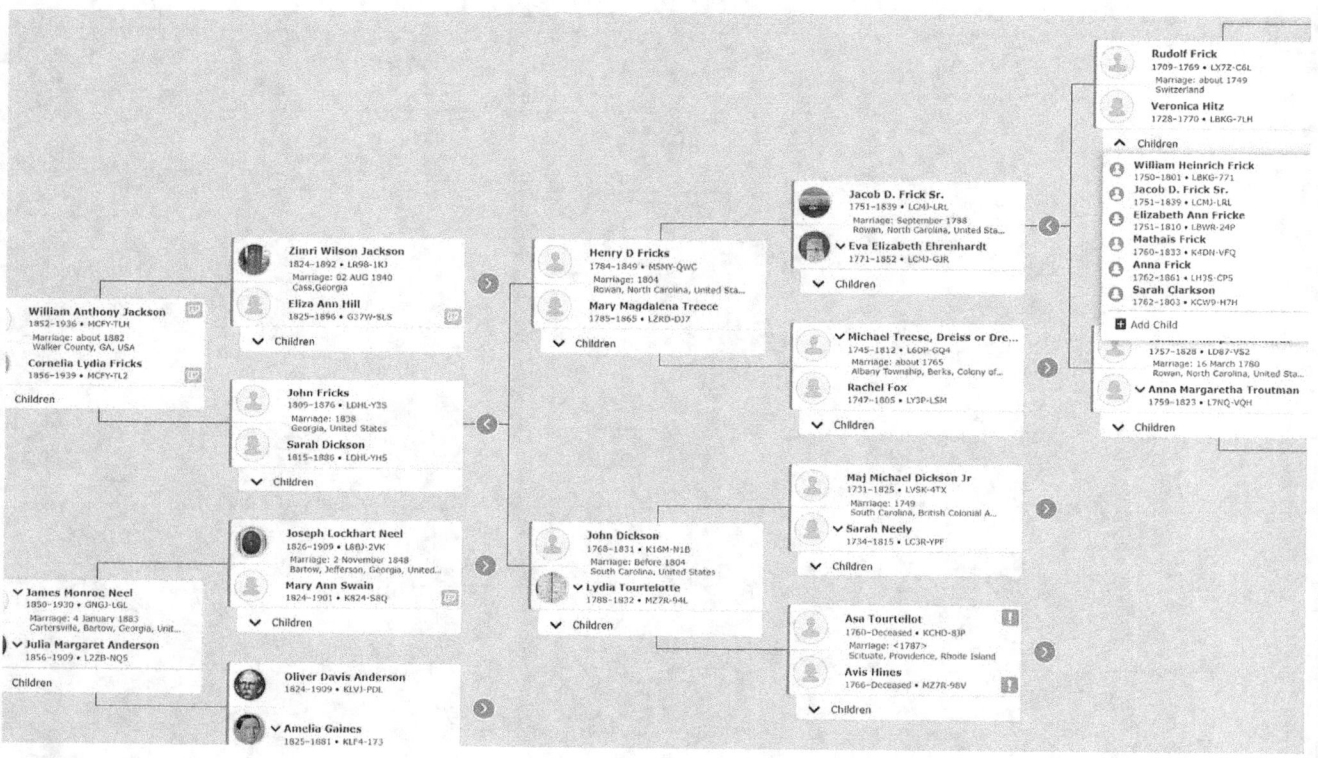

Jordan Family History
From Pennsylvania to California

Samuel Jordan's family immigrated to America during its founding years, settling in the vicinity of what eventually became officially designated by the U.S. Postal Service as "Dutch Hill," a pioneer community in Perry Township, Clarion County, Pennsylvania. One of Samuel's descendants – Alvin Gilmore Jordan – obtained a job with the westward-expanding railroad and embarked upon an adventure which introduced him to one of the most famous families in American history.

The surname "Jordan" has its origin in many different places, most notably from Greek and Hebrew name associations with the Jordan River in Israel. It also was returned to Europe by the Crusaders in ancient times after their reverent remembrances of that historic body of water. Accordingly, the name eventually made its way to America via European colonization there.

Among the first recordings of this surname in England were those of John *Jorden* of Cambridge in 1202 and Walter *Jurdan* of Sussex in 1327. An even earlier branch of adventurers with this nomenclature came to Ireland with the "English invaders" in 1168, reportedly accompanying "Strongbow Earl" of Pembroke and ultimately acquiring lands there in payment for their loyalty to King John.

Interestingly, these "Irish" Jordans – in order to also "acquire" an acceptable (and believable) "Irish heritage" necessary for easier assimilation into the Irish population – hit upon the idea of actually changing their name to "*MacJordan*," a surname still in existence in Ireland today.

In Normandy, France, the name was initially recorded as "*Jordanus*," and eventually became associated with the nobleman's class in that country. For unknown reasons today, the Jordan moniker also eventually emerged as an identity associated with nobility in Italy. Still later, it became a more common

name – as explained above – following introduction into Ireland, England, Germany, and Scotland, as well as numerous other locales.

In addition to these variables, the Jordan name eventually began appearing in various guises in the Spanish, Polish, and Hungarian languages. To say the least, though it is sometimes quantified as a somewhat rare name, the surname "Jordan" in actuality has "been around." The task therefore of determining the origin of one's particular branch of the Jordan ancestral pool can be quite tricky, not to mention frustrating. The research requires patience and determination.

It is unknown by this writer just when the father of *Samuel S. Jordan, Sr.* emigrated to America – or, from whence he originated – but the event undoubtedly occurred during the early days of colonial America, since it is a matter of record that Samuel S. Sr. was born in Huntingdon County, Pennsylvania, in 1797. Whether, in fact, his father was the original immigrant to the New World in this family line remains to be seen. Another possible source of entrance into the United States for this branch of the Jordans has been traced in more recent years to Virginia.

Samuel was married twice. His date of birth, as well as the names of his children with wife, *Susannah Truby*, are listed on a legal transaction with his second wife, *Elizabeth Silvers*, in property deeded to her. The union of Samuel and Susannah produced at

1870 JORDAN HEADSTONE, MT. CALVARY CEM, CLARION CO., PERRY TOWNSHIP, PA
Jordan, Samuel – Located in the community of Dutch Hill, Perry Township, Clarion County, PA.

least seven children, including *George Jordan*, who was born March 31, 1825 in Pennsylvania.

The Pennsylvania "Dutch"

For many years, some genealogists studying this "Pennsylvania-Dutch" branch of Jordans from the Samuel S. Jordan, Sr. family line have believed them to have immigrated to America by way of Holland – and this may even be accurate. Interestingly, the small Pennsylvania town in which most of the Jordans associated with Samuel S. Jordan, Sr. lived (and near which some still live today) in present-day Allegheny County even has an official United States Postal Service address of "Dutch Hill." This identity, however, could be a misnomer.

Beginning in the late 16th Century, Holland gained international dominance in the sea travel-trade industry. Many immigrants to the New World such as the Jordans therefore traveled to colonial America by way of Holland, fleeing as it were, religious persecution which was rampant upon those practicing the Protestant religion in France, Germany, England, Spain and Holland at that time. As such, these individuals fleeing to Holland for transport to the New World frequently became associated with Dutch nativity. Though understandable, this presumption of Dutch ancestry for all of these immigrants is not necessarily accurate.

In point of fact, most of the early "Pennsylvania Dutch" (including many still today) speak not "Dutch," but rather "German," just as do the Mennonites, the Amish, the Moravians, and any number of other similar cultural groups in this vicinity. They, therefore, must be presumed – and accurately so – to possibly be of German or Swiss origin instead of Dutch.

Due to their harsh persecution for their religious fervor, these very close-knit German cultural sects often chose to isolate themselves as much as possible in their new home, assuming in the process a somewhat unusual clannish identity. Ironically, though they sought only simple peace, survival and religious freedom, their clannish behavior earned them a certain amount of abuse even in their new home in America.

Jordan Family Lines in America by Country of Origin

Country	Numbers	Percent
Ireland	1,011	44
England	861	38
Germany	350	16
Scotland	55	2
Total	2,277	100

Part of the confusion regarding the origin of nativity of these "Pennsylvania Dutch" stems from the fact that they referred to themselves as "Deutsch," which is the German word for "German." English speaking Americans, hearing these Germans refer to themselves as "Deutsch," and knowing they traveled by way of Holland, therefore almost certainly mis-identified many of them for generations as "Pennsylvania 'Dutch.'"

As such, if the original settlers of "Dutch Hill," Pennsylvania, spoke German, this would obviously also lend strong credence to their German instead of "Dutch" nativity and the fact that the town's name had simply been corrupted originally by an otherwise unknowing populace.

Were the Jordans in the Samuel S. Jordan, Sr. family line also of German or Swiss heritage? Possibly. Possibly not. There were founding families in this "Dutch/Deutsch" community other than the Jordans, such as the Gravatts, who might also have been the actual connection with a German heritage. Further study is required before the nativity of the *Samuel S., Sr.* line of Jordans can be firmly established.

The late Goldie Evelyn Jordan of California (1890-1978) stated in correspondence that *"I have always supposed that my great-grandfather Samuel Jordan had come to western Pennsylvania* (when that area was first being settled) *from England, but* (others) *thought he had first come to Virginia."*

Samuel's son – *George Jordan* – who also hailed from Dutch Hill, Pennsylvania, was also married twice:

His first spouse was Catharine Horner (b. 03/31/1832 d. 03/12/1859) whom he married on October 18, 1849, at Dutch Hill, the marriage being performed by a "Rev. J. Walker." From this union came: Cassius Wallace (b. 05/02/1851), Alice Jane (b. 08/20/1855), Horace Wesley (b. 12/19/1857), and Harriet Ellen, whose recorded birthdate of 06/20/1859 in some records obviously conflicts with her presumed mother's death on 03/12/1859.

Interestingly, when Catharine died – possibly during childbirth with her final child on 03/12/1859 (also listed as 08/12/1859) – Horace, Alice, and Harriet (for reasons unknown today) went to live with relatives, instead of remaining with George. The *1860 Federal Census* shows them living with Andrew Horner, Sr. (Catharine's parents). It is known that some descendants of these children lived in North Carolina as recently as the 1970s. *(Per information from Essie Hudgins Jordan, wife of Guy Wilfred Jordan of Rockmart, Georgia. Some which Essie mentioned as being known are Laufer, Brady, and Hulda Jordan.)*

George Jordan's second marriage was to **Barbara (Barbary) Ann Polard/Pollard Ferguson/Feurguson** on 10/20/1861) in Pennsylvania, a widow (b. 06/21/1830, Pennsylvania, d. 06/25/1901) with children by a previous marriage. Barbara/Barbary and George fathered at least one child – *Alvin Gilmore Jordan* – in Dutch Hill, PA on August 12, 1863, but several more "Jordan" children are listed in George's *Last Will & Testament*. They all lived in the vicinity of Clarion County, PA most of their lives, with the exception of Alvin Gilmore.

1892 GEORGE JORDAN HEADSTONE, MT. CALVARY CEM, PERRY TOWNSHP, CLARION CO., PA

Though Alvin had half-brothers and half-sisters by his father's first marriage, it is unknown today if he and they ever lived together or even in the same vicinity – or if they even knew each other. Descendants of Horace, Alice and Harriet Jordan quite possibly still reside in the North Carolina area even today.

Alvin & "Linnie" Marry

Almost from the outset, Alvin Gilmore was an obviously ambitious individual. By the time he and *Mary Melinda "Linnie" Gravatt* – who also was a native of the Dutch Hill vicinity (and also of possible French or Dutch or German extraction) – were married in 1887, Alvin was already gainfully employed by the Santa Fe Railroad and living in Omaha, Nebraska.

The route Alvin took to gain employment with the railroad is unknown today, as are many facets of his life, but he had to have been a part of the original westward-expansion of the rail industry. He had already been employed by the railroad for a number of years by the mid-1880s, residing in the growing rail center of Omaha. The original trans-continental railroad was not completed to California until 1869, so Alvin may indeed have gained his initial employment with that westward rail expansion.

Mary Melinda, curiously, was living in Lincoln, Nebraska, at the same time as Alvin's residence in Omaha. Yet another inexplicable detail of their back-story involves the explanation of how these two individuals, who were born in the same close-knit neighborhood in Pennsylvania, would relocate – apparently independently of each other – to two quite separate cities in Nebraska, and then amazingly "find" each other for marriage.

A newspaper clipping announcing the couple's wedding appeared in the Lincoln, Nebraska, newspaper in 1887. It read as follows:

"Married, September 29, 1887, at the Christian parsonage by Elder J.B. Johnson, Mr. Alvin Gilmore Jordan and Miss Linnie Gravatt of this city. The wedding was a quiet one, only a few friends being present. The happy pair will make their home in Omaha, whither our best wishes accompany them."

Alvin Gilmore and Mary Melinda made yet another curious move too. Despite his assumed

BARBARA ANN POLLARD FERGUSON PHOTO
Barbara Ann was the second wife of George Jordan. She was a widow with children when she married George with whom she fathered at least one known child (Alvin Gilmore) and possibly four additional children (3 sons and 1 daughter). She died at the age of 71. She is pictured here circa age 60.

stable employment with the railroad at a time (circa 1888-1889) when such stable employment was fleeting, Alvin nevertheless left this job to return to the old Jordan home-place in Pennsylvania with Mary Melinda to live for a number of years. Was this move made to allow a pregnant Linnie to be near her parents in the birthing and early childhood of the couple's two children (a son, Guy Wilfred and a daughter, Goldie Evelyn)?

Or was this change of venue made in order to attend to aging parents who needed Alvin's and/or Linnie's assistance (George died in 1892; Barbara Ann died in 1901)? Or, was it made because Alvin had in fact lost his job with the railroad and therefore was without employment? We quite likely will never know the answers to these questions.

Whatever the reason, once the youngsters were up and growing, Alvin and Mary Melinda and family returned to the West where he took yet another

Downtown Colton, California - Dusty and quiet 8th Street in downtown Colton was photographed here circa 1890s. It was in this small close-knit community that Alvin Jordan lived and worked on the Santa Fe Railroad (which had a large rail yard nearby), and son, Guy, and daughter, Goldie, attended school and grew to young adulthood. It was also here that Wyatt, Virgil, Morgan, James, Warren, and their father, Nicholas Earp, lived and worked at bars and other enterprises at varying times and traveled by way of the Santa Fe Railroad.

job with the railroad – again, the Santa Fe – in sunny Colton, California, which was fast becoming one of the busiest "at-grade" railroad crossings in the United States, a circumstance that town still enjoyed as of 2022. While we don't know the exact date of this relocation to the West, we do know that Alvin and his family appear on the *1910 Federal Census* of Colton, San Bernardino County, California, where his occupation is listed as *"carpenter, railroad."*

It is quite possible that Alvin and Linnie moved to Colton – a suburb of the town of San Bernardino a mile or two away – somewhat earlier. If Alvin's mother died in 1901, and they had no other reason to remain in the East, it would not be unreasonable to assume he and Linnie had returned to the West as early as 1902. If one examines the *Last Will & Testament* of Alvin's father, George, it is clear that Alvin, somewhat surprisingly, was left no property by his

father in Pennsylvania, so perhaps he merely had little incentive to remain back East.

At that time, much of the interior and exterior structures of the "rolling stock" (passenger and freight cars, and sometimes even the large cabs on the steam locomotives) were, to a large degree, constructed of wood, much of it very ornately built, especially in the passenger club cars. Alvin's skills at carpentry must have been considerable, judging from his long tenure with the railroad (well over 20 years). He no doubt found steady employment at this profession with the railroad. Colton Crossing outside Colton was the site of one of the more notable "frog wars" in American railroad history. A frog war occurred when one private railroad company found itself in need of constructing its rail line across the tracks of another major rail line, a situation which inevitably resulted in hostilities between the two competing railroads.

Colton, California High School – Photographed here in 1903, Colton High was the home of the fighting "Yellow Jackets." Guy Wilfred Jordan and Goldie Evelyn Jordan both attended this uniquely-styled school in their formative years.

In the summer of 1882 (just a few months following the famed gunfight behind the O.K. Corral in Tombstone, Arizona Territory), tensions reached their boiling point when construction of the tracks for the California Southern Railroad reached Colton, California. In an attempt to forcibly prevent the competing California Southern crews from completion of their line which intersected the tracks of the Southern Pacific (SP), a SP locomotive and gondola were parked on the tracks at the location of the planned crossing. In addition, the SP hired armed men, including the by-then well-known Virgil Earp of Tombstone fame, to guard the tracks. Competition for control of the major east-west routes of the rails was big and valuable business.

Before the growing potential for violence at the Colton crossing could get out of hand, Governor Robert Waterman ordered San Bernardino County Sheriff J.B. Burkhart to enforce a state court order for completion of Cal Southern's route. Waterman informed Earp of the court order, causing the former lawman to acquiesce and instruct the SP engineer to remove its locomotive where it was blocking the intersection. The crossing then was built, ending the Southern Pacific's monopoly in Southern California.

The Earps in Colton

Though Alvin and Linnie Jordan did not know it

upon their arrival in the Colton environs, one of their neighboring families in that town was the famed Earps. At that time, however, the Earps were just another family associated with law enforcement in the West, but they would nevertheless later become one of the most famous in American history.

Did Alvin and/or Linnie personally know any member(s) of the Earp family? That circumstance cannot be positively confirmed or denied today, but in a town as small as Colton, California, (pop. 6,150 in 1900) it would be fair to say that Alvin Gilmore Jordan almost certainly knew of, and possibly interacted with, one or more members of the Earp family during his 20-plus years of residence in that vicinity.

It would, in fact, have been difficult for Alvin to have avoided the Earps. He not only worked for the Santa Fe – a favored mode of transportation of the Earp family – he also invested in, repaired and renovated real estate in the Colton/greater San Bernardino area, which put him in constant contact with the public, and no doubt quite possibly on occasion with various Earp family members as well.

Nicholas Earp and family had initially arrived in San Bernardino County, California, on December 17, 1864. They remained in the vicinity, living on a small farm for approximately four years until 1868 when they returned to their former home in Lamar, Missouri. The travels of the Earp family back and forth between California and Missouri were made via covered wagon, since there was no railroad or other mode of transportation from the eastern United States (or elsewhere) to California until 1869. These trips were made under extremely dangerous circumstances, since the western interior of the nation at that time was still an extremely wild and remote country largely controlled by hostile native Indians.

In 1877, the Earp patriarch and family returned to San Bernardino with youngest son *Warren* – who was twenty-three years of age at the time – in tow. Warren did not initially share the adventures of his older brothers, choosing instead to remain with his parents in California.

As a result of his very aggressive personality, the family referred to young Warren as "the tiger" in his early years. Unfortunately, this undesirable personality trait would gradually evolve into a bullying and very abusive treatment of almost everyone with whom he came into contact, particularly if Warren was under the influence of alcohol. It ultimately was largely responsible for ending his life prematurely.

According to the *San Bernardino Index* newspaper, *"Warren Earp of Colton, while intoxicated, entered the French restaurant on D Street and called for a supper. While his order was being prepared and before it was served, he became very noisy and tried to break the bottles in the caster. The night steward spoke to him politely and told him to keep quiet or else go out. At this Earp turned to and began to abuse the steward, raising up and striking him in the face at the same time. Earp struck the steward on the arm with a pickle jar, shattering the bottle and lacerating the waiter's arm and hand in a fearful manner. Officer Thomas was called in and placed Earp under arrest."*

Over the course of the next nine years, Warren reportedly was involved in at least three major bar fights at sites in San Bernardino County which were recorded as news items. In one incident, he shot off the right thumb of his antagonist – a man named

PHOTO OF THREE GENERATIONS OF JORDANS, POSSIBLY IN CALIFORNIA
Mary Melinda Gravatt Jordan, her daughter, Goldie Evelyn Jordan, and Barbara Ann Ferguson Jordan (George Jordan's second wife and Alvin Gilmore's mother) posed for a family portrait.

Jones. In another, he faced off against two Mexicans, waging war against them with a wooden club, reportedly seriously injuring one of the men.

All three participants in this wooden club melee were arrested, but as was often the case, father Nicholas was there to bail Warren out of jail that same night. That fatherly over-protection, it appears, was responsible to a great degree for Warren's dissent into unpredictable and unacceptable behavior. He seldom, if ever, was required to pay a price for his transgressions.

The other Earp siblings – **James**, **Virgil**, **Wyatt** and **Morgan** – had earlier departed from the family nest in San Bernardino to pursue various other occupational opportunities – usually in law enforcement, saloon operation, or mining – in neighboring states.

In 1880, **Nicholas** and wife, **Virginia**, and **Warren** moved yet again, this time to nearby Colton where the elder Earp purchased a farm outside of town which became the center of Earp operations for many years. He also purchased a saloon in Colton which he named the "Gem." Warren was a bartender in this saloon for a period of time.

Since he had a legal background – having served earlier in Missouri as a judge – Nicholas was able to apply this knowledge to several occupations associated with the legal profession in the Colton and San Bernardino areas, including service as justice of the peace in Colton. As such, he interacted on a regular basis with the Colton populace for many years.

All of Nicholas's sons and their various wives lived on and off in Colton from the 1870s through the 1930s, until their deaths or migrations to other locales eliminated their Colton residence.

On October 26, 1881, Virgil, Wyatt, and Morgan were involved in the now-famous and epic gunfight behind the O.K. Corral in Tombstone, Arizona Territory, which resulted in three deaths. Their lives were never the same from that point forward.

Following the Tombstone misfortunes and his later crippling wounds from an attempt on his life in that town on December 28 of 1881, **U.S. Deputy Marshal Virgil Earp** decided a change of venue was in order and moved from Tombstone to Colton where he resided with wife, Allie, at 528 West "H"

Street for a number of years. This home still stands in Colton as of this writing (2023).

Despite his devastated left arm which hung useless by his side for the remainder of his life, Virgil nevertheless was still effective as a law enforcement officer. He opened a detective agency in Colton, and in 1886 he was elected the town constable. When Colton was incorporated as a city, Virgil was elected as the first City Marshal on July 11, 1887. He was paid $75 a month and was re-elected to another term in 1888.

In later 1888, Virgil resigned as city marshal and he and Allie left Colton for nearby San Bernardino. Five years later, in 1893, he and Allie moved yet again to the short-lived mining town of Vanderbilt, California, where he owned and operated "Earp's Hall," a saloon, gambling hall, and meeting place used for public gatherings and even the town's weekly church services. His successes in the political arena in Vanderbilt, however, did not rise to the level of his business successes, since he lost the election for town constable in 1894.

In 1895, the San Bernardino City and County Directories carried the following listings: *San Bernardino Section: Earp, Warren – Capitalist. Earp, Virgil W. – Saloon Keeper. Colton Section: Earp, Nicholas P. – Book Agent.*

Final Days of the Earps

On March 18, 1882, in an attempt to eliminate what remained of the ever-vigilant and rigorous Earp law-enforcement cabal remaining in Tombstone, several members of the "Cow Boy" outlaw group assassinated *Morgan Earp* as he played billiards in Hatch's Saloon and narrowly missed placing a round in *Wyatt* as well as he sat watching the game. *James* and his wife, "*Bessie*," accompanied Morgan's body back to Colton where he was buried in that town's *Slover Mountain Cemetery*. When, five years later, quarrying operations encroached upon Morgan's remains in *Slover*, he was relocated to nearby *Hermosa Garden Cemetery*.

Morgan's beautiful wife, *Louisa "Lou" Houston Earp* reportedly had actually left Morgan earlier and traveled to Colton to live after discovering he had another consort in the Tombstone area, so she never

The Earp Family – Wyatt Berry Stapp Earp was born 1848 and died in 1929. He and his brothers had followed their father, Nicholas, to California, and were engaged in varying businesses at varying times in the Colton vicinity. They all eventually departed for other locales to seek their fortunes. Wyatt Earp is pictured here, circa 1870s, prior to his departure to Tombstone, Arizona Territory. One can only imagine his surprise and chagrin at what ultimately awaited him in that rough-and-tumble silver-mining mecca.

again saw him alive after leaving Tombstone. Louisa unfortunately died prematurely herself in 1894 in Long Beach, California, at age 39. She was buried in *Evergreen Cemetery* in Los Angeles.

No doubt sensing his brothers' need for support in Tombstone following the rising tensions there, *Warren* had relocated from Colton to Arizona during this period for a short time, but just as in Colton, his trouble-prone ways continued to follow him as he was involved in incident after incident. He, nevertheless, teamed up there with brother Wyatt and his law enforcement associates to support them as the outlaw element became more determined in their efforts to eliminate the Earp faction.

In later 1882, after ridding the southern Arizona Territory of many of the outlaws residing there, Wyatt and Warren, accompanied by *John Henry "Doc" Holliday*, *"Texas" Jack Vermillion*, *"Turkey Creek" Jack Johnson*, and one or two others departed that vicinity, traveling to New Mexico, Colorado, Idaho, California, and other locales, continuing to search for adventure and sources of income.

Warren eventually returned to the Colton/San Bernardino environs to live a short while with brothers Virgil, James, and other members of his family, but he shortly tired of Colton – or else had worn-out his welcome there – and returned, surprisingly, to Arizona, where he was hired by a cattle business near Willcox. In one of the last photos taken of him, he is pictured (either in Tombstone or Colton) with James's wife, Bessie.

In 1900, *Warren*'s penchant for trouble finally caught up with him in a fatal manner, resulting in his shooting death in a saloon in Willcox following a drunken argument. He and range boss Johnny Boyette had engaged in numerous violent confrontations in recent months, and had both become extremely hostile to the opposite party. Finally, following threats of violent harm by Earp, Boyette reportedly drew his revolver without provocation, and shot Warren in cold blood, killing him instantly.

Just as he had been in Colton, San Bernardino, and Tombstone, the youngest Earp was so roundly disliked in Willcox that no law enforcement authorities ever even attempted to arrest Boyette, nor were any charges filed against him nor even any investigation made of the shooting.

Warren Earp was buried in an unmarked grave in *Willcox Pioneer Cemetery*, no doubt to eliminate the possibility of a coroner's inquest to determine Boyette's guilt or innocence, since it was recorded by a number of sources that Warren was clearly unarmed at the time of the shooting. The exact site of his grave was never marked, and though the cemetery in which his remains reside is known, the specific site of those remains is a complete mystery today. A similar fate had befallen Earp associate and renowned Old West

figure John Henry "Doc" Holliday a few years earlier in Glenwood Springs, Colorado.

In 1901, *Virgil* and *Wyatt* attempted to open a gambling hall in Colton, but the town fathers voted down the enterprise, much to the two brothers' disappointment. The two continued nevertheless with other business endeavors in the Colton/San Bernardino area over the years, as well as in a number of other states and locales.

In 1905, *Virgil*'s hard life finally caught up with him when, at age 62, he came down with and died from pneumonia. As an inveterate cigar-smoker, his tobacco affinity had not aided his attempt at recovery from the pneumococcal bacteria with which his lungs were infected. Since his first wife and child lived in Portland, Oregon, Virgil's body was shipped there by rail for burial in that city's *Riverview Cemetery*.

In February of 1907, *Nicholas Earp*, patriarch of the Earp family who had lived to the ripe old age of 94, finally passed away in Colton. As a veteran of the Black Hawk and Mexican American wars, Nicholas was entitled to free burial at a nearby military cemetery.

Virgil Earp Home – The abode once occupied by Virgil and Allie Earp at 528 West "H" Street in Colton, California, is pictured. Virgil lived here for a number of years while serving as marshal of Colton and engaging in other business endeavors. Though crippled in his left arm by an assassination attempt in Tombstone, Arizona Territory, in 1881, he nevertheless was still a respected lawman and deadly pistol-shot.

PHOTO OF GOLDIE EVELYN JORDAN AND MOTHER, MARY MELINDA GRAVATT JORDAN

Photographed quite possibly in California, this photo offers an indication of the premature declination in health of Mary Melinda Gravatt Jordan.

Nicholas's wife – *Virginia Anne Cooksey Earp* – died in San Bernardino and is buried in the *Pioneer Memorial Cemetery* in that town.

In January of 1926, *James Earp*, the oldest full brother (half-brother *Newton* being the oldest) who had survived the U.S. Civil War, as well as the troubles in Tombstone, Arizona, where he had been a barkeeper, died quietly in San Bernardino at age 84. He was buried in that city's *Mountain View Cemetery*.

James's beautiful wife, *Nellie "Bessie" Bartlett Ketcham Earp* also died prematurely in January of 1887, in Colton, California, at the young age of 47. She was buried in San Bernardino's *Pioneer Memorial Cemetery* as well, not far from her mother-in-law, Virginia Anne Cooksey Earp.

In 1929, despite all the many dangerous engagements and gunfights in his life which he had survived, *Wyatt Earp* finally was himself felled, but not by an outlaw's or assassin's bullet. Prostate cancer took the lawman just short of his 81st birthday in Los Angeles, California. During his life he had been a buffalo hunter, lawman, gambling table manager, saloon keeper, miner, boxing referee, gambler, and brothel keeper, to name a few of his occupations.

Wyatt's famous last words as he passed away were *"Suppose. Suppose."* The cryptic last words were never explained. Wyatt was cremated and his ashes were interred in Colma, a suburb of San Francisco, California, in a Jewish cemetery where wife, *Josephine*, was later buried alongside him.

Virgil Earp's last wife – *Alvira "Allie" Packingham Sullivan Earp* – died in November of 1947. She had weathered all the tough years with the Earps, including the shoot-outs in Tombstone and elsewhere, outliving her husband by 42 years. She was one of the last original Earps in Colton, and was buried with a number of the other Earp family members in Colton's *Mountain View Cemetery*.

Alvin & Linnie in Colton

According to the *1920 Federal Census*, Alvin and Linnie Jordan were still living in Colton, where his profession was listed as *"carpenter foreman"* for the railroad. Alvin's talents in carpentry and wood-working for the railroad were well-established by this point.

San Bernardino Rail Yard - The Santa Fe Railroad Depot in San Bernardino was photographed here in 1915. Alvin Gilmore Jordan was headquartered here in his capacity as a master carpenter with the Santa Fe for many years. During his tenure, this site was one of the busiest rail yards in the Southwest, and it was from this depot that various members of the Earp brothers occasionally traveled via the railroad.

He eventually earned the designation of *"Master Carpenter"* before retiring from his railroad employment.

Alvin and Linnie's children – ***Goldie Evelyn*** and ***Guy Wilfred*** – spent the majority of their youth in Colton, attending the Colton schools while various members of the Earp family were active in that town. Guy was graduated from Colton Union High School in 1907. He continued his education at Stanford University where he was graduated with a Bachelor of Science degree in chemistry.

Guy no doubt was scholastically-inclined, because he almost certainly attended college on what must have been some type of academic scholarship, since his father's humble income undoubtedly would not have been enough to underwrite the expenses of board and tuition at a major college. Guy not only successfully completed his degree at Stanford, he also reportedly excelled there athletically in track & field sports, where he was very competitive in pole-vaulting.

During both high school and college, Guy was employed by both the Colton Portland Cement Company and the Calaveras Cement Company as the plant chemist. He also was later employed as plant chemist in a sugar refinery in Santa Domingo in Central America.

Guy's early professional endeavors no doubt became the basis for his later employment with the Portland Cement Company in Rockmart, Georgia, at which he was hired as Chief Chemist in 1919 following his military service in World War I.

Linnie's Death

By June 15, 1934, Alvin Gilmore Jordan's stationery listed his address as *415 North McClay Street,*

Colton, CA Cement Works – The cement production plant where a young Guy Jordan gained his first employment in the field of geology. He would go on to become Chief Chemist in the Southern States Portland Cement Plant in Rockmart, Georgia, in later years, where he died in a tragic industrial accident in 1946.

Santa Ana, CA. On that date he wrote the following letter to Guy in Rockmart:

"Dear Guy:

"Your letter received last week which found your mother somewhat improved. (At this time, Mary Melinda Gravatt, Alvin's wife and Guy's mother, suffered from a continuous debilitating illness, primarily involving heart disease.) *She goes around the house pretty well, but does not go out. Only to the doctor. Goes in a taxi. She has not been down for quite a while until today. She has not been feeling quite as well and has lost her appetite.*

"Our home we had when we left San Bernardino and which I sold to Mrs. Rebers (sp ?) *and took 3 lots as a payment and a mortgage for $2,500.00 came back. The mortgage was due a year ago last February. She had lost all the money she had when the San Bernardino County Bank closed* (This of course was during the height of the Great Depression) *and asked to have the mortgage renewed for 3 years longer. She said the taxes were paid to date.*

"We had so much sickness last fall and winter, I never got over to S.B. (San Bernardino) *to see about them* (the taxes on the house sold to Mrs. Rebers). *Did not think it necessary, but in May* (of 1934) *I wrote for a statement of the taxes and found they were not paid for 1932 or 1933, and the place was sold to the state for taxes in August of 1933. In fact, all of Mrs. Rebers' was. So I was up there last week trying to fix it up. It cost me about $155.00* (the equivalent of approximately $3,000.00 in 2023 dollars, which was a lot of money in 1934). *I still have the legal costs to pay when we get through with it. I don't know just what it will be. I did not like to take the house back as it is hard to rent, and rents are very low, and it is very hard for me to look after it, but it was the best thing I could do.*

"I guess Goldie (Goldie Evelyn Jordan, Alvin Gilmore's daughter and Guy Wilfred's sister) *is about the same. I have not seen her since about the 1st of March. She said she was coming home awhile after school was done, but I don't know when. It has been quite cool here all through June. Had nearly an inch of rain last week.*

"I have not been able to get away any place this spring except I go once a month to the hospital and was 2 days in San Bernardino last week. There are two bedrooms in the house up there that have to be renovated, but I think I can get it done without going up. I also have to get the house in Fullerton painted. (Alvin Gilmore apparently owned several homes which he used as rental properties in the general vicinity around Santa Ana where he was living in 1934.)

"We will be rather anxious about you and **Essie** (**Essie Hudgins Jordan**, wife to Guy) *next month, so write us as soon as all is over.* (Alvin apparently is referring to the impending birth of ***Patricia Carroll Jordan***, Guy's second daughter, who was born in Rockmart, Georgia, on June 25, 1934, just ten days from the date of this letter.)

"Love to you all.

"Father and Mother"

On June 6, 1937, Alvin Gilmore Jordan, whose stationery lists his home address at this time as *"Route 1, Box 1721, Tujunga, California,"* forwarded the following sad letter to his son, Guy Wilfred Jordan of Rockmart:

"Dear Guy:

"Just a few words to let you know that we laid your mother to rest on Friday, June 9ᵗʰ (1937), *in the Fairhaven Mausoleum in Santa Ana.*

"She always suffered a lot during all her sickness, but nothing comparable with the suffering during her last illness. She scarcely rested more than one or two hours out of the 24 unless under the influence of opiates, and the doctor we had nor Goldie were neither much in favor of them.

"One day we called in another doctor. He gave her relief for five hours. The regular doctor only gave her the hypodermics four times, and with the exception of the first and last one, they had very little effect. The day she passed away, she went to sleep about 10:00 am and passed away about 4:55 pm without ever waking up.

"She was very anxious to go from the beginning because she suffered so. Her sickness first started with angina pectoris, and then edema of the lungs and kidneys. There was a Mrs. Pardick stayed here all night. She, Goldie and myself nursed her through it all. The doctor was here about every day and several times

Alvin Gilmore and Guy Wilfred – Alvin Gilmore Jordan (standing) poses with his son, a young Guy Wilfred Jordan in San Bernardino, California, circa 1920. Since Alvin's father - George - left him no property or reason to reside in Pennsylvania, Alvin apparently chose the sunny climate of southern California for his permanent home.

during the night. Everything possible was done, but to no avail. She was in her usual health when I came home, but took suddenly sick when partly through eating breakfast the 4ᵗʰ day after I arrived home, and kept getting a little worse and weaker until the end came.

"Goldie expects to keep house for me, and as far as I know now, we will remain here where we are. Goldie may write more particulars to you. This is about all I feel able to write at the present time.

"Love to all.

"Father"

Alvin's & Guy's Deaths

The letters above offer a glimpse into the life of Alvin Gilmore following the decline and eventual loss of his wife, Mary Melinda "Linnie" Gravatt Jordan. Though he owned what seemed to be at least one home and two rental properties, Alvin Gilmore appears nevertheless to be struggling to get by on a meager income, just like millions of other Americans during the Great Depression.

On one hand, it seems mildly unusual that Guy Jordan did not travel from Rockmart, Georgia, to be with his mother in her last days, but circumstances during the Depression not only were extremely unpredictable, they were exceedingly dangerous for travelers – particularly those traveling long distances. Even though he was the Chief Chemist at a major cement production facility in Rockmart by that point, Guy perhaps felt the need to maintain constant control of his employment, since there were so many others in desperate straits seeking employment at virtually any payment rate.

The somewhat sadder letter below was written on January 31, 1947, by Hazel Dell Thompson of Los Angeles, California, shortly after the passing of Alvin Gilmore Jordan. It was written almost exactly ten years after Alvin Gilmore had written the letter to his son, Guy, announcing the death of Mary Melinda. The letter below is addressed to Guy's sister, *Evelyn Goldie Jordan Hill, 7 South Buena Vista Street, Redlands, California*. It reads as follows:

"My dear Goldie:

"Just a few lines to send you my blessing and very best wishes. It will always comfort you to know you were enabled to give your dear father the companionship and love that you and you alone could give. No one but just you could give him what he needed.

"I think toward the last he confused you a little with your darling mother. I kissed him goodbye at the hospital when we left him lying on the bed. Lillian also kissed him, and it seemed to make him happy and peaceful. I do not think he suffered much. In fact, he tried to get up to see us to the door. It was necessary to coax him just a little to remain quietly in bed.

"Goldie my dear you have what many others lack – a good conscience – and something to look forward to

Old San Bernardino, California - Photographed here in 1884, approximately 18 years prior to the arrival of the Jordan family, Old San Bernardino was a sleepy slow-paced community. Colton is a suburb of San Bernardino (separated by a couple of miles), and both the Jordans and the Earps resided in both locales at varying times. (Photo courtesy of San Bernardino Public Library)

with certainty in the future – a wonderful home with loved ones beyond all this uncertainty and strife. You may be sure that all is well with your dear ones, mother, father and brother Guy (By this point, Guy Jordan had been tragically killed in a terrible industrial accident at the Southern States Portland Cement Plant, Rockmart, Georgia, in 1946). *All their needs will be supplied.*

"The spirit world that lies all about us is no delusion, but a certainty. Many while yet living in the physical body have explored it, though in a quite limited sense of course. I, with my own eyes and other senses have long lived in the consciousness of this inner world. Verily indeed, there is "no dead," and we who are still in the body are in truth the ones who are nearest dead. The very body – or bodies – in which our spirits are confined restrict us every which way we turn.

"So we, who have consciousness of a wonderful future ahead should of all people be the most happy. It seems a little hard at times for us who are seemingly left alone in this world, and yet, we know we are never alone, for round about us on every hand, angelic hands reach out to support us.

"Love and very best wishes always –
"Hazel Dell Thompson"

Interestingly, the Chairman of the California Portland Cement Company in **Colton**, California, wrote to Essie Hudgins Jordan (Guy Jordan's wife) on September 9, 1946, as follows:

"Dear Mrs. Jordan:

"Mr. Harry Kaiser who was in my office when you visited here recently was out of town last week. He returned today and I told him about Guy. He feels just as I do and he asked me to express his sincere sympathy to both you and your daughters. You will remember that Guy and Harry both worked here with me when they were boys.

"If you can think of anything that I can do, please let me know. With my continued sympathy to you and your daughters, I am

"Sincerely,
"Wilson C. Hanna"

Guy W. Jordan (third row up from the bottom, third person from the left) is pictured with the Stanford University track & field team (1910-1913) on which he was a top participant in pole vaulting. As at most colleges and universities of that day, the sport of football had not reached the lofty status it enjoys at today's institutions. Track & Field, with its Olympic connotations, was a much more highly-regarded sport. (Photo courtesy of Stanford University)

"The Tiger" - Nellie "Bessie" Bartlett Ketcham Earp was married to oldest brother James Earp. She was an attractive female who had nevertheless lived a hard life, reflected in her no-nonsense uncompromising gaze. She is pictured here with the youngest Earp brother, Warren. Prior to (and possibly even after) meeting James, Bessie was a prostitute which was not uncommon in those days in the West. She, sadly, died prematurely at the age of 47 in January of 1887, in Colton, and was buried in San Bernardino's Pioneer Memorial Cemetery. Warren – nicknamed "The Tiger" – was so roundly disliked by virtually all his acquaintances that when he was murdered in 1900 in Willcox, Arizona, he was hastily buried in an unmarked grave and forgotten. The specific site of his grave today is unknown.

He still had his whole life in front of him when this photo of Guy Jordan was snapped with the Colton High School basketball team in 1907. To put this in perspective, the final episode in the so-called Indian Wars occurred just over 15 years earlier with the Sioux at the infamous Battle of Wounded Knee in South Dakota.

Guy's Rockmart Abode

Following Guy Wilfred Jordan's tragic death at the Southern States Portland Cement Company in Rockmart in 1946, his wife Essie continued to live in the large aged home which Guy had purchased for the couple circa 1927 at 215 Bluff Street, Rockmart. Guy had remodeled an older home on the site which had partially burned years earlier. Today, if one ascends the stairs to the attic of this old home which is now well over 100 years old, the charred exposed rafters and timbers may still be viewed.

Guy and Essie's first daughter, Marilyn, was born in this home. Though three other daughters were born to the couple, two of them died shortly after birth.

Essie maintained residence in the old home for the remainder of her life, helping to rear many grandchildren born in the 1950s and '60s, and serving as a beloved high school biology and chemistry teacher at nearby Rockmart High School from the late 1920s through 1970. She ultimately passed away peacefully in her sleep at this Bluff Street residence in 1999, one month shy of her 99th birthday.

Many happy gatherings of the Jordan, Jackson and Bradley families for special occasions such as birthday celebrations, Thanksgiving dinners, New Year's Day meals, Christmas Eve and Day events and much more were held over the years at this home. The receptions for the weddings of both of Guy's daughters – Marilyn and Patricia – were held at this site. Many happy memories were born here and will long be remembered with strong affection by those who enjoyed them all those years ago.

(The late Guy W. and the late Essie Hudgins Jordan were the parents of the late Marilyn Jordan Jackson of Rockmart, Georgia, and the late Patricia Jordan Nixon, (nee Bradley) of Doraville, Georgia. Many of the Jackson and Bradley children still reside in these areas as of this writing.)

Jordan Genealogical Line
(Ancestry of One Jordan Family Line in the United States)
(Country of Origin of Jordan Family Line: France)

The surname **"Jordan"** originates from a number of different locales, most notably from Greek and Hebrew name associations with the Jordan River in Israel. It also was returned to Europe as a surname by the Crusaders in ancient times after their reverent remembrances of that historic body of water. The name eventually made its way to America via European colonization. Among the first surname recordings in England were those of John **Jorden** of Cambridge in 1202 and Walter **Jurdan** of Sussex in 1327. An even earlier branch with this nomenclature came to Ireland with the "English invaders" in 1168, accompanying "Strongbow Earl" of Pembroke, ultimately acquiring lands there in payment for their loyalty to King John. These "Irish" Jordans – in order to "obtain" an immediate "Irish heritage" for easier assimilation into the Irish population – hit upon the idea of changing their name to "**MacJordan**," a surname still in existence in Ireland today. In Normandy, France, from whence also originated a Jordan family line, the name was initially recorded as "**Jordanus**," and ultimately became associated with the nobleman's class in France.

Great-great-great-great-grandfather: Frederick Jordan

b. 1780, Union, PA

m. Mary Polly Wilson. Issue: **Samuel** (b. 1797 d. 1870); Catharine (b. 1804 d. 1885); Sophia Ann (b. 1809 d. 1870); Israel (b. 1818 d. 1912); David William (b. 1819 d. 1874); Barbara (b. 1820 d. 1900); Emanuel (b. 1820 d. 1890); George (b. 1825 d. 1892); Mary Ann (b. 1827 d. 1903); and Catherine (b. 1828 d. 1893).

d. 1853, Perry township, Clarion Co., PA. Burial: Mt. Calvary Cemetery, Dutch Hill, Perry township, Clarion Co., PA

Great-great-great-grandfather: Samuel Jordan

b. 1797, sometime between June & October, Huntingdon Co., PA (Per *1850 & 1880 Censuses* and *1870 Mortality Schedule* for Perry Township, Clarion Co, PA, as well as 1906 *Death Certificate* for Mary Jordan Reichart)

m. **(1st)** Susannah Truby (b. 1800, Huntingdon Co, PA d. 1858) Issue: **George** (b. 03/31/1825 d. 02/17/1892), Harrison W. (b. 04/27/1827, d. 09/18/1891); Anna Mina "Jemima" (b. 1836); Mary (b. 04/17/1833, Clarion Co., PA, d. 05/18/1906, Perry, Clarion Co., PA); Samuel Jr. (b. 1834), William C. (b. 1838 d. 1904), and Rachel (b. 1842 d.   1914).

   (2nd) (1860) Elizabeth Silvers (or Silvis) Berry. Issue: Elizabeth had several children by her first husband, John Berry, including Miles A. (b. 1854) and Mary (b. 1857). Elizabeth and Samuel also had several more children.

d. June 3, 1870, Perry, Clarion, PA

   Note #1: The children of Samuel, Sr. and Susannah are listed on a deed to his second wife, Elizabeth, in which he granted property to her. These children and birthdays are also listed on the **1850 Federal Census** of Perry Township, Clarion Co., PA.

Great-great-grandfather: George Jordan

b. 03/31/1825 in Pennsylvania

m. **(1st)** 10/18/1849 in Pennsylvania, Catharine Horner (b. 03/31/1832, d. 03/12/1859), Dutch Hill, PA by Rev. J. Walker. Issue: Cassius Wallace (b. 05/02/1851); Harriet Ellen (b. 06/20/1854); Alice Jane (b. 08/20/1855, d. 1931); and Horace Wesley 12/19/1857, d. 1932).

   (2nd) 10/20/1861 in Pennsylvania, Barbary/Barbara Ann Polard (a.k.a. Pollard) Ferguson, a widow (b. 06/21/1830, Pennsylvania, d. 06/25/1901) with children by a previous marriage. She and George fathered at least one known child: **Alvin Gilmore**, and possibly three other sons – "Joseph" (?), "George W." (?) and "James" (?), as well as possibly a daughter named "Trudence M." (?), all of whom are listed in his *Last Will & Testament*. They all lived in the vicinity of Clarion County, PA most of their lives. Son, Alvin Gilmore is not mentioned in the *Will* unless he is the indecipherable name listed as George's *Executor*. By 1890 when George wrote his *Will*, Alvin Gilmore had already been living out West in Nebraska for several years. George's reasoning for his omission of Alvin from his *Will* is unknown today. He made substantial bequests to the above-mentioned Joseph, George W., James and Trudence.

d. February 17, 1892, Washington Township, Lawrence Co., Pennsylvania

   Note #2: When Catharine passed away in 1859, Horace, Alice, and Harriet (for reasons unknown today) went to live with relatives, instead of remaining with George. The **1860 Federal Census** shows them with Andrew Horner, Sr. (Catharine's parents).

   Note #3: It is known that some descendants of Alvin Gilmore's half-brothers and sisters lived in North Carolina as recently as the 1970s. *(Per information from Essie Hudgins Jordan, wife of Guy Wilfred Jordan of Rockmart, Georgia. Some of those named by Mrs. Jordan are Laufer, Brady, and Hulda Jordan.)*

Great-grandfather: Alvin Gilmore Jordan

b. 08/12/1863 in Pennsylvania, possibly near Dutch Hill

m. 09/29/1887 in Lincoln, Nebraska, Mary Melinda "Linnie" Gravatt (b. 10/23/1858 in Pennsylvania. d. 06/09/1937 in Colton, San Bernardino County, California). Issue: **Guy Wilfred** and Goldie Evelyn (b. 05/06/1890, Dutch Hill, PA. m. 06/02/1922, Santa Ana, CA, to Edward Hill by Rev. Robertson. d. 10/21/1978, Glendale, Los Angeles Co., CA. Buried in Glen Haven Memorial Park, San Fernando, CA). Guy was the father of the late Marilyn Jordan Jackson of Rockmart, Georgia.

d. 01/25/1947, San Bernardino Co., CA. Buried in Fairhaven Memorial Park, Santa Ana, Orange County, CA.

   Note #4: By the time he and Mary Melinda "Linnie" Gravatt were married in 1887, Alvin Gilmore apparently was already employed by the Santa Fe Railroad and living in Omaha, Nebraska. Mary Melinda's residence at that time was Lincoln, Nebraska. Alvin's residence in the **1920 Federal Census** is listed as *"Colton, San Bernardino, CA"* with a profession as *"carpenter foreman."* Interestingly, Alvin lived in the tiny community of Colton, San Bernardino Co., CA at the same time as a famous family by the name of Earp. Nicholas Earp – patriarch of James, Virgil, Wyatt, Morgan, and Warren – purchased a farm outside Colton in the 1870s, with various members of the immediate Earp family living there for the next 80 years.

Though he undoubtedly attended Stanford University in California on an academic scholarship, Guy Jordan was an outstanding athlete on the University's track & field and other teams. He is pictured here (standing, far right) with the baseball team.

1890 LAST WILL & TESTAMENT, GEORGE JORDAN (P1)

<u>Jordan, George</u> – Undoubtedly quite ill in 1891, George apparently realized the need to complete and finalize his Will. He passed away in 1892. He lists his address as "Washing Township, Lawrence Co." He appears to have been a prodigious businessman, having accumulated quite an estate for that day and time in Pennsylvania. He parcels out numerous tracts of property as well as hundreds of dollars to each of his numerous immediate family members. Curiously, he left these substantial bequests to four of his five children, choosing to deny son Alvin Gilmore entirely.

six acres more only further direct that my daughter Amanda Waddington get seven hundred dollars as follows which Joseph Jordan will pay in the folowin maner 2 hundred dollars in one year after my deth two hundred and fifty dollars in three after my deth and too hundred and fifty dollars in four years after my deth thes amounts draws no intrest if paid when due I farther direct that Sadie Patterson gets the McCune lot which she resids on part of now— I direct that my wife Elizabeth gets the south east room in the house and uses til the same and to bee kept in every thing to make her cumforte in this life which must come of the old homesed I further that my personal profiter be sold at public sale and if thare is any money left that my wife will have charg of the same and at her deth divided equaly amongs my children. I do affoint my sone Wm Jordan my exeautor in witness where of I George Jordan the testator have set my hand and seal this September 25 one thousand eight hundred and ninty

George Jordan [SEAL]

sined. scald. publickly and delivered by me George Jordan as his last will and testament in the freesence of us who have unto subscribe our names at his request as witnees thareunto and and in the foseno of the testator and of each other.

Attest

C. H. Martin
Luke V Martin

1890 LAST WILL & TESTAMENT, GEORGE JORDAN (P. 2)

Transcription
Last Will & Testament of George Jordan

September 18, 1890

I, George Jordan, of Washington Township, Lawrence, PA, being a farmer and of sound mind and understanding do make this my Last Will and Testament, revoking all former Wills.

Article 1 – I direct that all my just debts and funeral expenses be paid.

Second, I bequest to my son, James Jordan, the McLaron lot that he resides on now.

Third, I bequest to my son George H. Jordan the McCreary lot that he resides on now and further the timber on the Slater lot and five years to take same off after my death and a road across the old home sold to take it off.

Further, I direct that my daughter Trudence M. Fisher gets the Eddie lot and a hundred dollars paid her by Joseph Jordan in two years after my death. This will not draw any interest if paid when due.

I direct that Joseph Jordan get the old homestead and Slate lot making one hundred and six acres more or less.

I further direct that my daughter, Amanda Reddington, get seven hundred dollars (in payments) as follows which Joseph Jordan will pay in the following manner: 2 hundred dollars in one year after my death, two hundred and fifty dollars in three years after my death, and two hundred and fifty in four years after my death. These amounts draw no interest if paid when due.

I further direct that Sadie Patterson gets the McCain lot which she resides on part of now.

I direct that my wife, Elizabeth, gets the south east room of the house and access to the same, and to be kept in everything to make her comfort(able)) in this life which must come from the old homestead.

I further direct that my personal property be sold at public sale, and if there is any money left that my wife will have charge of same, and at her death divided equally amongst my children.

I do appoint my son Alvin Jordan my executor, in witness whereof I, George Jordan the Testator have set my hand and seal this September.

Note on Account, Pennsylvania

Jordan, Samuel – Samuel S. Jordan, Sr. (1797-1870) was Alvin Gilmore Jordan's grandfather. Pictured here is a page from an accounts book of long ago in Pennsylvania, which appears to identify a note or loan to Samuel with an original amount of $218.80, initiated October 1, 1813. Samuel has made payments on February 5 and December 18, 1846, but the note also has been periodically increased, leaving a balance due of $239.74 in 1847. As such, it appears this note, amazingly, has been carried for some 34 years. As of January, 1847, the account still has a balance due of $239.74. This may seem like an easily-payable sum today, but in actuality, it would be the equivalent of a debt of approximately $8,160.00 in 2022 dollars.

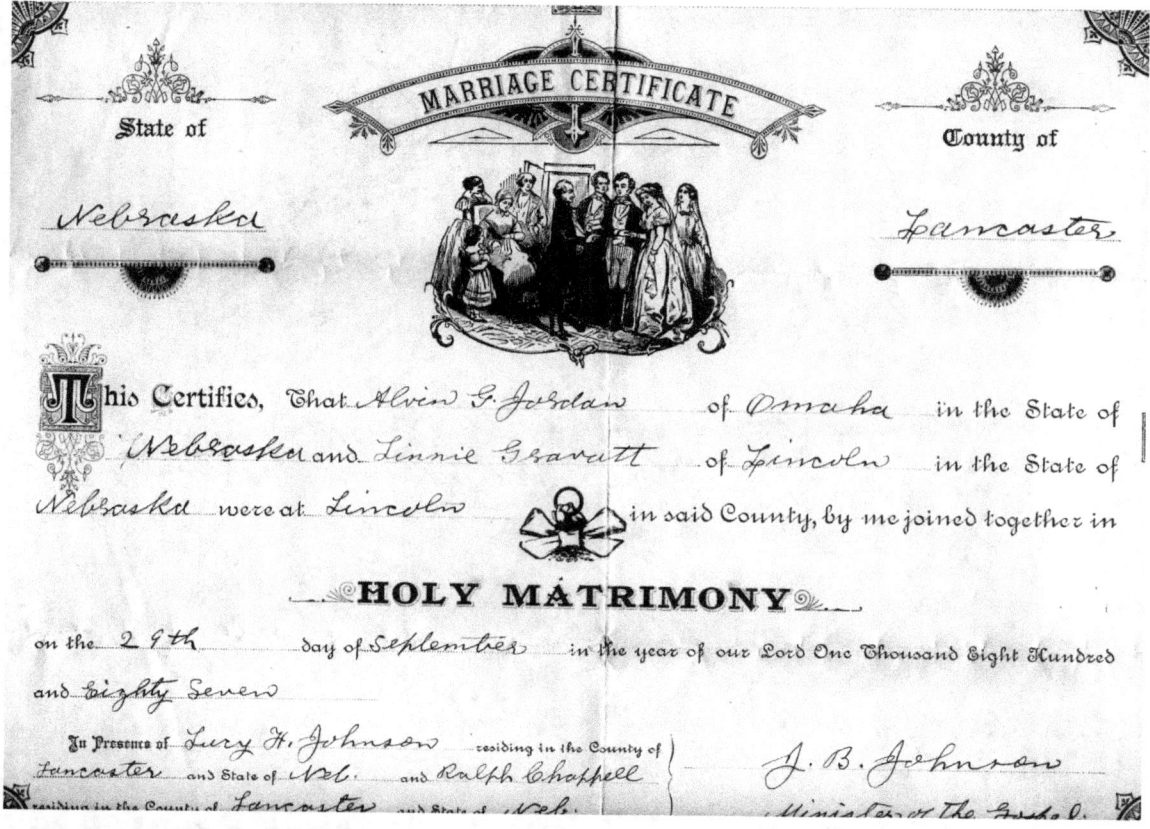

ALVIN GILMORE JORDAN MARRIAGE (1887)
After they both had departed Pennsylvania at separate times, Alvin and Mary Melinda "Linnie" Gravatt somehow were reunited in Nebraska where they were married on an autumn day in late September of 1887.

AT HOME ON THE ALLEGHENY
Alvin Gilmore's family had a farm in the Allegheny Valley of Pennsylvania not far from Pittsburgh. Alvin, his father, and his eventual wife, Mary Melinda Gravatt, were all born in that vicinity. The Jordan farm reportedly was approximately two miles over the hills from the river. When Guy and his sister – Goldie – were children, their family had another home quite near the river.

SCHEDULE of the whole number of Persons within the Division allotted to _William_

NAMES OF HEADS OF FAMILIES.	FREE WHITE PERSONS, (INCLUDING HEADS OF FAMILIES.)																						
	MALES.													FEMALES.									
	under 5	5 to 10	10 to 15	15 to 20	20 to 30	30 to 40	40 to 50	50 to 60	60 to 70	70 to 80	80 to 90	90 to 100	100 &c.	under 5	5 to 10	10 to 15	15 to 20	20 to 30	30 to 40	40 to 50	50 to 60	60 to 70	70 to 80
Samuel Jordan	2					1								1			1		2				
Philip Jordan	2	1				1												1		1			
Jacob Barger	2	1		1		1								1	1	1			1				
Frederick Jordan		1	2				1							1									
James Hogan		1	1	2	1		1							1	1		2						
David Young	1				1									1			1						
David White	1				1	1											1						
John Kerr							1													1			
Huston King	2				1												1						
Daniel Levien			2	1			1										4		1				
Thomas Knox	3	1			2	1	1															1	
John Beatty Esq.					2		1										1						
Philip Murrin	2	2			1									1									
James B Shepherd	1	2			1									1		1	1						
Abraham Smith	2	2			1									1	1	1							
Abel Springer	1	1			1									1									
John Marshall	1			1	3									1									
James Shaw	1	2	1			1								1			1						
Adam Stiren					2									2			2						
James McCarrin	1				1										1	1							
Benjamin Springer			2	8											1	1							
William Cartwright	2	1			1									2			1						
John Andris			1		1									1			1						
James Wilson			1	1										1									
Michael Connelly	1	1	1		1											2	1		1				
John E Hardin	1				1									1									
	27	15	8	8	21	9	4	4	3					16	7	5	5	20	7	4	3	1	

1830 FEDERAL CENSUS, ARMSTRONG COUNTY, PERRY TOWNSHIP, PENNSYLVANIA

Jordan, Samuel – This Census with Samuel as head of the household indicates it included two males under the age of five; one between 30 and 40 years of age; one female under five years of age; one female between 15 and 20 years of age; and two females between 30 and 40 years of age. These would be Samuel's children by his first wife, Susannah Truby. The "two males under the age of five" would be George (born 1825) and Harrison (born 1827). The "one male between 30 and 40 years of age" would be Samuel (born 1797). The "one female under five years of age" would be Anna Mina, also known as "Jemima," (born 1829). The "one female between 15 and 20 years of age" is unknown, as is one of the "two females between 30 and 40 years of age," the other of which would be wife, Susannah (born 1800). In these hard times, those families who were able often took in relatives who otherwise would have been homeless.

(No. 4.) **SCHEDULE of the whole number of persons**

FREE WHITE PERSONS, INCLUDING HEADS

NAMES OF HEADS OF FAMILIES.	Under 5	5 & under 10	10 & under 15	15 & under 20	20 & under 30	30 & under 40	40 & under 50	50 & under 60	60 & under 70	70 & under 80	80 & under 90	90 & under 100	100 & upwards	Under 5	5 & under 10	10 & under 15
Brot forward	27	27	19	13	33	22	13	7	4	3	1			34	26	25
Ebenezer Rankin				1										2		
Thos. Pollock	1	2	2				1							2		
Peter Hagan			1		1		1							1	2	2
Sarah Elder		2		1												
George Hagan					1	1										
James Hagan	2				1									1		
William Hagan	2	1			1									1		
Peter Latshaw	1	1	2			1										2
Stewart Hogan	1		1	1												
James Elder	1	2	2			1								1		
James Elder			1											1		
Thos. Elder		3	1	1										2	1	
Robt. McCall	2		1	1		1								1	1	1
Robt. McCarah				1											1	
Thos. Sneff	3		1											1		
Peter Cash		2	2			1								1		
Isreal Jordan				1												
Nathaniel Coulter	1	1	1			1								1	1	
Jonathan Sherletti	1					1								1		
James Davis				1												
Thos. Davis		2	1	3	2									1		
John McCall	3	1		1										1		
Jacob Edenburgh			1			1										
Joseph Everett			1	1		1										2
Hugh C. Young	1	1	1		1									2		
David Elder	1	1		1	1									1	1	
Saml. Jordan	3	1	1	1										1	1	
John Everett				1												
Joseph Everett		1		1										2		
Forwarded	56	44	43	15	14	19	20	16	7	3	1			56	56	52
	49															

Armstrong county, Perry township

1840 FEDERAL CENSUS, ARMSTRONG COUNTY, PERRY TOWNSHIP, PENNSYLVANIA

<u>Jordan, Samuel</u> – Samuel's household now indicates it includes "one male between 20 and 30 years of age" (which could possibly be Samuel, born 1797); "one female under five years of age" (who is unknown); and "one female between 15 and 20 years of age" (who might be Anna Mina, born 1829).

within this division allotted to *[signature: Henry Alderman?]*

	OF FAMILIES.									FREE COLORED PERSONS.											
	FEMALES.										MALES.						FEMALES.				
15 under 20	20 under 30	30 under 40	40 under 50	50 under 60	60 under 70	70 under 80	80 under 90	90 under 100	100 and up.	Under 10	10 under 24	24 under 36	36 under 55	55 under 100	100 and up.	Under 10	10 under 24	24 under 36	36 under 55	55 under 100	100 and up.
25	24	18	9	10	2	1															
		1																			
2			1																		
			1																		
2	1		1																		
				1																	
	1																				
	1																				
1	1		1																		
1		1																			
1																					
			1																		
		1																			
	1																				
	1																				
1			1																		
1																					
		1																			
1																					
1																					
2			1																		
	1																				
1					1																
						1															
1		1																			
		1																			
			1	1																	
	1																				
46	32	20	17	11	3	3															

Right portion of document on facing page

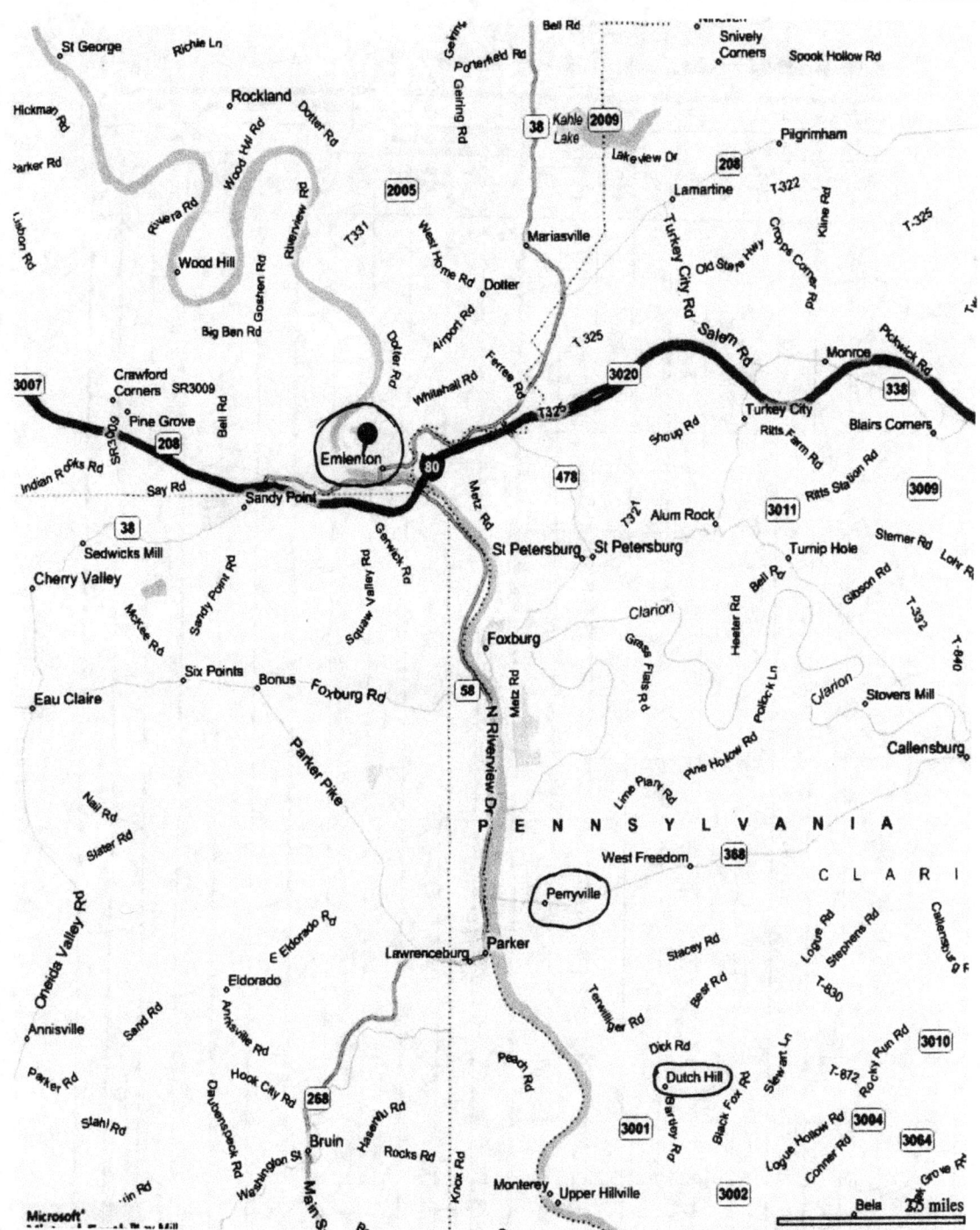

ALLEGHENY RIVER VALLEY, PENNSYLVANIA

Jordan Family Farm – Emlenton in Clarion County (For photo, see page 116) was the site of one of the Jordan family farms in Pennsylvania during the early youth of Guy Wilfred and sister Goldie (prior to the family's permanent move to California). It was here that Guy and Goldie were actually born according to a letter Goldie penned later in her life. A few miles south and east of the river at Dutch Hill, was the site of another Jordan farm at which Alvin Gilmore, Guy and Goldie lived for a short period of time and later claimed as the site of their nativity. Perry township in Clarion County is where Guy's grandfather – George Jordan – and wife Barbara "Barbary" Ann lived and probably are buried.

SCHEDULE I.—Free Inhabitants in *the Township of Perry* in the County of *Clarion* State of *Pennsylvania* enumerated by me, on the *5* day of *Oct* 1850. *David Wise* Ass't Marshal

Dwelling-houses numbered in the order of visitation.	Families numbered in the order of visitation.	The Name of every Person whose usual place of abode on the first day of June, 1850, was in this family.	Age.	Sex.	Color {White, black or mulatto.}	Profession, Occupation, or Trade of each Male Person over 15 years of age.	Value of Real Estate owned.	Place of Birth, Naming the State, Territory, or Country.	Married within the year.	Attended School within the year.	Persons over 20 y'rs of age who cannot read & write.	Whether deaf and dumb, blind, insane, idiotic, pauper, or convict.
1		George Thomas	15	m		labor		Pa				
2		Andrew	13	m								
3		William	8	m								
4		Emily	4	f								
5	2353	2414	Sam'l Snyder	52	m		farmer	1500				
6		Susannah	50	f								
7		Mary	19	f								
8		Samuel	16	m		"	"				✓	
9		Jemima	14	f							✓	
10		William	12	m							✓	
11		Rachel	8	f							✓	
12		Henry	23	m		Teacher						
13	2360	2415	George Jordan	25	m		labor					
14		Catharine	18	f							✓	
15	2361	2416	James Fox	27	m		" "	200				
16		Nancy	24	f							✓	
17		Emily	2	f								
18		Catharine	1	f								
19	2362	2417	Jacob Yates	23	m		b. Smith	100				
20		Isabella	26	f								
21		William	21	m								
22		Eliza	1	f								
23		Alex Cowder	19	m		" "						
24	2363	2420	William Cowder	63	m		farmer	1000				
25		Catharine	53	f								
26		John	16	m							✓	
27		Abigail	10	f							✓	
28		Eliza	8	f							✓	
29		Nancy	4	f							✓	
30		Eleanor	2	f								
31	2364	2421	Robert Johnston	26	m		"	3000				
32		Isabella	17	f								
33		John	2	m								
34		Elisabeth	1	f								
35		Elisabeth	55	f								
36	2365	2422	David Eldin	46	m		"	300				
37		Sarah	45	f								
38		Julyann	20	f								
39		Peter	16	m		"	"					
40		Catharine	14	f								
41	2366	2423	W. Stewart	38	m		"	4000				
42		Elisabeth	36	f								

1850 FEDERAL CENSUS, PERRY TOWNSHIP, CLARION CO, PENNSYLVANIA

Jordan, Samuel – Though very faded and difficult to read, one may still decipher the identities of the family members in Samuel's brood by their ages. Samuel is listed as the head of the family and identified as a "farmer." Listed below him are wife, Susannah Truby, age 50; Mary, age 17; Samuel, Jr., age 16; "Jemima," age 14; William, age 12; and Rachel, age 8.

Page No. _33_ .　　　　　　　OVI

SCHEDULE 1.—Free Inhabitants in _Perry Township_ in the County of _Clarion_ State of _Pennsylvania_ enumerated by me, on the _Fourth_ day of _August_ 1860. _S. S. Finney_ Ass't Marshal.

Post Office _Black Fox_ .

1	2	3	4	5	6	7	8	9	10	11	12	13	14	
Dwelling-houses numbered in the order of visitation	Families numbered in the order of visitation	The name of every person whose usual place of abode on the first day of June, 1860, was in this family.	Age	Sex	White, Color, black, or mulatto	Profession, Occupation, or Trade of each person, male and female, over 15 years of age	Value of Real Estate	Value of Personal Estate	Place of Birth, Naming the State, Territory, or Country.	Married within the year	Attended School within the year	Persons over 20 yrs of age who cannot read and write	Whether deaf and dumb, blind, insane, idiotic, pauper, or convict.	
202	202	Peter Taylor	45	M		Farmer	2000	872	Pennsylvania					1
		Eliza "	42	F					"					2
		Lot "	15	M					"		1			3
		Sarah A. "	12	F					"		1			4
		Peter "	10	M					"		1			5
		Stewart "	6	M					"		1			6
		William "	1	M					"					7
		Levi Wike	20	M		Laborer			"		1			8
		Hannah "	17	F					"		1			9
203	203	Jacob Cates	38	M		Blacksmith	1000	586	"					10
		Abigal "	20	F					"					11
		William A. "	13	M					"		1			12
		Eliza J. "	10	F					"		1			13
		Oliver N. "	7	M					"		1			14
204	204	Anthony Hoover	32	M		Farmer	1640	837	"					15
		Mary A. "	35	F					"					16
		Sarah C. "	7	F					"					17
		Minerva J. "	6	F					"		1			18
205	205	Adaline Fox	32	F		Widow			"					19
		Sarah J. "	14	F					"					20
		John N. "	12	M					"		1			21
		Clarissa A. "	10	F					"		1			22
		Christopher H. "	8	M					"		1			23
		Priscilla A. "	6	F					"					24
		Mary C. "	4	F					"					25
		George M. "	4	M					"					26
206	206	Peter Fair	67	M		Farmer	2000	703	"					27
		Mary "	6	F					"					28
		Malissa "	15	F					"					29
207	207	Jacob Stiges	28	M		Laborer		200	"					30
		Hannah "	24	F					"					31
		Peter "	2/12	M					"					32
208	208	Samuel Jordan	53	M		Farmer	2500	866	"					33
		Elizabeth "	40	F					"					34
		Rachael "	18	F					"					35
		Miles H. Berry	6	M					"					36
		Mary C. "	3	F					"					37
		Catharine Truby	67	F					"					Idiot	38

No. white males, _18_ No. colored males, ___ No. foreign born, ___ No. blind, ___ 9.140 9124 No. Idiotic, _1_ No. convicts, ___

No. white females, _20_ No. colored females, ___ No. deaf and dumb, ___ No. insane, ___ No. paupers, ___

1860 FEDERAL CENSUS, CLARION COUNTY, PERRY TOWNSHIP, PENNSYLVANIA

Jordan, Samuel – The dates and identities here, once again are ever so slightly non-conforming. If Samuel was born in 1897, he would be "63" in 1860, not "53" as stated in this census. He is listed as a "farmer" with $2,500.00 in real estate and $866.00 in personal assets. Listed with him are: his new (2nd) wife, Elizabeth Silvers Berry, age 40 whom he has just married this year (1860); daughter Rachel, age 18, by his first wife, Susannah Truby; one of Elizabeth's children – Miles H. Berry, age 6 – by her former marriage; another of Elizabeth's children by the former marriage, Mary, age 3; and then Catherine Truby, age 67. Catherine, perhaps, is sister to Susannah (1800-1858), since she is but 7 years older.

Page No. 43

237

SCHEDULE 1.—Free Inhabitants in _West Deer Township_ in the County of _Allegheny_ State of _Pennsylvania_ enumerated by me, on the _sixth_ day of _July_ 1860. _Edward Eberle_ Asst Marshal.

Post Office _Dorseyville_

1	2	3	4	5	6	7	8	9	10	11	12	13	14	
		William P Hemphill	18	M		Farmer	√ 1000		Pennsylvania					1
		Barbara Ann Ferguson	14	F					"					2
		John Edward Gibson	3	M					"					3
317	305	Robert Hemphill	29	M		Farmer	√ 1000	500	"	√				4
		Martha "	20	F		Wife			"	√				5
318	306	Adam Norris	60	M		Farmer	√ 2000	200	Ireland					6
		Effy "	63	F		Wife			Pennsylvania					7
		William "	24	M		Farm Laborer	√		"					8
		Adam J Miller "	9	M					"			√		9
		Rebecca Ferguson "	14	F					"			√		10
318	307	Adam Norris Jr	28	M		Farmer	√ 300		"					11
		Isabella "	27	F		Wife			Ireland					12
		Effyetta "	5	F					Pennsylvania					13
		Sarah Ann Sweing	13	F					"					14
319	308	John Montgomery	56	M		Farmer	√ 2500	726	Ireland					15
		Nancy "	54	F		Wife			Pennsylvania					16
		Elizabeth "	21	F		Domestic			"					17
		Thomas James "	19	M		Student	√		"			√		18
		John Ewing "	17	M		Farmer	√		"			√		19
		Agnes Ann Moran "	11	F					"			√		20
320	309	Eli Boyd	24	M		Farmer	√		"		√			21
		Catharine "	28	F		Wife			"		√			22
		Clara Virginia "	5	F					"					23
321	310	Henry Myers	30	M		Farmer & Carpenter	√ 3000	560	Hanover					24
		Eliza "	33	F		Wife			"					25
		George Henry "	7	M					Pennsylvania			√		26
		Christian "	4	M					"					27
		Eliza "	1	F					"					28
		Frederick Metes	19	M		Farm Laborer	√		Hanover					29
322	311	D S McKnight	59	M		Farmer	√ 3500	739	Pennsylvania					30
		Elizabeth "	45	F		Wife			"					31
		Robert "	22	M		Farm Laborer	√		"			√		32
		Margaret Emily "	15	F		Domestic			"					33
		Eliza Ann "	12	F					"			√		34
		Mary Elizabeth "	10	F					"			√		35
		John Albert "	7	M					"			√		36
		William Wrigley "	4	M					"					37
323	312	David Matthews	60	M		Invalid			Ireland					38
		Ann "	58	F		Wife			"					39
		Rebecca "	20	F		Milliner	√		"			√		40
		No. white males 20 No. colored males,				No. foreign born, No. blind,	12,300	2,725	No. idiotic,				No. convicts,	
		No. white females 20 No. colored females,				No. deaf and dumb, No. insane,			No. paupers,					

1860 FEDERAL CENSUS, ALLEGHENY COUNTY, WEST DEER TOWNSHIP, PENNSYLVANIA

Ferguson, Barbara Ann Pollard – Barbara was the second wife (m. 10/20/1861) of George Jordan. She is listed on this census at age 14, presumably a widow. This census reveals nothing other than the fact that she was born in Pennsylvania.

Schedule 2.—Persons who Died during the Year ending 1st June, 1870, in *Perry Township*, in the County of *Clarion*, State of *Penna*, enumerated by me, *J.S. Winkett*, Ass't Marshal.

Number of the Family, as given in the 2d column of Schedule 1.	Name of every person who died during the year ending June 1, 1870, whose place of abode at the time of death was in this family.	Age last birth day (If under 1 year, state months in fractions)	Sex—Male (M), Female (F)	Color—White (W), Black (B), Mulatto (M), Chinese (C), Indian (I)	Married (M) or Widowed (W)	Place of Birth, naming the State or Territory of the U.S., or the country, if of foreign birth.	Father of foreign birth	Mother of foreign birth	The Month in which the person died.	Profession, Occupation, or Trade.	Disease or Cause of Death.
1	2	3	4	5	6	7	8	9	10	11	12
10	Dunkle Infant	2/12	F	W		Pennsylvania			April		Epilepsia
24	Irwin Hannah	8/12	F	W		"			Feby		Inflamation of Liver
35	Kribs William	11	M	W		"			June		Kill'd falling Tree
37	Logue Infant	5/12	M	W		"			Feby		Whooping Cough
44	Boid Ellen	6	F	W		"			June		Croup
62	Stewart I.E.	9/12	M	W		Tennessee			March		acute Bronchitis
90	Crick Jesse T.	1	M	W		Penna			"		Lung Fever
105	Henshaw Joseph H.	18	M	W		"	1	1	May	Farm Hand	Consumption
118	Coon Minnie	5	F	W		"			Jany		Inflamation of Brain
140	Kingley Danil B.	64	M	W	W	"			June	Farmer	Kill'd by a Horse
153	Davis Martin	2	M	W		"			May		Drownd in Privy
171	Bayer Barbara	93	F	W	W	"			June		Lung Fever
174	Loranyh William	23	M	W		"			August	Farm Hand	Consumption
179	McKibbenMary	68	F	W	W	"			May		Typhoid Pneumonia
191	Henshaw Andrew	69	M	W		Ireland			June		Inflamation of Brain
201	Barr Hannah	25	F	W	W	Penna			April		Consumption
207	Kifer Jacob	6/12	M	W		"			March		Chronic Diarhoea
209	McCoy Sophia	62	F	W		"			"		Valvular disea. of the Heart
231	Davis Lizzie	1	F	W		"			Jany		Whooping Cough
247	Snyder Peter	53	M	W		"			Feby	Farmer	Chronic Bronchitis
250	Horner		M	W		"			May		Still Born
256	Gorden Samuel	72	M	W	M	"			June	Farmer	Softening of the Brain
260	Berry Mary	8/12	F	W		"			Jany		Lung Fever

I hereby certify that the foregoing Schedule No 2, was taken by me in accordance with the law and instructions and is correct to the best of my knowledge.

J. Winkett Ass't Marshal

Total number of deaths, 23	No. of white males, 13	No. of black males,	No. of mulatto males,	No. of married, 1	Total foreign born, 1
	No. of white females, 10	No. of black females,	No. of mulatto females,	No. of widowed, 4	

REMARKS:

1870 FEDERAL MORTALITY SCHEDULE, CLARION COUNTY, PERRY TOWNSHIP, PENNSYLVANIA

Jordan, Samuel - This mortality record for Perry Township indicates Samuel passed away in June of 1870, suffering from "softening of the brain." He was 72.

1880 Federal Census schedule, Schedule 1.—Inhabitants in Perry Township, in the County of Clarion, State of Penn, enumerated by me on the 10-11 day of June, 1880. R. G. [signature], Enumerator.

Page No. 19
Supervisor's Dist. No. 10
Enumeration Dist. No. 74

1880 FEDERAL CENSUS, PERRY TOWNSHIP, CLARION COUNTY, PENNSYLVANIA

Jordan, George – By 1880, Samuel had passed away (1870). George was now the head of the Jordan household in Dutch Hill. This census shows him listed as a farmer, age 55. His wife, Ann, age 50; and his son, Gilmore, age 16, are listed with him. Interestingly, a "May Snyder," age 9, identified as "adopted" is also listed with them.

125

TWELFTH CENSUS OF THE UNITED STATES.

SCHEDULE No. 1.—POPULATION.

109 A

1900 FEDERAL CENSUS, OIL CITY, VENANGO CO., PENNSYLVANIA

Jordan, Alvin Gilmore – Interestingly, in June of 1900, Alvin Gilmore, age 36, is living in Pennsylvania with wife, Mary Melinda Gravatt, age 41, with their two children, Guy Wilfred, age 11, and Goldie Evelyn, age 10. Despite his assumed stable employment with the railroad at a time (circa 1888-1889) when such a livelihood was rare, Alvin nevertheless left this job to return to the old Jordan home-place in Pennsylvania with Mary Melinda to live for a number of years. Was this move made to allow a pregnant Linnie to be near her parents in the birthing and early childhood of the couple's two children (a son, Guy Wilfred and a daughter, Goldie Evelyn)? Or was this change of venue made in order to attend to aging parents who needed Alvin's and/or Linnie's assistance (George died in 1892; Barbara Ann died in 1901)? Or, was it made because Alvin had in fact lost his job with the railroad and therefore was without employment? We quite likely will never know the answers to these questions.

1906 DEATH CERTIFICATE, PERRY TOWNSHIP, CLARION CO., PENNSYLVANIA

Reichert, Mary Jordan – Mary, full-sister to George Jordan, was the daughter of Samuel S. Jordan and his first wife, Susannah Truby. Mary was born 04/17/1831, Clarion Co., PA, and died 05/18/1906, Perry, Clarion Co., PA. She probably never left the county during her lifetime. She, also married an individual of German extraction, which would have been common in Dutch ("Deutsch") Hill, Pennsylvania.

FORM V. S., No. 5.

PLACE OF DEATH.

COMMONWEALTH OF PENNSYLVANIA.
BUREAU OF VITAL STATISTICS.
CERTIFICATE OF DEATH.

County of _Clarion_

Township of _Perry_
or
Borough of
or
City of

Registration District No. _363_

Primary Registration District No. _2429_

74856

File No.

Registered No. _35_

(No. _____ St.; _____ Ward)

[If death occurred in a Hospital or Institution, give its NAME instead of street and number.]

[If death occurs away from USUAL RESIDENCE give facts called for under "Special Information."]

FULL NAME _Elizabeth Jordan,_

PERSONAL AND STATISTICAL PARTICULARS

SEX _F._   COLOR _W_

DATE OF BIRTH _Apr 21 1821_
(Month) (Day) (Year)

AGE _87_ years, _4_ months, _7_ days

SINGLE, MARRIED, WIDOWED, OR DIVORCED _Widow,_

BIRTHPLACE (State or country) _Penna._

NAME OF FATHER _David Silvis,_

BIRTHPLACE OF FATHER (State or country) _Penna,_

MAIDEN NAME OF MOTHER _Mary Stewart,_

BIRTHPLACE OF MOTHER (State or country) _Penna,_

OCCUPATION _Invalid._

THE ABOVE STATED PERSONAL PARTICULARS ARE TRUE TO THE BEST OF MY KNOWLEDGE AND BELIEF

(Informant) _O. P. Berry (Son)_

(Address) _Petrolia, Pa._

Filed _Aug 31, 1908_   _____ Registrar

MEDICAL CERTIFICATE OF DEATH

DATE OF DEATH _Aug 28 1908_
(Month) (Day) (Year)

I HEREBY CERTIFY, That I attended deceased from _At Irregular Intervals,_ 190__ that I last saw her alive on _July 12" 1908_ and that death occurred, on the date stated above, at _2,_ P. M. The CAUSE OF DEATH was as follows:

General Debility Incident old age, _____ Days

(Duration)

Contributory _Congestion of lungs_ _____ Days

(Duration)

(Signed) _R A Wallace_ M. D.

_8/30_ 1908 (Address) _West Monterey_

SPECIAL INFORMATION only for Hospitals, Institutions, Transients, or Recent Residents.

Former or Usual Residence _____

How long at Place of Death? _____ Days

Where was disease contracted? _____

PLACE OF BURIAL OR REMOVAL _Dutch Hill Cem_

DATE OF BURIAL _Aug 30 1908_

UNDERTAKER _W. E. Homer_

ADDRESS _Dutch Hill_

1908 DEATH CERTIFICATE, PERRY TOWNSHIP, CLARION CO., PENNSYLVANIA

Jordan, Elizabeth Silvis Berry – Elizabeth was the second wife of Samuel S. Jordan. She and Samuel had several children, one of which was Abner Miles Jordan, who was George Jordan's half-brother.

DEPARTMENT OF COMMERCE AND LABOR—BUREAU OF THE CENSUS

THIRTEENTH CENSUS OF THE UNITED STATES: 1910 POPULATION

State: *California*
County: *San Bernardino*
Township or other division of county: *Colton township*
Name of incorporated place: *Colton city*
Enumerated by me on the *22nd* day of *April* 1910. *Pierre J. Hungate* Enumerator

Supervisor's District No. *8*
Enumeration District No. *94*
Sheet No. *12 A*

1910 FEDERAL CENSUS, COLTON, SAN BERNARDINO COUNTY, CALIFORNIA

Jordan, Alvin Gilmore – By 1910, Alvin, age 46, and his family had departed Pennsylvania permanently and moved back out West to California, where he was again employed by the railroad. He is described simply as "carpenter – railroad."

Certificate of Marriage
WITH MARRIAGE LICENSE

STATE OF GEORGIA

COUNTY OF HALL

TO ANY JUDGE, JUSTICE OF THE PEACE, OR MINISTER OF THE GOSPEL

You are hereby authorized to join

	AGE			AGE
G. W. Jordan	Not Given	*and*	Miss Essie Hudgins	Not Given

in the Holy State of Matrimony, according to the Constitution and Laws of this State and for so doing this shall be your License. And you are hereby required to return this License to me, with your Certificate hereon of the fact and date of the Marriage, within thirty days after the date of said Marriage.

Given under my hand and Seal, this 27 *day of* May 19 27

Arnold L. Bennett *Ordinary*

STATE OF GEORGIA **Certificate** COUNTY OF HALL

I Certify that

G. W. Jordan *and* Miss Essie Hudgins

were joined in Matrimony by me this 18 *day of* June 19 27

Recorded July 29 19 27

Arnold L. Bennett *Ordinary* Rev. L. L. Bennett **PARTY PERFORMING CEREMONY**

This is to Certify that the above is a true and correct copy of the Marriage Record of

G. W. Jordan

and Miss Essie Hudgins

as it appears in my office in Marriage Record, Book No. G *Page* 496

Witness my hand and Seal this 26 *day of* May 19 64

W. M. Jones

ORDINARY (PROBATE JUDGE) GAINESVILLE, GA.

GUY WILFRED JORDAN MARRIAGE (1927)
Guy had been employed as the chief chemist at Southern States Portland Cement plant in Rockmart, Georgia for several years before meeting and falling in love with Essie Hudgins of Clermont, Georgia. The couple ultimately were married at the Hudgins home in Clermont on a hot July afternoon in 1927.

STANFORD UNIVERSITY (1913)
Pictured is a view of Stanford University as it appeared in the early 1900s when attended by Guy Jordan.

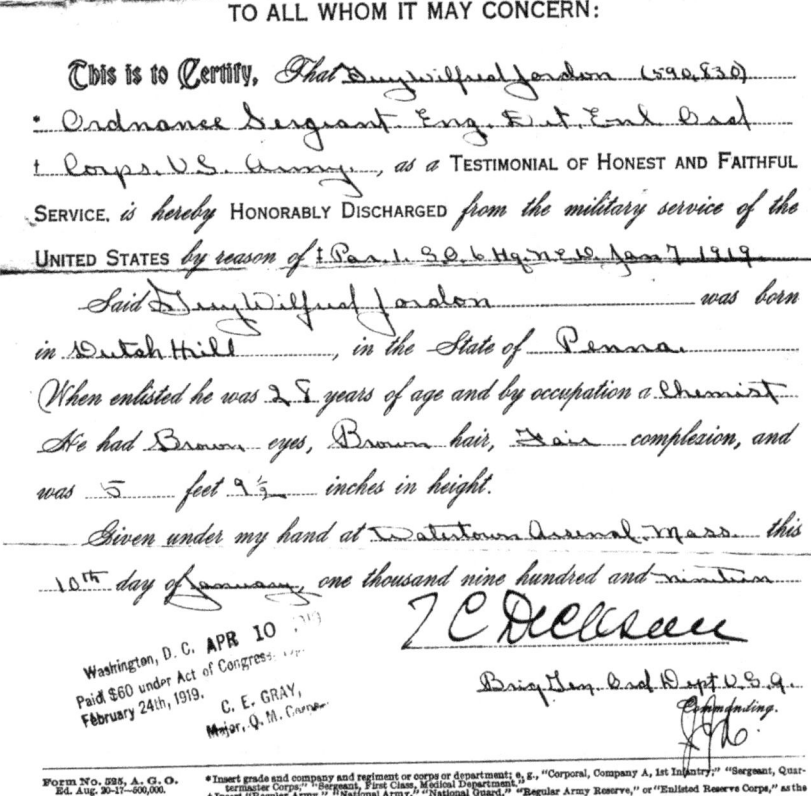

Honorable Discharge from the Army of the United States

TO ALL WHOM IT MAY CONCERN:

This is to Certify, That Guy Wilfred Jordan (590,830) *Ordnance Sergeant Eng. Det. Enl. Ord. †Corps. U.S. Army., as a TESTIMONIAL OF HONEST AND FAITHFUL SERVICE. is hereby HONORABLY DISCHARGED from the military service of the UNITED STATES by reason of ‡Par. 1. S.O. b Hg. N.P.D. Jan. 7 1919.

Said Guy Wilfred Jordan was born in Dutch Hill, in the State of Penna. When enlisted he was 28 years of age and by occupation a Chemist. He had Brown eyes, Brown hair, Fair complexion, and was 5 feet 9½ inches in height.

Given under my hand at Watertown Arsenal, Mass. this 10th day of January, one thousand nine hundred and nineteen.

Washington, D.C. APR 10
Paid $60 under Act of Congress
February 24th, 1919.
C. E. GRAY,
Major, Q. M. Corps

Brig. Gen. Ord. Dept. U.S.A.
Commanding.

Form No. 525, A. G. O.
Ed. Aug. 20-17—500,000.

Photographed circa 1918, Guy Jordan had reached the rank of staff sergeant in the U.S. Army Infantry. The actual location of his service, however, is unknown.

ARMY HONORABLE DISCHARGE (1919)

Guy Jordan enlisted in the U.S. Army on November 21, 1917 in New York City where he, interestingly, was immediately granted the rank of Ordnance Sergeant. With a specialty in Ordnance, he was attached to Watertown Arsenal in Massachusetts. He was honorably discharged on January 7, 1919 following the Armistice and conclusion of World War I.

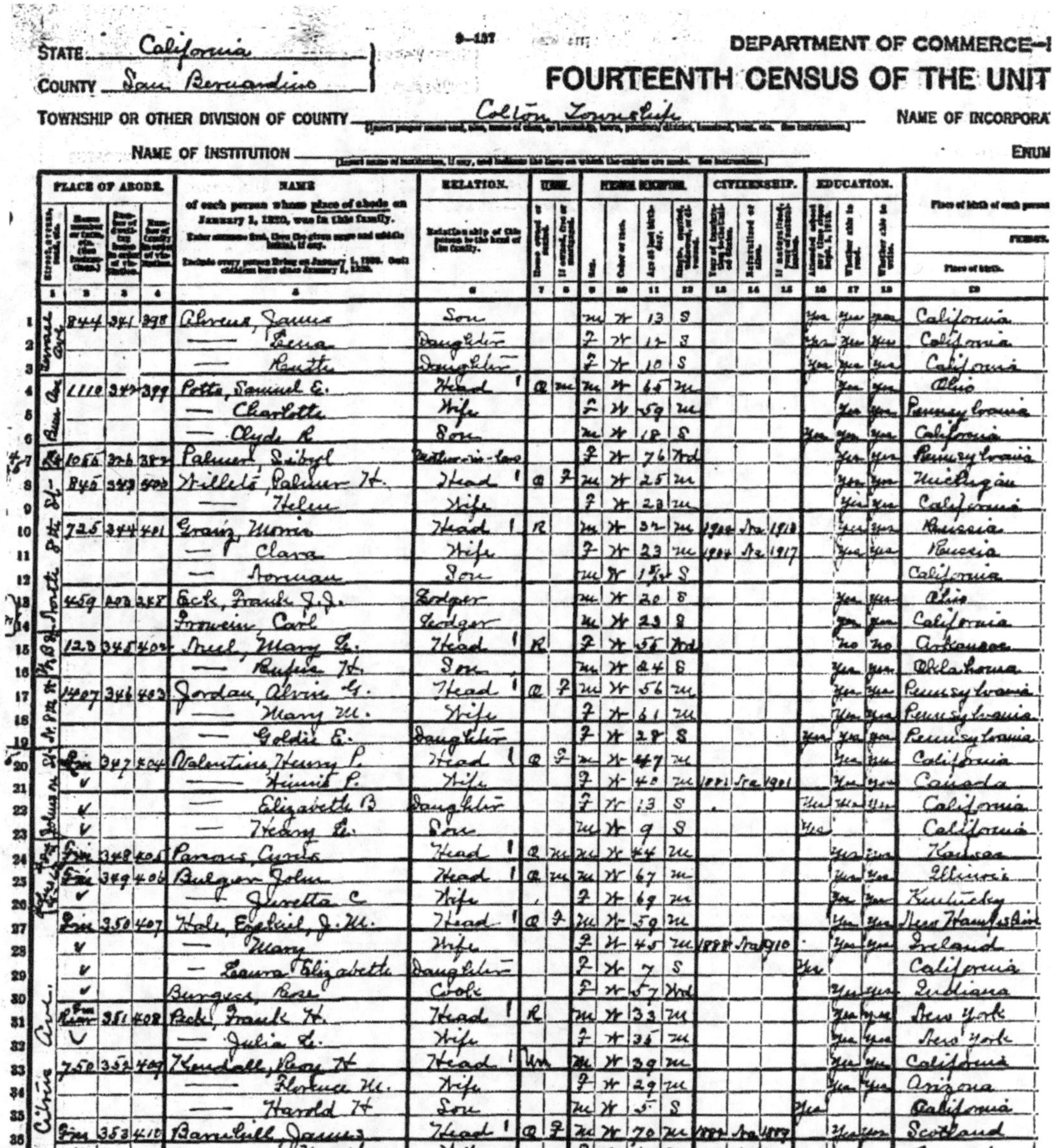

STATE _California_

COUNTY _San Bernardino_

TOWNSHIP OR OTHER DIVISION OF COUNTY _Colton Township_

NAME OF INSTITUTION ____

DEPARTMENT OF COMMERCE—I

FOURTEENTH CENSUS OF THE UNIT

NAME OF INCORPORA

ENUM

(handwritten census enumeration table — 1920 Federal Census schedule with columns for Place of Abode, Name, Relation, Home, Personal Description, Citizenship, Education, and Place of Birth)

1920 FEDERAL CENSUS, COLTON, SAN BERNARDINO CO., CALIFORNIA

Jordan, Alvin Gilmore – This census shows Alvin, at age 56, still the head of his household which includes wife, Mary Melinda, age 61, and daughter, Goldie Evelyn, age 29, still at home.

BUREAU OF THE CENSUS 1920   [D1—878]   SUPERVISOR'S DISTRICT NO. _9_   SHEET NO.

ED STATES: 1920—POPULATION 164 ENUMERATION DISTRICT NO. _150_ _15_ A

TED PLACE _Colfax City_   Precinct- WARD OF CITY _5_ 8830

ERATED BY ME ON THE _14th & 15th_ DAY OF _January_ 1920. _Julia M. Ward_ ENUMERATOR.

MOTHER TONGUE (20)	PLACE OF BIRTH (21)	Mother tongue (22)	PLACE OF BIRTH (23)	Mother tongue (24)	(25)	OCCUPATION Trade (26)	Industry (27)	Emp (28)	(29)	
	Germany	German	California		Yes	None				1
	Germany	German	California		Yes	None				2
	Germany	German	California		Yes	None				3
	Ohio		Ohio		Yes	Blacksmith	Pacific Fruit Co	W		4 136
	New York		Pennsylvania		Yes	None				5
	Ohio		Pennsylvania		Yes	None				6
	New York		New York		Yes	None				7
	Michigan		Michigan		Yes	Retail Merchant	Genl. Merchandise B...			8 766
	California		Illinois		Yes	None				9
Jewish	Russia	Jewish	Russia	Jewish	Yes	Merchant	Mens Furnishing...	Own		10 750
Jewish	Russia	Jewish	Russia	Jewish	Yes	None				11
	Russia	Jewish	Russia	Jewish		None				12
	Unknown	Un	France	French	Yes	Hatter Helper	Railroad	W		13 670
	Ohio		Switzerland	French	Yes	Hatter Helper	Railroad	W		14 630
	Arkansas		Missouri		Yes	None				15
	Tennessee		Arkansas		Yes	Boiler Maker	Railroad	W		16 140
	Pennsylvania		Pennsylvania		Yes	Carpenter Foreman	Railroad	W		17 148
	Pennsylvania		Pennsylvania		Yes	None				18
	Pennsylvania		Pennsylvania		Yes	Student Nurse	Hospital	W		19 872
	New York		Illinois		Yes	Salesman	Grocery Store	W	6	20 771
English	"English	English	Canada	English	Yes	None				21
	California		Canada	English	Yes	None				22
	California		Canada	English	Yes	None				23
	Vermont		Wisconsin		Yes	Ranch Laborer	Orange Grove	W		24 088
	Scotland	Scotch	Scotland	Scotch	Yes	Rancher	Own Grove	W	7	25 036
	Kentucky		Kentucky		Yes	None				26
	Massachusetts		New Hampshire		Yes	Rancher	Own Ranch	Own	8	27 036
English	Ireland	English	Ireland	English	Yes	None				28
	New Hampshire		Ireland	English		None				29
	Michigan		New York			Cook	Private Family	W		30 954
	New York		Michigan		Yes	Manager	Ranch	W		31 020
	New York		New York		Yes	None				32
	Vermont		California		Yes	Manager	Ranch	W	9	33 020
	England	English	England	English	Yes	None				34
	California		Arizona			None				35
Scotch	Scotland	Scotch	Scotland	Scotch	Yes	Rancher	Own Ranch	Own	10	36 136
					Yes	None				37
English	Canada	English	Canada	English	Yes	Chemical Engineer	Plant	W		38 872
	Scotland	Scotch	Canada	English	Yes	Driver	Bakery Wagon	O.a		39 716
	New Jersey		Connecticut		Yes	Nurse	Hospital	W		40 872
	Georgia		Connecticut		Yes	None				41
	Connecticut		Connecticut		Yes	None				42
	Connecticut		Connecticut		Yes	None				43
	Connecticut		Connecticut		Yes	Nurse	General	W		44 936
	New York		New York		Yes	Rancher	Own Ranch	O.a.	11	45 936
English	Scotland	Scotch	England	English	Yes	None				46
	Connecticut		Connecticut		Yes	Rancher	Own Ranch	O.a.	12	47 036
German	Germany	German	Germany	German	Yes	Rancher				48
	Germany	German	Germany	German	Yes	None				49
	Germany	German	Wisconsin		Yes	None				50
	United States		United States		Yes	Carpenter	House	W		51 148

Right portion of document on facing page

1930 FEDERAL CENSUS, ROCKMART, POLK COUNTY, GEORGIA

<u>Jordan, Guy Wilfred</u> – This census shows Guy, at age 41, with wife, Essie, age 30, and daughter Marilyn, age 2. Guy is listed as a "chemist" at the "cement plant" once located outside Rockmart.

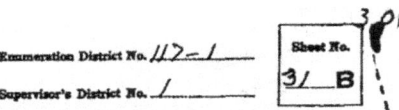

Form 15-6

MENT OF COMMERCE—BUREAU OF THE CENSUS

I CENSUS OF THE UNITED STATES: 1930

POPULATION SCHEDULE

Enumeration District No. 117-1

Supervisor's District No. 1

Sheet No. 31 B

Enumerated by me on _April 29_, 1930, _Mrs. P. V. Bray_, Enumerator.

MOTHER	MOTHER TONGUE (OR NATIVE LANGUAGE) OF FOREIGN BORN — CODE			CITIZENSHIP, ETC.			OCCUPATION	INDUSTRY	CODE			EMPLOYMENT		VETERANS			
20	21	A	B C	22	23	24	25	26	D	27	28	29	30	31	32		
Georgia		11				yes	Lawyer	Gen. Practice	X94	0	yes		yes	WW		51
Georgia		11				yes	None									52
Georgia		11					None									53
Georgia		11					None									54
Georgia		11					None									55
Georgia		11				yes	Teacher	Public School	494	W	yes					56
Georgia		11				yes	Merchant	Drug Store	8591	E	yes		40			57
South Carolina		11				yes	None									58
Georgia		11				yes	None									59
Georgia		11					None									60
South Carolina		11				yes	Manager	Warehouse	7388	W	yes		40			61
South Carolina		11				yes	None									62
Georgia		11				yes	Electrician	Cement Plant	1613	W	yes					63
South Carolina		11				yes	None									64
Georgia		11				yes	None									65
Georgia		11				yes	None									66
Georgia		11					None									67
South Carolina		11				yes	None									68
Georgia		11				yes	Cashier	Bank	8583	W	yes		40			69
Georgia		11				yes	None									70
Georgia		11					None									71
Georgia		11					None									72
New Jersey		11				yes	Barber	Barber Shop	8096	O	yes		40			73
Georgia		11				yes	None									74
Georgia		11				yes	None									75
Pennsylvania		11				yes	Chemist	Cement Plant	4803	W	yes		yes	WW		76
Georgia		11				yes	None									77
Georgia		11				yes	None									78
Georgia		11				yes	Foreman	Cement Plant	7403	W	yes		40		24	79
Georgia		11				yes	None									80
Georgia		11				yes	Manager	Retail Grocery Store	9X91	W	yes		40			81
United States		14				yes	Saleslady	Retail Grocery Store	9590	W	yes					82
Indiana		14				yes	Mechanic	Automobile	7623	O	yes		yes	WW		83
North Carolina		14				yes	None									84
Alabama		14				yes	None									85
Georgia		11					None									86
Georgia		11					None									87
Georgia		11				yes	Contractor	Construction	04X1	E	yes		40			88
Georgia		11				yes	None									89
Georgia		11					None									90
Georgia		11				yes	None									91
Georgia		11				yes	None									92
Georgia		11				yes	Salesman	Ford Place	9590	W	yes		40			93
Georgia		11				yes	Odd Jobs	Retail Grocery	7790	W	yes		40			94
Georgia		11				yes	Odd Jobs	Assembling	77X1	W	yes					95
Georgia		21				yes	Bookkeeper	Bank	6783	W	yes					96
Georgia		18				yes	None									97
Georgia		14				yes	Manager	Ga. Power Store	8V91	W	yes		40			98
Kentucky		14				yes	Merchant	Retail Dept. Store	83.91	E	yes		48			99
Georgia		21				yes	Saleslady	Dept. Store	9590	W	yes					100

Col. 11—World War .... WW
Spanish-American War .... SW
Civil War .... CW
Philippine Insurrection .... PhI
Boxer Rebellion .... Box
Mexican Expedition .... Mex

ENTRIES ARE REQUIRED IN THE SEVERAL COLUMNS AS FOLLOWS:

Cols. 6, 11, 12, 13, 14, 15, 18, 19, 20, and 23—For all persons.
Cols. 7, 8, and 10—For heads of families only. (Col. 8 required on every line for a large family.)
Col. 17—For married persons only.
Col. 18—For all persons 10 years of age and over.

Cols. 21, 22, and 23—For all foreign-born persons.
Cols. 24-26—For all persons 10 years of age and over.
Cols. 21, 22—For all persons 21 years of age, for whom an exception is reported in Col. 23.
Col. 30—For all males 21 years of age and over.

Right portion of document on facing page

135

State California

County Orange

Township or other division of county

Incorporated place Santa Ana

Ward of city #2 Prct of   Block No. _____

Unincorporated place _____

Institution _____

DEPART

FIFTEENTH

#	PLACE OF ABODE			NAME	RELATION	HOME DATA			PERSONAL DESCRIPTION						EDUCATION		PLACE OF BIRTH	
											Sex	Color	Age	Marital	Age at first marriage	Attended school	Able to read/write	PERSON	FATHER
1	528	1	1	Moore, James J.	Head	R		35	R	No	M	W	38	M 33	No		Kansas	Wisconsin
2				Grey W.	Wife-H				V		F	W	29	M 20	No	Yes	Oklahoma	Arkansas
3				Betty J.	Daughter				V		F	W	5	S	No		California	Tennessee
4				Caroline J.	Daughter				V		F	W	2	S	No		California	Tennessee
5	524	2	2	Morrison, Kenneth E.	Head	O	4500		R	No	M	W	35	M 12	No	Yes	Washington	Canada-English
6				Ina	Wife-H				V		F	W	36	M 14	No	Yes	California	Arkansas
7				Kenneth J.	Son				V		M	W	8	S		Yes	California	Washington
8	510	3	3	Hall, Edward W.	Head	O	7500		R	No	M	W	39	M 27	No	Yes	California	United States
9				Anita	Wife-H				V		F	W	37	M 25	No	Yes	California	Ohio
10				Milford W.	Son				V		M	W	10	S	Yes	Yes	California	California
11				Felitha J.	Daughter				V		F	W	7	S	Yes		California	California
12	508	4	4	Newell, Arthur E.	Head	R	6000		R	No	M	W	58	M 23	No	Yes	Minnesota	New York
13				Nellie A.	Wife-H				V		F	W	57	M 19	No	Yes	Nebraska	Wisconsin
14	426	5	5	Geren, Charles J.	Head	O	7000		R	No	M	W	41	M 24	No	Yes	Kansas	Indiana
15				Geren, Lois J.	Wife-H				V		F	W	36	M 20	No	Yes	Kansas	Indiana
16				Geren, Vincent E.	Son				V		M	W	14	S	Yes	Yes	Kansas	Kansas
17				Charles Jr.	Son				V		M	W	7	S	Yes		California	Kansas
				Squires, John E.	Servant				V		M	W	25	S	No	Yes	Kansas	Indiana
	422	6	6	Beebe, William M.	Head	R	35		R	No	M	W	32	M 30	No	Yes	California	England
				Virginia L.	Wife-H				V		F	W	27	M 25	No	Yes	Missouri	Missouri
				Gloria R.	Daughter				V		F	W	1	S	No		California	California
	?	7	7	Evans, Robert A.	Head	O	5500		R	No	M	W	42	M 29	No	Yes	Indiana	Indiana
				Florence	Wife-H				V		F	W	42	M 29	No	Yes	Maine	Maine
	151	8	8	Garner, Rob't A.	Head	O	7500		R	No	M	W	39	M 22	No	Yes	Nebraska	Illinois
				Jennie	Wife-H				V		F	W	40	M 21	No	Yes	Nebraska	Canada-English
				Dorothy	Adopted dau				V		F	W	4	S		Yes	California	Nebraska
	153	9	9	Bradley, Willie A.	Head	R	35		R	No	M	W	30	M 28	No	Yes	Arkansas	England
28				Mary O.	Wife-H				V		F	W	26	M 24	No	Yes	Missouri	Missouri
29				Mary	Daughter				V		F	W	1	S	No		California	Arkansas
30	411	10	10	Wright, James E.	Head	R	35		R	No	M	W	25	M 24	No	Yes	Nebraska	Illinois
31				Margaret	Wife-H				V		F	W	29	M 20	No	Yes	Illinois	Illinois
32	415	11	11	Jordan, Alvin S.	Head	O	5000		No		M	W	67	M 21	No	Yes	Pennsylvania	Pennsylvania
33				Mary M.	Wife-H				V		F	W	71	M 25	No	Yes	Pennsylvania	Pennsylvania
34	417	12	12	Smith, Harold W.	Head	O	5500		No		M	W	33	M 27	No	Yes	Virginia	U.S.
				Gertrude M.	Wife-H				V		F	W	27	M 21	No	Yes	Connecticut	Canada-English
				Eugene M.	Son				V		M	W	5	S		Yes	California	Virginia
				Donald C.	Son				V		M	W	1	S		No	California	Virginia
	481	13	13	Forder, Evan W.	Head	O	5000		No		M	W	31	M	No	Yes	Illinois	United States
				Claire L.	Wife-H				V		F	W	32	M 19	No	Yes	Michigan	Michigan
40				Fulton, Claire L.	Stepdaughter				V		F	W	9	S	Yes		Michigan	Ohio
41				McDowe, Teresa S.	Mother-in-law				V		F	W	55	S	No	Yes	Michigan	Michigan
42	435	14	14	Hunter, Edward A.	Head	O	4500		R	No	M	W	41	M 26	No	Yes	Nebraska	Pennsylvania
43				Ethel J.	Wife-H				V		F	W	51	M 36	No	Yes	Iowa	Illinois
44				Alta R.	Daughter				V		F	W	7	S	No		California	Nebraska
45				Graves, Philo	Father-in-law				V		M	W	86	Wd	No	Yes	Illinois	Vermont
46	421	15	15	Carroll, George S.	Head	O	5000		R	No	M	W	53	D	No	Yes	Australia	United States
47				Molly E.	Daughter-H				V		F	W	18	S	Yes	Yes	California	Australia
48				Eileen E.	Daughter				V		F	W	15	S	Yes		California	Australia
49	505	16	16	Robinson, John B.	Head	R	32.50		R	No	M	W	31	M 31	No	Yes	North Dakota	West Virginia
50				Ethel A.	Wife-H				V		F	W	31	M 30	No	Yes	Minnesota	Wisconsin

1930 FEDERAL CENSUS, SANTA ANA, ORANGE COUNTY, CALIFORNIA

<u>Jordan, Alvin G.</u> – By 1930, Alvin is 67 years of age and his listed occupation is "None." Listed with him is his wife, Mary Melinda Gravatt Jordan.

Form 15-6
ment OF COMMERCE—BUREAU OF THE CENSUS
CENSUS OF THE UNITED STATES: 1930
POPULATION SCHEDULE

Enumeration District No. 30-70
Supervisor's District No. 20
Sheet No. 1 A
90

Enumerated by me on April 3+4, 1930, Anita M. Stahl, Enumerator.

MOTHER TONGUE (OR NATIVE LANGUAGE) OF FOREIGN BORN				CITIZENSHIP, ETC.			OCCUPATION AND INDUSTRY				EMPLOYMENT		VETERANS		
Language spoken in home before coming to the United States (MOTHER)	CODE						OCCUPATION	INDUSTRY	CODE	Class of worker	Whether actually at work yesterday	If not, line No.	Whether a veteran of U.S. military or naval forces	What war or expedition	
20	A	B	C	22	23	24	25	26	D	27	28	29	30	31	32
Illinois	70					Yes	Engineer	Telephone	1X79	W	Yes		No		1
Oklahoma	86					Yes	None								2
Oklahoma	98						None								3
Oklahoma	98						None								4
California	96	43	1			Yes	Justice of Peace	Justice of Peace	8095	W	Yes		No	1	5
Tennessee	98					Yes	None								6
California	98						None								7
United States	98					Yes	Contractor	Grading + Sewer	0X81	E	Yes		No		8
Iowa	98					Yes	None								9
California	98					Yes	None								10
California	98						None								11
New York	64					Yes	Farmer	Farm	VVVO		Yes		No		12
Indiana	69					Yes	None								13
Indiana	70					Yes	Salesman	Insurance	8885	W	Yes		No		14
Iowa	70					Yes	None								15
Kansas	70					Yes	None								16
Kansas	98						None								17
Iowa	70					Yes									18
Ireland	98	00	0			Yes	Clerk	Title Company	7X92	W	Yes		Yes	WW	19
Missouri	66					Yes	None								20
Missouri	98						None								21
Indiana	60					Yes	Carpenter	Building	06X11	W	Yes		No		22
Maine	50					Yes	None								23
Illinois	69					Yes	Salesman	Furniture Store	4590	W	Yes		No		24
Canada-English	69	43	0			Yes	None								25
Nebraska	98						None								26
Ohio	94	00	1			Yes	Salesman	Paint Store	4591	W	Yes		No		27
Kansas	66					Yes	None								28
Missouri	98						None								29
Kentucky	69					Yes	Foreman	Factory	7469	W	Yes		No		30
Illinois	61					Yes	None								31
Pennsylvania	58					Yes	None								32
Pennsylvania	58					Yes	None								33
Pennsylvania	74					Yes	Salesman	Building	8286	W	Yes		Yes	WW	34
Canada-English	55	43	0			Yes	None								35
Connecticut	98						None								36
Connecticut	98						None								37
United States	61					Yes	Mechanic	Automobile	7623	W	Yes		Yes	WW	38
Michigan	62					Yes	Bookkeeper	Transfer	V78V	W	Yes				39
Michigan	62						None								40
Michigan	62					Yes	Accountant	News Paper	6649	W	Yes				41
Canada	69	43	2			Yes	Farmer	Farm	VVV	O	No	1	No		42
New York	65					Yes	None								43
Iowa	98						None								44
Vermont	61					Yes	None								45
United States	98					Yes	Manager	Manufacturing Co	7364	E	Yes		No		46
United States	98	ww	+			Yes	None								47
United States	98	ww	+			Yes	None								48
Michigan	67					Yes	Superintendent	Wholesale Slavery	99,91	E	Yes		No		49
Minnesota	64					Yes	None								50

Col. 31—World War ..... WW
Spanish-American War ... SP
Civil War Civ
Philippine Insurrection . Phil
Boxer Rebellion .... Box
Mexican Expedition ...... Mex

ENTRIES ARE REQUIRED IN THE
SEVERAL COLUMNS AS FOLLOWS:

Cols. 6, 11, 12, 13, 14, 16, 18, 25, 26, and 29—For all persons.
Cols. 7, 8, 9, and 10—For heads of families only. (Col. 9 requires an entry for a farm family.)
Col. 12—For married persons only.
Col. 13—For all persons 10 years of age and over.

Cols. 21, 22, and 23—For all foreign-born persons.
Cols. 24—For all persons 21 years of age and over.
Cols. 27, and 28—For all persons for whom an occupation is reported in Col. 25.
Col. 29—For all males 21 years of age and over.

Right portion of document on facing page

1940 FEDERAL CENSUS, ROCKMART, POLK COUNTY, GEORGIA

Jordan, Guy Wilfred – At age 50, Guy remains the chemist at the cement manufacturing plant outside Rockmart. Wife, Essie, is 40, and daughters Marilyn and Patricia are 12 and 5 years of age respectively. Six years hence, Guy will die tragically in a terrible industrial accident at the Rockmart cement manufacturing plant.

DEPARTMENT OF COMMERCE—BUREAU OF THE CENSUS

SIXTEENTH CENSUS OF THE UNITED STATES: 1940

POPULATION SCHEDULE

S. D. No. _7_   E. D. No. _115—1_   Sheet No.

Enumerated by me on _Apr. 9_ 1940:   _3_ **B**

Irene Moore, Enumerator.

State										No. weeks	Occupation	Industry		Code				Line No.
Georgia	XOXO	no	no	no	no	H	5										yes	41
Georgia	7813	yes	—	—	—	—	1	60		Owner, Operator	Retail dry goods	Pa	156	63	7	52	yes	42
Georgia	1513	yes	—	—	—	—	1	60		Owner, operator	Retail dry goods	Pa	156	63	9	52	yes	43
Florida	7935	no	no	no	no	U	7										no	44
Florida	717	no	no	no	no	U	7											45
Florida	713	no	no	no		H	5			House keeper	Own home	no					no	46
Florida	11	yes	—	—	—	—	1	84		Manager	Georgia P.	Pa	156	60	1	52		47
																		48
	XOXO	yes	—	—	—	—	1	78		Owner, operator	Retail liquor	Pa	156	74	4	52	yes	49
Georgia	1244	no	no	no	no	H	5			House keeper	House	no					no	50
Georgia	XX																	51
Georgia		yes	—	—	—	—	1	40		Textile worker	Cotton Mill	Pw	316	88	1	52	yes	52
Georgia		no	no	no	no	H	5											53
																		54
		yes	—	—	—	—	1			Lawyer	Private practice	Oa	V26	93	4	52	yes	55
		yes	—	—	—	—	1	40		Laborer	Cemetery	Pw	904	81	2	48	405	no	56
		yes	—	—	—	—	1	30		Boarding H. proprietor	Inn room	Pa	712	87	7	26	1370	yes	57
Georgia		yes	—	—	—	—	1	30		Teaching	Jr. high	Pw	V34	91	2	36	676	no	58
Georgia		yes	—	—	—	—	1	30		Teaching	Public s.	Pw	V34	91	2	36	630	no	59
Georgia		yes	—	—	—	—	1	30		Teaching	Public s.	Pw	V34	91	2	36	630	yes	60
Georgia		yes	—	—	—	—	1	30		Teaching	Public s.	Pw	V34	11	36	675	yes	61
Georgia		yes	—	—	—	—	1	30		Teaching	Public s.		V34	91	2	0	0	yes	62
N. Car.		yes	—	—	—	—	2	100		Civil engineer	W.P.A.	Pw	V16	89	2	52	3000	yes	63
N. Carolina		no	no	no	no	H	5											64
Georgia		yes	—	—	—	—	1	52		Cook	Boarding H.	Pw	720	87	1	52	170	yes	65
		yes	—	—	—	—	1	56		Chemist	Cement manufacture	Pw	V06	23	1	52	3000	yes	66
		no	no	no	no	H	5			House wife		no					no	67
							3											68
																		69
		yes	—	—	—	—	1	54		Furniture salesman	Furniture retail	Pw	298	67	1	52	1092	yes	70
		yes	—	—	—	—	1	10		Sales woman	Dry goods retail	Pw	248	6	1	4	48	no	71
		yes	—	—	—	—	1	40		Spooler	Fabric mill	Pw	496	88	1	52	817	no	72
		no	no	no	no	H	5			House wife	O. & home	no						73
Ala.		yes	—	—	—	—	1	84		Manager		Pw	156	67	1	52	624	yes	74
	XOXO	yes	—	—	—	—	1	92		Attendant	Institution	Pw	416	74	1	51	1275	yes	75
	XX	yes	—	—	—	—	1	40		Inspect	Fabric	Pw	496	88	1	51	837	no	76
	XOXO											no					no	77
Georgia	XOV3	no	—	—	—												no	78
Georgia	XOV3	yes	—	—	—		1	43		Dinner yarn spinner	Cotton Mill	Pw	496	88	1	51	696	no	79
	no	yes	—	—	—	—	H	5		House keeper	Home	no					no	80

IS 14 YEARS OLD AND OVER

FOR OFFICE USE ONLY—DO NOT WRITE IN THESE COLUMNS

TION	USUAL INDUSTRY		CODE								K	L	M	N	O	P	Q	R	S	T	U	V	W	X	Y	Z	Line No.
1	Private Pract.	Oa	V26	93	4						2		1	3	34	7	10		1		V26	93	4	9		1	59
											0	7	4		121	5											60

Right portion of document on facing page

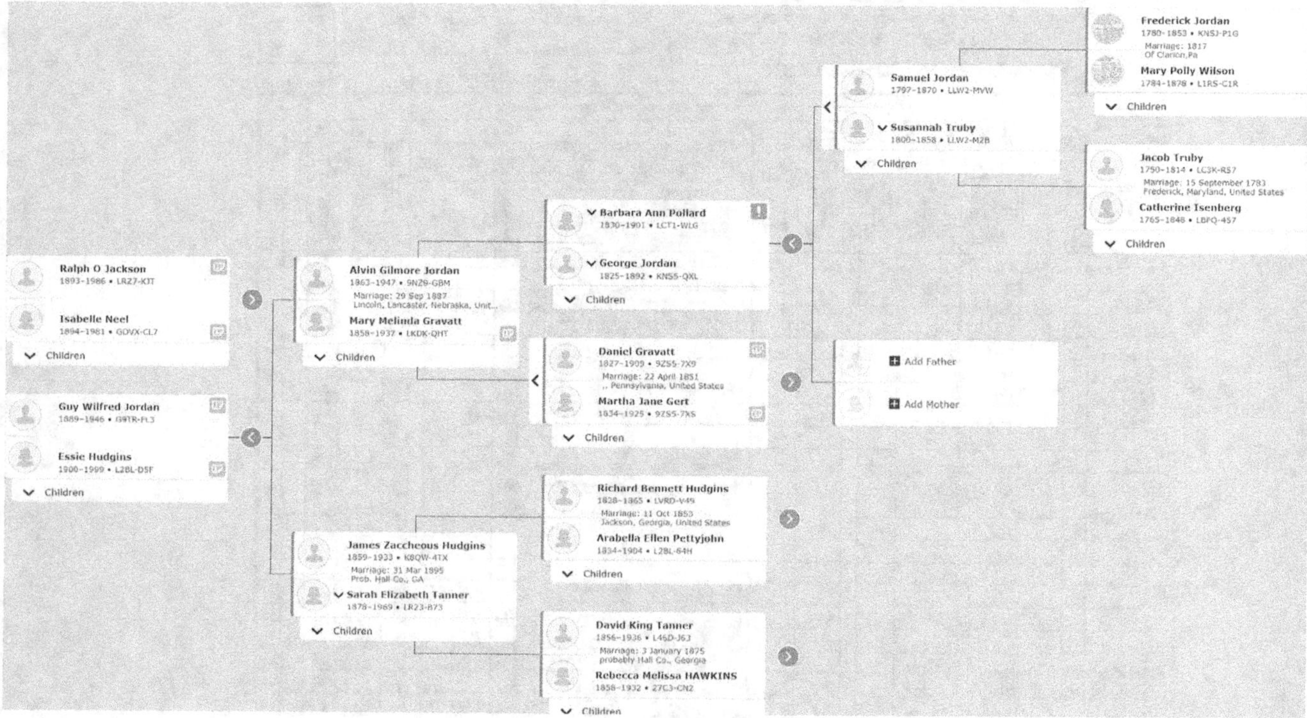

Frederick Jordan
1780–1853 • KNSJ-P1G
Marriage: 1817
Of Clarion,Pa

Mary Polly Wilson
1784–1878 • L1RS-C1R
∨ Children

Samuel Jordan
1797–1870 • LLW2-MVW
∨ **Susannah Truby**
1806–1858 • LLW2-M2B
∨ Children

Jacob Truby
1750–1814 • LC3K-RS7
Marriage: 15 September 1783
Frederick, Maryland, United States

Catherine Isenberg
1765–1848 • LBFQ-457
∨ Children

∨ **Barbara Ann Pollard**
1830–1901 • LCT1-WLG

∨ **George Jordan**
1825–1892 • KNS5-QXL
∨ Children

Ralph O Jackson
1893–1986 • LRZ7-KJT

Isabelle Neel
1894–1981 • GDVX-CL7
∨ Children

Alvin Gilmore Jordan
1863–1947 • 9NZ9-GBM
Marriage: 29 Sep 1887
Lincoln, Lancaster, Nebraska, Unit...

Mary Melinda Gravatt
1858–1937 • LKDK-QHT
∨ Children

Daniel Gravatt
1827–1909 • 9ZS5-7X9
Marriage: 22 April 1851
... Pennsylvania, United States

Martha Jane Gert
1834–1925 • 9ZS5-7XS
∨ Children

➕ Add Father

➕ Add Mother

Guy Wilfred Jordan
1889–1946 • G9TR-FL3

Essie Hudgins
1900–1999 • L2BL-DSF
∨ Children

James Zaccheous Hudgins
1859–1923 • K8QW-4TX
Marriage: 31 Mar 1895
Prob. Hall Co., GA

∨ **Sarah Elizabeth Tanner**
1878–1969 • LR23-873
∨ Children

Richard Bennett Hudgins
1828–1865 • LVRD-V49
Marriage: 11 Oct 1853
Jackson, Georgia, United States

Arabella Ellen Pettyjohn
1834–1904 • L2BL-64H
∨ Children

David King Tanner
1856–1936 • L46D-J6J
Marriage: 3 January 1875
probably Hall Co., Georgia

Rebecca Melissa HAWKINS
1858–1932 • 27C3-CN2
∨ Children

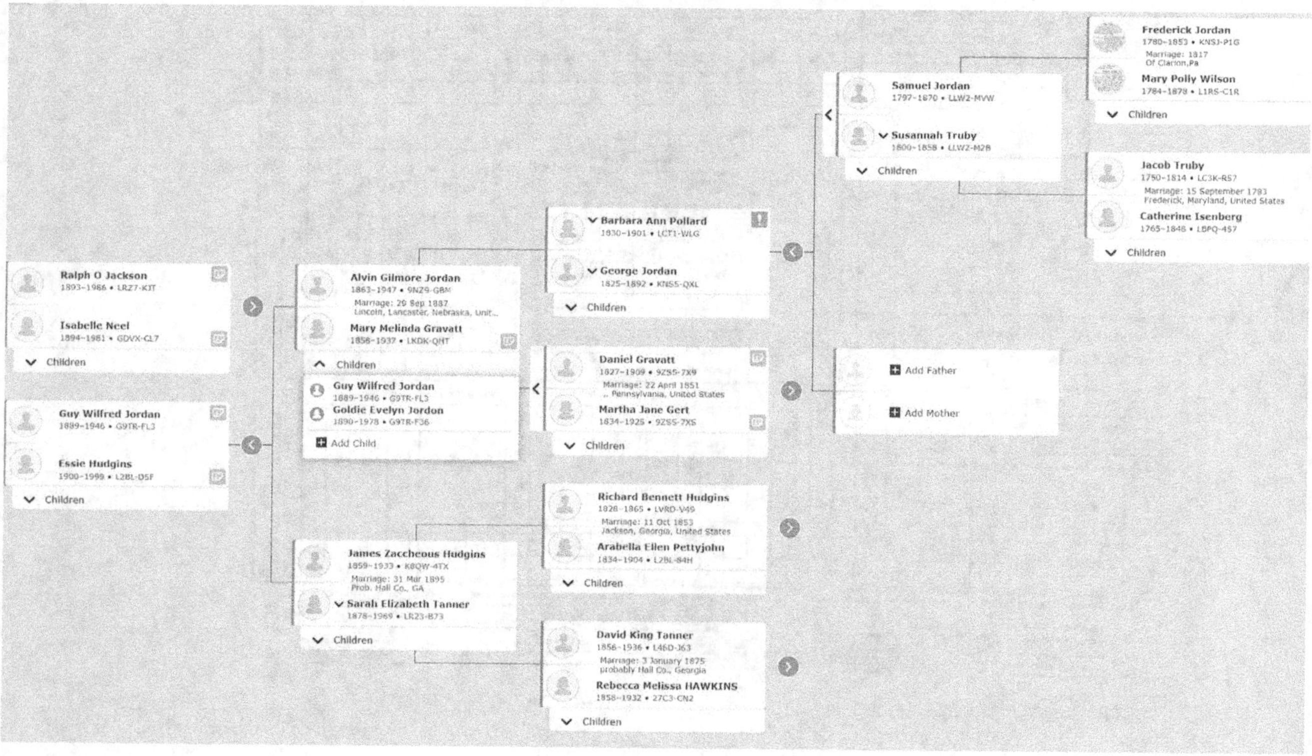

Frederick Jordan
1780–1853 • KNSJ-P1G
Marriage: 1817
Of Clarion,Pa

Mary Polly Wilson
1784–1878 • L1RS-C1R
∨ Children

Samuel Jordan
1797–1870 • LLW2-MVW
∨ **Susannah Truby**
1806–1858 • LLW2-M2B
∨ Children

Jacob Truby
1750–1814 • LC3K-RS7
Marriage: 15 September 1793
Frederick, Maryland, United States

Catherine Isenberg
1765–1848 • LBFQ-457
∨ Children

∨ **Barbara Ann Pollard**
1830–1901 • LCT1-WLG

∨ **George Jordan**
1825–1892 • KNS5-QXL
∨ Children

Ralph O Jackson
1893–1986 • LRZ7-KJT

Isabelle Neel
1894–1981 • GDVX-CL7
∨ Children

Alvin Gilmore Jordan
1863–1947 • 9NZ9-GBM
Marriage: 26 Sep 1887
Lincoln, Lancaster, Nebraska, Unit...

Mary Melinda Gravatt
1858–1937 • LKDK-QHT
∧ Children
👤 **Guy Wilfred Jordan**
1889–1946 • G9TR-FL3
👤 **Goldie Evelyn Jordan**
1890–1978 • G9TR-F36
➕ Add Child

Daniel Gravatt
1827–1909 • 9ZS5-7X9
Marriage: 22 April 1851
... Pennsylvania, United States

Martha Jane Gert
1834–1925 • 9ZS5-7XS
∨ Children

➕ Add Father

➕ Add Mother

Guy Wilfred Jordan
1889–1946 • G9TR-FL3

Essie Hudgins
1900–1999 • L2BL-DSF
∨ Children

James Zaccheous Hudgins
1859–1923 • K8QW-4TX
Marriage: 31 Mar 1895
Prob. Hall Co., GA

∨ **Sarah Elizabeth Tanner**
1878–1969 • LR23-873
∨ Children

Richard Bennett Hudgins
1828–1865 • LVRD-V49
Marriage: 11 Oct 1853
Jackson, Georgia, United States

Arabella Ellen Pettyjohn
1834–1904 • L2BL-84H
∨ Children

David King Tanner
1856–1936 • L46D-J63
Marriage: 3 January 1875
probably Hall Co., Georgia

Rebecca Melissa HAWKINS
1858–1932 • 27C3-CN2
∨ Children

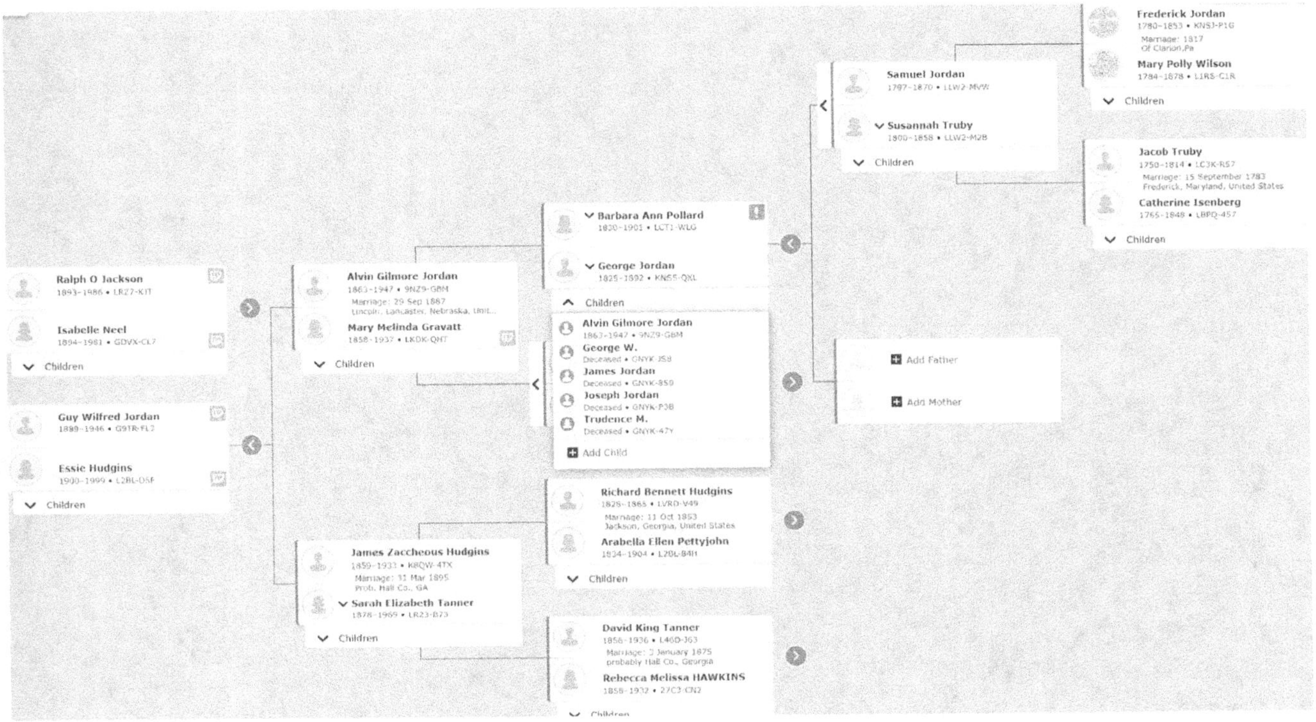

(Top chart)

Frederick Jordan
1780–1853 • KN53-P1G
Marriage: 1817
Of Clarion, Pa

Mary Polly Wilson
1784–1878 • L1RS-C1R
∨ Children

Samuel Jordan
1797–1870 • LLW2-MVW

∨ **Susannah Truby**
1800–1858 • LLW2-M2B
∨ Children

Jacob Truby
1750–1814 • LC3K-RS7
Marriage: 15 September 1783
Frederick, Maryland, United States

Catherine Isenberg
1765–1849 • L8PQ-457
∨ Children

∨ **Barbara Ann Pollard**
1830–1901 • LCT1-WLG

∨ **George Jordan**
1825–1892 • KN55-QXL

∧ Children

Alvin Gilmore Jordan
1863–1947 • 9NZ9-G8M

George W.
Deceased • GNYK-JS8

James Jordan
Deceased • GNYK-BS9

Joseph Jordan
Deceased • GNYK-P38

Trudence M.
Deceased • GNYK-47Y

➕ Add Child

Ralph O Jackson
1893–1986 • LRZ7-KJT

Isabelle Neel
1894–1981 • GDVX-CL7
∨ Children

Alvin Gilmore Jordan
1863–1947 • 9NZ9-G8M
Marriage: 29 Sep 1887
Lincoln, Lancaster, Nebraska, Unit...

Mary Melinda Gravatt
1858–1937 • LKDK-QHT
∨ Children

Guy Wilfred Jordan
1889–1946 • G9TR-FL3

Essie Hudgins
1900–1999 • L2BL-DSF
∨ Children

➕ Add Father

➕ Add Mother

Richard Bennett Hudgins
1829–1865 • LVRD-V49
Marriage: 11 Oct 1853
Jackson, Georgia, United States

Arabella Ellen Pettyjohn
1834–1904 • L29L-84H
∨ Children

James Zaccheous Hudgins
1859–1933 • K8QW-4TX
Marriage: 31 Mar 1895
Prob. Hall Co., GA

∨ **Sarah Elizabeth Tanner**
1878–1969 • LR23-B73
∨ Children

David King Tanner
1856–1936 • L46D-363
Marriage: 3 January 1875
probably Hall Co., Georgia

Rebecca Melissa HAWKINS
1858–1932 • 27C3-CN2
∨ Children

(Bottom chart)

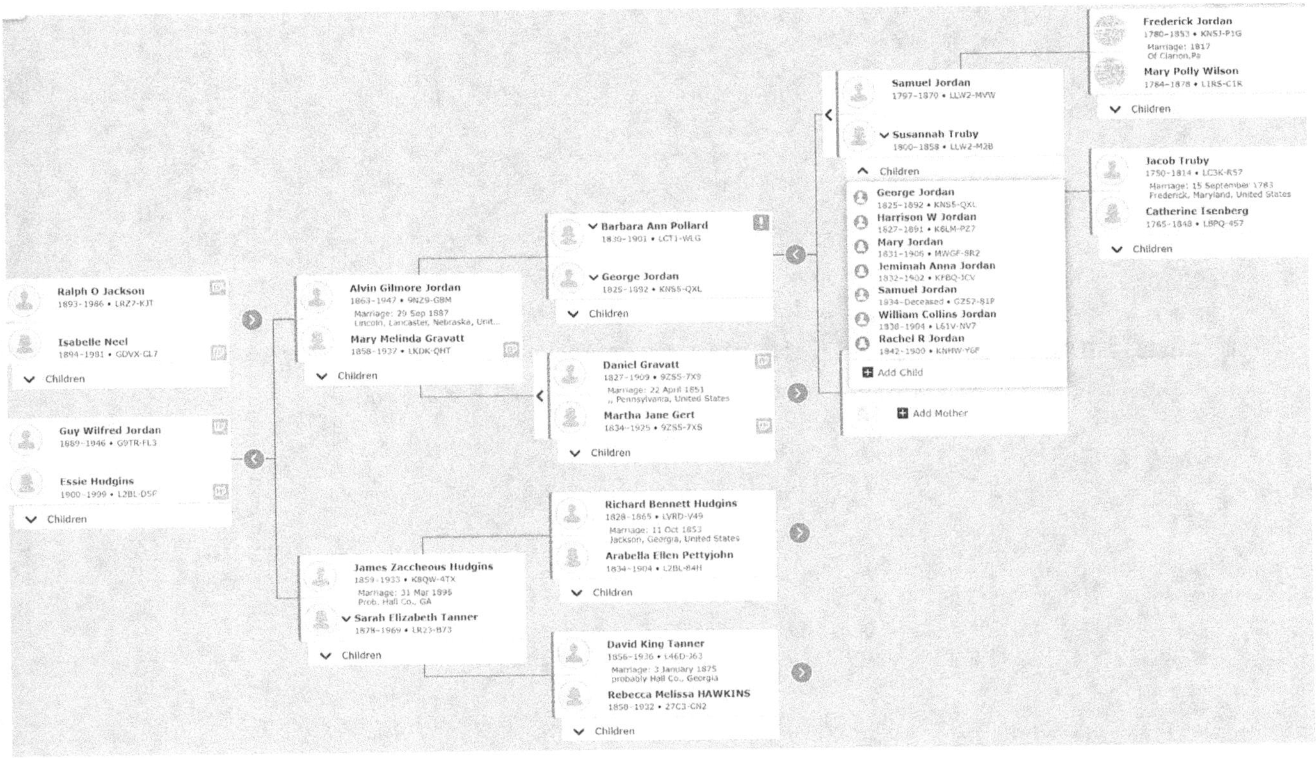

Frederick Jordan
1780–1853 • KN53-P1G
Marriage: 1817
Of Clarion, Pa

Mary Polly Wilson
1784–1878 • L1RS-C1R
∨ Children

Samuel Jordan
1797–1870 • LLW2-MVW

∨ **Susannah Truby**
1800–1858 • LLW2-M2B
∧ Children

George Jordan
1825–1892 • KN55-QXL

Harrison W Jordan
1827–1891 • K6LM-PZ7

Mary Jordan
1831–1906 • MWGF-8R2

Jemimah Anna Jordan
1832–1902 • KF8Q-3CV

Samuel Jordan
1834–Deceased • GZS2-81F

William Collins Jordan
1838–1904 • L61V-NV7

Rachel R Jordan
1842–1900 • KNHW-YGF

➕ Add Child

Jacob Truby
1750–1814 • LC3K-RS7
Marriage: 15 September 1783
Frederick, Maryland, United States

Catherine Isenberg
1765–1848 • L8PQ-457
∨ Children

∨ **Barbara Ann Pollard**
1830–1901 • LCT1-WLG

∨ **George Jordan**
1825–1892 • KN55-QXL
∨ Children

➕ Add Mother

Ralph O Jackson
1893–1986 • LRZ7-KJT

Isabelle Neel
1894–1981 • GDVX-CL7
∨ Children

Alvin Gilmore Jordan
1863–1947 • 9NZ9-G8M
Marriage: 29 Sep 1887
Lincoln, Lancaster, Nebraska, Unit...

Mary Melinda Gravatt
1858–1937 • LKDK-QHT
∨ Children

Daniel Gravatt
1827–1909 • 9ZS5-7XS
Marriage: 22 April 1851
, Pennsylvania, United States

Martha Jane Gert
1834–1925 • 9ZS5-7XS
∨ Children

Guy Wilfred Jordan
1889–1946 • G9TR-FL3

Essie Hudgins
1900–1999 • L2BL-DSF
∨ Children

Richard Bennett Hudgins
1828–1865 • LVRD-V49
Marriage: 11 Oct 1853
Jackson, Georgia, United States

Arabella Ellen Pettyjohn
1834–1904 • L29L-84H
∨ Children

James Zaccheous Hudgins
1859–1933 • K8QW-4TX
Marriage: 31 Mar 1895
Prob. Hall Co., GA

∨ **Sarah Elizabeth Tanner**
1878–1969 • LR23-B73
∨ Children

David King Tanner
1856–1936 • L46D-363
Marriage: 3 January 1875
probably Hall Co., Georgia

Rebecca Melissa HAWKINS
1858–1932 • 27C3-CN2
∨ Children

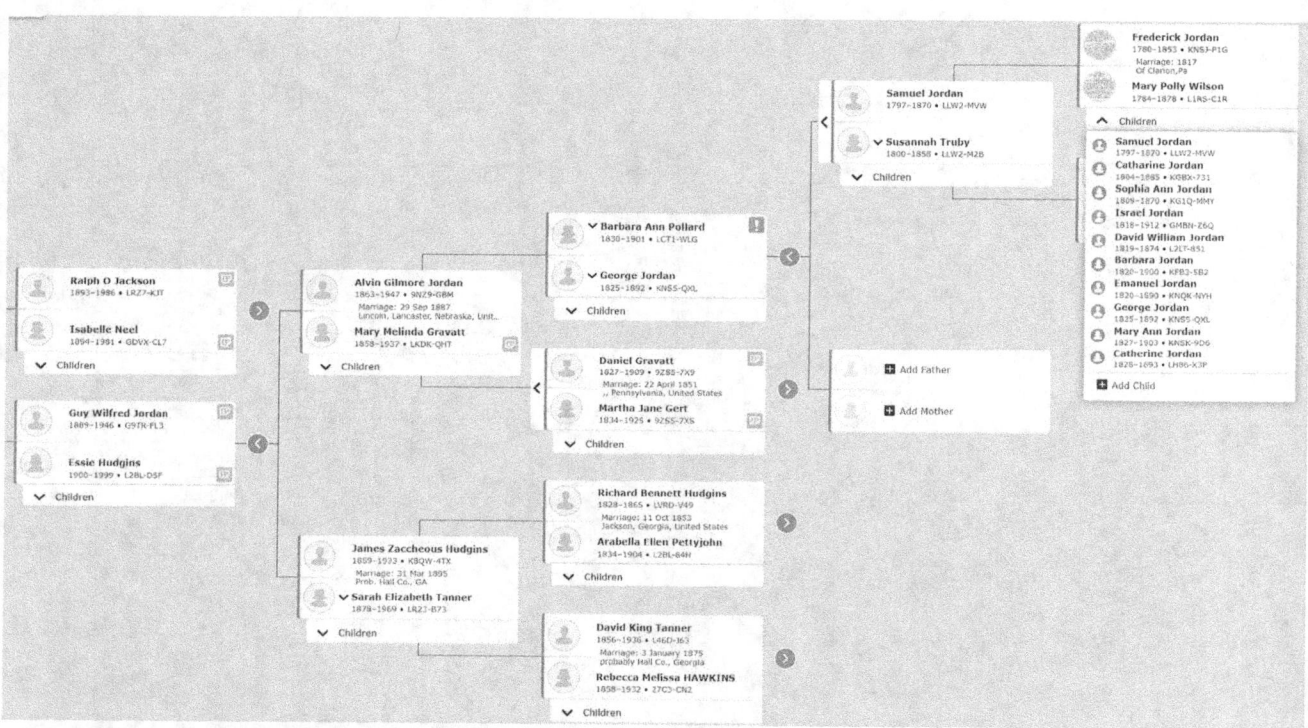

Family Tree of Jordam Family, pages 140-142 – laid out from the most recent to the most historic.

A Gravatt Family History
From Pennsylvania to Georgia

*The late Goldie Evelyn Jordan Hill of Sunland, California, stated emphatically
in a letter to her niece, Marilyn Jordan Jackson of Rockmart, Georgia,
on July 20, 1964, "My mother's family (Gravatt) is of French Huguenot ancestry."
Proof of this heritage, however has been difficult – if not impossible – to obtain.*

There has been ample speculation, genealogical research, and further investigations for decades into the origin of the Gravatt family which ultimately wound up in the Allegheny Valley north of Pittsburgh, Pennsylvania, in the 18th century. Much of this research and investigative effort by family descendants has been met with abject frustration, since the Gravatts were not avid records-keepers, but research is "on-going."

Recorded variously as "Grevatt," "Gravatt," "Gravet," "Gravat," and "Grevet," it has become accepted that this is an English surname, but in actuality, it quite likely is of Norman French origin. The name itself is somewhat rare, but there interestingly are a fair number of individuals with this name in Georgia.

Research indicates there are actually three possible origins for the name:

The first is that of a medieval diminutive of the occupational name "Graff," a derivative of the pre-7th Century French word "grafe," meaning "a quill," and therefore referring to "a clerk" or "scribe." To this has been added the diminutive suffix "-et," meaning "son of Graff."

A second possible origin of the name is from the ancient Germanic name of "Creiz." Also, in "Norman"-French this was "Grev," and again to this was probably attached the diminutive suffix "et" to also denote "son of Grev."

Other possibilities which cannot be dismissed are from the pre-7th Century Olde English words "graeve" or "graefe" or "greve," denoting a wood, or perhaps more likely referring to a steward, and hence an occupational name of medieval origin. This surname is amply-recorded as well in the surviving church registers of the diocese of Greater London from Elizabethan times.

It is into the vortex of all of these possibilities that any search for the accurate origin of this particular family line, and the reason(s) for their emigration to America, will fall. Such research is further complicated by the almost clannish nature of this family.

In one union, the Gravatts intermarried with the Jordan family, yet another line of possible Norman-French origin, and both ultimately found settlement in "the new world" north of Pittsburgh, Pennsylvania, in the Allegheny and Perry counties areas.

It is interesting to note that the township in Allegheny County in and around which the Gravatts and Jordans resided offers direct evidence that these families quite possibly hailed from Holland, or, from France by way of Holland (which is a more likely possibility), arriving in the fledgling United States prior to the U.S. Revolutionary War. That township in Allegheny County ultimately became known in county records as "Dutch Hill."

Many family researchers assume "Pennsylvania Dutch" automatically indicates an origin from Holland or the Netherlands – which could possibly be the case, but not necessarily. This Pennsylvania "Dutch" designation ironically could also refer to "Deutsch" instead of "Dutch," thereby indicating an origin from Germany – by way of Holland shipping – rather than Dutch or French ancestry. It is for this reason that many of the early settlers in Pennsylvania – including the Amish, Mennonites, and others of that area – speak *German*, not Dutch.

Allegheny County in which these Gravatts chose to settle was organized in 1788, but deeds to property and possessions did not begin to be officially recorded there until 1842. The Gravatt family farm near Logan's Ferry was recorded in 1846.

On October 24, 1967, Mrs. Goldie Evelyn Jordan Hill, a descendant of both the Jordans and the Gravatts of Pennsylvania, wrote to her niece – Marilyn Jordan Jackson of Rockmart (Polk County), Georgia – stating *"My cousin Mildred and her husband were here for a short visit. She is the one who has given me most of the information that I have about the Gravatt family. She had (conducted) rather extensive (research) about 25 years ago because she thought that she might become a member of the Daughters of the American Revolution.*

"Most of the information she (Mildred) collected I believe has come through word of mouth (and family lore) from one generation to the next," Hill added. *"The records in the Gravatt family Bible were obliterated by it becoming soaked (at some point) by water – I suppose during a flood which sometimes happens in the Allegheny Valley (where they lived in Pennsylvania).*

"There were three brothers (who originally immigrated to America), and the names of two of them were Robert and Samuel," Mrs. Hill said. *"These three brothers were driven from France at the time of the Huguenot persecution under Louis XIV. They went either to England or to Holland, and from there to New Jersey (perhaps stopping first in Nova Scotia). Evidence seems*

These families quite possibly hailed from Holland, or, from France by way of Holland

to indicate they came with Dutch colonists directly to New Jersey and settled in Monmouth County in Upper Friebold Township – a well-known Dutch settlement in America."

Here again, things are somewhat difficult to sort out. There is of course the obvious tie-in with the "Dutch," clearly reinforcing the known fact that Holland was a dominant force in the merchant shipping industry at this time, and that the Gravatts were taking advantage of this travel option to come to America. But again, were the Gravatts "Dutch," or "Deutsch," or "French," or what?

Robert Gravatt was born 1708 in Monmouth, New Jersey. According to family tradition and notes passed down by the late Mrs. Hill, a "Robert Gravatt" was brought across the mountains from New Jersey later in life to live with Johnson Gravatt at the Gravatt home at Logan's Ferry near present-day Kensington, PA (or possibly it was to the later Gravatt farm at nearby Fawn Township, Allegheny County, PA.) It is not known for certain today if this Robert Gravatt was Johnson's father or grandfather, but he quite possibly was his grandfather, since conflicting records seem to indicate Johnson's father died at a relatively young age and <u>was buried in New Jersey</u>. Johnson's grandfather, (Robert Gravatt the elder), who also was born in New Jersey, apparently died in Allegheny County, PA, and is believed to have been buried in the old Gravatt family cemetery in Fawn township, Allegheny County, PA.

Johnson (or "Johnston" on some census and other records) Gravatt was born in 1754 (some records indicate 1755) in Monmouth, New Jersey, and married Sarah Percy Pierce in 1780. Sources also indicate that both Johnson and his father, Robert, possibly served under Gen. George Washington during the Revolutionary War, participating in the Battle of Trenton.

"Records indicate that Johnson served in the army at the age of 24," Hill continues. *"It seems that at that time, soldiers enlisted for one or two months at a time.*

He served in the Monmouth County New Jersey Militia in April, May and June of 1778, and in July and August of 1780.

"Johnson migrated to western Pennsylvania, near the present-day town of Kensington, probably in 1780, since his son John was born there on August 25, 1781."

In the late 1700s, the shores of the Allegheny and the Monongahela Rivers were one vast wilderness, broken only by occasional patches of land cleared by the sparse settlers who braved that wilderness. Johnson Gravatt is credited with construction of the first schoolhouse in the Allegheny Valley which came to be known as "Percy School," after his wife, Sarah Percy.

In later years, being afflicted with asthma and wishing to move to higher ground, Johnson obtained title to land in Fawn Township about five miles north of Tarentum. This property ultimately became known as "the old Gravatt farm," and remained in the family until about 1870 when Johnson's grandson, Daniel, sold it.

Records indicate Johnson's son – John W. – served in the *War of 1812*. John, according to some records, died young at the age of 58 on January 7, 1839. He is buried in the third grave in old Gravatt Cemetery, Fawn Township, Allegheny County, Pennsylvania.

The *1860 Federal Census* for Salem, Mercer County, Pennsylvania (the correct location), however, seems to indicate John was still alive in 1860, since it includes a listing for a *"John Gravatt,"* age 78 (the correct age if he were born in 1781). This 1860 Census also lists the location of his birth as *"New Jersey"* (the more likely correct location), not Pennsylvania. It, however, includes only one other individual – *"Anne, age 74"* – in his household, which does not match up with his wife Sarah (unless perhaps Sarah's middle name was "Anne"). Despite the above information, the 1781 birth date conflicts with the *American Genealogical-Biographical Index*, a respected international online database accessed through *Ancestry.com* which indicates John W. Gravatt was in fact born in 1790.

John's son – Daniel Gravatt – and his twin sister were born to John and wife Sarah Kennedy Gravatt

on September 8, 1827, in Fawn Township, Allegheny County, PA. Daniel married Martha Jane Girt on April 22, 1851. The Girts came to the Pennsylvania area circa 1840. Daniel and Martha had eleven children, one of the older of whom was Mary Melinda Gravatt.

Daniel was a veteran of the U.S. Civil War, enlisting as a captain in 1864 and serving in Battery D, 6th Heavy Artillery Regiment, Pennsylvania until the end of the war. He died at the age of 82 on April 6, 1909 and was buried in Knox Chapel Cemetery at Cabot, Butler Co.

Daniel was the last heir to own the old Gravatt farm in Fawn Township, Allegheny County, PA. He sold it circa 1870, retaining title only to the old Gravatt family cemetery. It is unknown by this writer if this cemetery continues today to be owned by the Gravatt family. It is known, however, that it is located within private property in old Fawn Township (Brackenridge), Allegheny County, PA.

The following graves have been identified in the old Gravatt family cemetery:

1st Grave: Robert Gravatt. [It is not known for certain today if this grave is occupied by Robert the elder (Johnson's grandfather) or Robert the younger (Johnson's father).]

2nd Grave: Johnson Gravatt. (Died 1837)

3rd Grave: John W. Gravatt (Died January 7, 1839)

4th Grave: John Kennedy. (He was the father of John's wife, Sarah Kennedy, and has an interesting history of service in the Revolutionary War.)

5th Grave: Sarah Percy Gravatt (Mrs. Johnson Gravatt) (Died 1845)

6th Grave: Sarah Kennedy Gravatt (Mrs. John W. Gravatt) (Died circa 1872)

(The late Marilyn Jordan Jackson, formerly of Rockmart, Polk County, Georgia, and her children, Patricia, Olin, David, the late Mary Jackson Oettinger, and the late Guy Jackson of Rockmart (Polk County), Georgia, as well as the Bradley family of the Atlanta, Georgia metro area, Georgia, are among the Georgia descendants of the Allegheny Valley, Pennsylvania Gravatts and Jordans.)

Gravatt Genealogical Line
(Ancestry of One Gravatt Family Line in the United States)
(Country of Origin of Gravatt Family Line: Western Europe, likely France, Germany or England)

Recorded variously as "Grevatt," "Gravatt," "Gravet," "Gravat," and "Grevet," this is an **English surname**, but probably **of Norman French origins**. Literal origins of the name include: That of a medieval diminutive of the name "Graff," a derivative of the pre-7th Century French word "grafe," meaning "a quill," and therefore referring to a clerk or scribe. To this has been added the diminutive suffix "-et," meaning "son of Graff." A second possible origin lies in the ancient Germanic name of "Creiz." In "Norman" French this was interpreted as "Grev" and again to this was probably attached the diminutive suffix "et," again to denote "son of Grev." Other alternatives which cannot be dismissed are from the pre-7th Century Olde English words "graeve" or "graefe" or "greve," denoting a wood, or perhaps more likely referring to a steward, and hence an occupational name. This surname is well-recorded in Elizabethan church registers of the diocese of Greater London.

Great-great-great-great-great-great-great-great-grandfather: John Gravatt

b. 1628
m. Emlin Dinnis (St. Sidwell, Exeter, Devon, England) Issue: <u>**Samuel**</u>
d. (?)

Great-great-great-great-great-great-great-grandfather: Samuel Gravatt

b. 1670, Chesterfield, VA
m. Lydia Johnson Issue: <u>**John Robert**</u>
d. (?)

Great-great-great-great-great-great-grandfather: John Robert Gravatt

b. 1708, Monmouth, New Jersey
m. 1724, Thamy Holman (b. 05/10/1710, Upper Freehold, Monmouth, New Jersey; d. 1749), Monmouth, NJ. Issue: John (b. 03/06/1725, New Jersey, d.1780); Joseph (b. 10/05/1729, New Jersey, d. 1797); <u>**Robert**</u>; Martha (b. 09/19/1733, New Jersey); Patrick Kinnan (b. 1735, Scotland, d. 1820, New Jersey); Mary (b. 10/01/1735, New Jersey); William D. (b. 05/23/1739, Millstone, Somerset, NJ, d. 07/18/1826, Perrineville, Monmouth, NJ); Anna (b. 05/23/1739, Perrineville, Monmouth, NJ); Margaret (b. 04/20/1741, Monmouth, NJ); Phoebe (b. 03/03/1743, Monmouth, NJ); Aaron (b. 1745, Monmouth, NJ); Richard (b. 01/20/1747, Monmouth); Peter (b. 02/17/1749, Upper Freehold, Monmouth, d. 1808, Lower Freehold, Monmouth);
d. 1749, Pennsylvania. (Possibly the Robert Gravatt buried, Gravatt Cemetery, Fawn Township, Allegheny County, PA)

Great-great-great-great-great-grandfather: Robert Gravatt, Jr.

b. 02/26/1731 Monmouth, New Jersey
m. 1756, Margaret Elizabeth Johnson (b. 1736, New Jersey; d. 1795, Upper Freehold township, Monmouth, NJ), New Jersey. Issue: John (b. 1754, Shrewsbury, Monmouth, NJ, d. 1837 West Salem township, Mercer, PA); <u>**Johnson Gravatt (a.k.a. "Johnston")**</u>; Joseph (b. 1758, Monmouth, NJ); William (b. 1759, Monmouth, NJ); Hellena "Lena" (b. 12/4/1763, Mercer, PA, d. 1/26/1849, Monmouth, NJ); and Nancy Ann (b. 1770, Monmouth, NJ, d. 1860, Marshall, WV).
d. 1797, Upper Freehold Township, New Jersey. Buried Gravatt Cemetery, Brackenridge, Allegheny, PA

<u>Note #1:</u> According to Mrs. Goldie Evelyn Jordan Hill (sister of Guy W. Jordan) of California, Johnson Gravatt brought a "Robert Gravatt" to the Gravatt farm in Fawn Township, Allegheny County, PA to live. It is not known today if this was Johnson's father or grandfather. Some records seem to indicate it was his grandfather, since Robert the younger was born and died in New Jersey, and Robert the elder was born in New Jersey and died in Fawn Township, PA. According to Mrs. Hill, the Robert Gravatt brought to Fawn township was quite elderly and lived to an even older age. This, however, seems to conflict with the age information regarding Robert the elder, since, according to sparse records, he lived only to the age of 41. The oldest grave in the Gravatt cemetery in Fawn is engraved simply "Robert Gravatt," with no date information.)

Great-great-great-great-grandfather: Johnson (a.k.a. "Johnston") Gravatt

b. 1756, Monmouth, New Jersey
m. 1780, Sarah Percy (b. 11/23/1755, Shrewsbury, Monmouth, New Jersey, d. 1845, East Deer, Allegheny Co., Pennsylvania. Issue: <u>**John W.**</u>; Mary Polly (1785-1870); Nancy (1788-1849); James (1791-1810); Phoebe L. (1794-1843); Daniel (1796-1829); and Amanda (1802-1810).
d. 5 Sept 1826, East Deer Township, Allegheny Co., PA. Buried in the second grave in old Gravatt Family Cemetery, Fawn township, Allegheny Co., PA.

Great-great-great grandfather: John W. Gravatt

b. 08/25/1781 (or 1790), Monmouth, New Jersey
m. 06/25/1811, Fawn Township, Allegheny Co., PA to Sarah Kennedy (b. 4/8/1787, Pennsylvania, d. 9/3/1879, buried Old Gravatt Family Cemetery, Fawn Township, Allegheny Co., PA). Issue: <u>**Daniel**</u> & twin sister, Margaret (b. 1827, d. 1895); John (b. 1830).
d. 01/07/1839 (or post-1860), Fawn township, Allegheny Co., PA. Buried old Gravatt Family Cemetery, Fawn, Allegheny Co., PA.

<u>Note #2:</u> Records indicate Johnson's son – <u>John W.</u> – served in the *War of 1812*. John, according to some records, died young at the age of 58 on January 7, 1839. He is buried in the third grave in old Gravatt Cemetery, Fawn Township, Allegheny County, Pennsylvania. According to the *1860 Federal Census*, however, John quite possibly <u>was still alive in 1860</u>, since it includes a listing for a *"John Gravatt,"* age 78 (the correct age if he were born in 1781). This *1860 Census* also lists the location of John's birth as *"New Jersey"* (the more likely correct location), not Pennsylvania. It, however, includes only one other individual in his household – *"Anne, age 76"* – which does not seem to match the identity of John's wife Sarah (unless perhaps Sarah's middle name was "Anne"). This *Census* also lists the value of this John's personal property at a mere $100.00, with no listing for the value of any real estate. The 1781 birth date also conflicts with the *American Genealogical-Biographical Index*, a respected online database through *Ancestry.com* which indicates John W. Gravatt was in fact born in 1790.

Great-great-grandfather: Daniel Gravatt

- **b.** 09/08/1827, Fawn township, Allegheny Co., PA
- **m.** 04/22/1851 in Pennsylvania to Martha Jane Girt (b. 11/19/1834, Allegheny, PA; d. 01/20/1925, Winfield, Butler Co., PA; buried Knox Chapel Cemetery, Cabot, Butler, PA). Issue: William (1853-1931); **Mary Melinda**, Bell (b. 1860); James Alfred (1861-1947); Josephine Clare (1863-1908); Sarah Elizabeth (1865-1899); Ida (b. 1867); Thomas Barker (1870-1944); Harry Sylvester (1873-1913); Evaline (1876-1949) and one other unknown child.
- **d.** 04/06/1909; buried: Knox Chapel Cemetery, Cabot, Butler Co., PA.

> **Note #3:**   Daniel and Martha Jane had eleven children. Daniel was the last heir to own the old Gravatt farm in Fawn township, Allegheny Co., PA. He sold it circa 1870, retaining title only to the old Gravatt family cemetery. He was buried in Knox Chapel Cem, Cabot, Butler Co., PA, quite possibly beside his wife.

Great-grandmother: Mary Melinda Gravatt Jordan

- **b.** 10/23/1858, Fawn, Allegheny Co., PA
- **m.** 09/29/1887, Lincoln, Neb., to Alvin Gilmore Jordan (b. 08/12/1863, PA d. 01/25/1947, Colton, San Bernardino Co., CA). Issue: **Guy Wilfred** and Goldie Evelyn.
- **d.** 06/09/1937, Colton, San Bernardino Co., CA.

> **Note #4:**   By the time they were married in 1887, Alvin Gilmore apparently was already employed by the Santa Fe Railroad and living, at least temporarily, in Nebraska. The *1920 Federal Census* lists his residence as Colton, San Bernardino Co., CA, with an occupation as "carpenter foreman" for the railroad. Interestingly, he resided in Colton at the same time as a famous family by the name of Earp. Patriarch Nicholas Earp purchased a farm in Colton circa 1870s, where he and his family – including at various times, Virgil, Wyatt, Morgan et alle – lived until they died or relocated. Morgan Earp who was murdered in Tombstone, AZ Territory, is buried there. In a town as small as was Colton, Alvin Gilmore and Mary Melinda almost certainly were at least familiar and possibly even friends with members of the Earp family.)

Grandfather: Guy Wilfred Jordan

- **b.** 02/19/1889, Dutch Hill, PA (indicated as "West Monterey, PA" in some sources.)
- **m.** 06/18/1927, Clermont, Hall Co., Georgia, to Essie Irene (middle name later changed to "Carroll") Hudgins [b. 3/12/1900, Sugar Hill, Jackson (Gwinnett) Co., GA. Buried: Rose Hill Cemetery, Rockmart, GA.] Issue: **Marilyn** and Patricia.
- **d.** 09/05/1946, Rockmart, Polk Co., GA. Buried: Rose Hill Cemetery, Rockmart, GA.

Notes:

_____
_____
_____
_____
_____
_____
_____
_____
_____
_____
_____
_____
_____
_____
_____
_____
_____
_____
_____
_____
_____
_____
_____
_____
_____
_____
_____
_____
_____
_____
_____
_____
_____
_____
_____
_____
_____
_____

Names	State tax		EastPennsbro 1787
Galbreath John	5	9	10
Gravat Johnston	-	5	11
Grouse Jacob	-	-	11
Height Jacob	-	-	11
Holt John	-	-	6
Hartley Thomas	1	8	2
Huston Christopher	1	10	4
Huston John	2	19	9
Hoge John Rev	2	2	0
Hoge Jonathan Esqr	2	16	10
Hoge David	4	8	7
Hawk Michal	1	14	1
Hudson William	1	4	10
Hendericks Isaac	2	12	9
Herberger Widow	1	16	8
Huston John	1	1	11
Huston William	1	7	11
Humes James	1	12	6
Huling John	-	3	11
Heak Hervey	-	13	4
Junkin Joseph	2	9	4
Jones Benjamin	-	-	8
Johnston John	-	-	11
Junkins Widow	-	-	11
Junkins Benjamin	2	8	4
Kerr Widow	-	11	2
Kelso William	3	7	4
Lemmon John	-	11	7
Logan Widow	-	-	11
Longstaff Henry	2	-	1
Longstaff Martin	-	12	7
Lowdon Matthew	3	15	3

1768-1801 TAX & EXONERATION INDEX, PENNSYLVANIA
<u>Gravatt</u>, <u>Johnson</u> (aka "Johnston")

Names	Stat.[?] tax	E. Pennsbro' 1787	
Longstaff Philip	~	10	11
Laffery Isaac	~	1	5
Line Henry	1	17	1
Lance Philip	~	18	~
Levinston Jacob	1	4	10
Lincoln John	~	6	10
Longnecker Abram	1	9	2
Mulholmn James	~	1	5
McMullen Duncan	~	2	9
Martin John	~	1	3
Martin Joshheph	1	7	0
Morton Edward	9	15	3
McConnick James	1	13	3
Miller William	~	13	4
McConnick John	2	3	~
Martin Herman	1	11	7
McConnick Widow	~	1	~
Myves George	3	4	~
McGuire James	1	3	6
McGuire Francis	~	4	5
McConnick Jas. Jun.	1	3	2
Miller Jacob	1	7	11
Montgomery John	~	18	1
Martin Hugh	~	3	2
Martin James	~	7	8
McWhinie Robert	1	14	0
Miller Peter	~	3	8
Moore Howard	2	3	9
McEntreyJames	~	14	3
McDonald John	~	~	11
Monimith Conrad	~	~	5
McCollom Alexr.	~	~	5

Right portion of document on facing page

(67) Thos Strower	109	139	219		28	(62) Thos Strower	162	184	317		38
John Shipler 120	1		2			Nathaniel Cuningham	2		1		121
John Gording	1		1			John Brown	1		2		
Gasper Gare	3	3	3			Archebel Gardner	1	1	4		
Thomas Higgins	1	0	3		1	Willm Gardner	1	1	3		2
John Grevat	1	2	4			Susanna Porter	1	1			
John Anderson	1		2			Willm Willsey	1	3	3		
James Kelly	1	1	2			Alexander Morehead	1	3	4		5
Willm Kino	1		3			John Morehead	1				
Jacob Houseman	1		6			Alexander Morehead	1		1		
Mary Houseman	1	1	2			Peter Porter	1		1		
Christifer Houseman	1	1	2			John Porter	1		1		
Daniel Smock	2		1			Robert Thomson	1	1	2		
Garret Devor	2		4			Jacob Leek	1	3	4		
James McCamot	1		2			Ebenezer Walker	5	1	6		
James Finley	5		2		7	Willm Flasket	1	4	3		
John Powers	1	3	4		1	Joseph Burwell	3	2	1		
James Kelly	2		1			Leonard Smock	2	1	1		
Peter Shaw	1		1			Willm Morgin	1	1	6		
Alexander Hynes	1	4	3			Morgin Morgin	1		1		
James Ireland	1	2	4			Jery Vanmeter					
John Flack	3	2	5			John Baty	2	3	2		
Mikel Barr	1	1	4			James Maxwell	1	2	3		
Johnston Grevat	1	1	3			James Kirkland	1	2	4		
Thomas Morehead	3	4	2			John Alford		1	3		
Joseph Other	1	1	1			James Kilpatrick	1	4	4		
James Cuningham	1	1	1			Concelton Budd		2	2		
Edward Teel	2	3	4			Joseph Budd			3		
Jacob Vanmeter	1	4	5			Joshua Budd	1		3		
Thomas Patterson	1	3	2			Gilbert Budd	1	3	3		
Samuel Raggen	4	1	1			Thomas Thomas	1				
John Vanmeter	1	2	3			Niclas Linnerist	1	3	1		
Joseph Fulton	1		7			Thomas Bean	2				
Liddie Teel	2		2		1	Jesse Steward	1				
Willm Gardner	1	1	5			Joseph Lightbone	1	1	2		
Willm Gardner	1	3	5			Mary Grymes			3		
	162	184	317		38	Samuel Grymes	1				
						John Lommorvail	2	1	3		
						John Bacon	1	1	3		
						Richard Brickett	1	2	4		

1790 FEDERAL CENSUS, WESTMORELAND, ROSTRAVER, PENNSYLVANIA

Gravatt, Johnson (aka *"Johnston"*) – According to this census, it appears that Johnson had five children.

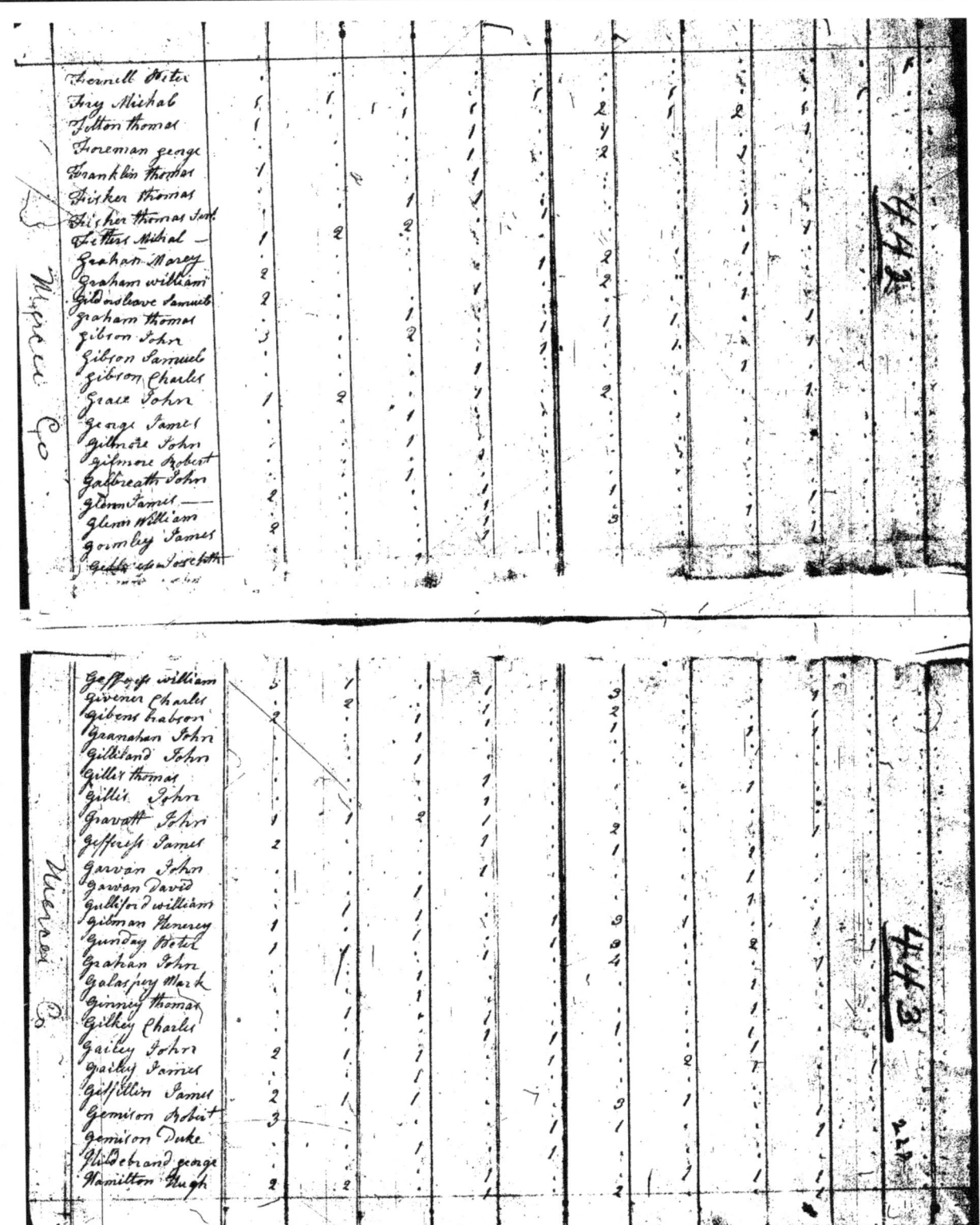

1800 FEDERAL CENSUS, MERCER COUNTY, PENNSYLVANIA

Gravatt, Johnson (aka *"John"*) – According to this census, Johnson again appears to have five children.

Deer Township (Page 1)

Name											
Barnabas Sweeney	"	"	"	"	1	3	"	1	"	1	"
Samuel Stulings	"	"	1	"	1	"	3	2	"	1	"
Daniel Wood	1	"	"	"	"	1	"	1	"	1	"
William Waddle	4	"	1	"	1	"	2	1	"	1	"
Thos. Armstrong	"	"	1	"	1	"	"	1	"	"	"
William Ralty	3	"	1	"	"	2	"	1	"	1	"
James Carnaghan	"	1	"	"	1	2	"	2	"	"	"
Thos. Kelley	"	"	2	"	1	"	"	1	"	"	"
John Henry	1	"	"	"	1	"	"	1	"	"	914
Andrew Williamson	9	"	1	"	1	"	"	1	"	"	"
Rosana Jones	2	1	"	"	1	"	"	1	"	"	"
John Glasgow	3	"	1	"	1	"	"	1	"	"	"
Clement Richason	2	2	2	"	1	"	"	1	"	"	"
Alex. Glasgow	"	"	1	"	1	"	"	1	"	"	"
John Duff	3	"	"	"	1	"	"	1	"	"	"
James Clendennen	"	"	2	"	1	"	2	1	"	"	"
Jacob Fox	2	"	"	"	"	"	"	3	"	"	"
David Ferguson	"	1	1	"	1	"	"	3	1	"	"
John Carnahan	1	"	1	"	1	4	"	3	1	"	"
Wm. Todhunter	"	"	1	"	1	1	"	"	"	1	"
Andw. Jack	2	1	"	1	"	2	"	"	"	"	"
James Haslet	4	1	1	"	1	1	"	"	"	"	"
James Leslie	2	1	"	"	1	2	1	"	"	1	"
William Leslie	"	1	2	"	1	"	"	"	1	"	"
William Juguro	"	1	1	"	1	"	"	"	"	1	"
Thomas Love	"	"	"	"	1	"	"	"	"	"	"
Henry Mckisnek	1	2	"	"	1	3	"	"	"	"	"
Robert Anderson	3	1	"	"	1	3	"	"	"	"	"
Thos. McConnel	3	1	1	"	1	2	1	"	"	"	"
Jane Russell	"	"	2	"	"	1	1	"	"	1	"
Thomas Stewart	"	1	1	"	1	1	1	"	"	"	375
Ezekiel Miller	1	2	1	"	1	3	2	1	"	"	"
Sinclair Gibson	2	1	3	"	1	1	"	1	"	"	"
John Simmons	1	1	"	"	1	3	"	1	"	"	"
Henry Hines	2	"	"	"	1	"	"	"	"	"	"
Johnston Graval	"	1	"	"	1	"	"	2	"	"	"
Ezekiel Day	"	"	2	"	"	"	"	"	"	"	"
George Summers	1	"	2	"	1	"	1	"	"	1	"
Abigail Hines	"	"	2	1	"	"	"	2	"	"	"
Rudolph Runin	"	"	1	2	"	"	"	1	"	"	"
Total Sheet	46	21	30	19	21	40	23	30	17	18	1

1810 FEDERAL CENSUS, DEER TOWNSHIP, ALLEGHENY COUNTY, PENNSYLVANIA

Gravatt, Johnson (aka *"Johnston"*) – Johnson appears to have six children according to this census ten years later.

1820 FEDERAL CENSUS, WEST SALEM, MERCER COUNTY, PENNSYLVANIA

Gravatt, Johnson (aka *"Johnston"*) – According to this census, Johnson has four male children under the age of eleven, one male child between 26 and 45 years of age, one female child under the age of eleven, one female between 16 and 26, and another female of indeterminate age, for a total of eight children.

(N° 4.) 21 2

SCHEDULE of the whole number of Pe[...]

Name of County, City, Ward, Town, Township, Parish, Precinct, Hundred, or District.	NAMES of HEADS OF FAMILIES.	MALES.									FREE WH[ITE]
		Under five years of age.	Of five and under ten.	Of ten and under fifteen.	Of fifteen and under twenty.	Of twenty and under thirty.	Of thirty and under forty.	Of forty and under fifty.	Of fifty and under sixty.	Of sixty and under seventy.	Of seventy and under eighty.
		under 5	5 to 10	10 to 15	15 to 20	20 to 30	30 to 40	40 to 50	50 to 60	60 to 70	70 to 80
		132	107	79	78	151	80	25	23	21	12
Penna	Geo: Burns		1			1	1				
	Jane Brown		1	1				1			
	Badly McLaughlin					1					
	Solomon Brown	3					1				
	John McNeely										
	Henry McLaughlin	3	2	2		1					
	Johnston Gravatt	1			1	1					
West Salem Township ~ Mercer County	William Alcorn							1			
	Jno Dundey		1					1			
	David W Thompson	2	3			2					
	Thomas Lawhead			1			1		1		
	Hannah Melvin						1				
	Wm Gravatt		1				1		1		
	Margarett Gravatt					1					
	Ruliff Gravatt	1	1				1				
	Jno Gravatt	2	1	1	2			1			
	Wm Westbay	2	2	2	1		1				
	James Westbay	1	1	1			1				
	Alex Hunter									1	
	Alex Hunter	2					1				
	Hiram Hunter	1					1				
	Jacob Loutzenhiser	1					1				
	James Hunter	2	1					1			
	Mathew Hunter			1			1				
	Jno Carson	2	1								
	Jno Gravatt						1				
		168	125	17	83	142	90	49	29	23	12

1830 FEDERAL CENSUS, WEST SALEM, MERCER COUNTY, PENNSYLVANIA

Gravatt, Johnson (aka "*Johnston*") – According to this census, Johnson Gravatt has one male child under the age of five, one male child between the ages of 15 and 20, one male child between the ages of 20 and 30 years of age, one female under the age of five, and one female between 20 and 30 years of age, for a total of five children. Since his son, John W. Gravatt was born in 1781, he would have been 49 years of age at the time of this census, living apart from Johnson, and have children of his own. John W. Gravatt's son, Daniel, was born in 1827, and died in 1909.

...rsons within the Division allotted to *James T.*

TE PERSONS, (INCLUDING HEADS OF FAMILIES.)

			FEMALES.											
Of eighty and under ninety.	Of ninety and under one hundred.	Of one hundred and upwards.	Under five years of age.	Of five and under ten.	Of ten and under fifteen.	Of fifteen and under twenty.	Of twenty and under thirty.	Of thirty and under forty.	Of forty and under fifty.	Of fifty and under sixty.	Of sixty and under seventy.	Of seventy and under eighty.	Of eighty and under ninety.	Of ninety and under one hundred.	Of one hundred and upwards.
80 to 90	90 to 100	100, &c.	under 5	5 to 10	10 to 15	15 to 20	20 to 30	30 to 40	40 to 50	50 to 60	60 to 70	70 to 80	80 to 90	90 to 100	100, &c.
3			196	98	8	13	120	60	38	31	19	7	-	1	
				2	2			1							
			1	2					1						
						1				1					
			1	1	1		1			1					
			1				1								
			1				1								
			1	1	1			1							
			1				1								
				1	1	1	2			1					
										1					
			2		3	2	1		1						
			2	1	1	1			1						
			1	1			1								
					1			1							
								1							
			1	1	2	1	1					1			
					1										
							1								
							1								
							1								
			1	1											
				1					1						
			2	2	2		1								
				1			1								
						1									
3			151	114	103	73	134	72	41	35	20	7	-	1	

Right portion of document on facing page

155

(No. 4.) SCHEDULE of the whole number of persons

NAMES OF HEADS OF FAMILIES.	Under 5	5 & under 10	10 & under 15	15 & under 20	20 & under 30	30 & under 40	40 & under 50	50 & under 60	60 & under 70	70 & under 80	80 & under 90	90 & under 100	100 and upwards	Under 5	5 & under 10	10 & under 15
Brought forward	33	31	20	17	43	32	12	8	2					40	34	16
Leroy Fleming	1				1									1		
Jacob Ryan			1		1			1						1	2	
James Borland				2	1											
Saml Morrison	2	1			1	1										
James Dickey	2				2	3										1
James Aryer							1									
John M Stewart				1	1											
Agnes Garrison		1	1													2
W. S. Funk	1	1			1	1									2	
James Mitchell		2				1								1		1
James Lazier	1						1							1	2	2
George Corbett		3	1	1				2						1		1
John English						1								1	2	
Russell Kennedy	1				1											
Peter Bedley	3															
Robt Connell	2	2	2			1									1	
Robert Day	1					1										
George Curry					2											
Robert Gillford		1				1								2	1	
Geo Morrison				1												
Geo Wyman	1															
Isaac T Brooks	1				1									1		
John Corb	1				1									1		
Saml Weaver					1											
Andrew Stryker							1									
John Toby				2	4	3		1								
Robt S Potter	1		1			1										
James Fulton	1		1	1			1									
James Kennedy						1								1	1	
John Kennedy		1	2	2												
Total	54 / 62	43	28	28	36	47	26 / 16	13	3					57	45	34

1840 FEDERAL CENSUS, EAST DEER, ALLEGHENY COUNTY, PENNSYLVANIA

Girt, John – John Girt was the father of Martha Jane Girt, the eventual wife of Daniel Gravatt. Daniel Gravatt was the son of John W. Gravatt who was the son of Johnson Gravatt. According to this census, John Girt has one male child under the age of five, one male child between 20 and 30 years of age, one female child under the age of five, and one female between 20 and 30 years of age. Since Martha Jane was born in 1835, she would have been the "female child under the age of five."

within the division allotted to *W. H. Smith*

	FEMALES.										FREE COLORED PERSONS.									
											MALES.						FEMALES.			
15 a under 20	20 a under 30	30 a under 40	40 a under 50	50 a under 60	60 a under 70	70 a under 80	80 a under 90	90 a under 100	100 and upwards	Under 10	10 a under 24	24 a under 36	36 a under 55	55 a under 100	100 and upwards	Under 10	10 a under 24	24 a under 36	36 a under 55
20	38	19	12	6	2		1												
	1		1																
	1																		
1	1		1																
1					1														
	1			2															
		1		1															
1		1																	
		1																	
2			2																
			1																
	1																		
	1																		
		1	0																
	1																		
	1																		
	1	1																	
	1																		
	1																		
1																			
1	1	2			1														
1		1																	
2	1		1																
1		1																	
		1	1																
32	54	30		0	4		1												

Right portion of document on facing page

SCHEDULE I. — Free Inhabitants in *East Deer Township* in the County of *Allegheny* State of *Penna* enumerated by me, on the *20th* day of *August* 1850. *John Magill* Ass't Marshal.

1	2	3	4	5	6	7	8	9	10	11	12	13
53	53	George S. Gibson	31	m		Farmer		pa				
		Mary	31	f				"				•
		Jessie E.	4	f				"				
		Adolph	2	m				"				
		Sarah B.	1	f				"				
54	54	Sarah Gravat	62	f			1000	"				
		Daniel "	26	m		Labourer		"			1	
		Margaret Eunrod	24	f				"				
		James "	22	m		Labourer		"				
		John Gravat	20	m		"		"			1	
		John G. Rodgers	15	m		"		"			1	
		Phebe J. Dobbs	5	f				"				
55	55	George Collet	56	m		Farmer	700	England				
		Sarah "	58	f				"				
56	56	John W. Hay	27	m		Farmer		pa				
		Rosanna Hay	22	f				England				
		George "	1	m				pa				
57	57	John Pratt	39	m		Farmer		Maryland				
		Anne "	35	f				pa				
		James "	19	m		Labourer		"			1	
		William "	16	m				"			1	
		John "	9	m				"				
		Catharine "	3	F				"				
		Thomas "	2	m				"				
		Margaret "	2/12	f				"				
58	58	David Thompson	48	m		Farmer	1.500	Scotland				
		Ann "	45	f				"				
		Catharine "	9/12	f				pa				
		James "	14	m				pa				
59	59	George Miller	50	m		Farmer	2.500	Ireland				
		Elizabeth "	50	f				"				
		Margaret A. "	15	f				pa			1	
		Elizabeth "	9	f				Ireland			1	
		Alex. Hunter	44	m		Labourer		"			1	
		John Ford	23	m		"		pa				
60	60	Joseph Gibson	52	m		Farmer	3.600	Ireland				
		Elizabeth "	53	f				pa				
		Samuel "	24	m		Labourer		"				
		Susanna "	22	f				"				
		Elizabeth A. "	18	f				"			1	
		Joseph Ritner "	12	m				"			1	

1850 FEDERAL CENSUS, EAST DEER, ALLEGHENY COUNTY, PENNSYLVANIA

Gravatt, Sarah – According to this census, Daniel Gravatt, age 26, is now effectively serving as the head of the household, still living at home with his mother Sarah. His father, John W. Gravatt, passed away in 1839, and was buried in the old Gravatt Family Cemetery. Daniel's occupation is listed as a *"laborer."* The other members of the family are: Margaret, age 24; her husband James Eunrod (?), age 22; John, age 20; John G. Rodgers, age 15; and Phoebe J. Dobbs, age 5.

SCHEDULE L.—Free Inhabitants in *Tarentum Borough* in the County of *Allegheny*, of *Penna* enumerated by me, on the *29th* day of *August* 1850. *Seth Thugile* Ass't Marsh

		The Name of every Person whose usual place of abode on the first day of June, 1850, was in this family.	Age	Sex	Color	Profession, Occupation, or Trade of each Male Person over 15 years of age.	Value of Real Estate	Place of Birth, Naming the State, Territory, or Country.			
27	27	George Dickey	35	m		Carpenter	1200	Pa		✓	
		Sarah A.	24	f							
28	28	James Clark	68	m		Merchant	1500				
		Agnes	67	f				Scotland			
		Angeline	28	f				Maryland			
		Isabella McMillen	63	f				Scotland			
29	29	Charles Hinkle	43	m		Carpenter	300	Maryland			
		Mary "	43	f				Pa			
		Emma "	13	f							
30	30	Jane Johnston	67	f			150	Ireland			
		Julia Frink	36	f				Pa			
		Sarah M. "	1	f							
31	31	John F. Courter	42	m		Carpenter	300				
		Mary "	33	f							
		Sarah A. "	11	f				"		1	
		John W. "	8	m				"		1	
		Isabella "	6	f				Iowa	1		
		Mary S. "	5/12	f				"			
32	32	John Grant	27	m		Butcher		Germany			
		Barbara "	28	f				Pa			
		John "	4/12	m				Germany			
		Ursalla "	66	f				"			
		Frederick "	23	m		Butcher					
33	33	Elizabeth Byers	70	f			800	Pa		1	
34	34	James Orr	66	m		Cooper	100	Ireland			
		Nancy "	65	f							
35	35	John Girt	38	m		Laborer		Pa			
		Sarah "	33	f				"			
		Martha J. "	15	f				"			
		John "	11	m				"		1	
		Joseph "	7	m				"		1	
		David "	6	m				"		1	
		Maria "	2	f				"			
36	36	James Kinsey	67	m		Shoes	1000	Ireland			
		Mary "	63	f							
		James "	32	m		Shitter					
		Hugh "	26	m		Student of Abst.					
		Mary "	25	f							
37	37	Robert "	34	m		Shitter					
		Margaret "	22	f							
		Margaret Dunston	12	f				unknown			

1850 FEDERAL CENSUS, TARENTUM BOROUGH, ALLEGHENY COUNTY, PENNSYLVANIA

Girt, Martha Jane – According to this census, Martha Jane is 15 years of age and living at home with her parents. In slightly more than eight months, she will be married to Daniel Gravatt. The other members of the family listed in this census are: her father, John Girt, age 38, listed as a *"laborer"*; her mother, Sarah, age 33; John, 11; Joseph, 7; David, 6; and Maria, 2.

1860 FEDERAL CENSUS, SALEM, MERCER COUNTY, PENNSYLVANIA

Gravatt, John W. (?) – Records indicate Johnson's son – <u>John W.</u> – served in the *War of 1812*. John W., according to other records, died young at the age of 58 on January 7, 1839. He reportedly is buried in the third grave in old Gravatt Cemetery, Fawn Township, Allegheny County, Pennsylvania. According to the *1860 Federal Census*, however, John quite possibly <u>was still alive in 1860</u>, since it includes a listing for a *"John Gravatt,"* age 78 (the correct age if he were born in 1781 as indicated in the 1860 Census). This 1860 Census also lists the location of John's birth as *"New Jersey"* (which, in fact, is the correct location according to his son Daniel's records). This Census, however, includes only one other individual – *"Anne, age 76"* – in his household, which does not seem to match the identity of John's wife Sarah who would have been 85 in 1860. This *Census* also lists the value of this John's personal property at a mere $100.00, with no listing for the value of any real estate. Compounding the confusion is the fact the 1781 birth date from the 1860 Census conflicts with the *American Genealogical-Biographical Index*, a respected international online database accessed through *Ancestry.com* which indicates John W. Gravatt was in fact born in 1790.

Battery L, Capt. Jos. B. Zeigler.

Battery M, Capt. John E. Alward.

Independent Battery C (Thompson's), Capt. Jas. Thompson.

Independent Battery E (Knap's), Capts. Jos. M. Knap, Chas. A. Atwell, Jas. D. McGill, Thos. S. Sloan.

Independent Battery F (Hampton's), Capts. Robt. B. Hampton, Nath. Irish.

Independent Battery G (Young's), Capt. John Jay Young.

Indpendent Battery H. (John J. Nevins), Capts. John J. Nevins, Wm. Borrowe, Edwin H. Nevin, Jr.

Two Hundred and Twelfth Regiment, Sixth Artillery—Col. Chas. Barnes. Lieut.-Col. Jos. B. Copeland. Majs. Robt. H. Long, Jos. R. Kemp, Frank H. White. Adjt. Sam. J. M. Farren. Q. M. C. C. V. Vandegrift. Surg. Wm. B. Hezlep. Asst. Surgs. Wm. Taylor, James L. Rea. Chap.

Wm. D. Moore. Sergt.-Majs. David S. Salisbury, Nelson P. Chambers. Q. M.-Sergts. Wm. L. Hunter, Wm. C. Rudyard. Com.-Sergt. Jas. J. Fowler. Hosp. Stew. Jas. M. Sprout.

Battery A, Wm. R. Hutchinson.

Battery B, Gustavus F. Braum.

Battery C, David Evans.

Battery D, Daniel Gravatt.

Battery E, Jos. B. Copeland, Jos. Keepers.

Battery F, Chas. Barnes, Wm. H. Obey.

Battery G, Frank H. White, Chas. F. Hadly.

Battery H, Malachi Leslie.

Battery I, Wm. H. McCandless.

Battery K, Thos. A. Stone.

Battery L, Robt. H. Long and David Cornelius.

Battery M, Jos. R. Kemp, Cornelius J. Watson.

1865 UNION ARMY IDENTIFICATION, HISTORY OF PITTSBURGH, PENNSYLVANIA

Gravatt, Daniel – This page (#258) from the *History of Pittsburgh & Environs, Volume II, Part 2,* lists the Union Army unit on which Daniel Gravatt served during the U.S. Civil War. He was a captain, assigned to the 212 Regiment, Sixth Heavy Artillery, Battery D. He served from September 13, 1864 to June 13, 1865.

Page No. 47

SCHEDULE 1.—Inhabitants in _Fawn Township_ , in the County of _Allegheny_ , State of _Pennsylvania_, enumerated by me on the _18_ day of _August_, 1870.

Post Office: _Tarentum_

R. P. McBall, Ass't Marshal

		The name of every person whose place of abode on the first day of June, 1870, was in this family.	Age	Sex	Color	Profession, Occupation, or Trade of each person, male or female.	Value of Real Estate	Value of Personal Estate	Place of Birth, naming State or Territory of U.S.; or the Country, if of foreign birth.	11	12	13	14	15	16	17	18	19	20	
1		Irwin Mary	2	F	W				Pennsylvania											1
2	122											✓								2
3	123 120	How Benjamin	61	m	W	Farmer	3000	850	Pa									1		3
4		— Rebecca	53	F	W	Keeping House			Pa											4
5		— Nancy	27	F	W	At Home			Pa											5
6		— Malinda	24	F	W	at Home			Pa											6
7		— Harriet	16	F	W	at Home			Pa											7
8	124 121	Grant Daniel	44	m	W	Farmer			Pa									1		8
9		— Martha	33	F	W	Keeping House			Pa											9
10		— William	17	m	W	Works on Farm			Pa											10
11		— Mary	13	F	W				Pa						1					11
12		— James	9	m	W				Pa						1					12
13		— Bell	9	F	W				Pa						1					13
14		— Josephine	6	F	W				Pa						1					14
15		— Sarah	4	F	W				Pa											15
16		— Ida	2	F	W				Pa											16
17		— Thomas	1/12	m	W				Pa			May								17
18	125 122	Grant Sarah	85	F	W	Keeping House			Pa											18
19	126 123	Dawson Ralph	25	m	W	Miller	1000	250	Pa									1		19
20		— Susan	20	F	W	House Keeping			Pa											20
21	127 124	Gilson Margaret	46	F	W	Keeping House	1500	375	Pa											21
22		— John	21	m	W	Works on Rail Road			Pa									1		22
23		— Newton	16	m	W	Works on Farm			Pa											23
24		— Free	14	m	W				Pa						1					24
25		— Lydia	11	F	W				Pa						1					25
26		— Maggie	9	F	W				Pa						1					26
27	128 125	Wilson Charles	62	m	W	Laborer		600	Ireland	1	1							1		27
28	129 126	Bruce Norman	57	m	M	Butcher	1200	200	Pennsylvania									1		28
29		— Mary	40	F	M	Keeping House			Pa											29
30		— Thomas	15	m	M				Pa						1					30
31		— Manerva	14	F	M				Pa						1					31
32		— Wilson	12	m	M				Pa						1					32
33		— Flora	9	F	M				Pa						1					33
34		— Harry	7	m	M				Pa											34
35		— Isabell	5	F	M				Pa											35
36	130 127	Coe Benjamin	47	m	W	Farmer	3000	1000	Pa									1		36
37		— Jane	46	F	W	Keeping House			Pa											37
38		— James	18	m	W	Student			Pa						1					38
39		— Mary	15	F	W				Pa						1					39
40		— Benjamin	13	m	W				Pa						1					40

No. of dwellings, _9_ No. of white females, _19_ No. of males, foreign born _1_
" of families, _8_ " colored males _4_ " females,
" white males, _13_ " females, _9_ " blind,

No. of homes,

1870 FEDERAL CENSUS, FAWN, ALLEGHENY COUNTY, PENNSYLVANIA

Gravatt, Daniel – According to this Census, Daniel Gravatt, age 44, is married to Martha Jane (Girt), age 33. In addition to Martha Jane, his household includes eight children: William, 17; Mary, 13; James, 9; Bell, 9; Josephine, 6; Sarah, 4; Ida, 2; and Thomas, one month. Daniel is listed as a "farmer." It notes that Mary, James, Bell and Josephine all attended school that year. A separate listing identifies Daniel's mother, Sarah, age 85, perhaps living alone. No valuation for personal property or real estate is listed for Daniel.

Page No. 121

Schedule 1.—Inhabitants in _Tarentum Borough_, in the County of _Allegheny_, State of _Penna_, enumerated by me on the _4_ day of _June_, 1870. Post Office: _Tarentum Pa_ _R C McBell_, Ass't Marshal.

			The name of every person whose place of abode on the first day of June, 1870, was in this family.	Age	Sex	Color	Profession, Occupation, or Trade of each person, male or female.	Value of Real Estate	Value of Personal Estate	Place of Birth, naming State or Territory of U. S.; or the Country, if of foreign birth.										
1	2		3	4	5	6	7	8	9	10	11	12	13	14	15	16	17	18	19	20
1			Cook William	12	m	W				Pennsylvania										1
2			— John	32	m	W	Cooper			Pa										2
3			— Sarah	21	F	W	Keeping House			Pa	11									3
4			— Lizzie	1	F	W				Pa										4
5	114	108	Mack Jacob	34	m	W	Laborer			Pa							1			5
6			— Anna	10	F	W				Pa			1							6
7			— Emma	9	F	W				Pa			1							7
8			— Mary	6	F	W				Pa			1							8
9			— Matilda	4	F	W				Pa										9
10			— George	1	m	W				Pa										10
11			Shuler Annie	21	F	W	Keeping House			Scotland	1	1								11
12	115	109	Kerroy John	57	m	W	Brickmaker			Ireland	1	1								12
13			— Agness	41	F	W	Keeping House			Pennsylvania	1									13
14			— Mary	20	F	W	Teaching School			Pa	1			1						14
15			— Joseph	18	m	W				Pa	1			1						15
16			— Sarah	14	F	W				Pa	1			1						16
17			— Agnes	16	F	W				Pa	1			1						17
18			— William	13	m	W				Pa	1			1						18
19			— James	11	m	W				Pa	1			1						19
20			— Martha	9	F	W				Pa	1			1						20
21			— Thomas	8	m	W				Pa	1			1						21
22			— Ford	4	m	W				Virginia	1									22
23			— Hugh	2	m	W				Missouri	1									23
24	116	110	Girt John	57	m	W		500		Pennsylvania							1			24
25			— Sarah	52	F	W	Keeping House			Pa							1			25
26			— Lizzie	15	F	W				Pa										26
27			— Bella	13	F	W				Pa			1							27
28	117	111	Shornhose Anna	25	F	W	Keeping House			Switzerland	1	1								28
29			— Samuel	3	m	W				Pennsylvania	1									29
30			— James	2	m	W				Pa										30
31			— Willie	4/12	m	W				Pa		1	Apr							31
32	118	112	Ross John	34	m	W	Works at Bone works			Pa							11			32
33			— Nancy	25	F	W	Keeping House			Pa	1	1								33
34			— Sadie	7	F	W				Pa										34
35			— Elizabeth	1	F	W				Pa										35
36	119	113	Moore Joseph	66	m	W	Undertaker	500		Pa	1	1								36
37			— Sarah	53	F	W	Keeping House			Pa										37
38			— Elizabeth	17	F	W				Pa				1						38
39			— Lida	15	F	W				Pa				1						39
40			— Willie	11	m	W				Pa				1						40

No. of dwellings 6   No. of white females 22   No. of males 500   500

1870 FEDERAL CENSUS, TARENTUM BOROUGH, ALLEGHENY COUNTY, PENNSYLVANIA

Girt, John – John Girt, 57 years of age, is listed as the head of his household which includes his wife, Sarah, 52, and: Lizzie, 15; and Bella, 13. John lists real estate he owns as valued at $500.00.

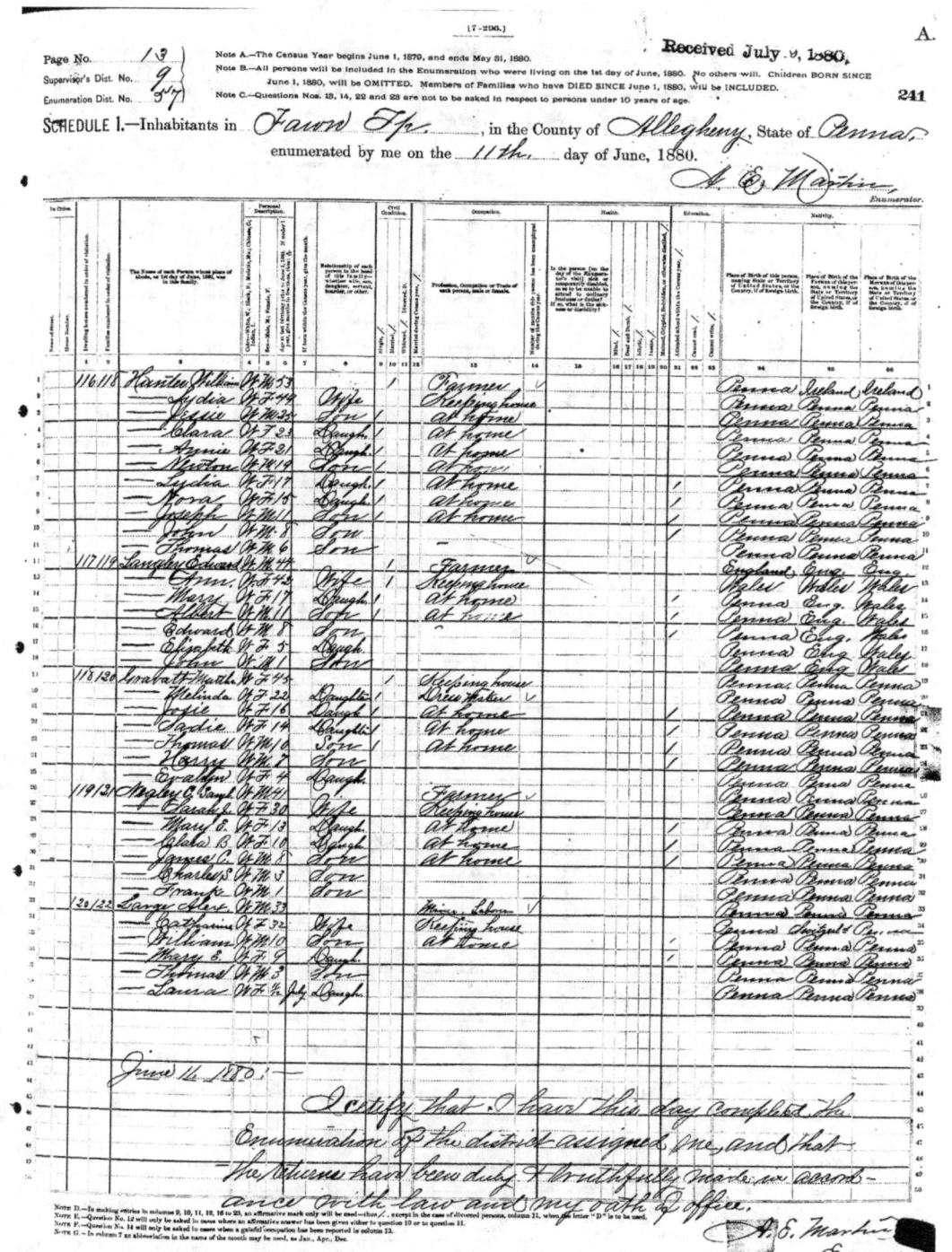

1880 FEDERAL CENSUS, FAWN, ALLEGHENY COUNTY, PENNSYLVANIA

Gravatt, Daniel – Though he would only have been age 53 and records indicate he did not die until 1909, Daniel Gravatt, for reasons unexplained, does not appear on this *1880 Census*. His wife, Martha Jane, age 45, is listed as the head of the household. The children still living at home included: Mary Melinda, age 22, who is listed as a *"dress-maker"*; Josie, 16; Sadie, 14; Thomas, 10; Harry, 7; and Eva Lynn, 4. No value for any personal property or real estate is listed, so one must assume they were living at poverty level, owning few if any possessions or real property. With no visible or known means of support, their life quite likely was extremely difficult.

[7-296.]

...ed Aug 2, 80

Note A.—The Census Year begins June 1, 1879, and ends May 31, 1880.

Note B.—All persons will be included in the Enumeration who were living on the 1st day of June, 1880. No others will. Children BORN SINCE 486
June 1, 1880, will be OMITTED. Members of Families who have DIED SINCE June 1, 1880, will be INCLUDED.

Note C.—Questions Nos. 13, 14, 22 and 23 are not to be asked in respect to persons under 10 years of age.

Page No. 22

Supervisor's Dist. No.

Enumeration Dist. No. 45

SCHEDULE 1.—Inhabitants in *Borough of Tarentum* , in the County of *Allegheny* , State of *Pennsylvania*
enumerated by me on the *16* day of June, 1880. *Carroll D. Evans*
Enumerator.

		Personal Description				Civil Condition			Occupation		Health				Education			Nativity		
		Mary Ca.	W F 32	Wife			Keeping House												Pennsylvania	Penna	Penna
		Elizabeth	W F 19	Daughter			At Home												Pennsylvania	Penna	Penna
		James A	W M 17	Son			Laborer												Pennsylvania	Penna	Penna
		Ida M	W F 13	Daughter			At Home												Pennsylvania	Penna	Penna
		Effie B	W F 11	Daughter			At Home												Pennsylvania	Penna	Penna
		Hanna M	W F 9	Daughter															Pennsylvania	Penna	Penna
		Samuel	W M 7	Son															Pennsylvania	Penna	Penna
13 207	Slacker Charles	W M 41					Laborer												Pennsylvania	Penna	Penna
		Lucinda	W F 35	Wife			Keeping House												Pennsylvania	Penna	Penna
		Elizabeth	W F 15	Daughter			At Home												Pennsylvania	Penna	Penna
		Lottie	W F 13	Daughter			At Home												Pennsylvania	Penna	Penna
		Samuel	W M 11	Son															Pennsylvania	Penna	Penna
		Smith James	W M 19	Nephew			Laborer												Pennsylvania	Penna	Penna
14 208	Brook George	W M 44					Carpenter												Pennsylvania	Penna	Penna
		Margaret	W F 41	Wife			Keeping House												Pennsylvania	Penna	Penna
		Jessie	W F 15	Daughter			At Home												Pennsylvania	Penna	Penna
		Addie	W F 12	Daughter			At Home												Pennsylvania	Penna	Penna
		Henry	W M 7	Son															Pennsylvania	Penna	Penna
		Annie	W F 4	Daughter															Pennsylvania	Penna	Penna
95 209	Girt John	W M 68					Laborer												Pennsylvania	Penna	Penna
		Sarah	W F 63	Wife			Keeping House												Pennsylvania	Penna	Penna
		Bell	W F 23	Daughter			Clerk in Dry Goods												Pennsylvania	Penna	Penna
	Gravatt Mary M	W F 22	Grand Daugh			Dress Maker												Pennsylvania	Penna	Penna
196 210	Timmons Joseph H	W M 51					Minister												W Virginia	Penna	Penna
		Raphel B	W F 43	Wife			Keeping House												Ohio	Ohio	Ireland
		Mary E	W F 19	Daughter			At School												Pennsylvania	W Virginia	Ohio
		Nathan E	W M 16	Son			At School												Pennsylvania	W Virginia	Ohio
		Joseph W	W M 12	Son			At Home												Pennsylvania	W Virginia	Ohio
		Rachel B	W F 8	Daughter															Pennsylvania	W Virginia	Ohio
		Jessie	W F 6	Daughter															Pennsylvania	W Virginia	Ohio
		William	W M 3	Son															Pennsylvania	Penna	Penna
197 211	Hanas Sarah	W F 36					Keeping House												Pennsylvania	Penna	Penna
		Beckie	W F 12	Daughter			At Home												Pennsylvania	Penna	Penna
		Mary	W F 4	Daughter															Pennsylvania	Penna	Penna
198 212	Smith Andrew	W M 33					Laborer												Pennsylvania	Germany	England
		Nancy	W F 32	Wife			Keeping House												Pennsylvania	Penna	Penna
		James M	W M 7	Son															Pennsylvania	Penna	Penna
		William	W M 5	Son															Pennsylvania	Penna	Penna
		Thomas J	W M ½ Nov	Son															Pennsylvania	Jersey	Penna
		Sarah	W F 57	Mother			At Home												Pennsylvania	Penna	Penna
195 213	Harris Sylvester	W M 34					Laborer												Pennsylvania	Penna	Penna
		Cathrine	W F 30	Wife			Keeping House												Pennsylvania	Penna	Penna
		Ella M	W F 12	Daughter			At Home												Pennsylvania	Penna	Penna
16 214	Scott James R	W M 32					Laborer												Pennsylvania	Penna	Penna
		Elizabeth	W F 25	Wife			Keeping House												Pennsylvania	Penna	Penna
		Hugh	W M 6	Son															Pennsylvania	Penna	Penna
		Nellie	W F 3	Daughter															Pennsylvania	Penna	Penna
		Josef M	W F 1	Col Daughter															Pennsylvania	Penna	Penna
199 215	Borland Joseph	W M 35					Laborer														

Note D.—In making entries in columns 8, 10, 11, 12, 13—21, an affirmative mark only will be used—thus / ; except in the case of divorced persons, column 11, when the letter "D" is to be used.
Note E.—Question No. 12 will only be asked in cases where no affirmative answer has been given either to question 10 or to question 11.
Note F.—Enumeration No. 14 will only be asked in cases where a painful incapacity have been reported in column 15.
Note G.—In column 7 an abbreviation for the name of the month may be used, as Jan., Apr., Dec.

1880 FEDERAL CENSUS, TARENTUM BOROUGH, ALLEGHENY COUNTY, PENNSYLVANIA

Gravatt, Mary Melinda – The pain of the poverty in the Gravatt and Girt families is now becoming even more evident as Mary Melinda is now living with her grandparents – the John Girt family. Mary Melinda, age 22, is still listed as *"dress-maker,"* and almost certainly continuing to struggle to make ends meet. John Girt, age 68, is the head of the household and still listed as a *"laborer"* for his profession. Family members listed are: wife Sarah, age 63, *"home-maker"*; and Bell, age 23, listed as *"clerk in dry goods store."*

(3-H-3)

NAME OF SOLDIER:	*Gravatt, Daniel*				

NAME OF DEPENDENT:	Widow,	*Gravatt, Martha J.*			
	Minor,				

SERVICE:	*D 6 Pa H A*				

DATE OF FILING.	CLASS.	APPLICATION NO.	CERTIFICATE NO.	STATE FROM WHICH FILED.
1890, Dec. 5	Invalid.	978858	734984	Pa.
1909 May 7	Widow,	919453	684238	Pa
	Minor,			

ATTORNEY:	*Claimant.*

REMARKS:	

1890 UNION ARMY VETERAN'S PENSION APPLICATION, PENNSYLVANIA

Gravatt, Daniel – On December 5, 1890, twenty-five years after the war had concluded, Daniel or his representative filed for a pension for his service in the U.S. Army during the Civil War. It is unknown today why he delayed so long in making application. He died almost 20 years later on April 6, 1909, and his wife Martha Jane then filed for his pension on May 7 of that year. She, no doubt, received benefits until her death. Beginning in 1862, a 100% disabled private was paid $8.00 per month – the equivalent of approximately $235.00 in 2023 dollars. A partially disabled veteran would obviously receive considerably less. Nevertheless, a hundred dollars or so went a long way in the poverty-stricken and oft-chaotic times in the 1890s.

7-224.

TWELFTH CENSUS OF THE UNITED STATES.

SCHEDULE No. 1.—POPULATION.

739 A
295

State _Pennsylvania_

County _Butler_

Supervisor's District No. _19_

Enumeration District No. _91_

Sheet No. _10_

Township or other division of county _Winfield Township_

Name of Institution, _X_

Name of incorporated city, town, or village, within the above-named division,

Ward of city,

Enumerated by me on the _20_ day of June, 1900, _Herman L. Bicker_ , Enumerator.

LOCATION			NAME of each person whose place of abode on June 1, 1900, was in this family.	RELATION. Relationship of each person to the head of the family.	PERSONAL DESCRIPTION							NATIVITY			CITIZENSHIP			OCCUPATION, TRADE, OR PROFESSION		EDUCATION				OWNERSHIP OF HOME				
												Place of birth of this Person.	Place of birth of Father of this person.	Place of birth of Mother of this person.														
1			Martha	Wife			Feb 1856	44	M	23	10	8	Pennsylvania	Pennsylvania	Pennsylvania						yes	yes	yes					1
2			Emma	Daughter			Nov 1881	18	S				Pennsylvania	Pennsylvania	Pennsylvania						yes	yes	yes					2
3			Pearl	Daughter			Nov 1883	16	S				Pennsylvania	Pennsylvania	Pennsylvania				At School		yes	yes	yes					3
4			Etta	Daughter			May 1887	12	S				Pennsylvania	Pennsylvania	Pennsylvania				At school		yes	yes	yes					4
5			Claud	Son			May 1892	8	S				Pennsylvania	Pennsylvania	Pennsylvania													5
6			Dale	Son			Aug 1895	5	S				Pennsylvania	Pennsylvania	Pennsylvania													6
7	188	89	Heasley Henry	Head			May 1849	51	M	17			Pennsylvania	Pennsylvania	Pennsylvania				Timber Dealer		yes	yes	yes		R	H		7
8			Fannie	Wife			Nov 1860	39	M	17	1	0	Pennsylvania	Pennsylvania	Pennsylvania						yes	yes	yes					8
9			Rine Rebeca	Servant			Feb 1874	26	S				Pennsylvania	Pennsylvania	Pennsylvania				House Keeper		yes	yes	yes					9
10	189	90	Saudenslager	Head			Aug 1830		M	4			Germany	Germany	Pennsylvania				Farmer		yes	yes	yes		O	F	146	10
11			E	Wife			1870	29	M	4	1	1	Pennsylvania	Ireland	Pennsylvania						yes	yes	yes					11
12			Mildred	Daughter			May 1898	1	S				Pennsylvania	Pennsylvania	Pennsylvania													12
13	190	91	Michal Henry	Head			Aug 1834	65	M	2	1	0	Germany	Germany	Germany	1848	51				yes	yes	yes		O	H		13
14	191	92	Cypher Charles	Head			May 1874	26	M	2			Pennsylvania	Pennsylvania	Pennsylvania				Day Labor	2	yes	yes	yes		R	H		14
15			Louella	Wife			Oct 1879	20	M	2	0	0	Pennsylvania	England	England						yes	yes	yes					15
16	192	93	Fair Clarence	Head			May 1868	32	M	4			Pennsylvania	Pennsylvania	Pennsylvania				Day Labor	3	yes	yes	yes		R	H		16
17			Maletta	Wife			Feb 1876	24	M	4	3	3	Pennsylvania	Pennsylvania	Pennsylvania						yes	yes	yes					17
18			Twila	Daughter			Oct 1896	3	S				Pennsylvania	Pennsylvania	Pennsylvania													18
19			Helen	Daughter			Dec 1897	2	S				Pennsylvania	Pennsylvania	Pennsylvania													19
20			Charley	Son			Oct 1899	7/12	S				Pennsylvania	Pennsylvania	Pennsylvania													20
21	193	94	Gravatt Daniel	Head			Sept 1827	72	M	49			Pennsylvania	New Jersey	Pennsylvania				Land Lord		yes	yes	yes		O	H		21
22			Martha	Wife			Nov 1834	65	M	49	11	7	Pennsylvania	Pennsylvania	Pennsylvania						yes	yes	yes					22
23	194	95	Baldauer Dionis	Head			Oct 1851	48	M	44			Italy	Italy	Italy	1888	11	AL	Day Labor	3					O	H		23
24			Barah	Wife			Jan 1839	61	M	44	9	2	Italy	Italy	Italy	1892	7											24
25			Agabito	Son			Aug 1860	40	M	21			Italy	Italy	Italy	1890	3	AL	Stone Cutter									25
26			Allice	Grin daugh			June 1887	12	S				Pennsylvania	Italy	Italy				At School		7	yes	yes					26
27			John	Gran Son			Oct 1889	10	S				Pennsylvania	Italy	Italy				At School		7	yes	yes					27
28			Susie	Gran daugh			Nov 1891	9	S				Pennsylvania	Italy	Italy						7	yes	yes					28
29	195	96	Heasley Nelson	Head			Feb 1856	44	M	10			Pennsylvania	Pennsylvania	Pennsylvania				Timber Dealer		yes	yes	yes		R	H		29
30			Rosabell	Wife			Jan 1873	27	M	10	9	3	Pennsylvania	Pennsylvania	Pennsylvania						yes	yes	yes					30
31			Perry	Son			Apr 1891	9	S				Pennsylvania	Pennsylvania	Pennsylvania						7							31
32			Freddie	Son			June 1895	4	S				Pennsylvania	Pennsylvania	Pennsylvania													32
33			Nelson	Son			Dec 1899	7/12	S				Pennsylvania	Pennsylvania	Pennsylvania													33
34	196	97	Huder Christed	Head			Mar 1827	73	Wd	1	1		Germany	Germany	Germany	1836	46		Painter Pipe Line	6		yes	yes		O	H		34
35			Harriet	Son			Feb 1848	52	M	12			Pennsylvania	Germany	Germany													35
36			Elizabeth	Wife			May 1855	45	M	12	4	9	Pennsylvania	Germany	Germany													36
37			Edward	Son			May 1885	13	S				Pennsylvania	Pennsylvania	Pennsylvania				At School		7	yes	yes					37
38			William	Son			Aug 1889	10	S				Pennsylvania	Pennsylvania	Pennsylvania				At School		7	yes	yes					38
39			Emma	Daughter			Mar 1894	6	S				Pennsylvania	Pennsylvania	Pennsylvania													39
40	197	98	Hall William	Head			Aug 1866	33	M	12			Pennsylvania	Pennsylvania	Pennsylvania				General Store	2	yes	yes	yes		R	H		40
41			Mary	Wife			Feb 1868	31	M	12	5	4	Pennsylvania	Pennsylvania	Pennsylvania						yes	yes	yes					41
42			Edna O	Daughter			Nov 1891	8	S				Pennsylvania	Pennsylvania	Pennsylvania						6							42
43			Berdella	Daughter			Dec 1893	6	S				Pennsylvania	Pennsylvania	Pennsylvania													43
44			William D	Son			May 1897	3	S				Pennsylvania	Pennsylvania	Pennsylvania													44
45			David E	Son			Mar 1899	1	S				Pennsylvania	Pennsylvania	Pennsylvania													45
46	198	99	Cruikshank David	Head			Feb 1853	47	M	3			Pennsylvania	Pennsylvania	Ireland				Farmer		yes	yes	yes		O	M	F 147	46
47			Maggie	Wife			Mar 1858	42	M	3	4	4	Pennsylvania	Pennsylvania	Pennsylvania						yes	yes	yes					47
48			Clark Ruth	Daughter			Jan 1879	21	S				Pennsylvania	W Virginia	Pennsylvania				Farm Labor									48
49			Frank	Son			July 1884	15	S				Pennsylvania	W Virginia	Pennsylvania						7	yes	yes					49
50			Stella	Daughter			Jan 1887	13	S				Pennsylvania	W Virginia	Pennsylvania						yes	yes	yes					50

1900 FEDERAL CENSUS, WINFIELD TOWNSHIP, BUTLER COUNTY, PENNSYLVANIA

Gravatt, Daniel – Daniel reappears in this Census. By this point, his household includes only himself at age 72 and wife, Martha, age 65. He lists his birth year as _1827_, and the place of birth of his father as _"New Jersey."_ Interestingly, he lists his occupation as _"landlord."_

Will
of
Daniel Gravatt

I Daniel Gravatt, give devise and bequeath to my Wife Martha Jane Gravatt all of my property, real, personal or mixed of which I shall die seized and possessed, or to which I shall be entitled at the time of my decease; the same to be used for her maintainance as she shall see proper. I hereby appoint my Wife Executrix of this my last Will and testament. In Witness Whereof, I have hereunto set my hand and seal, this 20th day of December in the year of our Lord one thousand nine hundred and two (1902)

Daniel Gravatt (ss)

The above instrument was signed in our presence by the testator Daniel Gravatt, he declared it to be his last Will and testament and requested us to sign our names as attesting witnesses.

H. S. Gravatt (ss)

Carbon Black
P.O.

Thos. Gravatt (ss)

State of Pennsylvania }
County of Butler }

Before me, the subscriber Register for the probate of wills and granting letters of administration, &c. in and for said county personally came Mrs E. A. Steetle and who being duly sworn according to law depose and say that they were well acquainted with H. S. Gravatt whose name appears as one of the subscribing witnesses to the above and foregoing last will and testament of Daniel Gravatt deceased dated the 20th day of December 1902 and this day offered for probate, that they are well acquainted with the hand writing of said H. S. Gravatt having frequently seen him sign his name, that to the best of their knowledge and belief the signature of said H. S. Gravatt as signed to said instrument is genuine and in his own proper handwriting. Deponents further testify that said H. S. Gravatt is now in California.

Sworn and subscribed before me this
20th day of April A.D. 1909.

Mrs. E. A. Steetle

Jillian A. Clark,
Register

Per E. J. Brugh,
Deputy

State of Pennsylvania }
County of Butler }

Register's Office April 20. A.D. 1909

Then personally appeared before me, the subscriber Register for the probate of wills and granting letters of administration in and for said county of Butler Thomas Gravatt one of the subscribing witnesses to the above and foregoing last will and testament of Daniel Gravatt deceased, who being duly sworn according to law, did

1902 LAST WILL & TESTAMENT, WINFIELD TOWNSHIP, BUTLER COUNTY, PENNSYLVANIA
Gravatt, Daniel – Daniel's will grants all his property and possessions to his wife, Martha Jane. The total lack of specifics in the Will, and uncomplicated nature of the instrument would lead one to believe that there was very little in the way of assets in his estate for him to contemplate leaving to his heirs, particularly since he apparently left nothing to his sons or daughters.

say that he was present and did see and hear Daniel Gravatt deceased, the testator therein named, sign, seal, publish, pronounce and declare the above and foregoing instrument of writing as and for his last will and testament, and that at the doing thereof he was of sound disposing mind, memory and understanding to the best of his knowledge and belief, and he, at his request, and in his presence and the presence of H. S. Gravatt did sign his names thereto as witness, and saw H. S. Gravatt sign as witness.

Sworn and subscribed before
me the day and year aforesaid.   Thos. Gravatt.
Julian A. Clark, Register
Per. E. I. Brugh Deputy

Now, Apr 20 A.D. 1909 the testimony of the above named witnesses being sufficient I do hereby admit the foregoing will to probate, and order the same to be recorded as such.
Given under my hand and seal the above date.
                          Julian A. Clark. Register.

State of Pennsylvania, County of Butler. SS:
Personally came before me the Register of Wills &c. in and for said County Thos Gravatt a resident of Cabot in said County, who being duly sworn according to law, deposeth and saith that to the best of his knowledge and belief Daniel Gravatt late of the Township of Winfield in said County departed this life on the 5th day of April A.D. 1909 about 3 o'clock P.M. of said day.
Sworn and subscribed to before me this   Thos Gravatt
20th day of April A.D. 1909.
        Julian A. Clark. Register
        per E. I. Brugh. Deputy

                  Recorded April 20, 1909.

Right portion of document on facing page

FORM V. S. No. 5.

PLACE OF DEATH.

COMMONWEALTH OF PENNSYLVANIA.
BUREAU OF VITAL STATISTICS.
CERTIFICATE OF DEATH.

County of _Butler_

Township of _Winfield_
or
Borough of_____
or
City of_____ (No._____ St.;_____Ward)

Registration District No. _292_

Primary Registration District No. _2293_

File No. _38529_

Registered No._____

[If death occurred in a Hospital or Institution, give its NAME instead of street and number.]

[If death occurs away from USUAL RESIDENCE give facts called for under "Special informaticn."]

FULL NAME _Daniel Gravatt_

WRITE PLAINLY, WITH UNFADING INK—THIS IS A PERMANENT RECORD.

N. B.—Every item of information should be carefully supplied. AGE should be stated EXACTLY. PHYSICIANS should state CAUSE OF DEATH in plain terms, that it may be properly classified. The "Special Information." for persons dying away from home should be given in every instance.

PERSONAL AND STATISTICAL PARTICULARS		MEDICAL CERTIFICATE OF DEATH

SEX _Male_ COLOR _White_

DATE OF BIRTH _September_ _6_ _1836_
(Month) (Day) (Year)

AGE _82_ years, _8_ months, _____ days

SINGLE, MARRIED, WIDOWED, OR DIVORCED _Married_

BIRTHPLACE (State or country) _Pa_

NAME OF FATHER _John Gravatt_

BIRTHPLACE OF FATHER (State or country) _New Jersey_

MAIDEN NAME OF MOTHER _Sarah Kennedy_

BIRTHPLACE OF MOTHER (State or country) _Pa_

OCCUPATION _Carpenter_

THE ABOVE STATED PERSONAL PARTICULARS ARE TRUE TO THE BEST OF MY KNOWLEDGE AND BELIEF

(Informant) _Martha Gravatt_

(Address) _Cabot Pa._

Filed _Mar 6_ 190 _9_
Apr, _W D Hoffman_
Registrar

DATE OF DEATH _Apr._ _6th_ _1909_
(Month) (Day) (Year)

I HEREBY CERTIFY, That I attended deceased from _March 22nd Apr_ 190 _9_ to _March 6th Apr._ 190 _9_
that I last saw him alive on _March 6 Apr,_ 190 _9_
and that death occurred, on the date stated above, at _3.57_

A. M. The CAUSE OF DEATH was as follows:

Pulmonary Gangrene

_529_ (Duration) _4_ Days

Contributory _Chronic Bronchitis_

Several years (Duration) _____ Days

(Signed) _Dr J M Scott_ M. D.

Apr 6 1909 (Address) _Cabot Pa._

SPECIAL INFORMATION only for Hospitals, Institutions, Transients, or Recent Residents.

Former or Usual Residence_____ How long at Place of Death?_____Days

Where was disease contracted?_____

PLACE OF BURIAL OR REMOVAL _Vox Chaple_ DATE OF BURIAL _April 7_ 190 _9_

UNDERTAKER _H G Koegler_ ADDRESS _Cabot Pa._

1909 DEATH CERTIFICATE, WINFIELD TOWNSHIP, BUTLER COUNTY, PENNSYLVANIA

Gravatt, Daniel – He was 82 years and 8 months of age when he passed away on April 6, 1909, of *"chronic bronchitis"* and *"pulmonary gangrene,"* which might be translated more simply to *"pneumonia and natural causes."* His listed occupation on the Death Certificate is *"carpenter."*

Commonwealth of Pennsylvania Department of Military Affairs	RECORD OF BURIAL PLACE OF VETERAN	.... County

NAME	DATE OF BIRTH	DATE OF DEATH
Gravatt , Daniel (Cravatt)	1827	1909

VETERAN OF		SERVED IN	
Rebellion	WAR	ARMY (X) NAVY ( )	MARINE CORPS ( )

DATES OF SERVICE	ORGANIZATION(S)	RANK
Sept. 13 1864 June 13 1865	Battery D. 6th Pa Artillery	Capt.

CEMETERY OR PLACE OF INTERMENT	NAME	Knox Chapel
	LOCATION	Winfield Twp.

LOCATION OF GRAVE IN CEMETERY	HEADSTONE
SECTION LOT No. RANGE GRAVE No. 4	GOVERNMENT ( ) COUNTY ( ) FAMILY (X)
INFORMATION GIVEN BY	REMARKS
DATE	

After being Recorded in the County Veterans' Grave Registration Record this card is to be sent
to THE ADJUTANT GENERAL'S OFFICE, Harrisburg, Pennsylvania, for final Record.

1909 VETERANS BURIAL, KNOX CHAPEL, WINFIELD TOWNSHIP, BUTLER COUNTY, PA
Gravatt, Daniel – Buried in Grave #4, Knox Chapel Cemetery, Cabot, Butler County, Pennsylvania.

THIRTEENTH CENSUS OF THE UNITED STAT[ES]

DEPARTMENT OF COMMERCE AND LABOR—BUREA[U]

STATE _____
COUNTY Butler
TOWNSHIP OR OTHER DIVISION OF COUNTY Winfield Township

NAME OF INCORPORATED PLACE X

NAME OF INSTITUTION X

ENUMERATED BY ME O[N]

Line	Number of dwelling	Number of family	NAME of each person whose place of abode on April 15, 1910, was in this family.	RELATION.	Sex	Color or race	Age at last birthday	Single/Married/etc.	Years married	No. children born	No. children living	Place of birth of this person	Place of birth of Father	Place of birth of Mother
51	9	9	Young, Samuel P	Head	M	W	45	M3				Pennsylvania	Pennsylvania	Pennsylvania
52			Elizabeth A. M	Wife	F	W	38	M3	3	3		Pennsylvania	Ger-German	Ger-German
53			William L	Daughter	F	W	11	S				Pennsylvania	Pennsylvania	Pennsylvania
54	10	10	Keepple, Charles J	Head	M	W	55	M16				Ger-German	Ger-German	Ger-German
55			Lizzie	Wife	F	W	44	M2	6	5		Pennsylvania	Ger-German	Ger-German
56			Fleming, Annie	Daughter	F	W	30	S				Pennsylvania	Pennsylvania	Pennsylvania
57			Keepple, Mahala	Daughter	F	W	10	S				Pennsylvania	Ger-German	Pennsylvania
58			Viola L	Daughter	F	W	9	S				Pennsylvania	Ger-German	Pennsylvania
59	11	11	Marks, William E	Head	M	W	47	M14				Pennsylvania	Pennsylvania	Pennsylvania
60			Lillie C.	Wife	F	W	43	M14	4			Pennsylvania	Pennsylvania	Pennsylvania
61	12	12	Hildebrand, John	Head	M	W	57	M35				Pennsylvania	Pennsylvania	Pennsylvania
62			Josephine	Wife	F	W	56	M35				Pennsylvania	Ohio	Ohio
63	13	13	Sarat, Martha	Head	F	W	75	Wd				Pennsylvania	Pennsylvania	Pennsylvania
64	14	14	Gravatt, Thomas B	Head	M	W	39	M19				Pennsylvania	Pennsylvania	Pennsylvania
65			Emma L	Wife	F	W	39	M19	5	5		Pennsylvania	Pennsylvania	Pennsylvania
66			Jesse H	Son	M	W	17	S				Pennsylvania	Pennsylvania	Pennsylvania
67			Lissa P	Daughter	F	W	15	S				Pennsylvania	Pennsylvania	Pennsylvania
68			Charles V	Son	M	W	12	S				Pennsylvania	Pennsylvania	Pennsylvania
69			James O	Son	M	W	7	S				Pennsylvania	Pennsylvania	Pennsylvania
70			Marguerit	Daughter	F	W	7/12	S				Pennsylvania	Pennsylvania	Pennsylvania
71	15	15	Lewis, William E	Head	M	W	69	M22				Pennsylvania	Pennsylvania	Pennsylvania
72			Rebecca	Wife	F	W	62	M2	3	3		Pennsylvania	Pennsylvania	Pennsylvania
73	16	16	Fleming, Charles	Head	M	W	38	M24				Pennsylvania	Pennsylvania	Pennsylvania
74			Mary A	Wife	F	W	49	M24	4	4		Pennsylvania	Ger-German	Ger-German
75			Clara C	Daughter	F	W	27	S				Pennsylvania	Pennsylvania	Pennsylvania
76			Matilda C	Daughter	F	W	26	S				Pennsylvania	Pennsylvania	Pennsylvania
77			Emma M	Daughter	F	W	23	S				Pennsylvania	Pennsylvania	Pennsylvania
78			Wilhamine L	Daughter	F	W	20	S				Pennsylvania	Pennsylvania	Pennsylvania
79	17	17	Cooper, Isaac E	Head	M	W	50	M25				Pennsylvania	Pennsylvania	Pennsylvania
80			Elizabeth	Wife	F	W	50	M25	4	4		Pennsylvania	Pennsylvania	Pennsylvania
81			Harry W	Son	M	W	23	S				Pennsylvania	Pennsylvania	Pennsylvania
82	18	18	Morris, John	Head	M	W	60	M34				Pennsylvania	Ger-German	Ger-German
83			Clara J	Wife	F	W	64	M34	7	6		Pennsylvania	Pennsylvania	Pennsylvania
84			Edgar L	Son	M	W	20	S				Pennsylvania	Pennsylvania	Pennsylvania
85			Emma B	Daughter	F	W	16	S				Pennsylvania	Pennsylvania	Pennsylvania
86			Minnie M	Granddaughter	F	W	11	S				Pennsylvania	Pennsylvania	Pennsylvania
87	19	19	Cooper, Nancy	Head	F	W	48	Wd				Pennsylvania	Pennsylvania	Pennsylvania
88			Margaret	Sister	F	W	65	S				Pennsylvania	Pennsylvania	Pennsylvania
89			Minder, Paul L	Grandson	M	W	7	S				Pennsylvania	Pennsylvania	Pennsylvania
90	20	20	Newport, Lewis H	Head	M	W	41	M23				Pennsylvania	Ger-German	Ger-German
91			Hattie M	Wife	F	W	41	M23	6	6		Pennsylvania	Ger-German	Pennsylvania
92			Edwin	Son	M	W	13	S				Pennsylvania	Pennsylvania	Pennsylvania
93			Cora A	Daughter	F	W	7	S				Pennsylvania	Pennsylvania	Pennsylvania
94			Leland O	Son	M	W	5/12	S				Pennsylvania	Pennsylvania	Pennsylvania
95			Lola E	Daughter	F	W	3/12	S				Pennsylvania	Pennsylvania	Pennsylvania

1910 FEDERAL CENSUS, WINFIELD TOWNSHIP, BUTLER COUNTY, PENNSYLVANIA

Gravatt, Martha Jane – Taken the year following Daniel's death, the 1910 Census indicates Martha Jane, now age 75, is still living in the family home she inherited from Daniel, since she is listed as the *"Head"* of the household. Interestingly, since her son Tom, age 39, is also apparently living in the same home, he also is listed as *"Head,"* undoubtedly since he now is the "bread-winner" of the family with a profession listed as *"carpenter."* His wife, Emma L. (?), age 39, is also listed with their children: Jesse H., 17; Lissa P., 15; Charles V., 12; James O., 7; and Marguerrie J., 7 months.

172

U OF THE CENSUS
ES: 1910—POPULATION

SUPERVISOR'S DISTRICT NO. _21_ SHEET NO. _1_ B
ENUMERATION DISTRICT No. _107_

WARD OF CITY

ON THE _16_ DAY OF _April_, 1910. _Edwin R. Feinley_, ENUMERATOR.

	Citizenship	Occupation			Education				

(Census population schedule — handwritten entries largely illegible; columns 15–32, lines 51–100. Occupations include "General farm," "Stone quarry," "Truck farm," "Carpenter," "House work," "Laborer," "None," etc.)

Right portion of document on facing page

173

STATE _Pennsylvania_

COUNTY _Butler_

9—387

DEPARTMENT OF COMMERCE—

FOURTEENTH CENSUS OF THE UNIT

TOWNSHIP OR OTHER DIVISION OF COUNTY _Winfield Twp. 1st Precinct_

NAME OF INCORPORA

NAME OF INSTITUTION ....

ENUM

	PLACE OF ABODE.			NAME	RELATION.	TENURE.	PERSONAL DESCRIPTION.					CITIZENSHIP.			EDUCATION.			Place of birth of each pers
1	2	3	4	5	6	7 8	9	10	11	12	13	14	15	16	17	18	19	PERSON / Place of birth.
51	✓			Mulcahy, Lillian	Wife			W	35	M					yes	yes	Pennsylvania
52	✓			— Edward	Son		M	W	14	S				yes	yes	yes	Pennsylvania
53	✓			— John	Son		M	W	12	S				yes	yes	yes	Pennsylvania
54	✓			Gravatt, Martha	Grandmoth		M	W	86	Wd					yes	yes	Pennsylvania
55	Fm	77	77	Heck, Philemon J.	Head	1 O Fr	M	W	62	M					yes	yes	Pennsylvania
56	✓			— Amanda J.	Wife		F	W	57	M					yes	yes	Pennsylvania
57	✓			— Vince	Daughter		F	W	37	S					yes	yes	Pennsylvania
58	✓			— Lillie	Daughter		F	W	32	S					yes	yes	Pennsylvania
59	✓			— Ada	Daughter		F	W	32	S					yes	yes	Pennsylvania
60	✓			— Martha	Daughter		F	W	14	S				yes	yes	yes	Pennsylvania
61	X	78	78	Pugh, George	Head	1 O Fr	M	W	62	M					yes	yes	Pennsylvania
62	✓			— Anna	Wife		F	W	52	M					yes	yes	Pennsylvania
63	✓			— Helen	Daughter		F	W	19	S					yes	yes	Pennsylvania
64	✓			— Myrtle	Daughter		F	W	17	S					yes	yes	Pennsylvania
65	Fm	79	79	Cooper, Nancy	Head	1 O H	F	W	59	Wd					yes	yes	Pennsylvania
66	✓			— Margaret	daughter		F	W	24	S					yes	yes	Pennsylvania
67	✓			Meeds, Paul	Grandson		M	W	16	S					yes	yes	Pennsylvania
68	Fm	80	80	Morris, George H.	Head	1 O Fr	M	W	38	M					yes	yes	Pennsylvania
69	✓			— Laura	Wife		F	W	36	M	1893		2 yr		yes	yes	Pennsylvania
70	✓			— John	Son		M	W	11	S				yes	yes	yes	Pennsylvania
71	✓			— Florence	Daughter		F	W	5½	S							Pennsylvania
72	Fm	81	81	Cooper, Isaac	Head	1 O H	M	W	64	Wd					yes	yes	Pennsylvania
73	✓			— Harry	Son		M	W	22	S					yes	yes	Pennsylvania
74	Fm	82	82	Flemming, Charles	Head	1 O Fr	M	W	68	M	1857				yes	yes	Pennsylvania
75	✓			— Mary	Wife		F	W	58	M	1857				yes	yes	Pennsylvania
76	✓			— Matilda	daughter		F	W	35	S					yes	yes	Pennsylvania
77	✓			— Emma	daughter		F	W	32	S					yes	yes	Pennsylvania
78	Fm	83	83	Lewis, William	Head	1 O Fr	M	W	77	M					yes	yes	Pennsylvania
79	✓			— Rebecca	Wife		F	W	70	M					yes	yes	Pennsylvania
80	Fm	84	84	Thompson, John	Head	1 O Fr	M	W	58	M					yes	yes	Pennsylvania
81	✓			— Hazel	Daughter		F	W	29	S					yes	yes	Pennsylvania
82	X	85	85	Keeller, Chester	Head	1 R	M	W	26	M					yes	yes	Pennsylvania
83	X	85	85	— Mary	Wife		F	W	21	M					yes	yes	Pennsylvania
84	✓			— Violet	Daughter		F	W	2½	S					yes	yes	Pennsylvania
85	✓			— Treeca	Daughter		F	W	½	S							Pennsylvania
86	X	86	86	Hildebrand, John	Head	1 R	M	W	69	M					yes	yes	Pennsylvania
87	✓			— Josephine	Wife		F	W	69	M					yes	yes	Pennsylvania
88	Fm	87	87	Cooper, James	Head	1 O Fr	M	W	34	M					yes	yes	Pennsylvania
89	✓			— Pearl	Wife		F	W	31	M					yes	yes	Pennsylvania
90	✓			— Charles	Son		M	W	9	S				yes	yes	yes	Pennsylvania
91	✓			— James	Son		M	W	5	S							Pennsylvania
92	✓			— Carrie	Daughter		F	W	2¾	S							Pennsylvania
93	✓			— May	Daughter		F	W	¾	S							Pennsylvania
94	Fm	88	88	Warnick, Albert	Head	1 O Fr	M	W	37	M					yes	yes	Pennsylvania
95	✓			— Margaret	Wife		F	W	32	M					yes	yes	Pennsylvania
96	✓			— Howard	Son		M	W	9	S				yes	yes	yes	Pennsylvania
97	✓			— Helen	Daughter		F	W	4½	S							Pennsylvania
98	Fm	89	89	Lewis, Robert	Head	1 R	M	W	34	M	R				yes	yes	Pennsylvania
99	✓			— Zelda	Wife		F	W	26	M					yes	yes	Pennsylvania
100	✓			— Violet J.	Daughter		F	W	5½	S					yes	yes	Pennsylvania

1920 FEDERAL CENSUS, WINFIELD TOWNSHIP, BUTLER COUNTY, PENNSYLVANIA

Gravatt, Martha Jane – It is unclear if, at this point, Martha Jane is still living in her and Daniel's home, but she quite likely is, though she is no longer listed as *"Head"* of the household. Now 86 years of age, Martha Jane no doubt is infirm and in need of daily help. She is listed as *"Grandmother,"* living with Lillian Mulcahy, age 35, and her children: Edward, age 14; and John, 12. The identity of this Lillian Mulcahy is unknown by this writer, as is the disposition of Martha Jane's son, Tom, and his family, who possibly no longer live in Winfield Township, since they do not appear in this page of the *1920 Census*.

BUREAU OF THE CENSUS   [D1—578]   SUPERVISOR'S DISTRICT No. 19   SHEET No. 4

'ED STATES: 1920—POPULATION   ENUMERATION DISTRICT No. 64   B

TED PLACE _____ [Insert proper name and, also, name of class, as city, village, town, or borough. See instructions.]   WARD OF CITY ____ 1151

HERATED BY ME ON THE 10.7.12 DAY OF January, 1920. James M. Cruckshank ENUMERATOR

	NATIVITY AND MOTHER TONGUE.				Whether able to speak English.	OCCUPATION.		Employee, salaried, or wage worker, or working on own account.	Number of farm schedule.	
	FATHER.		**MOTHER.**			Trade, profession, or particular kind of work done, as spinner, salesman, laborer, etc.	Industry, business, or establishment in which at work, as cotton mill, dry goods store, farm, etc.			
Mother tongue.	Place of birth.	Mother tongue.	Place of birth.	Mother tongue.						
20	21	22	23	24	25	26	27	28	29	
	Pennsylvania		Pennsylvania		yes	none				51
	Pennsylvania		Pennsylvania		yes	none				52
	Pennsylvania		Pennsylvania		yes	none				53
	Pennsylvania		Pennsylvania		yes	none				54
	Pennsylvania		Pennsylvania		yes	farmer	farm	OA	71	55 001
	Pennsylvania		Pennsylvania		yes	none				56
	Pennsylvania		Pennsylvania		yes	none				57
	Pennsylvania		Pennsylvania		yes	none				58
	Pennsylvania		Pennsylvania		yes	none				59
	Pennsylvania		Pennsylvania		yes	none				60
	Pennsylvania		Pennsylvania		yes	watchman	Stone Quarry	wg		61 80
	Pennsylvania		Pennsylvania		yes	none				62
	Pennsylvania		Pennsylvania		yes	none				63
	Pennsylvania		Pennsylvania		yes	none				64
	Pennsylvania		Pennsylvania		yes	farmer	farm	OA	72	65 00
	Pennsylvania		Pennsylvania		yes	none				66
	Pennsylvania		Pennsylvania		yes	none				67
	Pennsylvania		Pennsylvania		yes	farmer	in farm	OA	73	68 001
Germany	German	Pennsylvania		yes	none				69
	Pennsylvania		Pennsylvania		yes	none				70
	Pennsylvania		Pennsylvania		yes	none				71
	Pennsylvania		Pennsylvania		yes	farmer	farm	oa	74	72 001
	Pennsylvania		Pennsylvania		yes	none				73
Germany	German	Germany	German	yes	farmer	farm	oa	75	74 001
	Pennsylvania		Pennsylvania		yes	none				75
	Pennsylvania		Pennsylvania		yes	none				76
	Pennsylvania		Pennsylvania		yes	none				77
	Pennsylvania		Pennsylvania		yes	farmer	farm	oa	76	78 001
	Pennsylvania		Pennsylvania		yes	none				79
	Pennsylvania		Pennsylvania		yes	farmer	farm	oa	76	80 001
	Pennsylvania		Pennsylvania		yes	none				81
Germany	German	Pennsylvania		yes	toldresser	oil fields	wg		82 36
	Pennsylvania		Pennsylvania		yes	none				83
	Pennsylvania		Pennsylvania		yes	none				84
	Pennsylvania		Pennsylvania		yes	none				85
	Pennsylvania		Pennsylvania		yes	Logtrainer		wg		86 82
	Pennsylvania		Pennsylvania		yes	none				87
	Pennsylvania		Pennsylvania		yes	farmer	farm	oa		88 00
	Pennsylvania		Pennsylvania		yes	none				89
	Pennsylvania		Pennsylvania		yes	none				90
	Pennsylvania		Pennsylvania		yes	none				91
	Pennsylvania		Pennsylvania		yes	none				92
	Pennsylvania		Pennsylvania		yes	none				93
	Pennsylvania		Pennsylvania		yes	Boss	Stone Quarry	wg	79	94 076
	Pennsylvania		Pennsylvania		yes	none				95
	Pennsylvania		Pennsylvania		yes	none				96
	Pennsylvania		Pennsylvania		yes	none				97
	Pennsylvania		Pennsylvania		yes	laborer	Stone Quarry	wg	80	98 09c
	Pennsylvania		Pennsylvania		yes	none				99
	Pennsylvania		Pennsylvania		yes	none				100

Right portion of document on facing page

175

Form MAGO-41—200M—6-35 Commonwealth of Pennsylvania Department of Military Affairs	RECORD OF BURIAL PLACE OF VETERAN	Allegheny .... County

NAME Gravatt, Robert	DATE OF BIRTH	DATE OF DEATH

VETERAN OF Revolutionary WAR	SERVED IN ARMY (X) NAVY ( ) MARINE CORPS ( )

DATES OF SERVICE	ORGANIZATION(S)	RANK

CEMETERY OR PLACE OF INTERMENT	NAME Gravatt Cemetery, (Pvt.) LOCATION Brackenridge, Pa.

LOCATION OF GRAVE IN CEMETERY SECTION LOT No. RANGE GRAVE No.	HEADSTONE Small Stone GOVERNMENT ( ) COUNTY ( ) FAMILY ( )

INFORMATION GIVEN BY Co. Comm. 3/14/35 DATE	REMARKS

After being Recorded in the County Veterans' Grave Registration Record This card is to be sent to THE ADJUTANT GENERAL'S OFFICE, Harrisburg, Pennsylvania, for final Record.

1

1935 VETERAN'S GRAVE REGISTRATION, COMMONWEALTH OF PENNSYLVANIA

Gravatt, Robert – This official record was placed in the Pennsylvania Department of Military Affairs on March 14, 1935, to register the grave of Robert Gravatt as a U.S. Army veteran of the U.S. Revolutionary War. It notes the place of interment in *"Gravatt Cemetery (Pvt), Brackenridge, Allegheny County, Pennsylvania,"* and the fact that the grave is marked by a *"Small Stone."*

Form MAGO-41—200M—6-35 Commonwealth of Pennsylvania Department of Military Affairs	RECORD OF BURIAL PLACE OF VETERAN	Allegheny .... County

NAME Gravatt, Johnson (Son of Robert)	DATE OF BIRTH	DATE OF DEATH

VETERAN OF	Revolutionary WAR	SERVED IN ARMY (**X**) NAVY ( ) MARINE CORPS ( )

DATES OF SERVICE	ORGANIZATION(S)	RANK

CEMETERY OR PLACE OF INTERMENT	NAME Gravatt Cemetery, (Pvt.) LOCATION Brackenridge, Pa.

LOCATION OF GRAVE IN CEMETERY	HEADSTONE Shale Stone
SECTION LOT No. RANGE GRAVE No.	GOVERNMENT ( ) COUNTY ( ) FAMILY ( )
INFORMATION GIVEN BY Co. Comm. 3/14/35 DATE	REMARKS

After being Recorded in the County Veterans' Grave Registration Record This card is to be sent
to THE ADJUTANT GENERAL'S OFFICE, Harrisburg, Pennsylvania, for final Record.

1

1935 VETERAN'S GRAVE REGISTRATION, COMMONWEALTH OF PENNSYLVANIA

Gravatt, Johnson (son of Robert) – This official record was placed in the Pennsylvania Department of Military Affairs on March 14, 1935, to register the grave of Johnson Gravatt as a U.S. Army veteran of the U.S. Revolutionary War. It notes the place of interment in *"Gravatt Cemetery (Pvt), Brackenridge, Allegheny County, Pennsylvania,"* and the fact that the grave is marked by a *"shale stone."*

Form MAGO-41—200M—6-35 Commonwealth of Pennsylvania Department of Military Affairs	RECORD OF BURIAL PLACE OF VETERAN	Allegheny .... County

NAME Gravatt, John (Son of Johnson)	DATE OF BIRTH	DATE OF DEATH

VETERAN OF Indian WAR	SERVED IN ARMY (X) NAVY ( ) MARINE CORPS ( )

DATES OF SERVICE	ORGANIZATION(S)	RANK

CEMETERY OR PLACE OF INTERMENT	NAME Gravatt Cemetery, (Pvt.)
	LOCATION Brackenridge, Pa.

LOCATION OF GRAVE IN CEMETERY	HEADSTONE Small Stone
SECTION LOT No. RANGE GRAVE No.	GOVERNMENT ( ) COUNTY ( ) FAMILY ( )
INFORMATION GIVEN BY	REMARKS
DATE Co. Comm. 3/14/35	

After being Recorded in the County Veterans' Grave Registration Record This card is to be sent to THE ADJUTANT GENERAL'S OFFICE, Harrisburg, Pennsylvania, for final Record.

1935 VETERAN'S GRAVE REGISTRATION, COMMONWEALTH OF PENNSYLVANIA

Gravatt, John (son of Johnson) – This official record was placed in the Pennsylvania Department of Military Affairs on March 14, 1935, to register the grave of John Gravatt as a U.S. Army veteran of the Indian Wars. It also notes the place of his interment in *Gravatt Cemetery (Pvt)*, *Brackenridge, Allegheny County, Pennsylvania,* and the fact that the grave is marked by a *"small stone."*

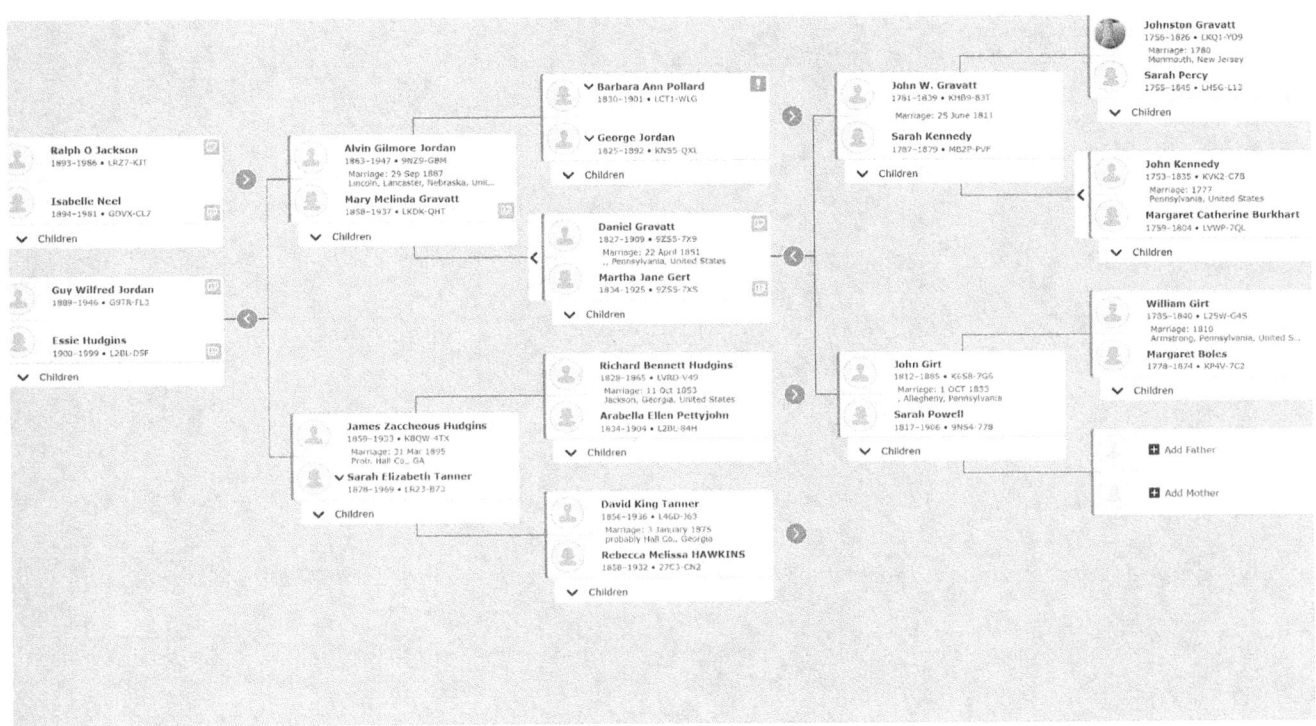

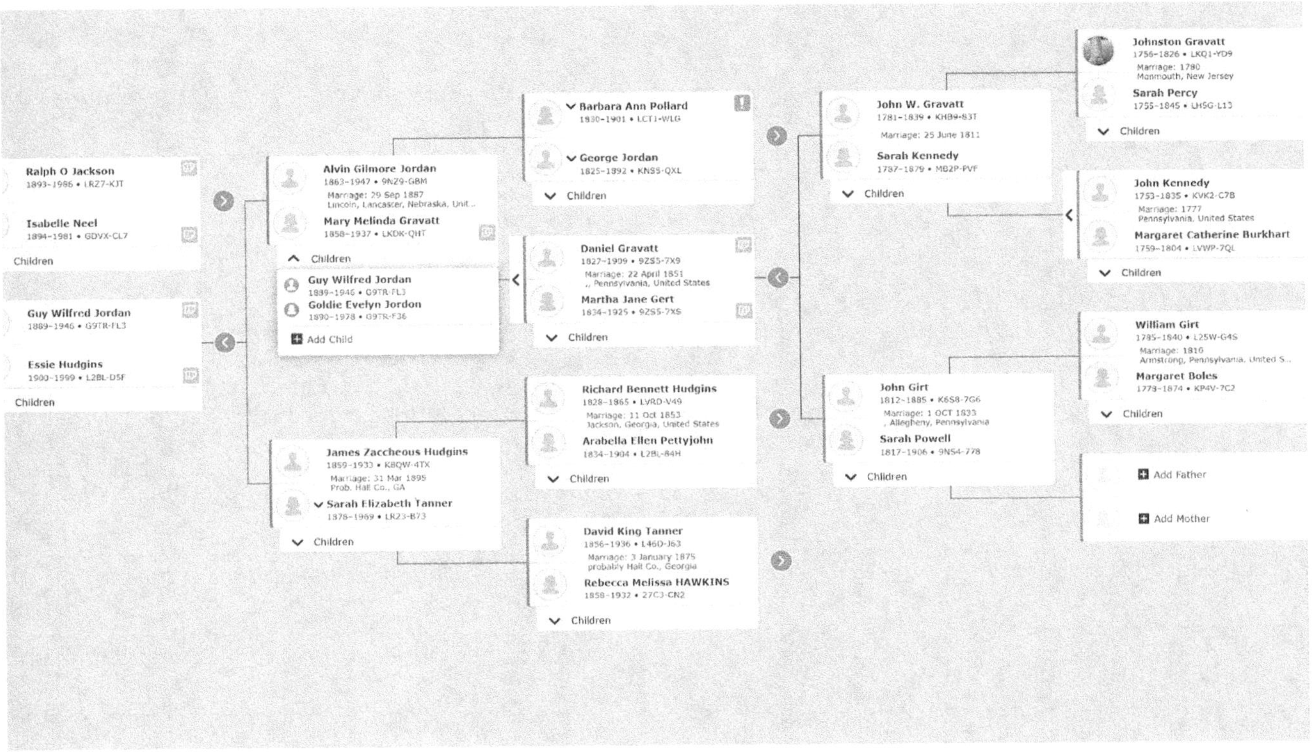

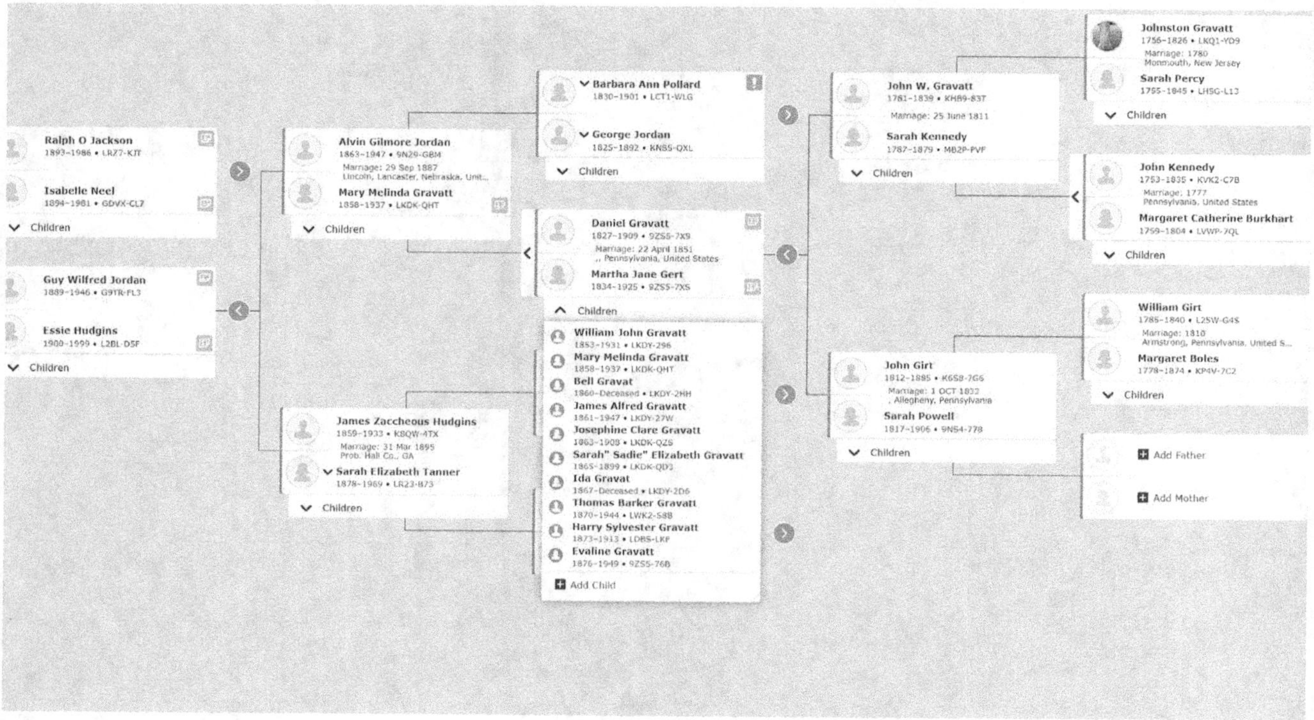

Ralph O Jackson
1893–1986 • LR27-KJT

Isabelle Neel
1894–1981 • GDVX-CL7
∨ Children

Guy Wilfred Jordan
1889–1946 • G9TR-FL3

Essie Hudgins
1900–1999 • L2BL-DSF
∨ Children

Alvin Gilmore Jordan
1863–1947 • 9N29-G8M
Marriage: 29 Sep 1887
Lincoln, Lancaster, Nebraska, Unit...

Mary Melinda Gravatt
1858–1937 • LKDK-QHT
∨ Children

James Zaccheous Hudgins
1859–1933 • K8QW-4TX
Marriage: 31 Mar 1895
Prob. Hall Co., GA
∨ Sarah Elizabeth Tanner
1878–1969 • LR23-B73
∨ Children

∨ Barbara Ann Pollard
1830–1901 • LCT1-WLG

∨ George Jordan
1825–1892 • KNS5-QXL
∨ Children

Daniel Gravatt
1827–1909 • 9ZS5-7X9
Marriage: 22 April 1851
,, Pennsylvania, United States

Martha Jane Gert
1834–1925 • 9ZS5-7X5
∧ Children

William John Gravatt
1852–1931 • LKDY-296
Mary Melinda Gravatt
1858–1937 • LKDK-QHT
Bell Gravat
1860–Deceased • LKDY-2HH
James Alfred Gravatt
1861–1947 • LKDY-27W
Josephine Clare Gravatt
1863–1909 • LKDK-QZ6
Sarah" Sadie" Elizabeth Gravatt
1865–1899 • LKDK-QD1
Ida Gravat
1867–Deceased • LKDY-2D6
Thomas Barker Gravatt
1870–1944 • LWK2-588
Harry Sylvester Gravatt
1873–1913 • LD8S-LKF
Evaline Gravatt
1876–1949 • 9ZS5-76B
➕ Add Child

John W. Gravatt
1781–1839 • KH89-83T
Marriage: 25 June 1811

Sarah Kennedy
1787–1879 • M82P-PVF
∨ Children

John Girt
1812–1895 • K6S8-7G6
Marriage: 1 OCT 1832
, Allegheny, Pennsylvania

Sarah Powell
1817–1906 • 9NS4-778
∨ Children

Johnston Gravatt
1756–1826 • LKQ1-YD9
Marriage: 1780
Monmouth, New Jersey

Sarah Percy
1755–1845 • LHSG-L13
∨ Children

John Kennedy
1753–1835 • KVK2-C7B
Marriage: 1777
Pennsylvania, United States

Margaret Catherine Burkhart
1759–1804 • LVWP-7QL
∨ Children

William Girt
1785–1840 • L2SW-G4S
Marriage: 1810
Armstrong, Pennsylvania, United S...

Margaret Boles
1778–1874 • KP4V-7C2
∨ Children

➕ Add Father

➕ Add Mother

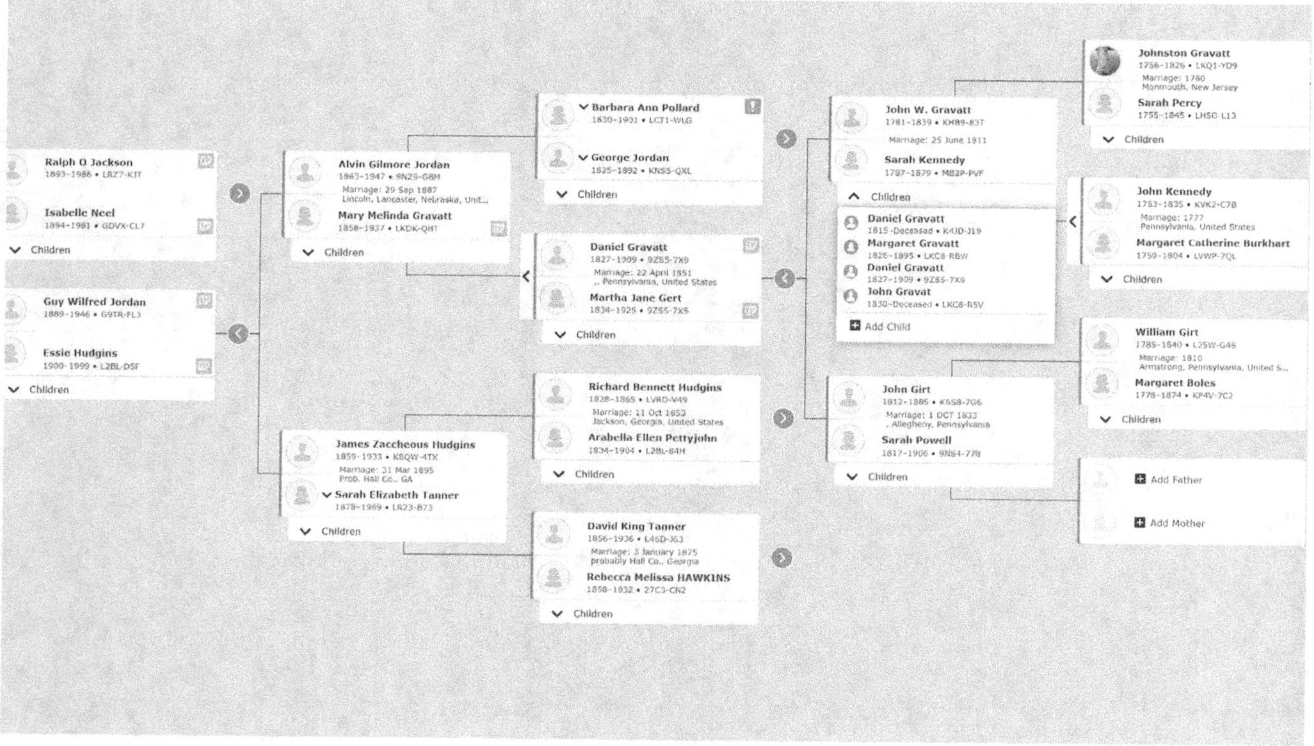

Ralph O Jackson
1893–1986 • LR27-KJT

Isabelle Neel
1894–1981 • GDVX-CL7
∨ Children

Guy Wilfred Jordan
1889–1946 • G9TR-FL3

Essie Hudgins
1900–1999 • L2BL-DSF
∨ Children

Alvin Gilmore Jordan
1863–1947 • 9N29-G8M
Marriage: 29 Sep 1887
Lincoln, Lancaster, Nebraska, Unit...

Mary Melinda Gravatt
1858–1937 • LKDK-QHT
∨ Children

James Zaccheous Hudgins
1859–1933 • K8QW-4TX
Marriage: 31 Mar 1895
Prob. Hall Co., GA
∨ Sarah Elizabeth Tanner
1878–1969 • LR23-B73
∨ Children

∨ Barbara Ann Pollard
1830–1901 • LCT1-WLG

∨ George Jordan
1825–1892 • KNS5-QXL
∨ Children

Daniel Gravatt
1827–1909 • 9ZS5-7X9
Marriage: 22 April 1851
,, Pennsylvania, United States

Martha Jane Gert
1834–1925 • 9ZS5-7X5
∨ Children

Richard Bennett Hudgins
1828–1865 • LVRD-V49
Marriage: 11 Oct 1852
Jackson, Georgia, United States

Arabella Ellen Pettyjohn
1834–1904 • L2BL-84H
∨ Children

David King Tanner
1856–1936 • L46D-363
Marriage: 3 January 1875
probably Hall Co., Georgia

Rebecca Melissa HAWKINS
1858–1932 • 27C3-CN2
∨ Children

John W. Gravatt
1781–1839 • KH89-83T
Marriage: 25 June 1811

Sarah Kennedy
1787–1879 • M82P-PVF
∧ Children

Daniel Gravatt
1815–Deceased • K4JD-J19
Margaret Gravatt
1826–1895 • LKC8-RBW
Daniel Gravatt
1827–1909 • 9ZS5-7X5
John Gravat
1830–Deceased • LXC8-R5V
➕ Add Child

John Girt
1812–1895 • K6S8-7G6
Marriage: 1 OCT 1832
, Allegheny, Pennsylvania

Sarah Powell
1817–1906 • 9NS4-778
∨ Children

Johnston Gravatt
1756–1826 • LKQ1-YD9
Marriage: 1780
Monmouth, New Jersey

Sarah Percy
1755–1845 • LHSG-L13
∨ Children

John Kennedy
1753–1835 • KVK2-C7B
Marriage: 1777
Pennsylvania, United States

Margaret Catherine Burkhart
1759–1804 • LVWP-7QL
∨ Children

William Girt
1785–1840 • L2SW-G4S
Marriage: 1810
Armstrong, Pennsylvania, United S...

Margaret Boles
1778–1874 • KP4V-7C2
∨ Children

➕ Add Father

➕ Add Mother

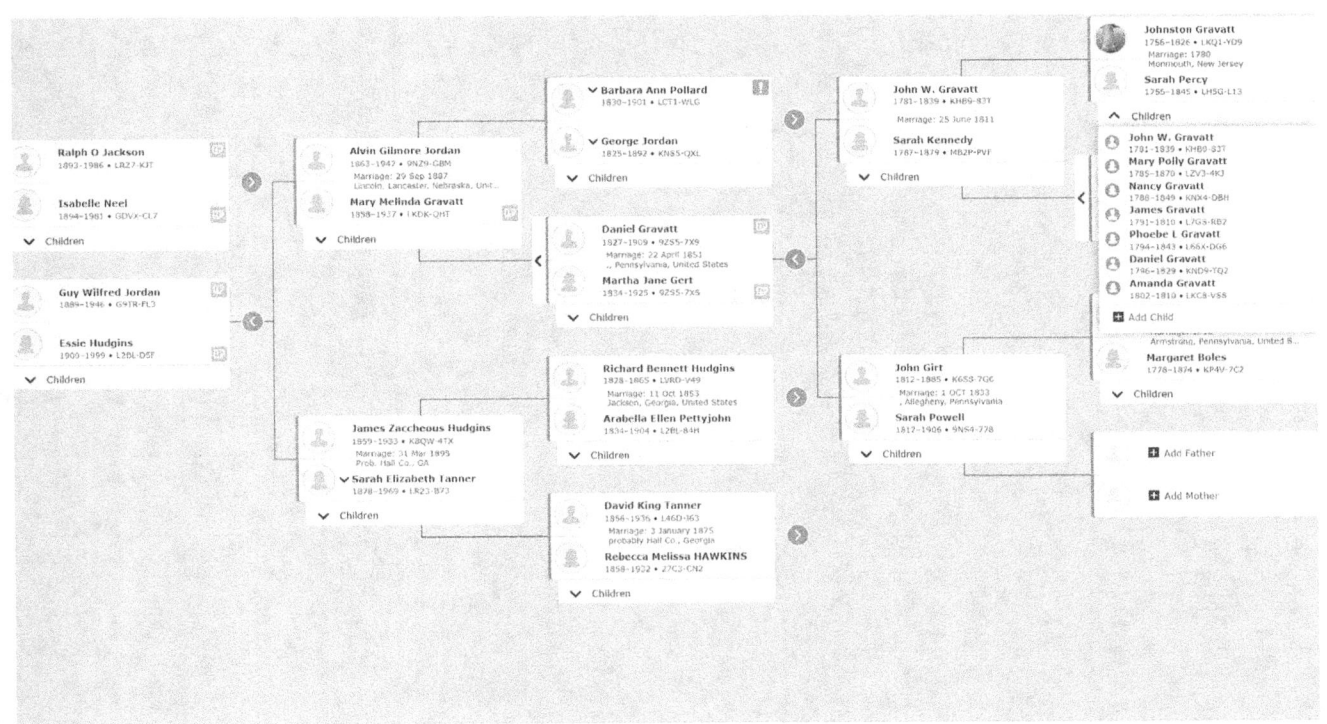

Top chart (upper section):

Ralph O Jackson
1893–1986 • LR27-KJT

Isabelle Neel
1894–1981 • GDVX-CL7

Children

Guy Wilfred Jordan
1889–1946 • G9TR-FL3

Essie Hudgins
1900–1999 • L2BL-D5F

Children

Alvin Gilmore Jordan
1863–1947 • 9NZ9-GBM
Marriage: 29 Sep 1887
Lincoln, Lancaster, Nebraska, Unit...

Mary Melinda Gravatt
1858–1937 • LKDK-QHT

Children

James Zaccheous Hudgins
1859–1933 • K8QW-4TX
Marriage: 31 Mar 1895
Prob. Hall Co., GA

Sarah Elizabeth Tanner
1878–1969 • LR23-BF3

Children

Barbara Ann Pollard
1830–1901 • LCT1-WLG

George Jordan
1825–1892 • KN85-QXL

Children

Daniel Gravatt
1827–1909 • 9ZS5-7X9
Marriage: 22 April 1851
.., Pennsylvania, United States

Martha Jane Gert
1834–1925 • 9ZS5-7XS

Children

Richard Bennett Hudgins
1828–1865 • LVRD-V49
Marriage: 11 Oct 1853
Jackson, Georgia, United States

Arabella Ellen Pettyjohn
1834–1904 • LZBL-84H

Children

David King Tanner
1856–1936 • L46D-963
Marriage: 3 January 1875
probably Hall Co., Georgia

Rebecca Melissa HAWKINS
1858–1922 • 27C3-CN2

Children

John W. Gravatt
1781–1839 • KHB9-93T
Marriage: 25 June 1811

Sarah Kennedy
1787–1879 • MB2P-PVF

Children

John Girt
1812–1885 • K6S3-7GC
1844 • , Allegheny, Pennsylvania

Sarah Powell
1812–1906 • 9NS4-778

Children

Johnston Gravatt
1756–1826 • LKQ1-YD9
Marriage: 1780
Monmouth, New Jersey

Sarah Percy
1755–1845 • LH5G-L13

Children

John W. Gravatt
1781–1839 • KHB9-93T

Mary Polly Gravatt
1785–1870 • LZV3-4KJ

Nancy Gravatt
1788–1849 • KNX4-QBH

James Gravatt
1791–1810 • L7GS-RB2

Phoebe L Gravatt
1794–1843 • L66X-DG6

Daniel Gravatt
1796–1829 • KND9-TQ2

Amanda Gravatt
1802–1810 • LKC8-VS8

Add Child

Armstrong, Pennsylvania, United S...

Margaret Boles
1778–1874 • KP4V-7C2

Children

Add Father

Add Mother

Bottom chart (lower section):

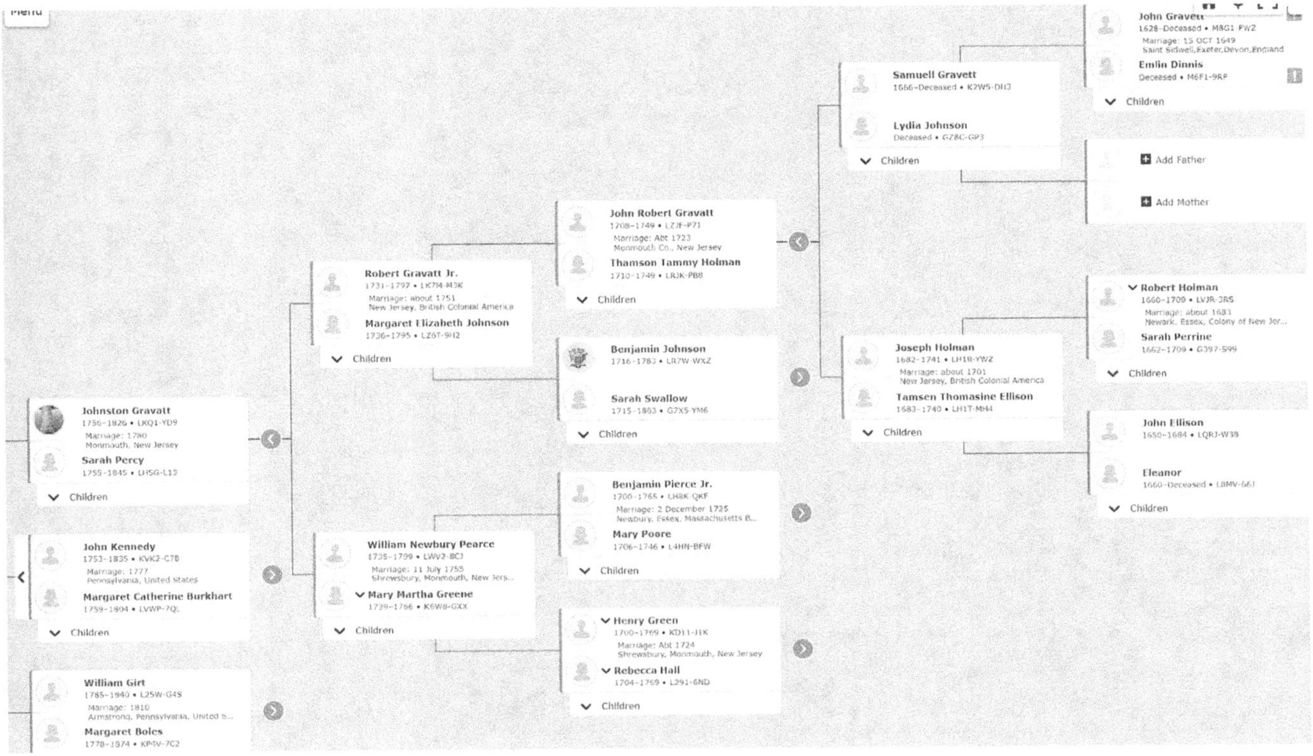

Menu

Johnston Gravatt
1756–1826 • LKQ1-YD9
Marriage: 1780
Monmouth, New Jersey

Sarah Percy
1755–1845 • LH5G-L13

Children

John Kennedy
1753–1835 • KVK3-C7B
Marriage: 1777
Pennsylvania, United States

Margaret Catherine Burkhart
1759–1904 • LVWP-7QL

Children

William Girt
1785–1940 • L2SW-G4S
Marriage: 1810
Armstrong, Pennsylvania, United S...

Margaret Boles
1778–1874 • KP4V-7C2

Robert Gravatt Jr.
1731–1797 • LK7M-M5K
Marriage: about 1751
New Jersey, British Colonial America

Margaret Elizabeth Johnson
1736–1795 • LZ9T-9H2

Children

William Newbury Pearce
1736–1799 • LWV2-BCJ
Marriage: 16 July 1755
Shrewsbury, Monmouth, New Jers...

Mary Martha Greene
1739–1766 • K6W8-GXX

Children

John Robert Gravatt
1708–1749 • LZ3F-P71
Marriage: Abt 1723
Monmouth Co., New Jersey

Thamson Tammy Holman
1710–1749 • LRJK-PB8

Children

Benjamin Johnson
1716–1783 • LR7W-WXZ

Sarah Swallow
1715–1863 • G7X5-YM6

Children

Benjamin Pierce Jr.
1700–1766 • LH8K-QKF
Marriage: 2 December 1725
Newbury, Essex, Massachusetts B...

Mary Poore
1706–1746 • L4HN-BFW

Children

Henry Green
1700–1769 • XD11-J1K
Marriage: Abt 1724
Shrewsbury, Monmouth, New Jersey

Rebecca Hall
1704–1769 • L291-6ND

Children

Samuell Gravatt
1666–Deceased • K9W5-DH3

Lydia Johnson
Deceased • GZ8C-GP3

Children

Joseph Holman
1682–1741 • LH3H-YWZ
Marriage: about 1701
New Jersey, British Colonial America

Tamsen Thomasine Ellison
1683–1740 • LH1T-MH4

Children

John Gravett
1628–Deceased • M8G1-FWZ
Marriage: 15 OCT 1649
Saint Sidwell, Exeter, Devon, England

Emlin Dinnis
Deceased • M6F1-9RF

Children

Add Father

Add Mother

Robert Holman
1660–1709 • LVJR-3RS
Newark, Essex, Colony of New Jor...

Sarah Perrine
1662–1709 • G397-599

Children

John Ellison
1650–1684 • LQR3-W39

Eleanor
1660–Deceased • L8MV-661

Children

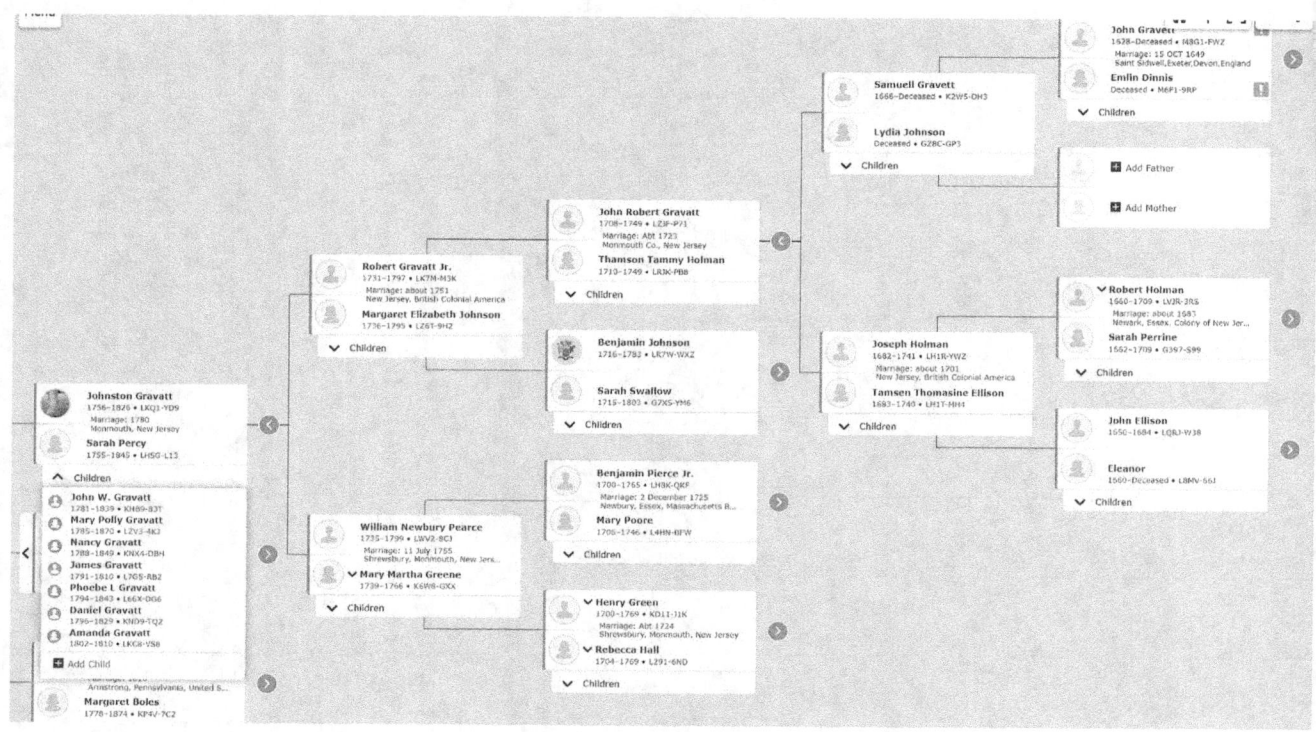

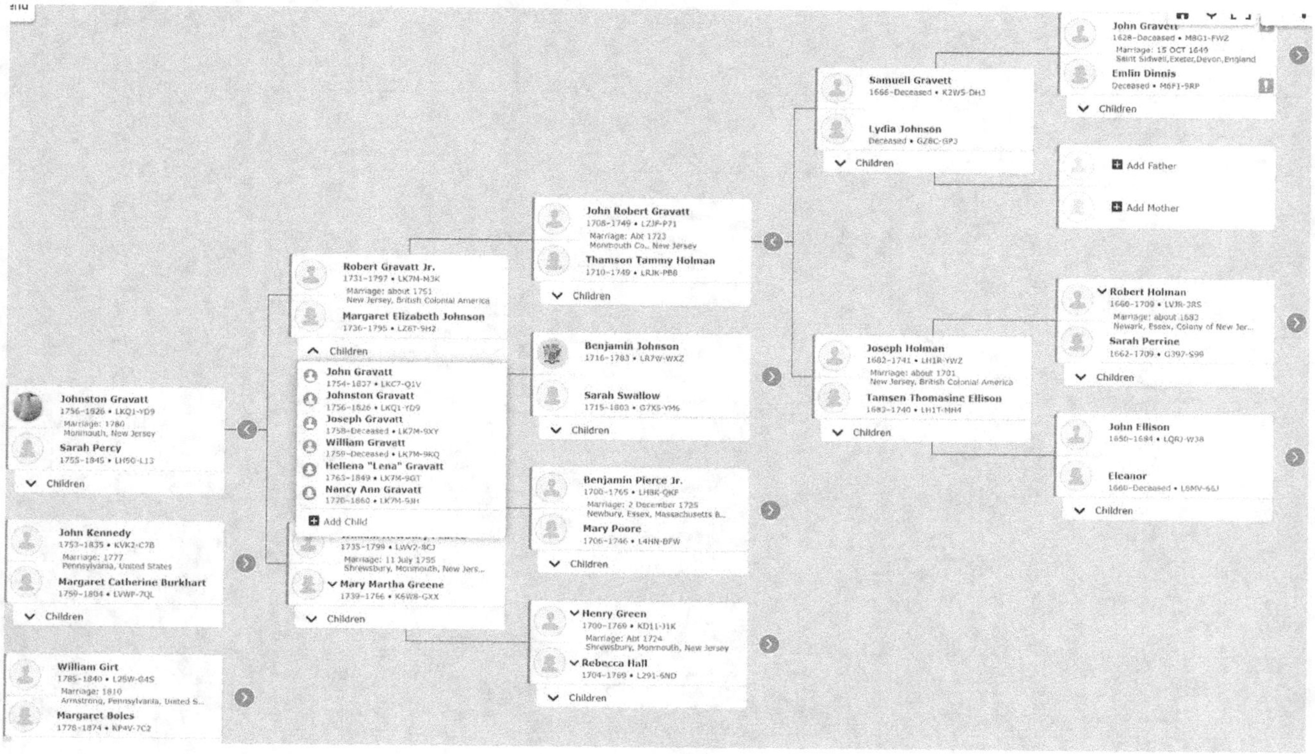

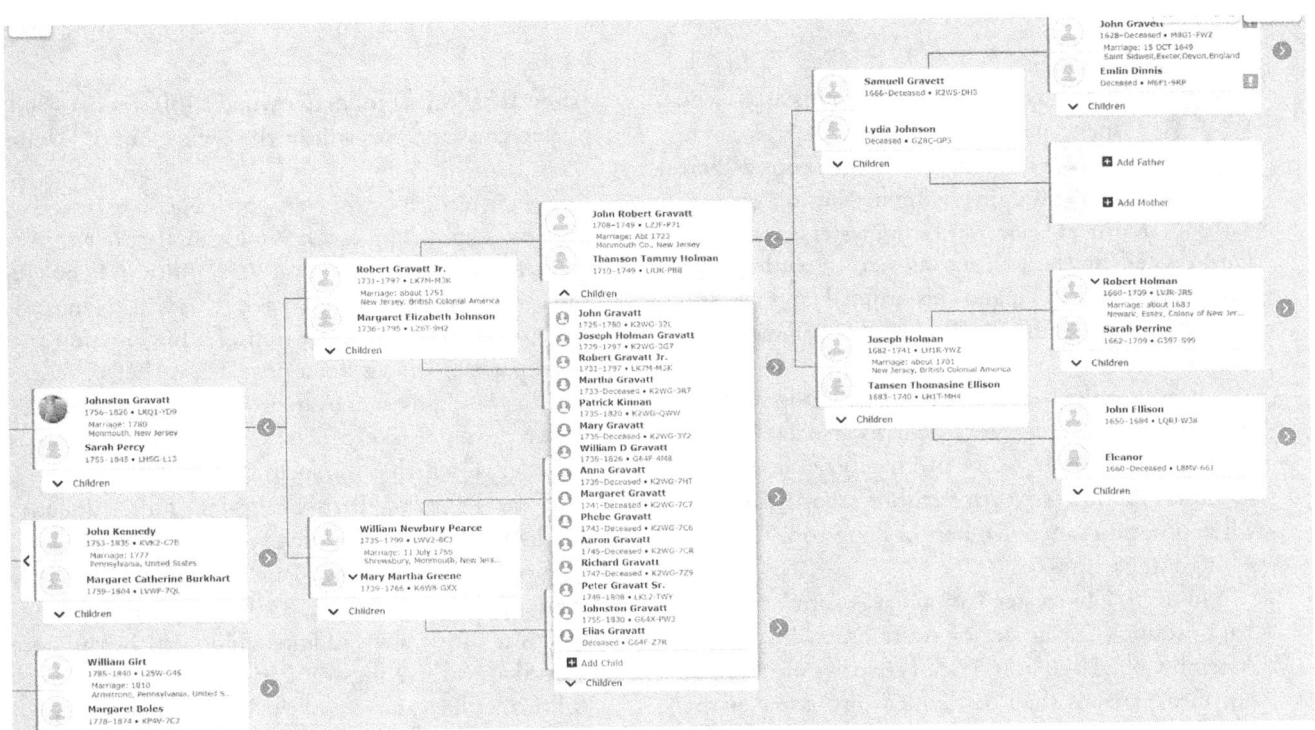

Family Tree of Gravatt Family, pages 179-183 – From the most recent to most historic.

The Hudgins Family
Of Jackson/Hall Counties

They were among the pioneers on this early dusty trail westward across Georgia from the eastern seaboard known as the Alabama Road. After reaching the northeastern vicinity of Cherokee Indian territory in what later became Jackson County, the Hudgins family put down roots which still exist today.

According to Dorothy Hudgins Shaw who spent many hours painstakingly researching the Hudgins family genealogy, there were Hudgins living in Virginia as early as 1642. Many of them were shipmasters. Grants of land owned by these Hudgins were recorded with deeds as early as 1634, and this original land was still owned by descendants of these hardy early settlers as recently as 1770.

It was only natural when the Hudgins family arrived in Virginia for them to associate themselves with a church. Some ultimately became active members of the Petsworth Parish Episcopal Church, while others became members of Kingston, Ware, or Abingdon Parishes.

In 1651 Gloucester County was formed out of York County. By an act of court order, the Grand Assembly of March 6, 1655, "all counties not yet laid out into parishes shall be divided into parishes the next county court." *(Hening, Statutes at Large, Volume 1, page 400).* The Church of England was the only church allowed in the new colony of Virginia, and it and its branches became the governing body in these early communities.

Petsworth Parish was west of Ware which was north of Abingdon Parish. Kingston Parish covered all the section east of North River. The first mention of Kingston Parish is found in the *Vestry Book*, dated November 15, 1679. At this time, the worship house was called North River Chapel. The land between North River and Blackwater Creek is still called Chapel Neck. This is the same area where records show that "John Hodden" owned 1,100 acres in 1643. Later, this land was still in the ownership of a John "Hudgins."

Few records of the Petsworth Parish exist today, but by some chance, the Kingston Parish Register survived the destruction of wars, time, and the elements, and is still preserved as of this writing in readable form (with the exception of a few missing and torn pages). In this document, the earlier instances of the Hudgins name are recorded as "Hudgen." Later, the name is recorded as "Hudgin," then later as "Hudgins," which is the spelling used today.

The Kingston Parish Register (KPR) includes births and baptisms for each year 1755 through 1777. The year 1778 is missing. Pages 167-170 (1779-1783) were recorded. After 1783 (and the Revolutionary War), very few Hudgins (Hudgen) births were recorded by the Kingston Parish. It is believed that, following the war, most of the Hudgins became associated with other churches, because they could then worship openly in any church of their choosing.

The Baptist faith, aided by the persistent ministrations of Robert Hudgins, had been brought to Gloucester County, Virginia, in 1775 by Iverson Lewis, pastor of Excel Church in King and Queen County. Robert had heard Elder Lewis preach, and had invited him to his home to preach to his family and friends. They had not been allowed to build a Baptist church prior to the conclusion of the Revolutionary War, because the Church of England was the only church allowed to exist in the colonies up to that point.

By 1790, the Baptists, led then by Robert Hudgins, had a sizeable congregation. After he was baptized, Hudgins was named their pastor. They then built a small church. They called it Petsworth Baptist Church. (This church was not in any way connected with Petsworth Parish.) Robert Hudgins led this church as pastor until his death in 1791. This church, built near Wolfe's Corner (present-day Meeting House Corner) is no longer standing.

In 1791, Kingston Parish was cut off to form Mathews County (*Colonial Churches of Tidewater Virginia by George Carrington Mason*). Some of the Hudgins descendants still live in Mathews County today. One small village in this county has a Baptist Church – Mathews Baptist – which was founded in 1777, shortly after the American Revolution. At that time, many Hudgins were active in this church, and their descendants continue to be active today. This little town is still known today as "Hudgins," Virginia (located at the intersection of VA 198 & VA 223).

Mathews Baptist was originally known as Kingston Church, and remained so until 1791, when the name was changed to Mathews Baptist. In 1905, the church was remodeled, leaving the balcony across the back.

Records of the church were not kept in the early years, but in 1790, it was recorded that Hugh Hudgins (probably a deacon) was ordered to cite two women – Mary Longest and Sister Westcombe – to appear before the church and account for their conduct in the practice of free communion. Also in 1833, it was recorded that Deacon Thomas Hudgins attended an Association meeting in Williamsburg.

In later years, Mathews Baptist was remodeled again and enlarged by adding a wing on both sides, as well as a new pastorium. Many Hudgins families still worship at this lovely church today in Hudgins, Virginia.

The early branch of the Hudgins family in Virginia from which the Hudgins in Hall County, Georgia, are derived today are descended as follows: John Hudgen, who married in Kingston Parish, Virginia, Mary Carney on 25 December, 1774; James Beverly (a.k.a. Bevely) Hudgen (b. 14 September, 1777) who married in North Carolina to Jane Bell; Zacharia (a.k.a. "Zacheus," "Zachus," and "Zaccharia") Hudgins (b. 1804 in Hall County, GA) who married Margaret (Peggy) Major (a.k.a. "Majors"); Richard Bennett Hudgins (b. 1831, Hall County, GA, d. January 4, 1865, during service in the Confederate Army, in Raleigh, North Carolina) who married Arabella Pettyjohn; and James Zacheus Hudgins who, in Hall County, Georgia, married first, Elizabeth Harris in 1882, and second, Sarah ("Sallie") Elizabeth Tanner in 1895.

James Beverly (Bevely) Hudgen (Hudgins) received land from his father-in-law, Francis Bell, in Hall County, Georgia, in the days when that area was still a pioneer country with most land still in possession of the native Cherokee Indians. James reportedly built a five-room log house there near a tiny settlement called "Macedonia." He is listed in the 1820 Hall County Census as "Beverly Hudgeons."

The settlement of James Beverly Hudgins' estate is listed in the Hall County Ordinary's office. James' sons, Zacharia (a.k.a. "Zacheus," etc.) and Holder, were administrators. In his will, James' farm was passed on to his wife, Jane Bell.

Upon Jane's death, the farm was passed to James' and Jane's son, Francis Bell Hudgins. Upon Francis' death, the farm was passed on to Francis' son, Jim. The property eventually came into the possession of a Mr. J.J. Lott, and was the site of frequent Hudgins family reunions over the ensuing years. It is not known who owns this property today.

The graves of James Bevely Hudgen (a.k.a. "Beverly Hudgins") and Jane Bell Hudgen (a.k.a. "Hudgins") can still be viewed today in Hall County near Chestnut Mountain. This small graveyard may have been no more than a family grave plot, since there are few, if any, other graves in the vicinity of these two Hudgen (Hudgins) graves. *(Note: To reach James Bevely Hudgins' grave today, travel to GA 53 South from Gainesville, past Lanier Raceway/Road Atlanta, to Macedonia Church (on left). Turn left just beyond this church onto J.J. Lott Road. Follow this road until it dead-ends into another road and then turn left again. The cemetery will be on the right just a short distance away. Be aware that the cemetery often is concealed from visibility by thick vegetation.)*

Zacharia (a.k.a. "Zacheus," "Zachus," and "Zaccharia") married Margaret "Peggy" Majors on 16 March, 1825, in Hall County, GA. They had ten children. Records on Zacharia are sketchy. He died 9 November, 1879, in Hall County, GA.

Richard Bennett Hudgins was 29 years of age when, on August 27, 1861, he departed to serve in the Confederate Army during the U.S. Civil War. He left behind his wife, Arabella Pettyjohn, two daughters – Mary and Margaret – and a young son, James Zacheus Hudgins. While still in service in the Confederate Army, Richard died in a Raleigh, North Carolina field hospital, after falling ill with pneumonia during the terrible winter of 1864. He passed away on January 3, 1865, and was buried January 4, 1865, in Raleigh's Oakwood Cemetery (Grave #356).

Family tradition maintains that Arabella, who had very straight black hair and other prominent Native American features, was possibly part Cherokee Indian, but no actual Native American blood connection has been establish for her. She was left destitute with three small children – Mary (1854-1885), Margaret Emmaline (1856-1934), and James Zacheus (1859-1933). Neither Margaret Emmaline nor James Zacheus (or "Jim-Zach" as he would later be known) would have any memory of their father, Richard Bennett.

After the war, Confederate money of course was worthless and anything worth owning had been pilfered or destroyed by marauding troops and other outlaws. Just as were most Southerners at that time, the Hudgins family was destitute. However, just as daylight follows darkness, "spring" soon followed the awful winter, and the family cow dropped a calf and the sow had a litter of pigs. The garden was planted from seeds hoarded from the previous year and there, thankfully, was enough to eat – at least for the time being.

Arabella had lost not only her husband, but also two brothers to the terrible war. It was not easy to carry on, but carry on she did. One way or another, just like the mythical "Scarlett" in **Gone With The Wind**, she was determined for her family to survive.

In 1872, Mary married, and in 1876, so also did Margaret. By 1880, Arabella was 46 years of age, and James Zacheus was the only child left at home. At that time, he was 20 years of age, and would soon be leaving the nest himself.

In 1882, James married Elizabeth Harris. From this union came five children. The first child was named Richard, in honor of his grandfather. A second son was named after his mother's father – Silas. The following two children – a boy and a girl – died in childhood. A fifth child, Lucy May, was the only female to survive.

The mother of these children – Elizabeth – died before Lucy was two years of age. The cause of her death is unknown today. Arabella, the grandmother, though feeling her years, took James' family in and did the best she could to take care of them for several years.

By the time the children were ages five, eight and ten, James knew they needed a full-time mother. After all, Arabella was 66 years old by that point and needed to slow down.

James had noticed a pretty young girl who lived nearby at Chestnut Mountain. She wasn't only pretty, she could sew expertly and cook the best biscuits James had ever tasted. Despite her beauty, she was a tom-boy of sorts, and even had her own beautiful black horse (a gift from her grandfather), but she loved children too, and this was of obvious importance to James. Her name was Sarah "Sallie" Elizabeth Tanner.

James, for his day and time, was moderately successful, and therefore of obvious interest to eligible ladies. He owned a small mercantile business and was respected by his peers. He also had a good reputation as a family man and provider for his family, and was active as well in his church. These qualities no doubt earned him high marks in the eyes of David Tanner, Sarah's father.

James ultimately popped the question to the vivacious 16-year-old beauty, and, after her father, Mr. Tanner, had agreed to the union, Sallie responded with a resounding "Yes!" After her acceptance of his proposal, James went shopping and bought the prettiest dress he could find for his new bride. The photograph of the two taken on their wedding day was made without Arabella, but did include James' three small children.

The marriage took place on March 31, 1895. Interestingly, there was no honeymoon after this marriage. There was no new home, nor even new furniture. James was a straight-forward practical man, and, being extremely frugal-minded, took his wife home to live in his mother's abode with his three children until he could provide them with a home of their own. And from the day she was married until the day he passed away, Sallie always referred to him as "Mr. Hudgins," and never as "James."

Both Sallie and James were devout Christians, and believed that the Bible meant that a wife submits herself to her husband, and if God meant for her to bear children, then she would have children. Sallie did not disappoint her husband either, and they were fruitful and multiplied.

While living in the house with Arabella, Sallie longed to have her own home. She wanted a kitchen that was hers and hers alone, so that she could bake good things without an "eye" looking over her shoulder. And if by chance her kitchen preparations didn't turn out right, she wouldn't then have to be concerned about any critical remarks either from the mother-in-law.

Interestingly, once while Arabella was napping, Sallie baked a cake and, for reasons unknown today, the cake didn't rise as it was supposed to. Sallie was so upset that she slipped out of the house and fed the cake to the hog. Arabella never knew of this little mishap, and Sallie never revealed it to anyone until many years later.

Sallie and James' first child was born one year and four months after the wedding. It was a beautiful baby girl. James thought she was the prettiest little girl he had ever seen, and he and Sallie named her "Daisy."

Two more children were born in quick succession while the family lived in Arabella's home: A son, Carl, and a daughter, **Essie**, were their names. Arabella's home was a log structure which once stood not far from the former community of Sugar Hill which once existed on the old Gainesville/Athens Highway

(formerly U.S. 129, but today called "Old Gainesville Highway," and officially re-identified as "GA 332" between Talmo and Pendergrass).

By this time, James could see that it was time to build a larger house to accommodate his growing family. He had purchased 181 acres of land in lower Hall County (still in the vicinity of Sugar Hill) from the estate of **George Washington Tanner** – Sallie's grandfather. On this property, an original log home, tenant houses, a gristmill, and a nicer home into which James temporarily moved his family, already existed. This temporary home had a large front porch with a separate room built at one end of the porch. This room was a tradition during the late 19th and early 20th centuries in the South. It was designed exclusively for traveling salesmen and itinerant preachers ("circuit riders").

This temporary home also had a large hall ("dogtrot") in the center of the house which led from the front porch to the rear porch. There in the rear, a large kitchen existed at the end of the porch. The kitchen had a huge fireplace and hearth with an oven built into one side. This fireplace was capable of burning very large logs, and this kitchen was where the cooking – as well as the eating – took place.

The remainder of this home was composed of two rooms. One large room was used for family gatherings, and it included a large fireplace for warmth in the winter. It also had two beds for sleeping. The other room was also for sleeping.

By 1900, James had completed the construction of a large house up on the main road *(originally identified as U.S. 129, but today called "Old Gainesville Highway," and officially re-identified as "GA 332" between Talmo and Pendergrass)*, still in the vicinity of Sugar Hill and his mother's home. At the same time that he was building this new home, he was also building a new store nearer to the main Gainesville to Athens road. This mercantile business carried most of the things needed by country residents of that day.

Inside the Hudgins store were oil for lamps, flour and meal for those who failed to visit the local miller, sugar, crackers, candy, bananas, cheese, nails, tacks, leather for new soles for worn-out shoes – and if the customer didn't have money, he or she could trade eggs, hens or fryers for what they needed. If they didn't have anything to trade, James, who was generous to a fault, would allow these individuals to charge their purchases until harvest time.

And if the harvest failed, James would even allow his customers to carry their debt over until the next harvest. Family records clearly demonstrated that some individuals never paid off their debts to James, but he would hardly ever mention these debts, preferring instead to be charitable. This very Christian-like trait endeared James to his neighbors, but it would later come back to haunt his family following James's death.

Hudgins Store in short order became the hub of life in the community of Sugar Hill. In the early 1900s, the U.S. mail was delivered there by a carrier riding on horseback. James' daughter, Daisy, would always run to the store when the mailman was arriving.

The mailman carried two steer horns and a gun along with his pouch of mail. After all, that was only 45 or 50 years after the War Between the States, and rural Georgia was still unpredictable and unsettled for the most part. One of the mailman's horns held gunpowder for his gun, and the other was used both to summon help (should he encounter an emergency situation) and to announce his imminent arrival in a community as he neared the outskirts of a town.

On one memorable occasion, the mounted mailman sounded his approach to the Hudgins' Sugar Hill home, and Daisy ran out to meet him. He handed her his powder horn and told her he would not need it anymore. It was his last mail run. "Rural Free Delivery" was scheduled to begin the following day, and the aged man was retiring. In 1990, Daisy Hudgins Giles gave that powder horn to her nephew, Richard Shaw (namesake of Richard Bennett Hudgins), to preserve and pass along to future generations.

The Sugar Hill home is where James' children by Elizabeth Harris – Richard Braselton, Silas and Lucy – grew up and left the fold. Lucy surprised the family by getting married July 25, 1908, to Az McNeal at the Hopewell Church Celebration on Candler Road in Hall County. Richard Braselton entered service in the U.S. Army and died from pneumonia on an Army base in California on January 12, 1919. He is buried at Concord Baptist Church Cemetery in Clermont, Hall County, GA. Interestingly, his grandfather (and namesake) – Richard Bennett Hudgins – also died of pneumonia, also while serving in the army – the Confederate States of America army – as described earlier in this article. Silas Arthur Hudgins was married to Mamie Major.

The new Sugar Hill home was also where most of the rest of James's and Sallie's children were born. A fourth child, David, was born soon after moving into the home. Then came Clyde, then Mary Lou. Soon, another baby was on the way. She was named Cora. Then came Ralph, Albert and Raleigh.

Before Sallie gave birth to Raleigh at Sugar Hill, she decided she would not have any more children. She felt ten children was a good number to "stop" on. However, shortly thereafter, Sallie became gravely ill with what ultimately was diagnosed as appendicitis. After being rushed to Downey Hospital in Gainesville, she was told that surgery was urgently required – immediately.

Following the removal of a ruptured appendix – an extremely serious condition – a tube was placed in Sallie's side for the drainage of fluid. In that day and age, most individuals would have died from such an illness. Sallie, however, later explained that she had prayed to the Almighty. It turned out to be a very poignant prayer. She revealed she had told God that if he would spare her life, she would never again complain about having children, and that she would have and love all the children he chose to allow her to conceive. The Almighty answered her prayer, and Sallie made good on her promise as well.

On June 19, 1904, Arabella Pettyjohn Hudgins, James's mother, finally passed away. She had endured an arduous life, and was not always pleasant to James' children during her later years, but by the same token, her life had never been easy. She was buried in Harmony Hall Baptist Church Cemetery in Hall County. *(Note: To reach Harmony Hall Baptist Church, take U.S. 129 east and turn left onto Blackstock Road in Hall County, then bear left onto Mangum Mill Road. Harmony Hall Baptist Church is on the left.)* Interestingly, Elizabeth Clementine Harris Hudgins (James'

1876 HOPEWELL BAPTIST CHURCH CEMETERY, HALL COUNTY, GAINESVILLE, GA

<u>Hudgins, Margaret "Peggy" Majors</u> – Pictured is Margaret's grave. She was Zacharia (a.k.a. "Zacheus" Hudgins' first wife and the mother of Margaret Marthena (1822-1912); Richard Bennett (1828-1865); Mary Jane (1834-1902); Esther L. (b. 1835); Nancy Evaline (b. 1837); Cindarella R. (1840-1910); Cleo E. (b. 1842); J.W. (b. 1844); Rebecca Emaline (1845-1927); and James Andrew Jackson (1847-1922).

first wife) and two of her children are also buried near to Arabella.

As the children matured, James Z. and Sallie had come to the realization that they needed to make yet another move – one of the most important moves of their lives. James was a strong advocate of a good education, and wanted his children to have the best education reasonably available to them.

By this point, Daisy and Carl were already enrolled at Chattahoochee High School in Clermont, Georgia, and the other children would shortly need higher education as well. James decided that instead of sending his entire brood away to the Clermont boarding school, he would simply move to that community so that the children could live at home and he could be more involved in their educations.

In order to accomplish this, James first rented a house near Clermont at Wauka Mountain. In the spring of 1913, he began moving his family and all their possessions to this new north Hall homestead. Some of the family rode in a wagon and some in a buggy. Others took turns walking and leading the milk cow.

Help was needed to move the furniture. It was a 25-mile trip from Sugar Hill to Clermont. Sallie had a small baby in her arms and luckily was not yet pregnant again. The trip started at first light and ended at sundown. The children of modern America have no idea of the many times difficult trials were endured by the children of pioneer America.

The Hudgins family had no sooner settled in their new home at Wauka Mountain before James got busy planning for the construction of a new home in downtown Clermont. It was to be the best and prettiest home he could build, and, as things turned out, he was successful. This lovely home – as of this writing in the year 2023 – still stands in Clermont on King Street.

This fifth house into which James moved his family was built with a large hall down the middle. It had a parlor (for receiving guests), six bedrooms, a large kitchen, and a dining room with a large table in order to accommodate the entire family for meals.

At the same time that he began building this new home, James set about also building a new store. It was located on Main Street just down the street from the hotel in Clermont, less than two blocks from the family home – and very near to the railroad tracks – for easy access to supplies and wares.

This new store carried all the same supplies that the store in Sugar Hill had carried, and some additional wares as well. The Gainesville and Northwestern Railroad had recently been completed to Robertstown in northeast Georgia where the huge supplies of virgin timber were being harvested. The tracks of this railroad passed directly through Clermont to the rear of James' new store. James also owned a warehouse near the railroad where additional supplies were stored.

Most of James' merchandise came by rail, but much of it also was supplied by mountaineers traveling through Clermont on their way to Gainesville where they annually sold the products they had grown and raised. James acquired many of their unique products seasonally each year to sell to the public. These included apples, sorghum, honey, chestnuts, turkeys, hogs, chickens, and many other unique mountain products. Most of these hardy mountain travelers simply camped out overnight in their mule- or ox-drawn wagons, but a privileged few were able to spend the night in the big hotel in Clermont.

After the big house on King Street was completed, the family was able to move in before the arrival of the eleventh child – Sarah – who was born 1914. Two more daughters were born in this home

1913 HUDGINS HOME IN CLERMONT, GA
Essie Carroll Hudgins (Jordan) – Only a very young adult at this point in her long life (she lived to be one month short of 99 years of age), the dynamo who later came to be known as "Miss Essie" in Rockmart (Polk), Georgia, sits (far right) with two of her sisters at the family's new home built by James Zacheus Hudgins in Clermont, Hall County, Georgia. This beautiful and somewhat historic home still stands (as of this writing in 2023) on King Street in Clermont.

in Clermont – Dorothy and Marjorie – bringing the family total to 13 children.

Two additional children were born, but did not survive birth. They were buried in the Concord Baptist Church Cemetery in Clermont where both James and Sallie would one day be laid to rest. Sallie, who was 43 by this time, was a strong lady, but time and nature were not on her side. From that point forward, she was never again able to conceive a child.

Remarkably, all 13 children were graduated from Chattahoochee High School which had become a respected Baptist-affiliated school in Clermont. Some of the children attended college as well, and some were graduated from college. In the early 1900s, this not only was a tremendously admirable achievement, it was a remarkable one as well. Of James' and Sallie's children, seven taught school at one time or another, and three retired as school teachers.

James and Sallie continued to prosper in the growing community of Clermont. New buildings had been added to the town to supplement the large hotel on the square. The Gainesville and Northwestern Railroad brought additional commerce to the community. Life was peaceful and harmonious for the Hudgins family.

Sallie was a good mother and a good doctor to her children. They all eventually fell victim to – and survived – chicken pox, measles, mumps, and a variety of other childhood sicknesses. Interestingly, not one of the children ever had pneumonia or extremely serious illnesses.

In September of 2000, Dorothy, the next to last child born to James and Sallie, remembered that on one occasion, a Dr. Homer Lancaster in Clermont had two little girls, one of whom – Martha – had fallen ill with an extremely high fever. The doctor had applied all his medical knowledge and expertise in an attempt to break the little girl's fever but she showed no improvement whatsoever.

"Dr. Lancaster, who was related to Mother, looked on her as a second mother to his children," Dorothy explained. "He came to her with tears in his eyes and asked her if she knew anything else to do to cure his precious daughter, because he had done all he could."

1914 CHATTAHOOCHEE HIGH SCHOOL – This rare photograph shows an early education center in northeast Georgia's Hall County. It once stood across the highway from Concord Baptist Church in Clermont. It was this school which, more than anything else, caused James Zacheus Hudgins to uproot his family and business in Sugar Hill, Georgia, and relocate to Clermont in north Hall County in 1913.

It is not known today what instructions Sallie gave the good doctor, but it is known that the following morning, Dr. Lancaster was at Sallie's door with a big smile on his face. The little girl's fever had finally broken during the night, and she was steadily improving.

Life in Clermont was idyllic not only for Mr. and Mrs. Hudgins, but for the children as well. A few years prior to her death in 1999 at the age of 98, daughter Essie remembered that "Father had a soda fountain in the store and made carbonated drinks for customers. My favorite was called 'peach phosphate,'" she recalled in delicious remembrance.

"I loved to play tennis on the hard clay courts behind the Miller's (Clermont) hotel," Essie added. "Jean Rogers and I used to play together in our middy blouses and box-pleated knee skirts. She later married my older brother, Carl, and the wedding was held in the hotel."

Dorothy, Essie's younger sister, was friends with Jean's younger sister, Frances. Prior to her death, she also described many happy memories of Clermont at the tennis courts behind the hotel, a duck pond, and a see-saw behind the hotel where the girls played as children. She also described many nights in the hotel with her childhood friend, and remembered crying her heart out when the Rogers family moved to Gainesville in the early 1920s.

Dorothy also remembered that when she walked from the Hudgins home on King Street, she had to cross the railroad tracks to get to her father's store. She was deathly afraid of the trains when she was five or six years old, but later, she says she enjoyed buying a ticket and riding the train to Gainesville to visit her friend Frances.

Trains weren't the only frightful experience for the Hudgins family in Clermont. They had only been living in their new home on King Street for approximately a year when a "cyclone" (actually a tornado) roared through the community causing damage. The front porch was blown off the hotel, but luckily the now-historic structure suffered little other damage that day. Other structures in town, however, were not so lucky.

In an interview in 1998, Essie Hudgins Jordan remembered the day all too clearly. Experiences with tornadoes are difficult to forget.

"Father had gone to the store, and Mother had gone to visit my grandmother, **Rebecca Hawkins Tanner**, who was ill," Essie explained. "My brothers and sisters and I were eating breakfast when we heard a strange noise. We ran to the window and saw things flying up high into the air. Our first thought was that we needed to get to our parents, but my older brother insisted that it was safer to stay right where we were."

As things turned out, Essie's brother's instructions were sound counsel, for neither the Hudgins children, nor their home suffered any ill effects from the tornado.

Life soon returned to normal in Clermont. James' business continued to thrive. He always wore a white long-sleeved shirt and a little black bow-tie at his business. He also carried a very businesslike appearance according to family members, but also had a knack for the sales of merchandise.

"All the stories you read which describe pioneer life and the little general store where saddles, sunbonnets, barrels of apples, cheeses, dry goods, animal traps, and such were sold – that was very similar to Father's store," Essie continued. "On cold winter days, men gathered around an old pot-bellied stove in the store to play checkers. Father loved to play checkers," she smiled conspiratorially.

Eventually, as the years passed and the children grew and began seeking their own lives in the world, the idealistic life in Clermont began fading away for the Hudgins family. James' health began failing

1923 GRADUATION PHOTO, GEORGIA NORMAL & INDUSTRIAL COLLEGE
Essie Carroll Hudgins (Jordan) – Photographed here in 1923, following her graduation from Georgia Normal & Industrial College in Milledgeville, Georgia, the late Essie Hudgins (Jordan) was one of the first female faculty members of Chattahoochee High School in Clermont, teaching there during the 1923-1924 school term. She also was an early graduate of the school. Her father, James Zacheus Hudgins, relocated his family and business in 1913 from Sugar Hill in Jackson County to the "up-and-coming" community of Clermont in north Hall County on the new Gainesville-Northwestern Railroad which had been built from Gainesville to Robertstown, Georgia. Essie and virtually all of her 12 siblings took full advantage of the education opportunities offered to them.

him, and he ultimately died from cancer of the liver in 1933. He was buried in Concord Baptist Church Cemetery with his two children who died in childbirth.

Following her husband's death, Sallie discovered there were outstanding uncollected debts owed by customers on accounts at James' store. She also discovered that sometime prior to his death, he had taken on a minor partner in his business – or at least that was the story she was given, and this "partner" claimed the outstanding uncollected accounts exceeded the value of the remaining assets of the store. It is unclear today why this "partner" was not just as responsible for these outstanding unpaid accounts as was James.

Sallie had strong doubts about the authenticity of the supposed partner's claim(s) to James' business, but with no firm knowledge of his business affairs, and no business acumen herself, Sallie was "out of her element" in fighting the lawsuit brought by the erstwhile "partner," and she ultimately lost the family business and source of income when the heartless individual foreclosed on the unpaid notes. It was a cruel fate.

Interestingly, however, it was also at approximately this same time that the Gainesville-Northwestern Railroad – the life-blood of tiny Clermont – entered into Receivership and the rails were taken up forever, eliminating the supply line to Clermont and the old Hudgins store. The loss of the rail line rendered the town and commercial district virtually worthless. It seemed almost like Providence had intervened to deal with the situation.

Sallie continued to live at the Clermont home for two more years until the last child – Marjorie – was graduated from Chattahoochee High School. Then, in 1935, she moved to live at 32 East Washington Street in Gainesville.

Around 1937, Sallie moved to Atlanta to live with daughter Daisy and husband Charles Giles. They had a large old home on Juniper Street with five bedrooms which they operated as a "rooming house." They rented rooms out to travelers and area residents. Sallie lived with them for a number of years.

By 1945, World War II was nearing an end, and Daisy and Charles decided to close down their rooming house. Sallie then moved in with daughter Marjorie and her husband "T," living with them for several years.

In the last 30 years of her life, Sallie lived with one daughter then another before eventually discovering a nursing home by coincidence in Austell, no doubt during one of her trips to see daughter, Essie, in the northwest Georgia town of Rockmart a few miles beyond Austell. At the time, Sallie was living with daughter Mary Lou in Powder Springs, and after some thought, she reportedly stated, "When this is finished, I want to move in here," pointing to the Austell nursing home.

The nursing facility was newly-constructed at that time, and affiliated with a local hospital. Sallie, always a prudent and wise individual, apparently knew she was getting up in years and didn't want to become a burden to any of her children, even though she had raised every single one of them from childhood to adulthood. In short order, Sallie had made good on her statement, and moved into the nursing facility, living there for the last years of her life until she passed away on December 22, 1969.

On a cold winter day on this earth, her mortal body was buried alongside that of James, her two stillborn babies and other relatives at Concord Baptist Church Cemetery in Clermont where their life had been so happy and content over half a century earlier. She no doubt smiled broadly as she entered Glory to rejoin husband James, and join hands with the Lord.

(Sarah Elizabeth Tanner Hudgins, descended from those pioneer Tanners who built such landmarks as Tanner's Mill at Chestnut Mountain, and James Zacheus Hudgins, descended from pioneers James Bevely Hudgins and wife Jane Bell, were all ancestors of the late Marilyn Jordan Jackson of Rockmart, and the late Patricia Jordan Nixon of Doraville, Georgia. Their children, grandchildren, and great-grandchildren – the Jacksons of Rockmart and Roswell; the Bradleys of Atlanta and Stone Mountain; and the Hughes of Rockmart, Marietta and Milton, Georgia, as well as the descendants of all the remainder of Sarah's and James' children, continue to grow the family today.)

A Hudgins Family History
At Chestnut Mtn (Hall) GA

Though it still shows up on maps even today, the actual original commercial district of this tiny former pioneer community disappeared long ago. Nevertheless, it is still well-known, and until 1986, included one of the oldest surviving gristmills in the state.

An 1895 map of Hall County identifies a community there called "Chestnut Hill." Old timers maintain that at one time, visitors to this spot could fill pockets and bags with the delicious fruit from the trees, lending an identity which has remained with this spot for the past 125 years, despite the fact the chestnut trees disappeared long ago (victims of a blight) just as the tiny town's once-vibrant little commercial district.

An old Gazette records that Chestnut Mountain was a postvillage of Hall County and in 1900 reported a population of 84 – quite a difference from the better than 25,000 in the community today, and the more than 200,000 living in surrounding Hall County today. *"It is located about four and one-half miles northeast of Flowery Branch and about 14 miles from Gainesville,"* the pioneer article explained.

Chestnut Mountain, to be certain, was one of the early communities in northeast Georgia, having been settled originally as a portion of Jackson County, established in 1796. Many early marriage and deed records for this community are still found today in the Jackson County Courthouse in Jefferson.

Chestnut Mountain was among a large portion of north Georgia counties originally parceled out in the 1820 Land Lottery. It became a farming district earlyon, and narrow roads through the community eventually linked Gainesville with Hoschton, Braselton and Jugtown (presentday Winder).

The first roads or lanes followed trails established ages earlier by native aboriginals. These early trails were usually little more than two or three feet wide, since the Indians traveled in singlefile, one after the other. This was often by necessity, since prior to European inhabitation and the harvesting (and sometimes outright decimation) of the original timber, the virgin forests contained thick growths of immense trees and almost impenetrable undergrowth.

The early trails used by the aborigines invariably had been originally created by migrating buffalo, antelope, deer and other wildlife who followed the routes of least resistance around hills, mountains and across bodies of water, and these trails ultimately were adopted by the natives.

The *Federal Road*, the first vehicular route in northeast Georgia, was opened in 1805 through what today is Hall County, an area which at that time was still included in the Cherokee Nation. When this occurred, the creation of Hall County was still thirteen years in the future.

The *Federal Road* soon became the main thoroughfare for pioneer travelers from Jackson County to west Georgia and the western territories, and was vitally important to early settlers. Many of these original travelers followed this route to Vann's Ferry on the Chattahoochee River before crossing and proceeding westward on the *"Alabama Road"* or northwestward on the *Federal Road.*

Old deed records show the *Federal Road* once passed the property of Irvin Strickland, Jr., and descendants say it also crossed the property of Jesse

Lott, Sr. Irvin (also spelled Ervin/Erwin) Strickland, Jr. of Chestnut Mountain was the son of Irvin, Sr. and the grandson of John Strickland.

Irvin, Sr. was married in 1807 in Jackson County, Georgia to Patsy Crow, and was enumerated in the *1820 Census of Hall County*. Loyd Strickland, the founder and owner of Crystal Farms in Chestnut Mountain, is a descendant of this family.

Native Indians At Chestnut Mountain – The early trails used by the aborigines who once inhabited the area known today as the southeastern United States, invariably had been created originally by migrating herds of buffalo, antelope, deer and other cloven-hooved wildlife. They followed the routes of least resistance around hills, mountains and across bodies of water, and these trails ultimately were adopted by the natives. Cherokee Indians once claimed the Chestnut Mountain area as their own. Pictured here are three who returned to northwest Georgia for a final visit to their former homeland a few years after the conclusion of the U.S. Civil War.

Jesse Lott, Sr. was born in 1771 in South Carolina, and died in Hall County in 1854. He was married to Nancy Martin who was born in Ireland. When Lott settled in Hall County in the Chestnut Mountain area, he bought 1,200 acres of land and an old log house which stood on the property.

In later years, Lott's house, which was two-storied, had a cellar which was used as a tavern or inn. Farmers who were driving livestock to market often overnighted at the spot, as did travelers along the road. Livestock shelters and fences were built to maintain the animals during the night.

A family story still related by Lott descendants maintains that Jesse, Jr. operated a store in the neighborhood. As the story goes, two men came in inquiring about buying meat one day. Jesse, who kept his money in a small wooden box under the stairway, was overpowered by the bandits who threw red pepper in his eyes and then robbed him.

After this experience, Jesse, according to family lore, buried his money for safekeeping. Some descendants today believe his hoard, which included gold coins, may still be buried near the old home site.

By the late 1820s, stagecoach lines operated over most of the main routes, including the route to Chestnut Mountain. Post riders, however, had begun traveling the *Federal Road* in 1819. Mail was delivered to the Carmel Mission (later called old Carmel Church and today known as Chestnut Mountain Baptist Church) and later to Chestnut Mountain on a weekly basis.

Ambrose Kennedy was named postmaster in 1865 and the old family cemetery is located along Highway 23. Kennedy was born in South Carolina and was married to Martha "Patsy" Gideon in Jackson County, Georgia. At one time he owned more than 5,000 acres in Hall and Jackson counties, operating a tanning yard and government distillery. He also served a term as sheriff of Hall County in 1850 and represented the county at the state capital in Milledgeville from 1863 to 1865.

Ambrose and Patsy were the parents of fourteen children. Sarah Jane, a daughter, was married to a gentleman named Thomas Jefferson Benton. Sarah Jane apparently did not know her husband had served with the Union Army during the U.S. Civil War until Thomas began receiving a pension. Sarah never quite forgave her husband for that. It is said that today, a fence still divides their graves in the Kennedy Cemetery. (Sarah also believed that marriage was a permanent bond.)

Ruth Smith Waters, a noted historian, has written that Chestnut Mountain once boasted a post office, an academy, and later, a three-story high school which also housed a masonic hall. The school burned in 1940 and the principal – George Dunagan – drove three miles to summon the Gainesville Fire Department – an effort which was in vain, as the structure was nevertheless completely destroyed. Two nearby churches – Baptist and Presbyterian – were then used to house students who continued to pursue studies at the site.

Three country stores were managed by W.A. McEver, J.T. "Thomps" Reed, and J.J. "Seif" Braselton. The names "McEver" and "Braselton," obviously familiar, would later become very prominent as identities of other nearby civic endeavors in later years.

A portion of Chestnut Mountain was included in Journey Cooper's farm and he planted cotton on the hill or "mountain" top. It is not known just how many mills (grist, etc.) existed from time to time in this area, but at least some of the operations were founded by Thomas Cooper and later operated by Journey. Thomas was married to Martha Meeks and son Journey married Mellie Bell.

Tanner's Mill, one of the oldest gristmills in Georgia and the oldest in Hall County, was located on the Walnut Fork of the Oconee River in the vicinity of Chestnut Mountain. It tragically was burned by vandals in 1986, erasing an important landmark forever in the blink of an eye.

Matthew Tanner, Jr. was one of the first Tanners to migrate to this section of the South, buying 250 acres in Jackson County from pioneer Elisha Winn. The property was located on both banks of the South Mulberry Fork of the Oconee River in Jackson.

A son of Matthew – David Tanner – purchased

the acreage where Tanner's Mill was built. David and his wife had eleven children, four of whom fought for the Confederacy in the Civil War.

Many old family and early church cemeteries are located in the Chestnut Mountain vicinity. One is the old Liberty Church Cemetery which was first established in Jackson County (later Hall County). It is believed that Francis Bell, a veteran of the American Revolution is interred here. He was the son of Thomas Bell and the family was originally from Virginia. Today, the grave of Francis Bell is unmarked, but many of his descendants in this same cemetery have headstones inscribed with family information.

Francis Bell married his first wife – Esther Montgomery – in 1770. Their daughter, Jane, born August 27, 1781, was married to James Beverly (also spelled Bevely) Hudgins (1777-1850) in January of 1801 (also recorded as June 6, 1801).

James Beverly Hudgins's *(Readers please see "The Hudgins Family of Jackson and Hall Counties" in the Hall County section of this book.)* father-in-law, Francis Bell, gave him property in Hall County, GA, in the days when the area was still an unsettled wilderness with most of the land still in the possession of the native Indians. James Beverly reportedly built a five-room log house on this land near a place called "Macedonia Settlement." He is listed in the *1820 Hall County Census* as *"Beverly Hudgeons"*, and again in the *1850 Hall Census*.

From the union of James Beverly and Jane Bell came Beverly, Jr.; Virginia B.; Gregory; Dessie; Mary Ann; Zacharia (a.k.a. "Zaccharia," "Zachus," and "Zacheus"); Holder; Esther; Francis Bell; and Iverson Delaprierre.

James Beverly and wife Jane Bell's graves may still be viewed in Hall County near Chestnut Mountain if one knows where to look. The small graveyard may have been no more than a family cemetery, and can be easily missed. To reach it: Travel to GA 53 South from Gainesville past Lanier Raceway/Road Atlanta to Macedonia Church on the left. Turn left just beyond this church onto J.J. Lott Road. Follow this road until it dead-ends into another road and then turn left once again. The cemetery will be on the right just a short distance away. Be aware that in the past, thick undergrowth has often concealed this tiny cemetery from the road.

Descendants of the Bell, Montgomery and Hudgins families still live throughout the Chestnut Mountain area today, as well as in many other parts of the state.

A descendant of Beverly and Jane Bell Hudgins – Iverson Daniel Hudgins – but for the interruption of World War I in 1914, would have been known as an international botanist. He was considered one of the foremost authorities on botany in America, and was visited at the time by botanists in the employment of King George of England and Kaiser Wilhelm of Germany.

The settlement of Beverly's estate is listed in the Hall County Ordinary's office. Sons Zacheus & Holder Hudgins were administrators. James Beverly Hudgins's old farm was passed to his wife, Jane, upon his death, and to their son, Francis Bell Hudgins, upon Jane's death, and to Francis's son, Jim, upon Francis's death.

In more recent years, Beverly's former property was owned by a Mr. J.J. Lott, and has been the site of frequent Hudgins family reunions over the years. Old Liberty Methodist Church at Chestnut Mountain disappeared long ago, as did the little community of Chestnut Mountain itself, though it (the community name of Chestnut Mountain) still may be found on maps even today.

As of this writing, pioneer James Beverly Hudgins's lonely grave – which was well-marked at last check – still amazingly exists with a handful of other graves today at Chestnut Mountain, Hall Co., Georgia.

[Zacharia/Zacheus Hudgins was the great-grandfather of the late Essie Hudgins Jordan – mother of the late Marilyn Jordan Jackson (both of Rockmart, Georgia) and the late Patricia Jordan Nixon (formerly of DeKalb County, Georgia). Marilyn's children: Patricia Jackson Hughes, Ralph Olin Jackson III, and David Anderson Jackson, have homes in the Rockmart (Polk County), Georgia, area as of this writing. Patricia Nixon's children: Hal, Eve, Dave and Melinda, reside in the Gwinnett, DeKalb, and Cobb County areas.)

Essie Hudgins Jordan and
A Christmas Reminiscence

ssie Hudgins Jordan was born March 12, 1900, in a log structure built by her grandfather near the tiny crossroads community of Sugar Hill in present-day Jackson County near the old Gainesville to Athens Highway (present-day U.S. 129). She lived 13 years of her life there, then seven years in equally quaint Clermont in North Hall County, before moving to Rockmart, Georgia in Polk County in the mid-1920s where she remained as a civic institution for some 75 years until her death in 1999. When all was said and done, she had lived just one month shy of her 99th birthday. She had come into this life during the last days of travel by horse and buggy and went out in the time of manned space flight into the heavens.

Needless to say, Essie Hudgins Jordan experienced quite a life, and ultimately had quite a story to tell of her experiences. As she approached her 99th birthday, the need to record her life experiences for posterity became painfully obvious to those who loved her. On a chill December evening in 1996 during the Christmas holidays, she sat down with a few members of her family to reminisce one final time about her experiences. That experience has proven to be very timely and valuable.

Essie hailed from hardy pioneer stock – the Hudgins and Tanners – both families which had migrated down the eastern seaboard of the United States before landing in northeast Georgia in the early 1800s. Her mother – Sarah Elizabeth Tanner Hudgins – was the great-granddaughter of David B. Tanner of Tanner's Mill fame. Her father – James Zacheus Hudgins – was the great-grandson of James Beverly (a.k.a. "Bevely") Hudgins who shows up time and time again in the history of northeast Georgia.

One of the places Essie remembered most fondly in her reminiscences was Clermont, Georgia, in

1909 Rockmart, Georgia Main Street – This view, looking south down Marble Street in Rockmart, Georgia, was photographed in 1909. Despite being the town's "Main Street," this was still an unpaved dirt road when Essie Hudgins (Jordan) arrived in the town to teach in 1924. The individuals facing the camera and standing in the middle of the road are W.T. Simpson and Cicero Waits. Simpson's well-known mare – "Old Nell" - is tethered (left).

north Hall County. The old Hudgins home on King Street in that still-tiny burg, yet stands (as of this writing in 2023), stark and dominant, just as it has for the past 108 years.

Construction on this home began in 1913 and was completed in 1914, by James Zacheus Hudgins. This home has weathered many disasters, not the least of which were immense tornadoes and mass pandemics, but still it stands, a testament to good fortune, its sturdy construction, a smiling Almighty, and the hardy family members who once lived there. Essie remembered this home fondly, just as she did her later experiences in Rockmart, in northwest Georgia, where she taught school for some 30 years.

Gathered with Essie on this December day in 1996 were her daughter – the late Marilyn Jordan Jackson – and her grandchildren – Patricia Jackson Hughes and her husband, Jimmy; Ralph Olin Jackson and his wife, Judy; and David Anderson Jackson and his wife, Judi. Essie's remembrances, digitally-recorded for posterity, are transcribed here as follows:

Olin: Do you remember any of your first Christmases? What is the earliest Christmas you remember?

Essie: Well, honey, I must have been about five or six (year 1906 in pioneer Sugar Hill), because the thing that I remember about that particular Christmas – what I remember most about that time was that we got "books," and I well remember that David got one, and Carl one and Clyde one, and me. We were the ones that got "books," and I got *"Little Red Riding Hood,"* and I remember that Clyde got *"Who Killed Cock Robin,"* and David got *"Black Beauty,"* and don't remember what Carl got. And one time my step-brother said that we weren't going to have Christmas that year because Santa Claus had broken a leg and wouldn't be able to come.

Marilyn: Why did he tell you that?

Essie: Oh just to tease us!

Olin: Was this in Clermont?

Essie: No. That was (when we lived) in Sugar Hill. But I think the times that I remember the most were when I used to come out here (the Jackson home in Rockmart) and sleep out here the night before Christmas, and Mary and Patricia would both have a fuss about who I was to sleep with. Do you remember that Patricia?

Patricia: I think you really wanted to stay at your house where you could actually "sleep," but we'd insist that you come out here.

Marilyn: She was "employed" to keep you all in bed!

Essie: And then what I remember the most of all was your Daddy (Ralph Jackson) would come in to light the fire, and those doors (double-doors

separating bedroom from living room) would be closed, and you'd all get against the door, and I remember Guy *(only four or five years old, but already the family comic)* laying down on the floor trying to see underneath the doors.

Olin: How did you decorate your house in Clermont at Christmas?

Essie: Well honey, we didn't do a lot of decoration back then.

Patricia: What kind of tree did you have?

Essie: It was always a cedar in the (front) hall.

Patricia: In the foyer? In that big foyer?

Essie: Yes.

Olin: How did you decorate the tree?

Essie: Out of the trees that I remember, they were decorated with live candles! And then we would light the candles! Imagine that!

Patricia: Weren't you afraid of them?

Judy: They caught fire sometimes...

Essie: Well... They could have, but you see we didn't let them stay on too long.

Patricia: What would you do? Would you light them for a special occasion then turn them back out? *(Author's Note: So accustomed are today's residents to "electrical" lighting, they are confusing "turning off" wax candles with electric lights.)*

Essie: The Christmas tree that I remember most when I was a child growing up was in that little one-room schoolhouse when the whole Sunday School had the Christmas tree and you exchanged gifts, and I remember my father had put so many gifts in there for different people in the community, and there was a show afterwards and it was a *"Magic Lantern."* Have you ever heard of a *"Magic Lantern?"*

Marilyn: It's one of these things that flashes pictures up on the wall.

Essie: That's right! And that was the thing that fascinated us. I couldn't understand how in the world that picture could be dancing across the wall.

Marilyn: These were the days before there were picture shows and motion pictures. (movies)

Judi: So what did ya'll do at your house on Christmas?

Essie: I don't remember a lot other than hanging up the stockings, and we always hung them in that middle room where nothing – we called it the "sitting room."

Olin: As you went in the front door?

Patricia: On the right?

Essie: That would have been.....You know Olin do you remember where that little porch had been built against the . . . .

Patricia: Where the fireplace was - the room we went into? *(Editor's Note: Patricia and Olin had obviously once accompanied Essie to revisit her old home in Clermont.)*

Essie: Yes. The one that we entered. Now that porch, our porch, had been taken off of our big house there, and that little one was built across the side if you remember Patricia. . . And that - we hung the stockings there. And we always got into the stockings. That was more fun than anything, because the stocking would be filled with all those goodies.

Judi: Did you get anything besides what was in the stocking?

Essie: Yes... Sometimes the girls would get dolls I don't remember what the boys got because evidently I wasn't interested in what they got. *(laughter)* I was only interested in what we got, but it was mostly just a doll or a simple toy of some kind.

Patricia: Did you get fruit and stuff?

Essie: Oh yes. We got fruit. Always.

Olin: Which room did you sleep in?

Essie: Oh I slept upstairs, in uh, oh, on the right. At the front. Uh huh. The right-hand side.

Patricia: As you go upstairs and take a right?

Essie: Yeah, to the right. That was my room and Daisy's room. We slept together. Now remember, all of us *(children)* were not at home at any one give time.

Patricia: Was Carl already gone at that time?

Essie: Yes. Carl was married by then. Well, not in the beginning of course.

Judi: But ya'll didn't have the young ones then.

Essie: No, we didn't have Margie and Sarah and Dorothy. They were the ones that were born there.

Olin: Did your father get special things in his general store for you at Christmas time?

Essie: Yes. Because he would have a lot of extra things, like uh, dolls, and toys of different kinds... and of course always food. Now, I've heard a lot of people say they never saw an orange except at Christmas time, . . . and that they seldom got bananas. . . and I can't remember a time that we didn't have apples, because Father would buy them by the *barrel* in the store.

Patricia: Well I wouldn't think apples would be all that original.

Essie: Well then too, the people from the mountains, the mountain folk, would bring down all kinds of things like chestnuts, and apples, sorghum, and peanuts to sell to father.

Patricia: But wasn't citrus special at Christmas?

Essie: Well yes. . . uh, citrus fruits I guess were special at Christmas.

Patricia: Oh I know what Mother said. It was raisins that were so special.

Marilyn: Raisins, and they were still on the stem too. . . .

Patricia: Because they probably came from California.

Essie: Oh yeah. . .Well that was the only kind that I ever knew of when I was a child growing up. Father got them in boxes and they were packed in layers and they were "on the stem;" they had been dried.

Olin: Did ya'll have a car so that you could drive to go down to Gainesville to go shopping?

Essie: No

Olin: Did you ever ride the train *(Author's Note: the Gainesville-Northwestern which passed through Clermont)* to Gainesville?

Essie: Yes. Numbers of times. But while I was still at home, the only car that my Father ever owned was a Buick, and I was in high school then, and David was teaching me how to drive, and I was coming out King Street, and he said "Slow down! It's time to turn in! Slow down! It's time to turn in. . . You're going to wreck the car!" And I turned the car so quick he said I did something to the front axel. I don't know what it was.

Olin: What was the hotel like back then.

Essie: Oh, Olin that old hotel looks pretty much like it always has, except on the lower floor. Part of it, uh, that was a dry goods store.

Olin: Did your father have any connection with that old hotel.

Essie: No. Father did not have any connection whatsoever with the old hotel.

Judy: Namma tell us what your first Christmases were like when you were first married to Mr. Jordan. *[Author's Note: Essie and her husband (Guy Wilfred Jordan) were married and lived in Rockmart, Georgia, where he was the chemist at the local cement manufacturing plant. Their home, built circa 1927 by Guy, still stands (as of this writing in 2022) at 215 Bluff Street, Rockmart, Georgia.]*

Essie: Oh. . . .Well, it'd been a long time since your grandfather Jordan had had a home – his own home – to live in. . . and we had a Christmas tree in the corner of the dining area. . . Marilyn do you remember that?

Judy: Okay, back to my question, How did you celebrate your first Christmas when you were married? *(Author's Note: Again referring to when they were married and living at the 215 Bluff Street, Rockmart address.)*

Essie: Well I just don't uh. . . I don't remember anything unusual except the Christmas tree, and the making of the cakes and the candies and everything like that – oh, I will tell you this,

Marilyn: You and Daddy stayed at home by yourselves?

Patricia: You didn't go down here and go home *(to Clermont)* by train?

Essie: Not that first Christmas, because you *(referring to Essie's first child, Marilyn)* were born in

March, and we did not go home that year, but we talked to them long-distance.

Patricia: Oh my word – improvised mental display. . . . *(Laughter at the thought not of "telephoning" long distance, but "talking" long distance.)*

Essie: Oh goodness. . . .We had a good time, I'll tell you that. . . And Olin your grandfather *(her husband, the late Guy W. Jordan)* was always the most gracious and courteous person that could possibly have existed at the time, and after we were married, he continued to bring me candy and flowers.

Patricia: Well Namma you told me that somewhere or other that you all went to get a turkey. Is that over there, uh, tell me where that is, because I think I remember the road. . . Wasn't there a little road that goes – what's the name of that little community down there? *(Editor's Note: Essie's pet-name among her multitude of loving grandchildren – and ultimately their husbands, wives and children – was always "Namma.")*

Essie: Well, going out to Taylorsville, if you will remember – out beyond, uh, the Hughes place – there's a little curve uh. . . Just before you get in to Taylorsville, well . . there's a little church in there, you remember *(Editor's Note: Taylorsville is a tiny country community east of Rockmart.)*

Olin: That's still a voting place, uh considered a voting precinct. . .

Patricia: It is, uh, uh, . .what do you call that Olin – Uh. . .no. . Well, there's a militia – It was, uh, I can't remember what you call that.

Essie: Anyway, before Thanksgiving, your daddy and Marilyn just a little girl, and I, would drive over the hills out toward uh, Taylorsville, and cut across to this man's house, and the turkeys would be roosting in the trees, and they would take one out for us. . . They'd have to climb a tree to get it.

Patricia: And then they'd, uh, they'd . . .Oh. Granddaddy would dress it?

Essie: Oh no. . . He never would ring its neck. . No. . . .uh, we would bring it in and we'd get somebody to "dress" it for us. . .

Patricia: Well, why didn't they do that out there when you bought it? . . . I thought they did all that out there. . .

Essie: No, they didn't. They just grew them, and they grew such nice turkeys. . .

Marilyn: They put it in a tow sack. . . .

Essie: Yeah, and every chicken that we got from the grocery store, it was alive when they brought them to us, and they'd have a hole cut in one end of the sack where the head could come out, and the feet and all would be tied to the sack. But, you got the lives. There was no such thing as buying a chicken or turkey ready-dressed.

Olin: Was it traditional for y'all to go back to Clermont in the early years for Christmas?

Essie: Uh after Marilyn was born, at Christmastime, we would try to make a trip back home, but in the wintertime, with the roads as bad as they were, and no pavement whatsoever, we did not go often. *(Editor's Note: Marilyn was born in 1928, so the vehicle they would be driving would not be terribly dependable, particularly on the muddy north Georgia dirt roads of the 1920s. However, quite surprisingly, Guy would later drive the family all the way to California in the family car in the 1930s, even, amazingly, across Death Valley.)*

Patricia: Did you go that first year when she was nine months old and a little baby? That second year, I mean?

Essie: I don't think so. I think we went in the summertime, but we did not go back at Christmastime.

Olin: And ya'll drove, you never took the train, did you?...

Essie: No. Never took the train. There was just one time, and your daddy carried me and Marilyn and Patricia when she was a baby, to the station out beyond Oglethorpe, and we got on the train and went to Gainesville and somebody met us and carried us to Clermont. *(Editor's Note: Many residents in Rockmart had become very reluctant to even consider rail travel as a result of witnessing a terrible disaster in 1926, when the Ponce de Leon and Royal Palm passenger trains collided at high speed in Rockmart, resulting in 26 deaths and massive destruction.)*

Patricia: Well I've heard mother say that she remembers that there was no electricity and they had gas lamps lit . . .

Essie: No...oil and gas.

Marilyn: There wasn't anything but the fire going, maybe, sitting in that front room waitin' on y'all. I remember somebody holding me because I had gone to sleep on the way...

Essie: Well Marilyn that was the year that you got the little white fluffy dog for Christmas. You remember that?

Patricia: Did you get it up there?

Essie: No, no. We bought it in Atlanta at a pet shop.

Patricia: So it was given to her for Christmas that year – in Rockmart?

Essie: Yes. . and we carried it with us. . .We had Christmas up there *(in Clermont)* that year. . .

Olin: What was it like driving up there? Do you remember about stopping along the way, or roads?

Essie: Don't remember anything except how

tiresome it was and that it took most of the day. We still had that little Ford coop when Patricia was born, and your mother, there was room . . . Do you know anything about those little Ford coops, . . Well, uh, we'd put a pillow up there and that's where Marilyn . . .She would lie down up there. . . . .and uh, we had to take the uh. . . .Patricia was a nuisance. . . . We had to take all that, uh, paraphernalia along because she could not take any liquid food – but her bottle. . . .She could only have four ounces at a time, and even that she would spit up, but uh, we had to take the sterilizer and everything else for both of the girls to Clermont every time that we went.

Olin: How come?

Marilyn: They had well water. . .

Essie: Not only that Marilyn, but no milk was homogenized or sterilized.

Patricia: Yeah I guess you would've had to do that...

Essie: You had cold milk. . . and it had to be prepared.

Patricia: Well did you ever take a picnic along the way? *(Editor's Note: In other words, since in those days, there was little more than wilderness in north Georgia, broken occasionally by mountain farms and a mountain community or two, one would have to pack along a meal to be eaten at some point either while driving or while parked in a cool spot somewhere along the way.)*

Essie: Evidently we did. . . . I should think that we had to have something along the way. . . .

Olin: Mother do you remember which route you took when you drove?

Marilyn: No. I have no earthly idea. . . .Probably cut up past Canton and across to Dawsonville

Essie: I think actually we went down to uh, to, across by Dahlonega and . . . I just don't remember.

Olin: And up old U.S. 19, probably . .

Essie: Yes.

Patricia: Well where did ya'll sleep in that house *(Essie's childhood home in Clermont)* when you were married?

Essie: Uh, mother had. . . Opposite where the uh, living room – we called it a parlor because that's what it was – and the front part of the hall was a reception hall, and there was a bedroom to the right, and that's where we slept. *[Editor's Note: Quite often, homes built in the 19th and early 20th centuries in the eastern United States included a room – usually built near the front hall and sometimes just off the front porch – for circuit-riding ministers and traveling salesmen ("drummers") to which reference as "the Parson's Room" usually was made. This undoubtedly is what James Zacheus Hudgins – being the highly religious man that he was – had built near the front door of his new home (constructed in 1913) in Clermont.]*

Patricia: When you returned you *all* stayed in there?

Marilyn: No I slept upstairs with Margie or somebody and the sheets scratched, and I itched and I cried and I went downstairs and Mother put *Mennen's Baby Powder* on me then told me to go back upstairs and lie down and keep my mouth shut. *(laughter)*

Essie: Well, she was disrupting the household, but I can understand now, because that would be kinda like Patricia. . .She was afraid. . .

Olin: Well tell me what you remember about your wedding there in the parlor.

Essie: Oh, that preparation required quite a little bit of effort, I remember that. But uh. . we made

– and I did most of it – I had seen an altar built in Riches *(Editor's Note: A well-known department store in Atlanta from 1867-2005)*, and I had decided that I wanted my altar where we were to be married done like that.

Olin: So the wedding actually took place in that old front left parlor room?

Essie: No. . In the hall . . Say for instance that this is the double-doors, the altar was built in front of the double-doors . . .and that's where we stood. . . .

Patricia: Yeah the people were out in the hallway. . .That's what I meant. . And the preacher stood to the back side of the altar there in the hall. I know. .That's what you told me. .

Essie: And father, uh. . I came down the back stairs with him. .and met the groom and the maid of honor. .

Patricia: Who was your maid of honor?

Essie: Evelyn Harris. . .who was uh. . .She wasn't really my cousin, but uh, I felt that she was, because she was the cousin of my half-brothers and sisters. .

Olin: Who was Granddaddy (Guy W.) Jordan's best man? . .

Essie: David, my brother. He came down from uh, Flint, Michigan, and was there. And one of my good friends there in Clermont played the piano and sang. . And I remember the songs that she sang were typical . . .They were just *"Oh Promise Me,"* and *"I Love You Too."* Those were two solos.

Olin: Tell me about when the tornado came through. Do you remember the cyclone? Now there was one that you said came through Clermont . . .

Essie: That's right! It did! Father had already gone to the store, and mother had gone to my grandmother's *(Arabella Pettyjohn Hudgins back at Sugar*

Hill in Jackson County) because she was ill. And we were having breakfast, and we heard this terrible noise. I went to the back door and don't remember anybody being there *(at home with them)* that was older than I was, but David, my brother who was just younger than me. We saw all these things flying up in the air. . . and I said *"Oh My goodness. Let's go across the street to our neighbor's. I'm afraid."* And David said *"No you won't. We're much safer to stay right here."* So we stayed, uh, there. And it *(the tornado)* went down the street that was just back of our house. . . Took off roofs (of houses) and blew up things. . Actually there were things flying up in the air. And it then went on out the street and took the whole porch off the old hotel. . . It then dipped down into a neighbor's house across the highway down in the lower part of the town, and did a quite a bit of damage down there, but it did not do one little thing to our house. It was just in the next block back of us, and that's how close we came to that. But I actually saw that thing moving in the air. . .

Patricia: How old were you?

Essie: Oh Honey. I can't remember how old I was. . . but I must have been about 15 or 16.

Marilyn: Well tell about when you and Aunt Daisy were cutting wood and she chopped your finger off.

Olin: Before you do that, let me ask you a quick question. Do you think that *(the Clermont tornado)* was the time the big tornado came through Gainesville?

Essie: No it wasn't honey. . .That one in Gainesville was after I was married.

Olin: There were several. There was one in 1906, and another one in 1936.

Essie: Well that earlier one was when we lived at Sugar Hill. And that was the one that destroyed so much of the New Holland area. But in 1936,

I was living in Rockmart, and your granddaddy called me from the plant *(the Rockmart Cement Plant where he was the plant chemist)* and told me that they had had a terrible storm in Gainesville, and that they weren't getting much news concerning it. And of course you know that made a nervous wreck out of me, because I knew that Mother lived right there and Dot and Margie and Albert *(Essie's sisters and brother)* and all were living *(in that same general vicinity)* with her. It happened at just the time that everyone was going to work or had just gone to work. And Dorothy and Margie were both working down on the Square *(Editor's Note: The Gainesville town square which was totally destroyed by the immense tornado, one of the worst in U.S. history)*, and one was working – I don't remember the stores that they were working in but they were working . . .and Albert had already gone to school because he was the principal out at River Bend. . and, uh Mother was at home, and she, her house was right across the street from the uh Baptist Church, First Baptist Church. . . .

Olin: What street was that on?

Essie: Uh, I think that's Brenau Avenue.

Patricia: Was that church destroyed?

Essie: No, uh. . .the uh . . .tornado didn't, it *(the church)* was made of Georgia marble and the tornado did not destroy it. It did something to the post office, but the old post office building is still there, isn't it Olin?

Olin: I don't know. . .

Essie: Well, anyway, the whole square downtown was just devastated, and all the buildings. . .and, uh, so many of the people were just fastened inside the buildings, and they couldn't get out, and fires were started, and a lot of the people that were killed were fastened in such a way in those old buildings that they could not escape and the fire was really what killed them. . but there was a big, big statue of one of the former generals of the Confederacy there in the square. . .

Olin: It's still there. .

Essie: Is it still there?? Uh huh. . .Well, the trees were blown down there. And, uh, I wanted uh my husband to come home and take me. I said *"Mother lives there where they are, and we must go over and help them,"* and he said *"You can do a lot more good because they are saying. 'Do not come.' and 'We'll do everything we can to find out about them.'"* Daisy my older sister was living in Atlanta, and she and Charles *(husband)* managed to get out and they went to Gainesville, and they got back to a place where they could call and let me know that they were all okay, so none of my family was hurt in any way. . .Uh, I don't remember the school where Albert was teaching, I don't think it extended all the way out there. . But, uh, the house where Mother was living, she knew it was a tornado that was coming, and

she told whoever was in the house with her – I don't know who it was – to get under the piano, crawl anywhere; get under anything you can; mother always would try to take care of whoever was there, and she herself would walk and watch the storm, and she saw this somebody back of the house, and he was holding onto oh, a kind of a bush of some sort, just lying down on the ground, and evidently he wasn't hurt, but the trees on the lot where mother's house was, were blown down, but they blew parallel to the house, not one of them went across the house. Windows were blown out, but nobody was hurt inside. After it was over with, she of course started trying to get to town – and that was just a couple of blocks away – to see about Dot and Marjorie. . .and everybody there was just trying to find out about their kinfolks who were in the section downtown. . .It must have been a terrible time, because it was terrible to be away and know about what happened. Matter of fact, Olin has in his book, he has a lot of the truth.

1936 TORNADO, GAINESVILLE, HALL COUNTY, GEORGIA
Sarah Elizabeth Hudgins – West Spring Street shows the devastation from the terrible twister which destroyed Gainesville, Georgia. It is still ranked today as one of the worst tornado disasters in U.S. history. Sarah Elizabeth Hudgins, wife of James Zacheus Hudgins, was living near this downtown section but miraculously escaped injury, as did three of her children (Dorothy, Margie and Albert) working downtown. From this date forward, Sarah Elizabeth was essentially homeless and lived with those of her children who had room until the last few years of her life when she passed away in a nursing home in 1969, but she lived a full and happy life.

Olin: The rest of it is all lies. . . *(laughter; Olin still teasing his grandmother mercilessly.)* Namma is Granny's former apartment in Gainesville still there?

Essie: No it's long gone.

Marilyn: To get back to the wood chopping incident. . Daisy was chopping kindling or something or other. . . .

Essie: I was just four years old, and when father got in some of these things in the grocery store, there were these big wooden tub-like things, and they had a top, and usually in the center, there was a hole, I guess that must have been crates in which he had gotten apples and things like that, and my older sister wanted to make – of all things – a churn-lid that a dasher could come up through to use in the play-house – so you could be churning milk. . . . You don't know a thing in the world about a churn do you???

Patricia: Yeah. . We understand this. . .but wait, this was just for play, right?

Essie: Yes. . . and I was the one that was elected – a four-year-old – to hold the lid. . . .Well she missed hitting in the right place (with the hatchet) and came down and cut my finger off completely.

Marilyn: Now the interesting part is what Granny did with that finger.

Essie: Oh yeah. . . .Well. . Uh, the uh, pharmacist – a traveling drug-man – a drummer, was selling drugs, and he had a horse and buggy, and father was not home. Father had gone to Gainesville that day to get supplies. Mother was taking care of the store. . ..Mother had me crying telling what had happened. The druggist had all these antiseptics and everything that father usually bought for the store. . . .Mother had a piece of wood – probably from a cigar box or something else. . . Anyway, she made a splint and put my finger back in place. . and they put all the antiseptics on it and we then had to wait. We had no doctor and no telephone to get to him. . . and we weren't able

to get him until that night. Well Mother and that salesman bandaged and took care of my hand and put the finger in that splint, and when the doctor did get there, the circulation had already started again in my finger. . .Now that's a miracle if you want to know the truth. . .The fact that mother had the presence of mind to put a splint on there and then bandage it and it was just "leather-guard sin" that the medicines man was there and that he helped her. When Father got there and they got the doctor there, I remember sitting on my father's knee, while they sewed my finger back on, and the circulation as I told you had already started. I guess you can still see where the stitches were to this day. . .The finger is in place, but the very end of it hasn't grown like the rest, and the middle joint is stiff. I can't bend it like the others.

Judy: How old were you?

Essie: I was about four years old.

Patricia: I heard another tale over Namma's birthday . . Was it Dot whose clothes caught on fire cause they had built a little fire to cook some mud-pies?

Essie: Yes. That was the first year that I had come to Rockmart to teach, and Dorothy and Margie *(Essie's youngest sisters)* were in the playhouse and they had made mud-pies and they decided that they were going to "bake" them, and Dot's clothes caught on fire

Patricia: But the funny *(if this could possibly be considered "funny")* part of this was that the family was all on the front porch having lemonade and not paying any attention while the children were out building a fire in the back yard. . .

Essie: Well she was burned so badly. . .

Patricia: Yeah she almost died. .. They didn't think she was going to live. . .

Essie: Yeah. . .That was another time that they

1920s Marble Hill Hotel – When Essie Hudgins (Jordan) first arrived in Rockmart (circa 1924) for her teaching position at Rockmart High School, she roomed at the Marble Hill Hotel on North Marble Street in Rockmart. This historic inn was built 1904-1906.

called me and I got on a train and came back home because she was crying and asking for me...

Olin: What do you remember about Rockmart back in the 1920s? Didn't you use to drive through Euharlee Creek and wash your car there?

Essie: Well Olin, there was no bridge except for a swinging bridge across Euharlee Creek on Church Street at the Methodist Church across to the other side going up toward the Youngs. You didn't drive across the creek there because it was too deep, but down on the lower side – which is Elm Street – all of it was dirt...There were no paved streets in Rockmart at all. But we did have a few paved sidewalks around town.. and uh, you'd drive your car through *(Euharlee Creek)* there on Elm Street – it was called a ford – and you'd just go in the water and go across and go up that rocky hill up toward the cemetery on the opposite side, and then it *(the road)* went out into the country..

Olin: How deep was the water?

Essie: It couldn't have been very deep – I guess maybe two feet..

Olin: The main streets were probably dirt back then too..

Essie: Oh yes.. All up and down town.. All the streets were dirt streets, and we'd get pot-holes in them during the wintertime and in rainy season.

Olin: Were there sidewalks?

Essie: When I first came to Rockmart there were sidewalks in town and there were sidewalks on Elm Street, and up Piedmont Avenue, in several areas of town, - all the way up Marble Street - but no paved streets.

Patricia: Were the sidewalks wood?

Essie: No they were concrete... You see we had the cement plant here then. *(Editor's Note: A Southern States Portland Cement Plant at which Guy W. Jordan was the plant chemist was newly-located a couple of miles outside Rockmart.)*

Olin: Tell me about the old theatre in Rockmart...

Essie: Oh.. the old Opera House? Well when I first went to Rockmart to teach, I spent the first month in the Marble Hill Hotel... and just down the street going toward town, across from where Guy Sloan's motor place used to be *(just north of the intersection of Marble and Elm Streets)* was a big two-story building they called *"the opera house,"* and it had a skating rink, and an auditorium where they had plays and things. While I was away one summer, that huge house burned, and I don't know how it caught on fire, but uh, it was terrible... it just made you cry. The devastation was so great.

Olin: Tell me about where Granddaddy Jordan lived when he first came to Rockmart..

Essie: Goodness me. I suppose when he first got here, he must have stayed in a hotel, and it would have been the Marble Hill Hotel. . until he had a room, and the only place that I know that he had a room for himself outside of the hotel was that big old two-story house which is now the Rockmart Florist (*the large home at the foot of the hill across Elm Street from Rose Hill Cemetery*).

Olin: Was that down there on the corner? Right across from the cemetery?

Essie: Yes. . On Elm Street.

Olin: I thought he also lived down there at the corner of Elm Street and Piedmont Ave.

Essie: No. . . Your granddaddy did not live there. I stayed in that house. That's where I boarded with the Burnettes for a year and a half. When I first came to Rockmart I lived at the Marble Hill Hotel for a month, and then we got a room. . a girl with whom I was in college went with me and we got a room in a lady's house downtown, but then she had peritonitis and died, and we had to move, so we moved down there across the street from the First Baptist Church in Mrs. Hartley's house. And then, uh, we moved to the Burnettes (*at the corner of Elm and Piedmont*).

Olin: Who were the Burnettes?

Essie: Uh, the Charles S. Burnettes. He was a hardware man in Rockmart. I roomed there for the rest of the time that I lived in Rockmart before I got married.

Olin: When you moved out of the Marble Hill Hotel and you lived down in the middle of town above one of those downtown buildings. . .,

Essie: Yes. . .That was in Mrs. Randall's house. . She had an apartment above one of those buildings downtown. . .I think it was called the telephone building.

Olin: And that was the building across South Marble from (*that big brick building at the corner of Marble and Church streets that was*) the old White's Department Store?

Essie: Yes. . . And she's the one who died from peritonitis, causing us to have to move again. That was when I packed my trunk knowing that I'd now moved two times since I'd been here and I was thinking it was just time for me to pack up and go home.

Olin: Yeah, there was something about someone with the school board saying you shouldn't be living there?

Essie: Yes. . the chairman of the school board came to us at the hotel at the end of the first month and said that young ladies who taught school were not supposed to live in a hotel, and we'd have to get a boarding place, but they did not provide us with a place to live. . . so that's why we had to hunt up another place to live.

Olin: What did they pay you when you first came to teach?

Essie: $70 a month, and out of that $70 I paid my rent and board and any other things that I needed.

Olin: Do you remember the old Piedmont Institute?

Essie: No. It wasn't there. It had burned, and the Rockmart High School had been built in the place where the Piedmont Institute used to be. . . but the old (Piedmont Institute) dormitory was still there, and in the old dormitory, the principal of the high school lived.

Olin: Where was the dormitory?

Essie: It was where the junior high building is now (*Editor's Note: This was the former junior high school building on Piedmont Avenue which was demolished for construction of the new Rockmart Library.*).

Olin: So they must have torn down the old dormitory to build the junior high school building…And the Institute was where the old high school building was – where the high school building is today?

Essie: That's right. . .but the old high school where I went to teach was a two-story building and it also burned – later – and the present one, I don't remember exactly when it was built, but it must have been built. *(Editor's Note: The present-day (2022) "new-old" high school building has been renovated and is used today as the Rockmart City Hall complex.)*

Olin: The 1940s.

Essie: No. . It had to have been built before then.

Olin: No. . It burned either in Daddy's last year or next to last year there. . . so that would have been, uh, 1939 or so. .

Essie: You're right. Your daddy didn't tell you that when he went to school there it was a two-story building, did he?

Olin: No, he didn't.

Essie: Well when your mother first started there it was a two-story building, so your daddy had to be in that building, because the auditorium was upstairs.

Olin: Tell me what you remember about that first high school building. It had a big auditorium upstairs?

Essie: Uh… the auditorium was upstairs, and a couple of classrooms on each end of the upstairs, and classrooms and offices were downstairs. . . and a little laboratory was at the end there next to the railroad, you know… It was a brick building, but it wasn't an up-to-date one like the next one was.

Olin: How many classrooms did it have?

Essie: Ten. . It had about ten classrooms. . Ten

or twelve at the very most. Twelve probably. And the auditorium.

Olin: What grades do you think it was through?

Essie: It was through the eleventh grade.

Olin: So it was 7th through the 11th grade?

Essie: Uh huh. Yeah. No. . .because that was where it started with the 1st. That was the only school, and it started with the first grade and went right on through the eleventh. After Mr. Scoggin came there, it was converted into a twelve-year school. But it was eleven grades up to that time. When your daddy was there, I think. .. Did he ever say that Mr. Scoggin was his principal?

Olin: I don't remember.

Essie: I guess he was. He had to be. So, uh, that was the building that your daddy went to high school in, and it was the building that your mother *started* to school in. . .It must have had a basement then. I don't even know how the fires got started.

Marilyn: I'm sure it had a basement because that was where the restrooms were and I was scared to go down there because of all those big ole boys and girls down there.

Olin: What do you remember about that building Mother? Do you remember it being two-story?

Marilyn: Oh yes.

Essie: It was only after Mr. Scoggin came there that it was changed to twelve grades.

Olin: Do you remember the auditorium up there? Did you ever see it there?

Essie: Oh yes. The students went to chapel every day up there, and they had to climb – those little girls – had to climb those stairs to get up there. *(Editor's*

Note: One can only imagine the consternation that would be created today by a public school requiring its students to attend chapel every day.)

Olin: Mother where did you go to school after the old high school building burned?

Marilyn: In the old Piedmont building – the same one to which you went to school. And I was in the 5th and 6th grades there, and then they had junior high school down there, and while they were building back the old (burned) building, they ran double-sessions or something or other down there (in the Piedmont building) . .

Olin: When you say "the old Piedmont School building," you mean the building that I attended for Junior High School? And that had been built there after they had torn down what Namma was referring to as "the old dormitory building?"

Marilyn: Yes.

Olin: Did you ever go to any gristmills around Rockmart to get flour back then?

Essie: No, but at home, father carried grain from our farm at Sugar Hill to the Gainesville Rolling Mill to grind into flour.

Olin: Did they use Tanner's Mill?

Essie: Tanner's Mill was for the corn. They ground corn down there. And it had two stones, you know – was a water-mill, but the Gainesville Rolling Mills were operated by electricity I guess.

Olin: Yep. They dammed up the Chattahoochee River outside town and generated electricity at Dunlap Dam.

Essie: I remember there were two big mills – there was the Gainesville Mill – cotton mill and then New Holland cotton mill…The New Holland Cotton Mill is still there – but how much it operates now I don't know. . . but, uh, the Gainesville Mill uh, went out of business years and years ago, and all that now is probably a business area. Used to be nothing between the square and the Southern Railway Station. You could ride a streetcar all the way down to the Southern Depot. Gainesville used to have street cars. Now I think I'm right about that…

Olin: Yeah. You're right. They did. You're right. I've got pictures of it.

1920s Rockmart Prior to Church Street – In earlier days in Rockmart, there were no bridges for vehicular traffic across Euharlee Creek. There was, however, a swinging bridge (pictured) across the creek at what today is Church Street at the Methodist Church. *"You didn't drive across the creek there because it was too deep,"* Essie Hudgins (Jordan) reminisced. *"There also were no paved streets in Rockmart at all. To cross the Euharlee, you'd just drive your car through it there at Elm Street (where it was shallow). It was called 'a ford.'"*

Historic Clermont, Georgia and the Gainesville-Northwestern RR

It was constructed as a transportation medium for the timber being harvested in northeast Georgia, and became a way of life for residents along the line from 1912 to 1935. When the seeming inexhaustible timber had all been harvested by the early 1930s, the little mountain short-line was necessary no more, and went out of business. When it disappeared, a way of life disappeared with it.

Just as occurred in the 1950s with a sister line – the Tallulah Falls Railroad – the Gainesville-Northwestern Railroad (G&NW) between Gainesville and Robertstown, Georgia, eventually depleted all the products which had originally given it life in 1912, and literally put itself out of business by 1935. The rails were pulled up and sold for scrap iron to Japan and the rights-of-way reverted back to ownership by the local landowners. It was a sad day for residents all up and down the picturesque little rail line into the mountains – but it had been really good while it lasted.

In the years preceding World War I, a group of businessmen had realized the value of the immense stock of forest products available in the northeast Georgia mountains. This same timber products industry also spawned a tiny community which would later grow to a far-greater prominence still in existence today – Helen, Georgia.

The Gainesville-Northwestern was incorporated on February 9, 1912, primarily to provide a viable and dependable mode of transportation for the timber products being harvested in northeast Georgia, and the wood products being produced from this timber by Byrd-Matthews Lumber Company in the present-day Helen vicinity. Passenger, freight, and mail service were provided by the G&NW which ran daily from Gainesville to Robertstown, passing thru numerous whistle- and flag-stops along the way.

Byrd-Matthews Lumber Company was one of the largest lumber mills east of the Mississippi in its day. It produced thousands of board feet of lumber every week which was shipped to Gainesville. After reaching that town, the lumber was transferred to other railroads for distribution throughout the United States as well as to a number of foreign countries. Lumber production was big business in north Georgia where virgin timber was still abundant in the early 1900s, and railroads such as the Gainesville-Northwestern Railroad were vital in the effort to harvest this timber.

The "passenger" aspect of the Gainesville-Northwestern Railroad featured what was known as "an excursion service" to and from Gainesville to and from Robertstown (above Helen), and also provided freight and postal service to these areas as well. The run began at the old Gainesville Depot (which still stands as of this writing in 2023) and made stops at Bradford Street Station (removed long ago), New Holland (also gone), Clark (gone), Autry (gone), Dewberry (gone), Brookton (the ruins of which survived until just recently), Clermont (long gone), County Line (gone), Mossy Creek Campground (long gone), Meldean (gone), Cleveland (long gone), Asbestos (gone), Mt. Yonah (gone), Nacoochee (still exists as of this writing in 2023), Helen (gone), and Robertstown (also gone). Gainesville, Brookton, Clermont, Meldean, Cleveland, Nacoochee, Helen, and Robertstown were what was known as "agency stations," and the train made regular stops at them. The others were known as "flag stops," (where stops were made only if the train was "flagged").

Clermont had existed as a community prior to the construction of the G&NW, springing up in part due to the town's strategic location on an aged travel route for traditional mountain products taken to market each year in Gainesville. When the railroad was constructed through the tiny town, Clermont gained a prime supply line and became a market destination from the more heavily populated cities of Gainesville and Atlanta to the south, factors which further enhanced its growth and fostered the commerce which sprang to life in Clermont from 1912 to the mid-1930s.

Another growth catalyst in Clermont which preceded the railroad was Chattahoochee High School, established around 1890. It became a Baptist Church-supported school which belonged to the Mercer University system of preparatory schools in 1919. It was a four-year school, with records indicating it produced its first graduating class in 1906.

Educational institutions of this nature were few in number in the north Georgia mountains at that time, and facilities such as Chattahoochee High became a strong incentive for the relocation of families interested in higher education for their children.

"My father and mother moved us to Clermont specifically so we could have the opportunity to go to a nine-month school," said the late Essie Hudgins Jordan, who was a graduate of Chattahoochee High. She was also a member of the faculty during the 1923-24 school year.

Miss Essie's father, James Zacheus Hudgins, had moved their family from Sugar Hill in South Hall County to Clermont in North Hall in 1913 when she was twelve years old. "Despite the fact that it meant wholly relocating a home and a profitable family

Byrd-Matthews Lumber Company was one of the largest lumber mills east of the Mississippi in its day.

business, it was important to Mother and Father that we children receive a good education," she added.

Miss Essie's beautiful old family home – built by her father in 1913 – still stands (as of this writing in 2023) on King Street in Clermont. It is one of a number of elegant turn-of-the-century homes which highlight the architectural beauty and scenic attractiveness of the town even today. While it was being constructed, the Hudgins family rented a home near Wauka Mountain.

In 1912, Clermont and the surrounding counties were still a very sparsely populated area, a type of pioneer country in many ways. "Father had a general store beside the railroad there in the center of town," Mrs. Jordan continued. "Clermont was a wonderful place for a child to grow up, and we had a large family – six brothers and six sisters.

"All the stories you read about pioneer life which describe the little general store where saddles, sunbonnets, barrels of apples, cheeses, dry goods, traps, and all the other staples of life in the mountains in that day and time, are very descriptive of what was sold in Father's store," she smiled. "On cold winter days, men gathered around an old pot-bellied stove to play checkers. 'Father loved to play checkers,' she stated in a conspiratorial whisper.

"Chattahoochee High School was a boarding school at that time," Miss Essie added. "The dormitory which housed both girls and boys was on the campus grounds. It had space for a music room and a library, as well as an apartment set aside for the school superintendent. Some of the students rented small cottages, going home on weekends and in the summer, when school was not in session."

The 1923-24 *"Annual Announcement"* booklet from Chattahoochee High offers a glimpse back in time at the school. It describes the institution as: *". . . located near the little town of Clermont, on the Gainesville-North Western Railroad, 16 miles from*

Gainesville....This puts Chattahoochee in a few minutes of Gainesville in one direction, and a few minutes of the mountains going north. For several miles in three directions, may be seen broad fields of corn and cotton and small grain. Much of this plateau section is yet wooded....Clermont is a thriving town, built up since the school was established. The town gives many advantages: one bank, post office, hotel, drug store, furniture store, five general mercantile stores, express office, two blacksmith establishments, and a telephone exchange.

As might be expected, social codes at the school were strict. Boys and girls were expected to refrain from all communication with each other except *"that which ordinary courtesy demands."* Boys and girls were not allowed the freedom of the town, except by special permission. They were expected to remain in their rooms at night. Boys were required to *"abstain from smoking cigarettes, playing cards, profanity, intoxicating liquors and the keeping of firearms."*

Before the railroad came through, and before Chattahoochee High School was constructed, Clermont's primary claim to fame had been its resort identity. The name *"Clermont"* is a shortened version of "Clear Mountains." The scenic location of the town in the shadow of nearby Wauka Mountain and the beginnings of the Blue Ridge Mountains in north Georgia, led to the construction of the Clermont Hotel in 1911-12. This structure, now over 110 years old, still stands on the old town square as of 2022.

Though not luxurious by any means, the Clermont Hotel was elegant for its day. The Gainesville-Northwestern Railroad passed right beside it and had its depot across the street. A tennis court (apparently one of the first in the north Georgia area) was available to the rear of the hotel, for guests.

Up toward what then was the tiny community of Helen, Mr. T.B. Henderson owned a general merchandise store next to the G&NW's Nacoochee Station. Both it and the Nacoochee Station still exist and are original to the community, being well over 100 years old as of 2022. *(Henderson's former General Store is the old brick building at the intersection of Highways 75 and 17, near the Indian mound. The former Nacoochee Station building stands across Highway 75 from the old general store building.)* Mr. Henderson's daughter, Mary Lula Henderson Davidson provided the following descriptive details concerning early life in turn-of-the-century Nacoochee:

"The Nacoochee Post Office was located in the general store and my father was postmaster there. He also served as rail agent at the Nacoochee Station. His duties included the issuance of tickets and the posting of freight bills. Most of the merchandise in his store came in by rail from Athens or Gainesville.

"Father was one of the few persons in the area who owned an automobile. Sometimes passengers coming in on the train would need transportation to one of the 'resorts' in the area or to a friend or relative's house. After arriving at Nacoochee Station, my brother - Bon - would drive the travelers to their destinations."

Mrs. Davidson also described how she helped her father in the store, post office and at the little railroad station. She remembers that in the store, they sold groceries, hardware, men's, women's and children's clothing, seeds and fertilizer, all mostly delivered by rail. She said that Mr. L.G. Hardman *(whose beautiful old home also still stands near the intersection of Hwy. 75 and 17, and was originally constructed by Civil War veteran Col. James Hall Nichols)* shipped butter and milk from his dairy by rail to Gainesville, and Mr. "Simp" Logan shipped asbestos from his asbestos mine by railroad.

Mr. Henry Davidson, who became the husband of Miss Mary Lula Henderson, was one of the many who helped to build the railroad from Gainesville to Robertstown. His brother, Mr. George Davidson, was an engineer on the train and Mr. Paul Westmoreland was fireman.

> *Boys and girls were not allowed the freedom of the town, except by special permission.*

The railroad brought many visitors to the White County area. Major resorts included the Alley House *(still in existence as the Old Sautee Inn today)* in Nacoochee; the Henderson Hotel in Cleveland (now long disappeared); and the Mitchell Mountain Ranch (also long gone) in Helen.

The Gainesville-Northwestern continued its 37-mile run from Gainesville to Robertstown until 1930. Shortly thereafter, when the once-inexhaustible supply of virgin timber had been depleted almost entirely, the railroad, with its life-blood gone, eventually became insolvent and service was discontinued. The tracks were taken up; the railroad rights-of-way reverted back to private ownership, and the Gainesville-Northwestern Railroad disappeared forever from the Hall and White County landscapes.

Chattahoochee High School Graduates (1906-1923)

1906 - J.T. Miller

1907 - Grover Miller

1908 - A.S. Kytle

1909 - George, Gearin, W.C. Grindle, C.W. Henderson, Fred Staton, W.L. Walker

1910 - H.W. Keith, U.A. Lawson, E.B. O'Kelley, M.K. Staton, Inez Spencer, Ruth Waters

1911 - F.L. Brown. B.J. Head, H.G. Hudgins, U.S. Lancaster, H.L. Lawson, R.H. Thomas, Minnie Head, Exer Head, Lola Staton.

1912 - H.E. Buffington, A.B. Eberhart, Claude Grindle, Hubert Haynes, W.H. Lord, B.H. Robinson, Beulah Hudgins, Vivian Jarrard, Liccie Payne, Lillie Payne, Nellie Whelchel

1913 - W.T. Evans, Charles E. Hawkins, W.P. Pettyjohn, W.A. Whitmire, John Haynes, A.B. Keith, C.H. Keith, F.P. Lockhart, Lena Hudgins, Mary Hulsey, Florence Ragan, Pink Standridge

1914 - C.J. Broom, H.T. Brookshire, O.G. Lancaster, G.F. Tyner, Salena Jarrard, Anna Belle Lockhart.

1915 - C.C. Jarrard, J.A. Meaders, M.D. Reed, Irene Bailey, Josephine Grogan, Chester Head, Iris Maddox.

1916 - Chesley Bennett, Harry Garrison, Richard Hawkins, Carl Lancaster, Elmira Grogan, Daisy Hudgins, Ethel Roark

1917 - W.E. Barnwell, R.L. Carter, Ernest Hulsey, J.L. Keith, D.T. Lawson, Y.W. Peck, H.H. Peyton, Beulah Greer, Myrtle Haynes, Ada Highsmith, Ethleen Jarrard, Florida Mauldin, Willie Staton.

1918 - Una Abercrombie, Laurie Truelove, Maude Logan, Esther Langford, Lillie Mac Culpepper, Annie Mae Haynes, Agnes Roark, Etta Chandler, Henry Reed, Clarence Puckett, Glenn Cooper, Edward Brown, Escoe Logan, Garnett Keith.

1919 - Valera Bowen, Bertie Mae Miller, Lillie Head, Sallie Hix, Hoke Grier, Homer Keith, Roy Martin, Bertha Waters, Essie Hudgins, Idell Haynes, Essie Tanner, Hester Tanner, Lucile Roark, Dewey Patten, Frank Cain, Howard Poole, Vassie Keith, Nell Whitmire.

1920 - Ernest Abercrombie, Clifton Bryson, Wallis Bennett, D.T. Buice, Nita Catlett, Callie Chandler, Adele Head, Vallie Hulsey, Floyd Hendrix, Avie Forrester, Jewell Keith, D.W. Lord, Ralph Miller, Clyde Maddox, Russell Marlow, Nellie Mae Pierce, Charlie Staton, Adelia Joe Staton, Clarence Walker, Julius Whitmire, Paul Whitmore, Edgar Hulsey.

1921 - Jarnet Carruth, Bonnie Carruth, Hugh Brice, Annie Brice, Henry Logan, Hortense Delong, Mabel Haynes, Mae Grant, Lee Grant, Herschel McGee, Seaborn Gilstrap, Y.D. Jones, Fred Moore, Ralph Thompson, J. Henry Lackey, Albert Martin, Nell Christopher, Mary Brown, Eugenia Rogers, Maudelle Pierce, Sylvia Gailey, Mary Elder, Price Bowen, Ruth Head, Michael McNeal, Texas Wallace, Herschel Davis, Laura Belle Culpepper, June Murphy, Ralph Murphy, Pearl Truelove, Pink Culpepper.

1922 - Ruth Crawford, Lee Buice, David Hudgins, Lucas Griffin, Willie Meaders, Cladith Simpson, Mozelle Marlowe, Hassie Mae Whitmire, Cordia Mullinax, Gertrude Kytle, Clarence Walker.

1923 - Cary Adams, Ernest Brown, Ralph Buffington, Lunie Mae Coker, Winnie Chandler, Kelsey Delong, Otis Dyer, Birdie Gailey, J.E. Grizzle, Clyde Hudgins, Mae Hooper, Mary Belle Jackson, Nina Keith, Vera Keith, Cora Belle Lancaster, Myrtle Moore, Fred Orr, Turner Quillian, Emma Haynes, Marilu Hudgins, Maggie Smith, Tony Walker.

Hudgins Genealogical Line
(Ancestry of One Hudgins Family Line in Georgia)
(Country of Origin of Hudgins Family Line: Wales and England)

In 1958, Houlder Hudgins IV wrote: *"In a collection of manorial documents in the estate of a Robert Blondell of Nottage Court in Llandaff, Wales, there is one dated 1505 which shows the original Welsh spelling of the Hudgins name as follows: 'Rhwwttchen'. At some point in time not now precisely known, an individual named Rhwwttchen moved from Wales to Liverpool in Lancastershire County, England. The English authorities reportedly found it difficult to pronounce the name as it was spelled . . . it started with a guttural Celtic rolling 'Rh' followed by a sound like 'udd' in the middle and ending with a soft sound like 'jinz.' As is often the case with settlement from one country to the next, the name was simplified by the English into 'Hudgins,' pronounced 'Hud-jinz,' and thus it has been ever since."*

Great-great-great-great-great-great-great-great-grandfather: Rhwwttchen

b. 1595, LLandoff, Wales

m. (?) Issue: **Thomas Hudgins** (b. 1620)

d. (?)

Great-great-great-great-great-great-great-grandfather: Thomas Hudgins

b. 1620, Liverpool, Lancashire, England

m. (?), Elizabeth Morgan (b. 1620, Glamorgan, Wales). Issue: **Robert Hudgins** (b. 1660)

d. (?)

Great-great-great-great-great-great-grandfather: Robert Hudgins

b. 1660, Liverpool, Lancashire, England

m. 1701, Charlotte Lewis (b. 1660 Glamorgan, Wales). Issue: William Hudgins (b. 01/18/1701, Llandaff, Monmouthshire, Wales, d. 10/12/1771, Gloucester, VA), **John Hudgen (Hudgins)** (b. 1705, England, d. 1784, Kingston Parish, Gloucester, VA), Lewis Hudgins (b. 1706, Gloucester, VA, d. 1799, Matthews Co. VA), and Robert Humphrey Hudgins (b. 1710, Liverpool, England, d. 1799, America).

d. (?)

Great-great-great-great-great-grandfather: John Hudgen (a.k.a. "Hudgins")

b. 1705, England

m. 12/25/1774, Mary Carney in Kingston Parish, VA. Issue: **James Beverly (a.k.a. "Bevely") Hudgen** (KPR)

d. 1784, Kingston Parish, Gloucester, VA

> **Note #1:** Many Hudgins lived in Virginia even before 1642. In 1790, the Baptist faith had a sizeable congregation in Virginia. One of the leaders of these Baptists was Robert Hudgins who became pastor of the church called Petsworth Baptist, leading this congregation until his death in 1791. (This church is in no way connected to Petsworth Parish, Virginia.) A Baptist church originally established in 1776, reportedly still exists in "Hudgins," Virginia. Known originally as "Kingston Baptist Church," a number of Hudgins have long been known to worship at this church, even in recent times. It remained known as "Kingston" until 1791, at which time the name was changed to "Mathews Baptist Church" after an act by the Virginia Assembly changed a portion of the former colony of Gloucester into Mathews County. Despite being changed to "Mathews Baptist," this church was still referred to by the Baptist Association as "Kingston Church" until 1804, and many references to the Hudgins family are found here.

> **Note #2:** "KPR" denotes "Kingston Parish Records, Virginia." The first U.S. records show the spelling as "Hudgen," then "Hudgin," then in the late 1700s, the name begins appearing in records as "Hudgins." Kingston Parish covered all of that section east of the North River in Virginia. In 1791, Kingston Parish was reconfigured to create Mathews County. A number of Hudgins descendants still live in Mathews County today, and a small community at the crossroads of VA 198 and VA 223 is still known as "Hudgins, VA" today.

Great-great-great-great-grandfather: James Beverly Hudgen/Hudgins

b. 09/14/1777 (also recorded as 10/26/1777), Kingston Parish, Gloucester, Virginia

m. 06/06/1801, Jane Bell, Jackson Co., GA (b. 08/27/1780, Guilford, NC, d. 1864, Hall Co., Ga) Issue: Beverly Jr. (b. 1800); Virginia B.; Gregory; Dessie; Mary Ann (b. 10/14/1801, Hall Co, d. 11/24/1885); **Zacharia (a.k.a. "Zaccharia," "Zachus," and "Zacheus")** (b. 03/04/1804, Hall Co., GA, d. 11/20/1877, Hall Co., Ga); Holder (b. 10/06/1806,, Hall Co., GA, d. 01/31/1881, Polk Arkansas); Esther (b. 08/18/1811, Hall Co., d. 05/30/1887, Walker Co., GA); Francis Bell (b. 09/29/1823, GA, d. 3/29/1905, Hall Co.); Iverson Delaprierre (b. 07/18/1826, GA, d. 10/07/1904, Chandler, Barrow, GA).

d. 1850, Chestnut Mountain (Hall Co.), GA. Buried Old Liberty Methodist Church, Chestnut Mountain, Hall Co., GA

> **Note #3:** James Beverly Hudgins's father-in-law, Francis Bell, gave him property in Hall County, GA, in the days when the area was still an unsettled wilderness with most of the land still in the possession of the native Indians. James Beverly reportedly built a five-room log house on this land near a place called "Macedonia Settlement." He is listed in the 1820 Hall County Census as "Beverly Hudgeons" (page 71), and again in the 1850 Hall Census (page 790). The settlement of Beverly's estate is listed in the Hall County Ordinary's office. Zacheus & Holder Hudgins were administrators. James Beverly Hudgins's old farm was passed to his wife, Jane, upon his death, and to their son, Francis Bell Hudgins, upon Jane's death, and to Francis's son, Jim, upon Francis's death. In more recent years, this property was owned by a Mr. J.J. Lott, and has been the site of frequent Hudgins family reunions over the years. Old Liberty Methodist Church at Chestnut Mountain disappeared long ago, as did the little community of Chestnut Mountain, though it (the community name of Chestnut Mountain) still may be found on maps even today. As of this writing, James Beverly Hudgins's lonely grave – which was well-marked – still amazingly exists with a handful of other graves in an isolated spot between several modern homes today at Chestnut Mountain, Hall Co., GA.

Great-great-great-grandfather: Zacharia (a.k.a. Zacheus) Hudgins

b.   03/04/1804, Hall Co., Georgia

m.   **(1st)** 03/16/1825, Hall Co., GA, Margaret "Peggy" Major (a.k.a. "Majors") (b. 03/20/1808, Hall Co., GA, d. 07/08/1876 (also listed as 07/08/1878), Hall Co., GA.) Issue: Margaret Marthena (b. 08/24/1822, Hall Co., GA d. 01/27/1912, Forsyth Co., GA). m. 09/24/1850, John I. Pirkle; **Richard Bennett** (b. 1828, Hall, d. 01/03/1865, N.C.); Mary Jane (b. 05/04/1834, Hall Co., d. 08/13/1902, Hall Co., m. 09/27/1857, Jacob Martin); Esther L. (b. 1835, m. 02/28/1856, Albert G. Pirkle); Nancy Evaline (b. 1837, m. 01/06/1863, C.M.C. Blackstock); Cindarella R. (b. 7/01/1840, d. 11/20/1910, m. 01/23/1866, James W. Lancaster); Cleo E. (b. 1842, m. 11/28/1877, William L. Lewis); J. W. (b. 1844); Rebecca Emaline (b. 1845, d. 01/28/1927, Hall Co., GA, m. 11/23/1860, Hugh C. Martin); and James Andrew Jackson (b. 06/05/1847, Hall Co., d. 04/10/1922, Hall Co., m. 12/22/1872, Sarah Elizabeth Blackstock).

    (2nd) 08/30/1876, Emily C. Whitworth Sexton (b. 10/06/1840, d. 07/26/1920).

d.   11/20/1877 (also listed as 11/09/1879), Hall Co., GA

    Note #4:   Richard Bennett Hudgins was a veteran of the War Between the States, serving in the Confederate infantry. During the final days of the war, with his unit (Company D, 27th Regiment, Georgia Volunteers, Army of Northern Virginia) in North Carolina, he fell ill with pneumonia and died and was buried in Oakwood Cemetery, Raleigh, North Carolina.

Great-great-grandfather: Richard Bennett Hudgins

b.   1828, Hall Co., GA

m.   10/11/1853, Jackson Co., GA, Arabella Pettyjohn [b. 04/03/1834, Jackson Co., GA, d. 06/19/1904, Hall Co., GA. Buried Harmony Grove Baptist Church *(also could be Harmony Hall Baptist Church)* Cemetery, Harmony Church Road, Hall, Co., GA]. *(Note: To reach Harmony Hall Baptist Church, take U.S. 129 east and turn left onto Blackstock Road in Hall County, then bear left onto Mangum Mill Road. Harmony Hall Baptist Church is on the left.)* Issue: Mary (b. 07/23/1854, d. 06/06/1885); Margaret Emmaline (b. 08/17/1856, Hall Co., GA, d. 10/16/1934, Jackson Co., GA); and **James Zacheus** (b. 12/30/1859, Jackson Co., GA, d. 02/01/1933, Clermont, Hall Co., GA).

d.   01/03/1865, Raleigh NC, from pneumonia while serving in Co. D, 27th Infantry Regiment, Georgia Volunteers, Army of Northern Virginia. Enlisted circa 08/27/1861. Contracted pneumonia near Goldsboro, NC, 12/27/1864. Sent to Confederate General Hospital #8, Raleigh, NC where he died. Buried 01/04/1865, Oakwood Cemetery, Raleigh, NC, Grave #356.

    Note #5:   Some of the extended Pettyjohn family, according to tradition, could possibly have been of Cherokee Indian lineage.

Great-Grandfather: James Zacheus Hudgins

b.   12/30/1859, Jackson Co., GA

m.   **(1st)** Elizabeth Harris, (07/22/1882) at Harmony Grove Baptist Church (Harmony Hall Baptist Church?), Hall Co., GA (b. 12/18/1867, Clayton Co., GA, d. 10/29/1892, Hall Co., GA. Buried Harmony Hall Baptist Church Cemetery, Hall County, GA). Issue: Richard B. (b. 02/18/1885, d. 01/12/1919); Silas A. (b. 09/05/1886); William J. (b. 08/01/1888, d. 04/13/1889); Mattie Bell (b. 01/20/1890, d. 06/26/1891); and Lucy May (b. 08/03/1891).

    (2nd) Sarah Elizabeth Tanner, (03/31/1895), (b. 12/07/1878, Chestnut Mountain, Hall Co., GA. Died 12/19/1969, Hiram, Paulding Co., GA.) Issue: Daisy Lee (b. 7/21/1896, d. 08/31/1996); Carl Washington (b. 08/28/1898, d. 12/27/1967, Lexington, KY); **Essie Irene (Carroll)**; David Bennett (b. 01/24/1902, d. 01/14/1983); Clyde Franklin (b. 11/06/1903, d. 02/18/1994); Mary Lou (Marilu) (b. 06/03/1905); Cora Estelle (b. 12/14/1906, d. 02/14/1992); Ralph Newton (b. 09/16/1908, d. 08/23/1970); Albert White (b. 04/21/1910, d. 02/01/1976); Raleigh (Raliegh) Edward (b. 06/05/1912, d. 07/11/1982); Sarah Rebecca (b. 07/14/1914, d. 12/10/1999, m. Herman Gibbs "Doc" Tankersley 11/18/1933 who was Justice of the Peace, Hall Co., GA for many years); Dorothy Belle (b. 11/23/1916, d. 05/15/2007, m. Ray Shaw); Marjorie Catherine (b. 10/23/1918, d. 07/20/2005).

d.   02/01/1933, Hall Co., GA. Buried Concord Baptist Church Cemetery, Clermont, Hall Co., GA.)

    Note #6:   James Zacheus Hudgins built a large elegant home in "downtown" Clermont, GA, and moved in with his family in 1914, just in time for the birth there of daughter Sarah. Two more children, Dorothy and Marjorie, were also born in this home, bringing the total number of children to 13. Two additional children were later born, bringing the total to 15, but wife Sarah was 43 years of age by this time, and these last two children did not survive. As of 2022, the fine old home built by James Z. in 1913 still stood on King Street in Clermont. The first ten Hudgins children were born in Sugar Hill, Hall Co., GA.

Grandmother: Essie Irene (Carroll) Hudgins Jordan

b.   03/12/1900, Sugar Hill, Jackson Co., GA. (Located on old Athens Hwy/U.S. 129 between Talmo and Pendergrass.)

m.   06/18/1927, Clermont, Hall Co., GA, Guy Wilfred Jordan (b. 02/19/1889, Dutch Hill, PA, d. 09/05/1946, Rockmart, Polk Co., GA. Buried Rose Hill Cemetery, Rockmart, Polk Co., GA) Issue: **Marilyn** and Patricia (b. 06/25/1934, Rockmart, Polk Co., GA, d. 12/29/2014, Doraville, DeKalb Co., GA.)

d.   02/11/1999, Rockmart, Polk Co., GA. Buried Rose Hill Cemetery, Rockmart, Polk Co., GA.

Notes:

_____

_____

_____

_____

NAMES of HEADS OF FAMILIES.	FREE WHITE PERSONS, (including heads of families.)																							
	MALES.													FEMALES.										
	under 5	5 to 10	10 to 15	15 to 20	20 to 30	30 to 40	40 to 50	50 to 60	60 to 70	70 to 80	80 to 90	90 to 100	100, &c.	under 5	5 to 10	10 to 15	15 to 20	20 to 30	30 to 40	40 to 50	50 to 60	60 to 70	70 to 80	80 to 90
William Harper	2	1	1	2			1							1		2	2		1					
Jacob Reames	1	1				1								2				1						
Richard Pinnell		2			1											1								
Samuel R. VanPresley	1					1								1										
Samuel Donaldson					1									1										
Charles Collins	2				1									1										
Ezekiel Pullman	1		2		1											1								
Daniel Pullman					1									1										
James Collins	1	1	1		1									2										
George Lumpkin			1	1	2		1							2						1				
Stephen Kennel		1	1	2										2										
William Williams																								
Abner McBell	1		1	2										2										
Beaufort Fister																								
Vincent Johnson	3		2																	2				
Harvey Thompson																								
Thomas Harvey	2													1	2	1				1				
Kesiah Bishop					1																			
Patsey Glaze		1																						
Frances Kesterly		2		2													2	1	1					1
John Collins				2	1	1		1						1				1						
William Murphy	1	1			1									1										
Samuel Pierce	1	1			1									1		1								
Beverly Hudgins	1	1		2			1							1		1	2	2	1					
Zacheus Hudgins	2		1											1										
John Scott	1	1		1										1										
	20	12	11	13	12	11	3	5	1	.	..	..	-	16	8	7	8	16	10	6	3	.	.	1

1830 FEDERAL CENSUS, HALL COUNTY, GEORGIA

Hudgins, James Beverly (a.k.a. "Bevely") – Listed on this 1830 Census are: "one male under five years of age"; "one male between ten and fifteen years of age"; "two males between twenty and thirty years of age"; "one male between fifty and sixty years of age"; "one female between five and ten years of age"; "one female between fifteen and twenty years of age"; "two females between twenty and thirty years of age"; "one female between thirty and forty years of age"; and one female forty to fifty years of age." In 1830, Bevely's son, Bevely, Jr., would have been 30 years of age, so he possibly was one of males between 20 and 30 years of age. Bevely's daughter, Mary Ann, born in 1801, would have been 29 years of age, so she possibly was one of the two females between 20 and 30 years of age. Zacharia/Zacheus born in 1804, would have been 26 years of age, so he could also have been one of the males "between 20 and 30 years of age," as could Holder, who, born in 1806, would have been 24 years of age. Another daughter, Esther, born in 1811, would have been 19, so she possibly was the female "between 15 and 20 years of age." Iverson Delaprierre, born in 1826, would have been the male "under five years of age."

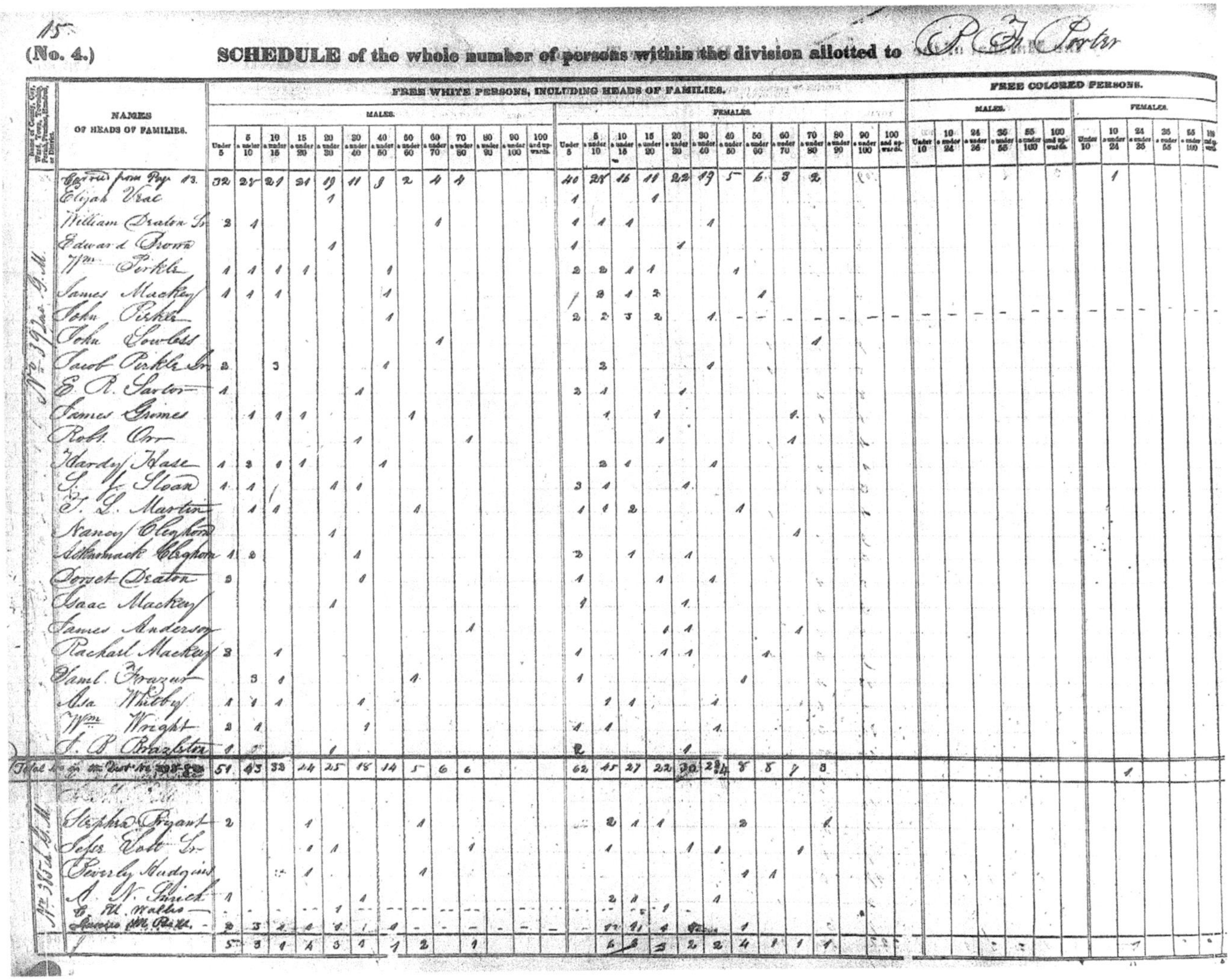
15
(No. 4.)
SCHEDULE of the whole number of persons within the division allotted to P. F. Porter
NAMES OF HEADS OF FAMILIES.
FREE WHITE PERSONS, INCLUDING HEADS OF FAMILIES.
MALES.
FEMALES.
FREE COLORED PERSONS.
Carried from Page 13.
Elijah Veal
William Draton Sr
Edward Brown
Wm. Pirkle
James Mackey
John Pirkle
John Lowless
Jacob Pirkle Jr
E. R. Sarter
James Grimes
Robt. Orr
Hardy Hase
S. Y. Sloan
T. L. Martin
Nancy Cleghorn
Sillamach Cleghorn
Dorset Draton
Isaac Mackey
James Anderson
Rachael Mackey
Saml. Frazier
Asa Whitby
Wm. Wright
J. B. Brazelton
Stephen Bryant
Peter Cole Sr
Beverly Hudgins
A. N. Smith

1840 FEDERAL CENSUS, JACKSON COUNTY, GEORGIA

Hudgins, James Beverly (a.k.a. "Bevely") – By 1840, Beverly's household has been considerably diminished. Listed this time are: "one male between 15 and 20 years of age"; "one male between 50 and 60 years"; "one female between 40 and 50 years"; and "one female between 50 and 60."

Georgia } By the Court of Justices of
Hall County } said County

To John H Hanson or his Deputy
County Surveyor of said County —
You are hereby authorized and required to admeasure
and lay out or cause to be admeasured and laid
out unto Zacheus Hudgins a tract of land
which will Contain   acres in said
County on the Waters of Allens fork of the
Oconee River adjoining lands of B D Majors
and the said Hudgins taking Special Care
that the same has not heretofore been laid out
to any other person or persons, And you also
hereby directed and required to record the plat
of the Same in your office. and transmit
a copy thereof together with this Warrant to
the Surveyor general within the time prescribed
by law —

Given under hands as Justices of
Said Court this 4th day of February
1851

J L Baugh J.I.C
G G Thompson I.I.C
E Goode I.I.C
James Roberts I.I.C

1851 HALL COUNTY HEADRIGHT AND LAND BOUNTY
Hudgins, Zacheus (a.k.a. "Zacharia") – In this document, Zacheus Hudgins is being granted a land bounty by Hall County adjacent to Allen Fork on the Oconee River.

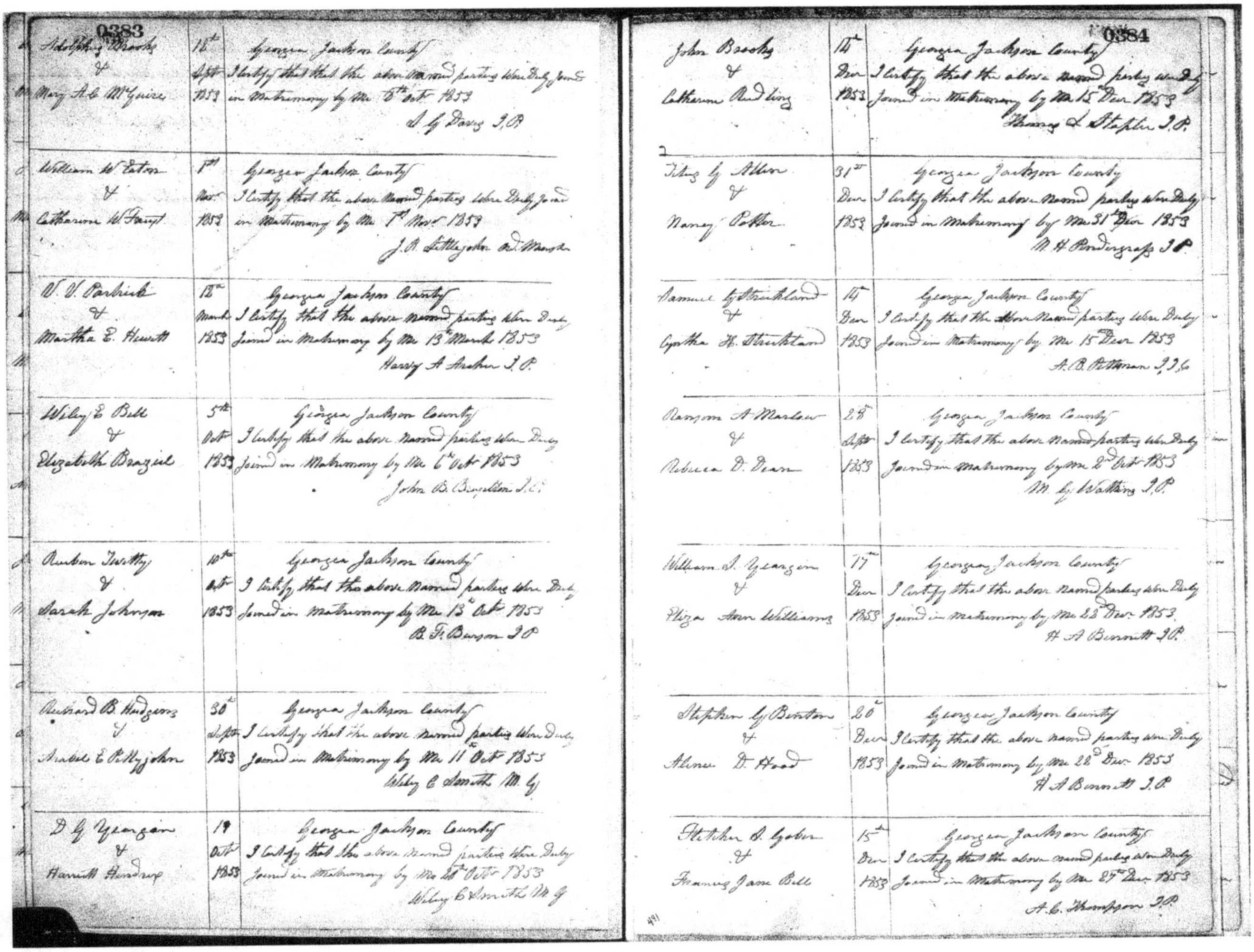

Parties	Date	Certificate
0383 Adolphus Brooks & Mary A. C. McGuire	18th Sept 1853	Georgia Jackson County. I Certify that the above named parties were Duly Joined in Matrimony by Me 6th Oct 1853 S. G. Davis J.P.
William W. Eaton & Catharine W. Fawcett	1st Nov 1853	Georgia Jackson County. I Certify that the above named parties were Duly Joined in Matrimony by Me 1st Nov 1853 J. R. Littlejohn Ord. Minister
V. V. Parrick & Martha E. Hewitt	12th March 1853	Georgia Jackson County. I Certify that the above named parties were Duly Joined in Matrimony by Me 13th March 1853 Harvey A. Archer J.P.
Wiley E. Bell & Elizabeth Brazeil	5th Oct 1853	Georgia Jackson County. I Certify that the above named parties were Duly Joined in Matrimony by Me 6th Oct 1853 John B. Bingeldon J.C.
Reuben Twitty & Sarah Johnson	10th Oct 1853	Georgia Jackson County. I Certify that the above named parties were Duly Joined in Matrimony by Me 13th Oct 1853 B. F. Burson J.P.
Richard B. Hudgins & Arabel E. Pettyjohn	30th Sept 1853	Georgia Jackson County. I Certify that the above named parties were Duly Joined in Matrimony by Me 11 Oct 1853 Wiley C. Smith M.G.
D. G. Yeargin & Harriett Hendrup	19 Oct 1853	Georgia Jackson County. I Certify that the above named parties were Duly Joined in Matrimony by Me 20th Oct 1853 Wiley C. Smith M.G.
0384 John Brooks & Catharine Rudling	14th Dec 1853	Georgia Jackson County. I Certify that the above named parties were Duly Joined in Matrimony by Me 15 Dec 1853 Thomas L. Stapler J.P.
Tilmon G. Allen & Nancy Potter	31st Dec 1853	Georgia Jackson County. I Certify that the above named parties were Duly Joined in Matrimony by Me 31st Dec 1853 M. H. Bondurant J.P.
Samuel G. Strickland & Cyntha H. Strickland	14th Dec 1853	Georgia Jackson County. I Certify that the above named parties were Duly Joined in Matrimony by Me 15 Dec 1853 A. B. Pittman J.I.C.
Ransom A. Marlow & Rebecca D. Dean	28 Sept 1853	Georgia Jackson County. I Certify that the above named parties were Duly Joined in Matrimony by Me 2d Oct 1853 M. G. Watkins J.P.
William J. Yeargin & Eliza Ann Williams	17 Dec 1853	Georgia Jackson County. I Certify that the above named parties were Duly Joined in Matrimony by Me 22 Dec 1853 H. A. Bennett J.P.
Stephen G. Benton & Aline D. Hood	20th Dec 1853	Georgia Jackson County. I Certify that the above named parties were Duly Joined in Matrimony by Me 22d Dec 1853 H. A. Bennett J.P.
Stephen D. Gober & Francis Jane Bell	15th Dec 1853	Georgia Jackson County. I Certify that the above named parties were Duly Joined in Matrimony by Me 27th Dec 1853 A. C. Thompson J.P.

1853 JACKSON COUNTY MARRIAGE RECORDS
Richard Bennett Hudgins – Richard and Arabella Pettyjohn are united in marriage.

Page No. _145_

SCHEDULE 1.—Free Inhabitants in _268th District_ in the County of _Hall_ State _145_ of _Georgia_ enumerated by me, on the _19th_ day of _July_ 1860. _O. Thompson_ Ass't Marshal.

Post Office _Sugar Hill_

		The name of every person whose usual place of abode on the first day of June, 1860, was in this family.	Age.	Sex.	White, black, mulatto.	Profession, Occupation, or Trade of each person, male and female, over 15 years of age.	Value of Real Estate	Value of Personal Estate	Place of Birth, Naming the State, Territory, or Country.				Whether deaf and dumb, blind, insane, idiotic, pauper, or convict.	
1	2	3	4	5	6	7	8	9	10	11	12	13	14	
1		James Lackie	9/12	M					Ga					1
2	1075 906	J. Thomas	75	M					"				1 Pauper	2
3		Mary "	50	F					"		1			3
4		Samuel "	7	M					"		1			4
5	1076 907	Z. Hudgins	56	M		Farmer	1500	1000	"					5
6		Margaret "	52	F		Tailorist			"					6
7		E. "	25	M		Farmer	200	175	"	*	1			7
8		Evaline "	23	F					"					8
9		Cindarilla "	19	F					"					9
10		Cloah "	18	F					"		1			10
11		Z. W. "	16	M					"		1			11
12		Rebecca "	15	F					"		1			12
13		J. A. J. "	12	M					"		1			13
14	1077 908	P. G. Major	41	M		Farmer	2000	10000	S.C.					14
15		Nancy "	36	F					"					15
16		Margaret "	14	F					"		1			16
17		James "	12	M					Ga		1			17
18		Mary "	11	F					"		1			18
19		Sarah "	9	F					"		1			19
20		Albert "	5	M					"					20
21		Robert "	3	M					"					21
22		Infant "	days	M					"					22
23	1078 909	J. C. Little	63	M		Farm Labrer	125	50	S.C.					23
24		Margaret "	18	F					"		1			24
25	1079 910	A. Little	39	M		Farmer		300	"					25
26		Elizabeth "	40	F					Ala		1			26
27		James "	15	M					Ga		1			27
28		John "	13	M					"		1			28
29		Benjamin "	9	M					"		1			29
30		Mary Ann "	6	F					"		1			30
31		Margaret "	4	F					"					31
32	1080 911	W. A. McDuffie	27	M		Farm Labrer		140	Ga		1			32
33		Jane "	26	F					Ireland					33
34		James "	10	M					Ga					34
35		Mary "	8	F					"					35
36		Wm. "	5	M					"					36
37		Robert "	3	M					"					37
38		Thomas "	7/12	M					"					38
39	1081	Unoccupied												39
40	1082	Do												40

No. white males _22_ No. colored males. No. foreign born. No. blind. No. idiotic. No. convicts.
No. white females _16_ No. colored females. No. deaf and dumb. No. insane. _3825 11665_ No. paupers.

1860 FEDERAL CENSUS, SUGAR HILL (268TH DISTRICT), HALL COUNTY, GEORGIA

Hudgins, Zacharia (a.k.a. "Zacheus") – Listed within this Census are Zacharia, age 56, a farmer with real estate valued at $1,500.00 and personal property valued at $1,000.00; his wife, Margaret ("Peggy" Majors), age 52, listed as a *"tailorist"*; "E," age 25, a male who is listed as a farmer with real estate valued at $200.00 and personal property valued at $175.00 and who is unable to read or write; Evaline, age 23; Cleo E., age 18; J.W., 16; Rebecca, 15; and J.A.J. (James Andrew Jackson), 12. For reasons unknown today, Richard Bennett and Mary Jane were not included in this Census. Richard served in the Confederate Army from 1861 to 1865, dying of pneumonia during the terrible winter of 1865. He was buried January 4, 1865, in Raleigh's Oakwood Cemetery (Grave #356).

1870 FEDERAL CENSUS, TADMORE DISTRICT, HALL COUNTY, GEORGIA
Hudgins, Zacheus (a.k.a. "Zacharia") – Listed in this census are: Zacheus, age 65, still the head of his household; his wife, Margaret ("Peggy"), age 50, "keeping house"; Clora, age 27, "assisting Mother"; James A., age 23, "laboring on farm"; and interestingly, an individual named "Samantha Chandler," age 17, listed also as "laboring on farm." As with Samantha Chandler, the identity of "Clora" is unknown.

1880 FEDERAL CENSUS, TADMORE DISTRICT, HALL COUNTY, GEORGIA

Hudgins, Arabella Pettyjohn – Arabella, age 46, is now the head of the household, even though she is listed simply as "keeping house." Her son, James Zacheus, age 20, is listed as "farmer."

Georgia, Hall County.

To any Minister of the Gospel, Judge or Justice of the Peace:

YOU ARE HEREBY AUTHORIZED TO JOIN

James Z. Hudgins and *Miss E. C. Harris*

in the Holy State of Matrimony, if they are such persons as are by law authorized to marry, and this shall be your License for so doing; and you are required to return to me this License, together with the accompanying Certificate properly certified to as to the facts, and date of said marriage.

Given under my hand and official signature, this _19th_ day of _July_ 188_2_

J. B. M. Winburn Ordinary.

I Hereby Certify, That _James Z. Hudgins_ and _Miss E. C. Harris_ were this day duly joined in Matrimony by me, this _23rd_ day of _July_ 1882

W. E. Smith, O. M. G.

1882 MARRIAGE LICENSE, HALL COUNTY, GEORGIA

Hudgins, James Z. and Elizabeth C. Harris – James Z. Hudgins and his first wife, Elizabeth Harris obtained this Marriage License on July 19 of 1882, and were duly married on July 23 of that year. From this union would be born Richard and Silas. Two other children would die in child-birth. A fifth child – Lucy Mae – would survive. Unfortunately, James' wife, Elizabeth, would die in 1892, a short ten years from the date of this marriage. The cause of her death is unknown today.

1900 FEDERAL CENSUS, TADMORE DISTRICT, HALL COUNTY, GEORGIA

Hudgins, James Z. – In 1895, three years after the 1892 death of his first wife, James Z. Hudgins married his second wife, Sarah "Sallie" Elizabeth Tanner of the nearby Tanner's Mill clan. James is first listed as "40" years of age in this Census, but this age was crossed out by the Census Taker and replaced with the age 39. Perhaps since he was born on December 30, 1859, there was some confusion in the matter. Whatever the circumstances, wife Sallie's age – which was actually 21 at the time – was also crossed out and replaced with an illegible number. This Census also lists the birth year incorrectly for both James and Sarah. It lists James's profession as *"farmer & merchant."* The birth year for a number of the other Hudgins children is also incorrect. The Census Taker does not even list a birth year or age for James's now-elderly mother, Arabella, who was born in 1834, while Cherokee Indians still inhabited north Georgia.

1910 FEDERAL CENSUS, TADMORE DISTRICT, HALL COUNTY, GEORGIA

Hudgins, James Z. – This Census shows James still the head of the family. It lists his age correctly as "50," but even though he was a well-known and prosperous general merchandise businessman on the town square until the day he died, his profession in this Census is listed as "farmer." His wife, Sarah Elizabeth, age 31, is listed in his household, as are: Daisy, 14; Carl, 12; Essie, 10; David, 9; Clyde, 7; Mary Lou, 5; Cora, 3; and a new-born "J.Z." (James Zacheus) Jr. is listed as one month old. The early 1900s in rural north Georgia were extremely hard times, and J.Z Jr. is one of several children born to James and Sarah who did not survive.

From The Mayor:

MUSINGS FROM MINUTES OF EARLY TOWN COUNCIL MEETINGS

The Town of Clermont received its charter from the State of Georgia on August 11, 1913. All indications are that Clermont was a bustling community before it was chartered as a town. The first recorded meeting of the mayor and council occurred on December 4, 1914, over a year after the town was chartered. December 1914 was a busy time for the new officers of Clermont. At the December 4th meeting, Mayor Mood Griffin swore in R. H. Ledford, George W. Grindle, Jim Haynes, and B. C. Haynes as Councilmen. The Council elected H. Tabor as the clerk of the Council, B. C. Haynes as Mayor-Pro-Tem, R. L. Kennimer as Treasurer, and Ferd Whelchel as marshal. The salaries of the officers were fixed as follows: Mayor $75 per annum, Councilmen $25 per annum, Clerk $25 per annum excluding $1.25 extra for issuing warrants, Marshal $60 per annum excluding $1.00 per day for working streets and $1.25 for each arrest with evidence to convict. The Council approved to require licenses for the following, along with their annual fee:

General Merchandise Line up $3,000 stock ($10.00)
Drug stores and Soda Fountains, etc up to $1,500 stock ($5.00)
Millinery Stores or Lines ($5.00)
Livery Business either by horses, mules, or automobiles ($5.00)
Guano Dealers ($5.00)
All persons owning or controlling Warehouses ($2.50)
Barber shop ($1.00)
Studios or Art Galleries ($1.00)
Hotels or Public Boarding Houses ($5.00)
Meat Markets ($2.50)
Public Machinery such as Cotton Gins, Planing Mills, etc ($2.50)
Blacksmith Shops ($2.50)
Medical Doctors ($5.00)
Opticians ($1.00)
Dentist or Dental Shops ($5.00)
Peddlers ($1.00)
Banks or Banking Institutions ($10.00)

There was also a fee of $2.50 to $5.00 per day or night for shows or public exhibitions according to size and for all persons subject to commutation pay $4.00 per year or 5 days work on the streets wherever the authorities shall require. Real and personal property taxes were set at $0.20 per hundred.

The next meeting was December 10, 1914. At this meeting a motion was carried to rescind the $0.20 property tax and reset at a more convenient Season. Motion was carried to post notices of business tax and make them payable January 15, 1915. Motions also carried to have the Town surveyed and to have necessary stationery printed. A street committee of Jim Haynes, Chairman, R. H. Ledford, and Dr. Pratt Cheek was appointed.

The Council met again on December 21, 1914. A motion carried to build a 10 foot by 12 foot calaboose with partitions. A committee of Jim Haynes, Chairman, G. W. Grindle, and B. C. Haynes was appointed to plan and have charge of building the calaboose. They were also to see J. T. Griffin and get a lease for 12 months for the calaboose. There was also a request to have the railroad clean up their right-of-way. The Council also noted that 3 fines totaling $12.25 had been imposed and collected.

December 29, 1914 a called meeting was held. C. T. Griffin was elected Mayor-Pro-Tem as H. Tabor had resigned. A motion carried for the Marshall to buy bucket, rope, windless, and whirl for public well and charge to Town.

January 4, 1915, the Council met. Motion was carried to employ the county surveyor to survey the Town. Committee of B. C. Haynes, Chairman, George W. Grindle, and Jim Haynes was appointed to get the survey done. Motion carried to require a license tax of $5.00 per year for all persons soliciting or writing insurance. Motion carried to have the Calaboose committee have a public closet built.

The Council met again on January 18, 1915. The Calaboose Committee presented the following bills. To G. L. Rudeseal, 29 hours labor @ 20 cents = $5.80; Ferd Whelchel, 15 hours work on calaboose @ 10 cents = $1.50 and 7 hours on road $0.70; T. E. Highsmith for 5 hours on calaboose @ 10 cents = $0.50; R. F. Whelchel 25 hours on calaboose @ 10 cents = $2.50; John Moose 5 hours on calaboose @ 10 cents = $0.50; J. T. Haynes 20 hours on calaboose @ 10 cents = $2.00; Silas Dunagan 2 hours work on road @ 10 cent = $0.20; T. C. Miller for hinges for calaboose $0.30 and Griffin Brothers $1.70 for nails.

At the February 8, 1915 meeting of the council it was moved and seconded that the doctor license and license for transporting passengers or baggage lag over until the parties have an opportunity of offering for business, especially autos, as the roads are in such conditions as not to justify their traveling, and as all interested have respectfully asked a little extension.

The calaboose committee reported that the calaboose and closet were completed and the following bills were presented to be paid. B. C. Haynes $3.30 for lumber; J. F. Haynes 64 cents for lumber; B. C. Haynes for 67 feet @ $1.10; T. T. Haynes one and three fourths days work; J. R. Delong $33.02 for lumber; T. E. Highsmith $1.40 for nails; the Marshall $1.45 for bucket and rope; and G. L. Rudeseal $1.50 for labor. The calaboose committee was dismissed.

1915 CLERMONT TOWN COUNCIL MEETINGS (P1)

The Survey Committee reported that Col. J O. Adams agrees to pay the surveyor for doing this work and that it would be done at his earliest convenience.

A committee of J. F. Haynes, Chairman, George Grindle, and Dr. Pratt Cheek was appointed to look into the sanitary condition of the Town. The Committee is to see that the Town is properly drained. Unsanitary swamps are to be investigated and reported as such at the next meeting. It was also moved to pay Tom Saxon $1.50 for work on King Street and for the ditch to be opened from closet at the expense of the Town.

Town Council met again February 22, 1915. The committee on sanitation reported that they had notified all persons having unsanitary swamps as pronounced unhealthy by the committee and that said swamps be thoroughly and in a satisfactory manner be drained. Work on said ditches to be commenced inside of 5 days and be completed inside of 30 days notice of said action being legally served them.

There was also a motion to post speed limits of 15 miles per hour at the corporate limits of Main Street. Another action considered by the Council was a warrant issued against a Mr. Marlow for being intoxicated. Appearance bond was fixed at $5.00. Mr. Marlow failed to appear in court and the bond was forfeited. A motion carried to pay Hudgins S. Gailey bill of $8.00 for roofing and nails.

At the March 8, 1915 meeting it was moved and seconded to pay Palmour Hardware Co. bill of $3.50 for nails and lock and Kytle Loggins bill of 2 days work ditching for Town. Motion carried to issue fi-fa against T. J. Faulkner for auto license. Motion approved to hire man to ditch Guy Bowens swamp at his expense, same being agreeable with Mr. Bowen. An ordinance was passed to force all persons having chickens to keep them on their own property.

At the March 22, 1915 meeting the Survey Committee was released as they had completed their work. Motion carried to pay the following bills for work in surveying: T. E. Highsmith $21.30; T. T. Haynes $1.50; Jim Haynes $1.00; T. M. Whelchel $3.00; J. F. Moorefield surveyor $10.96 as J. O. Adams refused to pay surveyor as promised. Approved payment of $9.00 to T. W. Staton for work on road. Appointed George Grindle, Jim Haynes, and Dr. Cheek to have road scrape made. The Marshall was ordered to warn all persons subject to  street tax to put in their spring term at once. The following were elected as the tax assessors and to be paid $1.50 per day. J. M. Haynes, T. W. Staton, and T. E. Highsmith. Marshall was to notify them of their election. The Town Council, at the April 5, 1915 meeting, adopted an ordinance that established public streets in the Town, named the streets, provided for a speed limit of 15 miles per hour, set fines for speeding, and prescribed what persons were responsible for work on the streets and provided penalties for those not doing the work. The fine for speeding was not less than $5 or more than $25 and was at the discretion of the mayor. Work on the streets was done at the direction of the marshal, and the mayor and council designated who was to do the work. Persons failing to do their street work were double taxed or fined not exceeding $3 per day or imprisonment in the "station house" for a period not exceeding 10 days at the discretion of the mayor.

Council had been searching for a place to hold its meetings, and at the April 19, 1915 meeting Mr. Hudgins reported that arrangements had been made with Mr. Adams to use the barber shop for 25 cents per month with lights and chairs furnished by the Town. Other business included the mayor agreeing to go to Staton and Cochran and ask them to pay warehouse tax and for the marshal to look into the matter of W. C. Ham writing insurance in town without a license. There was a report that not all the ditching work had been done. Also the street committee was to assist the marshal in getting a team and that King Street be worked at once and not to begin later than Wednesday of this week.

STATE _Georgia_

COUNTY _Hall_

9—137

DEPARTMENT OF COMMERCE—

FOURTEENTH CENSUS OF THE UNIT

TOWNSHIP OR OTHER DIVISION OF COUNTY _Clermont District 1745_

NAME OF INCORPORA

NAME OF INSTITUTION _____

ENU

Line	Street	Number of dwelling	Number of family	NAME of each person whose place of abode on January 1, 1920, was in this family.	RELATION. Relationship of this person to the head of the family.	Home owned or rented	If owned, free or mortgaged	Sex	Color or race	Age at last birthday	Single, married, widowed, or divorced	Year of immigration to the U.S.	Naturalized or alien	If naturalized, year of naturalization	Attended school	Whether able to read	Whether able to write	Place of birth of each person
51		28	31	Jackson George T.	Head	R	M	W	52	m					yes	yes	Georgia
52				— Mary E	Wife		F	W	37	m					no	no	Georgia
53				— Dicy	Daughter		F	W	10	S							Georgia
54				— Iver	Daughter		F	W	5½	S							Georgia
55		29	32	Griffin John T.	Head	O		M	W	63	m				yes	yes	South Carolina
56				— Bernice	Wife		F	W	61	m					yes	yes	Georgia
57				— Lucas	Son		M	W	18	S				yes	yes	yes	Georgia
58		30	23	Rudesal George L	Head	R	M	W	37	m					yes	yes	Georgia
59				— Louise	Wife		F	W	34	m					yes	yes	Georgia
60				— Lillian	Daughter		F	W	9	S							Georgia
61				— Rosavell	Daughter		F	W	4½	S							Georgia
62		31	34	Kildslel Amanda	Head	O		F	W	63	W				yes	yes	Georgia
63				— Nellie	Daughter		F	W	26	S				yes	yes	yes	Georgia
64		32	35	Grinelle Walter	Head	O		M	W	35	m				yes	yes	Georgia
65				— Claudie	Wife		F	W	31	m					yes	yes	Georgia
66				— Birdie May	Daughter		F	W	12	S				yes	yes	yes	Georgia
67				— Andrew J	Son		M	W	8	S				yes			Georgia
68		33	36	Hudgins James Z	Head	O		M	W	60	m				yes	yes	Georgia
69				— Sarah E	Wife		F	W	41	m					yes	yes	Georgia
70				— Daisy Lee	Daughter		F	W	23	S					yes	yes	Georgia
71				— Carl H	Son		M	W	21	S					yes	yes	Georgia
72				— Essie I.	Daughter		F	W	19	S				yes	yes	yes	Georgia
73				— David B.	Son		M	W	18	S				yes	yes	yes	Georgia
74				— Clyde F	Son		M	W	16	S				yes	yes	yes	Georgia
75				— Mary Lou	Daughter		F	W	14	S				yes	yes	yes	Georgia
76				— Cora E.	Daughter		F	W	13	S				yes	yes	yes	Georgia
77				— Ralph R	Son		M	W	11	S				yes	yes	yes	Georgia
78				— Albert K	Son		M	W	10	S				yes	yes	yes	Georgia
79				— Raleigh E	Son		M	W	7½	S				yes			Georgia
80				— Sarah	Daughter		F	W	5½	S							Georgia
81				— Dorothy	Daughter		F	W	3½	S							Georgia
82				— Marjorie	Daughter		F	W	1½	S							Georgia
83	Street	34	37	Turner Dave	Head	Rn		M	W	63	m				yes	no	Georgia
84				— Rebecca	Wife		F	W	60	m					yes	yes	Georgia
85				— Thomas	Son		M	W	16	S				yes	yes	yes	Georgia
86	Rway	35	38	Brown Ralph R.	Head	Rn		M	W	50	m				yes	yes	Georgia
87				— Emma	Wife		F	W	37	m					yes	yes	Georgia
88				— Myrtle	Daughter		F	W	25	S					yes	yes	Georgia
89				— Lily June	Daughter		F	W	19	S				yes	yes	yes	Georgia
90				— Ernest	Son		M	W	14	S				yes	yes	yes	Georgia
91				— Kermit	Son		M	W	11	S				yes	yes	yes	Georgia
92				— Louise	Daughter		F	W	10	S				yes			Georgia
93				— Libbie	Daughter		F	W	6½	S				yes			Georgia
94				— John W	Son		M	W	4½	S							Georgia
95				— O H.	Son		M	W	2¾	S							Georgia
96				— Blanche	Daughter		F	W	11/12	S							Georgia
97		36	39	Elder John G.	Head	O		M	W	53	m				yes	yes	Georgia
98				— Emma June	Wife		F	W	42	m					yes	yes	Georgia
99				— Mary E	Daughter		F	W	16	S				yes	yes	yes	Georgia
100				— Philip M.	Son		M	W	14	S				yes	yes	yes	Georgia

1920 FEDERAL CENSUS, CLERMONT, HALL COUNTY, GEORGIA

Hudgins, James Z. – James, now 60 years of age, is once again listed as the head of his family. Listed with him are wife, Sarah E., 41; and children: Daisy Lee, 23; Carl, 21; Essie I., 19; David B., 18; Clyde F., 16; Mary Lou, 14; Cora E., 13; Ralph, 11; Albert, 10; Raleigh, 7; Sarah, 5; Dorothy, 3; and Marjorie, 1. A sign of the hard times continuing into the years prior to the Great Depression is the fact that 20-plus-year-old children are still living at home – particularly male children.

BUREAU OF THE CENSUS [D1—578] SUPERVISOR'S DISTRICT No. 9 SHEET No. 39 44

'ED STATES: 1920—POPULATION ENUMERATION DISTRICT No. 105 r B 2251

ITED PLACE _Clermont Town_ WARD OF CITY _1_

MERATED BY ME ON THE _____ DAY OF _January_ 1920. _Sam Bu Hamer_ ENUMERATOR.

Father Mother tongue	Father Place of birth	Mother tongue	Mother Place of birth	Mother tongue	Able to speak English	Trade, profession	Industry, business	Employer etc.	Farm No.	No.
	Alabama		Georgia		yes	Section Hand	Railroad	W		51 640
	Georgia		Georgia		yes	none				52
	Georgia		Georgia		yes	none				53
	Georgia		Georgia			none				54
	South Carolina		South Carolina		yes	none				55
	Georgia		Georgia		yes	none				56
	Georgia		Georgia		yes	none				57
	Georgia		Georgia		yes	Carpenter	House	Em		58 18
	Switzerland	German	Switzerland	German	yes	none				59
	Georgia		Georgia			none				60
	Georgia		Georgia			none				61
	Georgia		Georgia		yes	none				62
	Georgia		Georgia		yes	none				63
	Georgia		Georgia		yes	Confection	Owner	OA.		64 747
	Georgia		Georgia		yes	none				65
	Georgia		Georgia		yes	none				66
	Georgia		Georgia			none				67
	Georgia		Georgia		yes	Retail merchant	Dry goods	OA.		68 758
	Georgia		Georgia		yes	none				69
	Georgia		Georgia		yes	teacher	Public school	W		70 862
	Georgia		Georgia		yes	none				71
	Georgia		Georgia		yes	none				72
	Georgia		Georgia		yes	Confection	Owner	OA.		73 747
	Georgia		Georgia		yes	Farmer	General Farm	OA.	7	74 000
	Georgia		Georgia		yes	none				75
	Georgia		Georgia		yes	none				76
	Georgia		Georgia		yes	none				77
	Georgia		Georgia		yes	none				78
	Georgia		Georgia			none				79
	Georgia		Georgia			none				80
	Georgia		Georgia			none				81
	Georgia		Georgia			none				82
	Georgia		Georgia		yes	Farmer	General Farm	OA.	8	83 000
	Georgia		Georgia		yes	none				84
	Georgia		Georgia		yes	none				85
	Georgia		Georgia		yes	Salesman	Dry good store	W		86 791
	Georgia		Georgia		yes	none				87
	Georgia		Georgia		yes	none				88
	Georgia		Georgia		yes	none				89
	Georgia		Georgia		yes	none				90
	Georgia		Georgia		yes	none				01
	Georgia		Georgia			none				02
	Georgia		Georgia			none				03
	Georgia		Georgia			none				04
	Georgia		Georgia			none				05
	Georgia		Georgia			none				06
	Georgia		Georgia		yes	Physician	General Practice	OA.		07 85
	Georgia		Georgia		yes	none				08
	Georgia		Georgia		yes	none				09
	Georgia		Georgia		yes	none				100

Right portion of document on facing page

231

State _Georgia_   Incorporated place _Town of Clermont_   DEPART...

County _Hall_   Ward of city _____ Block No. _____   FIFTEENTI

Township or other division of county _____   Unincorporated place _____   Institution _____

	PLACE OF ABODE			NAME	RELATION	HOME DATA			PERSONAL DESCRIPTION						EDUCATION		PLACE OF BIRTH	
																	PERSON	FATHER
51				Curtice	son				m	w	19	S			no	yes	Georgia	Georgia
52				Alvin	son				m	w	16	S			yes	yes	Georgia	Georgia
53				Melvin	son				m	w	16	S			yes	yes	Georgia	Georgia
54				James	son				m	w	9	S			yes	yes	Georgia	Georgia
55		53	53	Gilliland Joe	Head	R	8		m	w	45	M	27		no	yes	Georgia	Georgia
56				Belle	wife				f	w	39	M	20		no	yes	Georgia	Georgia
57				Mandell	daughter				f	w	14	S			yes	yes	Georgia	Georgia
58				Murrell	daughter				f	w	11	S			yes	yes	Georgia	Georgia
59		53	54	Gilliland Henry	Head	R	4		m	w	40	M	37		no	yes	Georgia	Georgia
60				Zera	wife				f	w	48	M	25		no	yes	Georgia	Georgia
61				Earnest	son				m	w	14	S			no		Georgia	Georgia
62		54	55	Monday J.B.	Head	R	5		m	w	41	M	27		no	yes	Georgia	Georgia
63				Mertey	wife				f	w	37	M	20		no	yes	Georgia	Georgia
64				Yvone	son				m	w	10	S			yes	yes	Georgia	Georgia
65				Annie	daughter				f	w	8	S			yes		Georgia	Georgia
66				Elyse	daughter				f	w	4	S			no		Georgia	Georgia
67				Francis	daughter				f	w	2¾	S			no		Georgia	Georgia
68		44	54	Thomas R.K.	Head	O			m	w	36	M	20		no	yes	Georgia	Georgia
69				Pearl	wife				f	w	31	M	17		no	yes	Georgia	Georgia
70				Bonnie Zoe	daughter				f	w	13	S			yes	yes	Georgia	Georgia
71				Clyde	son				m	w	8	S			no		Georgia	Georgia
72				Cleveland	son				m	w	1	S			no		Georgia	Georgia
73				Elizabeth	lodger				f	w	72	wd	20		no	yes	Georgia	Georgia
74				Goodman	lodger				m	w	53	wd	21		no	yes	Georgia	Georgia
75		56	57	Myers J.F.	Head	R	10		m	w	48	M	22		no	yes	Georgia	Georgia
76				Zida	wife				f	w	44	M	20		no	yes	Alabama	Alabama
77				Sylvester	son				m	w	18	S			no	yes	Alabama	Georgia
78				Wesley	son				m	w	16	S			yes	yes	Alabama	Georgia
79				Herd	son				m	w	13	S			yes	yes	Alabama	Georgia
80				Edmond	son				m	w	4	S			no		Georgia	Georgia
81		57	58	Payne J.S.	Head	R			m	w	27	M	21		no	yes	Georgia	Georgia
82				Olly	wife				f	w	19	M	14		no	yes	Georgia	Georgia
83				Bonnie Zoe	daughter				f	w	1 2/12	S			no		Georgia	Georgia
84		58	59	Hudgins J.Z.	Head	O	4000		m	w	70	M	20		no	yes	Georgia	Georgia
85				Sed Elizabeth	wife				f	w	51	M	16		no	yes	Georgia	Georgia
86				Rolly	son				m	w	17	S			yes	yes	Georgia	Georgia
87				Sara	daughter				f	w	15	S			yes	yes	Georgia	Georgia
88				Dorha Belle	daughter				f	w	13	S			yes	yes	Georgia	Georgia
89				Marjorie	daughter				f	w	11	S			yes	yes	Georgia	Georgia
90				Clyde	son				m	w	26	M	24		no	yes	Georgia	Georgia
91				Ellen	wife				f	w	20	M	18		no	yes	Georgia	Georgia
92				Martha	daughter				f	w	8/12	S			no		Georgia	Georgia
93		59	60	Chandler C.V.	Head	O			m	w	36	M	29		no	yes	Georgia	Georgia
94				Mae	wife				f	w	24	M	21		no	yes	Georgia	Georgia
95				Harold	son				m	w	4	S			no		Georgia	Georgia
96				Barbara	daughter				f	w	8	S			no		Georgia	Georgia
97		40	61	Simmons J.J.	Head	R			m	w	45	M	28		no	yes	Georgia	Georgia
98				Ida	wife				f	w	52	M	30		no	yes	Georgia	Georgia
99				Obel	daughter				f	w	19	S			no	yes	Georgia	Georgia
100				Ennis Bel	daughter				f	w	17	S			no	yes	Georgia	Georgia

ABBREVIATIONS TO BE USED IN COLUMNS INDICATED: [Use no abbreviations for State or country of birth or for mother tongue (Columns 18, 19, 20, and 21).] Col. 6.—Indicate the home-maker in each family by the letter "H," following the word which shows the relationship, as "Wife—H."; Col. 7.—Owned—O; Rented—R. Col. 10.—Male—M; Female—F. Col. 9.—Radio set—R. Make no entry for families having no radio set. Col. 12.—White—W; Negro—Neg; Mexican—Mex; Indian—In; Chinese—Ch; ... Col. 14.—Single—S; Married—M; Widowed—Wd; Divorced—D. Col. 25.—Naturalized—Na; First papers—Pa; Alien—Al. Col. 27.—Employer—E; Wage or salary worker—W; Working on own account—O; Unpaid worker, member...

1930 FEDERAL CENSUS, CLERMONT, HALL COUNTY, GEORGIA

Hudgins, James Z. – James, age 70, is the only name on the entire sheet which has indicated he owns his home in Clermont. He has listed the value as $4,000.00. In 1930, $4,000.00 was the equivalent of almost $65,000.00 in 2022 dollars, which was a fortune in those Depression-era days. Listed with James are wife, Sarah Elizabeth, age 51; Rollie (Raleigh), age 17; Sara, age 15; Dorothy Belle, age 14; Marjorie, age 11; Clyde, age 26, and wife, Ellen, age 20; and a child named Martha, eight months of age.

Hudgins Family

Form 15-6
MENT OF COMMERCE—BUREAU OF THE CENSUS
CENSUS OF THE UNITED STATES: 1930
POPULATION SCHEDULE

(8601)

Enumeration District No. 78-26
Supervisor's District No. 3
Sheet No. 3 B

Enumerated by me on 22 April, 1930, [illegible], Enumerator.

MOTHER (birthplace)	Language	Code A	B	C	22	23	24	Occupation	Industry	Code D	27	28	29	30	31	32	#
north carolina		78					yes	teacher in public school		9494	W						51
north carolina		78					yes	none									52
north carolina		78					yes	none									53
north carolina		78						none									54
Georgia		78					yes	shingle manufac		7744 8	yes		yes				55
Georgia		78					yes	none									56
Georgia		78					yes	none									57
Georgia		78					yes	none									58
Georgia		78					yes	shingle manufac		7744 8	yes		yes				59
Georgia		78					yes	none									60
Georgia		78						none									61
Georgia		78					yes	salesman mercantile		8590 8	yes		yes				62
Georgia		78					yes	none									63
Georgia		78					yes	none									64
Georgia		78					yes	none									65
Georgia		78					yes	none									66
Georgia		78						none									67
Georgia		78					yes	farming	Farm	VVVV8	yes		no		15		68
Georgia		78					yes	none									69
Georgia		78					yes	none									70
Georgia		78						none									71
Georgia		78						none									72
Georgia		78						none									73
Georgia		78						labor farm		VVVV8	yes		no				74
Georgia		78					yes	mercant mercantile		9891 8	yes		no				75
alabama		82					yes	none									76
alabama		82					yes	none									77
alabama		82					yes	none									78
alabama		82					yes	none									79
alabama		78						none									80
Georgia		78					yes	farming	Farm	VVVV8	yes		no		16		81
Georgia		78					yes	none									82
Georgia		78						none									83
Georgia		78					yes	mercantil		9891 0	yes		no				84
Georgia		78					yes	none									85
Georgia		78					yes	none									86
Georgia		78					yes	none									87
Georgia		78					yes	none									88
Georgia		78					yes	none									89
Georgia		78					yes	salesman Grocer Store		8590	W		yes				90
Georgia		78					yes	none									91
Georgia		78						none									92
Georgia		78					yes	agent railroad office		6277 8	yes		yes				93
Georgia		78					yes	none									94
Georgia		78						none									95
Georgia		78						none									96
Georgia		78					yes	farming	Farm	VVVV0	yes		no		17		97
Georgia		78					yes	none									98
Georgia		78					yes	none									99
Georgia		78					yes	none									100

Right portion of document on facing page

WRITE PLAINLY WITH UNFADING INK—THIS IS A PERMANENT RECORD. Every item of information should be carefully supplied. Cause of death should be stated in plain terms, so that it may be properly classified. Exact statement of occupation is very important. Was disease or injury caused by dangerous or insanitary conditions or occupation? .... Where was disease contracted if not at place of death?

CERTIFICA

GEORGIA DEPARTME

Bureau of

1. PLACE OF DEATH

County...... **Hall** ......Militia District (Number and

City or Town...... **Clermont** ......Length of residence in this

Street and Number (No.)...... **XX** ......(Street)......

2. FULL NAME ...... **JAMES ZACCHEOUS HUDGINS**

Residence (City or Town)...... **Clermont , Ga.** ...(

PERSONAL AND STATISTICAL PARTICULARS

3. SEX	4. COLOR or RACE	5. Single, Married, Widowed, Divorced (write the word)
Male	White	Married

6. DATE OF BIRTH (month, day, year)...... **Dec. 30, 1859**

7. AGE	Years	Months	Days	If less than one day
	73	1	2	Hours...... Minutes......

8. OCCUPATION

(a) Trade, profession or particular kind of work done, as spinner, sawyer, bookkeeper, etc. **Merchant**

(b) Industry or business in which work was done, as cotton mill, sawmill, bank, etc. **Merchandising**

(c) Date deceased last worked at this occupation (month and year) **December 1930**

(d) Total years spent in this occupation **52**

9. BIRTHPLACE

(P. O. Address) **Gainesville, Ga.**

FATHER

10. NAME

11. BIRTHPLACE

(P. O. Address)

MOTHER

12. MAIDEN NAME

13. BIRTHPLACE

(P. O. Address)

14. INFORMANT

(Signed) ......

(Address) **Athens, Ga**

19. BURIAL PLACE

(Cemetery) **Clermont, Ga.**

(Postoffice) **Clermont, Ga** Date **Feb. 2nd, 1933**

20. UNDERTAKER

(Signed) ......

(Address) ......

1933 DEATH CERTIFICATE, HALL COUNTY, GEORGIA

Hudgins, James Z. – James was one month beyond his 73rd birthday when he passed away somewhat prematurely and tragically from pancreatic cancer. He had been severely ill and unable to work for at least two or three years prior to his death. He had been a devout Christian, generous to a fault, carrying debts for many area residents for countless years and never asking for payment. According to his daughter, Essie, he provided gifts for most every member of his church and many in his community at Christmastime every year. Unfortunately, at the time of his death, a silent partner in his business called in all the debts which James had refused to collect, and assigned this indebtedness against ownership in the shared mercantile business in Clermont, and in doing so, gained, full ownership of the business, leaving James's wife, Sarah, and her family virtually destitute.

.TE OF DEATH   3-27
NT OF PUBLIC HEALTH   5786

Vital Statistics   33 5286 9
Registered No.

Name)............ Clermont 1745 ....State of Georgia

city or town: Yrs. 20 Mos. 1 Ds. 1 NON-RESIDENT (Yes or No)..........

.... Ward............
(If death occurred in a hospital, give its name instead of street and number)

Street and Number)..................... (State)..............

MEDICAL CERTIFICATE OF DEATH

16. DATE OF   Feb., 1st   19 33, at 7   A M
DEATH..
(Month, Day, Year)   (Hour)

17. I HEREBY CERTIFY, That I attended the deceased from Jan 10
to Jan 31st 1933 ....19.....to................19.....

I last saw h.. im alive on   Jan 31   19 33 death
is said to have occurred on the date and hour stated above.
The principal cause of death and related causes of importance in the
order of onset and duration of each:

My diagnosis was
Cancer of The
Pancras

Other contributory causes of importance:
Jaundice

What test confirmed diagnosis?....................................
(Specify whether autopsy, operation, laboratory or clinical)

If death was due to external causes (violence) fill in also the following:

Was injury an accident, suicide, or homicide?......................

Where did injury occur ....
(Specify city or town, if outside of limits, the county, and also the state)

Did injury occur in a home, public place or industry?...............

Manner of injury...

Nature of injury...

(Signed)......_G G Williams_......M.D.

(Address)......_Clermont Ga_

15. FILED   _Feb 16_   19 33

(Signed)...._A N Staton J.P._
(Local Registrar)

Right portion of document on facing page

235

State Georgia
County DeKalb

Incorporated place **Clarkston Town** Ward of city _____ Unincorporated place _____

Township or other division of county _____ Block Nos. _____ Institution _____

DEPARTMENT

SIXTEENTH C[ENSUS]

POP[ULATION]

LOCATION	HOUSEHOLD DATA	NAME	RELATION	PERSONAL DESCRIPTION	EDUCATION	PLACE OF BIRTH	CITIZENSHIP	RESIDENCE, APRIL 1, 1935			
								COUNTY	STATE		
1		Cummings, Mary	wife	w 29 m	Florida		Atlanta	Fulton	Georgia	
2		, Harold	son	w 7 S	Georgia		Atlanta	Fulton	Georgia	
3	147 R 25 no	Plowden, Edgar	Head	w 36 m	Georgia		Atlanta	Fulton	Georgia	
4		, Alice	wife	w 34 m	Georgia		Atlanta	Fulton	Georgia	
5	148 O 2500 no	McCord, Walter	Head	w 50 m	Georgia		same house			
6		, Katie	wife	w 53 m	Georgia		same house			
7	149 O 3500 no	Thompson, Fred	Head	w 50 m	Georgia		same house			
8		, Annette	wife	w 46 m	Georgia		same house			
9		, John	son	w 22 S	Georgia		same house			
10		, Lucian	son	w 15 S	Georgia		same house			
11		Marable, John	father-in-law	w 78 wd	Georgia		same house			
12	150 O 2000 no	Allen, Henry	Head	w 36 m	Georgia		same place			
13		, Betty	wife	w 38 m	Tennessee		same place			
14	151 R 18 no	Giles, Charles A.	Head	w 33 m	Georgia		Atlanta	Fulton	Georgia	no
15		, Daisy L.	wife	w 43 m	Georgia		Atlanta	Fulton	Georgia	no
16		Hudgins, Sara Elizabeth	mother-in-law	w 61 wd	Georgia		R	Hall	Georgia	no
17	152 O 2000 no	Rose, George M.	Head	w 62 m	Georgia		same house			
18		, Bessie A.	wife	w 60 m	Georgia		same house			
19		, Floyce	daughter	w 40 S	Georgia		same house			
20		McDaniel, Marie	daughter	w 32	Georgia		same house			
21		,		w 9 S	Georgia		same house			
22	153 O 1100 no	Malone, Almon C.	Head	w 60 m	Georgia		Atlanta	Fulton	Georgia	
23		, Cora	wife	w 30 m	Georgia		Atlanta	Fulton	Georgia	
24	154 R 15 no	Winslett, William J.	Head	w 24 m	Georgia		R	DeKalb	Georgia	
25		, India Jeanette	wife	w	Georgia		R	DeKalb	Georgia	
26	155 R 23 no	McCoy, John A.	Head	w 59 m	South Carolina		Anderson	Anderson	South Carolina	
27		, Dessie	wife	w 54 m	South Carolina		Anderson	Anderson	South Carolina	
28		, Margaret	daughter	w 17 S	South Carolina		Anderson	Anderson	South Carolina	
29		, Robert	son	w 15 S	South Carolina		Anderson	Anderson	South Carolina	
30	156 R 17 no	Holbrook, Joe	Head	w 44 m	Georgia		Atlanta	Fulton	Georgia	
31		, Etta	wife	w 42 m	Georgia		Atlanta	Fulton	Georgia	
32		, Glenn	son	w 18 S	Georgia		Atlanta	Fulton	Georgia	
33		, Myrtice	daughter	w 17 S	Georgia		Atlanta	Fulton	Georgia	
34		, Mary Jo	daughter	w 11 S	Georgia		Atlanta	Fulton	Georgia	
35		, Horace	son	w 8 S	Georgia		Atlanta	Fulton	Georgia	
36		, Karl	son	w 5 S	Georgia					
37	157 O 1000 no	Hollingsworth, Joseph	Head	w 68 m	Georgia		R	DeKalb	Georgia	
38		, Viola	wife	w 64 m	Georgia		R	DeKalb	Georgia	
39		, Frank	son	w 27 S	Georgia		R	DeKalb	Georgia	
40		, Frances	daughter	w 25 S	Georgia		R	DeKalb	Georgia	

SUPPLEMENTARY QUESTIONS

For Persons Enumerated on Lines 14 and 29

Line No.	NAME	PLACE OF BIRTH OF FATHER AND MOTHER		MOTHER TONGUE OR NATIVE LANGUAGE	VETERANS	SOCIAL SECURITY	USUAL OCCUPATION, INDUSTRY
		FATHER	MOTHER				USUAL OCCUPATION / USUAL INDUSTRY
14	Giles, Charles A.	Georgia	Georgia	English		yes yes both	assemblyman / Motor Co.
29	McCoy, Robert	South Carolina	South Carolina	English		no O	Student / High School

1940 FEDERAL CENSUS, DEKALB COUNTY, GEORGIA

Hudgins, Sarah Elizabeth Tanner – This census was taken four years after the massive tornado which struck Gainesville, Georgia in 1936 totally destroying the entire town and resulting in one of the worst disasters in U.S. recorded history. At the time of this tornado, Sarah had been living in an apartment in downtown Gainesville, as were several of her children. Though there were 165 to 200 deaths (the actual number was never known) and over 950 individuals seriously injured in this disaster, Sarah and her children escaped unscathed, but their homes were destroyed. At this point, Sarah was essentially homeless, and began a routine of life living with those of her children who had room to house her. She lived among her offspring in this manner for most of the remainder of her life. This 1940 Federal Census shows her living with her daughter Daisy and husband, Charles, near Atlanta. Under "Income and/or Salary," the census-taker records "0" for Sarah.

236

1940 United States Census – Population Schedule

S.D. No. 5 E.D. No. 44-42 Sheet No. 7 A

OF COMMERCE—BUREAU OF THE CENSUS

ENSUS OF THE UNITED STATES: 1940

ULATION SCHEDULE   676

Enumerated by me on April 12, 1940

Susie S. Pendley, Enumerator

31	22	23	24	25	E	26	27	OCCUPATION (28)	INDUSTRY (29)	F	31	32	33	34	Line No.
no	no	no	no	H							0	0	no		1
															2
yes	–	–	–			44		office Manager	automobile Association	Pw	52	2160	no		3
yes	–	–	–	·		44		Book Keeper	Plastering Contractor	Pw	52	936	no		4
yes	–	–	–	–		60		Truck jobber	wholesale meat	OA	52	0	yes		5
no	no	no	no	H							0	0	no		6
yes	–	–	–			28		manager	Poultry Farm	OA	52	0	yes		7
no	no	no	no	H							0	0	no		8
no	no	no	no	W							0	0	no		9
no	no	no	no	Q							0	0	no		10
no	no	no	no	W	/						0	0	no		11
yes	–	–	–			63		Clerk	Retail Grocery	Pw	52	988	no		12
yes	–	–	–			49		Saleswoman	Retail Jewelry	Pw	52	950	no		13
yes	–	–	–			32		assembly man	Motor Co	Pw	45	1500	yes		14
no	no	no	no	H	S						0	0	no		15
no	no	no	no	W	/						0	0	no		16
yes	–	–	–			44		carpenter	Building Construction		32	896	no		17
no	no	no	no	14							0	0	no		18
no	no	no	no	14	/						0	0	no		19
yes	–	–	–			44		Book Keeper	meat packers	Pw	52	1200	no		20
															21
yes	–	–	–			72		Barber	Barber Shop	OA	52	0	yes		22
yes	–	–	–			40		Inspector	manufacturing	Pw	0	0	no		23
yes	–	–	–			42		Truck Driver	Cleaning Company	Pw	52	800	no		24
yes	–	–	–			42		Sales Lady	Retail Department Store	Pw	52	700	no		25
yes	–	–	–			44		Carpenter	Building Construction	Pw	44	1100	no		26
no	no	no	no	H	S						0	0	no		27
no	no	no	no	S	/			Student	Book Store		0	0	no		28
no	no	no	no	S							0	0	no		29
no	no	no	no	ot				puller	Hat Factory	Pw	28	700	no		30
no	no	no	no	H	S						0	0	no		31
no	no	yes	–	–			20	Shipping Clerk	wholesale Bakery	Pw	8	80	no		32
no	no	no	no	S							0	0	no		33
															34
															35
															36
no	yes	–	–	–			40	Carpenter	WPA Recreation Project	Pw	26	360	no		37
no	no	no	no	H							0	0	no		38
no	no	no	no	W							0	0	no		39
no	no	no	no	S							0	0	no		40

FOR ALL WOMEN WHO ARE OR HAVE BEEN MARRIED — FOR OFFICE USE ONLY—DO NOT WRITE IN THESE COLUMNS

47	CODE	48	49	50	K	L	M	N	O	P	Q	R	S	T	U	V	W	X	Y	Z	Line No.
Pw																					14
Oc																					29

Right portion of document on facing page

Tanner Family History at Chestnut Mountain, GA

Though it still shows up on maps even today, the actual original commercial district of this tiny former pioneer community disappeared long ago. Nevertheless, it is still well-known, and until 1986, included Tanner's Mill, one of the oldest-surviving gristmills in the state.

An 1895 map of Hall County identifies a community there called "Chestnut Hill." Old-timers maintained that at one time, visitors to this spot could fill pockets and bags with the delicious fruit from the trees, lending an identity which has remained with this spot for well over 125 years, despite the fact the chestnut trees disappeared long ago (victims of a blight) just as did the tiny town's once-vibrant little commercial district.

The descendants of many pioneer families, such as Lott, Irvin, Strickland, Martin, Kennedy, Benton, **Hudgins**, **Tanner**, McEver, Reed, Braselton, Cooper, **Bell**, and **Montgomery** – just to name a few – can trace their roots to this tiny town.

An old Gazette records that Chestnut Mountain was a postvillage of Hall County and in 1900 reported a population of 84 – quite a difference from the better than 25,000 in the former town's vicinity today, and the more than 200,000 living in surrounding Hall County today. *"It is located about four and one-half miles northeast of Flowery Branch and about 14 miles from Gainesville,"* the pioneer article explained.

The unrestrained growth in northeast Georgia – particularly in Jackson, Hall, and Gwinnett counties, threatens to soon erase any remaining vestiges of this once-historic village. At one time, great forests, Native Americans, and herds of buffalo and elk frequented this vicinity, but they all have long since vanished into the mists of time.

Chestnut Mountain, to be certain, was one of the early communities in northeast Georgia, having been settled originally as a portion of Jackson County, established in 1796. Many early marriage and deed records for this community are still found today in the Jackson County Courthouse in Jefferson.

Chestnut Mountain was among a large portion of north Georgia counties originally parceled out in the 1820 Land Lottery. It became a farming district earlyon, and a very few rough, narrow roads through the community eventually linked Gainesville with Hoschton, Braselton and Jugtown (present-day Winder).

The first roads or lanes followed trails established ages earlier by native aboriginals, who had inherited many of the routes from migratory herds of buffalo, deer and antelope which instinctively sought the least arduous routes around hillsides, across the streams and through the mountains in their travels. These early trails were usually little more than two or three feet wide, since the Indians – and the hooved wildlife before them – traveled singlefile, one after the other.

This travel procedure was often by necessity, since prior to European inhabitation and the harvesting (and sometimes outright decimation) of the almost endless stands of virgin timber, the forests contained immensely-thick growths not only of towering trees, but almost impenetrable undergrowth.

The *Federal Road*, the first vehicular route in northeast Georgia, was opened in 1805 through what today is Hall County, an area which at that time was still included in the aboriginal Cherokee Nation. When this occurred, the creation of Hall County was still thirteen years in the future.

The *Federal Road* soon became the main

thoroughfare for pioneer travelers from Jackson County to west Georgia and the western territories, and was vitally important to early settlers. Many of these original travelers followed this route to Cherokee James Vann's Ferry on the Chattahoochee River before crossing and proceeding westward on the pioneer *"Alabama Road"* or northwestward on the *Federal Road*.

Old deed records show the *Federal Road* once passed the property of Irvin Strickland, Jr., and descendants say it also crossed the property of Jesse Lott, Sr. Irvin (also spelled Ervin/Erwin) Strickland, Jr. of Chestnut Mountain was the son of Irvin, Sr. and the grandson of John Strickland.

Irvin, Sr. was married in 1807 in Jackson County, Georgia, to Patsy Crow, and was enumerated in the ***1820 Hall County Census***. Loyd Strickland, the founder and owner of Crystal Farms in Chestnut Mountain, is a descendant of this family.

Jesse Lott, Sr. was born in 1771 in South Carolina, and died in Hall County in 1854. He was married to Nancy Martin who was born in Ireland. When Lott settled in Hall County in the Chestnut Mountain area, he bought 1,200 acres of land and an old log house which stood on the property.

In later years, Lott's house – which was two-storied – had a cellar which was used as a tavern or inn. Farmers who were driving livestock to market often overnighted at the spot, as did travelers along the road. Livestock shelters and fences were built to maintain the animals during the night.

A family story related for many years by Lott descendants maintained that Jesse, Jr. operated a store in the neighborhood. As the story goes, two strangers entered the store inquiring about buying meat one day. Jesse, who kept his money in a small wooden box under the stairway, was overpowered by the men who turned out to be bandits, who threw red pepper in his eyes and then robbed him.

After this experience, Jesse, according to family lore, buried his money for safekeeping. Some descendants today believe his hoard, which included gold coins, may still be buried near the old home site.

By the late 1820s, a number of stagecoach lines were active throughout Georgia and the Southeast.

Tanner's Mill – This photo of historic Tanner's Mill was taken prior to its demise by an arsonist's flames. It had been built in 1823 by David B. Tanner, and was one of the last gristmills still in existence in Georgia prior to its destruction. David B. Tanner was the great-grandfather of Sarah Elizabeth Tanner Hudgins and great-great-grandfather of Essie Hudgins Jordan.

One of the routes passed through Chestnut Mountain. Post riders, however, had begun traveling the *Federal Road* in 1819. Mail was delivered to the Carmel Mission (later called old Carmel Church and today known as Chestnut Mountain Baptist Church) and later to Chestnut Mountain on a weekly basis.

Ruth Smith Waters, a noted historian, has written that Chestnut Mountain once boasted a post office, an academy, and later, a threestory high school which also housed a masonic hall. The school burned in 1940 and the principal – George Dunagan – drove three miles to summon the Gainesville Fire

GAINESVILLE TANNERS DURING TORNADO OF 1936

<u>Tanner, Gladys</u> – The huge bell from the Hall County Courthouse was just one of countless bizarre and unbelievable results of the terrible Gainesville tornado of 1936. It was blown some 350 yards from the courthouse by the freak of nature. Miss Gladys Tanner of the Hall County Tanners poses beside the bell.

Department – an effort which proved to be in vain, as the structure was nevertheless completely destroyed. Two nearby churches – Baptist and Presbyterian – were then used to house students who continued to pursue studies at the site.

Three country stores were managed by W.A. McEver, J.T. "Thomps" Reed, and J.J. "Seif" Braselton. The names "McEver" and "Braselton" eventually became permanent fixtures, being attached to roads, villages, and other geographic mainstays in the vicinity in later years.

A portion of Chestnut Mountain was included in Journey Cooper's farm and he planted cotton on the hill or "mountain" top. It is not known just how many mills (grist, etc.) existed from time to time in this area, but at least some of the operations were founded by Thomas Cooper and later operated by Journey. Thomas was married to Martha Meeks and son Journey married Mellie Bell.

Tanner's Mill, one of the oldest gristmills in Georgia and the oldest in Hall County, was located on the Walnut Fork of the Oconee River in the vicinity of Chestnut Mountain. It tragically was burned by vandals in 1986, erasing a very historic state landmark in the blink of an eye.

Matthew Tanner, Jr. was one of the first Tanners to migrate to this section of the South, buying 250 acres in Jackson County from pioneer Elisha Winn. The property was located on both banks of the South Mulberry Fork of the Oconee River in Jackson.

A son of Matthew – **David Tanner** – moved to Hall County and purchased the acreage where Tanner's Mill was built. Tax records indicate he owned *"200 acres of hickory and oak land and 470 acres of pine lands."*

David and his wife, **Elizabeth Chamblee**, had eleven children, four of whom fought for the Confederacy in the U.S. Civil War. George Washington Tanner served with Col. Law's 43rd Regiment, Western Army; Thomas Langley Tanner served with

Wheeler's Cavalry, Western Army; William Floyd Tanner served with Lester's Company, 55th Georgia Regiment, Western Army; and Joseph Henry Tanner served with Dorsey's Company "D", Regular Virginia Army. Three of the sons returned home after the war. Joseph Henry Tanner was killed at the battle of Cedar Creek, Florida on March 1, 1864.

Many old family and early church cemeteries are located in the Chestnut Mountain vicinity. Old Liberty Church and Cemetery were early religious hallmarks. It is believed that **Francis Bell**, a veteran of the American Revolution is interred here.

Bell was the son of **Thomas Bell**, and the family – just as was the case with multitudes of Georgians – was originally from Virginia. Today, the grave of Francis Bell is unmarked, but many of his descendants in this same cemetery have headstones inscribed with family information.

Francis Bell married his first wife – **Esther Montgomery** – in 1770. Their daughter, **Jane**, born August 27, 1781, was married to **James Beverly** (also spelled Bevely) **Hudgins** (1777-1850) in January of 1801 (also recorded as June 6, 1801).

Bell granted property in Hall County to Hudgins in the days when the area was yet an unsettled wilderness with most of the land still in the possession of the native Indians. James Beverly reportedly built a five-room log house on this land near a place called "Macedonia Settlement." He is listed in the *1820 Hall County Census* as *"Beverly Hudgeons"* (page 71), and again in the *1850 Hall Census* (page 790).

From the union of James Beverly Hudgins and Jane Bell came Beverly, Jr.; Virginia B.; Gregory; Dessie; Mary Ann; **Zacharia** (a.k.a. **"Zaccharia," "Zachus,"** and **"Zacheus"**); Holder; Esther; Francis Bell; and Iverson Delaprierre.

James Beverly's and wife Jane Bell's graves may still be viewed in Hall County near Chestnut Mountain if one knows where to look. The small graveyard may have been no more than a family cemetery, and can be easily missed. *(To reach the graveyard: Travel to GA 53 South from Gainesville past Lanier Raceway/ Road Atlanta to Macedonia Church on the left. Turn left just beyond this church onto J.J. Lott Road. Follow this road until it dead-ends into another road and then turn left once again. The cemetery will be on the right just a short distance away. Be aware that in the past, thick undergrowth has often concealed this tiny cemetery from the road.)*

Descendants of the Bell, Montgomery and Hudgins families still live throughout the Chestnut Mountain area today, as well as in many other parts of the state.

A descendant of Beverly and Jane Bell Hudgins – Iverson Daniel Hudgins – but for the interruption of World War I in 1914, would have been known as an international botanist. He was considered one of the foremost authorities on botany in America, and was visited at the time by botanists in the employment of King George of England and Kaiser Wilhelm of Germany.

The settlement of Beverly's estate is listed in the Hall County Ordinary's office. Sons Zacharia & Holder Hudgins were administrators. James Beverly Hudgins's old farm was passed to his wife, Jane, upon his death, and to their son, Francis Bell Hudgins, upon Jane's death, and to Francis's son, Jim, upon Francis's death.

In more recent years, Beverly's former property was owned by a Mr. J.J. Lott, and has been the site of frequent Hudgins family reunions over the years. Old Liberty Methodist Church at Chestnut Mountain disappeared long ago, as did the little community of Chestnut Mountain itself, though it (the community name of Chestnut Mountain) still may be found on maps even today.

As of this writing, pioneer James Beverly Hudgins's lonely grave – which was well-marked at last check – still amazingly exists with a handful of other graves today at Chestnut Mountain, Hall Co., Georgia.

[Zacharia/Zacheus Hudgins was the great-grandfather of the late Essie Hudgins Jordan – mother of the late Marilyn Jordan Jackson (both of Rockmart, Georgia) and the late Patricia Jordan Nixon (formerly of DeKalb County, Georgia). Marilyn's extant children: Patricia Jackson Hughes, Ralph Olin Jackson III, and David Anderson Jackson, have homes in the Rockmart (Polk County), Georgia, area as of this writing. Patricia Nixon's children: Hal, Eve, Dave and Melinda, reside in the Gwinnett, DeKalb, and Cobb County areas.]

Tanner Genealogical Line
(Ancestry of One Tanner Family Line in Georgia)
(Country of Origin of the Tanner Family Line: Normandy, France and Ireland)

The Tanner name reportedly has many origins, but one of the most prominent derives from the ancient Anglo-Saxon culture of Britain. The occupational surname source is self-evident – that of a tanner of animal skins. The Normandy region off the coast of France holds the earliest records of this surname. There, Hugh de Tanur reportedly made grants to the Abbey of Culture in Normandy in 1082. At that time, there was a variety of early spellings including Tannour, Le Tannur, Tannator and Le Tanur. Some of the French Tanners later immigrated to Ireland where they became prominent in that culture.

Great-great-great-great-great-great-great-grandfather: Lewis Tanner

b.   1690, Bermuda Hundred, Henrico, VA

m.   1715, Margaret Haskins [b. 1700, Henrico Co. (present-day Chesterfield Co.) VA, d. 31 Oct 1765, Colony Laurel, KY] probably Henrico Co., VA   Issue: Lucius Matthew (b. circa 1700, Wake, NC, d. circa 1766, Mecklenburg Co., VA, British Colonial America); Thomas (b. 1716, Henrico, VA, d. 16 Nov 1802, Mecklenburg, VA); Lucius (b. circa 1720, Brunswick Co., VA, d. Oct, 1765, Lunenburg, VA); **Matthew Tanner, Sr.** (b. Oct 1730, Prince George, VA, d. Dec 1809, Pittsylvania, VA); Lewsirus [b. Lunenburg Co. (formerly Brunswick Co.), VA, d. 1 Oct 1765, Lunenburg Co., VA.]

d.   August, 1773, Amelia, VA

Great-great-great-great-great-great-grandfather: Matthew Tanner, Sr.

b.   Oct., 1730, Prince George, VA

m.   1753, Lucy Creed Haskins (b. 1735, Lunenburg, Lunenburg Co., VA, d.), Lunenburg, VA, Lucy Haskins Issue: Josiah (b. 10 Oct 1754, Mecklenburg, VA, d. 1 Nov. 1807, Oldham Co., KY); Martha W. (b. 1763, Seven Oaks Farm, Greenwood, Albemarle Co., VA, d. 11 Nov 1829, Hanover, Hanover Co., VA); Creed (b. 1765, Mecklenburg Co., VA, d. 15 July 1827, Pittsylvania, VA); **Matthew, Jr.** (b. 1765, Mecklenburg Co., VA, d. 15 Dec 1833, Hall Co., GA); Elizabeth Creed (b. 17 March 1774, Pittsylvania Co., VA, d. 3 Dec 1861, Troup Co., GA); Thomas (b. 1775, Pittsylvania Co., VA, d. 1 Nov 1807, Oldham Co., KY); Polly (b. 4 Jan 1779, Pittsylvania, VA, d. 8 July 1841, Bald Hill, Muscogee Co., GA); and Martha (b. 1873 Pittsylvania (?), VA).

d.   Dec, 1809, Mecklenburg, VA

Great-great-great-great-great-grandfather: Matthew Tanner, Jr.

b.   1765, Mecklenberg, VA. Listed in the 1782 Census of Pittsylvania County, Virginia. Property sold. Moved to North Carolina. Later moved once again to Oglethorpe Co., GA, purchasing two lots of land in 1806 and 1807. These properties were sold in 1818. On December 31, 1808, Matthew purchased from the sheriff – Elisha Winn – of Jackson County, 250 acres situated on both banks of the south Mulberry Fork of Oconee River, Jackson County, GA.

m.   (1st) Wife unknown. Issue: Two unknown daughters
(2nd) 01/20/1800, Alsey Langley [b. 1754, Caswell Co., NC, d. 15 Dec 1833 Hall Co., GA. Buried in Mt. Carmel Church Cemetery (unmarked).] Issue: Thomas (b. 21 March 1778, Scotland, United Kingdom, buried 1857, Pictou, Pictou, Nova Scotia, Canada); Lucinda (b. 15 Nov 1786, VA, d. 1853); **David Brannon Tanner** (b. 06/03/1801, Halifax Co., VA, d. 3 March 1876); Mary (b. circa 1802, Hall Co., GA); Moses T. (b. circa 1803, likely Halifax Co., VA); Thomas L. (b. 11 June 1803, NC, d. 18 Feb 1853, Dade Co., GA); Elizabeth (b. 13 Oct 1812, Hall Co., Ga, d. 2 Nov 1873, New Mexico, Carroll Co., GA).

d.   12/15/1833, Hall Co., GA. Buried in Mt. Mariah Church Cemetery (unmarked).

Great-great-great-great-grandfather: David B. (Brannon) Tanner

b.   06/03/1801, Halifax Co., VA (also listed as Caswell Co., NC)

m.   10/30/1823 in Hall Co., GA, Elizabeth Chamblee (b. 09/21/1806, Pendleton District, Pickens Co. SC, d. 08/03/1859, Hall Co., GA) Issue: **George Washington "Watt" Tanner** [b. 12/19/1824, m. 11/20/1845 in Jackson Co., GA to Sarah E. Mangum (b. 12/26/1827, d. 10/17/1912), d. 01/29/1912, Hall Co., GA]; Thomas Langley [b. 11/26/1826 in Hall Co., GA, (m. in Hall Co., GA on 09/08/1844 to Margaret Allbright) d. 6 Aug 1907, Tilton, Whitfield Co., GA]; William Floyd [b. 13 Nov 1830 (m. Cynthia Morgan on 04/27/1851) d. 6 April, 1910]; Christina Adeline (b. 30 June 1833, d. 28 Dec 1922, Hall Co., GA); David Brannon, (b. 10 June 1835, Hall, GA, d. 7 June 1878, Hall, GA); Elizabeth A. (b. 26 Jan 1837, Hall, GA, d. 8 Sept 1874, Acworth, Cobb, GA); Nancy Jane (b. 01/17/1839, Hall, GA, d. 21 Feb 1860, Hall, GA); Joseph Henry [b. 07/06/1841, (m. 05/09/1861 to Messinia Jane Bennett), d. 03/01/1864 at Battle of Cedar Creek, Baker, FL]; Mary K. (b. 4 Dec 1842, d. 12 Nov 1935, Gainesville, Hall, GA); Alsey Annie Louvina (b. 30 Dec 1843, d. 5 June 1930, Buford, Gwinnett Co., GA); Moses Taylor (b. 07/18/1849, Gainesville, Hall Co., GA, d. 14 May 1932, Gainesville, Hall Co.).

d.   03/20/1876, Tanner's Mill, Hall Co., GA

> **Note #1:** Elizabeth Chamblee was the daughter of George Washington Chamblee. The Chamblee property adjoined that of Matthew Tanner, Jr. Shortly after David and Elizabeth were wed, they moved to Hall County, GA, where they purchased the acreage where David constructed the Tanner's Mill of once-historic note. Before it was tragically destroyed by fire in the 1980s, Tanner's Mill, once located on the Walnut Fork of the Oconee River, Hall Co., GA, was one of the oldest gristmills remaining in Georgia. According to oral tradition, there also was a wool carding mill located on the opposite side of the Oconee River from Tanner's Mill which was also operated by the Tanners and which produced cloth during the U.S. Civil War to aid the Confederate cause. Tax returns for 1854 show that David Tanner was living in the 385th District of Hall. He owned 200 acres of land covered by huge stands of hickory and oak trees, and an additional 470 acres covered in towering pines.

> **Note #2:** David B. and Elizabeth Chamblee Tanner had four sons who fought for the Confederacy: George Washington, Thomas Langley; William Floyd; and Joseph Henry.

Great-great-great-Grandfather: George Washington "Watt" Tanner

b. 12/19/1824, Hall Co., Ga

m. 11/20/1845 in Jackson, Butts Co., GA, Sarah Elizabeth Mangum (b. 12/26/1827, Jackson, Butts Co., GA, d. 10/17/1912, Hall Co., GA). Issue: Mary Levinia (b. 10/26/1846, d. 01/25/1926); Elizabeth Sheppard (b. 11/04/1849, d. 10/03/1936, Stone Mountain, DeKalb Co., GA); William Thomas [(also listed as "Thomas F.") b. 18 May 1852, d. 28 March 1897, Parker, TX (also listed as d. 19 April 1926, Hardeman, TX)]; Sarah E. (b. 30 Sept 1854, Hall Co., GA, d. 30 Jan. 1855, Hall Co., GA); **David King** (b. 05/19/1856, Candler Hall, GA, d. 01/04/1936, Hall Co., GA); Sarah Irene (b. 20 June 1859, Hall Co., d. 24 Jan 1913, Hall Co.); John (b. 15 March 1864, Hall Co., GA, d. 31 Jan 1907, Gainesville, Hall Co.); Lucinda / Leeannah (b. 3 Oct 1866, Hall Co., d. 4 July 1950, Hall Co.); Frances Elizabeth (b. 12/31/1872); Joseph Mangum (b. 14 May 1873, Hall Co., GA, d. 8 April 1934, Wilkes Co., GA); James (b. 11/15/1876; Howell (b. 04/1880); and Ada (b. 10/1887).

d. 01/29/1912, Hall Co., GA

Great-great-Grandfather: David King Tanner

b. 05/19/1856, Hall Co., GA

m. 1875, Hall Co., GA, Sarah Rebecca (a.k.a. Rebecca Melissa) Hawkins (b. 04/11/1858, d. 02/06/1932, Gainesville, GA). Issue: Charles Washington (b. 02/13/1876, Gainesville, Hall Co., GA, d. 11/01/1954); **Sarah Elizabeth** (b. 12/07/1878); Lillian Ann (b. 04/07/1880, Gainesville, Hall Co., d. 08/31/1958, Gainesville); Benjamin Franklin (b. 06/11/1881, Gainesville, d. 10/23/1941, Doerun, Colquitt, GA); John Lelas (b. 01/02/1883, Hall Co., GA, d. 11/28o/1950, Americus, Sumter Co., GA); Mary Anna (b. 08/08/1886, Gainesville, d. 07/25/1977, Gainesville, Hall, GA); David Ernest (b. 04/23/1892, Gainesville, d. 01/23/1948); Pearl lee (b. 10/23/1893, Gainesville, d. 04/19/1977); and William Thomas (b. 11/29/1903, Gainesville, d. 05/13/1965, Hall Co., Ga).

d. 01/04/1936, Hall Co., GA

Great-grandmother: Sarah Elizabeth Tanner

b. 12/07/1878, Chestnut Mountain, Hall Co., GA

m. 03/31/1895, James Zacheus Hudgins [b. 12/30/1859 (also listed as 12/03/1859), Jackson Co., GA; d. 02/01/1933, Clermont, Hall Co., GA. Buried Concord Baptist Church Cemetery, Clermont. Issue: Daisy Lee (b. 07/21/1896, d. 08/31/1996); Carl Washington (b. 08/28/1898, d. 01/27/1967, Lexington, KY; **Essie Carroll (nee "Irene")**, (b. 03/12/1900, d. 02/11/1999); David Bennett (b. 01/24/1902, d. 01/14/1983, St. Ignace, MacKinac, MI); Clyde Franklin (b. 11/06/1903, d. 02/18/1994, Statesboro, Bulloch Co., GA); Mary Lou (Marilu) (b. 06/03/1905); Cora Estelle (b. 12/14/1906, d. 02/14/1992); Ralph Newton (b. 09/16/1908, d. 08/23/1970); Albert White (b. 04/21/1910, d. 02/01/1976); Raleigh Edward (b. 06/05/1912, d. 07/11/1982); Sarah Rebecca (b. 07/14/1914, d. 12/10/1999, m. Herman Gibbs "Doc" Tankersley, 11/18/1933. Tankersley was justice of the peace of Hall County, GA); Dorothy Belle (b. 11/23/1916); and Marjorie Catherine (b. 10/23/1918.).

d. 12/19/1969, Austell, GA. Buried 12/21/1969, Concord Baptist Church Cemetery, Clermont, Hall Co., GA.

Note #3: James Z. Hudgins contracted for the construction (1913) of a large elegant home in downtown Clermont, GA, into which he moved upon its completion in 1914, just in time for the birth there of daughter Sarah. Two more children, Dorothy and Marjorie, were also born in this home, bringing the total number of children in this family to thirteen. Two additional children were born later, bringing the total to fifteen, but wife Sarah was 43+ years of age by that point and nature simply was not on her side. These last two children did not survive. As of this writing (2022), this elegant home built by James in 1913 still stands on King Street in "downtown" Clermont. The first ten children in this family were born in Sugar Hill, Jackson County, GA.

Grandmother: Essie Irene (Carroll) Hudgins Jordan

b. 03/12/1900, Sugar Hill, Hall Co., GA (Located on old Athens Hwy/U.S. 139 between Talmo and Pendergrass.)

m. 06/18/1927, Clermont, Hall Co., GA, Guy Wilfred Jordan (b. 02/19/1889, Dutch Hill, PA, d. 09/05/1946, Rockmart, Polk, GA. Buried Rose Hill Cemetery, Rockmart, Polk, GA). Issue: **Marilyn** [(b. 03/20/1928, Rockmart, Polk, GA, m. 1948, Rockmart, Ralph Olin Jackson, Jr., (b. 12/08/1923, Rockmart, d. 12/11/2011, Rome, Floyd Co., GA) d. 2007. Issue: Patricia Carroll (b. 02/21/1950, Cedartown, Polk, GA); Ralph Olin Jackson III (b. 09/08/1951, Cedartown, Polk, GA); David Anderson (b. 11/06/1952, Cedartown, Polk, GA); Mary Lynne (b. 09/15/1954, Rockmart, Polk, GA, d. 05/12/2014. Ashes buried Rose Hill Cemetery, Rockmart); and Guy Jordan (b. 08/31/1957, d. 05/20/1980, Rockmart, b. Rose Hill Cemetery, Rockmart)]; and Patricia Carroll (b. 06/25/1934, Rockmart, Polk Co., GA, d. 12/29/2014, Doraville, DeKalb Co., GA. Issue: Hal, Eve, Melinda and David.)

d. 02/11/1999, Rockmart, Polk Co., GA. Buried Rose Hill Cemetery, Rockmart, Polk Co., GA

Marilyn Jordan Jackson

b. March 20, 1928, Rockmart, Georgia

m. 1948, Ralph Olin Jackson, Jr., Rockmart, Georgia. Issue: Patricia Carroll; Ralph Olin, III; David Anderson; Mary Lynne; and Guy Jordan.

d. 2007

Notes:

(No. 4.)   **SCHEDULE of the whole number of persons**

49

NAMES OF HEADS OF FAMILIES.	Under 5	5 & under 10	10 & under 15	15 & under 20	20 & under 30	30 & under 40	40 & under 50	50 & under 60	60 & under 70	70 & under 80	80 & under 90	90 & under 100	100 and upwards	Under 5	
Came from Page 171	25	18	20	16	12	8	9	7	3	3				2	
P. W. Martin					1										
Albert Green	2	2			1									1	
John Moreland			1	1		1									
S. B. M. Evans				1											
Jos. Howell				1		1								2	
Moses Sott					1										
David Tanner	1	1	1	1		1								2	1
J. J. Reynolds					1										
James Stone					1	1									
J. S. Simmons	2				1									1	
Geo. W. Sott					1										
Daniel Blackbird	2	1	1	1	1		1								
Ira Gaines	1				1										
Jas. Blackstock					1										
C. J. Simmons	1				1										
James Morgan	1	2	1		1									1	1
Wm. Miller				1	1		1								1
John Rouse		1	2	1		1									
Sevier Streete	2				1										2
Alex. McDuffie	1	1			1									2	1
Geo. Owen	1	2	1	1	1		1							1	1
John Simpson	1	1	2	1		1								1	2
Jas. Simpson														1	2
Jesse Simpson			1		2		1								1
Wm. Thomerson	1		1	1	1										1
Joshua R. Simmons	2	1		1	1										
Dempsey Melton	1	1		1										1	
Charles Wallis			1				1								
Thomas Cooper	1	2	1	1		1								1	1
John Martin				1											
	47	31	33	29	25	17	15	12	3	3					

1840 FEDERAL CENSUS, HALL COUNTY, GEORGIA

Tanner, David B. – Listed are: *"One male under the age of 5"* which would probably be David Brannon, born 1835; *"one male between 5 and 10"* which would probably be William Floyd, born 1830; *"one male between the ages of 10 and 15"* which would probably be Thomas Langley, born 1826; *"one male between 15 and 20"* which would probably be George Washington "Watt," born 1824; *"one male between 20 and 40"* which would undoubtedly be David B. Sr., born 1801; *"two females under 5"* which were probably Mary Elizabeth (1837) and Nancy J. (1839); *"one female between 5 and 10"* which was probably Christiana Adeline (1833); and *"one female between 30 and 40"* which undoubtedly is David's wife, Elizabeth Chamblee.

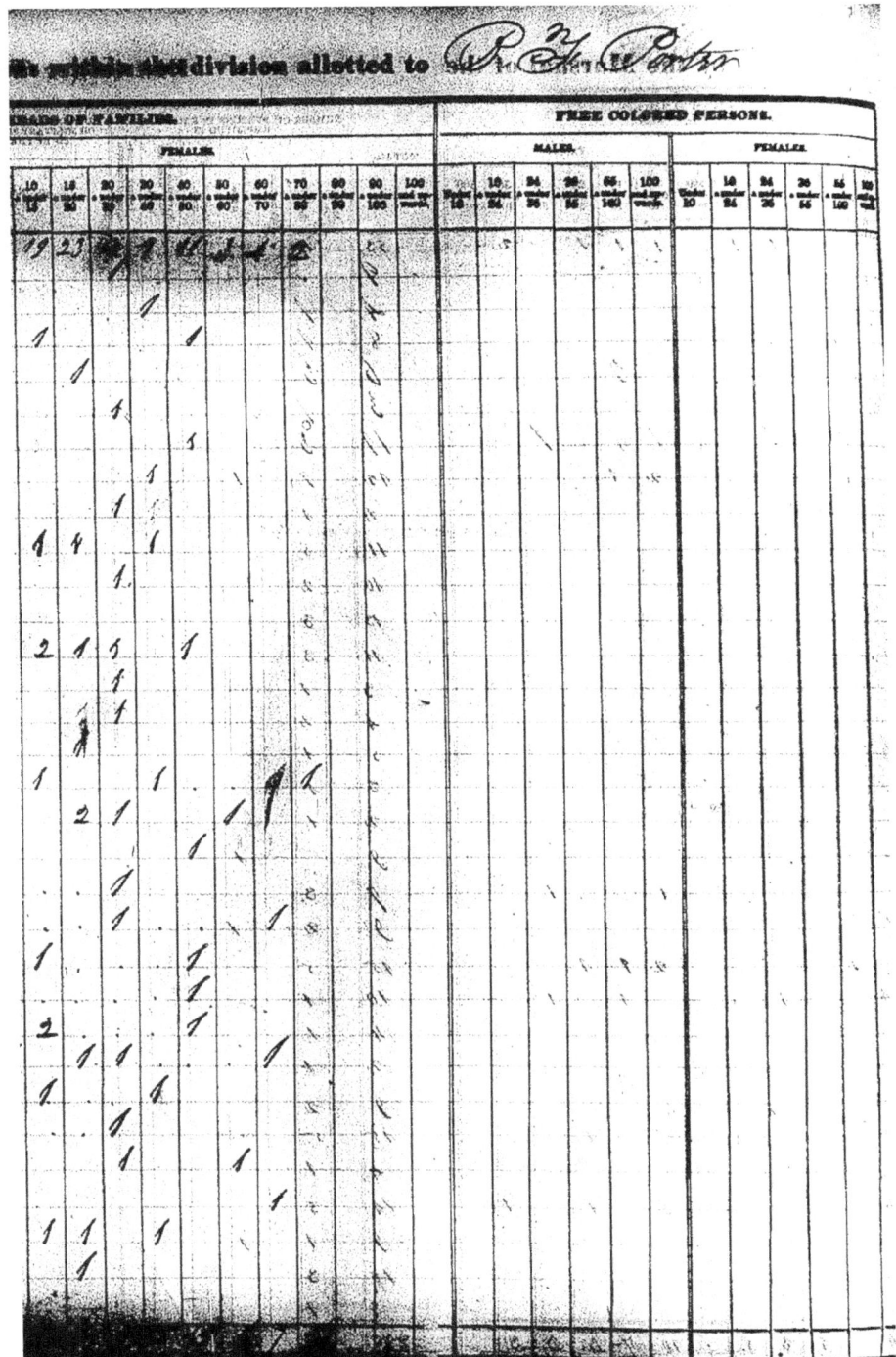

Right portion of document on facing page

SCHEDULE 1.—Free Inhabitants in *268th District* in the County of *Hall* State of *Georgia* enumerated by me, on the *19th* day of *July* 1860. *O. Thompson* Ass't Marshal

Post Office *Sugar Hill*.

	Dwelling-houses numbered in the order of visitation	Families numbered in the order of visitation	The name of every person whose usual place of abode on the first day of June, 1860, was in this family.	Age	Sex	Color	Profession, Occupation, or Trade of each person, male and female, over 15 years of age	Value of Real Estate	Value of Personal Estate	Place of Birth, Naming the State, Territory, or County	Married within the year	Attended School within year	Persons over 20 yrs of age who cannot read & write	Whether deaf and dumb, blind, insane, idiotic, pauper, or convict	
	1	2	3	4	5	6	7	8	9	10	11	12	13	14	
1			F. M. Newman	5	M					S.C.					1
2			F. I. "	3	M					Ga					2
3			I. R. "	4/12	M					"					3
4	1061	894	I. Hancock	55	M		Farmer	300	120	"			1		4
5			Esther "	36	F					"					5
6			Wm "	17	M					"		1			6
7			James "	15	M					"		1			7
8			Samuel "	12	M					"		1			8
9			Wilmuth "	11	F					"		1			9
10			Mary "	8	F					"					10
11	1062		Unoccupied												11
12	1063	895	G. W. Tanner	35	M		Farmer	4,000	1,000	"					12
13			Sarah "	32	F					"					13
14			Mary "	13	F					"					14
15			Elizabeth "	10	F					"					15
16			Thomas "	8	M					"					16
17			David "	5	M					"					17
18			Sarah "	4/12	F					"					18
19	1064	896	Tho. Kinney	30	M		Do	250	207	"					19
20			Martha "	24	F					"					20
21			Mary "	3	F					"					21
22			Sarah "	2	F					"					22
23	1065	897	W. Parker	47	M	1	Do		250	S.C.			1		23
24			Nancy "	41	F	1				"			1		24
25			Mary "	23	F					Ga			1		25
26			Wm "	20	M					"			1		26
27			Elizabeth "	18	F					"					27
28			Susan "	16	F					"					28
29			Nancy "	13	F					"					29
30			Sarah "	7	F					"					30
31			I. B. "	3	M					"					31
32	1066	898	I. H. Bennett	59	M	1	Do	550	200	S.C.					32
33			Matilda "	57	F	1				"					33
34			Matilda "	17	F					Ga		1			34
35			Sarah "	16	F					"		1			35
36	1067	899	R. B. Hargrove	28	M		Do	400	250	S.C.					36
37			Arabella "	26	F					"					37
38			Mary "	5	F					"					38
39			Margaret "	4	F					"					39
40			James "	7m/o	M					"					40

No. white males, *17* No. colored males, *3/2* No. foreign born, _____ No. blind, _____ No. _____

1860 FEDERAL CENSUS, SUGAR HILL, HALL COUNTY, GEORGIA

Tanner, George Washington – George, age 35, is listed as a farmer with $4,000.00-worth of real estate, which is not an insignificant estate in 1860. In five short years, however, his holdings will be reduced considerably after the devastation of the U.S. Civil War. Listed with George are: his wife, Sarah Elizabeth Mangum Tanner, age 32; daughters Mary, age 13, Elizabeth, age 10 and Sarah, 11 months; and sons Thomas, 8, David, 5, and Sarah, 11 months.

Tanner Family

1870 FEDERAL CENSUS, TADMORE, HALL COUNTY, GEORGIA

Tanner, George Washington – George, age 46, continues in the profession of farming. He is listed this time with real estate valued at $1,600.00. Though northeast Georgia avoided much of the devastation associated with the U.S. Civil War, the entire economic system of the South and its government was completely destroyed, and at this point five years beyond war's end, George is struggling like most of the remainder of the citizens of the South.

247

STATE OF GEORGIA,

Hall County.

To any Minister of the Gospel, Judge, or Justice of the Peace.

You Are Hereby Authorized

TO JOIN IN THE

Holy State of Matrimony,

David Tanner and _Miss Rebecca Hawkins_

ACCORDING TO THE

CONSTITUTION AND LAWS OF THIS STATE.

AND FOR SO DOING THIS SHALL BE YOUR SUFFICIENT LICENSE.

J. B. M. Winburn Ordinary

January 2nd 1875

GEORGIA,

Hall COUNTY.

I Certify, That the above-named parties were duly joined in MATRIMONY, by me,

This the _13_ day of _January_ 1875

John L. Ganus J.P.B.

1875 MARRIAGE LICENSE, HALL COUNTY, GEORGIA

Tanner, David King and Rebecca Hawkins – Joined in holy matrimony no doubt on a cold winter day, January 2, 1875.

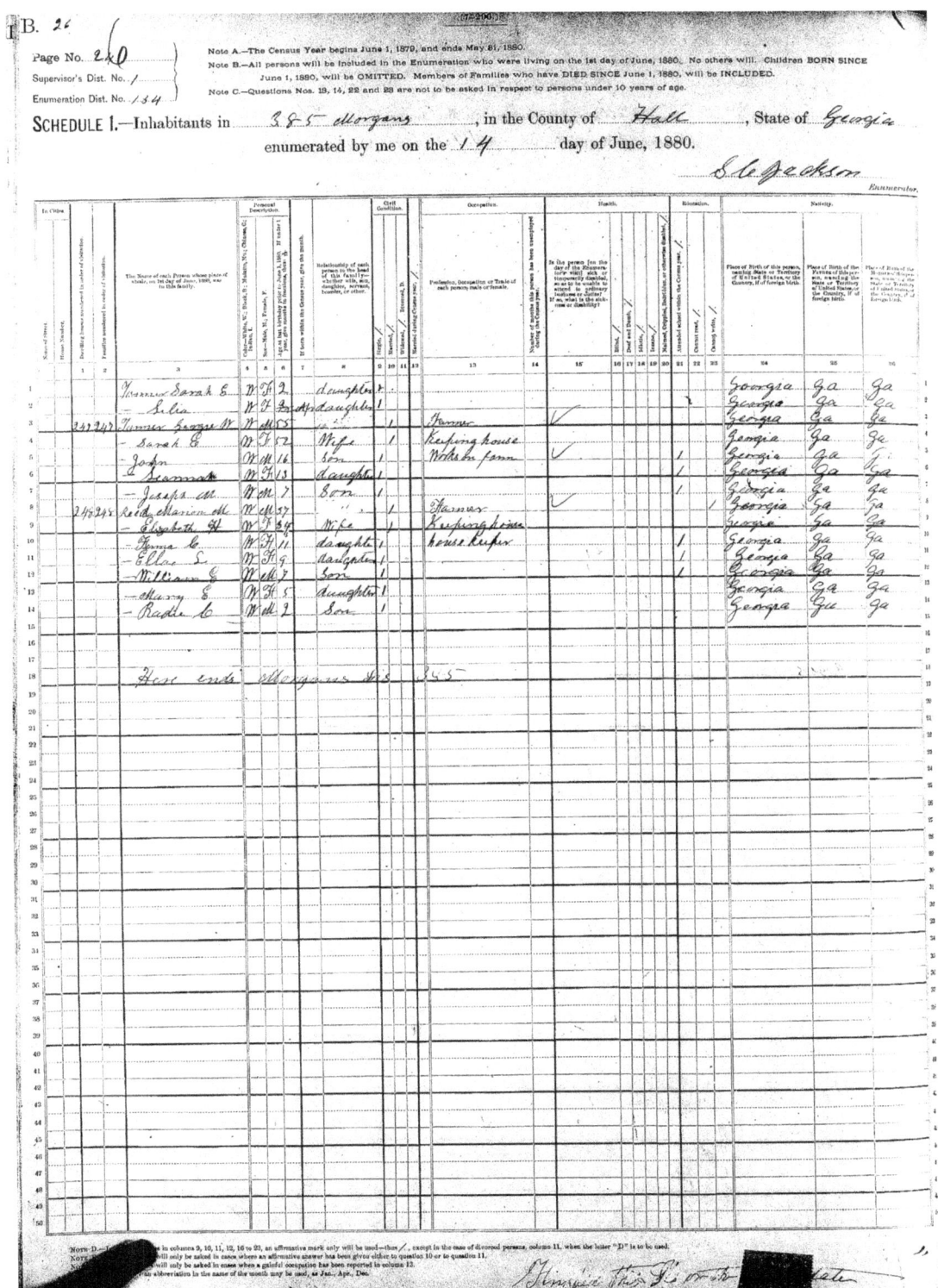

1880 FEDERAL CENSUS, TADMORE, HALL COUNTY, GEORGIA

Tanner, George W. – George, 55, continues farming the land which is the only way of life he has ever known. This census also lists his wife, Sarah Elizabeth, age 52; son, John, age 16; daughter, Sarah, age 13; and son Joseph, age 7.

7-294

TWELFTH CENSUS OF THE UNITED STATES.

B

SCHEDULE No. 1.—POPULATION.

State _Georgia_
County _Hall_
Township or other division of county _Candler Dist_

Name of incorporated city, town, or village, within the above-named division, _____

Name of Institution, _____

Ward of city, _____

Supervisor's District No. _39_ Sheet No. _13_
Enumeration District No. _74_

Enumerated by me on the _21_ day of June, 1900, _H. H. Towry_, Enumerator.

23

		NAME	RELATION	PERSONAL DESCRIPTION						NATIVITY			CITIZENSHIP		OCCUPATION	EDUCATION			OWNERSHIP			
51		Potts Henry T	Head	W m aug 1879 20 m 0						Georgia	Georgia	Georgia			Farmer				R	7	218	
52	243 243	Mary E	Wife	W f aug 1877 22 m 0 0 0						Georgia	Georgia	Georgia										
53	244 244	Ward William	Head	B m dec 1864 35 m 2						Georgia	Georgia	Georgia			Farmer				R	7	219	
54		Chaney	Wife	B f oct 1873 26 m 2 1 1						Georgia	Georgia	Georgia										
55		William B	Son	B m June 1899 ½ S						Georgia	Georgia	Georgia										
56	245 245	Law Sarah	Servant	B f may 1890 10 S						Georgia	Georgia	Georgia										
57	244 246	Collins George	Head	W m aug 1864 36 m 7						Maine	Maine	Maine							R	H		
58	346 345	Victoria S	Wife	W f mar 1860 40 m 7 0 0						Georgia	England	Georgia										
59	247 347	Little Ben T	Head	W m jan 1858 42 m 24						Georgia	S. Carolina	S. Carolina			Farmer				O	7	220	
60	250	Mary B	Wife	W f aug 1860 39 m 24 7 6						Georgia	N. Carolina	N. Carolina										
61		Kimmie W	Son	W m may 1881 19 S						Georgia	Georgia	Georgia			merchant							
62		William J	Son	W m aug 1883 16 S						Georgia	Georgia	Georgia			Farm Labors							
63		Charley F	Son	W m Jan 1888 11 S						Georgia	Georgia	Georgia										
64		Lelia A	Dau	W f dec 1890 9 S						Georgia	Georgia	Georgia										
65		Jamie L	Son	W m June 1893 6 S						Georgia	Georgia	Georgia										
66		Kinney D	Son	W m may 1897 3 S						Georgia	Georgia	Georgia										
67	247 248	Little James S	Head	W m mar 1835 65 m 81						Georgia	S. Carolina	Alabama			Farmer				O	7	221	
68		Amanda J	Wife	W f jan 1840 60 m 31						Georgia	N. Carolina	Georgia										
69	246 349	Brown William T	GrandSon	W m feb 1880 20 S						Georgia	S. Carolina	Georgia			Farm Labors							
70	244 250	Davis William	Head	W m dec 1860 39 m 13						Georgia	Georgia	Georgia			Merchant				O	H		
71		Janie	Wife	W f oct 1868 31 m 13 5 2						Georgia	Ireland	Georgia										
72		Florence	Son	W m mar 1886 12 S						Georgia	Georgia	Georgia										
73	357 353	Clifford	Son	W m dec 1896 3 S						Georgia	Georgia	Georgia										
74	246 354	Carter Butch B	Head	W m dec 1863 36 m 6						Georgia	Georgia	Georgia			Farm Labors				R	H		
75	253	Julia	Wife	W f nov 1874 25 m 6 3 3						Georgia	Georgia	Georgia										
76		Minnie	Dau	W f jan 1886 14 S						Georgia	Georgia	Georgia										
77		Florence	Dau	W f Nov 1897 2 S						Georgia	Georgia	Georgia										
78		Jewell	Son	W m apr 1900 2/12 S						Georgia	Georgia	Georgia										
79	244 254	Kinney James M	Head	W m feb 1874 26 m 4						Georgia	Georgia	Georgia			Merchant				R	H		
80		Lula	Wife	W f dec 1878 21 m 4 2 2						Georgia	Georgia	Georgia										
81		John M	Son	W m jan 1899 5 S						Georgia	Georgia	Georgia										
82	353 355	Gittie	Dau	W f apr 1899 1 S						Georgia	Georgia	Georgia										
83	456	Vandiver Sam	Head	W m July 1866 33 m 7						Georgia	S. Carolina	Georgia			Blacksmith				R	H		
84		Dora	Wife	W f dec 1873 26 m 7 2 2						Georgia	Ireland	Georgia										
85		Claud	Son	W m dec 1873 6 S						Georgia	Georgia	Georgia										
86		Bennett	Son	W m July 1895 4 S						Georgia	Georgia	Georgia										
87	254 257	Trout Thomas H	Head	W m may 1845 55 m 1						Georgia	Georgia	Georgia			Merchant				O	H		
88	257	Samantha	Wife	W f dec 1860 39 m 1 0 0						Georgia	Georgia	Georgia										
89	253 258	Lord James	Head	W m July 1869 30 m 2						Georgia	S. Carolina	Georgia			Farm Labors				R	H		
90		Sallie	Wife	W f June 1871 28 m 2 1 1						Georgia	Georgia	Georgia										
91	254 259	Hettie	Dau	W f oct 1899 7/12 S						Georgia	Georgia	Georgia										
92		Lancaster David	Head	W m aug 1836 60 wd						Georgia	N. Carolina	Georgia			Farmer				O	7	222	
93		Lela	Dau	W f may 1877 23 S						Georgia	Georgia	Georgia										
94		Charles	Son	W m feb 1882 18 S						Georgia	Georgia	Georgia			Farm Labors							
95	253 350	Mattie	Dau	W f mar 1884 16 S						Georgia	Georgia	Georgia										
96	256	Thomas	Son	W m aug 1886 13 S						Georgia	Georgia	Georgia										
97		Tanner David	Head	W m may 1856 44 m 24						Georgia	Georgia	Georgia			Farmer				O	m 7	223	
98		Rebecca Melissa	Wife	W f apr 1859 41 m 24 9 6						Georgia	Georgia	Georgia										
99		Benjamin	Son	W m mar 1881 19 S						Georgia	Georgia	Georgia			Farm Labors							
100		Mollie	Dau	W f oct 1885 14 S						Georgia	Georgia	Georgia										

1900 FEDERAL CENSUS, HALL COUNTY, GEORGIA

Tanner, David King – This Census lists David, age 44, and identifies him as a *"farmer."* With him are wife, Rebecca Melissa (Hawkins), 41, and son, Benjamin, 19, and daughter, Mollie, 14.

1910 FEDERAL CENSUS, HALL COUNTY, GEORGIA

Tanner, George Washington – George is now getting up in years at age 85. He and wife, Sarah, age 82, apparently are now living alone, since they have a separate listing in this census.

Tanner, David King – Listed below George's listing in this census is an entry for his son, David, age 53, with his wife, Rebecca, age 51, and sons Earnest, 17, and Thomas, 6. Also listed is a *"grandson," "Telford,"* age 2.

1930 FEDERAL CENSUS, HALL COUNTY, GEORGIA

Tanner, David King – Now 73 years of age, David is listed with wife, Rebecca, 70. In two years, she will pass away, and in six years, David also will be gone. Interestingly, David is actually listed on this census as a "miller," no doubt as a result of his work at Tanner's Mill which had been built by his grandfather, David B. Tanner, in 1823. It is unknown if he and Rebecca were "empty nesters" at this point, since their son, Thomas, has a separate listing right below them.

CERTIFICATE OF DEATH

GEORGIA DEPARTMENT OF PUBLIC HEALTH

Bureau of Vital Statistics

1511

1. PLACE OF DEATH

Registered No. *161*

County *Hall* Militia District (Number and Name) *1270 Flowery Branch* State of Georgia

City or Town *Flowery Branch* Length of residence in this city or town: Yrs. *2* Mos. Ds. NON-RESIDENT (Yes or No) *no*

Street and Number (No.) (Street) Ward
(If death occurred in a hospital, give its name instead of street and number)

2. FULL NAME *Mr David Tanner.*

Residence (City or Town) *Flowery Branch* (Street and Number) (State) *Ga*

PERSONAL AND STATISTICAL PARTICULARS	MEDICAL CERTIFICATE OF DEATH

3. SEX *Male* | **4. COLOR or RACE** *white* | **5.** Single, Married, Widowed, Divorced (write the word) *Widowed*

16. DATE OF DEATH *Jan 4* 19*36* at *6=00 a* M (Month, Day, Year) (Hour)

6. DATE OF BIRTH (month, day, year) *Sept 4 1856*

7. AGE Years *79* Months *4* Days *0* If less than one day Hours Minutes

17. I HEREBY CERTIFY, That I attended the deceased from *Dec 27* 19*35* to *Jan. 4* 19*36*

I last saw h— alive on *Jan 4* 19*36*, death is said to have occurred on the date and hour stated above. The principal cause of death and related causes of importance in the order of onset and duration of each: *Old Age Heart Trouble Labor Pneumonia*

8. OCCUPATION
(a) Trade, profession or particular kind of work done, as spinner, sawyer, bookkeeper, etc. *Retired*
(b) Industry or business in which work was done, as cotton mill, sawmill, bank, etc.
(c) Date deceased last worked at this occupation (month and year)
(d) Total years spent in this occupation

Other contributory causes of importance:

9. BIRTHPLACE (P. O. Address) *Gainesville Hall Co Ga*

What test confirmed diagnosis? *Clinical* (Specify whether autopsy, operation, laboratory, or clinical)

FATHER **10. NAME** *George Washington Tanner*

11. BIRTHPLACE (P. O. Address) *Dont Know.*

If death was due to external causes (violence) fill in also the following:

Was injury an accident, suicide, or homicide?

MOTHER **12. MAIDEN NAME** *Miss Sarah Mangum.*

Where did injury occur (Specify city or town, if outside of limits, the county, and also the state)

13. BIRTHPLACE (P. O. Address) *Dont Know.*

Did injury occur in a home, public place or industry?

14. INFORMANT (Signed) *C. W. Tanner.* (Address) *Flowery Branch Ga*

Manner of injury

Nature of injury

19. BURIAL PLACE (Cemetery) *Hopewell* (Postoffice) *Gainesville Ga* Date *Jan 6. 1936*

(Signed) *H. D. Liles* M.D. (Address) *Flowery Branch Ga*

20. UNDERTAKER (Signed) *B Vickers Son* (Address) *Gainesville Ga*

15. FILED *Jan. 20* 19*35*

(Signed) *D C Mooney,* (Local Registrar)

1936 DEATH CERTIFICATE, HALL COUNTY, GEORGIA

Tanner, David King – The cause of David's death is listed as "old age, heart problems, and pneumonia," the typical scourge of individuals in their later years, particularly in that era of no medicine and few skilled doctors in the South. David's wife, Sarah Rebecca, had preceded him in death.

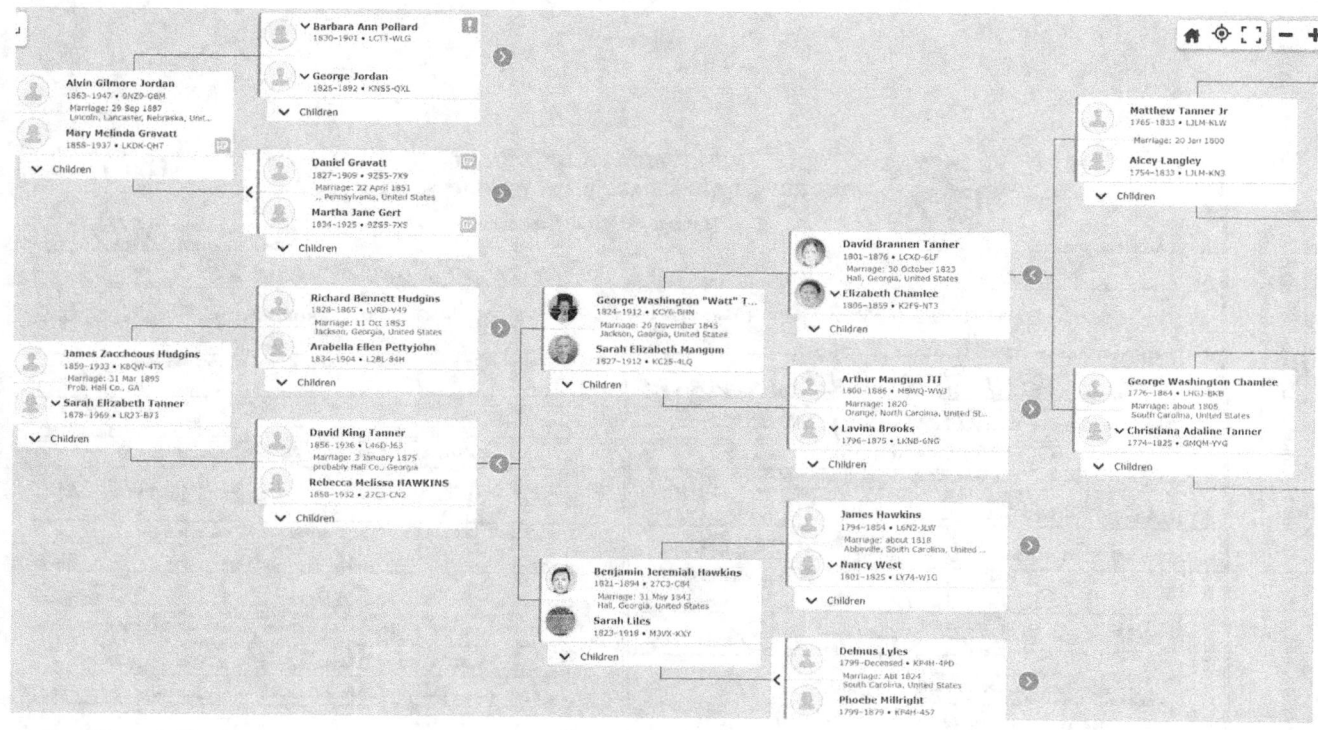

Top tree:

Barbara Ann Pollard
1830–1901 • LCT3-WLG

George Jordan
1825–1892 • KNSS-QXL
Children

Alvin Gilmore Jordan
1863–1947 • 9NZ9-G8M
Marriage: 29 Sep 1887
Lincoln, Lancaster, Nebraska, Unit...
Mary Melinda Gravatt
1858–1937 • LKDK-QH7
Children

Daniel Gravatt
1827–1909 • 9ZS5-7X9
Marriage: 22 April 1851
.., Pennsylvania, United States
Martha Jane Gert
1834–1925 • 9ZS5-7XS
Children

Richard Bennett Hudgins
1828–1865 • LVRD-V49
Marriage: 11 Oct 1853
Jackson, Georgia, United States
Arabella Ellen Pettyjohn
1834–1904 • L2BL-84H
Children

James Zaccheous Hudgins
1859–1933 • KBQW-4TX
Marriage: 31 Mar 1895
Prob. Hall Co., GA
Sarah Elizabeth Tanner
1878–1969 • LR23-B73
Children

David King Tanner
1856–1936 • L46D-363
Marriage: 3 January 1875
probably Hall Co., Georgia
Rebecca Melissa HAWKINS
1858–1932 • 27C3-CN2
Children

George Washington "Watt" T...
1824–1912 • KCY6-BHN
Marriage: 20 November 1845
Jackson, Georgia, United States
Sarah Elizabeth Mangum
1827–1912 • KC2S-4LQ
Children

Benjamin Jeremiah Hawkins
1821–1894 • 27C3-C84
Marriage: 31 May 1843
Hall, Georgia, United States
Sarah Liles
1823–1918 • M3VX-KXY
Children

David Brannen Tanner
1801–1876 • LCXD-6LF
Marriage: 30 October 1823
Hall, Georgia, United States
Elizabeth Chamlee
1806–1859 • K2F9-NT3
Children

Arthur Mangum III
1800–1886 • H8WQ-WWJ
Marriage: 1820
Orange, North Carolina, United St...
Lavina Brooks
1796–1875 • LKNB-6NG
Children

James Hawkins
1794–1854 • L6N2-JLW
Marriage: about 1818
Abbeville, South Carolina, United ...
Nancy West
1801–1925 • LY74-W1G
Children

Delmus Lyles
1799–Deceased • KP4H-4PD
Marriage: Abt 1824
South Carolina, United States
Phoebe Millright
1799–1879 • KP4H-457

Matthew Tanner Jr
1765–1833 • LJLM-KLW
Marriage: 20 Jan 1800
Alcey Langley
1754–1832 • LJLM-KN3
Children

George Washington Chamlee
1776–1864 • LHGJ-BKB
Marriage: about 1806
South Carolina, United States
Christiana Adaline Tanner
1774–1825 • GMQM-YYG
Children

Bottom tree:

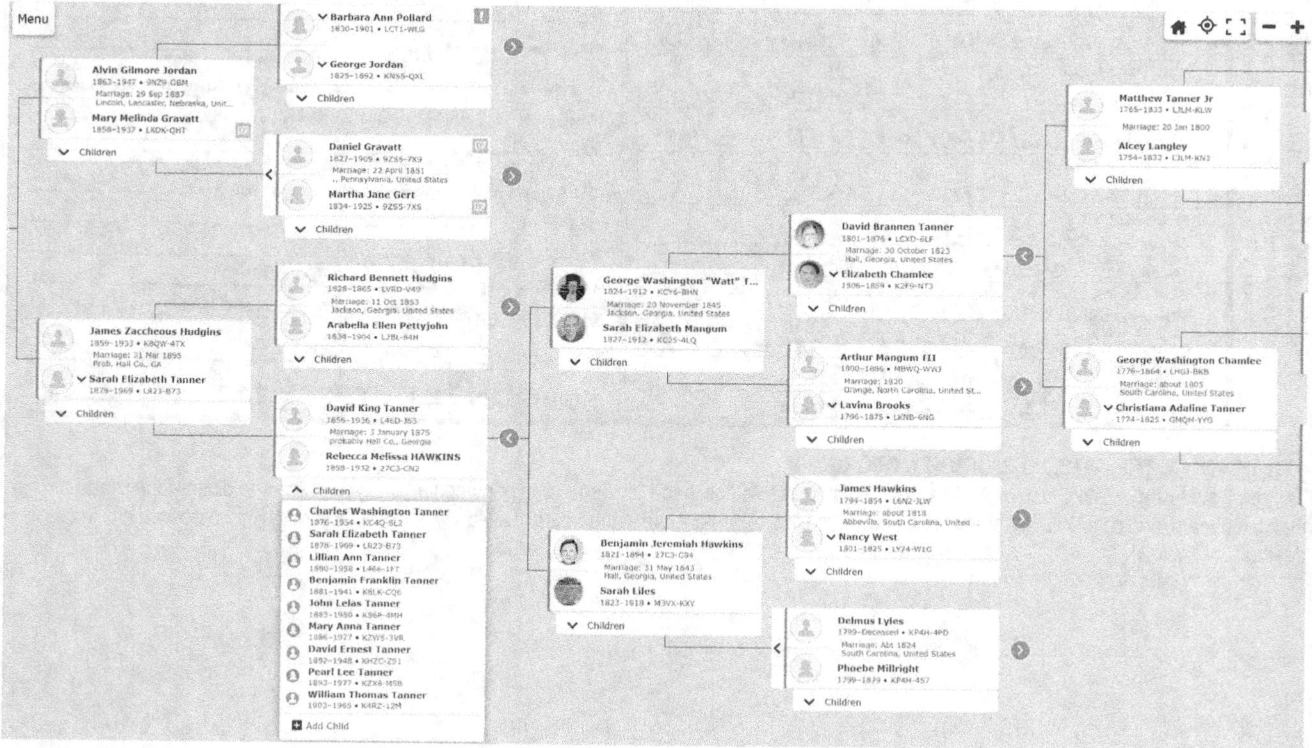

Menu

Barbara Ann Pollard
1830–1901 • LCT1-WLG

George Jordan
1825–1892 • KNSS-QXL
Children

Alvin Gilmore Jordan
1863–1947 • 9NZ9-G8M
Marriage: 29 Sep 1887
Lincoln, Lancaster, Nebraska, Unit...
Mary Melinda Gravatt
1858–1937 • LKDK-QH7
Children

Daniel Gravatt
1827–1909 • 9ZS5-7X9
Marriage: 22 April 1851
.., Pennsylvania, United States
Martha Jane Gert
1834–1925 • 9ZS5-7XS
Children

Richard Bennett Hudgins
1828–1865 • LVRD-V49
Marriage: 11 Oct 1853
Jackson, Georgia, United States
Arabella Ellen Pettyjohn
1834–1904 • L2BL-84H
Children

James Zaccheous Hudgins
1859–1933 • KBQW-4TX
Marriage: 31 Mar 1895
Prob. Hall Co., GA
Sarah Elizabeth Tanner
1878–1969 • LR23-B73
Children

David King Tanner
1856–1936 • L46D-363
Marriage: 3 January 1875
probably Hall Co., Georgia
Rebecca Melissa HAWKINS
1858–1932 • 27C3-CN2
Children

Charles Washington Tanner
1876–1954 • KC4Q-9L2
Sarah Elizabeth Tanner
1878–1969 • LR23-B73
Lillian Ann Tanner
1890–1950 • L46A-1F7
Benjamin Franklin Tanner
1881–1941 • K8LK-CQ6
John Lelas Tanner
1883–1986 • K36P-4MH
Mary Anna Tanner
1886–1977 • KZYS-3Y8
David Ernest Tanner
1892–1948 • XHZO-ZB1
Pearl Lee Tanner
1893–1977 • KZX4-M5B
William Thomas Tanner
1903–1965 • K4RZ-12M
Add Child

George Washington "Watt" T...
1824–1912 • KCY6-BHN
Marriage: 20 November 1845
Jackson, Georgia, United States
Sarah Elizabeth Mangum
1827–1912 • KC2S-4LQ
Children

Benjamin Jeremiah Hawkins
1821–1894 • 27C3-C84
Marriage: 31 May 1843
Hall, Georgia, United States
Sarah Liles
1823–1919 • M3VX-KXY
Children

David Brannen Tanner
1801–1876 • LCXD-6LF
Marriage: 30 October 1823
Hall, Georgia, United States
Elizabeth Chamlee
1806–1859 • K2F9-NT3
Children

Arthur Mangum III
1800–1886 • H8WQ-WWJ
Marriage: 1820
Orange, North Carolina, United St...
Lavina Brooks
1796–1875 • LKNB-6NG
Children

James Hawkins
1794–1854 • L6N2-JLW
Marriage: about 1818
Abbeville, South Carolina, United ...
Nancy West
1801–1925 • LY74-W1G
Children

Delmus Lyles
1799–Deceased • KP4H-4PD
Marriage: Abt 1824
South Carolina, United States
Phoebe Millright
1799–1879 • KP4H-457
Children

Matthew Tanner Jr
1765–1833 • LJLM-KLW
Marriage: 20 Jan 1800
Alcey Langley
1754–1832 • LJLM-KN3
Children

George Washington Chamlee
1776–1864 • LHGJ-BKB
Marriage: about 1806
South Carolina, United States
Christiana Adaline Tanner
1774–1825 • GMQM-YYG
Children

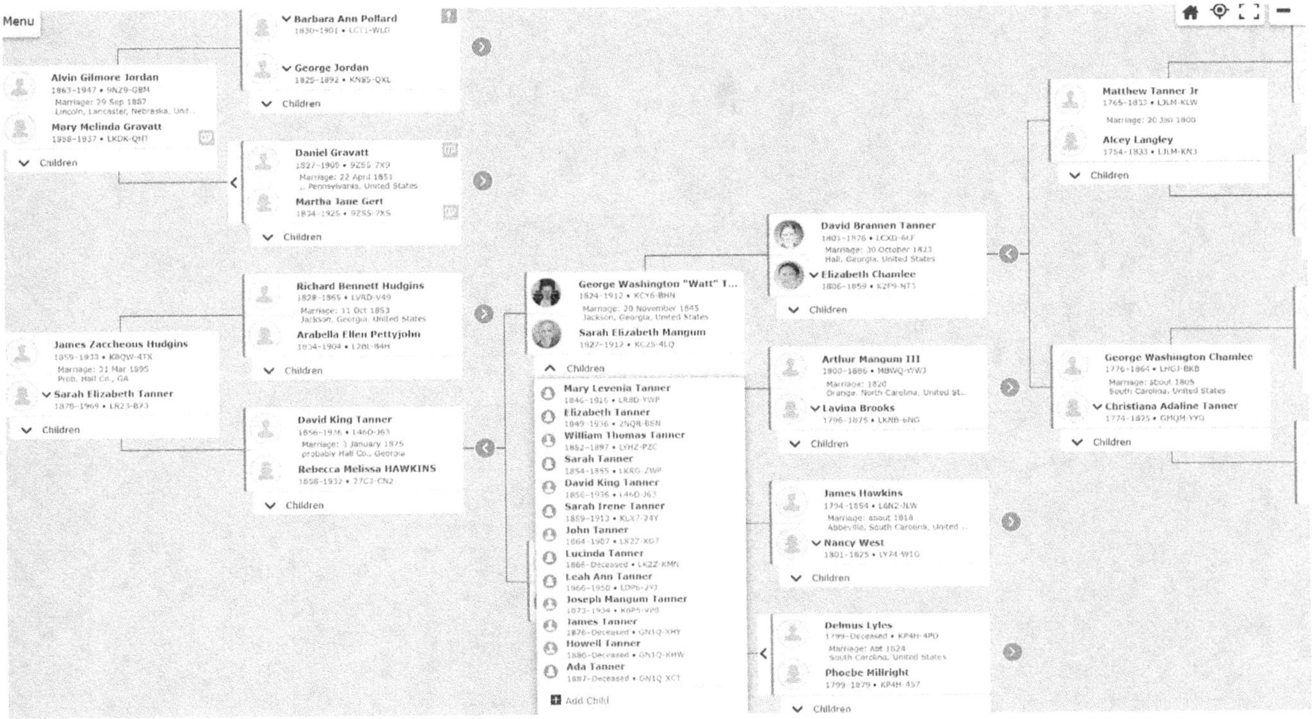

Top chart

Menu

Barbara Ann Pollard
1830–1901 • LC1T-WLD

George Jordan
1825–1892 • KN9S-QXL
∨ Children

Alvin Gilmore Jordan
1863–1947 • 9NZ9-GBM
Marriage: 29 Sep 1887
Lincoln, Lancaster, Nebraska, Unit...

Mary Melinda Gravatt
1858–1937 • LXDK-QHT
∨ Children

Daniel Gravatt
1827–1909 • 9ZSS-7X9
Marriage: 22 April 1851
,, Pennsylvania, United States

Martha Jane Gert
1834–1925 • 9ZSS-7XS
∨ Children

Richard Bennett Hudgins
1828–1865 • LVRD-V49
Marriage: 11 Oct 1853
Jackson, Georgia, United States

Arabella Ellen Pettyjohn
1834–1904 • L2BL-84H
∨ Children

James Zaccheous Hudgins
1859–1933 • K8QW-4TX
Marriage: 31 Mar 1895
Prob. Hall Co., GA

∨ **Sarah Elizabeth Tanner**
1878–1969 • LR23-B73
∨ Children

David King Tanner
1856–1936 • 146D-J63
Marriage: 3 January 1875
probably Hall Co., Georgia

Rebecca Melissa HAWKINS
1858–1932 • 27C3-CN2
∨ Children

George Washington "Watt" T...
1824–1912 • KCY6-BHN
Marriage: 20 November 1845
Jackson, Georgia, United States

Sarah Elizabeth Mangum
1827–1912 • KC25-4LQ
∧ Children
Mary Levenia Tanner 1846–1916 • LR8D-YWP
Elizabeth Tanner 1849–1936 • 2SQ4-BSN
William Thomas Tanner 1852–1897 • LYHZ-PZC
Sarah Tanner 1854–1855 • LKRG-ZWP
David King Tanner 1856–1936 • 146D-J63
Sarah Irene Tanner 1859–1913 • KLX7-24Y
John Tanner 1064–1907 • LK2Z-XGT
Lucinda Tanner 1866–Deceased • LK2Z-KMN
Leah Ann Tanner 1966–1950 • L3MS-2VJ
Joseph Mangum Tanner 1873–1934 • K6PS-V29
James Tanner 1876–Deceased • GN1Q-XHY
Howell Tanner 1880–Deceased • GN1Q-XHW
Ada Tanner 1887–Deceased • GN1Q-XCT
➕ Add Child

David Brannen Tanner
1801–1876 • LCXD-6LF
Marriage: 30 October 1823
Hall, Georgia, United States
∨ **Elizabeth Chamlee**
1806–1859 • K2F9-NT5
∨ Children

Arthur Mangum III
1800–1886 • M8WQ-YW3
Marriage: 1820
Orange, North Carolina, United St...
∨ **Lavina Brooks**
1796–1875 • LKMB-6NG
∨ Children

James Hawkins
1794–1854 • L6N2-JLW
Marriage: about 1818
Abbeville, South Carolina, United ...
∨ **Nancy West**
1801–1825 • LY74-91G
∨ Children

Delmus Lyles
1799–Deceased • KP4H-4PD
Marriage: Abt 1824
South Carolina, United States
Phoebe Millright
1799–1875 • KP4H-457
∨ Children

Matthew Tanner Jr
1765–1813 • LJLM-KLW
Marriage: 20 Jan 1800
Alcey Langley
1754–1833 • LJLM-KN3
∨ Children

George Washington Chamlee
1776–1864 • LHGJ-BKB
Marriage: about 1805
South Carolina, United States
Christiana Adaline Tanner
1774–1825 • GHQM-YYG
∨ Children

Bottom chart

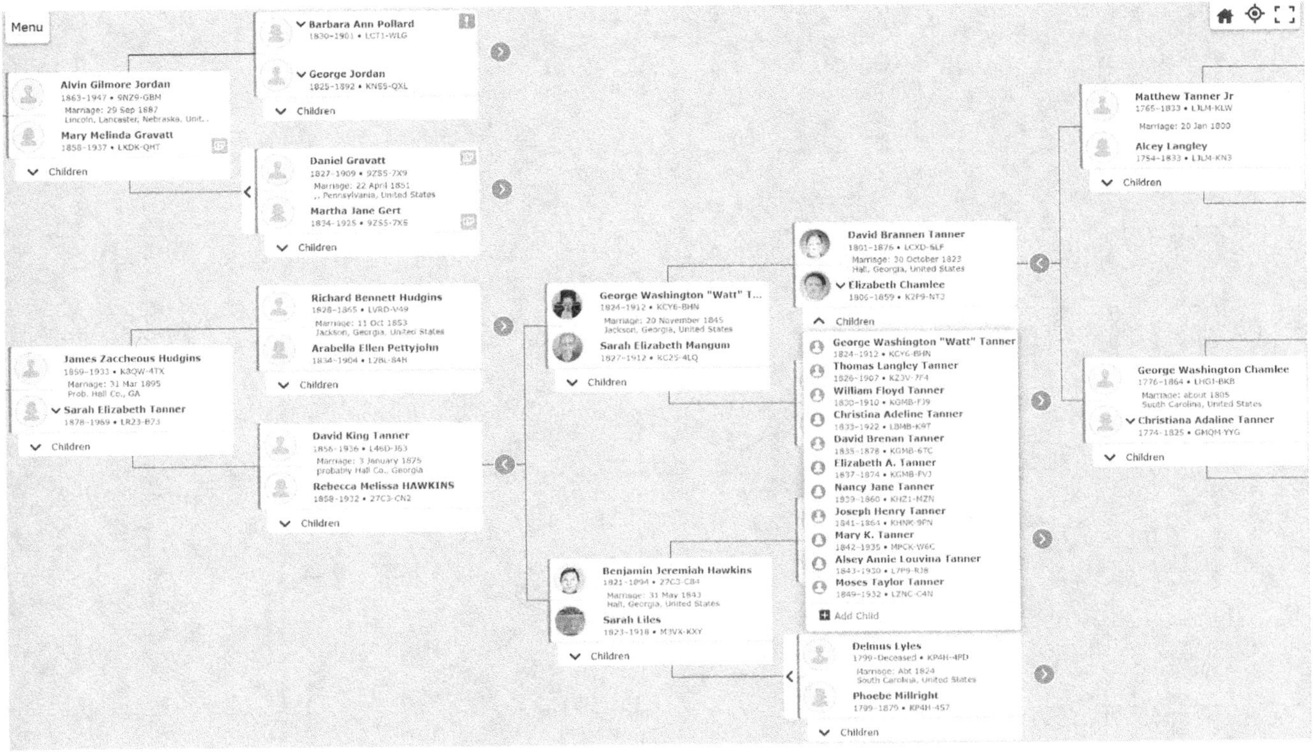

Menu

Barbara Ann Pollard
1830–1901 • LC1T-WLG

George Jordan
1825–1892 • KN9S-QXL
∨ Children

Alvin Gilmore Jordan
1863–1947 • 9NZ9-GBM
Marriage: 29 Sep 1887
Lincoln, Lancaster, Nebraska, Unit...

Mary Melinda Gravatt
1858–1937 • LXDK-QHT
∨ Children

Daniel Gravatt
1827–1909 • 9ZSS-7X9
Marriage: 22 April 1851
,, Pennsylvania, United States

Martha Jane Gert
1834–1925 • 9ZSS-7XS
∨ Children

Richard Bennett Hudgins
1828–1865 • LVRD-V49
Marriage: 11 Oct 1853
Jackson, Georgia, United States

Arabella Ellen Pettyjohn
1834–1904 • L2BL-84H
∨ Children

James Zaccheous Hudgins
1859–1933 • K8QW-4TX
Marriage: 31 Mar 1895
Prob. Hall Co., GA

∨ **Sarah Elizabeth Tanner**
1878–1969 • LR23-B73
∨ Children

David King Tanner
1856–1936 • 146D-J63
Marriage: 3 January 1875
probably Hall Co., Georgia

Rebecca Melissa HAWKINS
1858–1932 • 27C3-CN2
∨ Children

George Washington "Watt" T...
1824–1912 • KCY6-BHN
Marriage: 20 November 1845
Jackson, Georgia, United States

Sarah Elizabeth Mangum
1827–1912 • KC25-4LQ
∨ Children

Benjamin Jeremiah Hawkins
1821–1894 • 27C3-CB4
Marriage: 31 May 1843
Hall, Georgia, United States

Sarah Liles
1823–1918 • M3VX-KXY
∨ Children

David Brannen Tanner
1801–1876 • LCXD-6LF
Marriage: 30 October 1822
Hall, Georgia, United States
∨ **Elizabeth Chamlee**
1806–1859 • K2F9-NT3
∧ Children
George Washington "Watt" Tanner 1824–1912 • KCY6-BHN
Thomas Langley Tanner 1826–1907 • K23V-7F4
William Floyd Tanner 1830–1910 • KGMB-FJ9
Christina Adeline Tanner 1833–1922 • L8MB-K9T
David Brenan Tanner 1835–1878 • KGMB-67C
Elizabeth A. Tanner 1837–1874 • KGMB-FVJ
Nancy Jane Tanner 1859–1860 • KHZ1-MZN
Joseph Henry Tanner 1841–1864 • KH9R-9PN
Mary K. Tanner 1842–1935 • MPCK-W6C
Alsey Annie Louvina Tanner 1843–1930 • L7P9-RJ8
Moses Taylor Tanner 1849–1932 • LZNC-C4N
➕ Add Child

Delmus Lyles
1799–Deceased • KP4H-4PD
Marriage: Abt 1824
South Carolina, United States
Phoebe Millright
1799–1875 • KP4H-457
∨ Children

Matthew Tanner Jr
1765–1813 • LJLM-KLW
Marriage: 20 Jan 1800
Alcey Langley
1754–1833 • LJLM-KN3
∨ Children

George Washington Chamlee
1776–1864 • LHGJ-BKB
Marriage: about 1805
South Carolina, United States
Christiana Adaline Tanner
1774–1825 • GHQM-YYG
∨ Children

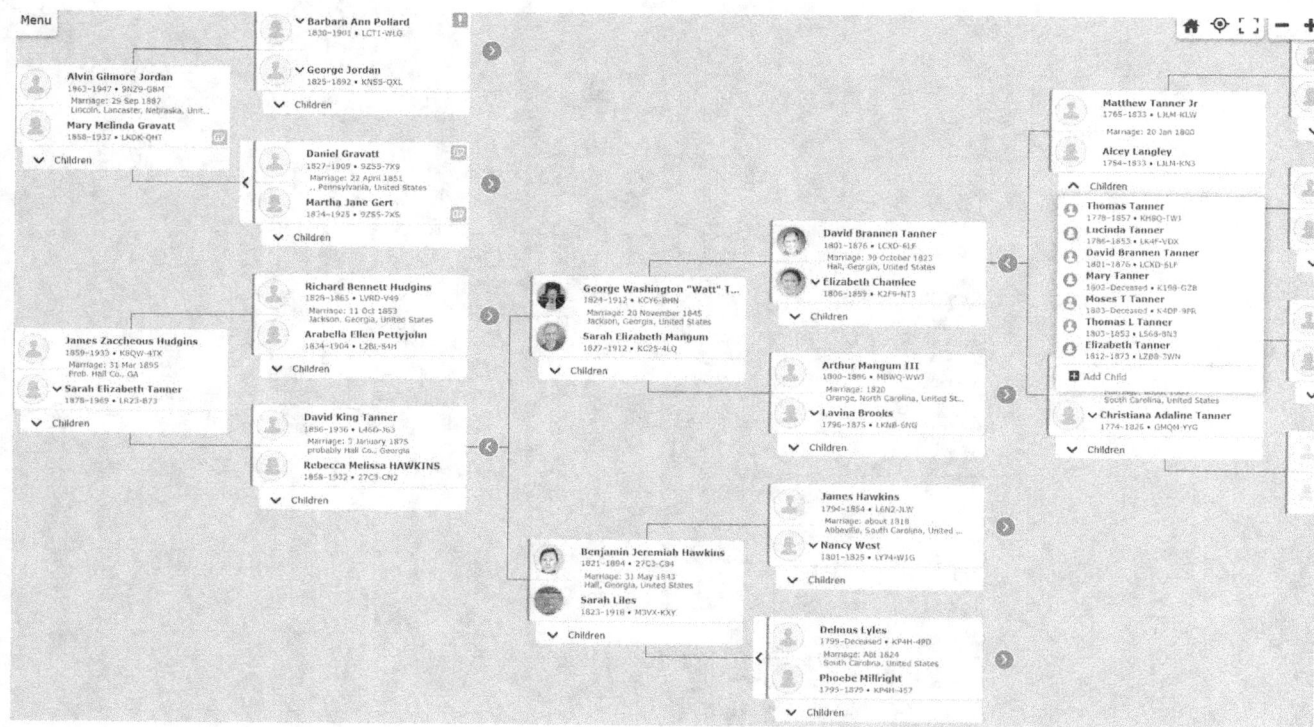

Menu

Alvin Gilmore Jordan
1863–1947 • 9N29-G8M
Marriage: 29 Sep 1887
Lincoln, Lancaster, Nebraska, Unit...
Mary Melinda Gravatt
1858–1937 • LKDK-QHT
⌄ Children

⌄ **Barbara Ann Pollard**
1830–1901 • LCT1-WLG

⌄ **George Jordan**
1825–1892 • KN55-QXL
⌄ Children

Daniel Gravatt
1827–1909 • 9Z55-7X9
Marriage: 22 April 1851
... Pennsylvania, United States
Martha Jane Gert
1834–1925 • 9Z55-7XS
⌄ Children

James Zaccheous Hudgins
1859–1933 • K8QV-4TX
Marriage: 31 Mar 1895
Prob. Hall Co., GA
⌄ **Sarah Elizabeth Tanner**
1878–1969 • LR23-B73
⌄ Children

Richard Bennett Hudgins
1829–1865 • LVRD-V49
Marriage: 11 Oct 1853
Jackson, Georgia, United States
Arabella Ellen Pettyjohn
1834–1904 • L2BL-84H
⌄ Children

David King Tanner
1856–1936 • L46G-J63
Marriage: 7 January 1875
probably Hall Co., Georgia
Rebecca Melissa HAWKINS
1858–1932 • 27C9-CN2
⌄ Children

George Washington "Watt" T...
1824–1912 • KCY6-BHN
Marriage: 20 November 1845
Jackson, Georgia, United States
Sarah Elizabeth Mangum
1827–1912 • KC25-4LQ
⌄ Children

Benjamin Jeremiah Hawkins
1821–1894 • 27C2-C94
Marriage: 31 May 1843
Hall, Georgia, United States
Sarah Liles
1825–1918 • M3VX-KXY
⌄ Children

David Brannen Tanner
1801–1876 • LCXD-6LF
Marriage: 30 October 1823
Hall, Georgia, United States
⌄ **Elizabeth Chamlee**
1806–1859 • K2F9-NT3
⌄ Children

Arthur Mangum III
1800–1886 • M8WQ-WW7
Marriage: 1820
Orange, North Carolina, United St...
⌄ **Lavina Brooks**
1796–1875 • LKNB-GNG
⌄ Children

James Hawkins
1794–1854 • L6N2-3LW
Marriage: about 1818
Abbeville, South Carolina, United ...
⌄ **Nancy West**
1801–1825 • LY74-W1G
⌄ Children

Delmus Lyles
1799–Deceased • KP4H-4PD
Marriage: Abt 1824
South Carolina, United States
Phoebe Millright
1799–1879 • KP4H-457
⌄ Children

Matthew Tanner Jr
1765–1833 • L3LM-KLW
Marriage: 20 Jan 1800
Alcey Langley
1784–1833 • L3LM-KN3
⌃ Children

👤 **Thomas Tanner**
1778–1857 • KH8Q-TW1
👤 **Lucinda Tanner**
1796–1853 • LK4F-VDX
👤 **David Brannen Tanner**
1801–1876 • LCXD-6LF
👤 **Mary Tanner**
1802–Deceased • K198-GZ8
👤 **Moses T Tanner**
1803–Deceased • K4DP-9P6
👤 **Thomas L Tanner**
1803–1853 • L568-B43
👤 **Elizabeth Tanner**
1812–1873 • LZ88-3WN
➕ Add Child

... South Carolina, United States
⌄ **Christiana Adaline Tanner**
1774–1826 • GMQM-YYG
⌄ Children

---

enu

Matthew Tanner Sr.
1730–1809 • LHX8-4VV
Marriage: 1751
Lunenburg, Virginia, United States
Lucy Creed Haskins
1735–1809 • L27K-WB5
⌄ Children

Thomas Langley
1732–1803 • L1P9-X6Q
Marriage: 1755
Caswell, North Carolina, United St...
⌄ **Mary Wiley**
1734–1823 • G664-SFF
⌄ Children

Jacob Chamlee
1752–1833 • KL77-SMF

Juda Chastain
Deceased • GF3Y-MCX
⌄ Children

➕ Add Father

➕ Add Mother

Lewis Tanner
1690–1773 • LTH9-DFF
Marriage: 1715
Prob.Henrico Co., Now Chesterfiel...
⌄ **Margaret Haskins**
1700–1765 • LTH9-JH5
⌄ Children

Thomas Edward Hoskins
1697–Deceased • LHGR-4X7
Marriage: Abt 1728
... Virginia
Elizabeth Giles
1701–Deceased • LHTR-T91
⌄ Children

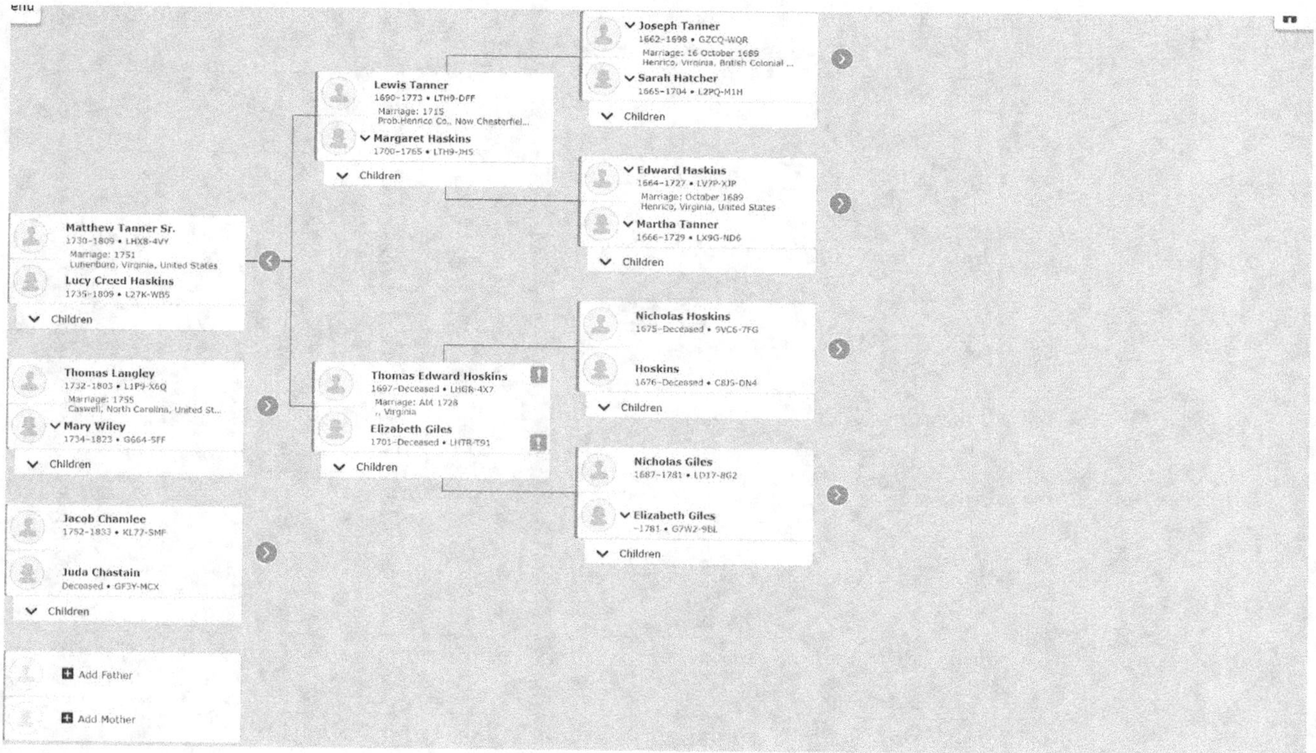

⌄ **Joseph Tanner**
1662–1698 • GZCQ-WQR
Marriage: 16 October 1689
Henrico, Virginia, British Colonial ...
⌄ **Sarah Hatcher**
1665–1704 • L2PQ-M1H
⌄ Children

⌄ **Edward Haskins**
1664–1727 • LV7P-XJP
Marriage: October 1689
Henrico, Virginia, United States
⌄ **Martha Tanner**
1666–1729 • LX9G-ND6
⌄ Children

Nicholas Hoskins
1675–Deceased • 9VC6-7FG

Hoskins
1676–Deceased • C8J5-DN4
⌄ Children

Nicholas Giles
1687–1781 • LD37-8G2

⌄ **Elizabeth Giles**
–1781 • G7W2-9BL
⌄ Children

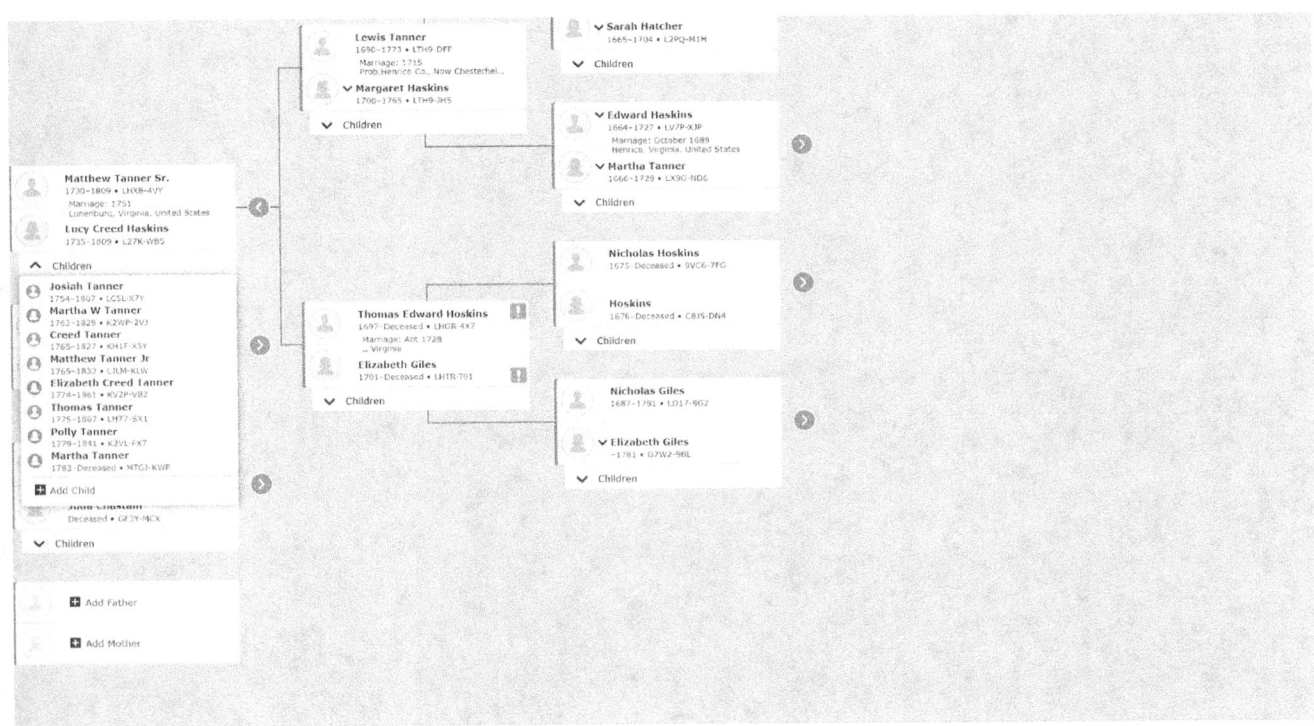

First tree (top)

Matthew Tanner Sr.
1730–1809 • LHX8-4VY
Marriage: 1751
Lunenburg, Virginia, United States

Lucy Creed Haskins
1735–1809 • L27K-WB5

∧ Children
- Josiah Tanner
  1754–1807 • LC5L-X7Y
- Martha W Tanner
  1762–1829 • K2WP-2VJ
- Creed Tanner
  1765–1827 • KH1F-X5Y
- Matthew Tanner Jr
  1765–1833 • LXJM-KLW
- Elizabeth Creed Tanner
  1774–1961 • KV2P-VBZ
- Thomas Tanner
  1775–1807 • LH77-SX1
- Polly Tanner
  1779–1841 • K2VL-FX7
- Martha Tanner
  1783–Deceased • MTGJ-KWP
- ➕ Add Child

Juda Chastain
Deceased • GF3Y-MCX

∨ Children

➕ Add Father
➕ Add Mother

Lewis Tanner
1690–1773 • LTH9-DFF
Marriage: 1715
Prob.Henrico Co., Now Chesterfiel...

∨ Margaret Haskins
1700–1765 • LTH9-JHS

∨ Children

Thomas Edward Hoskins
1697–Deceased • LHGR-4X7
Marriage: Abt 1728
.., Virginia

Elizabeth Giles
1701–Deceased • LHTR-T91

∨ Children

∨ Sarah Hatcher
1665–1704 • L2PQ-M1H

∨ Children

∨ Edward Haskins
1664–1727 • LV7P-XJP
Marriage: October 1689
Henrico, Virginia, United States

∨ Martha Tanner
1666–1729 • LX9G-ND6

∨ Children

Nicholas Hoskins
1675–Deceased • 9VC6-7FG

Hoskins
1676–Deceased • C8JS-DN4

∨ Children

Nicholas Giles
1687–1791 • LD17-9G2

∨ Elizabeth Giles
–1781 • G7W2-98L

∨ Children

Second tree (bottom)

Matthew Tanner Sr.
1730–1809 • LHX8-4VY
Marriage: 1751
Lunenburg, Virginia, United States

Lucy Creed Haskins
1735–1809 • L27K-WB5

∨ Children

Thomas Langley
1732–1803 • L1P9-X6Q
Marriage: 1755
Caswell, North Carolina, United St...

∨ Mary Wiley
1734–1823 • G664-SFF

∨ Children

Jacob Chamlee
1752–1833 • KL77-SMF

Juda Chastain
Deceased • GF3Y-MCX

∨ Children

➕ Add Father
➕ Add Mother

Lewis Tanner
1690–1773 • LTH9-DFF
Marriage: 1715
Prob.Henrico Co., Now Chesterfiel...

∨ Margaret Haskins
1700–1765 • LTH9-JHS

∧ Children
- Lucius Matthew Tanner
  1700–1766 • GSC3-KP1
- Thomas Tanner
  1716–1802 • 278F-VPJ
- Lucius Tanner
  1720–1765 • LHX8-4FB
- Matthew Tanner Sr.
  1730–1809 • LHX8-4VY
- Lewsirus Tanner
  –1765 • GVKF-CMG
- ➕ Add Child

Thomas Edward Hoskins
1697–Deceased • LHGR-4X7
Marriage: Abt 1728
.., Virginia

Elizabeth Giles
1701–Deceased • LHTR-T91

∨ Children

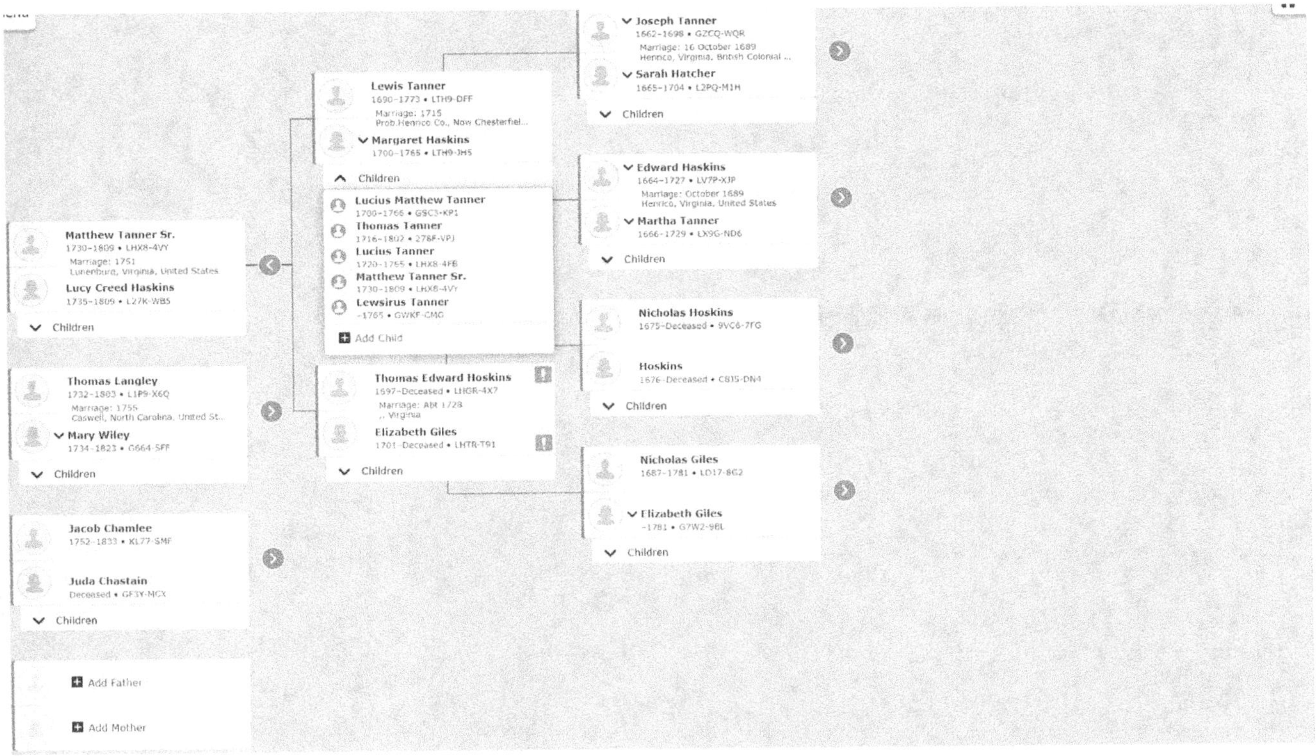

∨ Joseph Tanner
1662–1698 • G2CQ-WQR
Marriage: 16 October 1689
Henrico, Virginia, British Colonial ...

∨ Sarah Hatcher
1665–1704 • L2PQ-M1H

∨ Children

∨ Edward Haskins
1664–1727 • LV7P-XJP
Marriage: October 1689
Henrico, Virginia, United States

∨ Martha Tanner
1666–1729 • LX9G-ND6

∨ Children

Nicholas Hoskins
1675–Deceased • 9VC6-7FG

Hoskins
1676–Deceased • C8JS-DN4

∨ Children

Nicholas Giles
1687–1791 • LD17-9G2

∨ Elizabeth Giles
–1781 • G7W2-98L

∨ Children

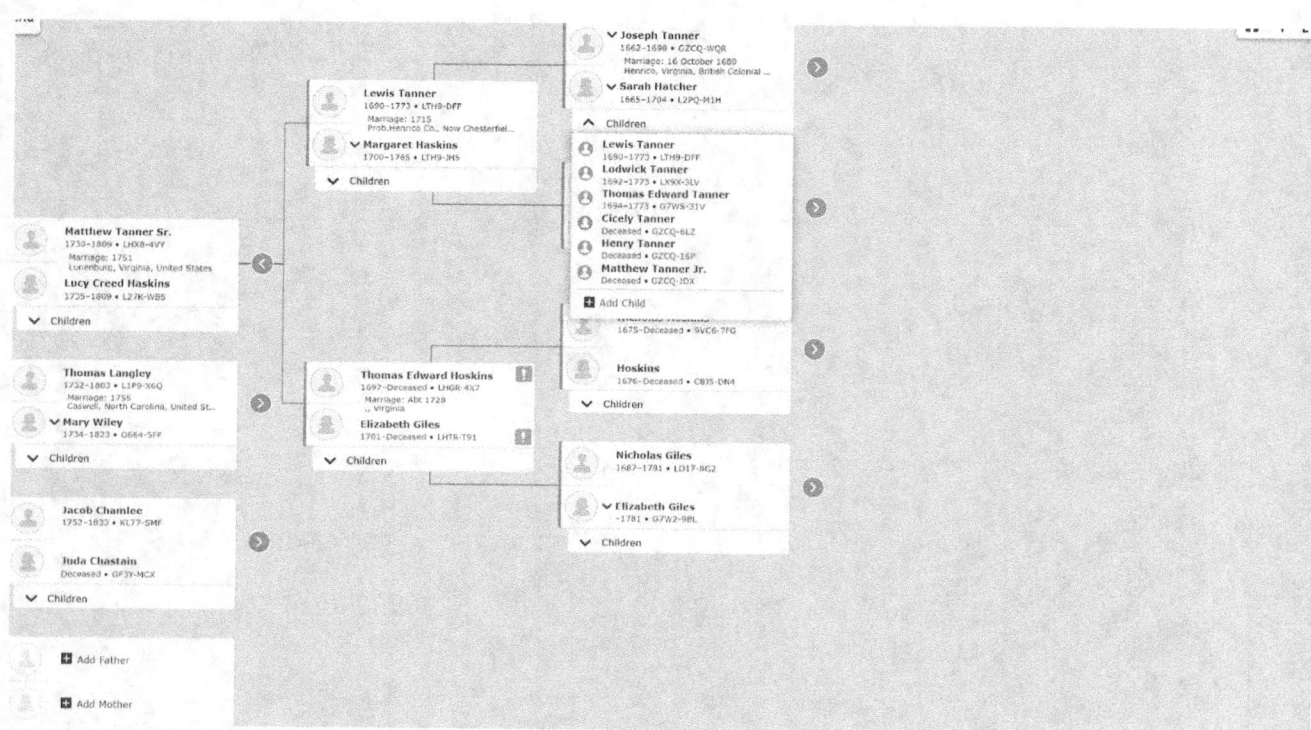

Family Tree of Tanner Family, pages 254-258 – From the most recent to most historic.

A Pettyjohn Family History
And Jacob Pettyjohn's Odyssey

Though he sought a normal, law-abiding life, Jacob Pettyjohn's existence turned out to be anything but ordinary. In 1859, at the age of 42, he was convicted of murder for failure to render assistance to a victim in need. After winning a "Stay of Execution," however, he did not wait around hoping for a reversed judgment. He had "seen the handwriting on the wall," and struck out for Texas, and a new life.

The Pettyjohn family from Virginia – just as most families – is not without its unusual twists and turns, even to the point of being implicated in a documented murder. Though the Pettyjohn lineage reportedly hails from early royalty in France, this stature was anything but obvious in the Georgia branch of this family.

James D. Pettyjohn (b. 1790 in VA) married *Temperance Rogers* (b. 1800 or 1806 in Jackson Co., GA) in 1815 or 1818. This group of Pettyjohns – either through the Pettyjohns themselves or through relations with the Rogers family – reportedly was part Native American.

The children of James and Temperance, all of whom were born in Jackson Co., Georgia, were: Nancy (b. 1816); *Jacob* (b. 11/01/1817 in Jackson Co., GA); Sarah Ann (b. 1819); Oliver Perry (b. 1821); John Rodgers (b. 1824); Elizabeth (b. 1827); Mary Evaline (b. 1828); Adaline Permilia and Addison Bainbridge (b. 1832); *Arabella (Arabel Ellen) (b. 1834)*; James Decatur (b. 1836); William Franklin (b. 1837); Thomas Jefferson (b. 1840); and Marion Gates (b. 1843).

Jacob Pettyjohn was destined to live a most unusual life, and he is central to the topic of this story. It begins in Forsyth County, Georgia, to which Jacob had moved sometime between 1840 and 1845, with his wife *Mary Mariah Whitmire* and their five children.

On the afternoon of August 7, 1858, Jacob, along with *Isaac Freeland, Levi Q.C. McGinnis, William R. Brannon, James McGinnis, Abraham Buice, William Buice, Claiborn Vaughan and his brother* were involved in a violent incident which ultimately resulted in Claiborn Vaughan's murder.

According to most accounts, *Jacob was not directly involved with the murder*, but by the simple fact that he was in the vicinity, aware of the situation, and did not render aid to the victim, he also was charged with and ultimately convicted of the crime of "Second Degree Murder" of Vaughan.

According to Forsyth County records, *Isaac Freeland was charged with the actual slaying of Vaughan,* using a knife with a one by four-inch blade – essentially a hunting knife – to cut a large gash on the left side of the victim's neck, severing the jugular vein. The other four defendants – Pettyjohn, Levi McGinnis, James McGinnis and William R. Brannon – were accused of *"feloniously, willfully, unlawfully, and of their malice aforethought. . . . aiding, helping, abetting, comforting, assisting, and maintaining the said Isaac Freeland"* in the commission of a violent crime.

The problems all started when court was held by the Justices of the Peace of Forsyth County for the Wildcat District on the first Saturday of August, 1858. The McGinnises, Vaughans, Buices, and several of their companions were in attendance at the courthouse. Like church camp meetings, "Court Week" was a very popular opportunity to meet and socialize with friends, relatives and neighbors.

By noon that day, several others had congregated

at the court ground: Isaac Freeland, Jacob Pettyjohn, Pinkney Lindsey, Ransom Barnes, Freeland's older sons, and others to watch the proceedings. Court week not only was a big event, it literally was the entertainment medium of that day, especially when serious trials were being heard in court. Little did these men know that they would themselves become the focus of intense attention in a Court Week of the not-too-distant future.

One of the standard "side attractions" during Court Week was a "liquor wagon" where corn and rye whiskeys were dispensed by the pint or quart for sale to the public. It was, in fact, a time-honored tradition which invariably – and ironically – led to trouble for the participants, and even though it was questionable legally, that circumstance was far out-weighed by the custom and popularity of the practice of "imbibing."

Out of the practice of imbibing grew other "side-line events" – such as competitive shooting matches – and the first Saturday in August, 1858, was no exception, with Abraham Buice and Archibald Martin competing against each other in one of the initial matches, and William Buice and Clayborn Vaughan placing side-bets against Jacob Pettyjohn and John Brannon, Jr.'s bets on the Buice-Martin match.

In order to find a place for the marksmanship contest, the group walked about a quarter of a mile southwest from the court grounds to a roadside clearing halfway between Wildcat Courthouse and Freeland's home. These events served as lead-ups to the later observation of whatever capital punishment might be meted out that day to the county's convicted criminals.

Though Abe Buice won the first match fairly, Martin was declared the initial winner of the second match before a loud argument from Buice declared that he had actually won that match also. With the outcome of the second match in question and a quarrel quickly in the making, the men decided to just return to the Wildcat Court ground, but that didn't help matters – not by a long shot. The ubiquitous whiskey which was readily available at the courthouse, along with several individuals who were particularly argumentative that day, served only to fan the flames of a quickly-building major quarrel.

Buice continued to insist he had won both matches, and demanded that Pettyjohn and Brannon turn over their illegitimate winnings to him. According to reports, Pettyjohn ultimately complied, stating "If I didn't win the money, I don't want it," and took the money out of his pocket and handed it to Buice.

According to the late Don Shadburn's **Pioneer History of Forsyth County**, *"Billy Buice, Jim McGinnis, Levi McGinnis, and Thomas Stone were standing nearby listening and watching. Several of the men soon fell into an argument, instigated by Jim McGinnis who sidled up to Pettyjohn and told him to knock Buice down. McGinnis then began walking around swearing under his breath.*

"Overhearing the remarks, Billy Buice started cursing McGinnis and Pettyjohn, and Levi McGinnis quickly stepped forward and offered his support. 'Jim (McGinnis), say what you please (to Buice),' he stated emphatically, rolling up his sleeves. 'If you can't whip him, I can.'

"At this point, cooler heads attempted to take control. Jacob Pettyjohn (to his credit) tried to calm the men and ease their tempers before serious trouble erupted, but his efforts were in vain.

"Sometime later, not long before sundown, Levi McGinnis suggested they 'go get something to drink and make friends.' Several of the men walked down to Ransom Barnes' wagon, tied up 'a little piece below the courthouse, and got a quart of liquor.' – each man contributing a few cents toward the purchase. The quart jar was passed quickly from hand to hand among the few who were eager to take it. The whiskey, however, only aggravated the still unresolved quarrel.

"Levi McGinnis, finding courage from the bottle, grew louder and bolder with his remarks about 'the South Carolinians.' Suddenly, he jerked Abe Buice's gun from his hand and hit him in the head with the breach, making Buice stagger."

"If I didn't win the money, I don't want it,"

According to later testimony, a general scuffling reportedly quickly ensued, with McGinnis grabbing Buice by the hair of his head and racing down the hill screaming *"G__ damn you! I'll jerk you as bald-headed as I did Pink Lindsey!"* The two soon fell to the ground panting and cursing, clawing, and ripping at each other like animals. After being broken up, Buice said he was leaving, and gathered his gun and hat.

About 15 minutes after the fight ended, as nightfall approached, the Buices and Vaughan departed. At this point, Levi McGinnis, weaving about with a bottle in his hand, loudly told the Buices and Vaughans to leave, otherwise he would *"kill the last damned South Carolinian of them."*

Witnesses said that Billy Buice, in his drunken state, made the mistake of bragging that he had been the bully in North Carolina and South Carolina, and that he would be the bully in Georgia too. He apparently intended to clearly indicate he was not intimidated in the least by McGinnis.

Claiborn Vaughan, however, had stayed clear of the fighting which seemed to have no logical genesis or intent. The Vaughans and Buices headed in the direction of Billy Buice's house. Buice, McGinnis and Freeland were all still fighting among themselves, with none of them really knowing or understanding what they were fighting about, or why. They were just mad as hornets in a drunken state, and nothing short of a state of unconsciousness was going to alter their lust for conflict.

By this point, still headed down the trail, Abraham Buice – no doubt was still stunned from the blow to his head – was not only confused, but also fearful of the way the situation was so quickly getting out of control. He was particularly frightened of another confrontation with the drunken Freeland whose actions could easily have been interpreted as being just short of insane.

According to later court testimony, in order to collect himself and avoid further conflict with Freeland, Abraham Buice said he *"ran off about forty yards from the place where Claiborne Vaughan later would be killed and sat down upon a log to hide."* As he sat in his hideaway, Buice later testified that he *"saw three men race down the darkened hill and hollow, toward the second branch across the old Mill Road."* Buice said it was much too dark for him to be able to make out the identity of the three phantom figures, and that soon, yet another individual gave a brief chase before suddenly stopping just short of the creek and turning back in the direction of the court ground.

According to further court testimony, after even more confusion and fighting and cursing and unfounded accusations, Levi McGinnis, Freeland, and Brannon, in the presence of Pettyjohn, confronted the unfortunate Claiborne Vaughan who was mounted upon a mare. This, no doubt, was precipitated solely by the fact that Vaughan had been identified and associated with the Buices as a "South Carolinian." Brandishing pocket knives, one or more of the men began dragging Vaughan off the mare, and, as evidence would later indicate, one or more of them also assaulted Vaughan with a knife – in a deadly manner.

Abe Buice further testified that while he was hiding nearby in the undergrowth and brush, he heard more scuffling sounds, shouting and cursing involving his friend, Vaughan. He stated that he distinctly recognized Vaughan's voice when the victim called out to his attackers *"I surrender! I surrender!"* Then in a louder voice Buice next heard Vaughan scream *"Murder! Murder!"*

Vaughan, after falling from his horse, continued to kick and struggle in vain, as his wails of anguish and pain grew weaker. Jeremiah Freeland who had been following the group saw the silhouetted figure of Vaughan lying in the road. He witnessed Vaughan raise himself on his hands and slowly crawl to the edge of the road moaning *"I'm a dead man . . . . dead man."* Pettyjohn, Jim McGinnis and Bill Brannon stood nearby, possibly in shock at what had occurred. They, however, had made the tragic mistake of failing to render assistance to a victim in dire need.

Later, after being identified as a suspect and being arrested and put on trial, Jacob Pettyjohn testified that he had gone along with the crowd merely as an "idle spectator," to watch Freeland and Buice fight.

He stated under oath that *"while following the Buices (who took to concealment) to the creek, he had heard the fighting and returned to the place where he earlier had passed Claib Vaughan."*

Pettyjohn added that he saw William Brannon again at that spot and that Brannon had staggered over to Vaughan, kicked him a few times, and demanded, *"Are you dead G__ damn you, old man? If Freeland has not whipped you, I can."*

The east-headed old Blackstock Mill Road on which the murder occurred was intersected north-south with what today would be old U.S. 19, an ancient Indian and game trail in pre-history. The Mill Road passed through three north-south flowing streams – which combine south of the road to form the main tributary of Dick's Creek.

Levi McGinnis and Isaac Freeland who had also been arrested and placed on trial for Vaughan's murder were both ultimately convicted of murder and sentenced to *"Death."* They were later hung on a gallows at the Forsyth County Jail. Freeland had the distinction of being the first person in recorded history to be hanged in Forsyth County.

William Brannon and Jim McGinnis were likewise found *"Guilty,"* but drew the lesser penalty of *"Involuntary Manslaughter,"* and sentenced to three years of hard labor at the state penitentiary in Milledgeville. By comparison, they "got off easy."

Meanwhile, a by-now totally crestfallen Jacob Pettyjohn who had heretofore been accustomed to being on the opposite end of the legal spectrum, was, on April 16, 1859, being tried for the capital crime of *"Murder"* of Claiborn Vaughan for his presence and failure to intercede in the matter. On the 23rd day of April, a jury found Pettyjohn *"Guilty"* of *"Second Degree Murder"* and sentenced him to be *"publicly hanged by the neck on a gallows until he is dead."* The reason for his being charged with and ultimately convicted of Second Degree Murder instead of Involuntary Manslaughter is unknown today.

To his great fortune, however, Pettyjohn – no doubt at least partially as a result of his previous unblemished record – won a *"Stay of Execution"* written by Judge Rice on May 21, 1859. The case was bound over to the State Supreme Court of Georgia,

and, also as a result of his otherwise sterling record and former law enforcement background, Pettyjohn was released on bail to await his new trial.

By this point, however, the previously-thunderstruck Mr. Pettyjohn had "seen the handwriting on the wall," and had no intention of waiting around for yet another verdict. He very shortly and quietly departed Georgia forever for the great state of Texas, where he began life anew and ultimately joined the Confederate Army where he reportedly *"served his country heroically during the war years as a high-ranking Confederate officer."*

According to the Texas State Archives, *"Jacob C. Pettijohn enlisted in the Confederate Army on April 20, 1861, for a period of 12 months."* He was *"a private in Company A, 1st Regiment, Texas Mounted Riflemen,"* commanded by Henry E. McCulloch.

Interestingly, according to his final mustering out information, *"Private Jacob Pettijohn left Ft. Pemberton April 11; arrived at Snyder's Bluff April 13, camped until the 19th when they reached Camp Timmins; 1 muster & payroll combined dated December 31, 1862 to February 28, 1863; 1 muster roll dated February 28, 1863 to April 30, 1863; Absent, left sick in hospital at Vicksburg February 18. Last paid August 31, 1862; bounty due him of $50.00; due him for clothing $33.83; Service 6 months at $11.00 = $66.00 plus $50.00 bounty, plus $33.83 commu. due him for 6 months & clothing. Total: $149.84."*

In 1863, $149.84 was the equivalent of $3,300.00, which was quite a bit of money in those days if Jacob had ever collected it. Unfortunately, the Confederate dollars in which this mustering out payment undoubtedly would have been made were dropping like a rock in 1863, and valueless by 1864 – unless he could have been fortunate enough to have been paid in gold or silver, which is doubtful. Since there are no further records on him, it is unknown today if he ever even collected the funds.

The ultimate resolution of the life of Jacob Pettyjohn is also unknown today. The one "known" final aspect of his life is that it appears he was fruitful and multiplied in his residence in Texas, since many Pettyjohn descendants reside there today. The site of Jacob Pettyjohn's burial is unknown today.

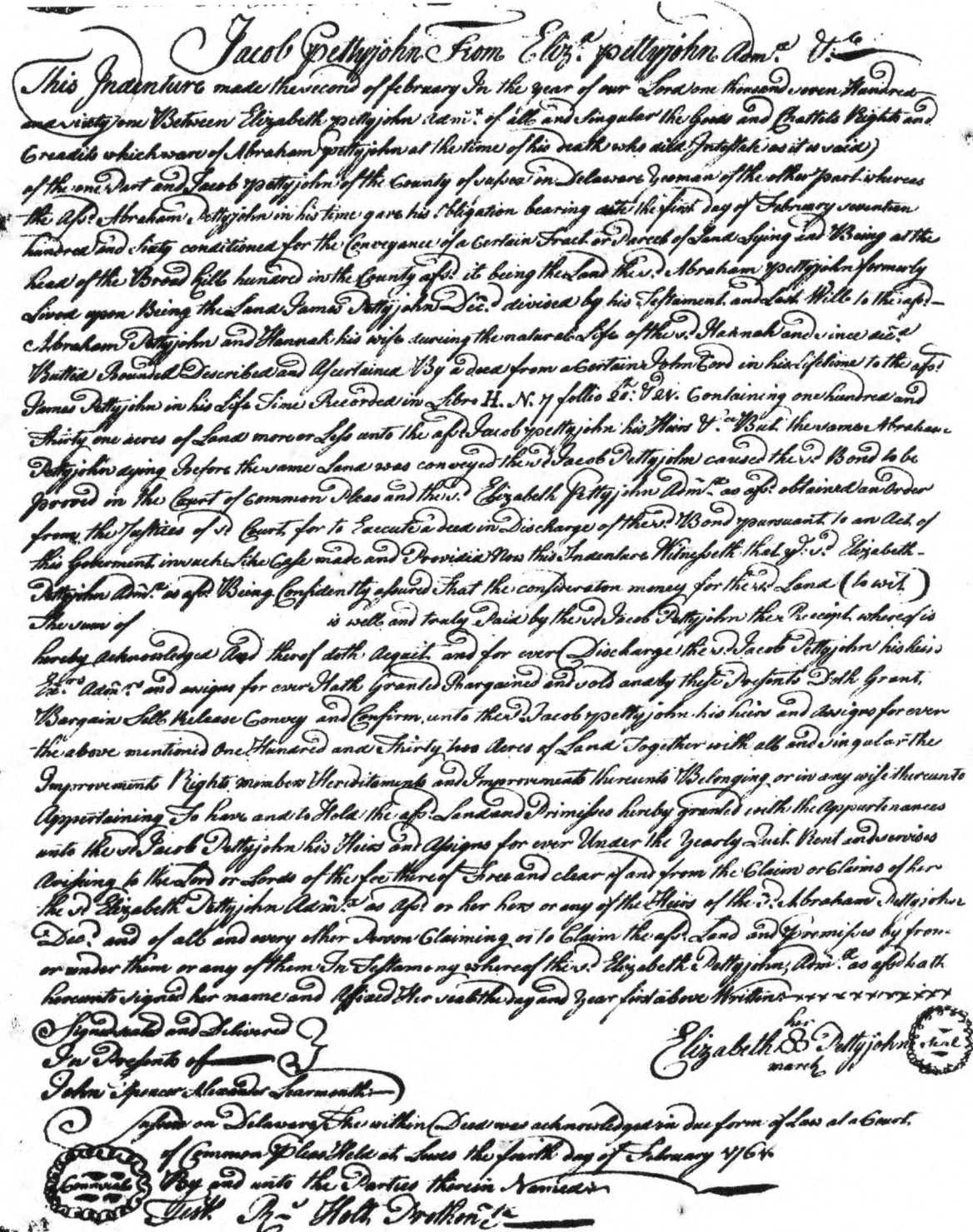

1761 LAND RECORDS, SUSSEX COUNTY DELAWARE

Pettyjohn, Jacob – In this document, written in beautiful penmanship which today is a lost art, Elizabeth Pettyjohn, wife of the deceased Jacob Pettyjohn (the elder) is attempting to gain legal title to a tract of land which had not been conveyed in Jacob's Last Will & Testament.

263

Transcription of Elizabeth Pettyjohn's Application for Legal Title to Jacob Pettyjohn's Delaware Property

Jacob Pettyjohn from Elizabeth Pettyjohn, administrator

This indenture made the second of February in the year of our Lord one thousand seven hundred sixty one between Elizabeth Pettyjohn, administrator, of all and singular the goods and chattel rights and credits which were of Abraham Pettyjohn at the time of his death who died intestate (as it is said) of the one part, and Jacob Pettyjohn of the county of Sussex in Delaware, yeoman of the other part.

Whereas the afo (aforementioned) Abraham Pettyjohn in his time gave his obligation bearing the first day of February seventeen hundred and sixty conditioned for the conveyance of a certain tract or parcel of land lying and being at the head of the broad hills hundred (?) in the county afo, it being the land this Abraham Pettyjohn formerly lived upon, being the land James Pettyjohn, dec (deceased), devised by his testament and last will to the afo Abraham Pettyjohn and Hannah his wife during the natural life of the afo Hannah and since dec'd (deceased).

Abetted, bounded, described and appertained by a deed from a certain John _____ in his lifetime to the afo James Pettyjohn, in his lifetime recorded in _____ H.N. _____ _____ _____ containing one hundred and thirty one acres of land more or less unto the afo Jacob Pettyjohn, his heirs, and/or _____, but the same Abraham Pettyjohn dying before the same land was conveyed to the afo Jacob Pettyjohn caused the afo bond to be _____ in the court of common pleas and the afo Elizabeth Pettyjohn, Adm (Administrator) as afo obtained an order from the justice of the courts to execute a deed in the discharge of their bond pursuant to an act of this government invokes in like cases made, and provided now this indenture witnesseth that the afo Elizabeth Pettyjohn, admst (administrator) as afo being confidently assured that the _____ money for the afo (to wit) the sum of _____ is well and truly paid by the Jacob Pettyjohn, the receipt whereof is hereby acknowledged and thereof doth acquit and forever discharge Jacob Pettyjohn his heirs _____ _____ and assigns forever, hath granted, bargained and _____ and by their agents doth grant, bargain, sell, lease, convey and confirm unto Jacob Pettyjohn, his heirs and assigns, forever the above mentioned one hundred and thirty two acres of land, together with all and singular the improvements, rights, privileges and improvements thereunto belonging or in any wise thereunto appertaining, to have and to hold the land and premises hereby granted with the appurtenances unto Jacob Pettyjohn his heirs and assigns forever under the yearly just rent and service as accruing to the Lord or Lords of the fee thereof free and clear of and from the claim or claims of heirs, Elizabeth Pettyjohn, adm as afo or her heirs or any of the heirs of Abraham Pettyjohn (dec.), and of all and every other person claiming or to claim the aforementioned land and premises by, from or under them or any of them.

In testimony whereof, Elizabeth Pettyjohn, Admin, as aforementioned oath, have unto signed her name and affixed her seal the day and year first above below written.

Xxxxxxxx

Elizabeth Pettyjohn

Her seal

Signed in the presence of John Spencer Alexander _____

_____ _____ _____ the within deed was acknowledged in due form of law at a Court of Common Pleas held at _____ the fourth day of February, 1761.

By and unto the parties therein named.

Justice _____ _____ _____

Pettyjohn Genealogical Line

(Ancestry of One Pettyjohn-Hudgins Family Line in Georgia)
(Country of Origin of Pettyjohn Family Line: France)

The surname Pettyjohn was first found in Burgundy (Bourgogne), an administrative and historic region of east-central France, where the Pettyjohns held a <u>family seat</u> in the seigneurie of Rotalier. This family eventually ascended to status among the nobility of Bourgogne, and Pierre Petitjean was a counselor in 1751 in the Chambre des Comptes de Bourgogne. From France this family immigrated first to England to escape religious and political oppression, and, from there, moved on quite likely to Holland and thence to America.

Great-great-great-great-great-great-grandfather: James Pettyjohn

b.   1687, Accomack, Virginia, Colony of Great Britain

m.   Hannah Wilson (b. circa 1695, Sussex, DE, d. Aug 1, 1788 to 12 December 1788, Sussex, DE) Issue: James (b. 1709, Sussex, DE, d. 3 May 1794, Sussex, DE); Thomas (b. 1711, Sussex, DE, d. 03 April 1782, Sussex, DE); John (b. circa 1714, Broadkill Hundred, Sussex, DE, d. bef 1749); Jacob (b. 1715, Sussex Co., DE); Sinderiah (b. circa 1717, VA); Elizabeth (b. 1720); Richard (b. circa 1720, Sussex, DE); Naomi (b. circa 1722, Hungars Parish, N. Hampton, VA); Patience (b. circa 1722, Sussex, DE); Marjorie (b. circa 1726, Sussex, Colony of Delaware, British Colonial America); Abigale (b. circa 1727, Sussex, Colony of DE, British Colonial America); Anzelah (b. circa 1728, Sussex, Col. Of DE); Lydia (b. circa 1728, Sussex, Col. Of DE); Elizabeth (b. circa 1730, Sussex, Col. Of DE); Samuel Molestein (b. 1732, Sussex, Col. Of DE); Mary (b. 1734, Sussex, Col. Of DE, d. 1844); **Abraham** (b. circa 1736, Hungars Parish, N. Hampton, VA, d. Feb, 1761, Sussex, DE); Sarah (b. circa 1746, Sussex, DE).

d.   11 Nov 1748, Sussex, DE

Great-great-great-great-great-grandfather: Abraham Pettyjohn

b.   circa 1736, Hungars Parish, North Hampton, VA

m.   5 November, 1752, Elizabeth Hardwick (b. 1724, Sussex, DE, d. 8 July 1772, Bedford, Bedford Co., VA) Broadkill Hundred, Sussex, DE Issue: **Jacob**; William (b. 1758, Broadkill Hundred, Sussex, DE, d. 15 May 1822, Amherst, VA); & Mary (b. circa 1760, Sussex, DE, d. circa 1808).

d.   Feb, 1761, Sussex, Delaware

> **Note #1:** In the 1820s, both Abraham Pettyjohn and Enoch Rogers moved to adjoining lands – Abraham into lower White County Georgia, and Enoch to upper Hall County. Abraham and Enoch both gradually migrated further westward (Abraham to Walker County in the 1830s) until they had both reached the old Indian Territory in what today is northwest Georgia. Some of Enoch's children migrated out to the West during the Indian removal from what today is the southeastern United States, but Enoch and Abraham decided they had traveled far enough and both eventually lived out their days in Walker County.

Great-great-great-great-grandfather: Jacob Pettyjohn

b.   1754, Broadkill Hundred, Sussex, Delaware

m.   circa 1777, Elizabeth Staton (b. circa 1740, Dinwiddie, VA, d. 01/07/1811, Jackson Co., GA), Amherst, VA. Issue: Reuben (b. 1778, Amherst, VA); Warren (b. 1779, Jackson Co., GA); Sarah (b. 1780, Amherst, d. 02/15/1863, Lima, Grant Co., WS); William (b. 1782, Amherst); Abraham (b. 1785, Amherst, d. 1870, Chattooga, GA); and **James** (b. 1790).

d.   18 July 1811, Jackson Co., GA

> **Note #2:** On January 7, 1811, Jacob Pettyjohn's Last Will & Testament was probated. In this document he names his son, James D. Pettyjohn, and *"my nephew Fleming Staton"* to whom he left *"all that part of my tract of land lying on the south side of Allen's Creek. . ."*

Great-great-great-grandfather: James D. Pettyjohn

b.   1790, Amherst, Virginia

m.   1815 (or 1818) Temperance Rogers (b. 1800, Jackson Co., Georgia; d. June or July, 1879 or 1880, buried Pendergrass, Jackson Co. GA) Issue: Nancy (b. 01/25/1816, Jackson Co, GA, m. Henderson Anglin, Jackson Co, GA, d. 12/10/1861, Forsyth Co., GA); **Jacob** [b. 11/01/1817, Jackson Co, GA, m. Mary Mariah Whitmire 12/17/1837, Jackson Co, GA, d. 1892, (Texas??) Heard Co., GA]; Sarah Ann (b. 10/17/1819, Jackson Co, GA, m. Alfred Gray, d. 12/16/1906, Forsyth Co., GA); Oliver Perry (b. 09/21/1821, Jackson Co, GA, m. Sarah A. Randolph, d. 08/18/1881, Hall Co., GA); John Rogers (b. 01/09/1824, Jackson Co., GA); Elizabeth (b. 03/17/1827, Jackson Co, GA, m. William J. Garrett); Mary Evaline (b. 09/02/1828); Adaline Permilia and Addison Bainbridge (twins?) (b. 01/04/1832, Jackson Co., GA, d. 1852); **Arabella** (Arabel Ellen) (b. 04/03/1834, Jackson Co., GA, m. Richard Bennett Hudgins, 07/30/1857, d. 06/19/1904, Hall Co., GA); James Decatur (b. 03/10/1836); William Franklin (b. 07/28/1837, Jackson Co., GA, m. Frances A. Smith 07/30/1857, d. 07/20/1862); Thomas Jefferson (b. 06/18/1840, Jackson Co., GA, d. 09/08/1861, Richmond, VA); Marion Gates (b. 09/23/1843, Jackson Co., GA, d. 06/01/1862).

d.   03/17/1866 b. Pendergrass, Jackson Co., GA

> **Note #3:** On November 5, 1866, James D. Pettyjohn's Last Will & Testament left everything to his wife, Temperance, daughter of John Rogers.

> **Note #4:** James D. Pettyjohn was an "ensign" in the Georgia Militia May 14, 1812, and, for his service, won two land draws in Jackson County, GA.

> **Note #5:** On a hot August evening in 1858, Arabella Pettyjohn's brother – Jacob Pettyjohn – suffered the misfortune of being present (and possibly indirectly facilitating) the murder of Forsyth County, Georgia, resident Claiborn Vaughan. Pettyjohn was later convicted of *Second Degree Murder* for being present at the incident and failing to render assistance to Vaughan. His two associates who actually committed the act were ultimately convicted of *First Degree Murder* and hung from the gallows in the old Forsyth County, Georgia Jail in 1858. Pettyjohn, who was likewise sentenced to die, won a *Stay of Execution* and his case was bound over to the State Supreme Court, due to questionable circumstances and his sterling record as a former sheriff. Interestingly, after winning his *Stay*, Pettyjohn decided "discretion" was the better part of valor, and lit out for Texas. After slightly more than a year, the U.S. Civil War was ignited, and Pettyjohn – who had joined the Confederate Army in Texas – became an after-thought in the Forsyth County legal system. His descendants live still today in Texas.

Great-great-grandmother: Arabella (a.k.a. "Arabel Ellen") Pettyjohn Hudgins

b.   04/03/1834, Jackson Co., GA

m.   **Richard Bennett Hudgins**, 07/30/1857 Issue: Mary (b. 07/23/1854, d. 06/06/1885); Margaret Emmaline (b. 08/17/1856, Hall Co., GA, d. 10/16/1934, Jackson Co., GA); and **James Zacheus** (b. 12/30/1859, Jackson Co., GA, d. 02/01/1933, Clermont, Hall Co., GA).

d.   06/19/1904, Hall Co., GA. Buried Harmony Grove Baptist Church *(also could be Harmony Hall Baptist Church)* Cemetery, Harmony Church Road, Hall, Co., GA). *(Note: To reach Harmony Hall Baptist Church, take U.S. 129 east and turn left onto Blackstock Road in Hall County, then bear left onto Mangum Mill Road. Harmony Hall Baptist Church is on the left.)*

> **Note #6:** Richard Bennett Hudgins departed in 1861 for service in the Confederate Army only two years after his son, James Zacheus was born. He died 01/03/1865, Raleigh NC, from pneumonia while serving in Co. D, 27th Infantry Regiment, Georgia Volunteers, Army of Northern Virginia. Enlisted circa 08/27/1861. Contracted pneumonia near Goldsboro, NC, 12/27/1864. Sent to Confederate General Hospital #8, Raleigh, NC, where he died. He was buried 01/04/1865, in Oakwood Cemetery, Raleigh, NC, Grave #356.

Great-grandfather: James Zacheus Hudgins

b.   03/04/1804, Jackson Co., Georgia

m.   **(1st)** Elizabeth Harris, 07/22/1882, Harmony Grove Baptist Church (Harmony Hall Baptist Church?), Hall Co., GA. (b. 12/18/1867, Clayton Co., GA, d. 10/29/1892, Hall Co., GA, buried Harmony Hall Baptist Church Cemetery, Hall County, GA) Issue: Richard B. (b. 02/18/1885, d. 01/12/1919); Silas A. (b. 09/05/1886); William J. (b. 08/01/1888, d. 04/13/1889); Mattie Bell (b. 01/20/1890, d. 06/26/1891); and Lucy May (b. 08/03/1891).

      (2nd) Sarah ("Sallie") Elizabeth Tanner, 08/31/1895 (this marriage date also could possibly be 03/31/1895), (b. /07/1878, Chestnut Mountain, Hall Co., GA, d. 12/19/1969, Hiram, Paulding Co., GA.). Issue: Daisy Lee (b. 7/21/1896, d. 08/31/1996); Carl Washington (b. 08/28/1898, d. 12/27/1967, Lexington, KY); **Essie Irene (Carroll)**; David Bennett (b. 01/24/1902, d. 01/14/1983); Clyde Franklin (b. 11/06/1903, d. 02/18/1994); Mary Lou (Marilu) (b. 06/03/1905); Cora Estelle (b. 12/14/1906, d. 02/14/1992); Ralph Newton (b. 09/16/1908, d. 08/23/1970); Albert White (b. 04/21/1910, d. 02/01/1976); Raleigh Edward (b. 06/05/1912, d. 07/11/1982); Sarah Rebecca (b. 07/14/1914, d. 12/10/1999, m. Herman Gibbs "Doc" Tankersley 11/18/1933); Dorothy Belle (b. 11/23/1916, Clermont, Hall County, GA, m. Ray Shaw, d. 05/15/2007, Gainesville, Hall Co.); Marjorie Catherine (b. 10/23/1918).

d.   02/01/1933, Hall Co., GA. Buried Concord Baptist Church Cemetery, Clermont, Hall Co., GA.)

> **Note #7:** James Zacheus Hudgins moved to Clermont, Georgia, in 1913, where he built a large home on King Street just in time for the birth there of his daughter, Sarah, in 1914. Two more children, Dorothy and Marjorie, were also born in this home, bringing the total number of children to 13. Two additional children were later born, but wife Sarah was 43 years of age by this time, and these last two children did not survive. As of 2022, the fine old Hudgins home – now well over 100 years old – still stood on King Street. The first ten Hudgins children were born in Sugar Hill, Hall County, GA.

Grandmother: Essie Carroll (nee Irene) Hudgins Jordan

b.   03/12/1900, Sugar Hill, Hall Co., GA. (Located on old Athens Hwy/U.S. 129 between Talmo and Pendergrass.)

m.   06/18/1927, Clermont, Hall Co., GA, Guy Wilfred Jordan (b. 02/19/1889, Dutch Hill, PA, d. 09/05/1946, Rockmart, Polk Co., GA. Buried Rose Hill Cemetery, Rockmart, Polk Co., GA). Issue: **Marilyn** [(b. 03/20/1928, Rockmart, Polk, GA, m. 1948, Rockmart, Ralph Olin Jackson, Jr. (b. 12/08/1923, Rockmart, d. 12/11/2011, Rome, Floyd Co., GA); Issue: Patricia Carroll (b. 2/21/1950, Cedartown, Polk, GA); Ralph Olin III (b. 09/08/1951, Cedartown, Polk, GA); David Anderson (b. 11/06/1952, Cedartown, Polk, GA); Mary Lynne (b. 09/15/1954, Rockmart, Polk, GA, d. 05/12/2014. Ashes buried Rose Hill Cemetery, Rockmart); and Guy (b. 08/31/1957, d. 05/20/1980, Rockmart, b. Rose Hill Cemetery, Rockmart)]; and **Patricia Carroll** (b. 06/25/1934, Rockmart, Polk Co., GA, d. 12/29/2014, Doraville, DeKalb Co., GA. Issue: Hal, Eve, Melinda and David.)

d.   02/11/1999, Rockmart, Polk Co., GA. Buried Rose Hill Cemetery, Rockmart, Polk Co., GA.

Marilyn Jordan Jackson

b.   March 20, 1928, Rockmart, Georgia

m.   1948, Ralph Olin Jackson, Jr., Rockmart, Georgia. Issue: Patricia Carroll; Ralph Olin, III; David Anderson; Mary Lynne; and Guy Jordan.

d.   2007

Notes:

_____
_____
_____
_____
_____
_____
_____
_____
_____

30											

SCHEDULE I.—Free Inhabitants in _Subdivision No 45_ in the County of _Jackson_ State _Georgia_ enumerated by me, on the _2nd_ day of _Oct._ 1850. _A.S. McCulloch_ Ass't Marshal 39

Families numbered in the order of visitation.	The Name of every Person whose usual place of abode on the first day of June, 1850, was in this family.	Age	Sex	Color	Profession, Occupation, or Trade of each Male Person over 15 years of age.	Value of Real Estate owned.	Place of Birth. Naming the State, Territory, or Country.	Married within the year	Attended School within the year	Persons over 20 y'rs of age who cannot read & write	Whether deaf and dumb, blind, insane, idiotic, pauper, or convict.	
1 571	George T. Pittman	35	m		Farmer ✓		Georgia					1
	Anna Pittman	30	f				"					2
	Sarah A. Read	19	f				"		1			3
	John B. H.	18	m				"		1			4
	William	7	m				"					5
	Elizabeth C.	5	f				"					6
	George L. H.	5/12	m				"					7
	Sarah Broxton	75	f				Virginia					8
2 572	John Roberts	38	m		Farmer ✓		S.C.					9
	Mary Roberts	33	f				"					10
	Martha A.	13	f				Georgia					11
	Leah C.	11	f				"					12
	John T.	9	m				"					13
	Mary C.	3	f				"					14
	David	1	m				"					15
3	Colmore Harrison	71	m		Farmer ✓	600	Maryland					16
	Frances Harrison	53	f				Georgia					17
	Levi J. Harrison	24	m		Farmer ✓		"					18
4	Allen White	63	m		Farmer ✓	1000	S.Carolina					19
	Sarah White	50	f				Georgia					20
	Cynthia	26	f				"					21
	Caroline	24	f				"					22
	Allen	23	m		Laborer ✓		"					23
	Andrew	18	m		" ✓		"					24
	Mary	16	f				"					25
	Sarah A.	14	f				"		1			26
	George W.	12	m				"		1			27
	Robert	10	m				"		1			28
	Anne E.	8	f				"		1			29
	Christopher C.	6	m				"					30
	John White	24	m		Carpenter		"					31
	James Pettyjohn	60	m		Farmer ✓	1000	Virginia					32
	Temperance "	50	f				Georgia					33
	Addison B.	18	m		Laborer ✓		"					34
	Arabella	16	f				"		1			35
	William F.	14	m				"					36
	Thomas H.	11	m				"					37
	Marion G.	7	m				"					38
	Paul R. Kimmingham	50	m		Farmer ✓	5000	Virginia					39
	Mary Kimmingham	57	f				S.C.					40
	Henry Burk	50	m		Farmer ✓	500	"					41
	Elizabeth Burk	48	f				S.C.					42

1850 FEDERAL CENSUS, JACKSON COUNTY, GEORGIA

Pettyjohn, James – In this census, James, age 60, and wife Temperance, age 50, are listed with their children Addison B., age 18; Arabella, age 16; William, age 14; Thomas, age 11; and Marion, age 7. In almost exactly three years, Arabella will marry Richard Bennett Hudgins. Eight years from the date of that marriage, he will enlist in the Georgia Volunteers to the Army of Northern Virginia and never return. Arabella, at the somewhat youthful age of 27, was left alone in a virtual wilderness to raise her children – Mary, age 7; Margaret Emmaline, age 5; and James Zacheus (not quite 2 years old). The 1860s and '70s in north Georgia were unbelievably harsh years, filled with outlawry, starvation, homelessness, and abject desperation. Arabella, to her credit, found a way to survive with her children, allowing this latter-day writer an opportunity to tell her story.

SCHEDULE I.—Free Inhabitants in _Thirtyfirst District_ in the County of _Forsyth_ 30 State of _Georgia_ enumerated by me, on the _10th_ day of _Augt_ 1850. _Saml Paxton_ Asst Marshal

154

	Dwelling-houses numbered in the order of visitation	Families numbered in the order of visitation	The Name of every Person whose usual place of abode on the first day of June, 1850, was in this family.	Age	Sex	Color	Profession, Occupation, or Trade of each Male Person over 15 years of age.	Value of Real Estate owned.	PLACE OF BIRTH. Naming the State, Territory, or Country.	Married within the year	Attended School within the year	Persons over 20 y'rs of age who cannot read & write	Whether deaf and dumb, blind, insane, idiotic, pauper, or convict.	
	1	2	3	4	5	6	7	8	9	10	11	12	13	
1	1		William Bagley	28	M		Farmer		Geo			1		1
2	2		John "	21	M		Farmer		"					2
3	3		Caroline "	19	F				"					3
4	4		G. A. "	17	F				"					4
5	5		Mary "	15	F				"					5
6	6		Aghas "	13	F				"					6
7	7	127	127	Joel Bradley	30	M		Chairs		S C				7
8	8		A. D. "	25	F				"			1		8
9	9		Almanza "	8	F				Georgia					9
10	10		Lucinda "	2	F				"					10
11	11	128	128	William H. Simmons	26	M		Farmer	900	Geo				11
12	12		A. E. "	20	F				"					12
13	13		Thomas G. "	1	M				"					13
14	14	129	129	Jacob Pettyjohn	32	M		Farmer	800	Geo				14
15	15		M. M. "	30	F				"					15
16	16		S. A. "	11	F				"		1			16
17	17		I. K. "	9	M				"		1			17
18	18		M. A. "	7	F				"		1			18
19	19		John J. "	5	M				"					19
20	20		S. J. "	3	F				"					20
21	21		Pettyjohn	1	M				"					21
22	22		Norish Green	27	M		Farmer		"			1		22
23	23	130	130	Alfred Owen	33	M		Farmer		Geo				23
24	24		Elizabeth "	19	F				S C					24
25	25		M. E. "	1	F				Geo					25
26	26	131	131	John Strickland	40	M		Farmer	500	N C			1	26
27	27		M. A. "	17	F				Geo					27
28	28		Levina "	1	F				"					28
29	29		M. A. Fernandes	19	F				"					29
30	30		E. E. "	13	M				"					30
31	31	132	132	R. W. Blackstock	29	M		Farmer	600	Georgia				31
32	32		C. A. "	20	F				N C					32
33	33		M. A. "	4	F				Geo					33
34	34		N. J. "	2	F				"					34
35	35	133	133	J. L. Blackstock	21	M		Farmer	175	Georgia				35
36	36		Ann "	18	F				"					36
37	37	134	134	Isaac Weeland	43	M		Farmer	2,500	Georgia				37
38	38		Hannah "	37	F				N C					38
39	39		John "	18	M		Farmer		Geo		1			39
40	40		Mary "	16	F				"		1			40
41	41		William "	14	M				"		1			41
42	42		Jeremiah "	12	M				"		1			42

An 19

18

1850 FEDERAL CENSUS, FORSYTH COUNTY, GEORGIA

Pettyjohn, Jacob – This census was the last in which Jacob Pettyjohn – brother to Arabel Ellen ("Arabella") Pettyjohn – appeared prior to his flight to Texas following his conviction for murder in Forsyth County in the summer of 1858. He is listed as a *"farmer,"* age 32, with his wife, Mary Mariah Whitmire, age 30, with their six children, ages 11, 9, 7, 5, 3, and 1. How his family survived after his departure is unknown today.

		The name of every person whose usual place of abode on the first day of June, 1860, was in this family.	Age	Sex	Color	Profession, Occupation, or Trade of each person, male and female, over 15 years of age.	Value of Real Estate	Value of Personal Estate	Place of Birth, Naming the State, Territory, or Country.	Married within the year	Attended School within the year		Whether deaf and dumb, blind, insane, idiotic, pauper, or convict.	
1	2	3	4	5	6	7	8	9	10	11	12	13	14	
1		Martha "	15	F					Georgia		(1)			1
2		William "	18	M					Do		(1)			2
3	366	366	Ciero C Bevel	32	M		Farmer	800	2050	Georgia					3
4		Sarah "	32	F					Do					4
5		Eveline "	11	F					Do		(1)			5
6		Andrew "	8	M					Do		(1)			6
7	367	367	William M Smith	48	M		Farmer	1500	1625	S Carolina					7
8		Clarisa "	38	F					Do					8
9		Helen "	14	F					Do		(1)			9
10		Joseph "	13	M					Do					10
11		Jane "	11	F					Do		(1)			11
12		Jefferson "	8	M					Do		(1)			12
13		Burnett "	6	M					Georgia		(1)			13
14		John "	3	M					Do					14
15		William Perry	20	M		Farm woman			Do		(1)			15
16	368	368	James Pettyjohn	70	M		Farmer	2500	3444	Virginia					16
17		Temperance "	60	F					Georgia		(1)			17
18		Thomas "	19	M		Field labor			Do					18
19		Marion "	16	M		Do			Do					19
20	369	369	Adam Wheeler	31	M		Farmer		50	Georgia					20
21		Mary "	25	F					Do		(1)			21
22		Webster "	3	M					Do					22
23	370	370	John R Brisentien	37	M		Farmer	1000	1125	Georgia					23
24		Matilda "	26	F					S Carolina					24
25		James "	12	M					Georgia					25
26		John "	8	M					Do		(1)			26
27		Antonett "	7	F					Do		(1)			27
28		Benjamin "	6	M					Do					28
29		Alfred "	4	M					Do					29
30	371	371	Thomas Morgan	63	M		Farmer	1200	652	Georgia					30
31		Lucy "	62	F					Virginia		(1)			31
32	372	372	John Ivy	28	M		Farm labour		70	Georgia		(1)			32
33		Mahala "	28	F					Do					33
34		Adeline "	5	F					Do					34
35		Joshua "	3	M					Do					35
36		Wiles "	1	M					Do					36
37	373	373	Jesse Morgan	30	M		Farmer	450	218	Georgia					37
38		Lurena "	25	F					Do					38
39		James "	6	M					Do					39
40		Andrew "	3	M					Do					40

1860 FEDERAL CENSUS, JACKSON COUNTY, GEORGIA

Pettyjohn, James D. – James is listed here at age 70 with wife Temperance, age 60. They both are getting up in years now but still have their two youngest children – Thomas, age 19 and Marion, age 16 – at home with them. James lists real estate valued at $2,500.00 and personal property valued at $3,444.00. In 1860, $3,444.00 was the 2023 equivalent of $123,157.00, and the cost of living in 1860 was exceedingly less than today. James therefore would have been considered at least modestly wealthy for his day and time, but it was wealth which would soon be *Gone With The Wind.* The U.S. Civil War with all its devastation would shortly make his "Confederate" dollars worthless, and the U.S. taxes newly-placed upon his property by Union tax assessors would be insurmountable.

1870 FEDERAL CENSUS, JEFFERSON, JACKSON COUNTY, GEORGIA

Pettyjohn, Temperance – James having passed away four years earlier, Temperance, age 70, is now the nominal head of the household. Living with her are a child named *"Mary,"* last name indecipherable, age 15; and an *"H"* Pettyjohn, a female of age 13 listed as *"house keeper."*

Pettyjohn, Arabel Ellen – Temperance's widowed daughter – Arabel Ellen or "Arabella" Pettyjohn Hudgins – receives a separate listing directly below Temperance's household. Whether Arabella was actually living in Temperance's home in those hard times is unknown today, but it was very likely. Listed with Arabella are her daughter Margaret Emmaline, age 13; and her son, James Zacheus, age 10. Arabella's husband – Richard Bennett Hudgins – contracted pneumonia while serving in Company D, 27th Infantry Regiment, Georgia Volunteers, Army of Northern Virginia, and died in Raleigh, North Carolina in 1864. During those extremely-lawless post-war days, the danger for females living alone in the wilds of north Georgia are indescribable today.

(3—H—11) 8—3271 **NAME OF SOLDIER:**	*Pettyjohn Jacob*	**INDIAN WARS.**		
NAME AND CLASS OF DEPENDENT:	*Pettyjohn Mary A. M.*		*widow*	
SERVICE:	*Rank* *Hollands + Buffington's Co Ga Vols* *Enlisted* (Florida War) *Discharged*			
ADDITIONAL SERVICE:				

DATE OF FILING.	CLASS.	APPLICATION No.	CERTIFICATE No.	FILE NO.	ACT.	STATE.
1892 Nov 19	*Ind. Wid.*	*2809*				*Ga.*

BOUNTY LAND:	
REMARKS:	

UATC

1892 INDIAN WARS PENSION APPLICATION, GEORGIA (?)

Pettyjohn, Mary Mariah – Filed on November 19, 1892, this application lists Mary as a *"widow,"* indicating her husband – Jacob Pettyjohn (1817-1892) – is deceased. In order for her to have that knowledge, it would seem that Jacob apparently had returned from Texas back to Georgia (from which he had fled in 1858 after his conviction for Second-Degree Murder). This would also indicate that he not only had died in Georgia, but that he was also buried in the state as well, although that site is unknown. Mary's application states that Jacob served in *"Holland's & Buffington's Company, Georgia Volunteers, Florida War"* (apparently during the Seminole Indian Wars).

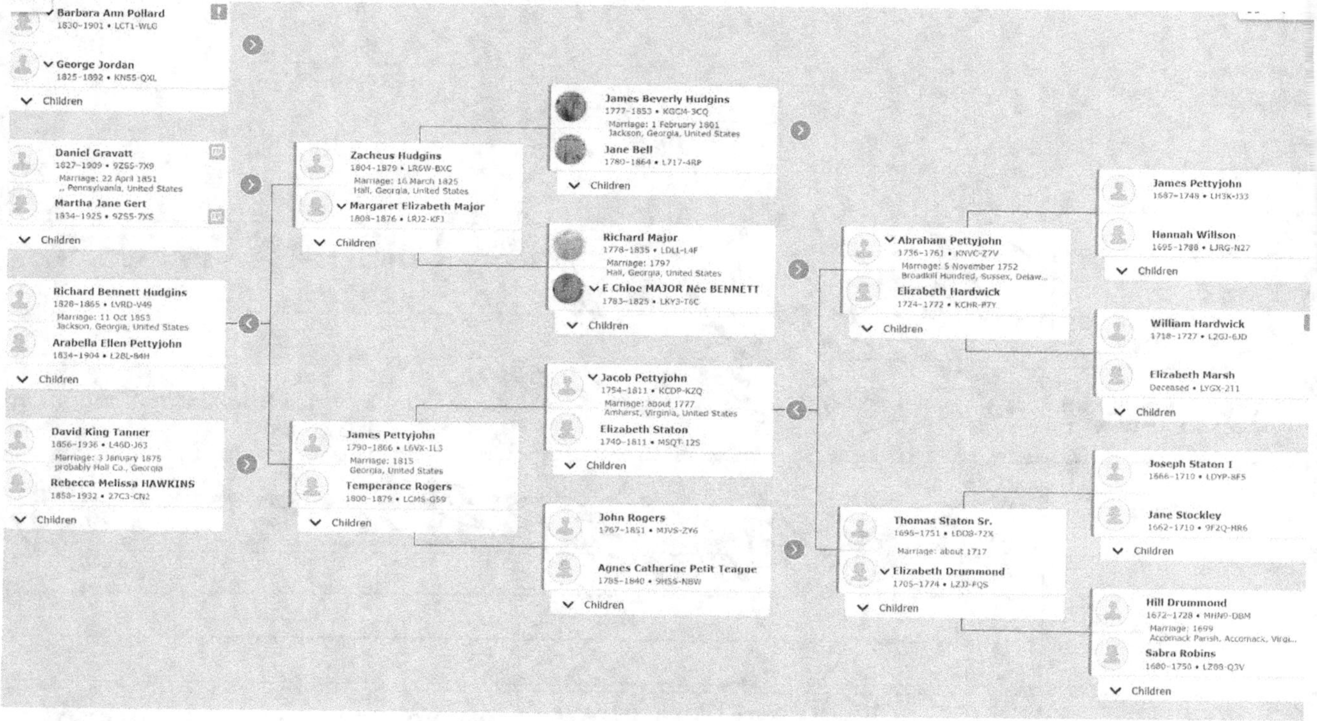

Family Tree (top chart)

- **Barbara Ann Pollard** 1830–1901 • LCT1-WLG
- **George Jordan** 1825–1892 • KN55-QXL
  - Children

- **Daniel Gravatt** 1827–1909 • 9Z55-7X9
  Marriage: 22 April 1851, Pennsylvania, United States
- **Martha Jane Gert** 1834–1925 • 9Z55-7X5
  - Children

- **Richard Bennett Hudgins** 1828–1865 • LVRD-V46
  Marriage: 11 Oct 1853, Jackson, Georgia, United States
- **Arabella Ellen Pettyjohn** 1834–1904 • L2BL-84H
  - Children

- **David King Tanner** 1856–1936 • L46D-J63
  Marriage: 3 January 1875, probably Hall Co., Georgia
- **Rebecca Melissa HAWKINS** 1858–1932 • 27C3-CN2
  - Children

- **Zacheus Hudgins** 1804–1879 • LR6W-BXC
  Marriage: 16 March 1825, Hall, Georgia, United States
- **Margaret Elizabeth Major** 1808–1876 • LRJ2-KFJ
  - Children

- **James Pettyjohn** 1790–1866 • L6VX-1L3
  Marriage: 1815, Georgia, United States
- **Temperance Rogers** 1800–1879 • LCMS-GS9
  - Children

- **James Beverly Hudgins** 1777–1853 • KGCM-3CQ
  Marriage: 1 February 1801, Jackson, Georgia, United States
- **Jane Bell** 1780–1864 • L717-4RP
  - Children

- **Richard Major** 1778–1835 • LDLL-L4F
  Marriage: 1797, Hall, Georgia, United States
- **E Chloe MAJOR Née BENNETT** 1783–1825 • LKY3-T6C
  - Children

- **Jacob Pettyjohn** 1754–1811 • KCDP-KZQ
  Marriage: about 1777, Amherst, Virginia, United States
- **Elizabeth Staton** 1740–1811 • MSQT-12S
  - Children

- **John Rogers** 1767–1851 • MJVS-ZY6
- **Agnes Catherine Petit Teague** 1795–1840 • 9HSS-NBW
  - Children

- **Abraham Pettyjohn** 1736–1761 • KNVC-Z7V
  Marriage: 5 November 1752, Broadkill Hundred, Sussex, Delaw...
- **Elizabeth Hardwick** 1724–1772 • KCHR-P7Y
  - Children

- **Thomas Staton Sr.** 1695–1751 • LDOB-72X
  Marriage: about 1717
- **Elizabeth Drummond** 1705–1774 • LZ3I-FQS
  - Children

- **James Pettyjohn** 1687–1748 • LH3K-J33
- **Hannah Willson** 1695–1788 • LJRG-N27
  - Children

- **William Hardwick** 1718–1727 • L2G3-6JD
- **Elizabeth Marsh** Deceased • LYGX-211
  - Children

- **Joseph Staton I** 1666–1710 • LDYP-8FS
- **Jane Stockley** 1662–1710 • 9F2Q-HR6
  - Children

- **Hill Drummond** 1672–1728 • MHN9-DBM
  Marriage: 1699, Accomack Parish, Accomack, Virgi...
- **Sabra Robins** 1680–1750 • LZ88-Q3V
  - Children

Family Tree (bottom chart — detail with children expanded)

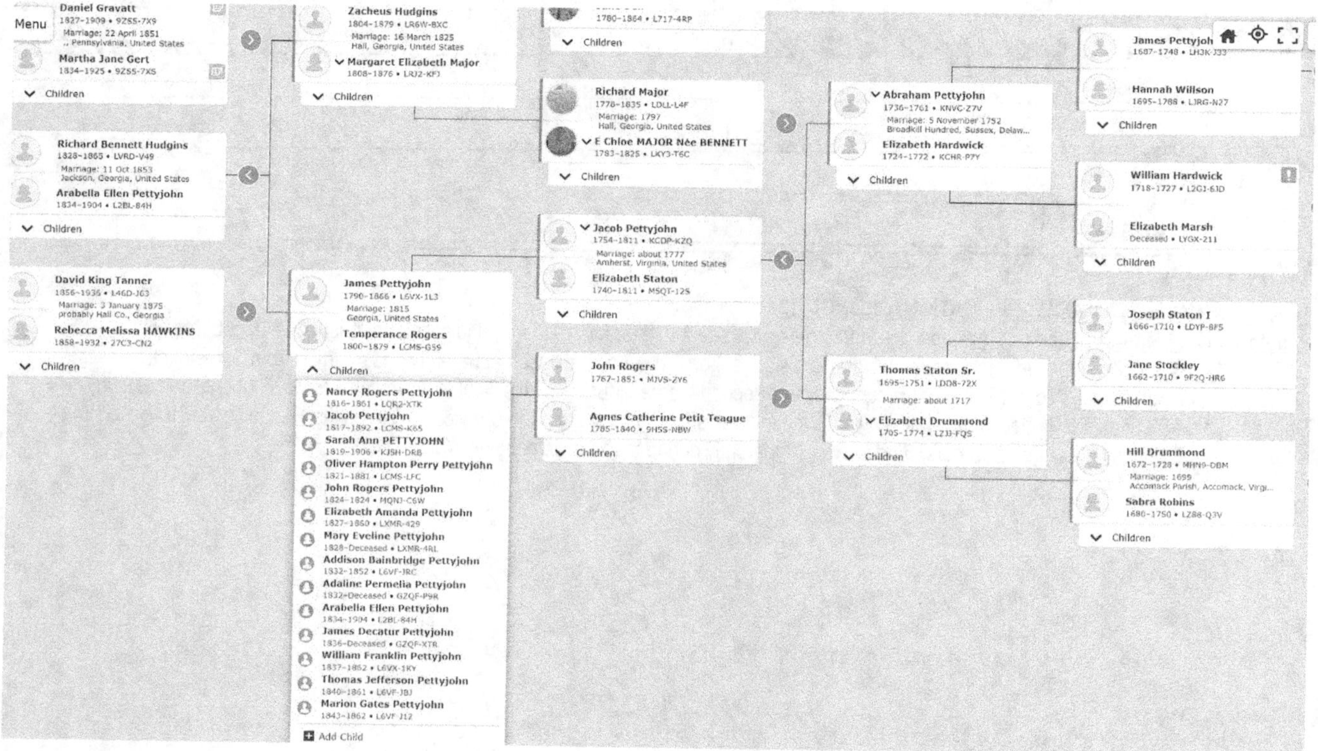

Menu

- **Daniel Gravatt** 1827–1909 • 9Z55-7X9
  Marriage: 22 April 1851, Pennsylvania, United States
- **Martha Jane Gert** 1834–1925 • 9Z55-7X5
  - Children

- **Richard Bennett Hudgins** 1828–1865 • LVRD-V49
  Marriage: 11 Oct 1853, Jackson, Georgia, United States
- **Arabella Ellen Pettyjohn** 1834–1904 • L2BL-84H
  - Children

- **David King Tanner** 1856–1936 • L46D-J63
  Marriage: 3 January 1875, probably Hall Co., Georgia
- **Rebecca Melissa HAWKINS** 1858–1932 • 27C3-CN2
  - Children

- **Zacheus Hudgins** 1804–1879 • LR6W-BXC
- **Margaret Elizabeth Major** 1808–1876 • LRJ2-KFJ
  - Children

- Jane Bell 1780–1864 • L717-4RP
  - Children

- **Richard Major** 1778–1835 • LDLL-L4F
  Marriage: 1797, Hall, Georgia, United States
- **E Chloe MAJOR Née BENNETT** 1783–1825 • LKY3-T6C
  - Children

- **Jacob Pettyjohn** 1754–1811 • KCDP-KZQ
  Marriage: about 1777, Amherst, Virginia, United States
- **Elizabeth Staton** 1740–1811 • MSQT-12S
  - Children

- **James Pettyjohn** 1790–1866 • L6VX-1L3
  Marriage: 1815, Georgia, United States
- **Temperance Rogers** 1800–1879 • LCMS-GS9
  - Children
    - **Nancy Rogers Pettyjohn** 1816–1851 • LQR2-X7K
    - **Jacob Pettyjohn** 1817–1892 • LCMS-KXS
    - **Sarah Ann PETTYJOHN** 1819–1906 • KJSH-D6B
    - **Oliver Hampton Perry Pettyjohn** 1821–1881 • LCMS-LFC
    - **John Rogers Pettyjohn** 1824–1824 • MQN0-C6W
    - **Elizabeth Amanda Pettyjohn** 1827–1863 • LXMR-929
    - **Mary Eveline Pettyjohn** 1828–Deceased • LXMR-4RL
    - **Addison Bainbridge Pettyjohn** 1932–1852 • L6VF-JRC
    - **Adaline Permelia Pettyjohn** 1932–Deceased • GZQF-P9R
    - **Arabella Ellen Pettyjohn** 1834–1904 • L2BL-84H
    - **James Decatur Pettyjohn** 1936–Deceased • GZQF-XTR
    - **William Franklin Pettyjohn** 1837–1852 • L6VX-1KY
    - **Thomas Jefferson Pettyjohn** 1840–1861 • L6VF-JBJ
    - **Marion Gates Pettyjohn** 1843–1862 • L6VF-J12
  - Add Child

- **John Rogers** 1767–1851 • MJVS-ZY6
- **Agnes Catherine Petit Teague** 1795–1840 • 9HSS-NBW
  - Children

- **Abraham Pettyjohn** 1736–1761 • KNVC-Z7V
  Marriage: 5 November 1752, Broadkill Hundred, Sussex, Delaw...
- **Elizabeth Hardwick** 1724–1772 • KCHR-P7Y
  - Children

- **Thomas Staton Sr.** 1695–1751 • LDOB-72X
  Marriage: about 1717
- **Elizabeth Drummond** 1705–1774 • LZ3I-FQS
  - Children

- **James Pettyjohn** 1687–1748 • LH3K-J33
- **Hannah Willson** 1695–1788 • LJRG-N27
  - Children

- **William Hardwick** 1718–1727 • L2G3-6JD
- **Elizabeth Marsh** Deceased • LYGX-211
  - Children

- **Joseph Staton I** 1666–1710 • LDYP-8FS
- **Jane Stockley** 1662–1710 • 9F2Q-HR6
  - Children

- **Hill Drummond** 1672–1728 • MHN9-DBM
  Marriage: 1699, Accomack Parish, Accomack, Virgi...
- **Sabra Robins** 1680–1750 • LZ88-Q3V
  - Children

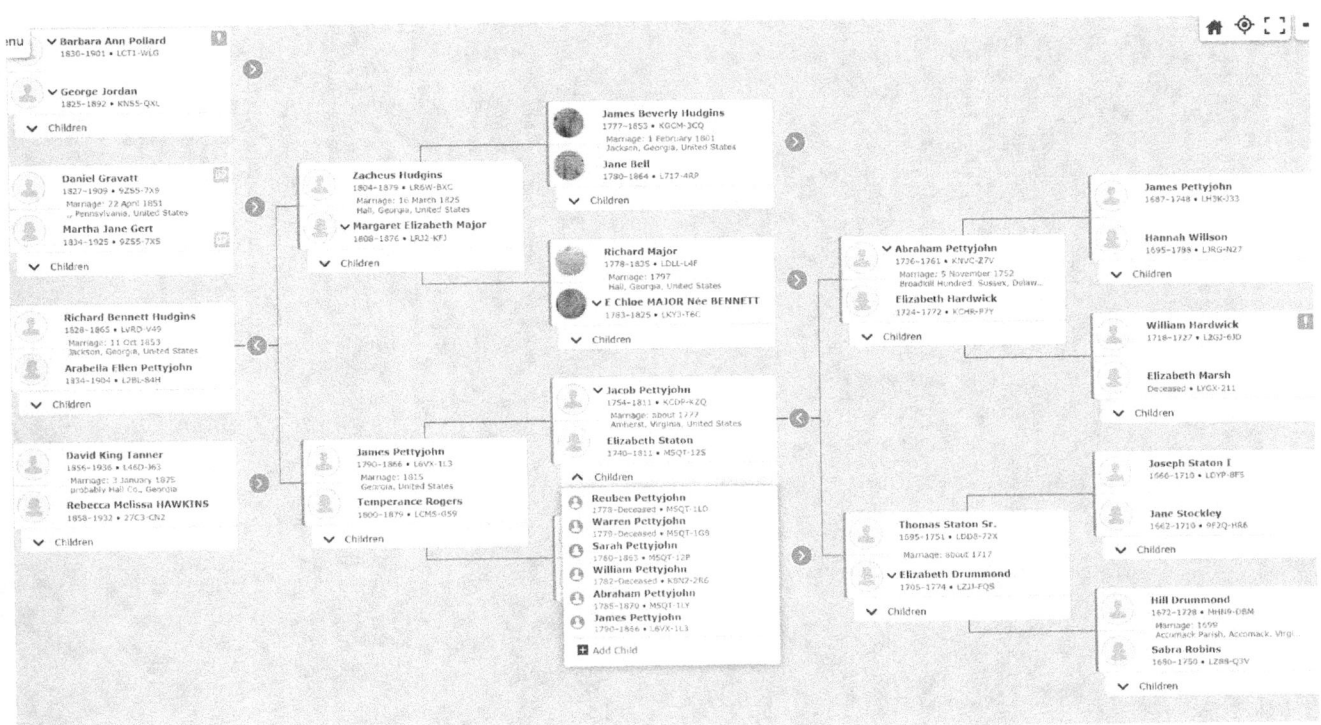

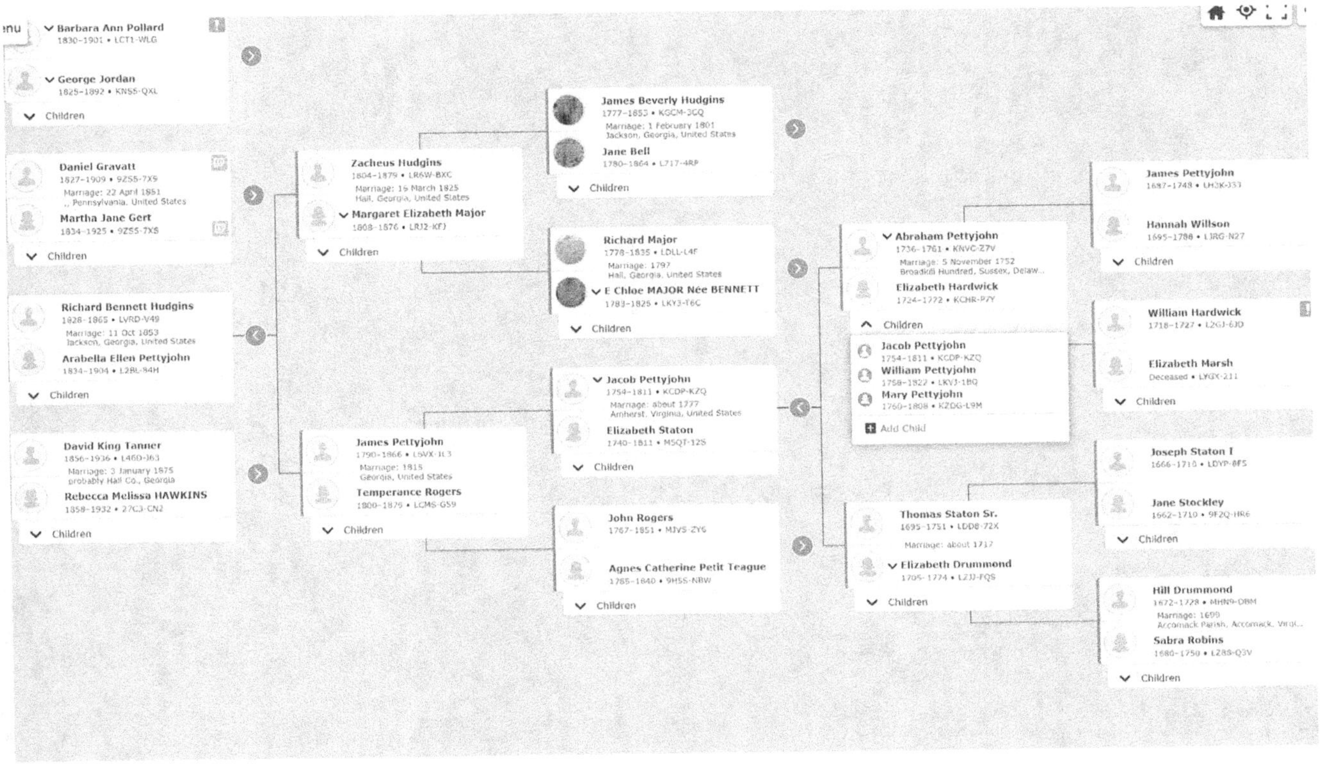

Some Genealogy Keys To Some Georgia Family Trees

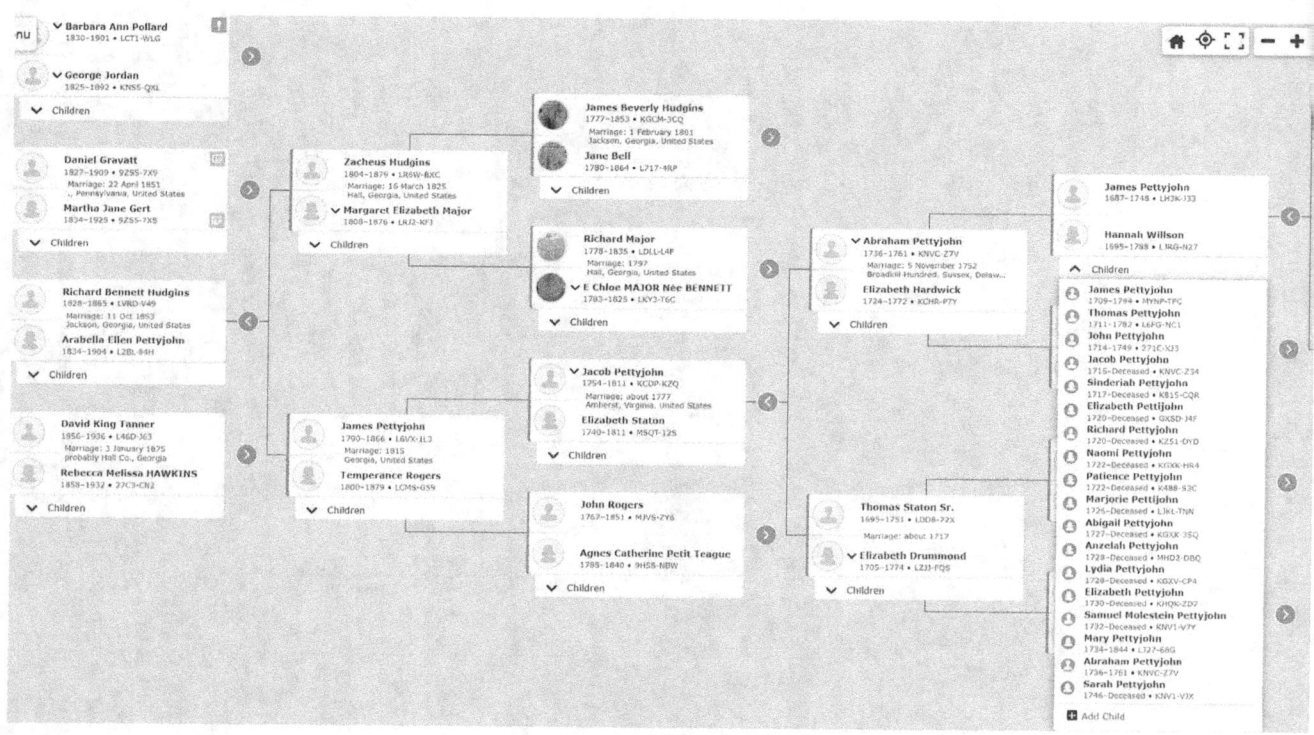

Top chart:

- Barbara Ann Pollard 1830-1901 • LCT1-WLG
- George Jordan 1825-1892 • KNSS-QXL
  - Children
- Daniel Gravatt 1827-1909 • 9ZS5-7X9
  - Marriage: 22 April 1851, Pennsylvania, United States
- Martha Jane Gert 1834-1929 • 9ZS5-7XS
  - Children
- Richard Bennett Hudgins 1828-1865 • LVRD-V49
  - Marriage: 11 Oct 1853, Jackson, Georgia, United States
- Arabella Ellen Pettyjohn 1834-1904 • L2BL-94H
  - Children
- David King Tanner 1856-1936 • L4GD-3G3
  - Marriage: 3 January 1875, probably Hall Co., Georgia
- Rebecca Melissa HAWKINS 1858-1932 • 27C3-CN2
  - Children

- Zacheus Hudgins 1804-1879 • LR6W-BXC
  - Marriage: 16 March 1825, Hall, Georgia, United States
- Margaret Elizabeth Major 1808-1876 • LRJ2-KF3
  - Children

- James Pettyjohn 1790-1866 • L6VX-JL3
  - Marriage: 1815, Georgia, United States
- Temperance Rogers 1800-1879 • LCM5-G5N
  - Children

- James Beverly Hudgins 1777-1853 • KGGM-3CQ
  - Marriage: 1 February 1801, Jackson, Georgia, United States
- Jane Bell 1780-1864 • L717-4RP
  - Children

- Richard Major 1778-1835 • LDLL-L4F
  - Marriage: 1797, Hall, Georgia, United States
- E Chloe MAJOR Née BENNETT 1783-1825 • LXYJ-T6C
  - Children

- Jacob Pettyjohn 1754-1811 • KCDP-KZQ
  - Marriage: about 1777, Amherst, Virginia, United States
- Elizabeth Staton 1749-1811 • MSQT-12S
  - Children

- John Rogers 1767-1851 • MJV6-ZY6
- Agnes Catherine Petit Teague 1785-1840 • 9HS8-NBW
  - Children

- Abraham Pettyjohn 1736-1761 • KNVC-Z7V
  - Marriage: 5 November 1752, Broadkill Hundred, Sussex, Delawa...
- Elizabeth Hardwick 1724-1772 • KCHR-P7Y
  - Children

- Thomas Staton Sr. 1695-1751 • LDD8-72X
  - Marriage: about 1717
- Elizabeth Drummond 1705-1774 • LZJJ-FQS
  - Children

- James Pettyjohn 1687-1748 • LH3K-J33
- Hannah Willson 1695-1788 • LR4G-N27
  - Children

  - James Pettyjohn 1709-1744 • MYNP-TPC
  - Thomas Pettyjohn 1711-1782 • L6FG-NC1
  - John Pettyjohn 1714-1749 • 271CJ-XJ3
  - Jacob Pettyjohn 1715-Deceased • KNVC-Z54
  - Sinderiah Pettyjohn 1717-Deceased • KB15-CQR
  - Elizabeth Pettijohn 1720-Deceased • GXSD-J4F
  - Richard Pettyjohn 1720-Deceased • KZ51-0YD
  - Naomi Pettyjohn 1722-Deceased • KGXK-HR4
  - Patience Pettyjohn 1722-Deceased • X4B8-63C
  - Marjorie Pettyjohn 1726-Deceased • L3KL-THN
  - Abigail Pettyjohn 1727-Deceased • KG3JK-3SQ
  - Anzelah Pettyjohn 1729-Deceased • MHD2-DBQ
  - Lydia Pettyjohn 1728-Deceased • KGXV-CP4
  - Elizabeth Pettyjohn 1730-Deceased • KHQK-ZD2
  - Samuel Molestein Pettyjohn 1732-Deceased • KNV1-V7Y
  - Mary Pettyjohn 1734-1844 • L327-6RG
  - Abraham Pettyjohn 1736-1761 • KNVC-Z7V
  - Sarah Pettyjohn 1746-Deceased • KNV1-VJX
  - Add Child

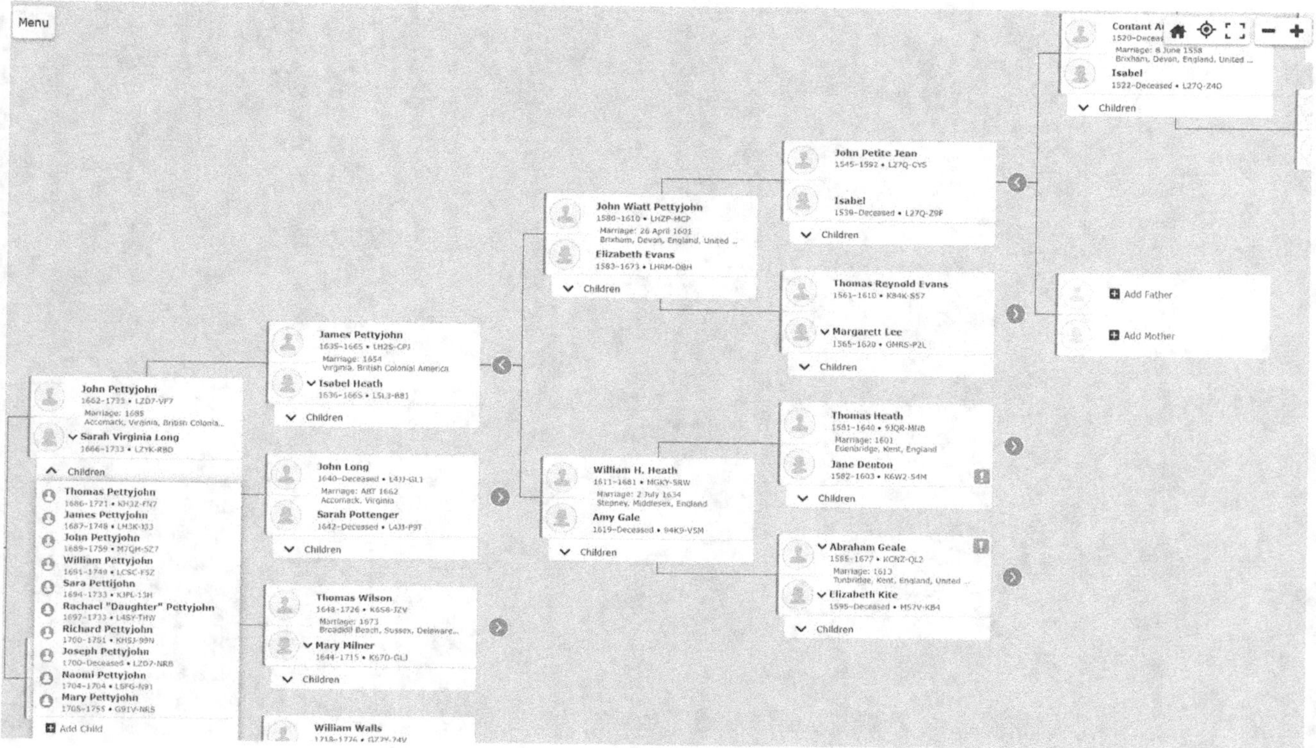

Bottom chart:

Menu

- John Pettyjohn 1662-1733 • LZD7-VF7
  - Marriage: 1685, Accomack, Virginia, British Colonia...
- Sarah Virginia Long 1666-1733 • L2YK-RBD
  - Children
    - Thomas Pettyjohn 1686-1721 • KFJ2-FN7
    - James Pettyjohn 1687-1748 • LH3K-J53
    - John Pettyjohn 1689-1759 • 397GH-SZ7
    - William Pettyjohn 1691-1749 • LCSC-FSZ
    - Sara Pettijohn 1694-1733 • KJPL-13H
    - Rachael "Daughter" Pettyjohn 1697-1733 • L4SY-THW
    - Richard Pettyjohn 1700-1751 • KHSJ-99N
    - Joseph Pettyjohn 1700-Deceased • LZD7-NRB
    - Naomi Pettyjohn 1704-1704 • LSPG-N91
    - Mary Pettyjohn 1705-1755 • G91V-NRS
    - Add Child

- James Pettyjohn 1635-1665 • LH2S-CPJ
  - Marriage: 1654, Virginia, British Colonial America
- Isabel Heath 1636-1665 • L5L3-RB1
  - Children

- John Long 1640-Deceased • L4JJ-GL1
  - Marriage: ABT 1662, Accomack, Virginia
- Sarah Pottenger 1642-Deceased • L4JJ-P9T
  - Children

- Thomas Wilson 1648-1726 • K6S8-JZV
  - Marriage: 1673, Broadkill Beach, Sussex, Delaware...
- Mary Milner 1644-1715 • K570-GLJ
  - Children

- William Walls 1718-1776 • GLZ7K-74V

- John Wiatt Pettyjohn 1580-1610 • LHZP-MCP
  - Marriage: 26 April 1601, Brixham, Devon, England, United ...
- Elizabeth Evans 1583-1673 • LHRM-DBH
  - Children

- William H. Heath 1611-1681 • MGKY-SRW
  - Marriage: 2 July 1634, Stepney, Middlesex, England
- Amy Gale 1619-Deceased • 94K9-VSM
  - Children

- John Petite Jean 1545-1592 • L27Q-CYS
- Isabel 1539-Deceased • L27Q-Z9F
  - Children

- Thomas Reynold Evans 1561-1610 • KB4K-SS7
- Margarett Lee 1565-1620 • GMRS-P2L
  - Children

- Thomas Heath 1581-1640 • 93QR-MNB
  - Marriage: 1601, Edenbridge, Kent, England
- Jane Denton 1582-1603 • K6W2-S4M
  - Children

- Abraham Geale 1588-1677 • KCN2-QL2
  - Marriage: 1613, Tunbridge, Kent, England, United ...
- Elizabeth Kite 1595-Deceased • M57V-KB4
  - Children

- Contant A... 1520-Deceased
  - Marriage: 8 June 1558, Brixham, Devon, England, United ...
- Isabel 1522-Deceased • L27Q-24D
  - Children

- Add Father
- Add Mother

274

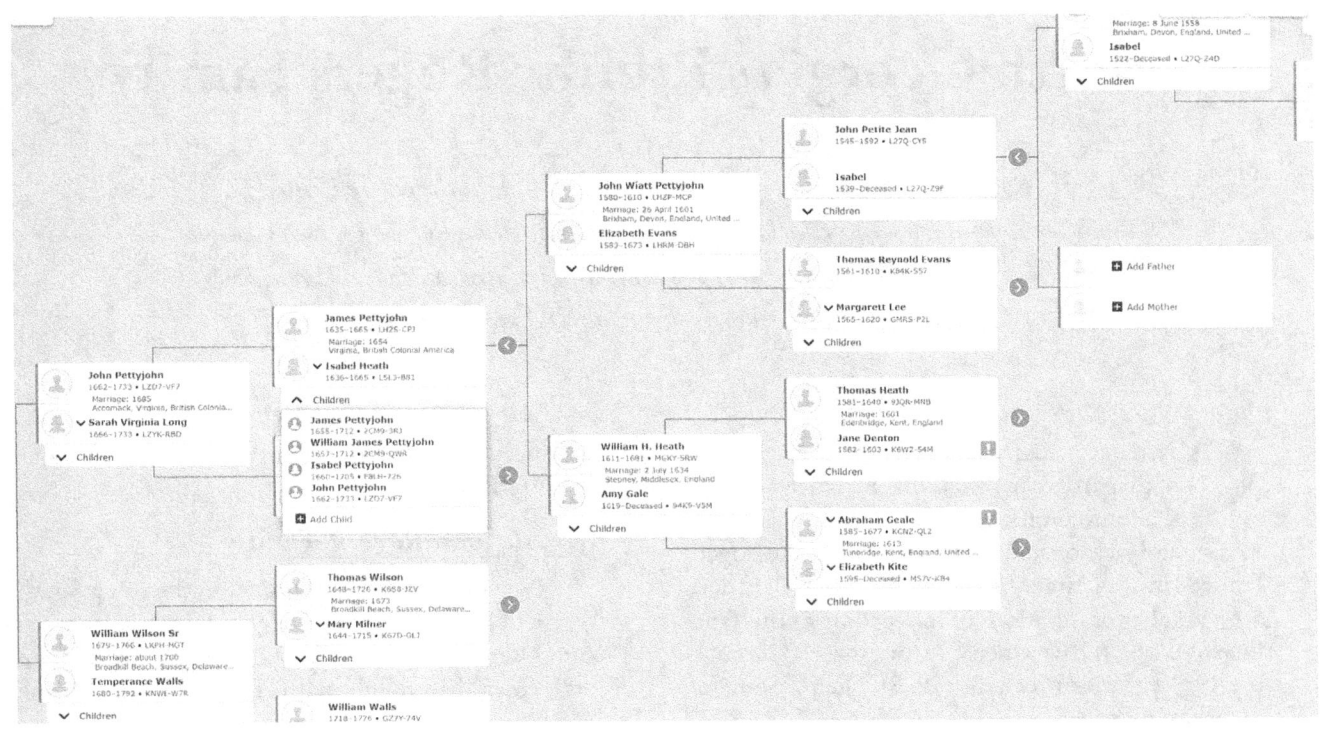

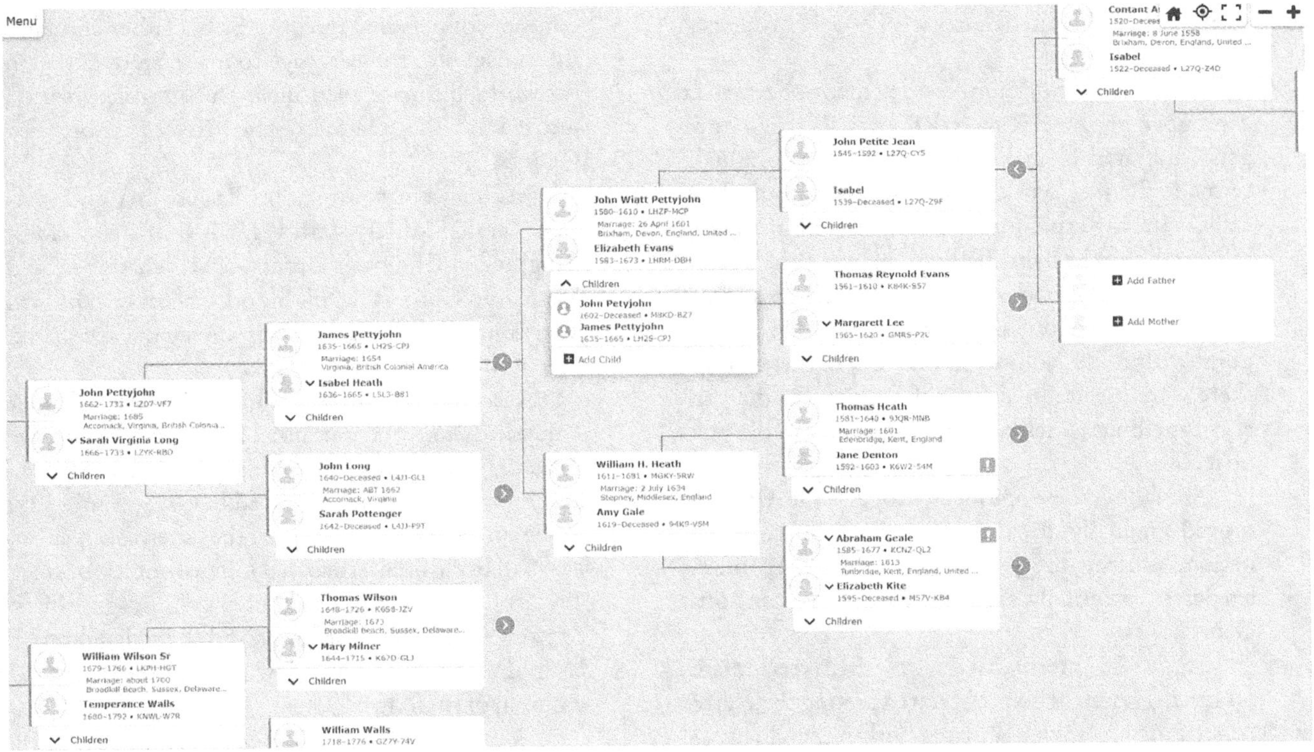

North Georgia's Prolific Rogers Family

The name "Rogers" is quite common in Georgia – and indeed the entire United States today.
The progenitor(s) and relations of this family line extending down into Georgia
have been much confused over the years and require considerable research
to arrive at or discern one's particularly correct Rogers ancestry.

Scattered across many areas in Georgia, and with particular attention on what today is the four-county area of Fulton, Forsyth, Hall and Jackson, one's relations within the Rogers family can sometimes be difficult to unravel. There are a number of variations of the spelling of this family name which have emerged from the 17th through the 19th centuries which also doesn't help. Some of the more common spellings are "Rodgers," "Rogers," "Rutgers," and "Rudigers" to name a few. "Rogers" – which is the most popular – is the 54th most popular surname in the United States with 305,901 bearers at last count.

In the course of pioneer settlement of America, a number of these Rogers/Rodgers/Rutgers/Rudigers emigrated from Europe to what was originally termed "the new world," an area known today basically as the eastern United States. As with many surnames, despite variant spellings, many of the bearers of these variant names are nevertheless genealogically interrelated, due simply to the fact that at some point within the evolutionary history of these names, there were inevitably mispronunciations and a variety of spellings which persisted thereafter in the public record.

Many of these pioneer Rogers subsequently moved gradually down the eastern seaboard of our nation, skirting the great Appalachian Mountains barrier to eventually arrive in what today in north Georgia.

Some also intermarried with Cherokee Indians, producing young who proliferated among the Native Americans. As they populated within the Cherokee culture, yet another aspect of this intertwined family was produced.

"Little John Rogers" Family

One of these Rogers families in the Deep South – that of John and Nancy Rogers – migrated from the Surry County section of Virginia into Georgia. John "the elder" had fought with the patriots during the U.S. Revolutionary War.

John the elder's son – *Little John Rogers* (1774-1851) – had been thoroughly indoctrinated with the concepts of personal freedom by his father and family. He set off at an early age to make his own way in the world, ultimately settling in the Cherokee Nation just east of the Chattahoochee River in northeast Georgia.

In this vicinity, this John Rogers met and married Sarah Cordery (circa 1785-1842), the eldest daughter of Thomas Cordery, a Scotch trader, and Sonicooie Cordery, a full-blood Cherokee who was later re-named "Susannah." By direct lineage, Sarah was of course a half-blood Cherokee.

According to the late Don L. Shadburn, former Forsyth County Historian and author of **Cherokee Planters in Georgia, 1832-1838**, *"Little John Rogers,"* also known as *"Tsan-Usdi,"* lived below Suwanee Old Town on the southern fringe of the Cherokee Nation, and had been an intermarried Cherokee citizen since 1802. His wife, Sarah, also known as "Susi," gave birth to twelve children – nine sons and three daughters – each of whom married and, with one exception, had children of their own.

"Rogers, and his mixed-blood sons, beginning

about 1819 when they moved from Gwinnett County, fenced and cultivated almost 200 acres of lowland and 125 acres of woodland on the west side of the (Chattahoochee) *river,"* Shadburn wrote. *"They also operated a public ferry for many years."*

Soon after John and Sarah's marriage, John reportedly built a fine home for them at the mouth of Suwanee Creek near what soon became the community of Sheltonville – once also known as "Shakerag," Georgia, founded circa 1820 (not far from present-day Suwanee, Georgia). At this site, John began what eventually became a remarkably profitable farming operation.

During a 50-year span of time, John reportedly amassed a small fortune, and was ultimately able to provide all his children – including his quarter-blood Cherokee sons William (1805-1870) and Johnson – good educations which they ultimately parlayed into advanced positions of leadership and prominence among both the Cherokees and Whites in north Georgia. Both William and Johnson were educated at the Lawrenceville Academy in what today is Gwinnett County, Georgia.

John Rogers was well-acquainted with several different governors of Georgia at varying times, as well as with the leadership of the Cherokee Nation. His two sons therefore also became very knowledgeable of governmental affairs at an early age.

During the *"Red Stick" Creek Indians Uprising* in what today is Alabama and south Georgia, John served on the staff of General Andrew Jackson. He rode a very dangerous mission from Fort Strother to Monticello, Georgia, and fought at the now-famous *"Battle of Horseshoe Bend."* One can only find this devoted association ironic in view of the fact that it was Jackson who eventually spearheaded the effort of disenfranchisement of all the Native Americans from their lands in what today is the eastern United States.

In 1832, in the wake of the Cherokee Land Lottery when official government appraisals of the Cherokee properties in Georgia were being conducted, it was determined that Little John Rogers (as the spouse of a half-blood Cherokee and therefore a "Cherokee countryman") owned *"200 acres, 23 houses, and 5,000 bushels of corn"* for which he was entitled to reimbursement by the federal government should he choose to voluntarily give up his property and move permanently to the West. His plantation and property were first assessed at a value of $2,000.00. This valuation was later increased to $3,800.00 by the federal commissioners assigned to this task.

John Rogers ultimately was paid this $3,800.00 for his property upon his voluntary move westward with wife Sarah. Despite the terrible and shameful circumstances of being dispossessed and faced with forced removal to a new home hundreds of miles away, one sometimes must keep these circumstances in perspective.

Those who might claim all Cherokees were "cheated" and their property "stolen" without just payment simply are not students of history. In point of fact, despite the injustice and associated miseries of such circumstances to the Native Americans, a payment of $3,800.00 (which John Rogers actually received for his property) in 1832 was the astounding equivalent of approximately $102,714.00 in 2022 dollars. In the 1830s, $3,800.00 was a breath-taking sum of money. Further, the cost of living in 1832 was infinitesimal compared to the cost in 2022, so the financial gain was far more than acceptable.

The possession problem lay in the fact that Native Americans believed they owned the land "naturally," and that it should not be taken from them at any price. There was no price which could be assigned to it as far as they were concerned.

Nevertheless, those Cherokees who had educated themselves and worked their way up the ladder of success were at least handsomely rewarded for the property taken from them, and even those Cherokees who were small property owners received just payment. Those who doubt this must simply check the historic record more closely. This, however, in no way pardons nor minimizes the illegal actions of the U.S. federal government in this matter.

It was at least partially for this reason that John Rogers was able to regain possession of his Georgia property after having lost it in the *Cherokee Land Lottery of 1832.* Even though he had to pay three times the lottery value of the property, he was able to repurchase the property through his then-advanced financial circumstances.

In a similar appraisal, it was determined that John's quarter-blood Cherokee son – William – *"owned a farm at Gilbert's Ferry with 100 acres, cleared and cultivated, 8 houses, and 1,500 bushels of corn"* for which he was also entitled to reimbursement. William also was handsomely reimbursed for his property and therefore able to later repurchase it from the lottery winner.

William was an important participant during the negotiations between the Cherokees and the White government for the Cherokee Removal in Georgia and the Southeast. He had been appointed as Cherokee Commissioner by Chief John Ross during the late 1820s, but their relationship was destined to sour as William eventually became an outspoken advocate of organized Cherokee removal (and the *Treaty of New Echota*) to the West, a proposition to which Ross was adamantly opposed. The circumstances ultimately became so harsh that Cherokee law imposed a death sentence upon any Cherokees who voted in favor of what came to be known as the *Removal Treaty*.

These circumstances, however, did not deter William, his brother Johnson, and many other prominent Cherokees in the least in their devout support for the Treaty. They envisioned the inevitability of the harsh circumstances which lay ahead for their Cherokee brethren in Georgia who refused to accept the Treaty and move westward.

William and Johnson felt it was much wiser for the Cherokee Nation as a whole to peaceably be reimbursed for their properties and accept re-location in the American West rather than to defy the U.S. government and invite violence. Ironically, they ultimately were proved to be correct in their analysis of the situation.

William & "Little John's" Homes

Interestingly, both John's and his son William's homes in north Georgia still stood prominently into the 21st Century, much to the surprise of many historians. This was due in no small measure to their preservation through continuous ownership by members of the Rogers family.

William's home – which he called *"Oakland"* – still stands prominently in present-day North Fulton County beneath towering oaks, some of which possibly took root in William's day as young trees. Though the ownership of this home is unknown today, it still remained in the control of the Rogers family as recently as the late 1990s. It had, in fact, been in the Rogers family from the date of its construction in the 1830s right up to the 1950s, when Nettie Rogers finally sold it to an individual outside the family.

"When the property came back on the market in 1980, our family repurchased it," explained Michael Rogers, a descendant of William, in an interview in the early 1990s. *"My father was born on this farm... not in this house, but in a house across the road that burned in the 1930s. So you can see how important the property is to us, and especially the structures still standing such as this house.*

"The old place needs a lot of work, but I'm getting there," Michael added at that time. *"I'm planting rows of trees to shield a new subdivision that is going in,"* he smiled distastefully, pointing eastward.

A Rogers family graveyard which dates from the 1830s, also exists near this home. In it rest the last remains of a number of stalwarts of this once-prominent family.

A short distance away, the home of William's father – John – also still stood in the early 1990s when it was owned by the Bowlin family, and is believed to still be standing as of this writing (2023). Built in 1828, it exists upon a tree-ensconced hilltop facing the wide floodplain of Suwanee Creek, the flatlands of which had proven so productive to Little John Rogers back in the 1830s and '40s.

"When we bought this house," said Cheryl Bowlin in a 1990s interview, *"it didn't have any plumbing or wiring. A fox lived in the basement, and the Shakerag Hunt Club in years past had routinely galloped their horses through the hallways to scare the fox out of the basement so they could chase him. The windows were all broken and the house was in a state of general disrepair, but it wasn't hard to see that it had been a startlingly beautiful home at one time."*

Interestingly, despite their subsequent intense preservation of the home, the Bowlins at that time were not aware of the immense historic significance of the structure when they purchased it. Following their investment in updating the home, they were thrilled when they discovered its actual historic background. To their good fortune – and that of posterity – they were wise enough to take great pains to preserve and renovate it as closely to its original configurations as possible. *"Last month, Will Rogers, Jr., was even here filming a bread commercial,"* Cheryl stated proudly at the time.

When the home's pedigree was discovered, the National Park Service even attempted to purchase the property from the Bowlins in order to add it to the park holdings in the Chattahoochee River corridor. The Bowlins, however, by then were savvy enough to understand that they were in possession of quite a jewel.

McNair-Rogers Family

Yet another former Cherokee who lived within several days' ride of John's and William's homes was David McNair (1774-1836) who also served on the staff of Andrew Jackson during the War of 1812. It was during the campaign against the *"Red Stick"* Creeks that McNair was introduced to John Rogers and they became good friends.

McNair was yet another prominent and respected leader in the Cherokee Nation, according to testimony recorded in 1829. He owned a beautiful farm in the rolling hills near the Conasauga River in Tennessee, approximately one and one-quarter miles beyond the boundary between that state and Georgia.

Here, David built his wife, Delilah Amelia (1785-1838) – the daughter of prominent and notorious Cherokee James Vann II and Elizabeth Thornton – a very handsome brick home, complete with intricate Indian-engraved fireplace mantles, brick smoke houses, and numerous other structures. Delilah was described as tall and beautiful, and bore David six healthy children.

If one searches for this once-impressive home today, he or she will be disappointed. A historic marker, at least, does mark the site as the former location of "McNair's Stand." The impressive home once stood upon a prominent knoll slightly west of Highway 411 in Tennessee. In American pioneer days, a "stand" was an overnighting spot, usually offering accommodations to travelers in the stagecoaches of that day.

A long gracefully-curving drive leads to the former site which is occupied today by a modern home. Near the entry of this drive, the graves of David and Delilah may be viewed today within the walls of the small family burial plot where they were buried back in the 1830s.

Despite the unlikelihood of its survival, McNair's home reportedly had in fact weathered many ensuing years and was still standing right up to the 1930s. In 1936, however, it reportedly was completely destroyed by a large tornado. Interestingly, this tornado quite likely was a portion of the huge tornadic storm which completely destroyed the Hall County, Georgia town of Gainesville to the south in 1936. It is still listed as one of the worst disasters in U.S. history.

Over his lifetime, David McNair reportedly maintained a friendship with many prominent members of the Cherokee Nation, including his old war companion, John Rogers. John's son, William, eventually became enamored with McNair's daughter, Mary Vann McNair, and ultimately took her for his wife.

By 1829, when the Georgia State Legislature passed a series of laws designed to remove the Cherokees' citizenship rights and then appropriate their land, William Rogers was 24 years of age. The previous year he had begun construction of his home named "Oakland" in what today is North Fulton County.

William and Johnson worked tirelessly for the Cherokee interests, both in Georgia and in Washington. In 1830, following passage of the Indian Removal Bill by the U.S. Congress, William and Johnson became outspoken critics of Cherokee Chief John Ross, joining what came to be known as the *"Treaty Party,"* along with Major Ridge, Elias Boudinot, Stand Watie, and numerous others. Boudinot was editor of the remarkable ***Cherokee Phoenix*** newspaper, the first of its kind for Native Americans.

Rogers & Cherokee Removal

By 1834, a storm of change had descended upon the Cherokees. William exerted all his influence and skills in an attempt to convince the other – *non-Treaty faction*-Cherokees – of the need to accept the Treaty, be reimbursed for their land and property, and move peaceably to the West, but his efforts were in vain.

Finally, the *Treaty of New Echota* (the Cherokee capital at that time) was signed on December 29, 1835, ceding all the Cherokee lands within the confines of what then was Georgia to the state of Georgia. It is difficult to envision this treaty as anything other than devastating to the Cherokee Nation as a whole.

William and his brother, Johnson, had joined the prominent Cherokee leader Stand Watie in signing the document, along with Elias Boudinot, Major Ridge, and many others. Cherokee Chief John Ross, however, considered the treaty signatures to be fraudulent, since they represented but a small percentage of the actual Cherokee population in the Southeast.

As a result of their signatures on and support for the Treaty, the lives of both William and Johnson were put in dire jeopardy. Numerous other prominent Cherokee leaders who had signed the treaty – including Major Ridge, Elias Boudinot, and others – were cruelly assassinated, and several attempts were made upon William's life.

Johnson Rogers ultimately chose to leave Georgia entirely, and take up residence in Washington, where he lived for the remainder of his life. Here, he worked diligently for the Cherokee cause until his death at age 61.

In spite of William's optimism, the Cherokee Removal of 1838 became a hallmark of horror for those Cherokees who had remained behind in Georgia in defiance of the Treaty. The illegality (it had been ruled as such by no lesser authority than the United States Supreme Court, a ruling which was then simply defied by President Andrew Jackson) of the removal became a stain upon White civilization in America which has lasted to the present day.

While awaiting transportation across the Hiwassee River on only the first leg of the removal westward, Delilah Vann McNair died of a stroke, becoming one of the first of over 4,000 Cherokees who ultimately perished during the terrible winter of the forced removal. The U.S. Army allowed the McNair children to return Delilah's body for burial next to her beloved husband who had perished two years earlier. The remains of the McNairs rest there today in quiet repose in their small graveyard just west of Highway 411 in Tennessee.

William Rogers paid $150.00 for inscribed grave markers for both the McNairs. A short time later on September 1, 1839, William himself suffered tragedy when his wife, Mary, was killed in a horse accident, leaving him with four small children to raise.

Like many other mixed-blood Cherokees and Indian "countrymen" (as the White spouses of the Native Americans were designated), William and his family had opted under the Treaty of New Echota – as was their right – to become citizens of Georgia and renounce their Cherokee citizenship. They were granted their citizenship on December 29, 1838, and by re-purchasing their property, were able to remain in Georgia.

William lived out his life at his home "Oakland," with his second wife – a Moravian teacher named Louisa Ruede. He died peacefully in his sleep at Oakland on April 12, 1870.

Enoch & John Rogers Families

According to researchers Mary Avilla Abel and Hall Farnsworth, one of the John Rogers of northeast Georgia – possibly one also related in some manner to the individuals detailed above – was enumerated in the *1820 Census of Jackson County, Georgia*. The name of this John's wife is not known today, since she disappeared from the census records prior to the *1850 Census of Jackson* in which wives' names finally began to be included.

The *1850 Census of Hall County* to which this John Rogers later moved lists him as 83 years of age, living in the household of his son, Jacob, in Hall, and as having been born in North Carolina. The parents of this **John Rogers** are not known, but the reasons detailed below indicate that the **Enoch Rogers** living near to him in the early 1800s was almost certainly his brother:

1/ John's name is listed as a witness to Enoch's purchase of land in Jackson County in 1802.

2/ John named one of his sons "Enoch," and Enoch named one of his sons "John."

3/ No other known researchers of the numerous individuals named "Rogers" in Jackson County included either the above Enoch or John in their family histories.

4/ When this Enoch relocated to Hall County, Georgia, in the 1850s, Jacob (son of Enoch's brother, John) moved to that location as well, and the two purchased adjoining property.

5/ Cherokee Indian records shown elsewhere verify that Enoch had a brother named "John."

Also in the same *1820 Census of Jackson County* which lists this John and Enoch Rogers and other members of this particular family, there is a **"Sally Rogers"** listed as the head of a household and identified as "over 45," with one female "10 to 15 years of age." **It is possible that she was the mother of John and Enoch.** Since she appears in no further census records after that date, she quite likely was deceased. She was not included in any other Rogers family histories of Jackson County.

Further indication that this Sally may have been the mother of John and Enoch Rogers is the fact that John named a daughter Sally and this name (or the name "Sarah" for which Sally was often a substitute) appears in the family periodically after that date.

The Will (dated May 15, 1849; probated October 1, 1851 in Jackson County) of the John Rogers identified above names his children. This Will, according to researchers Abel and Farnsworth, along with census records and some existing *Bible* records, is used to establish the descendants of this John Rogers.

This John Rogers, born circa 1767 in Cumberland County (later Moore County), North Carolina, is the father of a number of children, one of whom is **James Rogers**, his sixth child, who was born in 1808. James married Eliza Ann Whitmire (sister of Jane Whitmire who also married into this family) on January 17, 1833 in Jackson County.

Eliza Ann was born in 1818 and died 18 May, 1878. James died 12 April, 1877. **They were buried**

in clearly-marked graves in what in recent times became an overgrown (and ancient) section of the graveyard to the rear of old Academy Baptist Church in Jackson County, Georgia.

When the author of this work – Ralph Olin Jackson III – visited the Academy Church site in the 1990s, it was quite clear that this heavily-overgrown area of the church's cemetery had been abandoned for many years. If one looked carefully across what had become an overgrown forested hillside, numerous sunken graves were visible. **Since his son and other family members are buried in this site, it is quite possible that this is also the burial site of the original John Rogers of Jackson County note.**

Other children of this **John Rogers** include: Jacob, b. 01/12/1795 in North Carolina, m. on 06/18/1818, Mary Staton (b. 10/01/1800, GA, d. 09/28/1885), d. 04/19/1864; Enoch, b. ca. 1798 in North Carolina, m. Susanna Cunningham 10/21/1819, Jackson Co., GA, d. 1869, buried at his home-place in Cherokee Co., GA (present-day Fulton Co., GA); **Temperance, b. ca 1800, Jackson Co., GA, d. June, 1879 or 1880, buried Pendergrass, Jackson Co., GA, m. 1815 or 1818 James Pettyjohn, son of Jacob Pettyjohn;** Sarah ("Sallie"), b. ca. 1803, GA, m. Moses Redding 11/18/1822, Jackson Co., GA; Thomas, b. 12/29/1805, GA, m. Jane Whitmire 02/17/1833, Jackson Co., GA, d. 05/27/1876, Forsyth Co., GA; James, b. 1808, GA, m. Eliza Ann Whitmire 01/13/1833, Jackson Co., GA, d. 04/12/1877, Jackson Co., GA; Nancy, b. ca. 1810, GA, m. William R. Polk 12/20/1831; and Permilla, b. ca. 1813, GA, m. John B. Rowland 11/29/1835, Jackson Co., GA.

[Children of the above Temperance and James Pettyjohn: Nancy b. 01/25/1816, Jackson Co., GA, m. Henderson Anglin, Jackson Co., GA, d. 11/08/1838, GA; Jacob b. 11/01/1818, m. Mary Mariah Whitmire 12/17/1837, Jackson Co., GA, d. 1892 (Texas??) Heard Co., GA; Sarah Ann, b. 10/17/1819, Jackson Co., GA, m. Alfred Gray, d. 12/16/1906, Forsyth Co., GA; Oliver Perry, b. 09/21/1821, Jackson Co., GA, m. Sarah A. Randolph, d. 08/18/1881; Elizabeth, b. 03/17/1827, Jackson Co., Ga, m. William J. Garrett; Addison

Bainbridge, b. 01/04/1832, Jackson Co., GA, d. 1852; **Arabella (Arabel Ellen),** b. 04/03/1834, Jackson Co., GA, m. **Richard Bennett Hudgins,** 07/30/1857, d. 06/19/1904, Hall Co., GA; James Decatur b. 03/10/1836; William Franklin b. 07/28/1837, Jackson Co., GA, m. Frances A. Smith 07/30/1857, d. 07/20/1862; Thomas Jefferson, b. 06/18/1840, Jackson Co., GA, d. 09/08/1861, Richmond VA; and Marion Gates, b. 09/23/1843, Jackson Co., GA, d. 06/01/1862.]

(The Jacob Pettyjohn mentioned above as one of the children of Temperance Rogers and James Pettyjohn was quite a story unto himself. Please read about him in the Pettyjohn section of this book. In 1859, he was convicted (despite only being present during the commission of a crime and failing to render assistance) of Second Degree Murder in Forsyth County and sentenced to hang.)

Enoch Rogers who was the brother of the above John Rogers, was born in the 1760s, probably in North Carolina as was John. The *1830 Federal Census of Hall County*, Georgia lists his age as 60 to 70, and the *1840 Federal Census of Walker County*, Georgia to which he later removed lists his age as 70 to 80.

The first recorded indication of Enoch's presence in Georgia was in 1799, when he appears on a Jackson County Tax List which lists him as delinquent.

Enoch was married circa 1790 to Catherine "Katie" Teague, who was at least a half-blood Cherokee. At some point prior to October 7, 1809, this marriage was dissolved (or abandoned), since Enoch married Rachel Pettigrew on that date (*Marriage Records of Jackson County, Georgia*).

Enoch and Catherine Teague were the progenitors of a number of children. Their offspring are believed to have been: Robert, William, David, Polly, John, and Nancy.

Enoch and Rachel Pettigrew Rogers also had a number of children: a daughter born 1810; a son, probably James; a daughter born between 1810 and 1815; a son born between 1815 and 1820 named Thomas; a daughter born between 1815 and 1820; another daughter born between 1815 and 1820; a son born between 1820 and 1825 named Samuel; a

son born between 1825 and 1830; another son born between 1825 and 1830; a daughter born between 1830 and 1835; and a son born between 1830 and 1835 (which probably was Jacob).

For a listing and detailed description of all of these offspring, please see *"Kith and Kin of Georgia Ridge, Crawford County Arkansas"* by Mary Avilla Abel and Hall Farnsworth.

In 1802, **Enoch** is listed in the tax records of Jackson County with 65 acres of land.

In 1805, he is listed as living in Jackson County where he drew Land Lot #251, 2nd District of Baldwin County. This property was granted to him by the state of Georgia on 13 November, 1805. He also drew a number of other tracts of property around this same period of time.

On June 10, 1826, Enoch Rogers helped to organize the Holly Springs Baptist Church in Hall County where he served as the church's clerk from 1826 to 1835.

In 1828, Enoch was Justice of the Peace in Hall County. He subsequently appears in a number of records from that preoccupation.

On May 4, 1835, Enoch sold Land Lot #82, 12th District, Hall County, to Edward Hooper.

In 1837, Enoch was granted his letter from Holly Springs Baptist Church and migrated westward in the state. He is next found in the *1840 Federal Census of Walker County* in northwest Georgia where he apparently died during the 1840s. His second wife, Rachel, is listed in the *1850 Federal Census of Walker* as living with her son, Samuel and another son, Jacob, in that portion of Walker which became Catoosa County in 1853.

*(Grateful appreciation is expressed herewith to Mary Avilla Abel and Hall Farnsworth, authors of **Kith and Kin of Georgia Ridge, Crawford County, Arkansas,** and the late Dr. Branley Allan Branson, a former professor at Eastern Kentucky University in Richmond, Kentucky, and Don L. Shadburn, author of **Cherokee Planters in Georgia, 1832-1838,** for partial details related to this article. Dr. Branson is a descendant of Cherokees James Vann, David and Delilah McNair, and William Rogers.)*

Rogers Genealogical Line

(Ancestry of One Rogers-Pettyjohn-Hudgins Family Line in Georgia)
(Country of Origin of Rogers Family Line: Normandy, France or England)

Rogers is generally a patronymic surname of **English origin**, deriving from the given name of Roger commonly used by the natives of Normandy in France and meaning "son of Roger." The "**Rogers**" given name was probably first introduced to England after the Norman Conquest of 1066, and is first recorded as "Rogerus" in the Domesday Book of 1086.

Great-great-great-great-great-grandfather: Jacob Rogers

b.   1740

m.   Ruth Bunch b. 1728, d. 1775   Issue: **John**; Enoch, b. 1797, d. 1869; Elizabeth; Sarah; and Mary Ann.

d.   1774, Cumberland Co., NC

> **Note #1:** On page 149 of *Will Abstracts of Cumberland County, NC, 1754-1863* by Kate James Lepine and Anna Sherman, the *Last Will & Testament* of Jacob Rogers (d. 1774) is abstracted, mentioning his wife, Ruth, sons John and Enoch, and daughters Elizabeth Hancock, Sarah Rogers, and Mary Ann Rogers. Executors were wife Ruth and friend James Muse. Witnesses were William Manes, Charles Sherin and William Hancock.

> **Note #2:** On page 20 of Rassie E. Wicker's *Miscellaneous Ancient Records of Moore County, NC*, a 1761 deed to Jacob Rogers is abstracted. On page 460, Ruth Rogers is shown on a 1777 tax list of the part of Cumberland County, NC that became Moore County in 1784.

> **Note #3:** Ruth Rogers is listed in the *1790 Census of Moore County, NC*.

Great-great-great-great-grandfather: John Rogers

b.   circa 1767, Cumberland Co. (later Moore Co.), North Carolina

m.   ? Issue: Jacob, b. 01/12/1795 North Carolina, m. Mary Staton 06/18/1818 (Mary Staton b. 10/01/1800 GA, d. 09/28/1885), d. 04/19/1864; Enoch, b. ca. 1798 North Carolina, m. Susanna Cunningham 10/21/1819, Jackson Co., GA, d. 1869, buried at his home-place in Cherokee Co., GA (present-day Fulton Co., GA); **Temperance**; Sarah ("Sallie"), b. ca. 1803 GA, m. Moses Redling 11/18/1822 Jackson Co., GA; Thomas, b. 12/29/1805 GA, m. Jane Whitmire 02/17/1833 Jackson Co., GA, d. 05/27/1876 Forsythe Co., GA; James, b. 1808 GA, m. Eliza Ann Whitmire 01/13/1833 Jackson Co., GA, d. 04/12/1877 Jackson Co., GA; Nancy, b. ca. 1810 GA, m. William R. Polk 12/20/1831; Permilla, b. ca. 1813 GA, m. John B. Rowland 11/29/1835 Jackson Co., GA.

d.   1851 Buried: Probably Academy Church Cemetery, Jackson Co., GA

> **Note #4:** John Rogers was enumerated in the *1820 Census of Jackson Co., Georgia*.

> **Note #5:** Both Jacob Rogers and Mary Staton Rogers are buried in marked graves in old Holly Springs Cemetery, Hall County, GA.

> **Note #6:** Jackson County, GA records indicate that Mary Staton's mother was Mary Pettyjohn Staton, sister of Jacob Pettyjohn. She had a brother named Fleming Staton, b. circa 1793 in Virginia.

> **Note #7:** The *1850 Census of Hall County, Georgia*, lists John as 83 years old, and being born in North Carolina.

> **Note #8:** John Rogers' *Last Will & Testament*, dated May 15, 1849, probated October 1, 1851, in Jackson County, GA, names his children. This *Will*, along with U.S. Census records and existing family *Bible* records, are used to establish the descendants of John Rogers.]

> **Note #9:** Cherokee Indian records corroborate that Enoch had a brother named John.

Great-great-great-grandmother: Temperance Rogers Pettyjohn

b.   ca. 1800, Jackson Co., GA

m.   1815 or 1818 James Pettyjohn, son of Jacob Pettyjohn. Issue: Nancy b. 01/25/1816, Jackson Co, GA, m. Henderson Anglin, Jackson Co, GA, d. 11/08/1838, GA ; Jacob b. 11/01/1818, m. Mary Mariah Whitmire 12/17/1837, Jackson Co, GA, d. 1892, (Texas??) Heard Co., GA; Sarah Ann b. 10/17/1819, Jackson Co, GA, m. Alfred Gray, d. 12/16/1906, Forsyth Co., GA; Oliver Perry b. 09/21/1821, Jackson Co, GA, m. Sarah A. Randolph, d. 08/18/1881; Elizabeth, b. 03/17/1827, Jackson Co., GA, m. William J. Garrett; Addison Bainbridge, b. 01/04/1832, Jackson Co., GA, d. 1852; **Arabella** (Arabel Ellen) b. 04/03/1834, Jackson Co., GA, m. Richard Bennett Hudgins, 07/30/1857, d. 06/19/1904, Hall Co., GA; James Decatur b. 03/10/1836; William Franklin b. 07/28/1837, Jackson Co., GA, m. Frances A. Smith 07/30/1857, d. 07/20/1862; Thomas Jefferson, b. 06/18/1840, Jackson Co., GA, d. 09/08/1861, Richmond, VA; Marion Gates, b. 09/23/1843, Jackson Co., GA, d. 06/01/1862.

d.   June, 1879 or 1880, buried Pendergrass, Jackson Co., GA

> **Note #10:** Jacob Pettyjohn (1818-1892) brother to Arabella, was convicted (despite only being present during the commission of a crime by others) of murder in Forsyth County, GA in 1859. After being released on bond for a re-trial, he fled to Texas where he joined the Confederate Army.

Great-great-grandmother: Arabella Pettyjohn Hudgins

b.   04/03/1834, Jackson Co., GA

m.   Richard Bennett Hudgins, 07/30/1857 Issue: Mary (b. 07/23/1854, d. 06/06/1885); Margaret Emmaline (b. 08/17/1856, Hall Co., GA, d. 10/16/1934, Jackson Co., GA); and **James Zacheus** (b. 12/30/1859, Jackson Co., GA, d. 02/01/1933, Clermont, Hall Co., GA).

d.   06/19/1904, Hall Co, GA. Buried Harmony Grove Baptist Church *(Harmony Hall Baptist Church?)* Cemetery, Harmony Church Road, Hall, Co., GA). *(Note: To reach Harmony Hall Baptist Church, take U.S. 129 east and turn left onto Blackstock Road in Hall County, then bear left onto Mangum Mill Road. Harmony Hall Baptist Church is on the left.)*

> **Note #11:** Richard Bennett Hudgins enlisted in the Confederate Army on 08/27/1861, departing for service only two years after his son, James Zacheus had been born. He died 01/03/1865, Raleigh NC, from pneumonia while serving in Co. D, 27th Infantry Regiment, Georgia Volunteers, Army of Northern Virginia. He had contracted pneumonia near Goldsboro, NC, 12/27/1864, and was sent to Confederate General Hospital #8, Raleigh, NC, where he died. He was buried 01/04/1865, in Oakwood Cemetery, Raleigh, NC, Grave #356.

Great-grandfather: James Zacheus Hudgins

b.   03/04/1804, Hall Co., Georgia

m.   **(1ˢᵗ)** Elizabeth Harris, (07/22/1882, Harmony Grove Baptist Church (Harmony Hall Baptist Church?), Hall Co., GA. (b. 12/18/1867, Clayton Co., GA, d. 10/29/1892, Hall Co., GA). b. Harmony Hall Baptist Church Cemetery, Hall County, GA. Issue: Richard B. (b. 02/18/1885, d. 01/12/1919); Silas A. (b. 09/05/1886); William J. (b. 08/01/1888, d. 04/13/1889); Mattie Bell (b. 01/20/1890, d. 06/26/1891); and Lucy May (b. 08/03/1891).

   (2ⁿᵈ) Sarah ("Sallie") Elizabeth Tanner, 08/31/1895 (this marriage date also could possibly be 03/31/1895), (b. /07/1878, Chestnut Mountain, Hall Co., GA. Died 12/19/1969, Hiram, Paulding Co., GA.) Issue: Daisy Lee (b. 7/21/1896, d. 08/31/1996); Carl Washington (b. 08/28/1898, d. 12/27/1967, Lexington, KY); **Essie Carroll (nee Irene)**; David Bennett (b. 01/24/1902, d. 01/14/1983); Clyde Franklin (b. 11/06/1903, d. 02/18/1994); Mary Lou (Marilu) (b. 06/03/1905); Cora Estelle (b. 12/14/1906, d. 02/14/1992); Ralph Newton (b. 09/16/1908, d. 08/23/1970); Albert White (b. 04/21/1910, d. 02/01/1976); Raleigh (Raliegh) Edward (b. 06/05/1912, d. 07/11/1982); Sarah Rebecca (b. 07/14/1914, d. 12/10/1999, m. Herman Gibbs "Doc" Tankersley 11/18/1933 who was Justice of the Peace, Hall Co., GA for many years); Dorothy Belle (b. 11/23/1916, d. 05/15/2007, m. Ray Shaw); Marjorie Catherine (b. 10/23/1918, d. 07/20/2005)

d.   02/01/1933, Hall Co., GA. Buried Concord Baptist Church Cemetery, Clermont, Hall Co., GA.)

Note #12: James Zacheus Hudgins built a large elegant home in "downtown" Clermont, GA, and moved in with his family in 1914, just in time for the birth there of daughter Sarah. Two more children, Dorothy and Marjorie, were also born in this home, bringing the total number of children to 13. Two additional children were later born, bringing the total to 15, but wife Sarah was 43 years of age by this time, and these last two children did not survive. As of 2022, the fine old home built by James Z. in 1913 still stood on King Street in Clermont. The first ten Hudgins children were born in Sugar Hill, Hall Co., GA.

Grandmother: Essie Carroll (nee Irene) Hudgins Jordan

b.   03/12/1900, Sugar Hill, Jackson Co., GA. (Located on old Athens Hwy/U.S. 129 between Talmo and Pendergrass.)

m.   06/18/1927, Clermont, Hall Co., GA, Guy Wilfred Jordan (b. 02/19/1889, Dutch Hill, PA, d. 09/05/1946, Rockmart, Polk Co., GA. Buried Rose Hill Cemetery, Rockmart, Polk Co., GA). Issue: **Marilyn** and Patricia (b. 06/25/1934, Rockmart, Polk Co., GA, d. 12/29/2014, Doraville, DeKalb Co., GA.)

d.   02/11/1999, Rockmart, Polk Co., GA. Buried Rose Hill Cemetery, Rockmart, Polk Co., GA.

Mother: Marilyn Jordan Jackson

b.   03/20/1928, Rockmart (Polk Co.), GA

m.   1948, Rockmart, Polk Co, GA, Ralph Olin Jackson, Jr. (b. 12/08/1923, Rockmart, GA, d. 12/11/2011, Rome, Floyd Co., GA); Issue: Patricia Carroll (b. 02/21/1950, Cedartown, Polk Co., GA); **Ralph Olin III** (b. 09/08/1951, Cedartown, Polk Co., GA); David Anderson (b. November 6, 1952, Cedartown, Polk Co., GA); Mary Lynne (b. 09/15/1954, Rockmart, Polk Co., GA, d. 05/12 /2014. Ashes buried Rose Hill Cemetery, Rockmart, Polk Co., GA. Issue: Christopher and Alex); Guy Jordan (b. August 31, 1957, Rockmart, Polk Co., GA, d. May 20, 1980, Rockmart, GA. Buried Rose Hill Cemetery, Rockmart, Polk Co., GA).

d.   05/25/2007, Rome, Floyd Co., GA. Buried Rose Hill Cemetery, Rockmart, Polk Co., GA.

Notes:

_____
_____
_____
_____
_____
_____
_____
_____
_____
_____
_____
_____
_____
_____
_____
_____
_____
_____
_____
_____
_____
_____

1817 MARRIAGE ROLLS, JACKSON COUNTY, GEORGIA

Rogers, John and Cordery, Susannah / "Susie" – These primitive marital records preserve the happy occasion for *"Little John Rogers"* (1774-1851) (not to be confused with the original John Rogers of Jackson County note) and his new wife, Sarah (aka *"Susannah"*) (ca. 1785-1842). *Little John*, also known as *"Tsan-Usdi"* – was named as such to differentiate between himself and his father, "John the elder." *Little John* met and married Sarah Cordery (circa 1785-1842), the eldest daughter of Thomas Cordery, a Scottish trader, and Susannah Sonicooie, a full-blood Cherokee. Sarah or "Susie" Rogers (wife of Little John) was, by virtue of her parents' lineage, a half-blood Cherokee. According to the late Don L. Shadburn, former Forsyth County Historian and author of **Cherokee Planters in Georgia, 1832-1838,** *"Little John Rogers"* lived below Suwanee Old Town on the southern fringe of the Cherokee Nation, and had been an intermarried Cherokee citizen since 1802. His wife, Sarah/"Susie" gave birth to twelve children, each of whom married and, with one exception, had children of their own. Two of their sons – William and Johnson – became very important in Cherokee Indian affairs of the 1830s.

0106 ... & Elizabeth Hubbert	Aug 4th 1819	
Thos Reeves & Betsy Johnson	16th Aug 1819	
Silas Patton & Lucy Loy	12th Aug 1819	The within License executed by me the 19th of August 1819 John Stocks JP
Thomas Bishop & Lidda Brumbelow	6th Sept 1819	8th Sept 1819 The within was executed by me Thos C Barron JP
Anthony Baggett & Rebecca Ozburn	21st Sept 1819	
Henry Watkins & Elizabeth Sheffield	4th Oct 1819	
Robert Espy & Margaret King	6th Oct 1819	

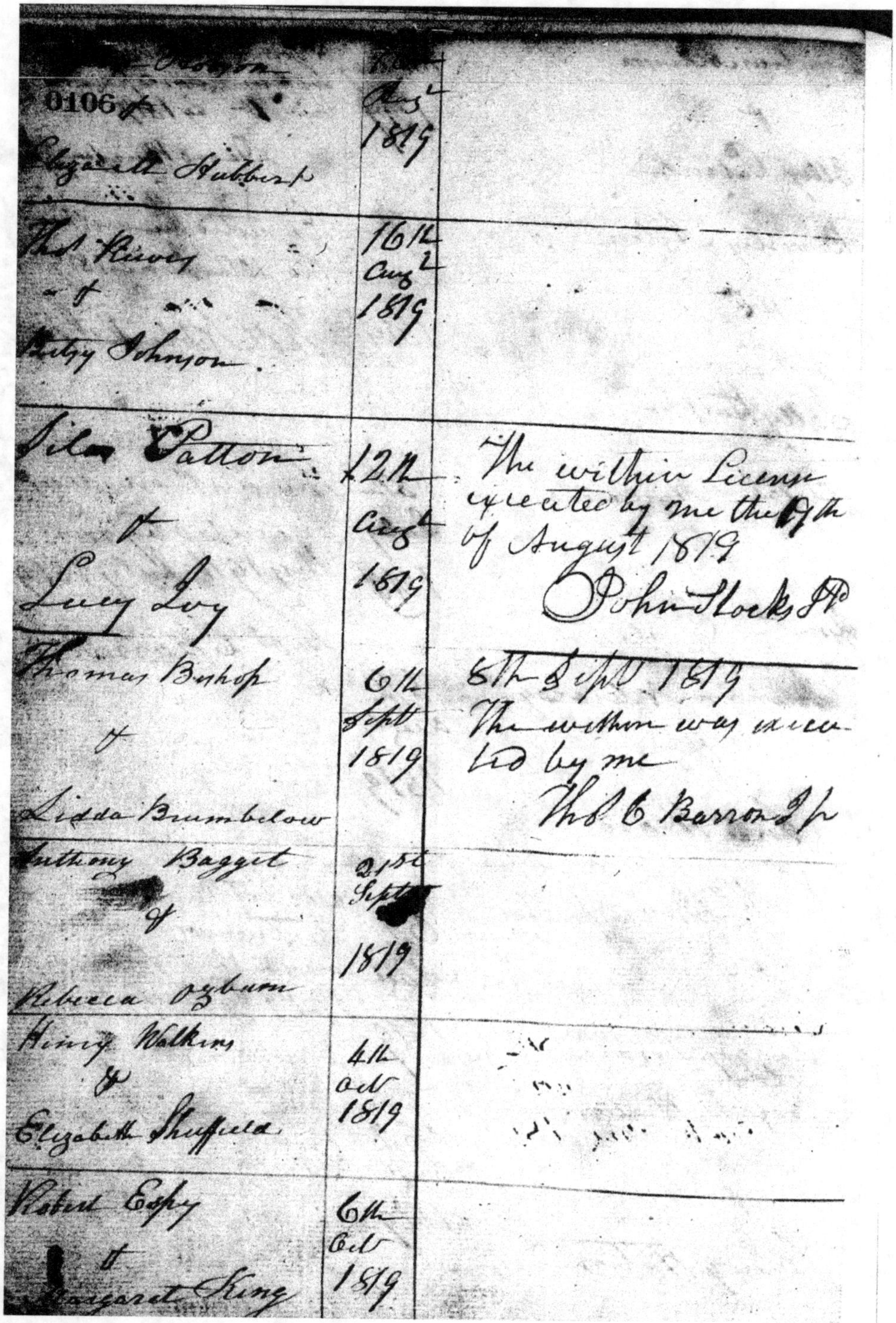

1819 MARRIAGE ROLLS, JACKSON COUNTY, GEORGIA

Rogers, Enoch and Susannah Cunningham – Pictured here is the Jackson County record for the marriage of Enoch and Susannah. This Enoch was the second child of the John Rogers of the Jackson County Rogers family. This Enoch was born circa 1798 in North Carolina. He married Susannah Cunningham on 21 October, 1819, in Jackson County and moved from there to Cherokee County, Georgia. He died there and was buried on his home-place in what today is North Fulton County, Georgia.

John King _v_ Elizabeth Johnson	6th Oct 1819	This certifies that ___ John King & Elizabeth ___ were duly joined ___ this 6th of Oct___ A.D. 1819 A.W.M. Cepher Washbourn M.G
Enoch Rogers _v_ Susannah Cunningham	21st Oct 1819	Executed 4th Oct 1819 John Holland Jp 010?
Amos Bradellon _v_ Elizabeth McMullen	20th Oct 1819	The within bond of ___ Matrimony was executed on the 21st of October 1819 by William Hill J.P.
Wm Armor _v_ Elizabeth Langley	27th Oct 1819	Executed the within by me this 28th October 1819 John Tacker J.P.
Beverly Parkerson _v_ Ansey Owens	2nd Nov 1819	
Lucy Kinnum _v_ Male Do Walling	8th nov 1819	Executed the within this 11th of November 1819 Stephen Boders Jp
Joseph Heath _v_ Maryan Wilson	8th nov 1819	Executed the within this 11th of November 1819 Stephen Bred

Right portion of document on facing page

1820 FEDERAL CENSUS, JACKSON COUNTY, GEORGIA

Rogers, Jacob and Enoch — Both Jacob and his brother Enoch are listed on this census. This Jacob was the first child of the John Rogers of Jackson County note, and this Enoch was John's second child. Jacob was born 12 January, 1795, in North Carolina. He married Mary Staton on 18 June, 1818; he died on 19 April, 1864. Mary was born 1 October, 1800, in Georgia, and died 28 September, 1885. They were both buried in marked graves in the old Holly Springs Cemetery in Hall County. Enoch was born in 1798 also in North Carolina. He married Susannah Cunningham on 21 October, 1819, in Jackson County and moved to Cherokee County, Georgia where he died and was buried in what today in North Fulton County.

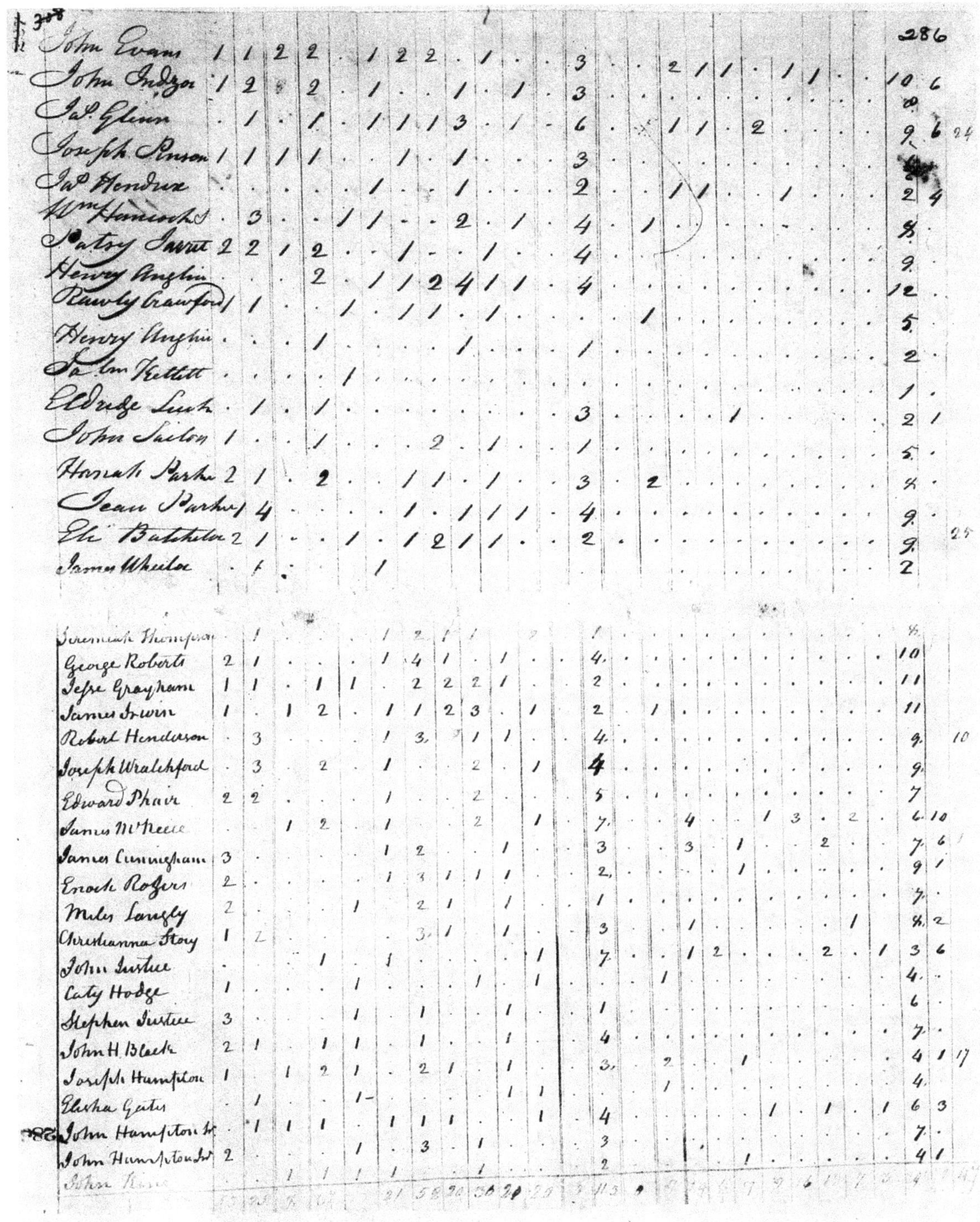
John Evans
John Indzor
Jas. Glenn
Joseph Penson
Jas. Hendrix
Wm Hancock
Patsy Jarrat
Henry Anglin
Rawly Crawford
Henry Anglin
Salm Kettett
Eldridge Lunk
John Sacton
Hanah Parker
Jean Parker
Eli Batchelor
James Wheeler
Jeremiah Thompson
George Roberts
Jesse Grayham
James Irwin
Robert Henderson
Joseph Wratchford
Edward Shaw
James McKeece
James Cunningham
Enoch Rogers
Miles Langly
Christianna Story
John Justice
Caty Hodge
Stephen Justice
John H. Black
Joseph Hampton
Elisha Gates
John Hampton Sr
John Hampton Jr
John Rice

1820 FEDERAL CENSUS, JACKSON COUNTY, GEORGIA

Rogers, Enoch – Listed on this census are Enoch (the elder, who was the brother of John Rogers of Jackson County note) and his children. Recorded are two males under 10 years of age (which would have been James and Thomas); one male over the age of 45 (which would have been Enoch); three females under 10 years of age (unknown); one female of 10 and under 15 years of age (unknown); one female of 16 and under 25 years of age (unknown); and one female of 26 and under 45 years of age (which would have been his wife, Rachel Pettigrew).

Name
John Rogers
Burwel Cook
Elgale Driskel
Flemin Huton
Andrew Armor
Robert Boyle
Joseph Cowdon
James Hemphill
Doris Barker
Isham Barker
Richard Majors
James Todd
Jerry Horton
Procer Horton
Ezekiel Price
Evan Polk
John Long
Reuben Pettijohn
Samuel Knox Senr
Samuel Knox Jnr
John Hobbs
James Pettijohn

1820 FEDERAL CENSUS, JACKSON COUNTY, GEORGIA

Rogers, John – Listed here is the John Rogers of Jackson County note with his eight children, Jacob (25); Enoch (22); Temperance (20); Sally (17); Thomas (15); James (12); Nancy (10); and Permilla (7). As is noteworthy from this census, there is no age bracket applicable to John's wife. For reasons unknown, she disappeared from the public record prior to 1820.

1820 FEDERAL CENSUS, JACKSON COUNTY, GEORGIA

Rogers, Sally – Also found in the 1820 Jackson County Census is one "Sally Rogers." She is listed as "over 45," with one female "Of 10 and under 15 years of age" in her household. Since she does not appear in later census records, it is possible that she was deceased after that point. It is not likely that she would have relocated alone to another area. It is possible she was the mother of the original John and Enoch Rogers of Jackson County note. John named a daughter "Sally," and that name appears in the family thereafter from time to time.

(No. 1.)
337

SCHEDULE of the whole number of Persons within the Division allotted to

Name of County, City, Ward, Town, Township, Parish, Precinct, Hundred, or District.	NAMES OF HEADS OF FAMILIES.	FREE WHITE PERSONS, (INCLUDING HEADS OF FAMILIES.)																								
		MALES.													FEMALES.											
		Under 5	5 to 10	10 to 15	15 to 20	20 to 30	30 to 40	40 to 50	50 to 60	60 to 70	70 to 80	80 to 90	90 to 100	100 &c.	under 5	5 to 10	10 to 15	15 to 20	20 to 30	30 to 40	40 to 50	50 to 60	60 to 70	70 to 80	80 to 90	91 to 100
	John Rogers			1			1											2		1						
	Hosea Martin		1	1		1										2	1	1								
	John McCarty				1	1	1	1									1	1		1						
	Middleton Brock					1									2				1							
	John T. Loves	3			1												1		1							
	Moss Wofford	1				1											1		1							
	Thos Burns				1			1											1		1					
	John Mars		1	1			1								2	1	1		1	2						
	Wm L Parr	2				1												1								
	Benjm Shelton				2			1							1	1	1	2	1	1						
	George B. Church	4	1			1													1							
	Baptist Park					1									2			1								
	Saml Hammon						1											1								
	David Nowlin			1		1									3											
	Benjm Roggins	1			1			1							1			1								
	Delanus Lyle				1			1												1	1	1				
	Cornelius Wright	1	3	2														1								
	Wm Mangrum	1													2	1		1								
	Alexr Batchelor	2				1									2	1	1	1								
	Jno Auglen	1		1	1										1	1										
	Robt Kirkham			1	2	1		1																		
	Ralph Huggins	1				1													1							
	Peter A. Auglen	3	3	1		1														1						
	John S. Rapp		3	1		1									1	2			1							
	Joseph Boyce	1			1										2	1		1								
	Charles Miller S.			2		1														1						
	Wm H. Trout	1		1											1		1									
		22	11	10	13	8	11	6	5	2					23	15	4	9	13	11	4	3	1			

86

82

1830 FEDERAL CENSUS, JACKSON COUNTY, GEORGIA

Rogers, John – Listed on this census is the original John Rogers of Jackson County note and five of his children: "Of 10 and under 15 years of age" (unknown); "Of 15 and under 20 years" (Permilla and Nancy); "Of 30 and under 40 years" (Temperance and Enoch). Temperance Rogers was John's third child and was born in 1800. She married James Pettyjohn and lived in Jackson County. One of her children was the Jacob Pettyjohn of Forsyth County who was convicted there of 2nd Degree Murder and sentenced to hang – a sentence which he managed to avoid (see the Pettyjohn section of this volume). Another of her children – Arabella Pettyjohn – married Richard Bennett Hudgins and the couple were the progenitors of a large clan of Hudgins in Jackson and Hall counties.

Thurston Anthony 0195 & Nancy Cruse	Jany 7 1833	Solemnized by me this 8th day of January 1833. Wm Burney J.P.
Wiley P. Warwick & Elizabeth M. Legg	23rd Jany 1833	Solemnized by me this 24th day of January 1833. J. W. Glenn M.G.
James C. Kerlin & Sarah Miller	3rd Nov 1832	Solemnized by me this 4th day of Nov 1832. Asa Varnum J.P.
Abel Stegler & Cynthia Miller	14th Dec 1832	the within was executed by me 16th of December 1832. Andrew Anthony M.G.
Howell M. Nunn & Elizabeth L. Stapler	7th June 1832	The above was solemnized by me this 7th day of June 1832. M.A. Brooks J.P.
Thomas J. Kidd & Martha Stockton	20th Feby 1833	Solemnized by me this 21st day of Feby 1833. Terry Bowen J.P.
Seth Jenkins & Jane Gilliland	26th March 1833	Solemnized by me this 23rd day of March 1833. Terry Bowen J.P.
James Ammons & Chaney Green	31st Jany 1833	Solemnized by me this 31st day of Jany 1833. James Millican J.P.
Mark Maldin & Matilda Holland	5th Nov 1833	Solemnized by me this 22nd Nov 1832. Jas H. David J.P.

Madison Umphries & Mary Ann Ivey	4th August 1831	Solemnized by me this 4th August 0197 Asa Varnum J.P.
D. M. Withite & Mahaly Wright	10th August 1832	Solemnized by me this 12th day of Sept 1832. Jas Millican J.P.
Green L. McBee & Nancy Saveall	9th April 1833	Solemnized by me this 2nd May 1833. Wm Burnas J.P.
William Moon & Agness Venable	15th July 1832	Solemnized by me this 16th July 1832 James Millican J.P.
James Thurmond & Susannah Benton	12th June 1832	Solemnized by me this 14 day of June 1832. M.A. Brooks J.P.
Fennel Wilson & Anna Key	19th April 1832	Solemnized by me this 19th April 1832. French Haggard J.P.
James Rogers & Elizabeth Whitmire	16th Jany 1833	Solemnized by me this 17th day of January 1833. Jno Whorton J.P.
Thomas Rogers & Jane Whitmire	15th Feby 1833	Solemnized by me this 17th Feby 1833. Jno Whorton J.P.
Alfred Butler & Catharine Gober	24th Jany 1833	Solemnized by me this 25th day of Jany 1833. French Haggard J.P.

1833 MARRIAGE ROLLS, JACKSON COUNTY, GEORGIA

Rogers, James – James, born in 1808, was the sixth child of the original John Rogers of Jackson County note. He (James) married Elizabeth "Eliza" Ann Whitmire on 17 January, 1833, in Jackson. She was born in 1818 and died 18 May, 1878. He died 12 April, 1877. They were both buried in marked graves in the pioneer section of the old Academy Baptist Church graveyard in Jackson County. When last checked by the author, R. Olin Jackson, this pioneer graveyard section was unmaintained and existed in an overgrown and heavily-forested area. Both James and his father – John – were listed in the minutes of Walnut Fork Baptist Church as members of Academy Baptist, so the original John Rogers of Jackson County note quite likely is also buried in this forested unmaintained section of the old Academy Baptist Church Cemetery.

(No. 4.) 9   **SCHEDULE of the whole nu...**

NAMES OF HEADS OF FAMILIES.	MALES														FEMALES		
	Under 5	5 under 10	10 under 15	15 under 20	20 under 30	30 under 40	40 under 50	50 under 60	60 under 70	70 under 80	80 under 90	90 under 100	100 and up		Under 5	5 under 10	10 under 15
John Woyles	1	2	1	0	0	1	0	0	0	0	0	0	0		1	0	2
Sterling White	1	0	1	1	1	0	0	1	0	0	0	0	0		0	1	1
Francis Nunn	0	1	1	0	1	0	0	0	0	0	0	0	0		0	0	2
Samuel Harlan	1	2	2	0	0	0	1	0	0	0	0	0	0		1	0	0
Aaron Sewell	0	1	0	0	0	0	1	0	0	0	0	0	0		0	0	1
Steven Justice	0	0	0	1	0	1	0	0	0	0	0	0	0		0	0	0
William Gilliland	0	0	0	1	1	1	0	1	0	0	0	0	0		0	0	0
Asaph Pollard	2	1	0	1	0	0	0	0	1	0	0	0	0		2	0	0
Jane Pollard	0	1	0	0	0	0	0	0	0	0	0	0	0		1	0	0
John Bailey	0	0	0	1	0	0	0	1	0	0	0	0	0		0	0	0
David Noyles	1	2	2	1	0	0	1	0	0	0	0	0	0		0	0	1
Gustavus Legg	0	1	1	0	0	0	1	0	0	0	0	0	0		0	1	1
James Rose	1	0	0	0	1	0	0	0	0	0	0	0	0		0	0	0
Sarah Justice	0	1	2	0	0	0	0	0	0	0	0	0	0		0	0	1
Nancy Bennett	0	1	1	0	0	0	0	0	0	0	0	0	0		0	0	0
Jonathan Williams	2	0	0	0	0	1	0	0	0	0	0	0	0		0	1	1
Powel R Kingenham	0	0	1	0	0	1	0	0	0	0	0	0	0		0	0	0
Wm A Long	2	0	2	0	0	0	0	1	0	0	0	0	0		0	1	0
Willis Long	0	0	0	1	0	0	0	0	0	0	0	0	0		0	0	0
John P Whitmire	2	1	0	0	1	0	0	0	0	0	0	0	0		0	0	0
John Whitmire	0	0	0	0	0	0	1	0	1	0	0	0	0		0	0	0
John Rogers	0	0	0	0	0	0	0	0	1	0	0	0	0		0	0	0
James Rogers	1	0	0	0	0	1	0	0	0	0	0	0	0		2	0	0
John Ward	1	1	0	2	0	0	1	0	0	0	0	0	0		1	1	2
Leroy Ethridge	0	0	0	0	0	0	1	0	0	0	0	0	0		0	1	1
Adam Williamson	1	0	0	0	0	0	0	1	0	0	0	0	0			2	1
Archie Mangum	0	0	0	2	0	0	1	0	0	0	0	0	0		0	0	1
Even Polke	0	0	0	1	1	0	0	1	0	0	0	0	0		0	0	0
Water Sims	2	0	0	0	1	0	0	0	0	1	0	0	0		0	1	0
John Reynolds	0	1	1	0	0	0	1	0	0	0	0	0	0		1	1	1
	18	16	15	10	9	4	8	6	2	2	0	0	0		9	10	16

1840 FEDERAL CENSUS, JACKSON COUNTY, GEORGIA

<u>Rogers, John & James</u> – Listed here are the original John Rogers of Jackson County note and his sixth child, James, born in 1808.

... division allotted to *[Holliday]*

FEMALES										FREE COLORED PERSONS — MALES						FEMALES					
15 under 20	20 under 30	30 under 40	40 under 50	50 under 60	60 under 70	70 under 80	80 under 90	90 under 100	100 and upward	Under 10	10 under 24	24 under 36	36 under 55	55 under 100	100 and upward	Under 10	10 under 24	24 under 36	36 under 55	55 under 100	100 and upward
0	0	1	0	0	0	0	0	0	0												
1	1	0	1	0	0	0	0	0	0												
1	0	0	0	1	0	0	0	0	0												
0	1	0	0	0	0	0	0	0	0												
0	0	2	0	0	1	0	0	0	0												
0	1	0	0	0	0	0	0	0	0												
0	0	0	0	1	0	0	0	0	0												
0	0	1	0	0	0	0	0	0	0												
0	1	0	0	0	0	0	0	0	0												
1	1	0	0	0	1	0	0	0	0												
1	0	0	1	1	0	0	0	0	0												
2	0	0	1	0	0	0	0	0	0												
0	1	0	0	0	0	0	0	0	0												
2	0	0	1	0	0	0	0	0	0												
1	0	0	1	0	0	0	0	0	0												
0	1	0	0	0	0	0	0	0	0												
1	0	0	0	0	0	0	0	0	0												
2	0	0	1	0	0	0	0	0	0												
1	0	0	0	0	0	0	0	0	0												
0	1	0	0	0	0	0	0	0	0												
0	0	0	0	1	0	0	0	0	0												
0	1	0	0	0	1	0	0	0	0												
0	0	1	0	3	0	0	0	0	0												
0	0	0	1	0	0	0	0	0	0												
2	0	0	0	1	0	0	0	0	0												
1	1	0	1	0	0	0	0	0	0												
0	0	0	1	0	0	0	0	0	0												
1	1	0	0	0	1	0	0	0	0												
0	1	0	0	0	0	0	0	0	0												
0	0	1	0	0	0	0	0	0	0												
17	12	6	10	5	4	2	0	0	0												

Right portion of document on facing page

1840 Federal Census, Walker County, Georgia — page image of the handwritten population schedule (No. 4), "SCHEDULE of the whole number..." with "NAMES OF HEADS OF FAMILIES" and "MALES" age-group columns.

1840 FEDERAL CENSUS, WALKER COUNTY, GEORGIA

Rogers, Enoch – By the late 1830s, various members of the Jackson County, Georgia Rogers clan had begun moving westward, but Enoch initially remained behind in Hall County. Whether this migration occurred in response to the Indian Removal Act is unknown today. In 1837, the year prior to the forced removal of the Cherokee Indians from north Georgia, records indicate that Enoch obtained his Letter of Dismissal from Holly Springs Baptist Church and moved shortly thereafter to Walker County in the northwest corner of the state where others of his family lived. By this point, however, Enoch's best days were behind him. At some point in the 1840s, he passed away in Walker and disappears from the public record. His second wife, Rachel, is listed in the *1850 Federal Census of Walker* in the household of her son Samuel, where another son, Jacob, also resided. Enoch's family appears in the 1820 (Jackson Co.), 1830 (Hall Co.), 1840 (Walker), and 1850 (Walker) Federal Censuses.

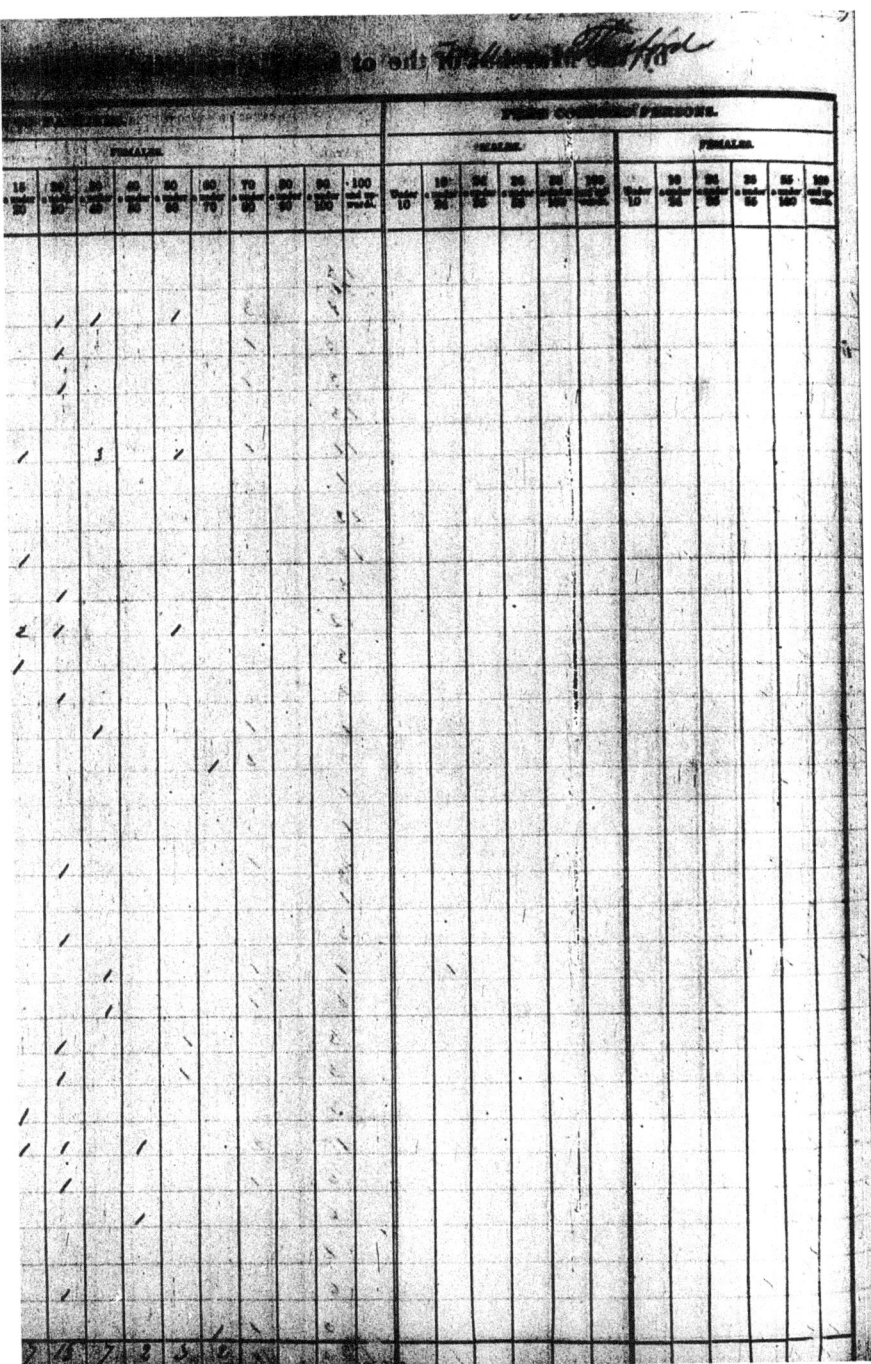

Right portion of document on facing page

Page No: 91

SCHEDULE 1.—Free Inhabitants in _Cunninghams District_ in the County of _Jackson_ State of _Georgia_ enumerated by me, on the 3ʳᵈ day of _July_ 1860. _William Bell_ Ass't Marshal

Post Office _Pot[?] fork_

Dwelling-houses numbered in the order of visitation	Families numbered in the order of visitation	The name of every person whose usual place of abode on the first day of June, 1860, was in this family.	Age	Sex	White, black, or mulatto	Profession, Occupation, or Trade of each person, male and female, over 15 years of age.	Value of Real Estate	Value of Personal Estate	Place of Birth, Naming the State, Territory, or Country.	Married within the year	Attended School within the year	Persons over 20 y'rs of age who cannot read & write	Whether deaf and dumb, blind, insane, idiotic, pauper, or convict.	
1	2	3	4	5	6	7	8	9	10	11	12	13	14	
		Joseph J Scott	9	M					Georgia					1
		Thomas "	7	M					Do					2
		Martha "	4	F					Do					3
		Alexander "	1	M					Do					4
338	338	Edward L Brooks	26	M		Farm laborer		700	Georgia					5
		Isabella "	18	F					Do					6
		Berian "	4/12	M					Do					7
338	338	William Guirard	37	M		Buggy maker	700	1225	Georgia	01				8
		Elizabeth "	25	F					Do	01				9
		Monye "	14	M					Do					10
		Mary "	12	F					Do					11
		Cornelia Oliver	7	F					Do					12
339	339	James Rogers	51	M		Farmer	1000	2692	Georgia					13
		Eliza Ann "	43	F					Do					14
		John "	17	M		Farm laborer			Do		01			15
		Eliza Ann "	14	F					Do					16
		Sarah "	11	F					Do					17
		Nancy "	8	F					Do					18
		Julia "	5	F					Do					19
		Jane "	3	F					Do					20
		Josa "	1	F					Do					21
340	340	Sarah Long	39	F		Farming	1500	3375	Georgia					22
		Thompson "	17	M		Farmer			Do					23
		Sarah "	16	F					Do					24
		John "	13	M					Do					25
		Martha "	11	F					Do					26
		Cinthia "	9	F					Do					27
		Eugenia "	7	F					Do					28
		Jefferson "	5	M					Do					29
		Eliza "	3	F					Do					30
		Nancy "	1	F					Do					31
341	341	William Williams	34	M		Miller		25	Georgia					32
		Aveline "	37	F					Do					33
		Mary "	11	F					Do					34
		Cinthia "	9	F					Do					35
		Ammanda "	7	F					Do					36
		Charles "	5	M					Do					37
		Jesse "	2	M					Do					38
342	342	Angus Simmion	41	M		Farmer	1000	275	N Carolina					39
		Mary "	31	F					Georgia					40

No. white males, 16   No. colored males,   No. foreign born,   No. blind,
No. white females, 24   No. colored females,   No. deaf and dumb,   No. insane,   4,200   7,792   No. idiotic,   No. paupers,   No. convicts,

1860 FEDERAL CENSUS, JACKSON COUNTY, GEORGIA

Rogers, James – This census records James – the sixth child of the John Rogers of Jackson County note – with all his family. James is identified in this census as a farmer with real estate valued at $1,000.00 and a personal estate valued at $2,692.00. In a brief five years of time, the economy of Georgia will be destroyed; the medium of trade – the Confederate dollar – will be worthless; the state in general will lie in ruins; and the residents of the state will be reduced to a survival by living off the land and fending off heartless and often deceitful tax assessors. Listed here with James are his wife, Eliza Ann, (43); and his children: John, (17); Eliza Ann, (14); Sarah, (11); Nancy, (8); Julia, (5); Jane, (3); and tiny Josa, (1). James will ultimately be buried – quite likely near to the gravesite holding his father, John Rogers – in the old Academy Baptist Church Cemetery in Jackson County, Georgia.

Supplemental Bibliographical References

1/ Bartow County Genealogical Society, ***Bartow County Heritage Book*** (1995)

2/ Cain, Andrew, ***History of Lumpkin County, 1832-1932*** (1979), The Reprint Company Publishers

3/ Church of Jesus Christ of the Latter-Day Saints, ***Family Search*** internet search engine (2022)

4/ Coulter, E. Merton, ***Auraria: The Story of a Georgia Gold Mining Town*** (1956), UGA Press

5/ Dabney, Joseph E., ***Mountain Spirits*** (1974), Bright Mountain Books

6/ Davis, Donald E., ***The Land of Ridge and Valley, A Photographic History of the Northwest Georgia Mountains***, (2000), Arcadia Publishing

7/ Dickens, Jr., Roy, ***Cherokee Pre-History*** (1976), University of Tennessee Press

8/ Ehle, John, ***The Trail of Tears*** (1988), Anchor Books

9/ Garrett, Franklin and Rice, Bradley, Atlanta Historic Society, ***Atlanta History, A Journal of the South*** (1980)

10/ Head, Sylvia Gailey, ***The Neighborhood Mint*** (1986), Gold Rush Gallery

11/ Hicks, John D., ***The Federal Union (Second Edition), A History of the United States to 1865*** (1952), Houghton Mifflin Company / The Riverside Press Cambridge

12/ Jackson, III, Ralph Olin, ***A North Georgia Journal of History, Vol. 1*** (1989), Legacy Communications, Inc.

13/ Jackson, III, Ralph Olin, ***A North Georgia Journal of History, Vol. 2*** (1991), Legacy Communications, Inc.

14/ Jackson, III, Ralph Olin, ***A North Georgia Journal of History, Vol. 3*** (1995), Legacy Communications, Inc.

15/ Jackson, III, Ralph Olin, ***A North Georgia Journal of History, Vol. 4*** (1999), Legacy Communications, Inc.

16/ Jackson, III, Ralph Olin, ***Moonshine, Murder & Mayhem in Georgia*** (2003), Legacy Communications, Inc.

17/ Jackson, III, Ralph Olin, ***Tales of the Rails In Georgia*** (2004), Legacy Communications, Inc.

18/ Kollock, John, ***These Gentle Hills*** (1976), Copple House Books

19/ McRay, Sybil, ***A Pictorial History of Hall County*** (1985), Taylor Publishing

20/ McRay, Sybil and James Dorsey, ***Windows of Memory, The Hall County That Was*** (1989) Chestatee Regional Library

21/ Ritchie, Andrew Jackson, ***Sketches of Rabun County History***, 1819-1948, Copple House Books

22/ Sargent, Gordon, Polk County Heritage Committee, 2000, ***The Heritage of Polk County, 1851-2000***

23/ Sawyer, Gordon, ***Northeast Georgia: A History***, (2001), Arcadia Publishing

24/ Shadburn, Don L., ***Cherokee Planters in Georgia, 1832-1838***, (1989), W. H. Wolfe Associates

25/ Shadburn, Don L., ***Pioneer History of Forsyth County, Forsyth County Heritage Series, Vol. 1*** (1981), W.H. Wolfe Associates, Roswell, GA

26/ Shaw, Dorothy Hudgins, Gainesville, Georgia, 2001

27/ Sherman, Gen. William T., ***The Capture of Atlanta and the March to the Sea*** (2007), Dover Publications, Inc., Mineola, New York

28/ Tate, Luke, ***History of Pickens County*** (1987), The Reprint Company Publishers

29/ Walker County Historic Society, ***Walker County, Georgia Heritage, 1833-1983*** (1984), Taylor Publishing Company

30/ Webb, J.A., ***History of New Holland, GA*** (1985)

31/ Wells II, Ridley, ***Old Enough To Die*** (1996), Hillsboro Press, Franklin, Tennessee

32/ Williams, Harry T.; Current, Richard N.; and Freidel, Frank; ***A History of the United States to 1876*** (1959), Alfred A. Knopf, New York

Subject Index

Name Index

Connally, Elizabeth 82,
Connally, Michael 117
Connell, Robert 156,
Conyers, Georgia 22,
Cook, John 163,
Cook, Sarah 163,
Cook, Lizzie 163,
Cook, William 163,
Coon, Minnie 124,
Cooper, Andrew J. 12,
Cooper, Carrie 174,
Cooper, Charles 174,
Cooper, Cornelia 40,
Cooper, Elizabeth 12, 172,
Cooper, Glenn 215,
Cooper, Hanny H. 224,
Cooper, Harry W. 172,
Cooper, Isaac E. 172,
Cooper, James 174,
Cooper, John 224,
Cooper, Josiah R. 12,
Cooper, Journey 196, 240,
Cooper, Thomas 196, 240, 244,
Cooper, Mark David 55,
Cooper, Matilda 224,
Cooper, Mary 224,
Cooper, May 174,
Cooper, Nancy J. 172,
Cooper, Pamela 12,
Cooper, Pearl 174,
Cooper, Ralph 40,
Cooper, William C. 12,
Cordery, Sarah "Susi" 276, 285,
Cordery, Sonicooie 276,
Cordery, Thomas 276,
Cotter, William 56,
Cotton, Alexander 62,
Coulter, Nathaniel 118
Cox, Adaline 86,
Cox, Alma D. 72,
Cox, Arthur L. 76,
Cox, Caroline 86,
Cox, Clyde W. 72,
Cox, Cora L. 72,
Cox, Edward 86,

Cox, Ernest 76,
Cox, Ezra A. 72,
Cox, Freeman 86,
Cox, George W. 76,
Cox, Henry 72,
Cox, Howard 76,
Cox, John W. 72,
Cox, Joshua 86,
Cox, Lois 76,
Cox, Luther E. 72,
Cox, Mary J. 76,
Cox, Mary L. 72,
Cox, Ollie L. 72,
Cox, Pearl 76,
Cox, Polly 86,
Cox, Sarah E. 72,
Cox, William 86,
Cox, William G. 72,
Clarke, Steve 71,
Craig, Cila 70,
Craig, Ida 70,
Crawford, D.A. 1,
Crawford, Ruth 215,
Culpepper, Laura Belle 215,
Culpepper, Lillie Mac 215,
Culpepper, "Pink" 215,
Cummings, Harold 236,
Cummings, Mary 236,
Cunningham, James 150,
Cunningham, Susanna 281,
   286,

D

Dahl, Anita W. 136,
Dahl, Edward W. 136,
Dahl, Lelitha I. 136,
Dahl, Milford W. 136,
Davidson, George 214,
Davidson, Henry 214,
Davidson, Mary Lula Henderson 214,
Davis, J. Anne 138,
Davis, Herschel 215,
Davis, James 118
Davis, Jonathan 85,
Davis, Lizzie 124,

Davis, Martin 124,
Davis, Miles 85,
Davis, Thomas 118
Dawson, Ralph 162,
Dawson, Susan 162,
Day, Ezekiel 152,
Day, Robert 156,
Deaton, Dorset 219,
Delong, Hortense 215,
Delong, Kelsey 215,
Demry, Mary J. 22,
Demry, Will 22,
Dickey, George 159,
Dickey, James 156,
Dickey, Sarah I. 159,
Dickson, John (Col.) 82, 84,
Dickson, Jr., Michael (Maj.) 92,
Dickson, Sarah 26, 79, 82, 83,
   84, 92,
Dillinger, Jane 66,
Dillinger, John 66,
Dillinger, Marcus 66,
Dillinger, Mary W. 66,
Dillinger, Sarah 66,
Dinnis, Emlin 146,
Dixon, Elizabeth 60,
Dixon, John 56,
Dixon, Penelope
Dixon, William 56,
Dobbs, Phoebe I. 158,
Drake, Isabella 38,
Drake, James G. 38,
Drake, Lusinda 38,
Drake, Newton 38,
Drake, Thomas J. 38,
Drake, William 38,
Dreiss, Michael 92,
Duff, John 152,
Dunaway, Ed 41,
Dunaway, G.L. 41,
Dunaway, L. 41,
Dunkle infant 124,
Durley, Horatio 56,
Dyar, Joseph L. 15, 39
Dyer, Otis 215,

Foxhall, William 60,
Franklin, Allen 18,
Franklin, Jim 18,
Franklin, Thomas 151,
Frazur, Samuel 219,
Freeland, Isaac 259, 260, 261, 262,
Freeland, Jeremiah 260, 261,
Frick, Alexander 84, 93,
Frick, Anna 84, 94,
Frick, Caleb 84, 93,
Frick, Catharine 84, 93,
Frick, Elizabeth 84, 93,
Frick, Elizabeth Ann 84, 94,
Frick, George 84, 93,
Frick, Gregor 81,
Frick, Henry 84,
Frick, Henry D. 84,
Frick, Isaac 84, 93,
Frick, Jacob 81, 82, 84,
Frick, Jr., Jacob 93,
Frick, Sr. Jacob D. 94,
Frick, Jacob D. 84,
Frick, Sr. John D. 92,
Frick, Mary 93,
Frick, Mathias 84, 94,
Frick, Nancy 84, 93,
Frick, Oswald 81,
Frick, Paul 84, 93,
Frick, Rudolf 84,
Frick, Sarah 84,
Frick, Susan 93,
Frick, Susanna 84,
Frick, Veronica 84,
Frick, William Heinrich 84, 94,
Fricks, Alexander Shaw 83, 84, 86, 87, 88, 92,
Fricks, Asa Tortoulette 83, 84, 86, 87, 92,
Fricks, Benjamin, 88, 89,
Fricks, Cassandra 87,
Fricks, Celia 89,
Fricks, Cornelia Lydia 26, 55, 70, 83, 84, 87, 88, 89, 92,
Fricks, Elizabeth 85, 86,
Fricks, Elizabeth J. 84, 93,

Fricks, Flavius Josephus 83, 84, 85, 86, 92,
Fricks, George 88,
Fricks, Henry 82,
Fricks, Henry D. 82, 84, 92, 93,
Fricks, Henry Reuben 84, 93,
Fricks, Isaac C. 84, 93,
Fricks, Jacob 82,
Fricks, Joel G. 82, 84,
Fricks, John 26, 79, 82, 83, 84, 85, 86, 87, 88, 92, 93,
Fricks, John D. 86, 87, 88,
Fricks, Sr. John 82, 83,
Fricks, Lucellieus W. 84, 93,
Fricks, Marcus Lafayette 84, 93,
Fricks, Martin Armstrong 84, 93,
Fricks, Mary A. 84, 93,
Fricks, Mary Elizabeth 83, 84, 87, 92,
Fricks, Michael Treece 84,
Fricks, N.B. 82,
Fricks, Napoleon B. 84, 93,
Fricks, Permelia 84, 93,
Fricks, Pleasant 93,
Fricks, Rose, 88,
Fricks, S. Davis 84, 93,
Fricks, Sarah (Sallie) 83,
Fricks, Sarah 84, 85, 86, 87, 88, 89, 93,
Fricks, Sela 88,
Frink, Julia 159,
Frink, Sarah M. 159,
Frix, Joel G. 93,
Frix, Michael Treece 93,
Fry, George 153,
Fry, Jacob 153,
Fry, John 153,
Fryer, James 156,
Fulton, James 156,
Fulton, Thomas 151,

G

Gailey, Birdie 215,
Gailey, James 151,
Gailey, John 151,
Gailey, Sylvia 215,
Gaines, Amelia 26, 28, 34, 35,

Gaines, James 42,
Gaines, Richard 42,
Gaines, Susan 34,
Galbreath, John 148, 151,
Galloway, Charlotte M. 17,
Galloway, Miles D. 17,
Galloway, Samuel H. 17,
Galloway, Thomas C. 17
Gardner, William 150,
Garner, Dorothy 136,
Garner, Jennie G. 136,
Garner, Robert D. 136,
Garrison, Agnes 156,
Garrison, Harry 215,
Gash, Joseph L. 38,
Gates, Abigail 122,
Gates, Charley R. 125,
Gates, Delilah E. 125,
Gates, Dickey 125,
Gates, Elijah J. 122,
Gates, George W. 125,
Gates, Huldy E. 125,
Gates, Jacob 122,
Gates, Jacob A. 125,
Gates, John B. 125,
Gates, Mary 125,
Gates, Oliver N. 122, 125,
Gates, William A. 122,
Gearin, George 215,
George, James 151,
George, John 56,
George, Thomas 56,
George, Michael 56,
Geren, Charles V. 136,
Geren, Jr., Charles V. 136,
Geren, Lois G. 136,
Geren, Vincent E. 136,
Gibbs, Frank 126,
Gibbs, Hattie 126,
Gibbs, Lottie 126,
Gibbs, Madeline 126,
Gibson, Charles 151,
Gibson, Elizabeth 158,
Gibson, Elizabeth I. 158,
Gibson, Free 162,

Tibbitts, Lane 76,
Towns, Mary 22,
Trammel, C.G. 40,
Trammel, Cherry 40,
Trammel, James 40,
Trammel, Lee 40,
Trammel, Mary 40,
Trammel, Nancy 40,
Trammel, Thomas 40,
Trammel family 50,
Treece, Mary 82, 84,
Treece, Mary Magdalena 92,
Treece, Michael 92,
Trippe, Judge Robert B. 4,
Troutman, Anna Margaretha 92,
Truby, Catharine 122,
Truby, Jacob 140,
Truby, John 156,
Truby, Susannah 95, 111, 117, 127, 140,
Truelove, Laurie 215,
Truelove, Pearl 215,
Tyner, G.F. 215,

U
Utrecht, Bishop of 81,

V
Valentine, Elizabeth B. 132,
Valentine, Henry P. 132,
Vann, II, Cherokee Chief James 279,
Vaughan, Alfred 22,
Vaughan, Claiborn 259, 260, 261, 262,
Vaughan, E.M. 41,
Vaughan, Francis J. 22,
Vaughan, Marie 22,
"Veach Guards" 1
Veal, Elijah 219,
Vermillion, Jack "Texas" 103,

W
Waddle, William 152,
Wade, Ronni 74,
Wade, William 74,
Waits, Cicero 198,
Walker, Clarence 215,

Walker, John 42,
Walker, Margaret 33, 42,
Walker, Tony 215,
Walker, W.L. 215,
Walker, William Ashford 42,
Wallace, Alice 73, 90,
Wallace, Texas 215,
Wallis-McElreath 51,
Ward, J.C. 24,
Ward, La Nelle 24,
Ward, Lud 24,
Ward, Merida 24,
Ward, Pauline 24,
Warriant, William 69,
Washington, Berry 70,
Washington, Clifford 18,
Washington, Hettie 18,
Waterman, Robert (Gov.) 100,
Waters, Bertha 215,
Waters, Ruth 215,
Waters, Ruth Smith 196,
Watie, Stand 279, 280,
Watkins, Sam 2,
Watson, Dusty 68,
Watson, Elliot 68,
Watson, Isabella 68,
Watson, John 68,
Watson, Mary 68,
Watson, Nancy 68,
Weaver, Sam 156,
Weeks, Gloria R. 136,
Weeks, Virginia R. 136,
Weeks, William M. 136,
Weems, Hattie 18,
Weems, Wiley 18,
Weir, Hugh I. 42,
Weir, Mary McKee 42,
Wells, Isaac 64,
Westmoreland, Paul 214,
Wheeler, Amelina 71,
Wheeler, Charles 71,
Wheeler, George 71,
Wheeler, Leeroy 71,
Wheeler, Louis 71,
Wheeler, Marcus 71,

Wheeler, Mary 71,
Whelchel, Nellie 215,
White, Bessie L. 134,
White, David 117, 120,
White, Evelyn H. 134,
White, J. Franklin 134,
White, Gaz 51,
White, Hattie 18,
White, Louise D. 134,
White, Mary 37,
White, Sarah 40,
White, Warren 40,
Whitehead, Eula 18,
Whitmire, Eliza Ann 281, 283, 293,
Whitmire, Hassie Mae 215,
Whitmire, Jane 281, 283,
Whitmire, Julius 215,
Whitmire, Mary Mariah 259, 265, 283,
Whitmire, Nell 215,
Whitmire, W.A. 215,
Whitmore, Paul 215,
Wike, Ann G. 125,
Wike, Hannah 122,
Wike, Helen 125,
Wike, Levi 122,
Wike, Mary J. 125,
Wike, Philip 125,
Wike, Sarah 125,
Wike, William 125,
Wikle, John E. 18,
Wiley, Sandy 88,
Wilkie, Francis M. 14,
Wilkie, Louisa C. 14,
Wilkins, Martin 62,
Williams, Elizabeth 57,
Williams, Jonathan 11,
Williams, William 64,
Williamson, Andrew 152,
Williamson, Dan Hugh 134,
Williamson, Jr., Dan Hugh 134,
Williamson, Latrelle 134,
Wilson, Augustus 67,
Wilson, Benjamin 64,
Wilson, Charles 162,
Wilson, Dorcas C. 67,

Wilson, Elizabeth 67,
Wilson, Hannah 265,
Wilson, Hiram W. 67,
Wilson, James 117
Wilson, Jane 67,
Wilson, Jane M.B. 67,
Wilson, Josephine 67,
Wilson, Margaret 160,
Wilson, Mary Polly 111, 140,
Wilson, N.A. 67,
Wilson, Robert I.J. 67,
Wise, Hannah 69,
Wise, Isaac E. 69,
Wise, Job E. 69,
Wise, John L. 69,

Wise, Lucy J. 69,
Wise, Margie 89,
Wise, Mary A. 69,
Wise, Mary E. 69,
Wise, William 69,
Wise, William L. 69,
Wofford, Ed 71,
Wofford, John 71,
Wofford, Gen. W.T. 4,
Wood, Daniel 66,
Wood, Elizabeth I. 66,
Wood, Julia A. 66,
Wood, Lydia A. 66,
Wood, Martha C. 66,
Wood, Mary A. 66,

Wood, Nancy L. 66,
Wood, Richard M. 66,
Wood, Silas B. 66,
Wright, James E. 136,
Wright, Louis B. 37,
Wright, Margaret 136,
Wyatt, Lettice Nicholl 26,
Wyman, George 156,

Y

Yancey, Elise 24,
Yancey, Eunice 24,
Yancey, Lawrence 24,
Young, David 117, 120,
Young, Hugh C. 118

About The Author

R. Olin Jackson began his studies in preparation for a professional career at the University of Georgia, later finishing an undergraduate degree in journalism at Georgia State University in Atlanta. He went on to achieve a master's degree in political science history from the University of North Georgia.

Professionally, Olin initially landed employment as a speechwriter for a Georgia politician in the late 1970s, moving on in the early 1980s with a return to the University of North Georgia where he served as Director of Media Services and Sports Information. When the opportunity presented itself, he advanced to employment as a senior account executive with a major public relations firm in Atlanta in the mid-1980s.

By 1987, Olin had decided to strike out on his own. He founded *Legacy Communications, Inc.*, where he was the award-winning executive editor and publisher of his flagship creations – *North Georgia Journal* and *Georgia Backroads* magazines – the premier travel and history publications of Georgia. He parlayed this endeavor into a long and fruitful career before selling it in 2005. *Georgia Backroads* is now in its 37th year (as of 2023) of publication.

In the interim, Olin also has written/co-written and edited a selection of books, including *Moonshine, Murder and Mayhem in Georgia* (2003); *Tales of the Rails in Georgia* (2004); *Georgia Backroads Traveler* (2005); *Georgia's Doc Holliday* (2006); *We Shall Die Together* (with Dan Roper) (2008); and *Traced with Fire, Written in Blood* (with Dan Roper) (2009).

Olin, more recently, has embarked upon a new business venture, founding Whippoorwill Publications, LLC in 2021. His current projects within that realm include *Mystery & History in Georgia, Volume I* (which was recently honored with a *Five-Star Award*

by *Readers' Favorite* book awards), and the companion to that book: *M&H in Georgia, Volume II*. Other works in progress include a captivating novel of historic fiction entitled *Whippoorwill Hill* (which is available at Amazon.com); and a selection of original poetry entitled *After All That We've Been Through*.

Olin is married to the former Judy Grizzle of Dahlonega, Georgia. The couple make their home in Roswell and Rockmart, Georgia. Olin also has a son – Burke – by a former marriage. Burke and his wife, Olga, have produced two wonderful grandchildren – Alexander and Catherine – who are the "apples" of Olin's eye.

www.ingramcontent.com/pod-product-compliance
Lightning Source LLC
Chambersburg PA
CBHW080837120626
46553CB00009B/2460